THE LIMITS OF SOVIET POWER IN THE DEVELOPING WORLD

The Limits of Soviet Power in the Developing World

Edited by Edward A. Kolodziej and Roger E. Kanet

The Johns Hopkins University Press
Baltimore

Published by
The Johns Hopkins University Press
701 West 40th Street
Baltimore, Maryland 21211

Library of Congress Cataloging-in-Publication Data
The Limits of Soviet power in the developing world/edited by Edward
A. Kolodziej and Roger E. Kanet.
p. cm.
Bibliography: p.
Includes index.
ISBN 0–8018–3762–6
1. Developing countries—Foreign relations—Soviet Union. 2. Soviet Union—
Foreign relations—Developing countries. 3. Soviet Union—Foreign relations—
1975– I. Kolodziej, Edward A. II. Kanet, Roger E., 1936–
D888.S65L55 1989
327.4701724—dc19   88–11716
                                                                            CIP

Contents

Acknowledgements

The editors wish to express their sincere appreciation to all of those who have made the project and the resulting study possible. An important element in the preparation of the study was a Soviet-Third World Workshop, held at the University of Illinois at Urbana-Champaign on 25–7 September 1986. Contributors and invited participants met to address the topic of US-Soviet Competition in the Third World: Probable Developments in the 1990s. In a series of sessions covering the global aspects of Soviet Third World policy, the policies of principal regional actors, and their implications for US policy, the fourteen primary contributors presented the first drafts of their papers for discussion and review. In addition to the primary contributors, revised copies of whose papers comprise the present volume, invited participants in the Workshop included:

Formal commentators:	David E. Albright, Air War College
	Robert S. Wood, Naval War College
Invited observers:	Robert Grey, Grinnell College
	George E. Hudson, Wittenberg University and Mershon Center
	Michael McGinnis, Indiana University
	Robin Alison Remington, University of Columbia-Missouri
	Dina Rome Spechler, Indiana University
	M. Crawford Young, University of Wisconsin-Madison
Rapporteurs:	Terry D. Clark, University of Illinois at Urbana-Champaign
	Daniel R. Kempton, University of Illinois at Urbana-Champaign

The editors wish to express their appreciation to all of these participants whose perceptive criticisms and suggestions resulted in greater clarity and precision in the final drafts of the individual papers. Moreover, they wish to give special thanks to David E. Albright, Robert Grey, George E. Hudson, Stanley Kochanek and Patrick Morgan for the detailed written comments they provided on revised drafts of portions of the manuscript and to Daniel R. Kempton and Kanti Bajpai who prepared the selected bibliography.

The editors are grateful, as well, for the financial support provided for the Workshop by the Program in Arms Control, Disarmament and International Security, the Department of Political Science, and the Russian and East European Center, all of the University of Illinois, and especially for the support of the US Department of Defense under contract no. MDA903-86-C-0112. Without this financial backing the project and the resulting study would have been impossible. However, the views, opinions, and findings contained in this book are those of the authors and should not be construed as an official Department of Defense position.

The editors also wish to thank all of the other authors for their willingness to revise their chapters, taking into account recommendations from Workshop participants and others. They also are grateful to Antje Kolodziej for final proofing and editing of the book. Finally, they wish to acknowledge the fact that without the essential role of Mary Hoffman the book would likely never have been completed. Not only has she managed the logistics of completing the volume, she has also rendered major assistance as a perceptive and demanding copy editor.

EDWARD A. KOLODZIEJ
ROGER E. KANET

Notes on the Contributors

Juan M. del Aguila is Associate Professor of Political Science at Emory University in Atlanta and Director of the Emory Center for International Studies. Included among his publications are *Cuba: Dilemmas of a Revolution* (1984), 'Cuba and the Soviet Union: Fishing in Troubled Waters', Canadian Institute of Strategic Studies (1985), and 'Central American Vulnerability to Soviet/Cuban Penetration', *Journal of Interamerican Studies and World Affairs* (1985). He is currently working on a second edition of *Cuba: Dilemmas of a Revolution* (1987).

Stephen P. Cohen is Professor of Political Science at the University of Illinois at Urbana-Champaign. He served as a member of the Policy Planning Staff of the Department of State during 1985–87. Dr Cohen is the author or co-author of six books, including: *The Indian Army* (1971), *The Pakistan Army* (1984), and (ed.) *The Security of South Asia: Asian and American Perspectives* (1987).

W. Raymond Duncan is Distinguished Teaching Professor of Political Science at the State University of New York, College at Brockport. During 1984–86 he was Scholar-in-Residence with the Central Intelligence Agency, where he worked on Soviet-Third World relations. Included among his publications is his most recent book, *The Soviet Union and Cuba: Interests and Influence* (1985). He is currently co-authoring a book on Soviet policy toward the Third World under Mikhail Gorbachev, while teaching at SUNY-Brockport and at Georgetown University.

Jerrold D. Green is Director of the Near East Center and Associate Professor of Political Science at the University of Arizona. Among his publications is *Revolution in Iran: The Politics of Countermobilization* (1982). At present he is at work on a study of the relationship between ideology and politics in the Middle East.

Roger E. Kanet is Professor of Political Science at the University of Illinois at Urbana-Champaign. Included among his publications are: (ed.) *Soviet Foreign Policy and East-West Relations* (1982), (ed.) *Soviet Foreign Policy in the 1980s* (1982), and (ed.) *The Soviet Union,*

Eastern Europe and the Developing States (1987). His current research interests focus on Soviet foreign policy in the Third World.

Edward A. Kolodziej is Research Professor of Political Science at the University of Illinois at Urbana-Champaign. His research and teaching interests focus on two interrelated concerns: the role of military force and threats in international relations and the arms control and security problems of the Atlantic Alliance. Among his major publications are: *The Uncommon Defense and Congress: 1945–1963* (1966), *French International Policy under De Gaulle and Pompidou: The Politics of Grandeur* (1974), and *Making and Marketing Arms: The French Experience and Its Implications for the International System* (1987).

Augustus Richard Norton is Associate Professor of Comparative Politics in the Department of Social Sciences, United States Military Academy, West Point, New York. Included among his publications are: *Moscow and the Palestinians* (1974), *Amal and the Shi'a: Struggle for the Soul of Lebanon* (1987), and (ed.) *The International Relations of the PLO* (forthcoming).

Thomas W. Robinson is Director of the China Studies Program at the American Enterprise Institute, Professor at Georgetown University, and Course Chairperson for China and Northeast Asia at the Foreign Service Institute. He is completing manuscripts on Chinese foreign policy, Soviet Asian policy, and Asian security, and has published over one hundred writings in these and the allied fields of Chinese politics, Korean politics, international relations theory, and the Strategic Triangle.

John Seiler is presently teaching courses at Mercy College and Dutchess Community College. His publications include (ed.) *Southern Africa since the Portuguese Coup* (1980). He is currently writing about the changing role of the military in the South African government and about the Namibian political situation. He is also completing a book on Kennedy-Johnson administration policy toward Southern Africa.

Sheldon W. Simon is Professor of Political Science and Director of Arizona State University's Center of Asian Studies. He also consults with the US Information Agency and the Department of Defense. He has written extensively on Asian foreign and security policies and is the author or editor of five books, including *The ASEAN States and Regional Security* (1982). Most recently, Professor Simon completed a book length study titled *The Future of Asian-Pacific Security Collaboration*.

F. Seth Singleton is Dean of the College of Arts and Sciences at Pacific University. His academic interests include Soviet foreign policy and the Soviet Union, Africa, and international security affairs. He has written extensively on these topics, including 'From Intervention to Consolidation: The Soviet Union and Southern Africa', in *The Soviet Impact in Africa*, R. Craig Nation and Mark V. Kauppi (eds) (1984).

Marvin G. Weinbaum is Professor of Political Science and Director of the Program in South and West Asian Studies at the University of Illinois at Urbana-Champaign. Among his recent publications are 'Afghanistan, International Responses and Responsibilities', in Ralph Magnus (ed.) *Afghan Alternatives* (1985) and *Egypt and the Politics of U.S. Economic Aid* (1986). He is currently working on a study of Soviet influence on the Afghan resistance movement and penetration into the refugee community in Pakistan.

Howard J. Wiarda is Professor of Political Science and of Comparative Labor Relations at the University of Massachusetts/ Amherst, and Resident Scholar and Director of the Center for Hemispheric Studies at the American Enterprise Institute for Public Policy Research. He is the author or editor of thirteen books, including (with Harvey Kline) *Latin American Politics and Development* (1984), (ed.) *Rift and Revolution: The Central American Imbroglio* (1984), *Dialogue on Central America* (1985), (ed.) *New Directions in Comparative Politics* (1985), and (with Mark Falcoff) *The Communist Challenge in the Caribbean* (1987). He is currently working on a book on American foreign policy making.

I. William Zartman is Professor of International Politics and Director of the African Studies Program at the Johns Hopkins School of Advanced International Studies in Washington, DC. He is the author of a number of books on North Africa: *Government and Politics in North Africa* (1963); *Destiny of a Dynasty* (1964); *Man, State and*

Society in the Contemporary Maghreb (1974); *Elites in the Middle East* (1980); and (ed.) *The Political Economy of Morocco* (1987). Dr Zartman has also written extensively on African politics and relations, with his latest work *Ripe for Resolution: Conflict and Intervention in Africa* (1985), and, as editor, *The Political Economy of the Ivory Coast, The Political Economy of Nigeria* (1983), and *The OAU after Twenty Years* (1984).

Preface

This volume has two principal objectives: to evaluate Soviet penetration of the developing world and to identify the implications of Soviet success and failure for US security and foreign policy. The two aims are linked since United States behaviour is a partial determinant of Soviet expansion or containment, although it is by no means the sole or in many instances the critical factor affecting Soviet choices. The constraints imposed by developing states, as this volume argues, must be given greater weight than they have until now in explaining Soviet policy toward the Third World.

Two general conclusions are reached. First, the divisions within the world society, composed of divergent religious and secular communities, of clashing nation-states, and of competing socioeconomic interests (cutting across ideological and national rivalries) inhibit significant Soviet expansion in the developing world. The global and regional diffusion of economic and military power further reinforces barriers to easy extension of Soviet influence in the near term. A decentralised world society, with autonomous centres of power and political initiative, also restrains, if not precludes, the Soviet Union from using force or coercive threats to promote its aims. Second, the external limits on Soviet power and internal imperatives pressing for socioeconomic and political reform within the Soviet Union favour a strategic Thermidor in the Soviet Union's quest to become a global power and to revolutionise the international system to suit its preferred values, needs, and interests.

LIMITS OF SOVIET POWER AND POLICY DILEMMAS

Soviet domination of the developing world is neither imminent nor inevitable. Notwithstanding the dramatic success of the Soviet Union in the 1960s and 1970s within the developing world, several constraints limit further Soviet expansion. In addition to the increasing ability of the developing states to resist subordination to Moscow and, conversely, to manipulate the Soviet Union for their advantage, Soviet influence is checked by the countervailing military and economic power of the United States and its Western allies, by the divisions within the socialist camp – most notably the Sino-Soviet split, by the receding relevance of the Soviet model to many Third World problems, and by the necessarily scarce economic and technological resources commanded by Moscow to project its power and purposes abroad. There appears to be little likelihood that these limitations will be fundamentally relaxed in the remainder of this century, however much the saliency of one factor or another may change in relative value.

Soviet planners and policy makers appear increasingly aware of their dim prospects, witnessed by the questions raised in the Soviet policy debate about the heavy costs, high risks, and dubious benefits of many Soviet commitments abroad. The mixed results of these efforts have bolstered doubts and reservations. The developing *and* developed worlds have not been as responsive to Soviet threats and blandishments as earlier Soviet regimes had hoped. The shortcomings of Moscow's policy instruments, which rest primarily on military power, have become progressively evident in the failure of the Soviet Union and its socialist partners in Eastern Europe and in the developing world to meet either their own modernisation and socioeconomic needs or, much less, those of the Third World.

The Soviet Union will confront a host of hard choices in the coming decade in the developing world. To which regimes should it commit its scarce resources? At what level and in what areas should these resources be committed? Where should previously extended commitments be revised to conform to limited Soviet power and competing aims? The latter are currently centered on internal socio-political and economic reform and on keeping pace in the arms competition with the United States, particularly in offensive and defensive nuclear systems. Here the dilemmas facing Soviet leaders are well known: to liberalise the economy and to decentralise resource allocation decisions risk weakening internal party control and downgrading military priorities, moves likely to be resisted by the party apparatus as well as by the military and elements of the civilian bureaucracies; to widen Soviet and socialist state economic ties and socio-cultural and diplomatic exchanges with Western capitalistic states threatens to increase demands for greater economic choice within the Soviet bloc, as well as to heighten pressures for greater political independence by bloc partners – after the Romanian example – and for the expression of greater political freedom within particular communist states, including the Soviet Union itself.

These choices are acutely felt in the developing world. At a global level, should the Soviet Union focus most of its attention and resources on socialist states within the Soviet camp? Or, should it widen its relationships with non-Marxist states, at the risk of dampening and dissipating revolutionary fervour and of weakening the incentives of Marxist-Leninist states to remain within the Soviet fold?

Soviet leaders also face a new dilemma in the developing world that compounds those with which we are all familiar. The choice is more complex than simply choosing between intra-party and state-to-state priorities. The choice confronting the Soviet leaders is whether to remain isolated within their own socialist system or to draw on the greater resources and stimulus of the non-socialist world to spur internal economic and technological reform and (what is likely to be more difficult) to accommodate themselves to a world in which the Soviet model of socialism appears fading – more for socioeconomic than for narrow military and internal security reasons.

Soviet leaders are being forced to limit the extension of Soviet commitments and resources to the developing world. Moscow is undergoing a fundamental reorientation toward the Third World as the object and instrument of its long-term policy. Whatever may be the attachment of Soviet planners to a revolutionary mission or to the goal of making the Soviet Union the equal of the United States as a global power, they have to define their aims in terms of the limitations of Soviet power.

Regarding the object of Soviet policy, Moscow appears prepared to devote whatever resources are necessary and to maintain and even increase its level of strategic and foreign policy commitments to keep what it has achieved in presence and influence in Cuba, Vietnam, and Ethiopia. These states appear to be integral parts of the Soviet bloc. As the focus shifts from these communist enclaves, the commitments of the Soviet Union appear less clear and certain between the superpowers. At this writing, Moscow has agreed to withdraw its military forces from Afghanistan, but resists defining the terms of political compromise to ensure its complete disengagement. The level of resources to be devoted to areas currently in dispute between the superpowers, principally Nicaragua and Central America as well as Angola and southern Africa, appears to be presently under serious examination, as the regional chapters suggest, with no fixed Soviet determination about the priority that they should or ultimately will be assigned in Soviet Third World policy.

The Soviet Union's costly successes – impressive when considered historically but still quite limited if global standards of influence are applied – and the intractability of the international environment, stubbornly resistant in a host of bewildering ways to Soviet designs, have introduced a new scepticism and soberness in Soviet thinking about creating a socialist world order. The conflicting needs and demands of Third World states advise a broader, more patient and pragmatic, and longer-term strategy toward the developing world than was once believed necessary or desirable. Soviet policy makers appear simultaneously more sensitive to the diverse and potentially insupportable claims of developing states on Soviet resources and commitments and more aware, partly informed by recent experience, that the states of the developing world are far less susceptible to Soviet manipulation or rapid modernisation than was previously believed, even in those cases where Soviet assistance has been substantial, as in China, Egypt, and Indonesia.

The developing world is increasingly being viewed more as an instrument than as an object of Soviet global policy. In the post-Brezhnev period, it has been progressively subordinated to Soviet needs for socioeconomic and technological development, to the exigencies of the US-Soviet arms competition, and to the requirements of better relations with developed states, especially those in Western Europe. Stronger ties with the West Europeans have the twin virtues of assisting the economic development of the Soviet Union and its bloc partners and of promoting greater independence in Western capitals from US leadership. These priorities are linked to the creation of a broader base of economic and political relations with the developing world to gain access to raw materials, trade outlets, and concessions needed for the modernisation of the Soviet economy as a prerequisite for long-term successful competition with the United States and the West.

These shifts in Soviet thinking and policy toward the developing world should not obscure the fact that Moscow or its partners have used force to get their way. Nor does this analysis suggest that they will forego armed intervention or support for revolutionary movements bent on overthrowing governments with which the Soviet Union may have formal diplomatic ties. The cases of Cuba, Vietnam, Angola, Ethiopia, and Afghanistan argue otherwise. But the limits of military force also appear apparent to Soviet decision makers. Marxist rule in Afghanistan, Angola, Mozambique, and Nicaragua has elicited greater resistance than appears to have been initially anticipated by Moscow. In Grenada, the Cuban-sponsored New Jewel Movement was overthrown and replaced by a US-backed regime committed to liberal principles of government. In addition, the Soviet experience in Southeast Asia, where ASEAN and China now contain Vietnam, suggests the lesson that too rapid an expansion of Soviet presence and influence can prompt countervailing responses which may eventually reverse short-run gains over the long-term, a kind of 'falling dominoes' in reverse. Third World states are also acutely aware of the limited utility of Soviet arms in addressing their rising socioeconomic needs – as much an imperative of survival as of the suppression of domestic opponents. There is, finally, a heavy burden placed on the Soviet Union in maintaining high defence expenditures and costly, not to mention risky, foreign military and security assistance programmes. These calculations and constraints cannot be – nor are they being – ignored by Soviet decision makers.

THERMIDOR IN SOVIET GLOBAL STRATEGY

At this juncture in the history of the international system and, specifically, in the evolution of the developing world, it would appear that Soviet leaders would prefer what might be termed a Thermidor in their competition with the West and the United States. It would appear that the Soviet Union cannot keep pace by relying on its existing military and economic base, including that of its bloc partners, nor, given the questionable attractiveness of segments of the developing world, does it have much incentive to try. Moscow needs time and better relations with the West to reform its outmoded and inefficient economic system, weighted down by excessive centralisation and bureaucratisation. Social ills – alcoholism, absenteeism, national and ethnic tensions – also need to be addressed. An unresponsive party structure needs to be revitalised, and tired personnel, attached to outmoded political notions and commitments, replaced.

In response to a period of Thermidor, the United States and its Western allies have an opportunity to affect Soviet choices in the developing world in ways, to be discussed in the final chapter of the volume, that are not only in their own interest but compatible in many areas with that of the Soviet Union. The East–West struggle will surely go on along a North–South axis – in deadly earnest and often with lethal consequences – but conceivably at less costly and risky levels, if both sides learn that, without any lessening of distrust, they can mutually moderate their aims, contain if not curtail their current levels of military and security commitments, and yet expand their competition in non-coercive ways within the developing world – without necessarily decreasing their own security or that of their closest partners.

Moving to more competitive, but less coercive, levels of conflict will not be easy, nor in some instances even desirable where concrete interests are at stake in key locales, as in the Middle East, but the conditions for a Thermidor and for a transition to more cooperative superpower relations are emerging if the superpowers wish to avail themselves of the opportunity. Neither side alone can effect such a transition; only in tandem will it work, since the benefits in shifting to lowered coercive conflict in the developing world are a partial function of superpower cooperation, not merely the result of unilateral initiatives which are not matched by corresponding confidence building measures from the other adversary.

APPROACH AND ORGANISATION

The principal findings and conclusions of the volume are the product of several complementary lines of systemic and regional analysis. First, the superpower conflict, however multifaceted and complex, is placed in the larger context of the international system within which this dynamic competition is viewed as the principal but not the only or, in many instances, the most significant force defining the global political community.

Chapter 1 argues that no state, including the Soviet Union, has the military power, will, or incentive to impose unilaterally its preferred values and interests on the international system. The developing states, moreover, have sufficient military forces and economic resources at their disposal in many cases to define regional security agendas, to determine the outcomes of intrastate and interstate conflicts, and to help or hinder efforts by the Soviet Union to create a global environment congenial to its opposing values and interests.

Chapter 2 outlines the evolution of Soviet policy toward the developing world. It stresses the Soviet perception of its revolutionary role in the international system. It underlines the determination of Soviet leaders to make the Soviet Union a global power and, ultimately, to organise a socialist-dominated world system. Sketched are successes of the Soviet Union in expanding its presence and influence abroad as well as the growing debate within policy-making circles of the limitations of Soviet power and that of its socialist brethren and the costs and risks of foreign adventures.

Part II, Chapters 3 to 14, adopts a regional approach. The primary focus is on those states in the developing world with which the Soviet Union has created special ties and commitments. The regional and Soviet specialists invited to contribute to this volume have been asked to address the following set of questions to facilitate comparison of Soviet behaviour across regions and to assist in generalising about the operational objectives and preferred instruments of Soviet policy: (1) Who are the principal actors in the region with close ties to the Soviet Union? (2) What are their principal aims, and how is the Soviet Union viewed as an instrument to facilitate the accomplishment of their objectives? (3) What overall strategy, if any, are these actors pursuing to elicit favourable Soviet responses? (4) What are the instruments used to manipulate Moscow? (5) How successful have the regional actors been? (6) What is their assessment of the costs, benefits, and future expectations of their relationship with the Soviet Union? (7) What are the principal problems and regional actors that are obstacles to the achievement of actor aims? and (8) To what extent is the United States a help or a hindrance?

Drawing on the answers to these questions and on the analysis of Part I, the final section elaborates on the two principal conclusions of this volume: the limits on Soviet power imposed by the international system and Moscow's need for a period of Thermidor in its competition with the West. Chapter 15 identifies current and emerging trends in Soviet thinking about the developing world. Chapter 16 summarises the constraints on Soviet behaviour, its tenuous position in the principal regions of the globe, and the incentives for the Soviet Union and the West to cooperate in a period of Thermidor. It also outlines a long-term strategy for the West to meet the Soviet challenge and to moderate the superpower struggle in the developing world.

As an aid to the hurried reader, the gist of this volume can be garnered from reading the summary introductions to all of the chapters. Each author has been asked to summarise his major arguments and conclusions. Within the limits of consistency and coherence, the editors have tried to retain as much as possible of the original style and substance of each contribution to preserve the richness of thought and insight brought to the volume by each regional expert. If we encouraged each flower to bloom in its own way, we felt obliged as editors to insist that each plant be seeded in the same conceptual field of analysis. Only the reader can judge whether we have struck the right balance. The editors assume full responsibility for Parts I and III. While Roger Kanet is the principal author of Chapter

15 and Edward Kolodziej of Chapter 16, both concur in the findings of these chapters. The contributors, however, should not be held personally responsible for these chapters, although the editors believe that their analyses of Soviet regional policy support the contributors' evaluations and recommendations.

EDWARD A. KOLODZIEJ
ROGER E. KANET

Part I

The Soviet Union and the Developing World: A Global Perspective

1 The Diffusion of Military Power Within a Decentralised International System: Limits of Soviet Power
Edward A. Kolodziej

INTRODUCTION

A splintered and fragmented world society,[1] including divisions within the communist camp, and the progressive diffusion of power throughout the international system limit the expansion of Soviet influence in the developing world. Specifically, the globalisation of the nation-state system with the end of colonialism and the collapse of the Eurocentric system and the spread of military capabilities, most notably to developing states, constrain Soviet aims and aspirations. These limitations are reinforced by others: the countervailing nuclear and conventional capabilities as well as the material and techno-scientific resources of the United States; the formidable military capacity and economic vitality of its West European allies and Japan; and the brittle strength of the economic and technological development of the Soviet Union and its bloc partners in Europe and elsewhere to sustain a strategy of global expansion. As the next chapter suggests and as succeeding chapters detail, Soviet ideology and expectations of increasing influence in the developing world have been forced to adjust, however slowly or reluctantly, to these parameters of power.

The Soviet Union lacks the military means and, accordingly, the incentive to organise unilaterally the world community on terms congenial to its values and interests primarily through the threat or use of force. The costs and risks of military intervention, the dubious benefits of continued high levels of military and economic assistance to clients and Marxist allies, and the offsetting forces at the disposal of opponent states blunt the prospects of Soviet success.

Conversely, the limitations of Soviet power do not imply an abandonment of military force as the key instrument of Soviet

diplomacy. The expansion of Soviet influence is attributable in no
small part to the military power of the Soviet Union and to the security assistance it has provided to others. On a more general level,
its struggle with the United States to shape a world that suits its
ideological preferences and national interests will almost certainly
persist, although the form, locale, scope, intensity, and stakes of
specific conflict points are likely to change over time and shift in focus
as they have since the conflict began in earnest at the end of the Second
World War.[2] The differences between the superpowers are too
profound, their interests and aspirations too pervasive, and the
perceived opportunities for gain often too tempting in the developing
world and elsewhere to induce their opponent to forego the use or
threat of military power, alone or in concert with others.

The interesting question is not whether Soviet leaders perceive
military force and security assistance in principle to be useful but in
which specific circumstances and to what extent force and military aid
should be used for what expected gains and at what costs and risks.
Expected gain is putatively estimated in terms of the expenditure of
scarce resources for the achievement of some strategic aim, valued by
the Soviets themselves, and for the acquisition of clients of varying
reliability and utility in advancing Soviet objectives. These gains also
have to be weighed against the likelihood of a direct confrontation
with the United States and the debilitating impact of regional and
global arms races and conflicts whose costs are calculated in terms of
their drain on other pressing foreign and domestic needs.[3] These
calculations must be made within a divided and increasingly decentralised international system resistant to Soviet force and entreaties.

A WORLD SOCIETY AT ODDS: THE DIVISIONS WITHIN

The incipient anarchy of the world society limits Soviet influence and
power. First, there exists no common historical, racial, cultural, or
linguistic heritage binding its members. There is no single historical
memory of the past or a unified conception of a future which the
peoples of the globe collectively share as equal members of an
integrated political system. There are no universally accepted values
or emotive symbols strong enough to hold the people of the globe
together. Those that exist divide the world society into fragmented,
particularist communities. It is within these communities that
individuals are socialised and binding loyalties forged. In exchange for

personal worth and identity, the world's populations are compartmentalised into groupings, separated by real, if invisible, humanly contrived barriers. If history is a guide, these groupings are at fundamental odds with each other about how the world should be ordered and the authoritative principles on which it should be based.

Second, and associated with the first condition, there exists no common religious or secular moral or legal code accepted by all peoples. Particular religions and ideologies have a tenacious hold on the minds and behaviour of the world populace. A host of confessional codes – Christian, Muslim, Hindu, Jewish – define alternative principles of legitimacy. These establish the final authority for political rule. In community-defined states, like Iran or Saudi Arabia, religious and secular authorities are almost indistinguishable. Community rules and norms regulate not only politics and government, but also the relations between adherents, and between them and outside groups. Similarly, ideological movements, like fascism or communism, perform functions primarily performed by communities based on religious principles. They lay down norms of conduct to ensure uniformity of behaviour. They are uneasy and uncomfortable – as often as not incompatible – with rival persuasions.

As long as the personal and collective loyalties of the world's population are bound by choice, socialisation, or coercion to one or the other of these systems of belief and differing conceptions of political and social authority, the preconditions of a global consciousness and shared sense of identity within a single, integrated world society cannot be met. Although divergent religious and secular communities need not necessarily be in perpetual competition and conflict with each other – through toleration, they can mutually prosper – efforts by any one or a group of them to impose a universal system are bound to be costly and futile exercises and an invitation to regional and global wars. The Second World War suggests the consequences of unlimited imperial expansion; the Middle Eastern and Southern Asian conflicts of the postwar era evidence the clash of irreconcilable communities bent on imposing their rule on adversaries.

Communities based on divergent religious or secular principles and ideologies have their own vision about how the world should be organised, who should rule, and on what terms. They also establish permissible boundaries for the formation of domestic political regimes, governmental institutions, and processes of decision. The objectives of the political community are also specified as well as guidelines for the scope and mechanisms of governmental authority.

At a global level, the Soviet-US conflict is not simply a matter of misperception over motives and intent, although misperceptions have certainly deepened hostility between the two states.[4] The discord is over which governmental and economic system should be the model for the global society and whose interests should prevail. Pakistani-Indian or Arab-Israeli differences are no less affected by chronic misperceptions, but these regional conflicts have deep religious roots nurtured by long centuries of mutual hostility and cumulative grievances. The Lebanese civil war is in many ways a microcosm of incipient global anarchy. Rival groups, associated with Muslim, Christian, and secular ideologies, struggle to prevail against their local adversaries. In the absence of an outside arbiter and regulator (a superpower, Israel or Syria), the civil war has become institutionalised as a way of life. These global and regional clashes – animated by incompatible visions of order and interest – create a fragmented mosaic of world society.

Not only do these ideological codes prompt communal and national clashes but they also fail to resolve differences even among adherents. Since the Renaissance, Christian unity has been shattered. For centuries Catholic–Protestant differences were a principal source of some of Europe's most internecine warfare. If they no longer spark wars between states, they still divide nations, evidenced by the persistent strife in Northern Ireland. In the Middle East, confessional differences – Shiite, Sunni, and other offshoots – pit Muslims against each other. Iran's attack on the secular values of the West and the Soviet bloc has been extended to an assault on the legitimacy of the Saudi Arabian regime's claim to be guardian of Islam's most sacred shrines. India, meanwhile, is split between Hindus and Sikhs as well as by other religiously based dissenting groups. Religious factionalism within Israel hinders the Middle East peace process since a ruling majority favouring a consistent policy on negotiations is difficult to form. Palestinians and the PLO are similarly unable to create a united front.

Most significant for Soviet prospects has been the breakup of the communist bloc. Soviet and Chinese approaches to the development of a socialist state and economy differ sharply and promise to diverge increasingly in the future. Their ideological clash is matched by equally significant sources of rivalry based on their national character and racial composition, not to mention the competition within which they are engaged for the favour of other states, most pointedly the United States, to enhance their relative positions. They also serve as different models for the development of socialist states. Chinese opposition precludes an imposed Soviet solution for the evolution of socialist regimes and economic systems. Their competition in the developing world, currently abated as each addresses its internal socioeconomic problems, is likely to grow as the resources at their disposal enlarge. The Chinese break reinforced the long-run trend, first begun by Tito's Yugoslavia after the Second World War, toward different nationally defined socialist states.

Third, the unequal distribution of wealth and productive resources around the globe divides the world society. Tensions arise at several levels. The economic disparity between the peoples of the North and South is the most obvious. In 1983 the developed North, with one billion people, approximately 20 per cent of the world's population, accounted for US $13 trillion of the global production of goods and services or 75 per cent of new wealth produced; the developing South, with 3.5 billion people or 80 per cent of the globe's population, produced only 25 per cent of new wealth.[5] This gap continues to widen. The South is organising itself into a permanent pressure group, committed to a redistribution of global wealth. The Group of 77 within the United Nations gives institutional form to these demands which are expressed along a wide continuous front, ranging from expropriation to requests for direct grants, favourable terms of trade, rescheduling of interest payments on foreign loans, debt renunciations and concessional arrangements.[6] While the West is the primary target of Third World critics, their demands now extend to the Soviet Union and the communist bloc as members of the economically favoured North.[7]

Within the developed world, economic and welfare issues which already bulk large are certain to increase in the future. Sharp differences are likely to widen and deepen not only over substantive issues concerning trade, monetary, investment, and fiscal policy, but also over the use of the West's economic and financial power to effect desirable change within the communist bloc and the developing world. The rancour within the West over a coordinated oil policy is well documented.[8] Wrangling is chronic over an increasingly wide range of trade problems, with agriculture currently topping the list, as well as over management of the international monetary system, interest rates and financial markets, and protectionist measures. Competition extends to military hardware sales within the Western alliance and to Third World states. Mounting trade surpluses submit Japan to pressures to shoulder a greater share of the burden of maintaining a liberal international economic system by opening its markets, by stimulating internal demand by competing on more favourable terms with other states (e.g. extending more leisure and greater social welfare benefits to its work force), by increasing its defence expenditures and foreign investments, and by providing more foreign assistance. As the global division of labour proceeds, newly industrialised countries (NICs) are also challenging the former hegemonial position of the United States and the older Western democracies.[9] Even Japan feels the pinch of growing competition from South Korea, Taiwan, Hong Kong, and India, all with large labour forces ready to accept lower wages and poor working conditions in their quest to wrest markets from their competitors.

Coordinating the economic policies of the liberal democracies for political purposes has proved difficult where competing interests are at stake. There is little likelihood that it will be easier in the future. The United States and Western Europe have different and competing interests in their economic dealings with the Soviet Union and the communist bloc. The quarrel between the United States and its NATO allies over the pipeline contract between West European governments and the Soviet Union in the early 1980s as well as over the transfer of technologically advanced equipment (computers, electronics, etc.) and over subsidies for agricultural sales to Eastern Europe illustrates the obstacles to developing a common Western position.[10]

In the race for markets, raw materials, investment opportunities, economic growth, and high domestic employment, the liberal democracies are in unremitting competition with themselves. No Western states or Japan can completely devolve responsibility for the economic welfare of their national societies to the vicissitudes of international competition. They are expected to use the political leverage at their disposal to bargain for economic advantage with other nations, including allies. These political imperatives impinging on Western governments place them at odds with each other. These capitalist states have evidenced remarkable resilience and enterprise in surmounting these competitive tensions in building a global economy that has produced unparalleled wealth. Past achievements do not assure future progress. The worldwide depression of the 1930s suggests otherwise. The absence of agreed goals and policies weaken the Western states in their efforts to preserve and promote a viable global economic order that undergirds their collective security and responds to the welfare and equity demands of their populations.

Soviet economic weaknesses hamper Moscow's ability to exploit Western competition. Moreover, the economic tensions within the West are paralleled by deep divisions within the communist camp. Post-Maoist China has initiated a revolutionary modernisation programme geared to greater access and closer ties with Western capitalist states. The Soviet Union is poised to move in the same direction, while attempting to maintain its economic grip on its satellites and clients and while still retaining its centralised modes of production and ownership. Whether these contradictory imperatives can be resolved is problematic. The Soviet Union, as the chapter on Southeast Asia (Chapter 6) suggests, has the incentive to moderate Vietnamese expansionist aims in order to improve its relations with the West and with ASEAN states. These economic and political incentives also impact on Hanoi. Within Eastern Europe strains are especially evident. East Germany chafes under Soviet restraints hampering its efforts to improve and strengthen its economic ties with West Germany and the European Community. Romania similarly resists incorporation into the Soviet economic sphere, paralleling its obstructionism within the Warsaw Pact. Hungary has unobtrusively geared its economy to Western needs and pursues internal policies that depart from central state practices. While the communist apparatus in Poland depends on the Soviet Union for its viability, Poland's economic future depends largely on the West. The Soviet Union and the Eastern bloc states are in competition with each other for Western favour and resources as well as for external stimulation of their sluggish economies.[11]

Fourth, the triumph of the nation-state as the principal unit for the political organisation of the global society ensures global division and disorder. Everyone is now Gaullist. Nationalism remains the dominant force in international society, and the nation-state is its political expression. There is no world political system. There is no acknowledged governmental authority with sufficient power to determine who gets what, how, when, and on what terms. The willingness of a state to adhere to widely observed international norms or to accept rules defined by others to guide its economic or political conduct depends fundamentally on its estimates of the costs and benefits, whether presumed or calculated, arising from compliance or non-compliance. These estimates will vary across states, depending on a wide range of internal and environmental considerations.

What makes the international society unique is the persistence of the nation-state as the political unit within which these calculations of power and purpose are made, however much internal decision making may be affected by regime, techno-economic resources, social organisation, or ideological factors.[12] No single state, including either superpower, can impose its will on the system and on the globe's diverse populations. Each state's claim to sovereignty and autonomy is backed by a monopoly of violence in the hands of a government which uses its power to resist external intervention and to arbitrate differences between individuals and groups within its domain. Depending on the degree of internal political and economic cohesion and centralisation within a state, governments also command national resources, as well as a panoply of coercive and non-coercive instruments, to project their will in competition with other regimes. Outcomes are rarely imposed as in Vietnam. Most are bargained or negotiated arrangements of an unstable and provisional character.

As more than one commentator has observed,[13] it is precisely this disorder of over 150 nation-states of various size and power capabilities that is a major determinant of the incipient anarchy of international society. The incentive of states to use coercive threats or force to support their claims is dictated not only by their own needs, their commitments to allies, and by the countervailing military power of rival states ready to enforce their own demands, but simply by the absence of a central authority capable of enforcing rules of behaviour on the states comprising the system. The Soviet Union has succeeded in creating an empire on its western borders. It dictates the socialist regimes of the East European states and binds them within a Soviet dominated economic system. Moscow's sway extends now to Afghanistan in Southwest Asia, to Vietnam in Southeast Asia, Cuba in the Caribbean, South Yemen in the Middle East, and Ethiopia and Angola in Africa. If measured against the distance travelled since the October Revolution, the Soviet Union has made impressive gains. Its success is less arresting if viewed against the backdrop of the world society. The piecemeal, incoherent sprawl of Soviet imperial rule suggests, ironically, that the Soviet Union's global grasp, however unlimited the sweep of its ambitions, is beyond its reach, as Afghanistan suggests. The principal obstacles to its expansion are the world society itself and the inexorable diffusion of power, particularly military force and economic and technological capabilities, within it.

MILITARY REINFORCEMENT OF GLOBAL DIVISIVENESS: DIFFUSION OF MILITARY POWER

The diffusion of military power around the globe since the Second

World War, and increasingly throughout the developing world, reinforces the nation-state as the principal unit of political organisation of the world society. The decentralisation of usable military power, however much the Soviet Union may have expanded its nuclear and conventional arsenals, also defines in general terms the limits and effectiveness of its military power or coercive diplomacy to impose its will on developing states. Viewed along several important dimensions of militarisation, as discussed below, Third World states dispose increasingly impressive military capabilities and know-how in designing, producing, and adapting weapons to their purposes. They also play key roles in deciding outcomes in interstate and intrastate conflicts and in facilitating or denying superpower access to the strategic assets under their control. Neither superpower can ignore these states as a potential hindrance or help in pursuing its aims and interests in the developing world.

Foremost among the assets of the developing states are the military capabilities they possess. More states have a greater amount and range of military destructive power in their hands than ever before. They are also capable of projecting this lethality at greater distances and with more calibrated effect than in the past. Diffusion may be measured along several dimensions: the level of absolute military expenditures (MILEX), the ratio of MILEX to GNP and to central governmental expenditures (CGE), the number of personnel under arms and their number per 1000 of population, and national arms production capacity as well as arms imports and exports. Along almost every one of these measures the developing states have registered discernible gains since the early 1970s. The rate of progress has tended to decline in the 1980s as military build-ups have approached saturation limits and as economic constraints and internal demands for welfare have limited governmental expenditures for the military. Increasing military assets have enhanced the capacity of developing states to play a larger number of roles, with greater weight and importance than in the past, in defining global and regional security arrangements.

Table 1.1 compares developed and developing states at successive two-year periods between 1973 and 1983 according to the amount of absolute spending on military forces, the ratio of MILEX to GNP and to CGE, and the number in the armed forces and the number per 1000 of population. Except for the ratio of MILEX to CGE and for the ratio of national armed forces to 1000 of population, all indicators point upward for world activity for developed and developing states. The developing states lead in the greatest percentage gains in expenditures for military forces, in percentage increases in GNP devoted to the

Table 1.1 World, developed, and developing states: comparisons by military expenditures (MILEX), MILEX/GNP, MILEX/CGE, Per Capita MILEX, armed force totals, and armed forces per 1000 of population, 1973–83

	1973	1975	1977	1979	1981	1983
Military expenditures (MILEX) (constant 1982 US $)						
World	564.9	618.9	643.8	671.7	726.6	778.9
– developed	469.7	489.7	505.9	526.2	568.3	616.3
– developing	95.3	129.2	137.8	145.6	158.3	162.6
MILEX/GNP						
World	5.7	6.0	5.7	5.6	5.8	6.1
– developed	5.8	6.0	5.7	5.6	5.8	6.2
– developing	5.4	6.2	5.8	5.6	5.7	5.8
MILEX/CGE						
World	24.1	21.8	20.5	19.5	19.0	19.2
– developed	24.5	21.6	20.6	19.5	18.9	19.4
– developing	22.5	22.2	20.2	19.5	19.1	18.4
Per capita MILEX						
World	144	151	152	153	160	166
– developed	458	470	479	491	521	557
– developing	32	42	43	44	45	45

Armed forces total (in thousands)						
World	25,580	25,960	26,125	26,878	27,864	28,355
– developed	10,484	10,320	10,365	10,448	10,634	10,827
– developing	15,094	15,640	15,760	16,330	17,230	17,528
Armed forces per 1000 of population						
World	6.5	6.4	6.2	6.1	6.1	6.1
– developed	10.2	9.9	9.8	9.8	9.8	9.8
– developing	5.2	5.1	5.0	5.0	5.0	4.9

Source: US Arms Control and Disarmament Agency, *World Military Expenditures and Arms Transfers: 1985* (Washington, DC: US Government Printing Office, 1985), p. 47. Errors due to rounding.

military, per capita military expenditures, and the number of personnel under arms. Beginning from a narrow base, percentage growth can be expected to be greater and more dramatic for developing states as they attempt to build and strengthen their military forces and as they assume the traditional role and attributes of nation-states.

What is interesting to note is the slowdown in MILEX growth rates between 1973 and 1983. In the decade 1963–73, developing countries spent, on the average, 4.94 per cent of their GNP on arms. This percentage grew slightly to 5.77 per cent on an annual average basis in the next ten years from 1973 to 1983. On the other hand, in the decade between 1973 and 1983, the MILEX to CGE ratio progressively favoured non-military expenditures as the data in Table 1.1 suggest. What these trends suggest is that for just a slight increase in the percentage of defence spending to GNP, developing states have been able to devote appreciably more resources to military purposes while increasing government spending for civilian needs. Developing states have been able to militarise to a substantial level of lethality, with more personnel under arms than ever before, while containing defence expenditures, on the average, to below 6 per cent of GNP. These same trends are reflected in the spending patterns of developed states.[14]

If the rate of growth of military expenditures and forces can be said to be increasing today at a slower rate than before, it does not necessarily follow that improvements in the arsenals of the developing states will not continue to enlarge in size and sophistication and to pose increased security problems for developed states and the superpowers. Table 1.2 identifies the number of developing states with advanced military systems since 1950. Advanced systems include supersonic aircraft, tactical missles of all types, armoured fighting vehicles, and modern warships, principally fast patrol boats with torpedo and guided missle capabilities. Dramatic increases in the number of states possessing these arms are recorded in all weapon system categories. In 1950, no developing state had either supersonic aircraft or tactical missiles; in 1985, 55 and 71 states, respectively, had one and usually several types of each system. Hand-held ground-to-air missiles, supplied to rebel forces by the United States and its allies in Afghanistan, Chad, Angola, and Nicaragua, have inflicted serious damage on Soviet or client forces. Over the same thirty-five year span, developing states also expanded their ground and naval capabilities. The Stockholm International Peace Research Institute (SIPRI) and

Table 1.2   Number of developing countries with advanced military systems

	1950	1960	1970	1980	1985
Supersonic aircraft	—	1	28	55	55
Tactical missiles	—	6	25	68	71
Armoured fighting vehicles	1	38	72	99	107
Modern warships	4	26	56	79	81

Sources: Stockholm International Peace Research Institute (SIPRI), *World Armament and Disarmament: 1978* (New York: Crane, Russak, 1978), pp. 238–53, for 1950, 1960, 1970; the International Institute for Strategic Studies (IISS), *The Military Balance: 1981–82* (London: IISS, 1981), for 1980; and *The Military Balance: 1985–86*, for 1985. IISS sources were supplemented by *Jane's Fighting Ships 1984–85* (New York: Jane's, 1984).

the International Institute for Strategic Studies (IISS) cite 107 states with advanced ground armour in 1985 in contrast to only one state in 1950, while 81 have modern naval vessels in 1985 against only four in 1950.

Table 1.3 also suggests that as these states industrialise and broaden their technological base, they also seek progressively to produce and even design their own weapons. The growth in indigenous arms production centres is as dramatic as the increase in the number of developing states with advanced weapon systems. In 1960 seven states produced 15 different types of military aircraft systems; in 1980 this number had more than doubled to 18 and the number of systems being produced more than quadrupled to 67. Over this period, 13 states produced 18 naval systems; twenty years later 25 were able to build 45 systems. The number of states capable of producing missiles rose to nine in 1980, covering 26 systems. In 1950 only one state was able to produce two types of missile systems. As for ground equipment, the story is the same but less spectacular. Six states have created ground production facilities for 17 different types of armoured systems, whereas none produced such material in 1960.

Despite these impressive strides, the developing world is still far behind the developed world in the value of arms produced. In 1983, according to a recent SIPRI study, the value of all arms produced by leading arms producers in the developing world (excluding the People's Republic of China) was slightly less than $2 billion, including indigenous and licensed production.[15] Diffusion of military

Table 1.3   Arms production in developing states

	Number of systems					
	1960		*1970*		*1980*	
Aircraft						
Fighters	1	2	3	4	6	10
Trainers (jet)	3	3	4	4	3	5
Trainers (basic)	6	7	5	6	11	13
Maritime (reconnaissance)	—	—	—	—	2	2
Transports	1	1	4	6	8	11
Aircraft (engines)	1	1	2	2	6	8
Helicopters	1	1	2	2	11	15
Avionics	—	—	—	—	3	3
Total[a]	7	15	8	24	18	67
Naval vessels						
Frigates	1	1	1	1	4	5
Corvettes	2	2	2	2	1	1
Patrol craft	8	8	13	13	20	25
Submarines	—	—	—	—	3	3
Amphibious craft	1	1	2	2	4	4
Support craft	6	6	4	4	7	7
Total[a]	13	18	15	22	25	45
Ground equipment						
Tanks	—	—	3	3	5	6
Armoured personnel carriers	—	—	1	2	5	6
Armored cars	—	—	2	2	2	2
Reconnaissance vehicles	—	—	—	—	2	2
Armoured bridgelayers	—	—	—	—	1	1
Total[a]	—	—	5	7	6	17
Missiles						
Surface-to-air	—	—	—	—	5	6
Air-to-ground	—	—	1	1	3	3
Air-to-air	1	1	2	2	5	5
Surface-to-surface	1	1	1	1	3	4
Antitank	—	—	1	1	7	8
Total[a]	1	2	5	5	9	26

Note: [a]Numbers of systems do not overlap; numbers of states frequently do.
Sources: Andrew L. Ross, *Arms Production in Developing Countries: The Continuing Proliferation of Conventional Weapons*, No. N-1615-AF, Rand Corporation Note (Santa Monica, CA: 1981), pp. 16–19. The Ross study was updated with data from the Stockholm International Peace Research Institute (SIPRI), *World Armament and Disarmament, 1974*, pp. 250–8; and *1980*, pp. 168–73 (New York: Crane, Russak, 1980). Publishers vary for *SIPRI Yearbooks*. A more comprehensive set of arms producing states (54), but grouped together in more general categories of production (i.e. ammunition, small arms, aircraft, armoured vehicles, missiles, and ships), is found in Michael Brzoska and Thomas Ohlson (eds), *Arms Production in the Third World* (London: Taylor & Francis, 1986), pp. 16–17.

production capabilities, while lagging behind other measures of militarisation, still reflects an upward bias as developing states continue to industrialise and broaden their technological and scientific infrastructures. Since 1950, the developing states (excluding China) are estimated to have produced major military systems within the four categories noted in Table 1.3 valued at almost $20 billion.

Most of the increases in the value of arms production in the developing world occurred in the decade between 1975 and 1984. During this period, both indigenous and licensed production approximately doubled from $349 million to $635 million and from $648 million to $1147 million, respectively.[16] If China were included, the value of arms production by developing states would be far greater. In excluding China from its calculations, SIPRI tends to depreciate the significance of Third World arms production. If ACDA figures for the arms imports and exports of developing states, including China, are relied upon, they suggest a higher level of effort and a gradual closing of the gap between developed and developing states over the last decade with respect to the value of arms exports.

Table 1.4, drawn from SIPRI data, lists the nine leading industrial arms producers in the developing world (excluding China) between 1981 and 1985. Israel is first, followed by India, Brazil, Taiwan, and Argentina as the top five producers. Measured in terms of Gross Domestic Product (GDP), military arms production is not large. Even in Israel, where the ratio of military production to domestic output is highest, it stood at only 2.6 per cent of GDP.[17] The economic size of the production effort is of less consequence than the gradual diffusion of military production facilities around the globe.[18] Following the pattern of leading developed states, the principal countries of the developing world are slowly broadening their control over those weapons systems important to their security interests and independence. These states possess a high degree of technical skill, reflected in India's explosion of a nuclear device in 1974 and in Brazil's and Israel's advanced aircraft and electronics industries.

What is occurring in developing states, even in those with large populations like India and Brazil where per capita income is low, is the development of highly paid and influential technocratic elites who are as talented and as competitive as their homologues in developed states. As it were, a Netherlands is emerging from India, a Belgium from China, and an Italy from Brazil. These military-industrial scientific-technical (MIST) complexes are linked to those in other developed states. They act as transmission belts for the diffusion of

Table 1.4 Rank order of the principal major weapon producing countries in the developing world, 1980–84 (in millions of constant 1975 dollars)

Country	Value
Israel	1,342
India	1,265
Brazil	566
Taiwan	562
Argentina	391
South Africa	380
South Korea	346
North Korea	265
Egypt	162

Source: Michael Brzoska and Thomas Ohlson (eds), *Arms Production in the Third World* (London: Taylor & Francis, 1986), ch. 2.

military technology. This phenomenon is particularly apparent in the growth of licensed production accords. These are increasingly preferred by developing states over direct arms purchases because they afford them not only new weapons but also the know-how to make them.[19] India assembles and produces key parts of the British-French Jaguar and French Mirage 2000; Israel has adapted Mirage technology to the Kfir. Even states which have not broken into the list of top arms producers have licences to co-produce advanced military equipment. These latter states include states like Indonesia, which recently has been granted a licence by General Dynamics to co-produce F-16s, one of the most sophisticated fighters in the world today.

The developing states are also slowly expanding their share of the world market in arms exports. Table 1.5 compares arms imports and exports of developed and developing countries over two-year intervals between 1973 and 1983. While the value of world arms exports, measured in billions of constant 1982 US dollars, was increasing by 34 per cent from $26.8 billion to $35.8 billion over this decade, developing states increased their share of arms exports in the world market from a little more than 2 per cent of the world total to over 11

Table 1.5   Value of arms deliveries: totals for the world and for developed and developing countries, 1973–83 (in billions of constant 1982 US $)

Year	Arms imports	Arms exports	Arms imports/ total imports (per cent)	Arms exports/ total exports (per cent)
World totals				
1973	26.8	26.8	2.3	2.4
1975	21.1	21.3	1.4	1.5
1977	29.0	29.1	1.7	1.8
1979	35.0	34.8	1.7	1.7
1981	38.8	38.9	1.8	1.9
1983	35.1	35.8	2.0	2.1
Developed states				
1973	6.7	26.2	0.7	3.0
1975	5.8	20.3	0.5	1.9
1977	6.3	27.9	0.5	2.3
1979	6.3	33.1	0.4	2.2
1981	7.2	35.4	0.5	2.4
1983	7.6	31.8	0.6	2.6
Developing states				
1973	20.1	0.6	8.7	0.3
1975	15.3	1.1	4.1	0.3
1977	22.7	1.2	5.4	0.3
1979	28.7	1.7	5.7	0.3
1981	31.6	3.5	5.3	0.6
1983	27.5	4.0	5.7	0.8

Source: US Arms Control and Disarmament Agency, *World Military Expenditures and Arms Transfers: 1985* (Washington, DC: US Government Printing Office, 1985), p. 89.

per cent between 1973 and 1983. During this ten-year period, the ratios of world arms imports and exports to total imports and to total exports also show a slight upward bias.

The evolution of arms imports and exports of the developed and developing world reveals a sharply contrasting pattern. Whereas the ratios of arms imports to total imports for developed states remained essentially unchanged, the developing states actually decreased the ratios of their arms imports to their total imports. This decline suggests not only the faster growth of non-military imports relative to arms exports in the developing world but also the impact of import substitution policies, reflected in higher levels of domestic arms production and licensing. At the same time, developing states (starting from a smaller base) more than doubled the ratio of their arms exports to overall exports, while the developed states increased their arms exports at a slower rate. The latter never attained the 3 per cent level of 1973. Almost a decade passed before they were able to increase their arms export ratio to 2.6 per cent of all exports in 1983.

One significant implication of these arms export figures is the multilateralisation of supply sources. Whereas the superpowers dominated the world market until the 1970s, they must now compete increasingly with suppliers from other developed and developing states. Based on ACDA figures, covering three four-year time periods between 1973 and 1983, the superpowers, together, controlled a decreasing share of the world market. Superpower shares fell from 70 per cent in 1973–76 to 60 per cent in 1977–80 and then again to 53 per cent in 1981–84. During this period, NATO countries, including France, progressively expanded their market shares from 18.1 per cent in the first period, to 21.8 per cent in the second, and to 25.6 per cent in the third. Largest gains were non-NATO and non-Warsaw Pact shares, which grew from less than one per cent of world arms exports between 1973 and 1976 to about 15 per cent between 1981 and 1984.[20] The supply of Chinese Silkworm missiles to Iran suggests how a third power can complicate superpower management of regional conflict to suit its individual or collective interests.

Two caveats should be kept in mind in assessing the prospects of Soviet (or US) use of force to promote its interests in the developing world. The aggregate figures cited above obscure major differences in regional military capabilities and the access of the Soviet Union to them. The regional chapters will discuss these differences in more detail. Notwithstanding the military assets of Soviet clients in the developing world – notably Cuba and Vietnam – there appears little evidence that the Soviet Union, alone or in league with its clients, has the resources or increasingly the incentive to impose its preferences through force on other than smaller states close to its borders, as in Eastern Europe, where historical ties are established. Where Soviet military power or assistance has been engaged in the developing world in the 1980s, Moscow has incurred heavy costs in just coping without having yet crushed indigenous opposition to client regimes (Angola, Afghanistan and Nicaragua). Apostate communist states, like China and Yugoslavia, give additional pause that even when socialist regimes are installed, they may be less than compliant.

Conversely, the capacity of developing states to resist foreign interference, as the Iranian case suggests, may be more formidable and daunting that a mere recitation of military capabilities and arms production facilities may convey. The ability of governments in the developing world to mobilise their populations, to enlist their support, to train loyal cadres (e.g. Iran's revolutionary guards), and to marshal the nation's material resources for war also diminish, and even nullify, the attractiveness of Soviet intervention.

IMPLICATIONS OF THE DIFFUSION OF MILITARY POWER: THE MULTIPLE ROLES OF DEVELOPING STATES IN DEFINING REGIONAL AND GLOBAL SECURITY

One obvious implication of the global diffusion of military power is the inability of any one state, including either superpower, to define, through the unilateral threat or direct use of military force, the global security system to its liking. The superpowers frustrate each other; counter-balance each other's nuclear arsenals; and in combination with their allies, they also roughly balance, particularly in central Europe, the conventional military power each bloc disposes. Whatever the difficulties confronted by the superpowers and their bloc partners in preserving these balances – and these are many and complex[21] – there appears no prospect that either will have a decisive military edge in the near future. Certainly neither superpower is presently capable of disarming the other's nuclear capabilities in a massive, surprise first strike without risking self-destruction. Both superpowers are also inhibited by the military resources at the disposal of developing states. Neither can determine the outcomes of conflicts (e.g. the Iran–Iraq War) or the modes of cooperation between them (e.g. ASEAN). They can certainly shape some of these patterns, most pointedly in areas where their vital interests appear to be at stake, but their influence is circumscribed – and increasingly so within the global society, although the absolute military and economic might of Moscow and Washington have, paradoxically, never been greater.

The greatest potential for uncertainty and instability in the superpower conflict would appear to arise in the developing world. Part of the explanation for this fluidity stems from three roles played by developing states as a consequence of their possession of increasingly greater usable military power. These include their ability (1) to define regional security agendas and, consequently, to influence the distribution of military capabilities and, by that token, the structure of the global security environment; (2) to decide the outcomes of interstate and intrastate conflicts; (3) to deny or grant the strategic assets under their control – military and non-military – either to the superpowers or to their clients.

Defining Regional Security Agendas

States or insurgent groups in the developing world have been the major source of armed conflict since the Second World War. The numerous wars of independence after 1945 and the decolonisation process testify to the ability of even poorly armed populations to wage successful local wars often against materially superior adversaries over long periods of time under adverse conditions. Since the Second World War, as Table 1.6 notes, 25 interstate and 32 intrastate armed conflicts have been initiated in the developing world. Over half of these in each category were begun since the middle 1960s after the decolonisation had been largely completed. The withdrawal of the European colonial powers did not produce the conditions for peace that many had expected. The period from 1965 to 1974 was particularly disruptive. Clashes between states or between factions competing for governmental power reached their highest peaks. Intrastate deaths approached almost two million, with the Vietnam War contributing the most to this total. This is also the period of three Arab-Israeli flare-ups (1967, 1970–71, 1973) and two Indian-Pakistani wars. The severity of these conflicts, measured by battlefield deaths and duration, evidences no clear pattern.

While the superpowers have been involved in some fashion in several of these wars – in southern Africa and the Middle East as well as in south, southwest, and southeast Asia – the primary sources of these armed conflicts were rooted in regional rivalries. These were insurgents seeking to create a new internal regime (e.g. Pol Pot in Cambodia) or governments attempting to enforce their claims on opponents (e.g. Syria and Egypt vs. Israel, or Iraq vs. Iran). Interstate and intrastate or civil wars were so fused in some instances that the distinction between one form of strife and another was all but effaced. The Vietnam War, the Middle East conflicts, and the Indian-Pakistani clash of 1971 illustrate the emergence of what may be viewed as zones of conflicts within which clashing regional and non-regional states and

Table 1.6   Wars in the Third World, 1945–80

Years	A. Interstate wars Number of wars initiated	Duration (months)	Battle deaths
1945–54	7	278.0	2,125,700
1955–64	3	38.1	44,230
1965–74	8	143.6	1,278.561
1975–80	7	182.4	77,500

Years	B. Intrastate wars Number of wars initiated	Duration (months)	Battle deaths
1945–54	2	49.4	1,001,000
1955–64	10	386.8	787,500
1965–74	14	510.1	1,821,626
1975–80	6	193.2	96.500

Source: Derived by Andrew Ross from data in Melvin Small and J. David Singer, *Resort to Wars: International and Civil Wars, 1816–1980* (Beverly Hills: Sage, 1982), pp. 92–9 and 229–32. See Andrew Ross, 'Dimensions of Militarization in the Third World', Occasional Paper of the Program in Arms Control, Disarmament, and International Security (Urbana: University of Illinois, 1986), pp. 17–18.

socio-political groupings – e.g. the PLO and Christian militia in Lebanon – vie for influence and dominance over a specified locale and its inhabitants. There is always the danger that the internecine conflicts within these zones will not be contained, and a superpower clash may erupt. They may escalate vertically, increasing in scope and lethality, or horizontally as conflicts spread to other regions and these become linked into an ever wider zone of hostility. The Vietnam War and successive Middle East wars exhibit these tendencies for expansion. As participants in these conflicts, the superpowers have often been prisoners of the initiatives of local rivals. There is no guarantee that Moscow and Washington will have the will and incentive to control their own competition sufficiently to establish the boundaries and intensity of these hostility zones – or have the means to do so.

Changes in the internal military power of a state – through its own efforts, through access to foreign assistance, or through shifts in regional alignment patterns – may also affect regional security relations. Depending on the scope and significance of these shifts in regional balances of power – only partly subject to superpower influence or control – perceptions of national threat can be heightened or diminished and the incentives to arm correspondingly weakened or strengthened. Whether some developing states, like Pakistan or India, will develop military nuclear programmes is a decision that lies progressively within their own technological capability.[22] As they gain increasing control over the nuclear fuel cycle through the development of their own scientific means and technical personnel, their decision to exercise a military nuclear option will depend more on political factors, including superpower pressures to restrain regional adversaries from going nuclear, than on the indigenous resources needed to develop a nuclear system. There is evidence that the Indian explosion of a nuclear device in 1974 was prompted by Indian perceptions that the superpowers could not be relied upon to establish an adequate basis for cooperation to contain Chinese political ambitions or the development of Chinese nuclear capabilities.[23] Indian fears are reinforced today by the Pakistani government's pursuit of a nuclear weapons programme which promises soon, unless arrested by strong external pressures, to add a Muslin bomb to the Christian, Communist, and Hindu bombs already exploded.[24]

Similarly, any decision of the Israeli government to break with its policy of ambiguity depends only partially on the superpowers. Since the 1960s Israel has professed that it does not have nuclear weapons and 'will not be the first to introduce them into the [Middle East] region'.[25] While there is no conclusive evidence that Israel does have nuclear weapons, there are repeated reports by informed observers of Israeli possession of an undisclosed number of nuclear devices.[26] As early as the late 1950s, Israel received technical assistance from France to build the Dimona reactor, which is purportedly capable of producing weapons grade plutonium. It also acquired French help in developing the Jericho surface-to-surface missile. Its supersonic aircraft, including F-15s and F-16s, can be fitted to carry nuclear weapons. Since the 1970s there has been extensive debate within the Israeli security community over nuclear policy.[27] Supporters of an open avowal state include such prominent figures as former Minister of Defence Moshe Dayan. The decision to go nuclear would not appear to be a technical one. Whether Israel decides to maintain or modify its current ambiguous position will depend on the evaluation of Israeli leaders of the security implications of staking Israel's future on publicly acknowledged nuclear weapons and the development of a doctrine to guide their design, deployment, and use.

Current Israeli behaviour is based on three general considerations: retention of US assistance and its implicit nuclear guarantee; containment of Soviet influence or presence in the Middle East; and the prevention of a nuclear arms race in the region that might challenge Israel's military dominance and threaten its existence.[28] A policy of ambiguity is calculated to have a deterrent effect on Arab states, without prompting potentially damaging reductions in US security commitments or stimulating US efforts to control Israeli initiatives in exchange for continued military and economic aid. There is also the fear that the Soviet Union will be induced to expand its military presence in the region by confronting Israel directly or by extending its military assistance and guarantees to its Arab clients. Finally, a nuclear arms race raises a host of new risks. Given the deeply seated animosities of regional rivals, it will be difficult to develop a stable nuclear balance. Technological asymmetries will increase pressures for preemption. The Israeli attack against Iraqi nuclear facilities in 1981 evidences the presence of these incentives. The likelihood that such weapons will fall into the hands of fanatical elements or terrorists also increases. Nuclear deterrence promises to be volatilised by the incessant domestic turmoil, religious fundamentalism, revolutionary fervour, and terrorism of Middle East politics. Superpower control over these forces, never firm and always tenuous, cannot be expected to improve in a nuclear Middle East.

The Middle East and South Asia illustrate the fragility of superpower control of events. They can shape and orient the security behaviour of regional states, but not dictate the course of their direction. While US mediation and material incentives were critical in the signing of the Camp David accord, the fact remains that both Israel and Egypt bore the final responsibility for having decided to take risks by cooperating with each other. The insurrection in West Pakistan that led to the creation of Bangladesh and to Indian military dominance in South Asia was neither initiated nor orchestrated by either superpower. Neither had much leverage over the Pakistani government whose oppressive policies instigated the rebellion, nor did either play a decisive role in India's decision to intervene and assert its hegemonic position. Neither superpower, moreover, can be said to have instigated the Iran–Iraq War, nor can either claim to have any decisive control over the outcome of the struggle. While superpower assistance enhanced the military prowess of these regional foes, the decision of when, where, how, and why these forces would be used was left essentially to local initiative.

Deciding the Outcomes of Interstate and Intrastate Wars

Once begun, developing states, acting often independently of the superpowers, have had a major impact on the outcomes of interstate and intrastate wars.[29] In Southeast Asia, Vietnam has established a hegemonial position over Laos and Cambodia. The border war with China which ended in a stalemate also suggests that Vietnamese forces remain formidable adversaries. No other military establishment since the Second World War has fought two major powers – China and the United States – with results as satisfying for its policy aims.

In the Middle East, neither superpower fully controls its clients despite large amounts of military and economic assistance sent to the region. Egypt launched its attack on Israel in 1973 after having first ordered Soviet military personnel to depart a year earlier. Israel's attack on the Arab states in 1967 and its massive victory, significantly achieved with French fighter aircraft, was in no way dictated by Washington. It was launched in spite of counsels of restraint emanating from the West and over the direct warning of French President Charles de Gaulle, whose government was Israel's major arms supplier.[30] The Lebanese invasion in 1982 was also launched on Israeli initiative without US consultation or approval.

Neither Iraq nor Iran has been responsive to the threats or blandishments of either superpower although the Persian Gulf War is threatening to the latters' interests. Even covert US and European arms shipments to Iran have not softened the tough stance adopted by the Khomeini regime in rejecting Western influence of any kind. An Iranian victory would strengthen Muslim fundamentalism throughout the Gulf region, potentially destabilising to governments allied with the West (Saudi Arabia, Kuwait, Jordan) and potentially disturbing the Kremlin's control of its large Muslim population.

In South Asia, India has retained its preponderant military status by solidifying Pakistan's division through its support for the independence of Bangladesh and through its defeat of Pakistani forces. Its superiority may well be threatened by a Pakistani decision to go nuclear, but it is not likely, in the immediate future, that Pakistan will be able to counter-balance Indian military capabilities. The Indian nuclear programme is well advanced and is poised for militarisation if Islamabad should cross the nuclear threshold. While it cannot be denied that Indian military power has been significantly assisted by concessionary arms sales from the Soviet Union and that its explosion of a nuclear device in 1974 was aided by access to fissionable materials and know-how from Canada and the United States, much of its progress in these areas was due to its own resources. Were superpower assistance to be abruptly stopped – an unlikely prospect given India's attractiveness as a strategic partner – India would still be the dominant power in South Asia, a tribute to its present and future military strength and to its success on the battlefield.[31] And in Africa, Cuban troops proved decisive in Ethiopia's defeat over Somalia in the Ogaden, a Soviet coup partially offset by Somalia's switch to the West. South African troops, meanwhile, freely operate against the military forces of Angola and Mozambique and frustrate the United Nations.

The armed forces of the developing states have been especially significant in deciding who wins civil wars. Cuban troops ensured the victory of the MPLA in Angola and continue to maintain that regime in power, but they, in turn, as surrogates for Soviet power, are checked by Jonas Savimbi's UNITA, based on strong tribal ties opposed to the Luanda regime. Tanzanian troops were also responsible for the overthrow of Idi Amin's regime in Uganda. Chadian troops under Hissène Habré, supplied and supported by France and the United States, have not only frustrated Libya's determination to install its clients in Djamena but, worse, drove Qaddafi's forces from much of the Aozou strip in 1987. On the other hand, Libya has been a disruptive force in Sudan and Tunisia and is one of the principal supporters of the Polisario in their armed revolt against Moroccan rule in the western Sahara. In turn, Morocco saved the Mobutu regime in Zaire when its troops were transported in US military carriers to put down rebel forces, an operation partially financed by Saudi Arabia.

Middle East policies have been fundamentally shaped by the military interventions of indigenous states in the domestic affairs of their neighbours. Lebanon's civil war elicited Israeli and Syrian interventions. Parts of the country remain under the sway of both countries. The split within the PLO is as much attributable to Israeli pressures as to Syrian support for an anti-Arafat faction within the organisation. Pakistani military assistance to Jordan was also partially responsible for the defeat of Palestinian insurgents in 1970. Adding to confused alignments is Syria's support for Iran in its war against Iraq, a move which is partly aimed at toppling the Hussein regime, although Syria and Iraq are ruled by rival factions of the Baath Socialist Party.

In Asia, third state invervention has been crucial in determining the outcomes of internal strife. Vietnam rules through client regimes in Cambodia and Laos. India is implicitly the guarantor of the Bangladesh regime. Assistance from Pakistan and other Muslim states is also critical for the Afghanistan insurrection against the Soviet supported government in Kabul.

Developing States as Strategic Assets

The increasing military power of developing states makes them attractive allies of other states. Cuba and Syria are valued Soviet clients as are Israel and Egypt within the Western camp. Indian hegemony in South Asia buttresses Soviet interests, while the Islamabad government of President Zia-ul-Haq is relied upon by Washington, in exchange for military assistance, to pressure the Soviet Union in Afghanistan by aiding rebel forces. Israel's military prowess has made it the dominant power in the Middle East.

Developing states also afford third states a wide array of assets useful for their strategic purposes. These include access to their sea lanes, airspace, and territory; arms sales and retransfers; military personnel as advisors or as intervention forces; and financial aid. They are also go-betweens where formal contacts may be disrupted. Algeria and Saudi Arabia have at different times played intermediary roles in negotiating between Iran and the United States over hostages and arms. The superpower global struggle depends on their access to foreign bases; over-flight, landing, and refuelling privileges; supply depots; command, control, and communication sites; and repair and rest facilities for their forces.

Developing states are also conduits for arms to other states, not infrequently against the wishes and over the opposition of a superpower. Israel and Brazil are important suppliers. Brazil has supplied armoured planes to Gabon, Uruguay, and Chile, and its armoured vehicles have been sold to Iraq in support of its war against Iran. Israel has also supplied arms to Iran and is a major supplier to governments in Central America, providing a mechanism by which to circumvent internal opposition within the United States to military assistance in support of authoritarian regimes or rebel forces in the region. Vietnam is also alleged to have sent captured stores of US equipment to Iran to replenish its stocks of US-supplied arms. Libya also delivered French Mirage fighters to Egypt in support of the 1973 Yom Kippur assault despite contractual assurances signed with France forbidding such retransfers.

Third World states have both military manpower and, in the case of oil-rich Middle East states, financial resources to help other governments in distress or to assist insurgency movements. Israeli military advisors were once welcome throughout Black Africa. Pakistani troops have served or are serving in Jordan, Abu Dhabi, and Saudi Arabia. As Muslims, they blend easily with the local populations in their countries. Well disciplined and trained, they afford other Muslim states with a relatively inexpensive means to upgrade the military forces at their disposal. They perform a variety of roles, ranging from flying advanced aircraft in Abu Dhabi to serving as an elite guard for the Saudi Arabian regime. The Saudi, Libyan, and Iranian governments have also reportedly furnished funds to a variety of governments and insurrectionist forces. Riyadh financed the purchase of arms for Egypt (before Camp David), Jordan, Sudan, North Yemen, Morocco, and Tunisia and assisted the Moroccan intervention in Shaba. Libya and Iran under Ayatollah Khomeini have proven to be disruptive forces throughout the Middle East and North Africa. Their revolutionary brand of Islamic fundamentalism challenges moderate Arab elements aligned with the United States and the West. Their support of terrorist activities, along with that of Syria, is a chronic source of disruption.

Implications of a Decentralised International System and the Diffusion of Military Power

The world society is at sixes and sevens, split by racial, communal, ideological, and national differences. The diffusions of military force throughout the international system since the Second World War has reinforced these divisions. The principal beneficiaries, but by no means the sole gainers, of this diffusion process have been nation-states and the governments in control of these states. They exercise a monopoly of violence and possess presumptive authority over the territories that are under their rule. International movements, based on religion or ideology, are mediated through the nation-state system, as the cases of Iran and Cuba, respectively, suggest. Successful insurgencies in the developing world against colonialism and, later, against indigenous governments share the characteristic of presenting themselves as champions of national self-determination, whether, respectively, the claim of unacceptable domination was being made directly against a foreign occupier or against a discredited local government whose survival depended on external assistance. Algeria illustrates the former; Ethiopia and Nicaragua, the latter. The drive toward national autonomy is a key component of the global political society and the critical determinant of its ethnocentric orientation.

Second, the diffusion of military force and organised means of violence among states and insurgent groups precludes any one state from coercively imposing its will and preferences on the global system. Countervailing force is too great an obstacle. Alignments between a superpower and a client state further raise the stakes of a confronta-tion with a developing state, evidenced in the limits confronted by US policy makers both in the Korean and Vietnamese wars or by the Soviet Union in its dealings with Israel. Even attempts by a superpower to control directly the behaviour of a regional state, where the superpower opponent is absent or peripheral to a contest, is not without unacceptable cost and escalatory risks, measured not only in terms of expended military assets but also in terms of elite and public willingness to maintain an operation. US military intervention in Lebanon had no appreciable impact on ending the civil war or on stabilising Middle East politics. Lives were lost – over 250 marines in a terrorist attack – and confidence in US commitments suffered. US influence with local factions, which must play some role in any peaceful solution to the strife, eroded. The Soviet Union faces similar problems in Afghanistan and Angola where local insurgencies have proven costly and intractable. While the Soviet regime does not confront either allied or domestic resistance to its interventions, it must still pay a material and political cost of engaging in these conflicts where positive benefits of military intervention are arguably less impressive than the material resources and diplomatic assets expended in maintaining them.

Third, the decentralisation of, and the diffusion of power within, the international system fundamentally inhibit Soviet expansionism at a regional level. In East and Southeast Asia, the Soviet Union's principal instrument, Vietnam, is counter-balanced by the ASEAN states, by a modernising China, and by an economically powerful and military proficient Japan. North Korean forces are offset by South Korean and United States military capabilities. Soviet security ties with India are based on calculations of mutual interest. They may not be a reliable measure of Soviet penetration. Soviet presence does not equate with influence. There is increasing evidence of Indian autarchy in producing its own weapons and in multiplying the sources of its arms supplies while New Delhi progressively orients its trade and investment policies toward the West to meet its economic needs.

Soviet opportunities in the Middle East appear circumscribed. Syria is Moscow's principal window on the Middle East. Iraq, its former major ally, is preoccupied with its war with Iran and needs assistance from the West as well as from Moscow to avoid defeat. Revolutionary Iran is as much opposed to the Soviet Union as to the United States. Arab divisiveness, the Israeli-Egyptian peace treaty, and Israeli military predominance defines Soviet weakness in the region, something that is very likely to continue throughout this century.

While the Soviet Union has established beachheads in Africa and the Western Hemisphere, it is likely to be essentially confined to them in the near future. It is likely to retain its hold on its Ethiopian enclave, but its prospects elsewhere for expansion are uncertain. It may hold Angola, but only at a high cost. Zimbabwe and Mozambique depend on Western assistance. Other African states offer little in the way of strategic assets. The upheaval in South Africa is a target of opportunity. Whether it is exploitable depends more on Western political vision, deft diplomacy, economic assistance, and reaction to Black demands than on Soviet military capabilities and armed assistance.

Cuba, on the other hand, is an important strategic asset – useful in advancing Soviet interests in Africa and on the southern tier of the United States. Whether it will add Nicaragua to its clients remains an open question. The outcome of the Nicaraguan revolution is still in doubt. Moscow confronts a dilemma in Central America. If it increases its assistance and commitment to the Sandinista regime in Nicaragua, it risks overextending itself in areas peripheral to its core interests and in a region of preponderant US and Western influence. If it fails to support Managua, its credibility with Marxist allies elsewhere is undermined. Even if the Sandinista regime prevails, with or without Soviet aid, its destabilising impact on Central America is potentially containable. Meanwhile, the remainder of Latin America is essentially outside the Soviet Union's sphere of interest.

Fourth, the diffusion of military power in an unstable developing world creates incentives for implicit and explicit Soviet-American cooperation. These incentives, while not negligible, essentially derive from the global competition of the superpowers and are limited in the extent of their possible exploitation by the conflict. Both superpowers have an incentive to define the rules of armed intervention and assistance to clients and to restrain their dependencies from taking initiatives that might increase the risks of escalation and a superpower confrontation. Both also have an incentive to maintain their nuclear preeminence and to discourage nuclear proliferation in the developing world. Acting on these incentives cannot be expected to transform the superpower conflict. Failing to respond to these problems threatens superpower control over their global competition to their mutual disadvantage and at the cost of what reliability derives from the currently fragmented and refracted global and regional security arrangements that provisionally regulate state behaviour.

The succeeding chapter traces the general evolution of Soviet policy toward developing countries up to the 1980s; the chapters of Part II explore Soviet penetration of the developing world from a regional perspective. They provide a worm's-eye view of the limits and prospects of Soviet power to complement the bird's-eye survey attempted in this chapter. The concluding chapters of Part III review the perception of Soviet leaders and analysts of the mixed experience of the Soviet Union in the Third World and of the constraints on its behaviour as well as the implications of both for Western policy.

Notes

1. For a discussion of the notion of a world society within an anarchical political system composed of rival nation-states, see Hedley Bull, 'Society and Anarchy in International Relations', in Herbert Butterfield and Martin Wright (eds.), *Diplomatic Investigations*, (Cambridge: Harvard University Press, 1966), pp. 35–50. The notion of world society presented here is drawn from Bull's argument that there exists a global society, composed of the world's population, whose diverse aims and interests are increasingly interdependent. The US-Soviet conflict is a characteristic feature of contemporary global society but only one of its constituent elements. As this chapter argues, it is not always a key determinant of cooperation and conflict among members of the world society. Both superpowers are compelled to adapt to the demands arising from their environment and, accordingly, to define their conflict in ways compatible with these imperatives.

2. The superpower conflict as a global struggle has been chronicled by a rich literature which need not be repeated here. The perspective of a struggle to define the political order of the world community is adopted from George Modelski, 'The Theory of Long Cycles and US Strategic

Policy', in Robert E. Harkavy and Edward A. Kolodziej (eds.), *American Security Policy and Policy-Making* (Lexington, MA: Lexington Books, 1982), pp. 3–20.

3. The paradigm adopted in this chapter to explain Soviet behaviour is essentially that of a 'rational actor' who, weighing the costs and benefits of alternative courses of action, chooses at the margin to maximise gains. It does not assume, however, that this process of decision making is unaffected by resource constraints, competitive aims, or domestic political and organisational factors that skew perceptions and priorities. See Graham Allison, *Essence of Decision* (Boston: Little, Brown, 1971) for an extended analysis of alternative decisional paradigms to explain behaviour.

4. See Louis J. Halle, *The Cold War As History* (New York: Harper, 1976). He develops the misperception argument. The Modelski perspective appears more relevant to an explanation of hegemonic struggle between the superpowers (see note 2).

5. US Arms Control and Disarmament Agency, *World Military Expenditures and Arms Transfers: 1985* (Washington, DC: US Government Printing Office, 1985), p. 47. Hereafter cited as WMEAT.

6. See Stephen A. Krasner, *Structural Conflict: The Third World against Global Liberalism* (Berkeley, LA: University of California Press, 1985) for a discussion of the Third World attack on the Western-dominated trade and monetary system.

7. Elizabeth Kridl Valkenier, 'East–West Competition in the Third World', in Marshall D. Schulman (ed.), *East–West Tensions in the Third World* (New York: Norton, 1986), pp. 158–180.

8. Robert Lieber, *Will Europe Fight for Oil: Energy Relations in the Atlantic Area* (New York: Praeger, 1983).

9. Robert O. Keohane, *After Hegemony: Cooperation and Discord in the World Political Economy* (Princeton: Princeton University Press, 1984).

10. See, for example, Stephen Woolcock, *Western Policies on East–West Trade* (London: Routledge & Kegan Paul, 1982); Zbigniew M. Fallenbuchl, 'East–West Economic Relations since the Beginning of the 1970s', in Roger E. Kanet (ed.), *Soviet Foreign Policy and East–West Relations* (New York: Pergamon, 1982), pp. 77–93.

11. For a discussion of tensions within the Warsaw Pact, see, for example, the articles appearing in Ingmar Oldberg (ed.), *Unity and Conflict in the Warsaw Pact* (Stockholm: Swedish National Defence Research Institute, 1982).

12. See note 3.

13. Kenneth Waltz, *A Theory of International Politics* (Reading, MA: Addison-Wesley, 1979), and, earlier, Herbert Butterfield, *History and Human Relations* (London: Collins, 1951).

14. For comparison, see ACDA, *WMEAT*, 1985, p. 47 and ACDA, *WMEAT*, 1963–73, p. 14.

15. Michael Brzoska and Thomas Ohlson (eds.), *Arms Production in the Third World* (London: Taylor and Francis, 1986), pp. 291–304.

16. Ibid., p. 8.

17. For 1983, Andrew Ross calculated the ratios of military production of major systems to gross domestic product for seven of the nine leading arms producers: Argentina (0.2); Brazil (0.1); Egypt (0.4); India (0.3); Israel (2.6); South Korea (0.1); and South Africa (0.2). Percentages for North Korea and Taiwan are not available. Andrew L. Ross, 'Militarization in the Third World', Table 4, Armed Forces and *Society*, vol. 13, no. 4, summer, 1987, p. 571. Note that Brzoska and Ohlson (see note 15) treat Israel as a developing state.

18. In addition to the recent Brzoska and Ohlson volume, cited in note 15, there are several well-documented studies of arms production facilities and MIST complexes in the developing world: Stephanie G. Neuman (ed.), *Defense Planning in Less Industrialized States* (Lexington, MA: Lexington Books, 1984); 'International Stratification and Third World Military Industries', *International Organization*, vol. 38, no. 1, 1984, pp. 167–97; James E. Katz (ed.), *Arms Production in Developing Countries: An Analysis of Decision Making* (Lexington, MA: Lexington Books, 1984), especially the article by Neuman, pp. 15–38; and Milton Leitenberg and Nicole Ball (eds.), *The Structure of the Defense Industry* (London: Croom Helm, 1982).

19. The interest of developing states in licensed arrangements is suggested in the listing of such accords in Appendix I of Brzoska and Ohlson, pp. 291–304 (see note 15).

20. ACDA, *WMEAT*, 1985, p. 43.

21. For a discussion of the issues, see John M. Collins, *US-Soviet Military Balance, 1980–1985* (Washington, DC: Pergamon-Brassey, 1985); International Institute for Strategic Studies, *The Military Balance, 1985–1986* (London: IISS, 1985), pp. 182–94; NATO, *NATO and Warsaw Pact: Force Comparisons* (Brussels: NATO Information Service, 1984); and William Baugh, 'The American-Soviet Strategic Balance', in Patrick Morgan and Edward A. Kolodziej (eds.), *International Security and Arms Control: A Reference Guide to Theory and Practice* (Westport, CN: Greenwood Press, forthcoming). The conventional balance in Europe between the two blocs may, arguably, not be as tilted in favour of the Warsaw Pact as many believe. See Jonathan Dean, *Watershed in Europe* (Lexington, MA: Lexington Books, 1987). The cautious assessment of the International Institute for Strategic Studies (IISS) is also relevant: 'our conclusion remains that the conventional military balance is still such to make general military aggression a highly risky undertaking for either side ... The consequences for an attacker would still be quite unpredictable and the risks, particular of nuclear escalation, remain incalculable.' IISS, *Military Balance: 1986–87* (London: 1986), p. 225.

22. This is a generally shared conclusion of two leading experts in nuclear proliferation: Leonard S. Spector, *Nuclear Proliferation Today* (New York: Vintage, 1985); and Lewis A. Dunn, *Controlling the Bomb* (New Haven, CT: Yale University Press, 1982).

23. See R. V. R. Chandrasekhara Rao, 'Strategic Thinking in India in the 1970s: Prospects for the 1980s', in Robert O'Neill and D. M. Horner (eds.), *New Directions in Strategic Thinking* (London: Allen & Unwin, 1981), pp. 153–68.

24   For a discussion of the Pakistani nuclear programme, see Spector, *Nuclear Proliferation*, especially pp. 70–110.
25.   Quoted in Louis René Beres (ed.), *Security or Armageddon* (Lexington, MA: Lexington Books, 1986), p. 191.
26.   See Robert E. Harkavy, *Spectre of a Middle Eastern Holocaust: The Strategic and Diplomatic Implications of the Israeli Nuclear Weapons Program* (Denver, CO: University of Denver Monograph Series in World Affairs, 1977); *Times* (London), 5 October 1986; and Spector, *Nuclear Proliferation*, pp. 117–48.
27.   For example, see Shai Feldman, *Israeli Nuclear Deterrence: A Strategy for the 1980s* (New York: Columbia University Press, 1982); and Slomo Aronson, 'The Nuclear Dimension of the Arab-Israeli Conflict: The Case of the Yom Kippur War', *Jerusalem Journal of International Relations*, vol. 7, no. 1–2, 1984, pp. 107–42.
28.   See Avner Yaniv, 'Israeli's Conventional Deterrence: A Re-Appraisal', in Beres (ed.), *Security or Armageddon*, pp. 45–60 (see note 25).
29.   An elaboration of these points is found in Edward A. Kolodziej and Robert E. Harkavy, *Security Policies of Developing Countries* (Lexington, MA: Lexington Books, 1982), pp. 331–65.
30.   Michael Bar-Zohar, *Suez Ultra-Secret* (Paris: Fayard, 1964).
31.   See Raju G. C. Thomas, 'India's Nuclear and Space Programs: Defense or Development?', *World Politics*, vol. 38, no. 2, January 1986, pp. 315–42.

2 The Evolution of Soviet Policy Toward the Developing World From Stalin to Brezhnev
Roger E. Kanet

INTRODUCTION

The substantial 'successes' registered by the Soviets in the Third World in the 1970s that led some observers to see a qualitative shift in the relative positions of the USSR and the United States have not led to comparable gains in the 1980s. In fact, a number of Soviet clients now face serious internal challenges.

This chapter will examine the role of Soviet policy toward the Third World as part of the efforts of the Soviet Union to influence the development of the international system in ways favourable to its interests. Special emphasis will be given to factors that have been most important in determining Soviet policy, including the influence of Third World countries and the relevance of the Third World to overall Soviet foreign policy.

During the Stalin years the Soviets paid little attention to developments in the colonial areas. Only with the shift in policy under Khrushchev did they attempt to play the role of a global power. During this period, however, Soviet aspirations exceeded capabilities, especially in the area of military force. Not until after 1970, when the Soviets had reached relative nuclear parity with the United States and had acquired substantial power projection capabilities, were they able to extend effectively their involvement throughout the Third World. However, their accomplishments depended primarily on their ability to provide military/security support to Third World regimes facing internal or external security threats. By the end of the Brezhnev era the Soviets had become a global power – though one that relied heavily on a single, military, instrument for its superpower status.

The most important factor that has motivated Soviet policy in the Third World has been the global competition for influence with the United States – whether the immediate objective was to eliminate perceived security threats, as in the Middle East since the mid-1950s, or to weaken US and Western positions of influence more distant from Soviet territory. Other objectives have included increased competition with China for influence, justification of the claim of the Soviet system to represent a revolutionary future, and economic development through improved trading arrangements.

Soviet involvement in the Third World has depended heavily on developments over which Soviet leaders have exercised little or no control, such as the overthrow of the Batista regime in Cuba, the ongoing Arab-Israeli conflict, and the collapse of the Portuguese dictatorship; moreover the establishment of close ties with a number of developing countries has resulted in the latters' ability to exercise at least some influence over the evolution of Soviet policy.

Even prior to Brezhnev's death in late 1982, the Soviets had begun to reassess their policy toward the Third World. Concern was voiced about the drain on Soviet resources and about the bleak prospects for 'progress' in many client states. Although the reassessment has expanded since Brezhnev's death, there is no evidence to support the argument that the Soviets are about to withdraw from competition in the Third World.

Despite the expansion of Soviet capabilities over the past thirty years and the new role that the USSR has been able to play in international affairs, its power and influence remained limited at the time of Brezhnev's death. First, its position in the Third World depended heavily on the coincidence of Soviet interests with those of client states – especially in security affairs. Just as important was the inability of the Soviets to respond to the economic development needs of Third World states. Given the state of the Soviet domestic economy, this limitation is not likely to be overcome in the foreseeable future. Although the ability of the USSR to act globally is still quite limited, the availability of extensive military capabilities has enabled the USSR to challenge Western interests throughout the world in ways that would have been unthinkable twenty years ago.

THE SOVIET UNION AND THE DEVELOPING WORLD

At the beginning of the 1980s many US observers maintained that the Soviet Union had achieved such major successes in its policies in the Third World[1] during the preceding decade as to mark a qualitative shift in the relative positions of the USSR and the United States in their competition for influence throughout Asia, Africa, and Latin America. A listing of only the most important Soviet 'gains' in the Third World included the unification of Vietnam under a Soviet-backed communist regime; the establishment of Soviet-oriented communist governments in Laos and Kampuchea; the creation of self-proclaimed Marxist-Leninist states (in most cases with at least some Soviet military support) in Angola, Mozambique, Ethiopia, South Yemen, and Afghanistan; and the increasing influence that Cuba and other Soviet dependents were able to play in the Non-Aligned Movement.[2]

From the Soviet perspective these accomplishments were but evidence of the 'changing international balance of forces' and resulted from both the growing nuclear and conventional military capabilities of the USSR and the insoluble conflicts between the interests of the industrialised West and the developing countries.[3]

The Soviet successes of the 1970s, however, have not been followed by comparable gains in the 1980s. In fact, from the perspective of Moscow the roster of 'losses', disappointments, and increased costs suffered since the beginning of the decade are arresting. In the Middle East serious setbacks had occurred already in the 1970s, when the Soviets lost their major ally, Egypt, and were, for all practical purposes, frozen out of the peace process and forced to focus their efforts increasingly on peripheral actors such as South Yemen, the PLO, and Libya. Although the Soviets welcomed the collapse of the US position in Iran when the Shah was overthrown, the implacable hostility of the Khomeini regime toward the USSR has prevented the latter from benefiting substantially from past US failures.[4] In Sub-Saharan Africa the dramatic Soviet gains of the 1970s in countries such as Angola and Ethiopia have been followed by a significant decline in Soviet relations – even with some of its closest Marxist-Leninist allies.[5]

In Latin America and the Caribbean the Soviet expectations that the Sandinista victory in Nicaragua and the leftward shift in Jamaica and Grenada would be precursors of the further undermining of US influence in the region have yet to be fulfilled – in part because of the US intervention in Grenada and changes in the political and military situation in El Salvador.[6] After seven years of direct military intervention in Afghanistan the Soviets still find themselves unable to consolidate their dominant position or to turn over political or military control to the local communists.[7] By early 1988 they had agreed to abandon their efforts to impose a solution on the country. In Southeast Asia the ongoing efforts of their Vietnamese allies to pacify Kampuchea remain a major impediment to renewed Soviet efforts to normalise relations with China, although the expansion of Soviet military facilities in Vietnam is an important component of the growing military strength of the USSR in East Asia and the Western Pacific. Yet, Soviet political influence in the Far East has not matched the dramatic extension of its military power.

In outlining the negative side of Soviet relations with the Third World since the beginning of the decade, Harry Gelman has stated: 'there is evidence of a variety of Soviet disappointments and frustrations in the Third World, particularly over the last five years and in some cases going much further back, and there is also evidence that at least a somewhat more sour and chastened mood has evolved in Soviet thinking in response to this experience.'[8]

However, what we have noted to this point concerning the problems and disappointments that the Soviets have experienced with their Third World policy in recent years deals with only one side of the relationship. It is essential to recall, as well, the shift that has occurred over the past three decades in the Soviet role in the Third World. The power base from which Mikhail Gorbachev and his colleagues in the Soviet leadership operate is immeasurably stronger than that which Nikita Krushchev inherited from Stalin in 1953 or that which Leonid Brezhnev took over from Khrushchev eleven years later. The Soviet Union in the late 1980s is a global power with interests that stretch across most of the developing world. It has also managed to create a power projection capability – primarily of a military nature – that enables it to affect developments in regions where, only a short time ago, Soviet behaviour was irrelevant to the outcome of events.

In this overview chapter we shall be interested especially in examining the crucial role that Soviet policy toward the Third World played in Soviet efforts to influence the development of the international system in competition with the United States in the years up to the death of Brezhnev in 1982. As a part of that examination we shall trace the evolution of Soviet policy toward the Third World, with special consideration given to the factors that appear to have been most important in determing Soviet policy, of the relevance of the Third World to overall Soviet policy, and of the influence that Third World allies/clients have apparently exercised on the evolution of Soviet policy.

SOVIET POLICY FROM STALIN TO BREZHNEV

Soviet policy in the developing world in the years since the Second World War can be divided into at least three sub-periods, based on Soviet capabilities and behaviour.[9] During the first of these periods, the last eight years of Stalin's rule in Moscow, the Soviets were preoccupied with reconstruction of their war ravaged economy and consolidation of their control over areas that had come under the domination of the Red Army in 1945. With only few exceptions little attention was given to the colonial areas of the world that were soon to evolve into what we now refer to as the Third World.

Stalin's death in 1953 and the coming to power of Nikita Khrushchev ushered in a second period in Soviet policy toward the Third World that was characterised by a growing awareness of the importance of the developing world and an almost frantic effort to break out of the political isolation that had characterised the late Stalin era. In a significant attempt to benefit from the growing conflicts between the West and national liberation movements or recently independent states in the Third World, the Soviets offered economic and political assistance and attempted to establish a wide range of political ties with Third World leaders. During this period, which extended through the 1960s, a major weakness in Soviet relations with developing countries stemmed from their inability to project military power much beyond the confines of the territory that they dominated. This meant an inability to provide effective support to allies or clients – as in the Middle East wars of 1956 and 1967 or when Patrice Lumumba requested support against separatist elements in the Congo (now Zaire) in 1960. In addition, however, the limited economic base from which the Soviets competed with the United States represented another long-term weakness.

A third period in Soviet relations with the Third World began about 1970, at the time when the Soviets had reached relative strategic nuclear parity with the United States and had created the military infrastructure that would permit them to use military power effectively in the attempt to determine the outcome of events outside Soviet dominated territory. Throughout the 1970s military power, including military support to clients, became the single most important element in the Soviet drive to expand its role throughout the Third World. The introduction of Soviet (and Cuban) military support into local conflicts in Angola and Ethiopia were decisive to their initial outcomes. Soviet arms transfers to countries such as Syria and Libya were also essential to the efforts of the leaders of those countries to accomplish their own international objectives.

During the three periods in Soviet foreign policy the USSR has gone from the position of a predominantly regional power with regional interests and limited capabilities to that of a global superpower. Almost immediately after the end of the Second World War the Soviet Union and the United States were involved in a struggle for influence that focused initially on Europe. Within a few years the Soviet Union managed to create along its Western borders a zone of dependent states which it effectively dominated; in Asia communist parties allied to the Soviet Union came to power in North Korea, China, and North Vietnam prior to Stalin's death. Despite the increase in influence in the regions bordering Soviet territory and the growth of Soviet military power during the decade after the Second World War, when Stalin died in 1953 the Soviet Union was still substantially inferior to the United States in its ability to influence events in the international system. It remained a regional power whose major international competitor commanded far superior resources and, with its allies, dominated the international system politically, militarily, and economically. Postwar Soviet expansion had played a prominent role in stimulating the creation of a US-centered system of alliances in Europe and Asia oriented toward containing the further extension of Soviet power and influence. As a result of this alliance system, US military forces were stationed around virtually the entire periphery of the Soviet-dominated communist world, from Germany in the west, through the Middle East, to Korea and Japan in the east.

Not only had the United States greatly expanded its political, economic, and military role in international affairs in the years since the Second World War, but its British and French allies remained global powers with interests and capabilities scattered throughout most of Asia and Africa. With the exception of its political and economic contacts with other recently established communist states, the Soviet Union remained isolated from the remainder of the international community. Relations with newly independent states in Asia were virtually non-existent, in large part as a result of Stalin's refusal to view the leaders of these new countries as more than mere puppets of Western imperialism. In spite of the improvement in its relative military position in the postwar period, the USSR remained politically isolated and militarily and economically inferior.

Rather than reducing the security concerns of the Soviet leadership, postwar developments had, in fact, fed the traditional Russian paranoia concerning security. The Soviet Union remained, in the eyes of its leaders, a beleaguered bastion of socialism surrounded by a hostile – and militarily superior – capitalist world that was dominated by the United States. Stalin's primary approach to the problem of security had followed the long-standing Russian policy of expansion and consolidation of control over regions adjacent to Soviet territory. But limited capabilities, the eventual reaction of the West, and the internal demands of the Soviet system itself had prevented the Soviet Union from expanding its zone of control beyond those territories occupied by the Red Army at the conclusion of the Second World War, although the communist victory in China in 1949 appeared to extend Soviet influence over the largest country in Asia. In the years immediately following the war the Soviets had focused their efforts mainly on consolidating their position in Eastern Europe, although even here they continued to face resistance, as developments in the years 1953–56 indicated.[10]

Among the initial changes introduced by the post-Stalin leadership at the beginning of the second period in postwar Soviet policy were those concerning the overall policy of the Soviet state toward the outside world. In Europe efforts were made to reestablish relations with Yugoslavia and to reduce the level of tension in East–West relations. 'Peaceful coexistence' replaced the 'two-camp' thesis as the foundation of Soviet relations with the members of the NATO alliance in part, at least, to reduce the isolation of the Soviet Union and as a prelude to an eventual Western recognition of the existing political realities in postwar East-Central Europe. In its policies toward the developing world the new Soviet leadership introduced comparable innovations. No longer were countries such as India and Egypt viewed as mere appendages of Western imperialism, but rather as independent states whose interests overlapped in many areas with those of the Soviet Union and the other members of the redefined 'socialist community'.[11]

Under Khrushchev's leadership the Soviets initiated their attempt to expand their overall role in international affairs. In the Middle East, for example, the beginnings of Soviet military and economic support in Afghanistan, Egypt, and later in other radical Arab states, effectively challenged Western dominance and reduced Soviet isolation in that region of strategic significance for Soviet security. The wave of decolonisation that swept over Africa in the decade after Ghanaian independence in 1957 found the Soviets willing to provide assistance to a variety of new African states. The attempted deployment of missiles in Cuba in the fall of 1962 was probably the high point of Khrushchev's efforts to challenge the dominant position of the United States in the international system; however, it also indicated most dramatically the continuing inferiority of the position from which the Soviet Union was operating.

In the early 1960s the Soviet Union still lacked the economic, military, and political capabilities necessary to compete effectively in most regions of the world. The United States commanded substantial strategic superiority, and this superiority forced the Soviets to move especially cautiously – and even to retreat – in situations of direct conflict such as the Cuban Missile Crisis. Moreover, the absence of an effective Soviet capability to project conventional military power outside its own area of control meant that Soviet leaders had great difficulty in supporting clients or allies in areas outside the core region of Soviet power. In 1956, for example, it was primarily US opposition to the joint British-French-Israeli attack of Egypt – not Soviet threats to intervene – that brought the Suez War to a conclusion. In 1960 the closing of the airport in Leopoldville by UN officials in the Congo effectively cut off Soviet support for the forces of Patrice Lumumba. In the mid- to late-1960s Soviet-oriented political leaders in Ghana and Mali were overthrown with virtual impunity. In sum, in this period the Soviet Union was unable to provide the type of effective support that would permit it to stabilise throughout the Third World regimes which it viewed as friendly and generally supportive of Soviet interests.

The Khrushchev era in Soviet politics witnessed a major break from the past in terms of the expansion of Soviet interests and the attempt of the USSR to play a greater role in the international system. However, the results of this change in orientation were mixed. Even though the Soviet Union had begun to close the military gap between itself and the United States and had established the foundations for the development of relations with a number of Third World countries – and was, therefore, no longer isolated – these relations remained fragile and provided the Soviets with few concrete returns on their investment of support. Moreover, the Soviet empire itself was beset with serious internal fissures. The Albanians and Chinese had already withdrawn completely from the Soviet-oriented 'Socialist Community'; in addition, the Romanians successfully resisted Soviet pressures to follow a joint line in foreign affairs, and other East European countries were experimenting with their domestic political and economic systems. The accession of Cuba to the Soviet network of states and the reduction of the Western monopoly of contacts with the developing states, though clearly beneficial to Soviet interests, did not balance these losses.

In late 1964, as the Brezhnev leadership team came to power in the Soviet Union, the position of the USSR in the non-communist international system was stronger than it had been a decade earlier. Still, the USSR remained primarily a regional power. Its interests and, in some cases, its commitments had expanded beyond the confines of Stalin's empire, but inadequate capabilities severely limited its ability to affect significantly events in other areas of the world.

Even prior to Khrushchev's overthrow several developments had occurred that would prove to have a major impact on the growth of the role of the Soviet Union in the international system in the 1970s. The first of these which would prove to be of great importance for the expansion of the Soviet role in international affairs related to the collapse of the European colonial empires and the 'radicalisation' of many of the newly independent states. Conflicts of interest between the industrial West and the less developed countries provided the Soviet leadership with possibilities to expand their involvement in countries or regions that earlier were closed to them. Related to this was the reduction of Western power – and involvement – in much of the Third World, as evidenced by the British withdrawal from the regions 'east of Suez'.

More important was the initiation by the early 1960s – reinforced by the débâcle of the Cuban Missile Crisis – of a programme of military build-up in both the nuclear and conventional areas and the Soviet military expansion into areas that until that time were outside the range of Soviet military capabilities. Initially the Soviets concentrated on developing their nuclear strategic capabilities, in order to offset the superiority of the United States that still existed at the beginning of the 1960s. During the early years of that decade efforts were made to assure the survivability of Soviet nuclear forces with construction of reinforced missile silos, placement of missiles at sea, and development of a first-generation missile defense system. By the mid-1960s the Soviets were making progress in increasing their own strike capabilities and at the end of the decade had reached something approximating strategic parity with the United States.[12] Since the beginning of the 1970s, therefore, the strategic nuclear power of the United States has been largely neutralised by countervailing Soviet strategic capabilities.

Besides the expansion of Soviet strategic capabilities begun in the Khrushchev era and continued until the present, the Soviets have also built up their conventional military power – both in Europe and throughout Asia and Africa and even Latin America – to the point where they are now capable of projecting power throughout a substantial portion of the world. Among the most important aspects of this development has been the construction of both an ocean-going navy and a worldwide merchant fleet that also engages in military-related logistical support and reconnaissance. Although the development of the Soviet fleet became most visible only after Khrushchev's fall from power, the decision to develop a surface fleet was made prior to the Cuban Missile Crisis.[13] By the 1970s the Soviets had created a naval capability that permitted them to play an important military role in various international crisis situations, such as the 1971 Indo-Pakistani War, the Middle East War of 1973, and other conflicts.[14]

Moreover, they had also created a network of agreements with a number of developing countries that gave them access to the naval facilities necessary for the maintenance of this new ocean-going fleet. The production of long-range transport aircraft and the signing of agreements for overflight rights and the use of landing facilities provided an important complement to the expanded naval power. Yet, Soviet power projection capabilities are generally less fully developed than those of the United States and are probably limited in effectiveness to providing support for established clients.[15]

Another important aspect of the expansion of the Soviet Union as a global power in the post-1970 period has been the continuing commitment of the Soviet leadership to the extension of the Soviet role in world affairs. In the mid-1970s, for example, the Soviet Minister of Defence enunciated the broadened view of the role of the Soviet military when he stated that 'the historic function of the Soviet armed forces is not restricted merely to their function in defending our Motherland and the other socialist countries' and that aggression by the Western 'imperialist' states should be resisted 'in whatever distant region of our planet' it occurs.[16] The changed correlation of forces in international affairs, the Soviets have argued, permitted the USSR to provide support to the just cause of national liberation and to 'progressive' regimes threatened with intervention by the Western imperialists or their reactionary 'stooges' in the developing world. No longer was the capitalist West able to act with impunity in undermining progressive regimes or in supporting revolutionary movements.

Finally, at least since the overthrow of the government of Salvador Allende in Chile in 1973, the Soviets have expanded their support for 'national liberation movements' and various terrorist organisations. Even though their ideological orientation and immediate goals may not coincide with many of these organisations, the Soviets have apparently decided that support for terrorism undermines the long-term interests of pro-Western states in the Third World and of the West itself.[17]

Since the beginning of the 1970s the Soviet leadership has continued to view Europe and East Asia as areas of crucial significance to its security and has, therefore, pursued efforts to expand the USSR's military capabilities *vis-à-vis* both NATO and the People's Republic of China, especially by deploying a new generation of intermediate-range nuclear missiles. At the same time, however, Soviet policy toward the West has been oriented toward reducing the tensions that characterised relations during the 1950s and 1960s. The *détente* policy of the 1970s fit well with the USSR's overall drive to expand its worldwide role, since part of its purpose was to reduce the likelihood of Western – especially American – response to the extension of Soviet involvement throughout the Third World. The Soviets hoped to be able to convince Western leaders that improvements in direct bilateral relations between East and West were far more important for the latter than developments in other regions of the world. They expected that the leaders of the Western alliance system would be unwilling to risk the benefits of *détente* – in particular economic benefits for countries that were suffering from the effects of 'stagflation' – by attempting to counter Soviet activities elsewhere in the world.

In many respects this Soviet objective benefited from events in the Third World over which the Soviets themselves exercised only minimal influence. First of all, the continuing drive toward independence in the developing world and the inability of moderate governments in many developing countries to deal effectively with the problems of economic backwardness and political instability combined to bring to power throughout portions of Asia, Africa, and the Western Hemisphere a group of governments more strongly anti-capitalist and anti-Western than their predecessors. This provided the Soviets and their Cuban and East European allies with opportunities to gain access to – if not always influence over – leaders in a substantial number of developing states. At the same time the position of the United States and its Western allies deteriorated throughout the Third World.

Associated with the relative change of position of the Soviet Union and the West in developing countries during the 1970s was the unwillingness or inability of the West, including the United States, to pursue a coherent course of action in its policies. The US defeat in

Vietnam, the Watergate scandal, and the exposure of various CIA operations all contributed to an environment in the mid-1970s that made it virtually impossible for Washington to initiate an effective response to Soviet activities in the Third World. Moreover, given the political environment of *détente* and the apparent conviction of some US leaders that the period of US-Soviet conflict characteristic of the Cold War had come to an end, the political atmosphere in the United States was not conducive to checking Soviet attempts to expand their international role by taking advantage of conflict situations throughout the Third World. In both Angola in 1975–76 and in Ethiopia two years later the Soviets assumed correctly that they would be able to intervene without incurring an effective US counteraction, since the United States did not have the will to challenge the expansion of Soviet involvement in regions then considered far from the centres of primary US interest.

In the Third World itself the Soviets indicated during the 1970s that the political and military foundations that they had laid during the prior decade, or so, provided them with the capabilities to project power to support outcomes deemed favourable to their own interests. In Angola, Ethiopia, and Southeast Asia, for example, Soviet (and Cuban) support was essential in either bringing to power or consolidating regimes that were friendly toward and dependent on the USSR. By the middle of the 1970s the Soviet Union had become a state with both global interests and global capabilities. In Angola and again in Ethiopia it demonstrated the capability of providing allies with significant military assistance and proved that this assistance could be adequate to change the local balance of power in favour of the recipients of Soviet support. In return, the Soviets acquired access to naval and air facilities that are useful to them in potential conflicts with the West.[18]

Since the early 1970s the Soviets have continued to provide substantial support to political movements or countries of potential importance to their strategic and global interests, despite what seems to be a preference for supporting 'progressive' regimes and movements. Although an upsurge of Soviet involvement in Sub-Saharan Africa occurred in the mid-1970s, Soviet interest is still concentrated heavily in the arc of countries that border the southern flank of the USSR. Here the Soviet goal has remained the reduction of Western influence and military capabilities and the concomitant expansion of the military and political capabilities of the Soviet state. This has meant that the Soviets have continued to provide military and political support to such countries as Iraq, Syria, and South Yemen. In several cases they have signed treaties of friendship and cooperation with important South Asian, Middle Eastern, and African countries, for example, Iraq and India. In fact, during the 1970s they also increased their efforts to improve relations with countries formally allied with the West, such as Turkey and Iran (prior to the overthrow of the Shah) by offering economic assistance and even military hardware as a means of reducing these countries' dependence on their Western allies – in particular the United States. Another important element in Soviet policy has been the search for access to both naval and airport facilities that would enable them to expand the reach of their military capabilities.

From the initial establishment of contacts with Third World states more than thirty years ago, the Soviets have relied heavily on the provision of economic and military assistance as means of developing and consolidating relations.[19] In general the terms of Soviet assistance are favourable when compared with commercial loans available to emerging nations on the international market, though the Soviets offer virtually no non-repayable grants, and all aid is provided in the form of credits for the purchase of Soviet goods and equipment. Soviet trade with Asia and Africa has grown rapidly as well, though an important aspect of this trade has been the degree to which it has been related to the provision of economic assistance. With relatively few exceptions (e.g. the purchase of rubber from Malaysia and grain from Argentina) trade has resulted from agreements between the Soviet leaders and their Afro-Asian counterparts which include the commitment of Soviet economic and technical assistance. Examples of this type of agreement have been those with Egypt and India which called for the Soviet Union to provide capital equipment on the basis of long-term credits. These loans were to be repaid with the products of the recipient country over a period of twelve years at an interest rate of 2.0–2.5 per cent. Such agreements have been especially attractive to those countries which have had problems obtaining the convertible currency necessary to purchase on the world market machinery and equipment needed for economic development projects.

By the end of the 1970s, then, the relative position of the two major power blocs in the Third World had changed markedly. The collapse of the Western colonial empires and the ensuing rise of numerous anti-Western regimes in the developing world, Western military retrenchment, and various other developments resulted in the contraction of the Western military presence and of Western political influence throughout most of Asia and Africa. At the same time the Soviets were able to establish a network of economic, political, and military relationships that permitted them for the first time in their history to play the role of a global power with worldwide interests and the capabilities to pursue many of those interests effectively. The change in the relative position of the Soviet Union in the international political system stemmed in part from the continued build-up of Soviet military power and the willingness and ability of the Soviet leadership to take advantage of the conflicts between the less developed states and the major Western powers.[20] Already in the 1970s the Soviets were able to employ their newly developed military power – including an ocean-going fleet and long-range transport aircraft – in conjunction with access to port and air facilities in order to support distant and dispersed political and strategic goals.

By the beginning of the present decade the Soviet Union had become a true superpower with the ability to influence developments in areas far from Soviet territory. Although the primary means available to them in their attempts to accomplish their short- and long-term objectives throughout the Third World has been the provision of various forms of military support, that support has been accompanied by a wide range of other Soviet activities — relations with revolutionary movements and political parties, modest amounts of economic assistance, political support in various international forums, and a vast assortment of propaganda activities.

Yet, as will be discussed in more detail below and in the remaining chapters of this study, even while they increased their ability to project power and to extend their influence in important regions of the world, the Soviets faced the growth of countervailing forces that continue to limit their effectiveness in accomplishing their overall objective of reshaping the international system. Their new clients were, for the most part, among the weakest and most backward of the developing countries. Moreover, increased Soviet involvement in several regions of the Third World acted as a stimulus to other Third World states to improve their relations with the West.

THE PLACE OF THE THIRD WORLD IN SOVIET POLICY

Before concluding the review of Soviet policy in the Third World up to the death of Brezhnev, we will attempt to respond to the questions posed at the beginning of this chapter concerning the factors that influence Soviet policy toward the developing countries, including the needs and demands of the developing countries themselves, and the significance of the Third World in overall Soviet policy. Ever since the first efforts under Khrushchev to establish a major presence in the developing world, the primary Soviet objective has been directly related to the global competition with the United States. As we have already noted, the initial immediate target was in countries along the southern borders of the Soviet state where the United States in the mid-1950s was in the process of creating an alliance system to contain the Soviet Union. The presence of US military facilities in Iran, Iraq, Pakistan, and Turkey and the efforts to incorporate into the Baghdad Pact (later CENTO) the other major countries of the Middle East represented from the perspective of Moscow a potential threat to the long-term security interests of the USSR. The primary Soviet objective in this region over the past thirty years has been the loosening or destruction of the ties that bound the states of the region to the United States, and the West in general, and the eventual removal of US military power from the area.

Elsewhere in the Third World, even in regions of significantly less importance for Soviet security interests *vis-à-vis* the United States and the West, the global competition with the United States has also been of crucial importance in determining Soviet behaviour. In both Sub-Saharan Africa and in Latin America, Soviet policy has been closely associated with efforts to undermine Western positions of influence, as in West and Central Africa in the early 1960s and, more recently, in southern Africa. In addition, since the break in relations with the People's Republic of China a quarter of a century ago, competition for influence with China in the Third World has also played a role in influencing Soviet policy. This has been most evident in South and Southeast Asia, where the Soviets have committed themselves to supporting countries such as India and Vietnam as a means of 'containing' Chinese influence.

For the Soviet leadership the success of their policy in the Third World is viewed as likely to bring with it several important benefits. First of all, it would reduce the overall military and economic strength of the West by depriving the United States and its allies of military facilities and sources of important industrial raw materials. Conversely, as we have already seen, the acquisition of overseas basing facilities by the Soviet Union itself provides the capacity to respond to the security needs of client states and to monitor the military activities of the United States in regions as far from Soviet territory as the South Atlantic and the Southwest Pacific.

In addition, ever since the Bolshevik Revolution in 1917, Soviet leaders have justified their claim to rule on the basis of the inevitable march of history and on the success of the revolutionary process throughout the world. The extension of communist rule into Eastern Europe and Asia in the 1940s, it was claimed, was evidence of this revolutionary process. The creation of Marxist-Leninist regimes in the Third World in the 1970s and the conflicts between other developing states and the West, the Soviets have argued, provide evidence of the shifting 'correlation of forces' in international affairs and of the continuing success of the revolutionary process in the long-term struggle with capitalism. In short, revolutionary 'successes' in the developing world have been used, in part, as justifications for the claims of the Soviet leadership to maintain their dominant position.

Once the Soviets have succeeded in establishing close ties with individual countries in the Third World, the internal requirements of maintaining those ties has become an operative factor in influencing Soviet behaviour. For example, the lessons learned by the Soviets in their relations with African leaders such as Kwame Nkrumah, Modibo Keita, and Sékou Touré in the late 1960s have influenced Soviet policies in Africa since the mid-1970s. First of all, they recognise the inherent instability of politics in most African states and the drawbacks of basing their position primarily on cordial relations with individual leaders alone. Thus, since the late 1960s they have strongly encouraged client states – e.g. Egypt under Nasser, Angola, Ethiopia – to 'institutionalise the revolution' by establishing cadre parties modeled on the Communist Party of the Soviet Union. In conjunction with the Cubans and the East Germans, they have also emphasised the creation of domestic security forces to strengthen the position of radical regimes. Finally, the creation of a network of basing facilities provides them with the capability of providing security support to client regimes threatened by either internal or foreign opposition. Thus, as the Soviets have succeeded in breaking out of the isolation of the Stalin era and in establishing close ties with a number of developing states, the objective of solidifying relationships and of protecting client states has become an important factor in determining their policies.

Before proceeding to a discussion of the impact of the policies of client states on Soviet policy, it is important to note that there is evidence of the growing importance of economic factors in Soviet relations with the Third World. During the late 1970s and early 1980s the sale of armaments in the Third World for hard currency covered the substantial deficit in Soviet trade on the world market. Increasingly, Soviet economic relations with some developing countries have been based on economic, rather than primarily political, criteria – as evidenced by Soviet grain imports from Argentina and Brazil, and the substantial credits provided to Morocco to expand the latter's ability to produce phosphates for the Soviet market. However, overall the Soviet Union remains only a marginal actor in the international economy; for only a very few countries, such as Cuba and Vietnam, does it serve as a major source of development assistance or as a significant market for exports.

However, despite the apparent increase in importance of economic factors in Soviet relations with the developing countries, the primary factor movitating Soviet behaviour over the past thirty years has been the global competition with the United States. During the 1970s the Third World became the focal point for that competition for several reasons. First, the nuclear stalemate and the possibility of direct Soviet-US conflict resulting in nuclear war precluded a frontal challenge to the United States in Europe. Moreover, by the mid-1970s it was clear to decision makers in Moscow that the United States was not likely to respond to increased Soviet involvement in areas of only secondary or tertiary concern to the United States – e.g. Angola, the Horn of Africa, Southeast Asia. Added to this was the fact that the United States and its European allies were committed in the mid-1970s to efforts to improve bilateral East–West relations in Europe. Thus, they were not likely to risk the emerging *détente* relationship over disputes about Soviet involvement in the Third World. Finally, developments within the Third World itself – the collapse of the Portuguese colonial empire, the overthrow of the emperor in Ethiopia, and serious political instability in other countries – provided opportunities for Soviet intervention now made possible by the expansion of Soviet military capabilities over the prior decade or so.

To this point we have tended to discuss Soviet policy in the Third World primarily from the perspective of Moscow – with primary emphasis placed on Soviet objectives, Soviet policy, and Soviet capabilities. Yet, the evolution of Soviet policy over time has depended heavily on developments in the Third World and on the objectives and behaviour of individual developing countries. Although the Soviets have created the general outlines of an approach to the developing world, their actual policy initiatives have depended primarily on events over which they exercised little or no control (e.g.

the overthrow of the emperor in Ethiopia or the collapse of the Portuguese dictatorship). In other words, the policy of the Soviet Union has been largely reactive and has responded to some of the opportunities provided it. Over time the successes, failures, and actual evolution of Soviet policy have been influenced by the goals, interests, and concerns of Third World partner or client states.

Since the regional chapters of this book will detail this aspect of the Soviet-Third World relationship, it is sufficient at this point merely to note some of the examples of the impact of Third World actors on Soviet policy. First, it should be noted that in virtually every case where the Soviets have managed to establish a medium- or long-term relationship with developing countries, this relationship depends heavily on the Soviet willingness and ability to respond to the interests and concerns of the developing states. Of greatest important over the course of the past thirty years has been the Soviet ability to provide a wide range of developing countries (or revolutionary movements) with military and security support. This was true in the case of Egypt under Nasser and of Somalia prior to 1977; it remains true in Cuba, Angola and in Vietnam today.

However, as has been evident in a number of cases, the security demands of the recipient of Soviet support may well increase. The Soviets are then faced with the prospect of increasing their support, as they did during the 'war of attrition' in Egypt in the late 1960s and, more recently, in Syria after the Israeli military victory of 1982, when Soviet forces were brought in to man air defence systems. Although heightened Soviet direct involvement may bring with it other benefits (e.g. access to military bases in Egypt), it also increases the prospects for direct confrontation with the United States. As the security demands of the client state increase, it is likely that the interests of the USSR and its client may diverge. Then the Soviets are faced with the prospect either of continuing to expand their military involvement or of denying the requests of the client and risking the relationship that they had worked to establish. This has occurred on at least three occasions in the past decade or so: in Egypt, where the policies and demands of the new government of Anwar Sadat after 1971 increasingly conflicted with Soviet policy; in Somalia, where the Soviets were unable to control a client and, moreover, where they saw greater long-term advantages in backing Ethiopia; and, most recently, in Mozambique, where their unwillingness to increase internal security support and to meet economic needs resulted in Mozambique's negotiating a security arrangement with South Africa and its diplomatic tilt towards the West.

Elsewhere one finds other examples of the impact of the policy objectives of Third World states on the evolution of Soviet policy. This has been especially evident in the Soviet relationship with India which, in many respects, is at the centre of Soviet policy in the non-communist developing world. This relationship, which, unlike Soviet involvement with some other Third World states, is not based on a coincidence of revolutionary ideological objectives, has been by far the strongest and most stable over the past three decades. It is founded, to a substantial degree, on a coincidence of security and political interests of the two states (especially concerning possible Chinese expansion in Asia and on the role of the United States and its major regional ally, Pakistan, in the subcontinent). Yet the demands of the relationship have constrained Soviet efforts to regularise relations with Pakistan (in the early 1970s) and increasingly result in India's ability to extract from the USSR very favourable terms for the purchase of sophisticated armaments.

Despite the central role that India plays in overall Soviet policy in the Third World, the Soviets find themselves in a situation in which their long-term relevance for India's interests and concerns is likely to wane. As the threat to Indian security posed by both China and Pakistan has lessened and India's overall economic performance has expanded, the Soviets have found themselves in a weakened bargaining position in their relations with India. The Indian economy requires little that is readily available from the Soviet Union; in fact, India now runs a substantial balance-of-trade surplus in its bilateral 'barter' trade with the USSR. Moreover, the Indian government is able, because of improvements in its hard currency balance-of-trade situation, to purchase weapons on the world market. These developments have resulted in the reduction of the overall relevance of the USSR for the long-term interests of India. The recent Soviet willingness to provide India with the most sophisticated weapons (Mig-29 aircraft that were not yet in production in the USSR) on very favourable terms suggests evidence of a Soviet recognition of their need to find ways to enhance their continuing relevance to India's needs.

Overall it is important to recognise that Soviet policy in the Third World has not been carried out in a vacuum. It has represented Soviet responses to explicit opportunities offered it by developing countries – or to constraints placed on its behaviour, in part at least by developing countries. As we shall see below in the discussion of Soviet policy since the death of Brezhnev (Chapter 15), the Soviets are well aware of recent changes in the Third World environments to which their policy must respond and of the constraints that continue to limit their ability to restructure the international system.

THE BREZHNEV LEGACY IN SOVIET-THIRD WORLD POLICY

When Brezhnev died in autumn of 1982 Soviet policy toward the Third World had already entered a period of reassessment. In a number of countries with which the Soviets maintained close ties, insurgencies undermined internal stability and required the continued provision of Soviet (as well as Cuban and East European) security support.[21] Moreover, the Reagan administration had already initiated efforts to counter what many of its members viewed as the unchallenged expansion of Soviet involvement in and domination over areas of strategic importance for the long-term interests of the United States and its allies. Finally, the Soviet invasion of Afghanistan in late 1979 had prompted widespread condemnation among Third World states and had tarnished the 'anti-imperialist' image that the Soviets had so assiduously cultivated. By the 1980s Soviet analysts had already begun to question the optimism of the prior decade concerning likely developments in the Third World.[22] As we shall see in some detail below (Chapter 15), in the brief period since Brezhnev's death this reassessment has resulted in a downplaying of the central position acquired in the 1970s of the Third World in overall Soviet policy.

Soviet activism in the Third World in the latter stages of the Brezhnev era had resulted in large part from a coincidence of several favourable factors already discussed above: the achievement of strategic nuclear parity; the growth of Soviet power-projection capabilities; the opportunities presented to the USSR by the collapse of the Portuguese empire in Africa; demands for socioeconomic reforms in the Third World; the radicalisation of several developing states; and the malaise that engulfed the United States in the wake of Vietnam and Watergate. The Soviets took advantage of these factors to extend significantly their involvement in various Third World conflict situations where their ability to provide military support was important in the successful acquisition or retention of power by their new-found clients. This was all part of the much heralded 'changing international correlation of forces' in favour of socialism and the

Soviet Union which was referred to in virtually all Soviet assessments of global developments in the late 1970s.[23]

As a result of their support for revolutionary movements and governments, the Soviets obtained some important military advantages through access to military facilities in strategically significant regions of Southeast Asia, Africa, and the Middle East. However, most of their new clients were small, weak, and dependent upon continued Soviet support for their very existence. While this weakness represented an asset for the Soviet's ability to exert influence and even control, it also meant that these countries soon became a substantial drain on Soviet resources. Even prior to the death of Brezhnev, Soviet commentators and analysts began to recognise that the benefits that the USSR had gained from their 'successes' in the Third World were counter-balanced, in part at least, by a new series of problems – all of which have become even more evident under Brezhnev's successors.

The first of these problems derived from the growing cost of supporting clients. A group of US analysts, has estimated that the costs of Soviet empire – including subsidies to Eastern Europe and the growing subsidies to Cuba and Vietnam, plus the outlays in places like Ethiopia and Afghanistan – had reached somewhere between $35 billion and $46 billion annually by 1980.[24] It is essential to recall that the growing costs of Soviet overseas commitments occurred precisely at the time that the Soviet economy had begun to suffer from falling economic growth rates.

In addition to the concerns about the economic drain on the Soviet economy resulting from growing commitments to Third World clients, Soviet analysts have recognised the fact that the successes of national liberation movements in coming to power in the 1970s have not been matched by successful efforts to create viable political-economic systems. In most of these countries economic production has fallen off since the mid-1970s, and most of the governments are faced by continuing indigenous challenges to their authority (in part, as in Nicaragua, Afghanistan, and Angola, supported from the outside). As recent Western surveys of Soviet literature on the Third World have demonstrated, the Soviets have been quite frank in recognising the difficulties facing the vanguard parties that have come to power with Soviet assistance.[25]

A third set of problems facing the Soviets, in part as a result of their Third World 'successes' of the 1970s, derived from the deterioration of their relations with the United States. The US grain embargo, for example, was a direct response to Soviet military intervention in

Afghanistan, and the policies of the new Reagan administration were strongly influenced by what was viewed as virtually unrestricted Soviet aggression in various Third World areas.

Despite Soviet concerns about the cost of their involvement in the Third World and about the weakness and instability of most of their major Third World clients, there was no major shift in actual Soviet behaviour prior to Brezhnev's death – nor is there evidence that Gorbachev and his associates are likely to initiate a policy of wholesale withdrawal from prior commitments. As will be evident in the following regional studies, although the Soviets refused to provide the economic and security backing required by the embattled regime of President Machel of Mozambique and his successor, elsewhere they have continued to extend substantial new support to establish Third World clients and allies.

Overall the post-Brezhnev leadership of the USSR has continued the policies toward most Third World clients that were initiated under Brezhnev. If anything, the costs of supporting established clients (such as Cuba, Angola, and Vietnam) and of maintaining ties with important allies (such as India) have risen. Although the desire to reduce costs has been voiced increasingly, the immediate demands of retaining and consolidating the Soviet positions in the Third World have overridden this desire. Although they have been unwilling to make major new commitments, they have fulfilled and even expanded commitments made earlier, as in Angola and Cuba.

They have also increased their efforts to improve relations with large capitalist states in the Third World. Their continued cultivation of relations with India is an example of this aspect of their policy, as have been their attempts to expand relations with countries such as Brazil and Argentina, even when those countries were ruled by the military. Yet the problem that the Soviets face as they attempt to court these countries results from the relative lack of economic resources with which to compete with the West. In the 1970s they were able to capitalise on their major strength – the ability to provide security support – as they established close ties with countries in Asia, Africa, and the Middle East. As they attempt to expand relations with the large, basically stable, Third World states, the overall weakness of their economy represents a major drawback. Not only do they lack the investment capital and the technology sought by these countries, but increasingly they are in competition with them for export markets in the West. Thus, prospects for Soviet success in this area are not at all clear.

Despite the expansion of Soviet capabilities and the new role that the USSR has been able to play in international affairs, its power and influence were still limited at the time of Brezhnev's death in late 1982. While the Soviet Union had succeeded in breaking out of the international isolation of the late Stalin years and had increased its regional influence and its ability to project power, relative to the countervailing power that it confronted throughout the world, its successes remained quite limited. The United States and its major allies remained far more influential than the USSR throughout most of the Third World. This was especially true in the economic realm for most of the regionally important Third World states. Moreover, as will be discussed in more detail in Chapter 15, internal demands for socioeconomic and political reform within the USSR and the continued need for access to Western trade and technology as a stimulus to the domestic economy are likely to result in policies in the near term that emphasise consolidation rather than further expansion.

In the regional chapters that follow these themes will be developed as they relate to Soviet policy toward specific areas of the Third World. Moreover, we shall return to them in the concluding section of the book when we examine developments in Soviet policy since Brezhnev's death.

Notes

1. For lack of a better alternative, the term 'Third World' is used here to refer to all non-communist countries of Asia, Africa, and Latin America except Japan, South Africa, and Israel. The author is well aware of the lack of precision of the term and that it includes countries with a wide range of political and economic characteristics – rapidly industrialising states of East Asia and Latin America, the rich oil-producing states, countries making only modest progress in expanding their economies, and those that are, in fact, regressing. The terms 'developing countries' and 'developing world' are also used here interchangeably with 'Third World'.
2. See William M. LeoGrande, 'Evolution of the Nonaligned Movement', *Problems of Communism*, vol. 29, no. 1, 1980, pp. 35–52. See also Mark N. Katz, 'Anti-Soviet Insurgencies: Growing Trend or Passing Phase', in Roger E. Kanet (ed.), *The Soviet Union, Eastern Europe and the Developing States* (Cambridge: Cambridge University Press, 1987).
3. See, for example, Sh. Sanakoyev, 'The World Today: Problem of the Correlation of Forces', *International Affairs* (Moscow), no. 11,

November 1974, pp. 40–50; for a Western assessment of the Soviet concept see Michael J. Deane, 'The Correlation of World Forces', *Orbis*, vol. 20, no. 3, 1976, pp. 625–37.

4. See, for example, Alvin Z. Rubinstein, *Soviet Policy toward Turkey, Iran, and Afghanistan* (New York: Praeger, 1982); Muriel Atkin, 'Soviet Influence in Contemporary Iran', in Walter Laqueur (ed.), *The Pattern of Soviet Conduct in the Third World* (New York: Praeger, 1983), pp. 109–33. See also the regional chapters of the present study for evidence supporting the assessment presented here.

5. For a recent discussion of Soviet policy in Africa, see Daniel R. Kempton and Roger E. Kanet, 'Soviet Policy in Africa: Prospects and Problems for Model and Ally Strategies', in Jane Shapiro Zacek (ed.), *The Gorbachev Generation*, vol. 2, *Major Foreign Policy Issues Facing the New Leadership* (New York: Paragon Books, 1988).

6. See, for example, Jiri Valenta and Herbert J. Ellison (eds), *Grenada and Soviet/Cuban Policy: Internal Crisis and U.S./OECS Intervention* (Boulder, CO: Westview, 1986); Cole Blasier, *The Giant's Rival: The USSR in Latin America* (Pittsburgh: University of Pittsburgh Press, 1983); and Robert S. Leiken, *Soviet Strategy in Latin America*, Washington Papers, No. 93 (New York: Praeger, 1982).

7. See Henry S. Bradsher, *Afghanistan and the Soviet Union*, 2nd edn (Durham, NC: Duke University Press, 1986).

8. Harry Gelman, *The Soviet Union in the Third World: A Retrospective Overview and Prognosis* (Santa Monica, CA: Rand/UCLA Center for the Study of Soviet International Behavior, Occasional Paper OPS-006, March 1986), p. 3.

9. For a similar periodisation of Soviet policy in the Third World based on capabilities and behaviour see the excellent recent study by Rajan Menon entitled *Soviet Power and the Third World* (New Haven/London: Yale University Press, 1986), pp. 1–18. Soviet policy toward the Third World since the Second World War can also be divided into periods based on stated Soviet perceptions and policy statements. The resulting 'periods' differ slightly from those presented here.

10. See Zbigniew Brzezinski, *Game Plan: How to Conduct the US–Soviet Contest* (New York: Atlantic Monthly Press, 1986).

11. For a discussion of Soviet policy in this period see Roger E. Kanet, 'Soviet Attitudes Toward Developing Countries Since Stalin', in Roger E. Kanet (ed.), *The Soviet Union and the Developing Nations* (Baltimore, MD: Johns Hopkins, 1972), pp. 26ff.

12. For a discussion of these points see Carl G. Jacobsen, *Soviet Strategic Initiatives: Challenge and Response* (New York: Praeger, 1979), pp. 1–8.

13. See Norman Polmar, *Soviet Naval Power: Challenge for the 1970s*, revised edn (New York: Crane, Russak, for National Strategy Information Center, 1974), pp. 40–45.

14. For a number of studies of the use of the Soviet fleet in international conflict situations see Michael MccGwire, Ken Booth, and John McDonnell (eds), *Soviet Naval Policy: Objectives and Constraints* (New York: Praeger, 1975); Michael MccGwire and John McDonnell (eds),

Soviet Naval Influence: Domestic and Foreign Dimensions (New York: Praeger, 1977); Bradford Dismukes and James M. McConnell (eds), *Soviet Naval Diplomacy* (New York: Pergamon, 1979); and Bruce W. Watson and Susan M. Watson (eds), *The Soviet Navy: Strengths and Liabilities* (Boulder, CO: Westview, 1986). For an excellent analysis of the political role of Soviet military power see Stephen S. Kaplan *et al.*, *Diplomacy of Power: Soviet Armed Forces as a Political Instrument* (Washington, DC: Brookings Institution, 1981).

15. For a discussion of the new Soviet capabilities see Jacobsen, *Soviet Strategic Initiatives*, especially pp. 51–72 (see note 12). For a reasoned argument that one must be careful not to exaggerate the facilities that have been made available to the Soviets, see Richard Remnek's appendix in Dismukes and McConnell (eds), *Soviet Naval Diplomacy* (see note 14). See, also, Menon, *Soviet Power*, especially pp, 90–128, concerning the limitations that still exist in Soviet power projection capabilities. See also Francis Fukuyama, *Soviet Civil-Military Relations and the Power Projection Mission* (Santa Monica, CA: Rand Corporation, 1987), especially pp, 30–49.

16. Andrei Grechko, 'The Leading Role of the CPSU in Building the Army of a Developed Socialist State', *Problemy istorii KPSS* (May 1974), translated in *Strategic Review*, vol. 3, no. 1, 1975, pp. 88–93.

17. For a brief recent overview of the place of support for international terror in Soviet foreign policy see Samuel T. Francis, *The Soviet Strategy of Terror* (Washington, DC: Heritage Foundation, 1985), revised edn. See also Claire Sterling, *The Terror Network* (New York: Holt, Rinehart & Winston, 1981) and Uri Ra'anan, Robert L. Pfaltzgraff, Jr., Richard H. Shultz, Jr., Ernest Halperin, and Igor Lukes (eds), *Hydra of Carnage: International Linkages of Terrorism* (Lexington, MA: Lexington Books, 1985).

18. For a discussion of the importance of basing rights in Soviet Third World Policy see Robert E. Harkavy, *Great Power Competition for Overseas Bases: The Geopolitics of Access Diplomacy* (New York: Pergamon, 1982), especially pp. 173–204, 233–9.

19. See Roger E. Kanet, 'Soviet Military Assistance to the Third World', in John F. Copper and Daniel S. Papp (eds), *Communist Nations' Military Assistance* (Boulder, CO: Westview, 1983), pp. 39–71.

20. Several recently published books examine Soviet involvement in Third World conflicts in some detail. See, for example, Stephen T. Hosmer and Thomas W. Wolfe, *Soviet Policy and Practice toward Third World Conflicts* (Lexington, MA: Lexington Books, 1983); Joachim Krause, *Sowjetische Militärhilfepolitik gegenüber Entwicklungsländern* (Baden-Baden: Nomos Verlagsgesellschaft, 1985); and Bruce D. Porter, *The USSR in Third World Conflicts: Soviet Arms and Diplomacy in Local Wars 1945–1980* (Cambridge-London-New York: Cambridge University Press, 1984).

21. For a discussion of guerrilla insurgencies targeted against Soviet-supported states see Katz, 'Anti-Soviet Insurgencies' (see note 2).

22. Among the most comprehensive recent treatments of changing Soviet interpretations of the Third World are Jerry F. Hough, *The Struggle for*

the Third World: Soviet Debates and American Options (Washington, DC: Brookings Institution, 1986); Daniel S. Papp, *Soviet Perceptions of the Developing World in the 1980s: The Ideological Basis* (Lexington, MA/Toronto: Lexington Books, 1985); Thomas J. Zamostny, 'Moscow and the Third World: Recent Trends in Soviet Thinking', *Soviet Studies*, vol. 36, 1984, pp, 223–35; Francis Fukuyama, *Moscow's Post-Brezhnev Reassessment of the Third World* (Santa Monica, CA: Rand Corporation, 1986), Report No. R-3337-USDP; and Elizabeth Kridl Valkenier, *The Soviet Union and the Third World: An Economic Bind* (New York: Praeger, 1983).

23. For an overview of the Soviet view of 'correlation of forces' see Deane, 'The Correlation of World Forces' (see note 3).
24. See Charles Wolf *et al.*, *The Costs of the Soviet Empire* (Santa Monica, CA: Rand Corporation, No. R-3073/1-NA, September 1983), p. 19.
25. See items referred to in note 22.

Part II

The Soviet Union and the Developing World: A Regional Perspective

Latin America

3 Cuban-Soviet Relations: Directions of Influence

W. Raymond Duncan

INTRODUCTION

Havana and Moscow share a relationship of mutual benefits and costs, where each side values the other's assets. Havana relies on Moscow's economic and military aid – about US $4–5 billion annually – as vital support facilitating Cuba's key policy goals: defence against US threats, economic survival, and prominence in the Third World. Moscow uses Cuba's geostrategic proximity to the United States and backing of Third World revolutionary movements to undermine US power in Latin America and other Third World arenas. Neither Moscow nor Havana dominates the other, but each strives to maximise its benefits and minimise costs in their relations.

Havana is not without leverage in dealing with Moscow. Given Soviet perceptions of Cuba as a valuable ally, Fidel Castro has acquired manoeuvring room – admittedly circumscribed by Cuba's dependent position – to pursue Cuban interests in ways that do not challenge those of the USSR. His strategy has been to cooperate with the Kremlin in Third World interventions, promoting communist causes and supporting Soviet foreign policy guidelines. These efforts have kept Soviet economic and military aid flowing since the early 1960s.

Castro frequently uses public diplomacy as an influencing tactic to highlight Cuba's utility to the Soviets or to pressure Moscow –notably at the 27th Congress of the CPSU (February–March 1986) where he told Mikhail Gorbachev not to forget the Third World. Indeed, in some cases – Angola and Central America – Castro appears to have led the USSR toward policies they might otherwise not have pursued. Still, Cuba's ability to influence the Soviets is limited, and Moscow has taken a number of steps to keep the fiery Cuban leader in line.

HISTORICAL SETTING

The Cuban-Soviet relationship was not love at first sight. Moscow demonstrated neither much faith in Fidel Castro's revolutionary movement against Fulgencio Batista during 1957–8, nor strong belief in its staying power against US opposition when victory was achieved in 1959.[1] These views stemmed from Soviet perceptions of Latin America generally, which prior to Castro's Revolution, occupied a low priority in Soviet-Third World interests when Nikita Khrushchev was busily wooing other developing countries closer to Moscow's borders.[2] From the Soviet perspective, Cuba's geographic proximity to the United States made Castro's revolution highly susceptible to Latin America's basic 'geographic fatalism', a term referring to US regional dominance and drive to protect its 'strategic rear' against threatening radical nationalist and leftist movements.[3] US actions that removed a leftist movement in Guatemala in 1954 seemed to pre-ordain Castro's revolution to a similar fate.[4]

For Castro's part, he and his revolutionary guerrilla fighters were not especially interested in the Soviets. When Castro assumed power in January 1959, the coalition government did not represent Cuba's communists of the Popular Socialist Party (PSP), and when the Soviet government recognised the new Cuban government on 10 January 1959, the Cubans did not reciprocate. Castro's early policy statements made clear that he 'was not a communist' and that the Moscow-line PSP would not be running the country, because his revolution's thrust was distinctly nationalist.[5] Philip W. Bonsol, US Ambassador to Cuba at the start of Castro's rule, points out that Castro did not admire the old line pro-Soviet communists for their past passivism, including their reluctance to support Castro until late in his struggle with the Batista regime.[6] At this time it was not yet clear to Castro that pursuing his revolutionary agenda would progressively alienate the United States, thereby creating economic and security vulnerabilities that would require a powerful external ally.

Compatible interests – shaped by each country's perception of the United States as the key adversary – eventually brought Havana and Moscow together.[7] Cuba's deteriorating relations with the United States during 1959–60 led Castro to reevaluate the nature of Cuban-US relations, which resulted in his seeking outside economic aid and military support.[8] Cuba's attraction to the Soviets stemmed from Moscow's economic and military capabilities, competition with the United States for global power, and demonstrated interest in Third World national liberation movements.[9] The US-backed April 1961 invasion convinced Castro that Moscow could meet his need for an external guarantor to lessen the risk of another US invasion as he pursued the radical transformation of Cuban society and his foreign policy mission of aiding other revolutions elsewhere in the Third World.[10]

As Cuba's relations with the United States deteriorated during 1959–61, Khrushchev's initial low-level interest in Castro's revolution began to shift. Rather than from Moscow's pursuing Havana, however, relations jelled more as a result of Castro's actions, which influenced Khrushchev to reassess the promise of Castro's 26th of July Movement.[11] Castro's invitation to Moscow to open a Soviet trade exhibition in Cuba, for example, led to the Cuban-Soviet trade pact of February 1960, while Cuba's expropriation of North American private industries during 1959–61, and defeat of the US-backed Bay of Pigs invasion in April 1961, stirred Soviet interest in Castro's staying power.[12] When Castro described his revolution as 'Marxist-Leninist' in December 1961, and eventually merged the old Cuban Communist Party (PSP) with his own radical nationalist 26th of July Movement, he further consolidated his anti-American and anti-imperialist credentials in the eyes of the Soviet Union.[13]

By 1962 Moscow was looking at a potential client which was breaking the region's 'geographic fatalism' by proving its ability to sustain a leftist Latin American national liberation movement only 90 miles off US shores in a region traditionally dominated by the United States.[14] Backing Cuba provided a stunning opportunity to introduce Soviet power and presence into the Western Hemisphere directly in the US 'strategic backyard', thus undermining traditional US power and forcing the United States to divert resources and attention to the security of this region – away from those geostrategic areas closer to Soviet borders.[15] These considerations lay behind Moscow's decision to solidify ties with Havana, a determination which led Khrushchev in 1962 to place missiles in Cuba to protect the island, enhance Soviet prestige in guaranteeing Cuban security, and advance Moscow's strategic competition with the United States.[16]

NATURE OF THE CUBAN-SOVIET RELATIONSHIP

The view adopted in this chapter argues that the nature of Cuban-Soviet ties is not one of complete control by the Soviets or by the Cubans. It is more complex, providing benefits and costs for both sides, where neither patron nor partner completely controls the other. Given Cuba's dependence upon Soviet economic and military aid in order to survive, however, Moscow occupies the predominant position, forcing the Cubans, as one analyst puts it, 'to operate within the outer parameters set by the Kremlin'.[17] The trick in probing Cuban-Soviet relations is to try to capture the rich complexity of the relationship, discerning the kinds of benefits and costs experienced by both parties and understanding the ways in which each partner attempts to use its influence in maximising the benefits while minimising the costs.[18]

The value of this approach to understanding Cuban-Soviet relations is its conceptualisation of benefits and costs for both parties, the range of issues susceptible to influence, and the notion that both Havana and Moscow at times exert influence over each other.[19] This model avoids the pitfall of assuming axiomatically that the large Soviet presence in Cuba translates into total influence over Cuban domestic and foreign policy – an assumption that seems incorrect upon close examination of Cuban-Soviet relations in a number of settings as discussed below. Rather, it defines influence as a two-way proposition: how and in what ways one state is able to shape the behaviour of another. On some issues, the Soviets have clearly influenced Cuban actions, but on other issues, Cuba has been successful in modifying or changing Soviet behaviour.[20]

BENEFITS AND COSTS IN CUBAN-SOVIET RELATIONS

Cuba and the Soviet Union have been able to weather many ups and down in their relationship since the early 1960s.[21] Events of the 3rd Party Congress of the Communist Party of Cuba (4–7 February 1986) and the 27th Congress of the Communist Party of the Soviet Union (25 February–6 March 1986), for example, followed a period of chilled relations, which set in following the 1983 US intervention in Grenada. Moscow sent its second-ranking man in the Politburo, Yegor Ligachev, to the Havana Congress, and he used the occasion to praise Cuba's international prestige and its social and economic advances.[22] Ligachev assured Castro that Cuba could 'rely upon the Soviet Union' for continued support, while Castro described Moscow as 'our closest friend and our best political ally', stressing that Cuban relations with the Soviet Union 'enjoy priority and special attention'.[23] Accorded a place of honour later at the 27th Congress, Castro hailed Mikhail Gorbachev's 'brilliant and valiant main report', which showed 'the immense glories ... of the ... Soviet people's historic deeds'.[24] These testimonies highlight the scope and length of Cuban-Soviet ties, which make this relationship the strongest and most important of Soviet links to Third World partners.[25]

Benefits from Cuba's Perspective

Castro's drive to establish and sustain relations with the USSR is based on Soviet economic and military assistance, so necessary to shore up Cuba's failing economy, defend against the United States, and carry out Cuba's sense of 'proletarian internationalism'. Soviet help remains vital to Cuba's economic survival, for without the annual $4–5 billion pumped in by the USSR, Cuba's economy is hardly likely to stay afloat.[26] Soviet economic cooperation with Cuba has been notably valuable in terms of direct and indirect subsidies, most dramatically Cuba's purchase of oil from the USSR typically at below world market prices for home consumption and for resale for hard currency.[27] The Soviets also have been buying Cuban sugar at above world market prices and have allowed Cuba – unlike Grenada (1979–83) or Nicaragua – entry into the Soviet-sponsored Council for Mutual Economic Assistance (CMEA), which provides additional trade benefits and technical assistance from East European countries.[28]

Cuba's military relations with the Soviet Union have yielded tremendous dividends for the Castro regime, primarily deliveries of Soviet military hardware free of charge and training for Cuba's Revolutionary Armed Forces (FAR).[29] The enormity of Soviet military assistance since the early 1960s has converted Castro's once small guerrilla army of about 4000 personnel, with no capability to reach beyond Cuba's shores, into an armed force of about 295 000.[30] A military machine organised along the lines of the Soviet armed forces, Cuba's FAR has become a key factor in ensuring the survival of the Castro regime against domestic and foreign opponents and a significant actor on the world stage capable of serving Cuban and Soviet interests.

Thanks to Soviet assistance, Cuba has acquired the second largest armed force in the Western Hemisphere, excluding the United States. In a population of approximately 10 million, Cuba has an estimated 160 000 men on active military duty, 135 000 in a finely-honed ready reserve, and about 1.3 million serving in the part-time Territorial Militia Troops, with an additional 100 000 in civil defence.[31] While Soviet weapons deliveries began to arrive in Cuba in late 1960, helping make possible Castro's victory in the April 1961 Bay of Pigs operation, Soviet assistance and the quality of weapons sharply increased when

Castro abandoned his criticism of Moscow's policies in 1968 and again after Cuban troops saw action in Angola (1975) and Ethiopia (1977).[32] Soviet arms deliveries again increased sharply during 1981–84, reaching levels unmatched since the 1962 missile crisis, following Castro's efforts in backing the Sandinista rebel forces in Nicaragua after they overthrew Anastasio Somoza in July 1979.[33] Although Havana does not have a formal treaty of alliance and mutual defence with the USSR, nor a treaty of friendship like other Soviet partners in the Third World, sustained Soviet aid has carried a sense of commitment to Cuba's defence needs.[34]

Cuba's relations with the USSR have produced numerous political benefits. Close ties with the Soviets have provided Havana with a 'progressive' identity, contrasting with its pre-revolutionary status as a capitalist dependency, and membership in a world socialist system advancing with history on its side.[35] Partnership with the USSR has brought with it the diplomatic backing of the world's second superpower, with its economic, military, political resources advancing Cuba's own foreign policy objectives in the Third World. Soviet assistance has been vital in providing Castro with the resources to play a significant political role on the world stage – in backing revolutionary regimes and movements– well beyond what this socialist *caudillo* could have achieved without Soviet support.[36] Soviet party-to-party ties meanwhile have been instrumental at home in institutionalising Castro's revolution, consolidating the power of Castro's 26th of July Movement, and allowing Cuba's charismatic leader to proceed with socialising Cuba's population.

The View from Moscow

Soviet benefits derived from sponsoring Castro's revolution are numerous and, from Moscow's perspective, well worth the costs. Cuba's geostrategic location provides the Soviet Union with unique leverage in the Caribbean Basin – an opportunity to project power into the US 'strategic rear' and therefore a major asset in Soviet bilateral competition with the United States for superpower status.[37] In this sense, Cuba's location close to the United States parallels Vietnam's proximity to China, Moscow's other world class adversary. Cuba's key role in advancing Soviet competition with the United States is underscored by the Soviet military and intelligence gathering presence in Cuba.[38] In return for the $4–5 billion economic aid and free military aid invested in Cuba, the Soviets receive numerous strategic benefits for an annual cost less than that required to support a single aircraft carrier task force.[39] Cuba's location has led Moscow to establish the Lourdes intelligence gathering facility near Havana, the most sophisticated intelligence complex outside the Soviet Union.[40] From this facility the Soviets monitor US commercial satellites, the NASA space programme activities at Cape Canaveral, and US military and merchant shipping communications.[41] Approximately 2100 Soviet technicians staff the Lourdes operations.[42]

Another military benefit for Moscow's investment in Cuba is the leverage gained in flying spy and training missions along the East coast of the United States with Soviet BEAR-D long-range reconnaissance aircraft.[43] These aircraft collect intelligence on US military installations on the East coast and US naval activities in the Atlantic and Caribbean, including those of US nuclear submarines.[44] In addition, the Soviets have used Cuba as a port to deploy naval task forces to the island and the Caribbean for training and demonstrations of power in an area that is a major US trading route.[45] The Caribbean and Gulf of Mexico maritime trading routes carry approximately 55 per cent of US imported petroleum and about 45 per cent of all US seaborne goods.[46] Additionally, the traditionally significant Panama Canal lies within this important geographic arena.[47]

The Kremlin's pervasive military presence in Cuba, while not mounting a direct military challenge to the United States in the Caribbean Basin, nevertheless preoccupies US attention and diverts it away from more sensitive geostrategic regions closer to Soviet shores. In capitalising on this opportunity, the Soviets have stationed at least 7700 military and intelligence personnel in Cuba. They include a 2800 military advisory group to train and help maintain the huge Cuban military machine and a 2800 man mechanised infantry brigade, which help reassure Cuba that it can rely on Soviet support in deterring US threats against Castro's power.[48]

From Moscow's perspective, its massive presence in Cuba probably provides the Kremlin with some influence and control of the FAR, helping insure its continuing loyalty stemming from the benefits of Soviet investments.[49] The Soviets cannot fully trust Fidel Castro, given the record of Cuban-Soviet relations and Castro's foreign policy ambitions, strong sense of national identity, and previous erratic policies.[50] In addition to seeking control and influence over the FAR by stationing a large Soviet presence on the island, Moscow has worked closely with Raúl Castro, Fidel's brother, Defence Minister, and head of the FAR, while seeking to create pro-Soviet lobbies within the FAR, notably among its officer corps.[51]

Cuba, while pursuing its own Third World foreign policy objectives, has worked closely with the Soviet Union to bring to power or protect Marxist-Leninist regimes in Angola (1975–76), Ethiopia (1977–78), Grenada (1979) and Nicaragua (1979).[52] Without Cuba's internationalist roles in Africa and the Caribbean Basin, it is doubtful that Moscow could have acquired its extensive Third World empire which came into being from the mid-1970s onward.[53] Castro's willingness to provide ground forces and advisors in Africa and the Caribbean Basin became indispensable to Moscow's foreign policies in these regions.[54] In Africa, for example, the Soviets were cautious in commiting their own troops directly, which might have promoted a counter-productive US response, and in the Caribbean Basin Cuba's interest and knowledge were key factors in exploiting revolutionary opportunities in Grenada and Nicaragua.[55] Additional factors favouring the use of Cuban troops were the large number of blacks and mulattos in the FAR, which blended in with the African setting, and Cuban language facility in helping the Sandinistas come to power and consolidate their position in Nicaragua.[56] Soviet personnel are notorious for not mixing well with Third World populations – from ethnic, linguistic, and cultural perspectives.[57]

The size of Cuban military contingents sent abroad to aid leftist regimes and movements illustrates huge Soviet gains resulting from its Cuban investments.[58] As a willing participant to intervention in Angola on behalf of the Popular Movement for the Liberation of Angola (MPLA) – with which Cuban ties date back to the early 1960s – Havana dispatched some 20 000–25 000 personnel who became engaged in the Angolan civil war.[59] By 1983–84, the rebel UNITA forces in Angola estimated Cuban combat forces and civilian advisors at 30 000–40 000.[60] When the Cubans became involved in Ethiopia, they shipped an estimated 16 000–17 000 troops, a figure which peaked in 1978 and eventually declined by several thousand during the 1980s.[61] By 1985, Cuba's Third World military presence was estimated at over 35 000–37 000 troops in Africa, 2500–3500 in Latin America, and 500 in the Middle East and North Africa.[62] During the October 1983 Grenada crisis, Cuba revealed that 784 Cubans were on the island, of whom 43 were members of the armed forces: 22 army officers and the rest translators and support personnel.[63]

Moscow enjoys political benefits from its ties to Cuba, especially in the various roles Cuba has played as leader of anti-United States causes and in portraying the USSR as the Third World's 'natural ally'.[64] As a leader in the Third World, Havana has stressed the need to break dependency on Western capitalism, urged the importance of socialist economic development, created a highly touted socialist ethic of achievement, struggle and work, assumed a radical leadership position within the Non-Aligned Movement and at the United Nations, and taken the diplomatic leadership in Third World internationalism.[65] While promoting Cuba's own Third World objectives in playing these roles, Havana has also advanced Soviet foreign policy aims in bolstering leftist causes in developing countries.[66]

In advancing its own and Soviet interests in the Third World, Cuban policy instruments include significant health, education and construction assistance which earn it good will, hard currency – although the bulk of Havana's programme is offered free of charge – and credibility regarding its Third World credentials.[67] Nicaragua is a case in point, where approximately 4500 Cuban civilians were present by 1985, involved in construction, teaching, medicine, and similar activities. The majority of these Cuban civilians, as in other Third World countries, have received some military training.[68]

Rising Costs for Havana and Moscow

The mutual costs of Cuban-Soviet relations have been increasing over the past years, bringing discernible strains in the relationship.[69] On the economic front, the Cubans are known to experience on-and-off frictions with Moscow, owing to their economic dependency, which restricts Cuba's freedom of economic decision making.[70] While Soviet aid has been substantial, it brings with it unpleasant pressure for doing things the Soviet way and for effective economic management, which the reform-minded Gorbachev regime is likely to address even more strongly in coming years due to Cuba's sagging economy.[71]

Signs of evident Cuban discontent with its position as traditional agricultural supplier to the USSR and East European states, and with Moscow's lacklustre backing in allowing more rapid and diversified Cuban industrialisation, surfaced during the mid-1980s. Castro, for example, refused to attend the June 1984 CMEA summit meeting in Moscow – claiming that he was preoccupied with domestic matters at home – nor did he attend Chernenko's funeral in March 1985. A 50 per cent increase in Soviet economic and trade aid to Cuba for the five-year period 1986–90, with its approximately $3 billion in new credits, announced in April 1986, may have eased some of Cuba's frustrations, at least temporarily.[72] Still, this new aid agreement raised even higher the costs for Moscow in supporting its Cuban partner.

Other costs are associated with the difficult tasks of consolidating and keeping Marxist clients in power in far-flung locations like Angola. Serving abroad for extended periods and the seemingly unending wars in Angola and Ethiopia have created rising popular discontent in Cuba, especially as the number of Cubans killed in action has increased over the years.[73] In addition, Castro's government has experienced a loss of Third World prestige since the Soviet invasion of Afghanistan, which undermined its non-aligned credentials.[74] Following Moscow's invasion of Afghanistan in 1979, Havana opposed the United Nations resolutions condemning the USSR's invasion and, as a consequence, lost its bid for a seat on the UN Security Council.[75]

Cooperative intervention with the Soviets has produced another type of cost for Havana: frictions with Moscow over Cuba's differing perception of its geopolitical role in backing Third World clients.[76] Moscow has been stressing East–West issues, while Havana is more concerned with North–South and regional issues.[77] These policy differences came to the fore in Cuban and Soviet approaches to Grenada's New Jewel Movement and have produced Cuban annoyance with Moscow's low profile in Nicaragua before, during, and after the Grenada crisis.[78] The marked difference in geostrategic perspectives – Moscow's global East–West perceptions and Havana's North–South priorities – surfaced at the 1986 Third Party Congress in Havana and the 27th Congress of the CPSU in Moscow.[79]

Following Castro's main address to Havana's Third Party Congress, which stressed Third World and Latin American issues in its foreign policy segments, Cuban leaders put together a hastily-drafted resolution more pointed in its pro-Soviet positions.[80] In contrast to Castro's strident language regarding Third World positions, the new resolution stressed Cuba's backing of the Soviet interest in using 'dialogue and constructive negotiations' to solve international conflicts and emphasised Cuba's 'unchangeable attitude in favor of a solution of the historic differences with the United States'.[81] And later in Moscow, where Gorbachev stressed East–West relations in his main address, virtually ignoring the Third World, Castro reminded the delegates that Third World issues demanded attention, and the national liberation struggles in 'Vietnam, Nicaragua, El Salvador,

Angola, Namibia, South Africa, Western Sahara, Palestine, Afghanistan, and Kampuchea' were fought with great costs and should not be relegated to 'so-called low level conflicts'.[82] These differences are not likely to disappear in the near future.

From Moscow's perspective, rising costs are associated with Cuba's persistent problems of economic inefficiency, low worker productivity, absenteeism, and even corruption.[83] Far from a model of socialist efficiency, Cuba's continued food rationing and black market are embarrassments to the USSR, while its inability to meet its export requirements to the USSR and other CMEA partners are costs the Soviets must continue to bear as part of their Cuban investment.[84] In contrast with Gorbachev's economic liberalisation, moreover, Castro has moved in the opposite direction: closing popular farmers' markets and exhorting Cubans to work harder as morally inspired revolutionaries.

The rise in Soviet economic aid to Cuba – from $1–2 billion annually during the 1960s to $4–5 billion in the mid-1980s – attests to the rising costs in supporting Moscow's Caribbean outpost.[85] By the mid-1980s Cuba was receiving over 50 per cent of all economic aid Moscow provided to communist and non-communist clients in the Third World.[86] Additionally, Moscow's trade subsidies to Cuba in oil sales and sugar purchases amounted to rising costs associated with the loss of potential hard currency.[87]

Additional costs in outfitting Cuba's armed forces are associated with the relationship. Military deliveries to Cuba, which reached unprecedented levels during 1981–84, indicate hard currency losses to the USSR in so far as these weapons were provided free, rather than earning hard currency income, as in the cases of other Soviet partners in Syria or Libya.[88] It is conservatively estimates that the Soviets provided about $3.8 billion in military aid to Cuba during 1961–79; other estimates indicate a higher figure of $4.5 billion through 1975.[89] Because Moscow relies on hard currency earnings from Third World weapons sales, its free-of-charge policy with Cuba is a distinct rising cost, especially because Cuba is requiring more weapons to meet perceived threats from the United States and to facilitate its cooperation in bolstering Soviet-Cuban clients in Angola, Ethiopia, and Nicaragua, who face serious internal security threats to their rule.[90]

CUBAN INFLUENCE ON SOVIET FOREIGN POLICY

The complexity of the Cuban-Soviet relationship, with its mutual benefits and costs, has led Havana and Moscow over the years to use their different brands of influence to maximise benefits and minimise costs.[91] Toward this end, each side has used available leverage to exert influence on the other's behaviour, trying to produce outcomes favourable to both parties.[92] Although the Soviets have resorted at times to a form of assertive influence, using sanctions to punish Cuba – especially denying economic aid or petroleum supplies as in the 1960s – the most frequently used form of influence by both partners has been of a cooperative variety.[93] Cooperative influence seeking is signalled by bargaining, inducing, persuading, or cajoling one another to cooperate on an issue of mutual interest rather than compelling or coercing one side to shift its actions owing to sanctions imposed by the other.[94]

A close look at Cuba's relations with the Soviet Union, dating back to their genesis in the early 1960s, indicates considerable evidence of Havana cooperatively influencing Soviet behaviour.[95] Castro, for example, held out in committing Cuba to either side of the Sino-Soviet rift in the 1960s, stressed the role of armed struggle as a key path to change in Latin America, and publicly criticised the Soviets for giving insufficient aid to Vietnam.[96] These tactics were effective after the 1962 missile crisis, because they produced the desired end of extracting more economic and military assistance from the USSR.[97] Castro's tactic of using public diplomacy – verbally chastising or in other ways seeking to cajole the Soviets into increased aid – appears to have worked again in 1986, when, following distinct public signals of displeasure from Havana during 1984–85 about the level of Soviet economic assistance (Castro did not attend the 1984 CMEA summit meeting; nor did he attend Chernenko's funeral, thus snubbing the new Soviet leader, Mikhail Gorbachev), Moscow increased trade and aid assistance by 50 per cent.[98]

Cuba's valued resources in aiding Third World national liberation movements have led to a number of instances of Cuban influence on Soviet decision making concerning its policies toward the Third World. Analysis of Cuban-Soviet cooperative intervention in Angola strongly suggests that Cuba led the way into the intervention, making the decision to increase its intervention independently of the USSR – at a time when the Soviets were reluctant to become too deeply involved lest the situation draw them into a direct confrontation with the United States.[99] Although the Soviets provided increasing logistical support as the campaign got underway, the Cubans and MPLA commanders planned the campaign, and Cuba's ground forces were committed in direct combat against MPLA opponents.[100] The Angolan experience indicates more influence flowing from Havana to Moscow than the reverse, stemming from Cuba's close historic ties with the MPLA, uninterrupted consistency in supporting this movement compared to the Soviets, and readiness to dispatch ground forces as opposed to Soviet cautions and cold reception to the MPLA's initial request for additional weapons and supplies in mid-1975.[101]

Cuban-Soviet influence relations in Ethiopia during 1977–78 contrast with the Angolan case of 1975–76. While Cuban soldiers were found under Cuban command in Angola, in Ethiopia overall command of the fighting remained under Soviet control.[102] A number of factors accounted for the more predominant Soviet leadership role in Ethiopia. Among them must be included the Horn of Africa's strategic interest to Moscow, dating back to the days of Peter the Great, compared to Cuba's minimal involvement before 1976.[103] Cuba did not become directly interested in Ethiopia until 1977, when Castro visited Africa and attempted to mediate a settlement between Ethiopia and Somalia over the Ogaden dispute – which failed. Still, Cuban influence on the Soviets, stemming from Havana's role as an indispensable ally in the Soviet Union's African posture, was by no means non-existent in Ethiopia. Owing to its role in Angola and Ethiopia, Cuba gained the status of privileged ally, which yielded increased leverage in insisting on increased economic and military aid from the USSR.[104]

In Grenada and Nicaragua in 1979, as discussed in more detail in the next chapter, it was Cuba – the actor with the strongest interest and most knowledge of the Caribbean Basin – that initially led in establishing relations with Grenada's New Jewel Movement (NJM) and in supporting Nicaragua's Sandinistas before they defeated Somoza in July 1979.[105] Cuba arguably drew the Soviets into a Grenada connection because not until over a year after the NJM coup did the Soviets initiate formal relations between the CPSU and the NJM during a visit by Deputy Prime Minister Bernard Coard to Moscow, and the Soviets did not make a formal commitment until two years after the coup, in July 1982, during a visit to Moscow by Prime Minister Bishop.[106]

In the case of Nicaragua, the Cubans were even more advanced in revolutionary developments because they directly aided the Sandinistas in coming to power.[107] The Sandinista National Liberation Front

(FSLN) received little Soviet attention during its struggle against Somoza in 1978 – although Moscow did extend some verbal support. In sharp contrast, Cuba helped train the FSLN, and Cuban military advisors from Havana's Department of Special Operations were with FSLN columns fighting in the final offensive in mid-1979.[108] Of extreme importance in the Sandinista victory was Cuba's insistence that the three competing Sandinista factions – divided by personal rivalries and tactical disputes – unify their efforts as a condition of continued Cuban support.[109] Leaders of the three factions – Prolonged Popular War, GPP; Proletarian Tendency, TP; and Terceristas – became the members of the Sandinista National Directorate after Somoza's fall, and they eventually removed the non-Marxist-Leninists from power and assumed total control of the Revolution.[110] Havana's commitment to the victorious Sandinista armed struggle and revolutionary changes in Nicaragua, as discussed in the next chapter, in all probability influenced Moscow to revise its position on the efficacy of armed struggle in Central America.[111]

Cuban-Soviet relations in Angola (1975–76), Grenada (1979), and Nicaragua (1979) illustrate that Soviet involvement stemmed largely from Cuban initiatives and other opportunities afforded the USSR over which it had little or no prior influence. Soviet African and Caribbean policies – aiding Marxist-oriented leaders to take, and begin to consolidate, power – were largely dependent on the willingness and leadership provided by Fidel Castro in committing ground forces, military trainers and advisors, organisational advice, political skills, and social services to revolutionary regimes and movements. For the Soviets' part, they demonstrated caution, restraint, and unwillingness in taking unacceptable risks that might raise the possibility of counterproductive US responses drawing Moscow into an unwanted direct confrontation with Washington.[112]

Cuba's Influence Building in the 1980s

In determining Cuba's role in influencing the Soviets, however, it would be inaccurate to overstate Havana's part in fomenting the instability leading to revolutionary situations. Civil wars and revolutionary situations, which created initial openings for an expanded Cuban presence in Angola, Ethiopia, Grenada, and Nicaragua, were home-grown. In Angola it was fuelled by the collapse of the Portuguese empire; in Ethiopia, by a Somali external threat in the disputed Ogaden region; in Grenada and Nicaragua, by repressive political regimes, crystallising mass discontent, and emerging Marx-ist-oriented revolutionary elites.[113] Once in power, leftist elites in Angola, Ethiopia, Grenada, Nicaragua, and elsewhere have conti-nued to face internal and external threats to their rule, leading them to seek additional assistance from Cuba and the USSR. This regime vulnerability in the 1980s has created new opportunities for Cuba to gain influence in its Soviet relations by demonstrating Havana's capabilities in maintaining pro-Soviet clients in power.

Many of the Third World regimes that the Soviets and Cubans have helped bring to power since the mid-1970s are pre-industrial societies, economically weak, Marxist-oriented, narrowly based politically, and under attack from externally backed indigenous insurgents.[114] While these vulnerabilities have created opportunities for continued Soviet and Cuban presence, they have raised the stakes of Moscow's Third World commitment, because the Soviets – who traditionally back national liberation movements – now run the risk of seeing their brand of 'national liberation' partners overthrown by opposing national liberation movements. All this comes at a time when Moscow's determination to pay the price of maintaining its established position with preferred clients is squeezed by other costs associated with developing its own economy.[115] From this perspective, the Soviets probably feel impelled to depend on Cuba's continued willingness to commit ground troops, military advisors, and social help on behalf of pro-Soviet Marxist-Leninist regimes. In addition to Cuba's huge overseas military contingents, its 16 000 teachers, doctors, construc-tion engineers, and other aid workers in 22 Third World countries also serve Soviet interests – and thereby become a source of Cuban leverage with the USSR.[116]

Cuba's role in backing Third World pro-Soviet Marxist-Leninist regimes – as Moscow also steps up support for these embattled Third World partners – helps maintain Havana's status as a privileged ally. In Angola, where the Soviets have replaced the war material the army lost in the 1985 offensive against South African- and US-backed guerrilla forces, top Cuban military advisors have worked with Soviet counterparts in planning new government efforts to defeat Jonas Savimbi's forces in southeast Angola.[117] Cuban military strength in Angola, which fell to about 17 000 after the MPLA victory, began to rise steadily in the face of Savimbi's successes, reaching 25 000 to 35 000 troops by late 1984, including some troops transferred from Ethiopia.[118] An additional 5000 Cuban workers stationed in Angola round out Havana's presence, performing roles simply unavailable to

Soviet personnel, given their ethnic, cultural, and linguistic differences.[119].

In Ethiopia, Cuban troop strength dropped from approximately 12 000 at the end of the Ogaden War to around 3000 in 1985.[120] The Ethiopians may have requested this reduction, in so far as the Cubans did not normally take part in joining the more direct Soviet military assistance to Ethiopia's struggles with Eritrean and Tigrean national liberation movements.[121] Still, as the Soviets pumped in additional technicians and pilots to back government offensives against rebel insurgent groups in 1986, Cuba's presence as another Third World country standing behind Moscow's efforts was of no small political significance to Kremlin leaders.[122] While the Cuban presence may not translate into direct influence in tactics and strategy against rebel insurgents, it does signal Havana's continuing utility as a cooperative partner in meeting the rising costs of consolidating Moscow's Third World empire with its strategic benefits in East–West competition.

Cuban activities in Nicaragua, as noted in Chapter 4, illustrate another case of Cuba demonstrating its utility to the USSR and gaining leverage as Moscow's key Third World ally, while keeping the pressure on the Soviets to provide the strongest possible backing for the Sandinistas – who represent Havana's sole success in 25 years of supporting revolutions in Latin America.[123] Of special significance are Cuba's efforts in consolidating the Sandinista nine-man National Directorate, which occupies the apex of power in the Nicaraguan political system.[124] With the consolidation of National Directorate power has come a political system roughly mirroring the Cuban system – replete with grass roots mass organisations and political socialisation to Sandinista values through education, cultural activities, and the public media.[125]

By playing a major role in the National Directorate's command of Nicaragua's military, security, and political resources – and by helping institutionalise a more controllable political system – Havana has helped create a setting for the effective use of Soviet material resources. In the Nicaraguan Ministry of the Interior, for example, Cuban influence appears exceptionally strong. The public record indicates four Cuban advisors assigned to the minister and his three vice-ministers; one assigned to the chief of the central general staff; one each to three chiefs of directorates general; one each to the 13 chiefs of directorates; and 43 at the level of chiefs of departments.[126] Of the estimated 4500 Cubans present in Nicaragua in 1987, about 2000–2500 personnel are found throughout the Nicaraguan decision-making machinery, including the armed forces and intelligence organisations. The remaining personnel work in nonmilitary fields such as education and health.[127] Moscow undoubtedly appreciates that Cuban military security advisors have made possible the rapid development of Nicaragua's Soviet-backed military security machine – thus enhancing Cuba's leverage with the Soviets in advising them on how to deal with Nicaragua.[128]

In seeking to influence Soviet foreign policy in the Third World, Havana was pursuing other policy guidelines by the mid-1980s. Castro strongly supported the new Soviet conceptualisation of US 'neoglobalism', by which is meant US anti-communist activities against Moscow's Third World Marxist-Leninist clients in countries like Afghanistan, Angola, Libya, and Nicaragua.[129] 'Neoglobalist' actions, as classified by Moscow and Havana, include US backing of the Contras against Nicaragua's Sandinistas, Jonas Savimbi's UNITA organisation against Angola's MPLA, and direct bombing of Libyan territory.[130] 'Neoglobalism', in a nutshell, is the Soviet version of a new US doctrine of the Third World designed to 'roll back' communism.

Second, Castro has taken an active effort in regaining prestige that has been tarnished in Latin America since the Soviet invasion of Afghanistan in 1979. Toward this end, Cuba established diplomatic relations with Uruguay in 1985 and with Brazil in 1986. Meanwhile, other governments in South America, like Ecuador and Peru, have been moving toward expanded ties with Cuba. These improved relations have resulted from Castro's reducing Cuba's previous high visibility in revolutionary causes in Latin America and seeking to build credibility as a legitimate state actor with Latin America's new democracies.[131] The Cuban leader's backing of the Contadora process, seeking negotiated political settlements to Central America's conflicts, and his reduced public emphasis on the merits of El Salvador's guerrilla groups during 1984–85 are key elements of Havana's improved image building. Cuba, as might be expected, endorsed the Central American peace agreement signed in early August 1987 by the governments of Nicaragua, El Salvador, Honduras, Costa Rica, and Guatemala. By accentuating Cuba's credentials as a legitimate state actor, Castro has placed Cuban foreign policy closely in line with that of his Soviet patrons.

Third, Castro has seized new issues to highlight Cuba's leadership within the Third World Non-Aligned Movement, one of Cuba's traditional bases of leverage in dealing with the Soviets. Havana has taken the lead in stressing the Latin American debt issue, with all the anti-US elements that issue possesses.[132] In addition, it increasingly has stressed Latin America's imbalance of trade and the need for a New International Economic Order – a North–South concern dating back to the early 1970s. And Castro has moved toward improved church-state relations in Cuba, while expressing his fondness for Latin America's liberation theology with its anti-imperialist overtones.[133] Significantly, Castro's deepening concern with international issues has led observers to speculate that he has been turning over day-to-day domestic policies to his brother, Raúl, so that he can instead concentrate on crafting a more dynamic foreign policy.[134]

Fourth, in a move which affects Cuba's influence in foreign relations with the Soviets, Castro has been attempting to revive the island's sagging economy, albeit in directions more consistent with Castro's infatuation with 'moral incentives' than Gorbachev's experiments with economic liberalisation.[135] Castro's main report to the Third Party Congress stressed the need to improve Cuba's 'insufficient', 'undisciplined', and 'mediocre' economy, trying to convince the Soviets that Cuba would be able to produce a Cuban version of Soviet economic reform efforts.[136] Taking his cue from Gorbachev, Castro delivered the most systematic attack on Cuba's economy since 1970 – hitting hard the island's poor record in economic planning and notorious bureaucratic inefficiency. In addition, by mid-1986 a number of Cuban Politburo members were fired and replaced, and significant changes occurred in the Cuban Central Committee.[137] These signals sent to Moscow did not go unnoticed, for Gorbachev soon notified Castro that Cuba could 'be sure of the unfailing solidarity of the Soviet Union', a point underscored by the 50 per cent increase of Soviet economic and trade aid which followed the Cuban Party Congress.[138]

Finally, Castro is capable of using the public arena to pressure the Soviet Union not to reduce its focus on the Third World in deference to East–West issues. In his closing remarks to the Third Party Congress, Castro lashed out at increased US aid to the Contras in Nicaragua, stating that 'we will do everything possible for the Nicaraguan people'.[139] Regarding renewed US aid to the UNITA forces under Savimbi in Angola, Castro stressed that Cuban troops would stay there '10 years, 20 years, 30 years … if necessary'.[140] Moscow did not give these remarks much prominence.[141]

Later, at the 27th Congress of the CPSU, Castro again drew attention to different emphases in Soviet and Cuban foreign policy. Gorbachev dwelled on East–West strategic issues, the correlation of forces between capitalism/imperialism and socialism/communism,

and global issues such as the pollution of the world's environment –
omitting references to national liberation movements in Africa, the
Middle East, or Latin America and not mentioning economic needs of
the developing countries.[142] In response to Gorbachev, Castro first
paid tribute to his main report and the strength of Cuban-Soviet ties,
but then reminded his audience that Third World issues also
demanded attention. He forcefully argued that 'the fruit of the blood
and lives of many of the best sons of our peoples' should not be
reduced in global affairs to 'so-called low-level conflicts'.[143] Castro left
no doubts about Cuba's position by noting that 'the Third World
countries expect and are sure they will receive maximum solidarity
from the socialist community in their struggle for just economic gains'.

Limits to Cuban Influence

While the nature of Cuban-Soviet relations underscores that Cuba is
far from a strict proxy or surrogate of the USSR, Havana's overall
influencing capabilities naturally are limited.[144] Moscow possesses
economic and military resources vital to Cuba's survival, not the other
way around, which means that outer parameters of acceptable
behaviour are established by Moscow, not Havana. Cuba's arena of
influence lies within the domain where Soviet and Cuban interests
intersect – which includes undermining US power in the Third World;
aiding national liberation movements; consolidating Third World
Marxist-Leninist governments; encouraging new 'socialist-oriented',
revolutionary, anti-American regimes; and promoting the cause of
regional and international leftism. In so far as most of these foreign
policy issues are not vital to Soviet national security, the room for
Cuban manoeuvring is greater than would be the case on more central
Soviet policy issues.

Cuba cannot coerce the Soviets to do something they may not wish
to do through private or public pressure.[145] In March 1984, for
example, Castro apparently became profoundly annoyed with Konstantin Chernenko's conciliatory approach to the United States,
especially the late Soviet leader's low-level response to US pronouncements aimed at the leftist Sandinista government in Nicaragua.
Castro's ire was especially piqued in March 1984 when the Soviet
leader refused to allow a Soviet naval flotilla to approach Nicaraguan
waters. The flotilla was on its way to Nicaragua when a Soviet tanker
was severely damaged by a mine at the entrance to Nicaragua's Pacific
harbour of Peurto Sandino. The point is that Castro's apparent

insistence that Moscow have the flotilla proceed to Nicaragua as a demonstration of Soviet military backing for the Sandinista government fell upon deaf ears – an example of failed Cuban influence seeking.[146]

SOVIET CAPABILITIES TO INFLUENCE CUBAN FOREIGN POLICY

Soviet influence on Cuban actions, as its counterpart, is best assessed in the context of the nature of the relationship which serves both sides' interests. Because Moscow gains so much from Havana in projecting power and presence into the Third World and in competing with the United States for superpower status, the Soviets have rarely resorted to sanction-backed coercive pressures on the Castro government.[147] Because Cuban and Soviet strategic interests tend to be so compatible, Moscow's influence on Havana's foreign policy is less directed at radically altering Havana's directions than at managing policy decisions in ways that keep them in line with Soviet objectives. What we have here is the reverse side of Cuba's influence seeking, that is, Moscow's exerting its own brand of cooperative influence on the Cubans.[148] Cooperative influence is sought, for example, through Moscow's reinforcing Havana's military and security assistance capabilities to Third World regimes – sustaining economic and military aid flows, brokering weapons transshipped through Cuba to Nicaragua, or providing Soviet logistical support, coordination, and transportation in Angola, Ethiopia, and Nicaragua.

While the Cuban and Soviet views on the nature of their military cooperation and on the role and mission of the Cuban Armed Forces coincide, the Soviets are probably determined to make certain that these views continue to coincide and that Castro not undertake foreign policy activities adverse to Soviet interests.[149] The more prominent Soviet interests include avoiding actions that greatly risk pulling Moscow into direct confrontation with the United States, that upset the balance between strong state-to-state relations with the developing countries and support for revolutionary movements and regimes, or that undermine caution and restraint in bolstering armed struggle movements in the Third World.

Toward this end, the Soviets have granted neither a formal defence alliance with Cuba nor a treaty of peace and friendship, which gives Moscow more leverage in preventing the Cuba from undertaking actions which could trigger a counter-productive US response or, worse, a direct confrontation with Washington.[150] The Soviets also have exercised a kind of counter-influence on Cuba: despite Havana's stress on the need for Moscow to show a more determined backing of the Sandinistas, for example, Moscow has not introduced sophisticated Mig-21s into Nicaragua, and it rejected Castro's argument that Soviet naval squadrons should visit Nicaragua to act as a deterrent to the Contras' mining of Nicaraguan harbours.[151] Until 1980, moreover, the Soviets continued to resist the export of Cuba's model of armed revolutionary struggle in Latin America.

In so far as Cuba's Revolutionary Armed Forces (FAR) are a major instrument of Cuban foreign policy, it comes as no surprise that Moscow has attempted to insure that the FAR stay within acceptable confines of behaviour.[152] Given Castro's history of independent actions, Cuba's radical nationalist past, and the Cuban enthusiasm for supporting armed struggle revolutionary movements, it is reasonable to expect that Moscow wishes to avoid Cuba's FAR triggering an unwanted crisis. The Soviets have followed several policies in attempting to influence Cuba's FAR in desired directions. They entail:

1. Making certain the FAR remains completely dependent on the Soviet Union for weapons, equipment, supplies, and training in their use.
2. Restricting Cuba's ability to manufacture spare parts and equipment.
3. Permeating the FAR with Soviet military tactical and strategic doctrine, organisational concepts, political control systems, and instructional methods.
4. Training Cuban officers in the USSR and using Soviet military advisors and instructors in Cuba.
5. Closely coordinating Soviet advisory activities with the Cuban Intelligence Service (DGI) by utilising Soviet military and KGB intelligence organisations.
6. Exerting Soviet influence over the organisation of Cuba's military schools and curriculum development.
7. Reinforcing these activities by teaching as many Cubans as possible, military and civilian, the Russian language.
8. Cultivating close cooperative relations with Raúl Castro, second man in the Cuban political hierarchy and Minister of Defence, and with the *Raulistas* who support him.

These activities – directly conditioning Cuba's chief foreign policy instrument – insure that the Soviets will not be caught by a surprise Cuban military action, and they go far in preventing over-manipulation by Castro.

A general method of Soviet influence seeking over Cuban foreign policy is systematically to socialise the Cuban population, military and civilian, young and old, party cadres and the average citizen, to Cuba's fraternal ties with the USSR. Toward that end, the Soviets emphasise – through speeches by resident diplomats and visiting dignitaries, radio and television broadcasts, reading materials, cultural exchanges, scholarship-backed training in the USSR, awards and ceremonies, anniversary celebrations, etc. – those themes tying Cubans and Soviets together. They range from praise of Cuban accomplishments, benefits of Cuban-Soviet cooperation, and the glorious histories of Soviet-Cuban 'combat cooperation' to the future benefits of following the Marxist-Leninist path in domestic and foreign policies.

As an extra step in controlling conditions of Soviet influence on Cuban foreign policy Moscow has used its time-tested format of KGB operations within the FAR. Operations of this type are not astounding, because one of Moscow's chief capabilities in aiding Third World clients, including Cuba, has been the provision of a national security model – including internal security – to help Third World leaders overcome their vulnerabilities to internal opposition groups and external threats. This standard policy provides Moscow with opportunities to use KGB officials not simply to help set up internal security mechanisms for the host country, but to infiltrate host country military and non-military institutions. Cuba is no exception. Indeed, given the exceptionally large number of Soviet personnel in Cuba, 14 000–15 000 civilian and military, opportunities abound for KGB personnel to be placed throughout the Cuban military, as well as government, security, political, and economic institutions. The classic example of KGB control occurs within the Cuban intelligence agency, the DGI, which came under KGB supervision after 1968. Still, limits to Soviet influence on Cuban foreign policy exist.

Limits to Soviet Influence

Among the limits to Soviet influence on Cuban foreign policy not previously identified is the power of Cuban nationalism and Castro's uniquely independent personality.[153] As evidenced by the 3rd and 27th party congresses in Havana and Moscow, the Cubans and Soviets continue to disagree over a number of issues in foreign policy –

among others, North–South versus East–West commitments, levels and degrees of support for Third World clients, Cuba's discomfort with Moscow's occupation of Afghanistan – and Cuba is still capable of undertaking unilateral foreign policy actions, as it did in Angola in 1975. And while Cuba knows that it has no real alternatives to dependence on the Soviets for economic and military support, Castro and his followers are not sanguine about the degree of Cuba's dependence on the Soviets, which they are likely to resist whenever possible.

Students of the Cuban FAR point to other limits to Soviet influence.[154] One factor is the difference in attitudes and perceptions of those trained in the USSR and those trained in Cuban military institutions. It is difficult to assess the extent to which Cubans become 'pro-Soviet' when trained in the Soviet Union, outside of the advantages they may gain in assignments or promotion. Another potential limit to Soviet influence is the result of negative military attitudes formed through service in foreign countries, like Angola or Ethiopia.[155] Loss of life, adverse working conditions, and separation from relatives and friends have created morale problems in many a military situation; Cuba's military is now exposed to these conditions in what appears to be unending African wars and a permanent presence in Nicaragua.[156] While Cuba's involvement in Angola, Ethiopia, or Nicaragua has not produced the kind of internal dissent experienced in the United States during its Vietnam involvement, Havana's military adventures probably are not without their costs in terms of unsettling the Soviet connection in the minds of some Cubans.[157]

TRENDS AND PROSPECTS

Given the durability and nature of compatible interests served by this most important of Soviet-client relationships, a straight line projection of the trends previously discussed is most likely. Each side will continue to try to maximise benefits and lower costs, and each will try to cooperate with the other in ways to achieve these ends. It seems unlikely that either the Cubans or the Soviets will perceive the costs of the relationship outweighing the gains, triggering a destabilising downturn in Havana's ties with the Soviets. For this to occur a dramatic turn of events would have to happen, such as a serious decline in Soviet economic and military assistance to Cuba or a split in the Angolan MPLA or Nicaraguan Sandinista ranks, with Havana and Moscow falling out over divided loyalties, or a surprise diplomatic or military foreign policy move by Castro which threatened drawing Moscow into direct confrontation with the United States. Escalating frictions, while also unlikely, could ensue, under conditions conceivably different from the present. The most serious issue triggering heightened conflict is Cuba's economic performance. If it becomes more ineffective than it has been, Gorbachev could become increasingly frustrated at a time when economic reform, effectiveness, and rising productivity are being pressed on the Soviet domestic front. Sharpened complaints from Moscow's CMEA partners about Cuba's economy and the diversion of CMEA resources to Cuba could stimulate this type of future. Additional sources of friction might occur from Castro's more heatedly accentuating Cuban foreign policy differences with the Soviets – over Soviet intervention in Afghanistan, *détente* efforts with the United States at possible Cuban expense, or lack of attention to North–South economic development issues. Conversely, the Soviets could become displeased should Castro, for one reason or another, get too far out front in directly supporting revolutionary movements in Central or South America, thus undermining Moscow's efforts to build state-to-state relations.

Notes

1. On Soviet caution regarding Castro's 26th of July movement, see Jacques Levesque, *The USSR and the Cuban Revolution: Soviet Ideological and Strategic Perspectives* (New York: Praeger Special Studies, 1982), introduction; also Edward Gonzalez, *Cuba under Castro: The Limits of Charisma* (Boston: Houghton Mifflin, 1974), pp. 121–2.
2. Soviet perceptions of Latin America before the Cuban Revolution are examined in Stephen Clissold (ed,.), *Soviet Relations with Latin America* (London: Oxford University Press, 1970); and 'Soviet Relations with Latin America between the Wars', in J. Gregory Oswald and Anthony J. Strover (eds), *The Soviet Union and Latin America* (New York: Praeger, 1970), ch. 1.
3. Joseph Whelan, *The Soviet Union in the Third World, 1980–8: An Imperial Burden or Political Asset?*, report prepared for the US House of Representatives, Committee on Foreign Relations, by the Congressional Research Service, Library of Congress (Washington, DC: US Government Printing Office, 1985), p. 255.

4. Herbert Dinerstein, *The Making of a Missile Crisis: October 1962* (Baltimore, MD: Johns Hopkins University Press, 1976), ch. 1.

5. Gonzalez, *Cuba under Castro*, pp. 96–100 (see note 1).

6. Philip W. Bonsol, *Cuba, Castro and the United States* (Pittsburgh: University of Pittsburgh Press, 1971), p. 67.

7. See W. Raymond Duncan, *The Soviet Union and Cuba: Interests and Influence* (New York: Praeger, 1985), ch. 2.

8. *Survey of International Affiars, 1959–60* (London: Oxford University Press, 1964), pp. 489–90.

9. Ibid.

10. Duncan, *The Soviet Union and Cuba*, pp. 34–8 (see note 7).

11. Ibid.

12. On the Soviet-Cuban trade pact of 1960, see the joint communiqué issued by the USSR and Cuba, *Pravda*, 16 February 1960.

13. See *Cuba, the US, and Russia, 1960–63* (New York: Facts on File, 1964).

14. Ibid.

15. On the evolution of Soviet perceptions regarding Cuba's utility to Moscow's foreign policy, see Leon Gouré and Morris Rothenberg, *Soviet Penetration of Latin America* (Coral Gables, FL: Center for Advanced International Studies, 1975).

16. Dinerstein, *Making of a Missile Crisis*, ch.5 and 6 (see note 4).

17. See William J. Durch, 'The Cuban Military in Africa and the Middle East: From Algeria to Angola', in *Studies in Comparative Communism*, vol. 11, Summer 1978, pp. 34–74.

18. For other versions of this third interpretation, see Edward Gonzalez, 'Cuba, the Soviet Union and Africa', in David Albright (ed.), *Communism in Africa* (Bloomington: Indiana University Press, 1980), pp. 147–65; Jorge Domínguez, 'Cuban Foreign Policy', *Foreign Affairs*, vol. 57, no. 1, 1978, pp. 91–98.

19. Issues of sanctions, influence, and power are discussed in David V. J. Bell, *Power, Influence, and Authority: An Essay in Political Linguistics* (New York: Oxford University Press, 1975); see also Harold Lasswell and Abraham Kaplan, *Power and Society: A Framework for Political Inquiry* (New Haven, CT: Yale University Press, 1950), pp. 48–9.

20. See Alvin Z. Rubinstein (ed.), *Soviet and Chinese Influence in the Third World* (New York: Praeger, 1975).

21. See Duncan, *The Soviet Union and Cuba*, ch. 1–4 (see note 7).

22. For coverage of the 3rd Party Congress in Havana, see daily entries for 3–12 February, 1986, in the Foreign Broadcast Information Service's Daily Report: Latin America (Washington, DC, hereafter FBIS-LAM), and Daily Report: Soviet Union (Washington, DC, hereafter FBIS-SOV); *New York Times*, 9 February 1986; and *Washington Post*, 5 February 1986.

23. Moscow TASS in English, 5 February 1986; in FBIS-LAM, 6 February 1986, p. Q/2; and FBIS-SOV, 6 February 1986, p. K/1.

24. Havana Tele-Rebelde Network, 26 February 1986; trans. in FBIS-LAM, 27 February 1986, p. Q/1.

25. See W. Raymond Duncan, 'Castro and Gorbachev: Politics of Accommodation', *Problems of Communism*, vol. 35, no. 2,

March–April 1986, pp. 45–57.

26. See Cole Blasier, 'COMECON in Cuban Development', in Cole Blasier and Carmelo Mesa-Lage (eds), *Cuba in the World* (Pittsburgh: University of Pittsburgh Press, 1979), p. 225.
27. *Washington Post*, 5 June 1985; also *Financial Times* (London) 1 March 1986.
28. Blasier, 'COMECON in Cuban development', pp. 225–56 (see note 25).
29. See International Institute for Strategic Studies, *The Military Balance 1985–86* (London: IISS,, 1985), pp. 140, 146–7.
30. Ibid.
31. US State and Defense Departments, *The Soviet-Cuban Connection in Central America and the Caribbean* (Washington, DC, 1986), pp. 3–10.
32. See Jorge Domínguez, 'The Armed Forces in Foreign Relations', in Cole Blasier and Carmelo Mesa-Lago (eds), *Cuba and the World* pp. 54ff.; and Gonzalez, 'Cuba, Soviet Union and Africa', p. 163 (see note 18).
33. State and Defense Departments, *Soviet-Cuban Connection*, p. 9.
34. Ibid., pp. 8·10.
35. Duncan, *The Soviet Union and Cuba*, ch. 4 (see note 7).
36. Ibid.
37. Whelan, *The Soviet Union in the Third World*, pp. 305–18 (see note 3).
38. State and Defense Departments, *Soviet-Cuban Connection*, pp. 3–10; and *The Challenge to Democracy in Central America*, (Washington, DC, 1986), pp. 10–13.
39. State and Defense Departments, *Soviet-Cuban Connection*, p. 4.
40. Ibid., *Challenge to Democracy in Central America*, pp. 10–12.
41. Ibid.
42. Ibid.
43. Ibid.
44. Whelan, *The Soviet Union in the Third World*, pp. 271–7 (see note 3).
45. Ibid.
46. Ibid.
47. Ibid.
48. State and Defense Departments, *Soviet-Cuban Connection*, p. 3.
49. See Leon Gouré, 'Soviet-Cuban Military Relations', paper prepared for Radio Marti Program, VOA/MR (Washington, DC: US Information Agency, August 1985), p. 1.
50. Ibid., p. 16.
51. Ibid., p. 9.
52. Whelan, *The Soviet Union in the Third World*, parts 4 and 5 (see note 3).
53. Ibid.
54. Durch,'The Cuban Military in Africa and the Middle East: From Algeria to Angola', (see note 17).
55. Ibid.
56. Ibid.
57. See Bruce D. Porter, *The USSR in Third World Conflicts: Soviet Arms and Diplomacy in Local Wars, 1945–1980* (New York/London: Cambridge University Press, 1985), -pp. 224–5.

58. Ibid., pp. 54–6, 134–5, 229–30, 164–70, and 203–5.
59. Whelan, *The Soviet Union in the Third World*, p. 315 (see note 3).
60. Ibid.
61. Ibid.
62. US Department of Defense, *Soviet Military Power* (Washington, DC: US Government Printing Office, 1985), pp. 116–17.
63. *New York Times*, 31 October 1983, p. A10.
64. See H. Michael Erisman, *Cuba's Internatinal Relations: The Anatomy of a Nationalistic Foreign Policy* (Boulder, CO: Westview, 1985), ch. 1.
65. Ibid.
66. Ibid.
67. Ibid., pp. 77–80.
68. State and Defense Departments, *Soviet-Cuban Connection*, pp. 24–7.
69. Duncan, 'Castro and Gorbachev', *Problems of Communism*, vol. 35, no. 2, March–April 1986, pp. 45·57.
70. Ibid.
71. Ibid.
72. Ibid.
73. See Erisman, *Cuba's International Relations*, ch. 5 (see note 64).
74. Ibid.
75. Ibid., p. 129.
76. Duncan, 'Castro and Gorbachev', pp. 48–50 (see note 69).
77. Whelan, *The Soviet Union in the Third World*, pp. 339ff (see note 3).
78. Duncan, 'Castro and Gorbachev', pp. 53–57 (see note 69).
79. Ibid., pp. 53–4.
80. Ibid., p. 53.
81. Ibid.
82. Havana Tele-Rebelde Network, 26 February 1986; in FBIS-LAM, 27 February 1986, pp. Q/1–2.
83. Whelan, *The Soviet Union in the Third World*, pp. 305ff (see note 3).
84. Duncan, *The Soviet Union and Cuba*, ch. 7 (see note 69).
85. Cole Blasier and Carmelo Mesa-Lago (eds), *Cuba in the World* (Pittsburgh: University of Pittsburgh Press, 1979), p. 44.
86. Ibid.
87. Ibid.
88. Whelan, *The Soviet Union in the Third World*, p. 311 (see note 3).
89. Ibid.
90. State and Defense Departments, *Challenge to Democracy in Central America*, pp. 7–15.
91. Duncan, *The Soviet Union and Cuba*, ch. 1 (see note 7).
92. Ibid.
93. See *New York Times*, 24 March 1968.
94. See Gonzalez, *Cuba under Castro* (see note 1).
95. See Andres Suarez, *Cuba: Castroism and Communism, 1959–1966* (Cambridge: MIT, 1967).
96. Levesque, *The USSR and the Cuban Revolution* (see note 1).
97. Ibid.
98. Duncan, 'Castro and Gorbachev', p. 57 (see note 69).

99. Duncan, *The Soviet Union and Cuba*, p. 130 (see note 7).
100. Ibid.
101. Ibid.
102. See Harry Brind, 'Soviet Policy in the Horn of Africa', *International Affairs* (London), vol. 60, no. 1, Winter 1983–84, pp. 78ff.
103. Ibid.
104. Gonzalez, 'Cuba, Soviet Union and Africa', pp. 145–67 (see note 18).
105. Jiri and Virginia Valenta, 'Leninism in Grenada', *Problems of Communism*, vol. 33, no. 4, July–August 1984, pp. 1–23.
106. Ibid.
107. See Jiri and Virginia Valenta, 'Sandinistas in Power', *Problems of Communism*, vol. 34, no. 5, September–October 1985, pp. 1–28.
108. Duncan, *The Soviet Union and Cuba*, p. 164 (see note 7).
109. Ibid.
110. See David Nolan, *FSLN: The Ideology of the Sandinista and the Nicaraguan Revolution* (Coral Gables, FL: Institute of Inter-American Studies, University of Miami, 1984), 1–5.
111. Whelan, *The Soviet Union and the Third World*, pp. 324ff (see note 3).
112. Ibid.
113. Ibid.
114. See Jerry Hough, *The Struggle for the Third World: Soviet Debates and American Options* (Washington, DC: Brookings Institution, 1986), ch. 1, 2, 7, and 8.
115. Ibid.
116. *New York Times*, 22 January 1985.
117. *Washington Post*, 11 June 1986.
118. *New York Times*, 10 May 1984; 22 June 1985
119. Erisman, *Cuba's International Relations*, pp. 78–9 (see note 64).
120. Ruth Leger Sivard, *World Military and Social Expenditures, 1985* (Washington, DC: World Priorities, 1985), p. 13.
121. Duncan, *The Soviet Union and Cuba*, pp. 32–36 (see note 17).
122. State and Defense Departments, *Soviet-Cuban Connection*, pp. 8–10.
123. Ibid., pp. 19–30.
124. Ibid.
125. Ibid.
126. *Latin America Regional Reports* (London), 'Mexico and Central America', RM86-01, 10 January 1986.
127. *Washington Post*, 13 August 1987, p. A32.
128. Ibid.
129. Moscow Domestic Radio Service in Russian, 3 April 1986; in FBIS-SOV, 8 April 1986.
130. Ibid.
131. See Jorge Domínguez, 'Cuba in the 1980s', *Foreign Affairs*, vol. 65, no. 1, Fall 1986, pp. 118–35.
132. See Castro's speech to Havana's Third Party Congress, Havana Domestic Radio in Spanish, 4 February 1986; in FBIS-LAM, 7 February 1986, pp. 55ff.
133. Ibid., pp. 53–4.
134. Duncan, 'Castro and Gorbachev', pp. 54–7 (see note 69).

135. *Washington Post*, 24 April 1987.
136. Havana Domestic Radio in Spanish; in FBIS-LAM, pp. 14–19.
137. Duncan, 'Castro and Gorbachev', pp. 52–3 (see note 69).
138. Ibid.
139. Havana International Service, 8 February 1986; in FBIS-LAM, 10 February 1986, p. Q/36.
140. Ibid.
141. See coverage of Nicaragua and Cuba in FBIS-SOV, 8–13 February, 1986.
142. Moscow Television Service, 25 February 1986; in FBIS-SOV, 26 February 1986, pp. Q/1–46.
143. Havana Tele-Rebelde Network, 26 February 1986; in FBIS-LAM, 27 February 1986, pp. Q/1–2.
144. Duncan, *The Soviet Union and Cuba*, ch. 1 (see note 7).
145. Ibid.
146. *Washington Post*, 24 March 1986.
147. Erisman, *Cuba's International Relations*, ch. 4 (see note 64).
148. Duncan, *The Soviet Union and Cuba*, ch. 1 (see note 7).
149. Gouré, 'Soviet-Cuban Military Relations', pp. 20ff (see note 49).
150. Ibid., p. 14.
151. *Washington Post*, 24 March 1985.
152. Gouré, 'Soviet-Cuban Military Relations', pp. 20ff, from which much of the following discussion of the FAR is drawn (see note 49).
153. Erisman, *Cuba's International Relations*, ch. 1 (see note 64).
154. Gouré, 'Soviet-Cuban Military Relations', pp. 29ff (see note 49).
155. Ibid.
156. Whelan, *The Soviet Union in the Third World*, part 4 (see note 3).
157. Ibid.

4 The Soviet Union, the Caribbean, and Central America: Towards a New Correlation of Forces
Howard J. Wiarda

INTRODUCTION

In terms of Soviet relations with Third World client states, the region of Central America and the Caribbean provides a particularly interesting and complex case study area. Cuba was the first of the Latin American countries to declare itself a Marxist-Leninist state; to fall, rather like an overripe plum, into Soviet hands; and to become a Soviet client. But then the client state took on a life of its own; and over the last ten years we have seen Cuba, with its limited resources and only ten million population, emerge as something of a global power, with interests, missions, and experienced fighting forces, trainers, and technical personnel operating in some two dozen Third World nations. This is not in any sense to minimise Cuba's continuing economic and military dependence on the USSR or to suggest that Cuba operates entirely independently of the USSR and not at its behest.

But it is to say that among the Soviets' Third World clients Cuba plays a unique and particularly important role. The client itself has become a patron, almost a global power if judged by its extensive military activities abroad. In Central America and the Caribbean, especially, the Cubans have been operating ahead of and with greater commitments of manpower and resources than have the Soviets. The Nicaraguan and Grenadan revolutions were more 'Cuban projects' than they were the result of Soviet machinations. The Soviet Union relies heavily on the Cubans not just to provide the military personnel for various overseas adventures, but in Latin America it seeks Cuban advice and guidance as well, while not itself taking a large or direct role. It works through the Cubans and uses Cuba as something of an 'advance party', as 'shock troops' in an area where the Soviet Union does not want itself to become heavily involved or to overly antagonise the United States. In the process the client state, Cuba, has seen its power and prestige enhanced to the point where it has now acquired clients of its own. In this chapter we seek to unravel these complex relations among the Soviet Union, Cuba, and the newer revolutionary states of the region: Grenada (1979–83) and Nicaragua (1979–present).[1]

CONCEPTUAL AND THEORETICAL CONSIDERATIONS

Several methodological and theoretical points need to be made by way of preface. First, we accept in general terms the theoretical orientation and assumptions offered by Edward Kolodziej and Roger Kanet in the introductory chapters to this volume. These include the fundamentally anarchic nature of the world system, the primacy of nation-states within that system, the essentially bipolar (United States, Soviet Union) nature of the competition and rivalry between the superpowers, and the increased capacity of other actors, including a number of Third World client states, to manipulate and manoeuvre within that context. We further accept the notion that while the Soviet Union does not likely have a 'grand design' for the 'conquest' of Latin America and other world areas, it does have a set of goals and tactics to advance its interests while simultaneously frustrating, tying up, and embarrassing the United States.[2]

Second, a comment needs to be offered about dependency theory and its application within the socialist bloc. Dependency theory has most often been used to describe the relations between Third World client states and the 'imperial powers' – i.e. the United States. But there is no reason why dependency cannot also exist between socialist nations that are unequal in size and resources; and in a recent pathbreaking analysis,[3] dependency theory has been applied to the relations between Cuba and the Soviet Union. That is, Cuba was found to be heavily dependent on the Soviet Union – politically, economically, diplomatically, militarily. But within that context, as in the dependency relations between the United States and its clients, the Cuban client may have considerable independence of movement and capacity to manipulate the superpower, just as the superpower manipulates Cuba – although these relations remain asymmetrical and therefore quite one-sided.

A third preliminary comment deals explicitly with the relations between clients and superpowers. Unlike the East European countries that are on the Soviet border and into which Soviet troops have been sent almost as an occupation army, Cuba is separated from the Soviet Union by six thousand miles of ocean.[4] There are two extreme interpretations of Cuba's relations with the Soviet Union: one that sees it as absolutely dependent and the other that views it as completely autonomous. My position on this issue, which is similar to that of W. Raymond Duncan in Chapter 3 of this volume,[5] is that Cuba is both dependent on the Soviet Union in some senses and independent at the same time, a 'junior partner' in the relationship, a client but not really an occupied, proximate satellite in the same way the East European countries are. There is a convergence but not always an identity of interests between Cuba and the Soviet Union, a situation in which the Soviet Union is a major presence in Cuba but in which its influence is not always as great as it might seem. At the same time the asymmetries of power and wealth between Cuba and the Soviet Union provide the latter with immense leverage *vis-à-vis* Cuba.

Within this framework, the chapter proceeds to an analysis of the Central American and Caribbean context and its 'ripeness' for revolutionary upheaval, of the rising Soviet presence and influence in the region, of Cuba's role (covered in more detail in the previous chapter) as a Soviet proxy and intermediary, of case studies of Grenada and Nicaragua and the Cuban/Soviet role in these revolutions, and finally to some conclusions and implications on the Soviet presence and the US policy response in the Caribbean Basin.

THE CARIBBEAN/CENTRAL AMERICAN CONTEXT

The countries of the Caribbean and Central America have been modernising gradually – now at an accelerated pace – over the past fifty years.[6] Since the partial breakdown of the old order in the great depression of the 1930s, economic take-off has begun to occur, social change has accelerated, new social and political groups have formed, the traditional isolation of these countries has given way under the impact of what Lucian Pye called the 'world culture',[7] political mobilisation has gone forward, and the Cold War and international conflict have come to the area. A new business and commercial class has grown up alongside the traditional landed elites, a strong middle class (both civilian and military) has emerged, urban lower class elements have become increasingly organised and politicised, and rural peasants and Indians are being mobilised and brought into the political process for the first time. These trends render obsolete the popular image of Central American and Caribbean countries as wholly traditional and backward, still dominated by 'the oligarchy', and therefore presumbly 'ripe for revolution'.

Actually, a number of these countries may be ripe for revolution, but not necessarily because they are so poor and backward. The literature, from Crane Brinton to the present,[8] is clear in saying that revolutions do not occur in the poorest and most backward of countries. If that were the case, most of Africa plus Haiti and parts of Asia would be in constant upheaval. Rather, revolutions tend to occur in countries that have begun the great ascent to modernity, where the traditional, backward, and lethargic past has been put behind, but where the process either is proceeding too slowly or is going in such unacceptable directions (as in Cuba under Batista or Nicaragua under Somoza) that it is anathema to the bulk of the population. Revolution is therefore a product not so much of backwardness but of change, not so much of poverty *per se* but of raised hopes and expectations that were then dashed or frustrated. Revolutions tend to occur not in affluent countries nor in wholly traditional ones but in those that have begun a process of change. In this sense (although one need not accept the hyperbole involved) W. W. Rostow in his pathbreaking *The Stages of Economic Growth* was correct in calling communism (and also fascism) a 'disease of the transition'.[9]

By all indices the nations of Central America and the Caribbean fit this description quite precisely. That is, they are *transitional nations*, no longer backward, having begun the modernisation process, but not quite fully modern either. In this region a great deal of social and economic modernisation has gone forward in the last half century, but this has not been accompanied in all countries by corresponding political change. Instead, political institutions have remained vulnerable; they are often fragmented, with a weakly developed infrastructure. It is precisely in these kinds of societies, where socioeconomic modernisation has occurred but political development has not gone forward apace, that violent, society-wide revolution is liable to occur. The history of US neglect, on the one hand, and interventionism, on the other, which tend to fan the flames of nationalism and anti-Americanism,[10] lend a further ingredient to the revolutionary fires. US interventionism (and the anti-Americanism it engenders) tends to be more frequent in the weak, vulnerable states of the Caribbean and Central America than in the generally larger and more institutionalised polities of South America.[11] That helps explain why the only successful Marxist-Leninist revolutions in Latin America have occurred in Central America and the Caribbean (what we will here term the Caribbean Basin, encompassing both the islands and the mainland) and not in South America. Poverty and backwardness are of course important factors in explaining revolution, but they are not the only factors and may not even be the most important. Political variables may be at least as critical as social or economic ones. In the case of the Caribbean Basin countries here under review, one is struck by the same sequential political processes in all the revolutionary contexts. That category includes the countries that have had successful revolutions (Cuba, Grenada, Nicaragua) as well as those in which there may be a 'revolutionary situation' (Guatemala, El Salvador). In all of them there first came socioeconomic modernisation and, with it, something of an early political opening to greater democracy and pluralism. But then, as change accelerated and some of the more traditional groups began to feel threatened, the crackdown began. Political cloture or sclerosis began to set in and the regimes-in-power tried to turn the clock back to an earlier and simpler time, using extensive political repression. In the case of Batista the regime became so brutal and so corrupt that it was no longer acceptable to the majority of Cubans. Much the same happened in Nicaragua: increased corruption and brutality at a time of expectation for political opening. Moreover, the Somoza regime opted to monopolise the corruption rather than to share it with the country's elites. These forces – political opening and then cloture at a time of heightened expectations, corruption and brutality at levels that are no longer tolerable – these are the elements that have caused revolution in the Caribbean Basin, not just poverty *per se*.[12]

Several further distinctions need to be kept in mind lest we paint the picture with too broad a brush. One involves the distinction between the English-speaking countries of the region, with their strong democratic traditions steeped in the Westminster model, and the Spanish-speaking countries that generally lack that tradition. Another is to distinguish between those countries of the area that have experienced the heavy hand of US interventionism (Cuba, Nicaragua, Guatemala), where anti-Americanism and nationalism are particularly potent, and those that have not felt the US presence heavily. A third distinction must be drawn on the basis of size: the larger nation-states of the area such as Colombia, Mexico, or Venezuela; the medium-sized 'city-states' of Central America and the Caribbean; and the smaller islands and 'mini-states' of the Caribbean in which (as the case of Grenada illustrates) it may be possible to carry out a sucessful revolution with only a dozen or so fighters. These distinctions are important, as we shall see, both in providing additional explanatory factors in our understanding of Caribbean Basin revolutions and in assessing the Soviet and US interest in, and response to, them.[13]

THE SOVIET PRESENCE IN THE CARIBBEAN BASIN

The Soviet Union traditionally has not been a strong player in the Caribbean Basin.[14] The Caribbean is far away, from the point of view of Soviet strategic planners; it lies within the United States orbit; the Soviets have not in the past had the naval or other resources to be more than a minor presence there; and the region has not been of significant economic or strategic importance to the Soviet Union itself. Through the 1950s the idea of Stalinist legions, military or political, playing a serious role anywhere in Latin America could be dismissed as ludicrous, as indeed it deserved to be.

There have long been communist parties, trade unions, and leftist university student groups in Latin America, dating back to the 1920s and 1930s. But such groups never enjoyed much popular support and had very little influence. By the 1950s and 1960s most of them had become old and rather tired bureaucracies, with no hope of ever achieving power.[15] There were exceptions of course: Brazil and Chile have long had communist parties of some influence, and in the early 1950s in Guatemala some communists had infiltrated and were occupying some key positions in the government of Jacobo Arbenz.[16]

The Cuban Revolution altered the situation considerably. For the first time there was an openly Marxist-Leninist state in the Western Hemisphere. Also, Cuba demonstrated that it was possible for a Latin American state to break out of the US orbit – and get away with it – which helps explain Cuba's continuing popularity among Latin American nationalists despite the manifest failures of the revolution itself. Moreover, after 1961 Cuba allied itself closely with the Soviet Union. The Soviets had not been strongly involved in the Cuban Revolution; in fact they had worked out a marriage of convenience with the Batista regime and denounced Fidel Castro as a *'petit bourgeois* reformer' – a strong epithet in the Marxian lexicon. Cuba joined the socialist bloc not as a result of any effort or clever planning on the Soviets' part but as a product of sheer luck and fortuitous circumstances. But from this point on the Soviets had a base of operations in Latin America, a centre for propaganda and indoctrination, a training centre, a naval, air, and military base, and a Spanish-speaking country on which it could rely for advice and access.[17] The Soviets' initial forays into Latin America in the 1960s, following Cuba's lead, example, and own orientation, were not overly successful. The strategies of fomenting guerrilla revolutions failed in country after country. The culmination to this embarrassing period came with the failure and death of Ché Guevara in Bolivia, which some say was instigated by the Soviet Union itself. In any case, with the failure of the guerrilla strategy the Soviets turned to a longer-term and more nuanced plan to build up gradually their presence and influence in the region. Here we can only summarise some of the main components of the expanded Soviet strategy, as well as the more subtle and complex tactics that have evolved along with the strategy.[18]

1. *Diplomatic and normal state-to-state relations.* By now the Soviet Union has established normal diplomatic relations with 16 Latin American countries. This has given the Soviet Union a diplomatic and a political presence throughout the hemisphere it had lacked before. In addition, it provides a legitimacy to the Soviet presence and activities; it further provides a sense of 'normalcy' to Soviet activities and has helped remove the ogre stigma that accompanied the earlier strategy of subversion and guerrilla tactics.

2. *Military presence.* Although by no means a match for the United States in the Western Hemisphere, the Soviet Union has significantly increased its naval and air presence in the Caribbean region, using Cuba as its base and advance post.

3. *Trade relations.* The Soviet Union has significantly increased its level of commerce with Latin America to a point where it compares with other industrial countries (Japan or West Germany, but not the United States); moreover, the Soviets have *regularised* their trade with quite a number of countries, enabling them to maintain extensive relations despite changes of regime.[19]

4. *Quality of personnel.* The quality of Soviet representation in Latin America has improved dramatically. More Soviet officials speak Spanish and have experience in Latin America; Soviet study centres focused on Latin America have also improved considerably.

5. *Cultural exchanges.* Soviet cultural contacts and exchanges have expanded significantly, surpassing US efforts in many countries.

6. *Propaganda offensives.* These too have been stepped up, and the quality and sophistication of the efforts have greatly improved. Because Latin America is often inclined to believe the worst about

the United States, Soviet disinformation campaigns have similarly been effective.

Not only does the Soviet Union show a rising presence in Latin America, albeit not at a level yet that comes close to matching that of the United States, but its strategies and tactics have become more sophisticated as well.[20] To begin, Soviet policy is now far more focused and active in the region than was the case in 1960. Second, there is a new emphasis on long-term goals – building contacts, access, sympathy – rather than pursuing short-term (revolutionary) objectives. Third, the Soviets have become far more clever at playing upon nationalistic sentiments and using the widespread anti-Americanism throughout the region for their own advantage. Fourth, their strategies, have become far more flexible, ranging from normal state-to-state relations in some countries to destabilisation and subversion in others (or with both tactics pursued at the same time in a single nation). Fifth, the emphasis on the '*foco* theory' as championed by Ché Guevara of a peasant-based guerrilla insurgency that serves as the *focus* of the revolution has given way to a strategy emphasising broader anti-imperialist tactics and the building of more broadly based opposition coalitions. That strategy proved successful in Nicaragua and is being attempted in El Salvador and Guatemala.

In the sixth place, the Soviets have been instrumental in such revolutionary contexts as Nicaragua and El Salvador in forcing the several anti-regime groups to come together for the common struggle. Seventh, they have been clever and skillful in building international support for their causes and in undermining and discrediting US-favoured groups and regimes. Eighth, as the Soviets have grown more sophisticated in their analyses of Latin America, they have also taken a stronger and more direct role in devising overall strategy for the region. And lastly, the Soviets have become much more realistic in their assessments. They recognise that the entire region is not about to become ripe for revolution. But they do see situations to take advantage of – to embarrass the United States, and to score partial gains – all without expending many resources of their own.[21]

While the overall Soviet presence has certainly increased in Latin America over the last quarter century and while the tactics and strategies have become more sophisticated, there are also severe limits on the Soviet role and possibilities there. These limits include the fact that the Soviets do not always like or get along very well in Latin America, that there is not a base of good will toward the Soviet Union in the region, and that communist party and other organisations are often weak and without popular support. Then there is geography – distance and logistics make a more activist Soviet role difficult. The strong US presence and its overwhelming local advantage in the Caribbean Basin make the Soviets reluctant to challenge the United States in its own backyard and where fundamental Soviet interests are few. Finally, there are Soviet domestic pressures, chiefly economic, which would seem to rule out a much vaster Soviet commitment to Latin America in the foreseeable future. Cuba is already an immense drain on the Soviet economy, Nicaragua has been told it cannot expect a great deal more in the way of economic assistance, and other revolutinary regimes and movements would likely get even less. These comments are not meant to imply the Soviets will curtail their activities in Latin America or that they would reject another plum like Cuba or Nicaragua if it fell into their lap. But it is to say that resources are limited and so too will be Soviet commitments.[22]

This brief review of the Soviet presence in the Caribbean Basin highlights several features: (1) the new opportunities available to the Soviet Union in that region; (2) the rising and multidimensional Soviet presence in the area over the last 25 years; (3) the more sophisticated strategies and tactics employed by the Soviets; and (4) the limits on the Soviet role and future possibilities. We turn next to Cuba's important role in this context.

THE CUBAN ROLE

Cuba's relations with the Soviet Union have been thoroughly and admirably treated by W. Raymond Duncan in Chapter 3.[23] What requires brief elaboration here is Cuba's role as an intermediary between the Soviet Union and the rest of Latin America. For Cuba is not just a Soviet outpost and base in a military sense – another Soviet 'satellite' – it also functions as a guide and interpreter of Latin American politics for the Soviet Union, as an advisor on political and political-cultural affairs, and, through its highly trained and experienced military and socioeconomic assistance missions, as the advance arm of the Soviets throughout the region. And in the process the Cubans have begun to take on 'projects' of their own, such as Nicaragua and Grenada.

The island of Cuba has been converted over the years into a major military, air, naval, and intelligence base offering numerous advantages to the Soviet Union. Cuba is a refuelling station, an arms depot, a training base, a propaganda centre, a launch pad for naval operations and reconnaissance flights – in short, a large 'aircraft carrier' floating ninety miles from US shores. Cuba acts, to a degree independently and also as a proxy,[24] to further Soviet (as well as Cuba's own) military/strategic and political objectives in such critical regions of conflict as Southern Africa, the Horn of Africa, the Arabian Peninsula, Southeast Asia, to say nothing of Central and South America. The relationship is enormously advantageous to the Soviet Union in that it can rely on a now faithful and proven ally without itself seeming to be directly involved.[25] In addition, Cuba has enabled the Soviet Union to augment considerably its paramilitary presence, including spy and communication ships, agents, flyovers, 'fishing boats', channels for arms and training. This vast Cuban *cum* Soviet military presence in such far-flung areas of the globe has given rise to the charge that the Cubans are 'Gurkhas' – paid mercenaries known for both their efficiency and their brutality.

Cuban contributions to Soviet expansionism in the Caribbean Basin have gone beyond a mere military role. They include methodological and political lessons that they have taught the Soviet Union as well as strictly military assistance.[26] Methodologically, the Cubans have evolved away from the *foco* theory of the 1960s, which was nurtured by a misreading of their own revolution. Their approach is now far more realistic and sophisticated. The Cubans have discarded the sharp distinction between rural and urban bases in favour of a strategy that encompasses both (thus recognising the explosive potential of Latin America's cities where misery, overcrowding, and unemployment are almost endemic); they have abandoned their ideological rigidity in favour of a subtler strategy that incorporates a variety of non-Marxist, Catholic, and independent socialist groups without relinquishing control of them; they have become far more accomplished in the use of front organisations; and they have devised a strategy for unifying the left-wing and anti-regime movements into a broad 'anti-imperialist' and 'popular' movement.[27] The most successful case of the application of these new principles, as we shall see, is Nicaragua.

Politically, the Cubans have served to orient the Soviets in Latin America, providing them with information and understanding regarding an area about which the Soviet Union has but limited experience, understanding, or empathy.[28] The Soviets are, in a sense, Weberians, rationalists, and Europeans in their expectations and understandings of political behaviour – as are Americans – and they have not had a history of understanding, liking, or getting along very well in the more informal, clientelistic, personalistic, clan- and family-based politics of Latin America. The Cubans have thus introduced them to the subtleties of and taught them how to operate in Latin America, and thereby contributed significantly to the more recent Soviet successes there.

But while emphasising the ideological and political roles, one should not neglect the Cuban military role. Under this category should be included the extensive Cuban intelligence system, the network of Cuban guerrilla training camps, the extensive and now highly experienced Cuban military units, tens of thousands of Cuban labourers and technical personnel with paramilitary training sent to a variety of Third World countries, and vast logistics (aircraft) capabilities, able to reach all the countries of the Caribbean Basin (albeit not yet sufficient to reach Africa, the Middle East, and Asia for which the Cubans are still dependent on Soviet aircraft).[29]

In all these ways the Cubans have acted as a 'broker', and interlocutor, or perhaps a 'surrogate' for the Soviet Union, on the one hand, and revolutionary regimes and movements in the Caribbean Basin, on the other. The Cubans played such a role as intermediaries in the Nicaraguan Revolution and were probably more influential in shaping the direction of that revolution than the Soviet Union itself. The Cubans provided the entrée for the Salvadoran guerrilla groups into Soviet-bloc embassies in Mexico City, to the Soviet Union itself, and to such other sources of guerrilla and terrorist assistance as Ethiopia, Libya, and Vietnam. And it was the Cubans, as we shall see, who adopted the Grenadan Revolution as their project, providing massive support and assistance and showing the less-experienced Grenadans around the labyrinthian corridors of Moscow, to say nothing of the equally complex *salons* of European and Socialist International sympathy.

THE SOVIET UNION, CUBA, AND THE NICARAGUAN REVOLUTION

The Somoza regime in Nicaragua was seldom the unabashed monster entirely holding back change that has become the popular image since the Sandinista Revolution. Nor was the United States quite its unwavering supporter that is part of the same picture. As usual, the situation is far more complex than the propaganda would have us believe.

Anastasio Somoza, Sr., was a rather traditional Latin American man-on-horseback in a long Nicaraguan and Latin American tradition of men on horseback. His regime was authoritarian rather than totalitarian. Somoza used some brutal methods, particularly in the early years of his regime, but this seldom took the form of systematic terror or torture found in more 'total' systems. Rather, Somoza practiced a form of generally mild authoritarianism as distinct from a Batista or a Trujillo, to say nothing of a Mussolini or a Hitler.[30]

While Somoza was clearly a dictator, his regime could also be considered somewhat reformist, quasi-populist, and developmentalist. In the mid-1930s Somoza brought with him into power for the first time the new *mestizo* middle-class, both civilian and military, thus ushering in a major class and racial change in Nicaraguan society and politics. He carried out a large number of economic and social programmes that brought considerable progress to his tradition-bound country. He had, during most periods, considerable popular support as a strong leader and could undoubtedly have won an honest election had he chosen to hold one. Nor was the United States an unswerving supporter. If we can go beyond that famous quip regarding Somoza attributed to FDR and always cited in the literature ('He may be a SOB but at least he's our SOB'), the fact is the United States rather consistently sought to use its influence to push the Somoza regime toward greater reform and democracy.[31]

The process of reform was accelerated in the 1960s under Somoza's son and heir, Luís. Greater reforms were stressed as part of President John F. Kennedy's Alliance for Progress, the economy grew rapidly, new social programmes were introduced, the human rights situation improved considerably, and for a time the Somozas actually stepped down from the presidency – though not giving up much real power. Had these liberalising trends continued, it is unlikely the Somoza regime would have been overthrown.[32]

The real problem came in the 1970s. Luís had died and was replaced by the second son, Anastasio, Jr, or 'Tachito'. Tachito Somoza was more brutal than his father or brother had been, greedier, and more corrupt. He refused to allow the processes of social and economic development occurring inexorably in the country to have any political expression, ruling out any form of greater pluralism and democracy. When such expressions arose, he brutally snuffed them out. His greed and corruption exceeded the permissible bounds even of a Nicaraguan society which historically has not been excessively Calvinistic about such things; worse, he refused to share the corruption as his father and brother had wisely done, preferring to monopolise it for himself and thereby lose the support of even those upper- and middle-class Nicaraguans who had earlier supported the regime. In the end, when the United States also got off his bandwagon, Somoza was left with no support whatsoever.

There had long been a quasi-clandestine, Moscow-oriented communist party in Nicaragua, which had virtually non-existent popular support and was something of a laughing stock. The party, or at least some of its members, was thought to be in the pocket of Somoza – a strange-bedfellow arrangement that was the best evidence of its weakness. When Somoza wanted to impress junketeering US congressmen with his staunch anti-communism, he would throw the local communists in his pay in jail. When he wanted to impress other congressmen with his democratic credentials, Somoza would let the communists out to demonstrate that *all* groups enjoyed political freedom in Nicaragua. This farce does not leave one impressed with the strength or sagacity of the Nicaraguan Communist Party.[33]

As the opposition to Somoza mounted during the 1970s, and as the guerrilla struggle spread, the comic opera features took on deadly seriousness.[34] But it is essential to know that among the nations – both communist and non-communist – aiding the Nicaraguan guerrilla forces, it was Cuba, not the Soviet Union, that took the lead. The Soviets, still remembering the aborted guerrilla campaigns of the 1960s, tended to look on the Sandinista revolutionaries as romantic, unreliable, *petit-bourgeois*, with little chance of succeeding. Although Moscow gave some verbal support to the revolution in its last phase, up to that point the Soviet Union had paid almost no attention to Nicaragua or the Sandinistas.

Cuba's role in the revolution was instrumental in its success. Cuba helped train the leadership of the *Frente Sandinista de Liberación Nacional* (FSLN) and also provided the revolution with the arms to take on and overcome the Somoza military. Cuban military advisors were fighting with the FSLN in its final campaign in 1979. In addition, Cuba forged the critical unity agreement among the three contending Nicaraguan guerrilla factions that enabled the revolution to succeed.[35] Virtually the entire system of intelligence and security in Nicaragua is modelled after that of Cuba. The Cubans taught the Nicaraguans how to avoid alienating their entire middle class, how to influence US domestic opinion, how to manipulate European opinion and the Socialist International, how to impress outsiders by maintaining the appearances of democracy even while its substance was being undermined, how to handle and use to best advantage the hordes of 'political pilgrims' who now flocked to Nicaragua.[36]

The Cuban presence is most visible in the military realm. Some 3000 Cuban military personnel are stationed in Nicaragua; approximately 2000 others serve in paramilitary capacities. The Cuban effort has been directed chiefly at training a new and revolutionary Nicaraguan army and developing all facets of security and intelligence. In addition the paramilitary personnel work as technical advisors, in construction, and in handling heavy equipment. They have received military training and are prepared and equipped to fight – rather like the Cuban paramilitary construction workers who were building the famous airport in Grenada.

Cuba's impact on Nicaragua is of course primarily political.[37] There is an affinity and convergence between the two nations' revolutions in terms of ideological persuasion, political and social institutionalisation, modus operandi, and even revolutionary style – a revolutionary *Weltanschauung*, if you will. Cuba represents, after all, a successful transition of a Latin American state out of the US orbit and in the direction of a new model of revolutionary socialism – an ideal that is attractive to the Nicaraguan and other hemispheric revolutionary elites. The responsibility is both a heavy one and attractive to the Cubans.

As Raymond Duncan has emphasised in the preceding chapter, the Soviet Union lagged far behind Cuba in seizing the opportunities afforded by the revolutionary upheaval in Nicaragua. Nicaragua's regular pro-Moscow Communist Party was not involved in the early phases of the revolution against Somoza and echoed the then-Soviet line of opposition to armed struggle. The Soviet Union stayed aloof from political developments in Nicaragua and apparently played no direct role in the victory by the Sandinistas. Only in mid-1981, two years after the revolutionary regime had come to power and even longer from the time the Cubans had become heavily involved, did the Soviet Union become heavily committed. At this point the Soviets, who are not always eager to embrace quickly what they perceive as shaky and possibly unreliable Third World regimes, began to give their full support to the Sandinista regime. And even today, although the level of Soviet assistance especially in the area of arms transfers is crucial, it is Cuba that has by far the largest number of personnel in Nicaragua. The Soviet Union has preferred what Duncan calls a 'low-risk, low-profile, cautious and restrained role'.[38]

The Soviet Union has by now come to the conclusion that it appreciates and wants to maintain the Nicaraguan regime. But it is unwilling to commit vast resources to it. The Soviets welcome the emergence of a socialist Nicaragua into their camp. They see Nicaragua as a springboard for scoring additional gains elsewhere in Central America. They also recognise the utility of Nicaragua in sowing further divisiveness in the United States and of causing the latter no end of trouble, embarrassment, money, and military resources. But in both the economic and the military spheres, the rules of thumb for the Soviets have been caution, prudence, and only limited commitments.

Economically, the Soviets have provided considerable assistance to Nicaragua, particularly in the area of military equipment. However, they have clearly told the Nicaraguans that they will not subsidise their revolution to anywhere near the degree they have underwritten the Cuban revolution for twenty-five years – that is massively, in the amount of about $5 million per day, more than the United States provides in assistance to any other country in the world. The Soviet Union, given the problems and continuing hardships in its own domestic economy, is not eager to take on still another Third World 'basket case'. Nicaragua has been told that economically it is largely on its own, to sink or swim, and that the Soviet Union will not rescue it. Hence with US aid cut off and not much coming from the Soviets or anyone else, it is understandable why the Nicaraguan revolution has not succeeded economically, why standards of living are declining, why there are so many shortages, and why the economy is close to being a failure.

Militarily, there are also limits. The Soviets and Cubans have helped build up the Nicaraguan armed forces, militia, and security organisations to a point where they now outnumber by several times those of any of Nicaragua's neighbours – and may outnumber those of all their neighbours combined. Moreover, the Nicaraguan forces are very well trained, and equipped with modern socialist bloc (chiefly Czechoslovak) equipment. But while there has been a massive flow of equipment and training into Nicaragua, there are bounds here as well.

First, the Soviets have not committed more than a handful (30–40) of their own military personnel to Nicaragua, preferring to use the Cubans instead. Second, the Soviets know that they should not provide Mig fighter planes to Nicaragua. They, the Cubans, and the Nicaraguans have all been told in no uncertain terms – the ultimatums already given – that the United States will not tolerate Migs in Nicaragua. Should there prove to have been Migs in those mysterious packing crates that were once shipped to Nicaragua, or should the Migs be shipped at some later point, there is no doubt the United

States would take swift military action to remove them – all the parties understand this. The issue therefore is not Migs – that has been decided – but rather from the US point of view what to do about all the other heavy equipment and sophisticated armaments (tanks, helicopter gunships, small missiles) that Nicaragua *is* receiving. The third limit concerns the Soviets' willingness to come to the defence of Nicaragua if it is attacked by the United States. The Soviet Union has told Managua that it would not come to its defence militarily, that in this area too Nicaragua was on its own. Particularly in the wake of the US invasion of Grenada in 1983, such reluctance on the part of the Soviets has added to the Sandinistas' already acute sense of paranoia.[39]

All this has introduced some considerable tension in the relations among these socialist bloc countries. The tension is disguised by the rhetoric of fraternity and socialist brotherhood, but it is there none the less. The Soviet Union obviously welcomes new Marxist-Leninist states into its camp, but it wants to achieve these gains without commiting much in the way of its own resources, and without these activities provoking US military retaliation in an area where the United States is strong and the USSR weak. The Cubans, with their ambitious and 'global' foreign policy, have special interests in expanding their sway in their own, Latin American, part of the world. They therefore walk a fine line between their dependence on the Soviet Union, and hence the need not to antagonise their patron, and their desire to expand both Cuba's sway and that of socialism by persuading or perhaps sucking the Soviets into a larger commitment in the Caribbean Basin. The Nicaraguans, who have become quite skilled players in these games in their own right, still find themselves dependent on both the Cubans and the Soviets, a double dependency that leaves them particularly vulnerable and weak and often playing the role of eager supplicant to an often unenthused Soviet Union.

THE SOVIET UNION, CUBA, AND THE GRENADAN REVOLUTION

If this situation of double dependency and of eager, almost self-abasing supplication to the Soviet Union for recognition and assistance is true for Nicaragua, it was even more true for the small, island, mini-state of Grenada.

Grenada and Nicaragua were not necessarily unique cases; rather, they were part of an evolving Soviet strategy that had come into play by the late 1970s.[40] The Soviet Union, which as we have seen had become during that decade wary of underwriting romantic, costly, and unsuccessful guerrilla struggles, began to alter its view in 1979 when the revolutions in Nicaragua and Grenada succeeded. The Soviets determined that they could achieve significant gains with relatively little commitment by assisting broad-based popular front and anti-imperialist forces in contexts where right-wing dictatorships were wobbly and hence vulnerable. But the Soviets also determined that they would build more 'quality controls' into their commitment so as to avoid the frustration, defeats, even humiliations of the several aborted guerrilla struggles they had sponsored in the 1960s. These controls included greater selectivity in the quality and reliability of the client, greater willingness to exercise veto power over their clients' activities, greater use of trustworthy proxy forces (Cuba) who know the local terrain, greater use of local intermediaries so that in case of defeat the Soviet Union itself is not embarrassed, close supervision of client state 'adventurism', avoidance of direct Soviet involvement so as not to provoke the United States, less commitment of Soviet economic and military resources, and closer control over the key military, intelligence, and security apparatus of the client state. Nicaragua and Grenada were the first to experience this more cautious but sophisticated Soviet posture; indeed they provided the cases upon which the new policy was based.[41]

The Grenadan Revolution was a much more planned, prepared, sophisticated, and serious affair than has generally been portrayed.[42] Grenada has been treated in the Western media as rather 'comic opera'. How could a revolution on a small island with only 100 000 population whose chief export is nutmeg be taken seriously? But a close reading of the treasure trove of documents captured by the US military forces in Grenada reveals a revolution with dedicated leaders, serious issues, intense debates, wrenching decisions, and finally a horrible denouement in the events leading to the murder of the revolution's leader Maurice Bishop and his replacement by a more reliable and orthodox pro-Soviet leadership.[43]

The Grenadan Revolution was not only more serious but considerably more Marxist-Leninist than previously thought.[44] If one had read only the popular press accounts, one would have had the image of a carefree and relaxed revolution, fun-loving and rather indolent. The minutes of the Grenadan Revolution's Political Bureau, however, show not a bunch of fuzzy-minded, romantic, and peace-loving social democrats but a dedicated leadership of Marxist-Leninists with very clear aims and goals.[45] They fought with skill and comsummate determination to ally themselves with Cuba and the Soviet Union, to undermine US positions in both the area and in international bodies, and to spread their revolution to neighbouring islands and even the mainland. Even more so than in Nicaragua, Cuba was the key to the success of the revolution. Cuba was the chief external driving force behind the revolution, not the Soviet Union. Grenada may in a sense be viewed as Cuba's 'project' in the Caribbean. Cuba was involved in all aspects of the Grenadan Revolution, its chief mentor, inspiration, and revolutionary guide. It served as the go-between for Grenada with both Nicaragua and the Soviet Union. Cuban technicians built the airport that was designed to accommodate the largest military transports, bombers, and fighter jets; Cuba also provided doctors, technical advisors, social workers, and teachers. Cubans often sat in on meetings of the Grenadan New Jewel Movement's (NJM) Central Committee and its Political Bureau. Grenadan leaders were constantly in Havana for advice. The Cuban Communist Party and the NJM had signed a far-reaching plan of cooperation and exchange. It is clear that the Grenadans did practically nothing without consulting first their Cuban advisors. The Cubans were also busy preparing the Grenadans to take on 'cases' of their own – just as Grenada itself had been a Cuban case – in Belize, Guyana, and the numerous former British islands of the Caribbean.[46]

By contrast, the Soviet Union appeared to keep a certain distance from the Grenadan Revolution and the New Jewel Movement. The NJM was considered by Moscow a 'fraternal party', but it was not treated on the same level of other, what the Soviets considered to be more regular and orthodox, communist parties. The Soviet Union seemed not to trust fully the NJM leadership, which may also have been a ploy to force the NJM to demonstrate its loyalty and unquestioning orthodoxy. Other than the visits of Bishop to Moscow, a brief meeting of the two countries' military commanders, and a single visit by a Soviet official to Grenada, the Soviet Union paid scant attention to Grenada. Grenada was a small and sometimes rather pathetic supplicant in the intricate corridors of Moscow, and the Soviets seldom listened or paid Grenada serious consideration.[47]

Soviet levels of assistance and contacts were similarly meager. Perhaps two dozen Grenadans had received some advanced training in Moscow, but they were unhappy being lumped together with the

Canadians and the '*gringos*' in the same 'American' study group. The Soviet Union provided little if any economic assistance to Grenada; what there was of it came through Cuba. The representative of the Grenadan Revolution in Moscow had a devilishly frustrating time gaining access to Soviet officials and usually got behind the closed doors only when accompanied by a Cuban representative. The Soviets gave some verbal encouragement to the Grenadans and paid lip service to their plans to export their revolution, but the Soviets did not press the Grenadans on this and apparently had only modest expectations of what the revolution could accomplish. In fact, one senses from the captured documents that the Soviets were sceptical of the Grenadan Revolution and were waiting for the leadership to demonstrate its loyalty and trustworthiness. Until then, few commitments could be made.

The Soviet Union both kept its distance from the Grenadan Revolution and chose to work through a proxy, Cuba. Even the well documented Grenadan case, however, does not enable us to resolve fully the issue of the degree of central control over these activities emanating from Moscow as opposed to autonomy on the part of the proxy. Though it is clear that ultimate authority rested with the Soviets, the documents show considerable leeway and autonomy for the Cubans. That means Cuba had quite a lot of independence in pursuing its Grenadan case. But it also served to protect the Soviet Union and provided it with the best of all possible worlds. The Soviets could claim credit for the successes achieved, guard against being exploited by the unproven Grenadans, and shield themselves from the potential for failures while also blaming them on the Cubans. If the regime got in trouble and disaster loomed, the Soviets could wash their hands of the affair and leave the Cubans there holding the bag. That is ultimately what happened when Bernard Coard took over from Bishop, Bishop and his followers were murdered, and the United States intervened. The Cubans were left to fight the invading Americans while the Soviets were able to avoid being blamed for what went wrong and also managed to avoid confronting the United States in a disadvantageous locale.

In the Grenadan case again, Cuba emerges as the real linchpin of revolutionary activities in the Caribbean, the essential hub from which other activities radiate. Cuba's central role is made abundantly clear in the captured documents. We have seen that Nicaragua is one of the 'spokes' in the Cuban 'wheel' and Grenada another. The Soviet Union, meanwhile, keeps a low profile aiding, assisting, and exercising overall supervision but benefiting from having Cuba up front and as its leading edge.

The US intervention in Grenada left an ambiguous legacy. The short-term effects were quite dramatic: the Marxist-Leninist regime on the island was ousted, the Cubans were sent home (in some disgrace, for not fighting hard enough against the Americans), and democracy in Grenada was resurrected. There were equally dramatic results elsewhere in the area: Suriname's left-leaning dictatorship unceremoniously sent most of its Cuban advisors packing, the El Salvadoran guerrillas were forced to reassess their prospects downward in the face of US resolve and commitment, and the already paranoid Nicaraguans – convinced that they were next on the US hit list – saw their anxieties increase. The strong US action also forced the Soviets and the Cubans to rethink their position and strategy in the region, to reassess the region's ripeness for revolution, and to reconsider the resolve and strength of the United States.[48]

The US intervention in Grenada, however, may not have been the unadulterated defeat for the Soviet Union and Cuba that is often portrayed. The Soviets and Cubans did reap some propaganda advantage from portraying the United States as an interventionist power. In some quarters the US invasion may have strengthened the 'moral equivalency' argument that sees the USSR in Afghanistan and the United States in Grenada pursuing essentially equivalent policies. Nor do the Soviets suffer long from pique or guilt; they have already reassessed and redesigned their strategies accordingly. Grenada in this sense may be only a temporary setback.

But the case of Grenada may lead the prudent and quite pragmatic Soviets to conclude that the United States has raised the costs of their adventurism in the Caribbean Basin – an area where the US has overwhelming local advantage politically, militarily, economically, and logistically – to a level the Soviets see as too risky, too uncertain, and too costly. There are abundant signs that the Soviets are reassessing their Caribbean strategies and that they may decide to concentrate their efforts on areas closer to their home base where they have the advantage.[49] If that is the case, then the Grenada intervention may have been a real and significant triumph for US policy in the region – though it does not more than marginally affect the global balance of power or mean that the Soviet Union is just a paper tiger. Instead, the Soviets may simply decide to concentrate on other areas – Pakistan, let us say – where the risks are less and the potential returns, from their point of view, more significant.

CONCLUSION

The Soviet Union has not long had a compelling or major strategic interest in Central America, or in the rest of Latin America, but that situation has changed considerably in the last quarter century. The Soviet presence in the region has increased significantly in the diplomatic, political, military, cultural, and economic realms. Soviet strategies and tactics have similarly become more sophisticated. And at the same time the Soviet strategic interest in the area has grown. It is not that Latin America has become a vital trading partner with the Soviet Union (although that is changing too), or that the Soviet Union is desperate for Latin American resources, or that Latin America is crucial to Soviet strategic interests. Latin America is more important to the Soviets for what it can *deny* to the United States than for what it contributes to the Soviet Union. Latin America can be used to embarrass the United States, it can cause the US a host of problems and troubles, and in the event of a crisis it can tie up US resources – including military resources – that might otherwise be directed against the Soviet Union. This last may well be the main strategic interest of the Soviets in Latin America.

What makes the Latin American case particularly interesting in the larger context of this study is the role of Cuba as the Soviets' agent, advance arm, and guide in the region. In this relationship, which carries with it a considerable degree of bargaining between the superpower and its proxy and sometimes sharp disagreement, both Cuban and Soviet interests (not always identical) have been served. Cuban troops, aid, and personnel have been critical in scores of Third World conflicts. One is tempted to say Cuba has become a regional proxy for the USSR in Latin America, just as Brazil and Iran were for the United States in their respective regions in an earlier era – except that Cuba also plays a global role, through its actions and military presence in Africa, the Middle East, and Southeast Asia. In the Latin American area, however, it is significant that it was Cuba, not so much the Soviet Union, that was instrumental in the triumph of the Grenada and Nicaraguan revolutions. Cuba took on these countries as *its* cases; the Soviet Union exercised overall guidance but none the less worked through Cuba as its intermediary and interlocutor. In turn Cuba has sought to inspire the Nicaraguans to greater efforts to export their revolution in Central America and, until the denouement in 1983, tried to get the Grenadans to carry their revolution to both other islands and the English-speaking mainland.

It is a complex and fascinating story of the Soviet Union's using Cuba as its proxy, Cuba in turn playing a decisive role in Grenada and Nicaragua, and these two countries attempting – thus far unsuccessfully – to develop their own 'cases' in their respective sub-regions. Moreover, in this situation of what we have called 'double dependency', the capacity of those small states at the lower rungs of the revolutionary hierarchy – Grenada and Nicaragua – to extract much assistance, let alone concessions, from their patrons has been negligible. Cuba is valuable to the Soviets, but Grenada and Nicaragua may be expendable – a situation that does not give these latter two much bargaining power in Moscow. Indeed, they are often left with making rather strained efforts to gain an audience from a not overly sympathetic Soviet officialdom, an embarrassment that is compounded by having to employ the Cubans to open the doors of the Kremlin.

But, particularly in the aftermath of the Grenada invasion and the strong and continuing US commitment in the Caribbean Basin, a major reevaluation of what the Marxist literature calls the 'correlation of forces' in this entire region has been under way.[51] The lesson has become clear to all, including the Soviet Union, as well as other Marxist-Leninist regimes and movements. The United States is willing for the time being to use force and other concerted means to ensure its security interests (1) where it has the overwhelming local advantage (i.e. the Caribbean as distinct from Southeast Asia), and (2) against small and vulnerable states (i.e. Grenada) where the mission can be accomplished quickly and relatively painlessly. Such circumstances would stand in contrast to those of larger, more difficult countries (i.e. Cuba, Nicaragua) where a battle would likely be bloody, protracted, and perhaps unsustainable from the viewpoint of US public opinion. However, the recent revelations that Nicaragua might be more vulnerable than earlier anticipated, coupled with enhanced US military preparedness for such an encounter, mean that the possibility of US action against that country should not be entirely ruled out. These trends have by no means been lost on the Soviet Union, which does not wish to challenge the United States in a region where its interests are limited and where the US would have the advantage of fighting in its own backyard. In addition, while we cannot at this moment (1987) predict the outcome of the Arías Central American Peace Plan, it seems likely that the Plan will (1) perpetuate the already ambiguous situation in the region with regard to outside actors like the United States, Cuba, and the Soviet Union; and (2) result in added pressure being placed on the Sandinista regime.

These and other lessons are currently being absorbed by Soviet strategic planners and their implications analysed. Whereas in 1979 Central America and the Caribbean looked ripe for revolution, today that seems less likely. The revolution has not spread, the political situation in Grenada has been reversed, the Sandinista government in Nicaragua is in trouble, the guerrillas in Guatemala and El Salvador have suffered strong reversals, the traditional forces in these countries now enjoy an enhanced position and have proved more resilient than expected, the Left has not proved as popular as thought, and the United States has proved not to be a paper tiger. The Soviets know their own inefficient and bureaucratic model is not very attractive in the region and that there are unlikely to be soon many more Marxist-Leninist states in the region. The Soviet Union will continue to be a significant presence in Latin America, but there are signs that its emphasis may now be placed on other regions where the chances of gain are higher. This does not mean the Soviets have been defeated and will abandon the region; rather it is part of the ebb and flow of Soviet foreign policy. Today may well be a period of ebb, representing a significant, though still limited, victory for US foreign policy signaled by the recent cease fire accord between the Contras and the Sandinista regime.

Political developments elsewhere in Latin America have not been reassuring from a Soviet perspective. There is a new spirit of prudence and pragmatism throughout the area. The older, more radical development models (Cuba, Peru, Chile, Jamaica, Nicaragua) are dead or severely challenged. They have few admirers anymore. With the new pragmatism has come the practical recognition on the part of Latin America's leaders of the need for a realistic, working relationship with the United States. That was probably the great mistake of the Nicaraguan Revolution: the belief that a small, weak Central American state whose logical markets are in North America could have its revolution *without* or *against* the United States. That is impossible, and it is one of the major lessons that came out of the last five years of Latin American economic depression. The West Europeans, East Europeans, Chinese, Soviets, and Socialist International all *talk* a great deal about aid and trade but actually provide very little. Hence when the chips are down, like it or not, Latin America remains dependent on the United States for markets, capital, tourism, technology, investment, aid, and protection from inside and outside foes. That is a powerful lesson, one that works to the disadvantage of the Soviet Union and that has forced a host of Latin American states back into a continued and very pragmatic realisation of the need to modify some of their desires for greater independence and toward a more realistic and mature relationship with the United States. Finally, US strategic policy is also undergoing reformulation.[52] The old doctrine of hegemony, containment, and economy of force is now being modified in favour of a broader strategic doctrine. The new doctrine encompasses development as well as purely crisis response as in the past, building long-term relations with Latin America instead of merely responding to short-term events, a broader and more sophisticated conception of security rather than the narrow one of the past. To the extent this sorely-needed, updated strategic doctrine is implemented, the US position in Latin America is likely to be enhanced. That will also enter into Soviet considerations of the possibility of securing further gains in Latin America, of how the Soviets use their Cuban proxy in the future, and of whether Latin America is worth the added costs that will be required.

Notes

1. For further elaboration see Howard J. Wiarda and Mark Falcoff, *The Communist Challenge in Central America and the Caribbean* (Washington, DC: University Press of America, 1987).
2. The analysis here derives from Dennis L Bark (ed), *The Red Orchestra: Instruments of Soviet Policy* in *Latin America and the Caribbean*, (Stanford, CA: Hoover Institution Press, 1987).
3. Robert A. Packenham, 'Capitalist Dependency and Socialist Dependency: The Case of Cuba', paper prepared for delivery at the Annual Meeting of the American Political Science Association, New Orleans, 29 August–1 September 1985.
4. On Cuban foreign policy and Cuban-Soviet relations see Jorge Domínguez, 'Cuba's Relations with the Caribbean and Central American Countries', in Alan Adelman and Reid Reading (eds), *Confrontation in the Caribbean Basin* (Pittsburgh: Center for Latin American Studies, University of Pittsburgh, 1984), pp. 165–202.
5. W. Raymond Duncan, 'Cuban-Soviet Relations: Directions of Influence', Chapter 3 of this volume.
6. See the analysis in Howard J. Wiarda and Harvey F. Kline, *Latin American Politics and Development* (Boulder, CO: Westview, 1984).
7. Lucian W. Pye and Sidney Verba (eds), *Political Culture and Political Development* (Princeton: Princeton University Press, 1965).
8. Crane Brinton, *Anatomy of Revolution* (New York: Random House, 1965).

9. W. W. Rostow, *The Stages of Economic Growth* (Cambridge: Cambridge University Press, 1960).
10. On the roots of anti-Americanism in Latin America see Irving Louis Horowitz, 'Latin America, Anti-Americanism, and Intellectual Hubris', in A. Z. Rubinstein and Donald E. Smith (eds), *Anti-Americanism in the Third World* (New York: Praeger, 1985).
11. Howard J. Wiarda (ed.), *Rift and Revolution: The Central American Imbroglio* (Washington, DC: American Enterprise Institute, 1984).
12. See Howard J. Wiarda, 'The Internal Dimensions of the Crisis in Central America', *Occasional Paper*, Center for Latin American Studies, University of Connecticut, Fall 1985, pp. 1–23; and *Dialogue on Central America* (Washington, DC: Roosevelt Center for Public Policy Studies, 1985).
13. For further discussion Wiarda, *Rift and Revolution* (note 11); also James R. Greene and Brent Scowcroft (eds), *Western Interests and US Policy Options in the Caribbean Basin* (Boston: Oelgeschlager, Gunn & Haim, 1984).
14. For the background details see Howard J. Wiarda, 'Soviet Policy in the Caribbean and Central America: Opportunities and Constraints', in John Garrard and S. Neil MacFarlane (eds), *Soviet Policy in the Third World* (forthcoming).
15. Luis Mercier Vega, *Roads to Power in Latin America* (New York: Praeger, 1969).
16. Ronald C. Schneider, *Communism in Guatemala 1944–1954* (New York: Praeger, 1959).
17. Tad Szulc, *Fidel: A Critical Portrait* (New York: Morrow, 1986).
18. These themes are considerably elaborated in the author's previously cited paper, 'Soviet Policy in the Caribbean and Central America', (see note 14) and Wiarda and Falcoff, *Communist Challenge* (see note 1).
19. A recent assessment focused on Soviet relations with Argentina is in the *Washington Post* (4 November 1986), p. A12.
20. The best analysis is Ernest Evans, 'Revolutionary Movements in Central America: The Development of a New Strategy', in Wiarda (ed.), *Rift and Revolution*, pp. 167–93 (see note 11).
21. Jiri Valenta and Virginia Valenta, 'Soviet Strategies and Policies in the Caribbean Basin', in Wiarda (ed.), *Rift and Revolution*, pp. 197–252 (see note 11). Revised versions of this important paper and of that of Evans are published in Wiarda and Falcoff, *Communist Challenge* (see note 1).
22. These points are elaborated in Wiarda, 'Soviet Policy in the Caribbean and Central America' (see note 14).
23. Duncan, Chapter 3, this volume.
24. A good collection on these themes is Jorge Domínguez (ed.), *Cuba: Internal and International Affairs* (Beverly Hills, CA: Sage, 1982).
25. M. R. R. Frechette, 'Cuba-Soviet Impact on the Western Hemisphere', *Department of State Bulletin*, vol. 80, July 1980, pp. 77–80; and Morris Rothenberg, 'Latin American in Soviet Eyes', *Problems of Communism*, vol. 32, no. 5, September–October, 1983, pp. 1–18.
26. Mark Falcoff, 'Cuba: First among Equals', in Bark (ed), *The*

Red Orchestra (see note 2).
27. Evans, 'Revolutionary Movements' (see note 20).
28. Wiarda, 'Soviet Policy in the Caribbean and Central America' (see note 14).
29. Documented in Falcoff, 'Cuba' (see note 26).
30. Richard Millett, *Guardians of the Dynasty* (Maryknoll, NY: Orbis, 1977). For a comparative and theoretical perspective see Howard J. Wiarda, *Dictatorships and Development* (Gainesville, FL: University of Florida, 1968).
31. Mark Falcoff, 'Somoza, Sandino, and the United States: What the Past Teaches – and Doesn't', *This World*, vol. 6, Fall 1983, pp. 51–70.
32. Based on field research by the author in Nicaragua during this period. See also Shirley Christian, *Nicaragua* (New York: Vintage, 1986).
33. Millett, *Guardians* (see note 30); Bernard Diedrich, *Somoza* (New York: Dutton, 1961); David Nolan, *The Ideology of the Sandinistas and the Nicaraguan Revolution* (Coral Gables, FA: University of Miami Press, 1984).
34. The best account is that of Christian, *Nicaragua* (see note 32).
35. Falcoff, 'Cuba' (see note 26).
36. The reference is to the book by Paul Hollander, *Political Pilgrims* (New York: Harper & Row, 1983).
37. The analysis here follows that of Falcoff, 'Cuba' (see note 26).
38. See W. Raymond Duncan, *The Soviet Union and Cuba: Interests and Influence* (New York: Praeger, 1985).
39. Based on interviews with US and Nicaraguan officials. See also Howard J. Wiarda, 'The Impact of Grenada in Central America', in Jiri Valenta and Herbert J. Ellison (eds), *Grenada and Soviet/Cuban Policy* (Boulder, CO: Westview, 1986), pp. 105–22.
40. Jiri and Virginia Valenta, 'Leninism in Grenada', *Problems of Communism*, vol. 33, no. 4, July–August 1984, pp. 1–23.
41. The best and most complete study is that of Valenta and Ellison (eds), *Grenada* (see note 39).
42. The analysis here follows the author's earlier paper, 'The Impact of Grenada' (see note 39).
43. The author has had access to the documents captured in Grenada and has based his conclusions on them. An early evaluation of the documents is by Michael J. Ledeen, *Grenada: A Preliminary Report* (Washington, DC: US Departments of Defense and State, 1984).
44. Valenta, 'Leninism in Grenada' (see note 40).
45. Memo from the Grenada embassy in Moscow on NJM relations with the CPSU, Grenada Documents Log No. 012329. For additional documentation see the notes cited in Wiarda, 'Impact of Grenada' (see note 39).
46. Memo from Bernard Coard to Maurice Bishop of 30 June 1982, Grenada Documents Log No. 104262; especially valuable are the minutes of the NJM's Political Bureau and Central Committee.
47. Cooperation and Exchange Plan between the Cuban CP and the NJM, Log No. 100016; Protocol to the 27 October 1980, Grenada-USSR Agreement on Arms Deliveries, Log. No. 000193.

48. Wiarda, 'Impact of Grenada' (see note 39).
49. W. Raymond Duncan, 'Soviet Union Opportunities in Latin America: New Opportunities and Old Constraints', *Journal of Interamerican Studies and World Affairs*, vol. 26, May 1984, pp. 163–98.
50. See the discussion in Howard J. Wiarda, 'Updating US Strategic Policy: Containment in the Caribbean Basin', *Air University Review*, vol. 37, July–August 1986, pp. 26–38.
51. Duncan, 'Soviet Union Opportunities' (see note 49); Wiarda, 'Soviet Union Policy' (see note 14); David E. Albright, 'Latin American in Soviet Union Third World Strategy: The Political Dimension', in Eusebio Mujal-León (ed.), *USSR-Latin American Relations* (Princeton: Princeton University Press, 1987).
52. Wiarda, 'Updating US Strategic Policy' (see note 50). This paper is part of a larger project undertaken by the American Enterprise Institute on this subject.

5 The Soviet Union in South America: Accent on Argentina, Brazil, and Peru
Juan M. del Aguila

INTRODUCTION

A growing web of shared interests between the Soviet Union and key South American countries stems from Moscow's need to do business with industrial and commercial powers like Brazil and Argentina, as well as from Moscow's desire to maintain links to Peru, where the Soviets have a modest military presence. Soviet strategy in South America is acquiring a political character, but the economic and commercial dimension is still paramount. The Soviet Union is not perceived as posing a major threat to any of these countries, and Argentina in particular may look to Moscow for political support in its continuing dispute with Britain over the Falkland Islands. Each of these states follows a foreign policy that is relatively independent from Washington, a trend the Soviets encourage. Argentina, Brazil, and Peru capitalise on trends towards polycentrism in the international system, and each actor values the diversification of its foreign economic and political relations.

Soviet strategy in South America is hardly driven by ideology, and Moscow subscribes to a conventional state-to-state model of relations with these countries. Suspicions about Moscow's revolutionary goal linger on, particularly in Brazil, but the Soviets appear to be constrained in their pursuit of long-term revolutionary goals by the fear that they would lose valuable commercial and political relationships if they are found to be promoting subversion. Democratic regimes in all three countries suffer from high debt, but Moscow cannot offer effective relief on this front. Still, the Soviets reap political and propaganda dividends from the economic crises. Relations between Moscow and each of these key South American states are maturing, and the long-term Soviet presence in South America is expected to stabilise and grow.

121

Regime changes in key South American countries in the 1980s stem largely from the failure of the military-authoritarian model to produce lasting political legitimacy in the face of growing social and economic pressures. Processes of democratisation are moving the region – with the exception of Chile and Paraguay – away from authoritarianism and into a new cycle of rulership under civilian-democratic governments. Since 1980 Argentina, Brazil, Uruguay, and Peru have instituted democratic rule, and their respective political systems are becoming stable and remarkably mature.[1] Constitutional government under civilian authority is now the rule in South America, but the new regimes differ among themselves in political orientation, in developmental outlook, and in foreign policy strategies. Still, historically and culturally, the nations of South America form part of the Western world.

With democratisation, new sources of pluralism are emerging and the region's elites are conscious of the need to manage properly 'the new interdependence' by pursuing options that would improve their respective nation's position in the regional and world systems. There is a growing recognition that Argentina, Brazil, and Peru, among others, can benefit from a diversification of their political, commercial, and even strategic relationships, and that such a process does not mean a repudiation of traditional ties to the United States or the West in general. The leadership in these countries is sympathetic to some of the demands associated with the North–South struggle, without losing sight of the peculiar security considerations that could make the region a focal point for East–West tensions.[2] Nationalism shapes the outlook of the new democratic leaders, particularly in the case of Peru's president, Alan García, and its expression reflects an intense desire for recognition and autonomy.

For different reasons, these countries are expanding ties to the Soviet Union and other communist states, which in some cases build on relations developed over the last two decades.[3] The Soviet Union's rise to world power status has had an impact on the thinking of the region's strategic elites, and is recognised as having changed the character of the postwar world. Local communist parties are a conduit for Soviet influence in the region and are a factor in national politics, though their strength varies from country to country and in no case is it overwhelming. A desire to reduce Washington's real or perceived hegemony over the region also helps to explain why some countries see contacts with the Soviet Union positively, despite the fact that regimes are aware that crossing certain thresholds – especially in the security area – could complicate relations with Washington. Finally, the Soviet Union is not perceived as a major strategic threat by Argentina, Brazil, or Peru, and there is little fear in these countries that the Soviet Union would begin to destabilise the region if the opportunity arose. Anti-communism is no longer the driving force behind any of these nations' foreign policy, and the divisions and strategic rivalries between Moscow and its adversaries are well understood.

Argentina, Brazil, and Peru perceive the Soviet Union to be less of an ideological actor and more of a conventional great power. Respectively, their policies toward Moscow aim to reduce the weight of US hegemony in each case, and increase each actor's bargaining power. In brief, Argentina, Brazil, and Peru are not looking for a comfortable kind of clientelism, but rather for a relationship with Moscow that improves each actor's economic and political standing in the international system without jeopardising their integrity or national security. Moscow is interested in expanding normal inter-state relations with Argentina, Peru, Brazil, Colombia, Venezuela, and other countries, and does so pragmatically and with little regard for a regime's political orientation. The Soviets did business with successive military regimes in Brazil during the 1960s and 1970s, and with a repressive military junta in Argentina in the early 1980s. At the same time, Moscow pursued a convenient military relationship with military regimes in Peru that sought to change the traditional norm of Peruvian foreign policy in order to expand ties with several Western countries and those of the socialist bloc.[4] Soviet writers note the importance of such relations, and reaffirm the need for 'developing interstate relations with those newly-free countries which are following the capitalist road', based on the principle of peaceful coexistence.[5] The coming to power of democratic forces creates new incentives for the Soviets, and it is clear that the shift away from military rule introduces some qualitative differences in how the Soviet Union perceives the political balance inside a particular country. Social Democrats are favoured over more moderate Christian Democratic forces, and traditional conservatives are still viewed with ideological suspicion, particularly in Brazil. Moscow also recognises that leaders like Raúl Alfonsín in Argentina and Alan García in Peru are popular and on occasion, anti-American. The latter tendency could be encouraged. In short, Moscow remains committed to a 'a state to state model of relations with the countries of the region',[6] and to a particularistic rather than a uniform assessment of those relations. Such an approach enables Moscow to cope with rapid shifts – should these come – and to minimise potential losses if the area were once again to turn rightward.

CATEGORISATION OF REGIMES

The Soviets' categorisation of regimes suggests that there is a continuum upon which regimes are differentiated, and that such depends on the class-base of a particular regime, the internal conditions which brought a regime to power, the level of development found in a particular country (and the development model followed), and even foreign policy orientation. Consolidated Marxist-Leninist regimes such as Cuba's are the Soviets' principal allies, followed by those where a revolutionary vanguard party like the *Frente Sandinista de Liberacíon Nacional* (FSLN) is leading the process of social transformation. Of particular significance here is the fact that no South American country is taking 'the socialist path', and Argentina, Brazil, and Peru are clearly capitalist, even if the state is a major economic force in trade, finance, and overall development. All three have a growing private industrial sector, welcome foreign investment, and do billions of dollars worth of foreign trade with Western capitalist states. There is much evidence to suggest that in each case, a global, rather than a regional, outlook, shapes foreign policy behaviour. Argentina and Peru are members of the Non-Aligned Movement (NAM).

According to Daniel Papp, 'Soviet analysis asserts that the developing world is gradually becoming more differentiated, with more and more states choosing either the socialist or capitalist path of development', which means that categorisation is more subtle and sophisticated. Still, the major South American countries would be categorised as 'broadly capitalist', because they are all democratic, variably anti-imperialist in intensity, relatively large and with considerable economic potential, and 'their internal development strategies were not determined by multinational corporations, the World Bank, or the International Monetary Fund.'[7] This would be the case even if international lending organisations were to pressure governments into a monetarist or more fiscally conservative strategy, because each country, especially Brazil, retains some leverage of its own.

Though clearly capitalist, these countries would more specifically be viewed as 'bourgeois-democratic' in character, because the middle and upper classes are the key to the stability of the political regime, and formal democracy prevails. Strands of populism are part of the domestic policy agenda, but the working class is not assigned 'a historical mission'. The Soviets must realise that, in each case, the potential for revolutionary transformations is quite low, and that in fact what is being contemplated is the institutionalisation of 'state-managed' capitalism alongside the expansion of democratic notions of rights and social responsibility. This is so recognised by leading South American communists, like Rodney Arismendi of Uruguay, who writes that 'those Latin American countries that employ democratic forms of government have reached particularly high levels of capitalist development'.[8]

Moscow perceives Argentina and Brazil to be the most powerful states in South America, quite able to resist US pressures in specific issue areas. Consequently, the nature of the economic or political system is not as important as each local actor's pursuit of a strategy that takes advantage of the superpowers' global rivalries. Moscow has capitalised on 'official Washington's concentration on perceived threats in the rest of Latin America, growing local capabilities and national assertiveness that tended to reject US leadership'.[9] By doing business with Moscow, key South American states enhance their status in the system and force each superpower to realise the limits of their actual or potential influence.

Statements from the 27th Congress of the Communist Party of the Soviet Union (CPSU) suggest that Moscow is ready to expand relations with social democratic governments in Latin America, as well as with moderately nationalistic governments which on occasion resist Washington's hegemony. Argentina and Peru are ruled by social democrats, and Brazil is under a centrist regime which allows pro-Moscow elements on the left such as the Brazilian Communist Party to participate in domestic politics. Specifically, the Congress declared that 'the Soviet Union's foreign policy is that of solidarity with the forces of social emancipation and national liberation, close interaction with socialism-oriented countries, with revolutionary democratic parties and the Non-Aligned Nations Movement, and development of contacts with social democracy.'[10] Moscow is signalling a willingness to broaden contacts in the region and throughout the Third World, and recognises that in Latin America, social democracy is a force to be contended with. Moscow is well-positioned to take advantage of radical trends in social democracy and has to some extent already benefited from some of the anti-American positions taken by organisations like the Socialist International, to which Peru's *Alianza*

Popular Revolucionaria Americana (APRA) and several other Latin American social democratic parties belong. In sum, Moscow's categorisation of several South American regimes as 'bourgeois-democratic' is realistic, because it recognises that for the medium term, the internal balance of forces has shifted from military-technocratic to elected civilian-managerial elites with populist inclinations.

On the other hand, the same regimes that are now viewed as bourgeois-democratic were not too long ago controlled by the military, but that made little difference when it came to Moscow's interest in them. Except for brief interludes of civilian rule, Argentina was ruled by anti-communist generals from 1966 until 1983; Brazil's military government lasted from 1964 until 1984; and Peru was under successive military regimes from 1968 until 1980. The Peruvian military's leftist tendencies were more pronounced that those of either the Argentine or Brazilian military regimes, which were distinctly 'bureaucratic-authoritarian'. A paradox lies in the fact that the military regimes in Brasilia and Buenos Aires cracked down on the revolutionary left at a time when relations with Moscow started to mature. Moscow was not seen as the source of Argentina's or Brazil's domestic agitation, and in fact its ideological influence over the insurrectional and terrorist left was marginal. Moscow took advantage of opportunities offered by these regimes and largely refrained from meddling in the respective country's internal affairs for the sake of future political gains. Paradoxically, the Soviets have not suffered a heavy political price for their association with repressive governments and have had little difficulty in continuing relations with democratic regimes.

Moscow's relationship with Argentina during the last years of military rule illustrates how pragmatic its approach was, and how little attention Moscow pays to how a regime treats its citizens. For example, the Soviets willingly reciprocated the Argentine military's shift to a policy of 'ideological pluralism' in the early 1970s by signing trade and other agreements with the Lanusse regime. Subsequently, Moscow refrained from criticising the Videla administration's widespread violations of human rights or its repression of the radical left during the dirty war against subversion and terrorism. In addition, Moscow made huge purchases of Argentine grain and other goods in the early 1980s and viewed Argentina's refusal to join the embargo imposed by the Carter administration quite positively. Finally, Moscow supported Argentina during the Falklands War in 1982, but refrained from selling military hardware to Buenos Aires even as it encouraged Argentina to defy US and British interests in the South Atlantic. As Aldo César Vacs concluded, 'The Soviet-Argentine relationship became, in the course of the decade, among the most cordial ever established between the Soviet Union and a Latin American country',[11] and both nations appear to be committed to its preservation. President Alfonsín's visit to the Soviet Union in October 1986 suggests that political issues are becoming more salient in the bilateral relationship.[12] A stable relationship handled pragmatically suits each country well.

State interests led Moscow to emphasise trade and commerce in relations with successive military regimes in Brazil despite the anti-communist outlook of those regimes and their clearly pro-American attitude. Ideological incompatibility did not prevent Moscow from doing business with governments that took Washington's view of the Cold War, and in this case, had broken diplomatic relations with Cuba. Brazil's economic and long-term political importance made a difference in the way its military governments were perceived in Moscow, and Brazil's gradual de-emphasis of a foreign policy based on 'ideological frontiers' meant that it too welcomed its ties to Moscow. The Soviets have an abiding interest in expanding their presence in Brazil, but must do so in a manner that does not threaten Brazilian security interests in the South Atlantic or even in west-central Africa. If Moscow's ties to Argentina expand into the security and defence areas, that could raise some worries in Brazil; the latter is already known to be concerned with Soviet-Cuban gains in Angola, and may at some point resist new Soviet entreaties.[13] In its relations with Brazil, the USSR has struck a delicate balance between its state interests and the ideological and expansionist aims of its foreign policy, but the urge to deepen its penetration has not disappeared. Moscow's new leadership is committed to 'the cultivation of key capitalist-oriented Third World countries' in South America, and Brazil figures prominently in Gorbachev's agenda.[14]

To recapitulate, Soviet categorisations of regimes do not offer definitive guides to Soviet behaviour, because such categorisations often fail to account for substantive differences among regimes and at times create contradictions for policy makers and technocrats more interested in practical matters. At least one influential Soviet writer is known to have been disillusioned with semantic and conceptual flaws in the manner through which categorisation is effected, and has suggested critical revisions.[15] Moscow's interests in the major South American countries stems from its own economic needs, as well as from a desire to reduce US influence in the region and increase its own. As Cole Blasier, Morris Rothenberg, Vacs, and others point out, pragmatism and realism, rather than strict ideological criteria or revolutionary imperatives, go a long way in shaping Moscow's relations with key South American countries. The absence of any moralism is also quite striking.

DIMENSIONS OF SOVIET POLICY

Soviet foreign policy toward the region has two dimensions: a formal one between governments based on state-to-state relations, and an extra-governmental one between the CPSU and the non-ruling but pro-Soviet communist parties of various countries.[16] In the 1980s Moscow has been more interested in expanding state-to-state relations with key South American countries than in throwing its weight behind local communist parties, because the political situation in most countries is not favourable to the communists. Moscow supports parties that call for armed struggle (as is the case now with the Chilean Communist Party), but also those that operate legally (i.e. the Peruvian Communist Party). The lessons of Allende's débâcle in Chile are still fresh in Moscow, and in its dealings with local parties it must avoid the dangers of 'ultra-leftism' as well as the charge of 'being left on the sidelines' by revolutionary forces making a bid for power.[17]

On the other hand, having allies in all of the major countries of South America is clearly advantageous to Moscow, because it establishes a communist presence in key political systems, multiplies the channels through which Moscow can exercise influence, and opens up direct lines of communication between Moscow and the locals. In addition, local communist parties are potential strategic assets that can be mobilised in times of crisis, or be used to pressure governments on behalf of Soviet goals. Local parties are potentially a front wedge of Soviet influence in Latin America, and through its financial, organisational, and ideological support for them, Moscow can keep abreast of local issues and trends.

Argentina's Communist Party is the largest in South America, with some 70 000 members. Its status is legal, but the party does not have legislative representation.[18] The party still suffers from the fact that it collaborated with the military on some issues in the late 1970s, and was charged with political opportunism. The party has given tacit approval to some of Alfonsín's proposals in foreign policy, particularly those that call for a restoration of Argentine sovereignty over the Falklands and support for a negotiated solution to the crisis in Central America.

The Brazilian left includes Trotskyites, pro-Moscow and pro-Beijing elements, as well as new groupings of former Castroite and insurrectional groups. The *Partido Comunista Brasileiro* has some 20 000 members. The *Partido Comunista do Brasil* has switched its loyalty from the People's Republic of China to Albania, and it remains rooted in orthodox communism. These parties have legal status, but quarrels among parties and factions have weakened their political prospects.[19] In fact, Riordan Roett notes that the Brazilian 'communists are expected to be a negligible force in the political arena', because moderate parties on the left have much broader popular support and have been more effective in aggregating working-class interests.[20] Moscow's ability to influence local politics through the now legal communist parties is thus limited. As it has had to do in the past, Moscow must resolve local quarrels between its supporters. In any event, the Brazilian government has little to fear from the communists at this point, and one can be relatively certain that the military and the security forces are watching the communists' behaviour.

Peru's Communist Party (PCP) operates legally and has some 2000 members. It participated in the 1984 congressional elections as a member of the United Left coalition, and the coalition received 26 per cent of the vote. The United Left has 48 out of 180 deputies in the Peruvian congress, and the PCP has six of the 48 leftist deputies.[21] The party has some support in the organised working class and among intellectuals, but finds its efforts to expand its support constrained by president Alan García's popularity and by APRA's historical enmity toward the communists. The leadership has demonstrated satisfaction with the workings of the United Left coalition, and the party is now committed to playing by the rules of the democratic game. At times, the party supports García, and it did so when in 1987 he announced the nationalisation of the banking system. Still, its long term goal is 'for the national and social liberation of Peru', which can be interpreted to mean a number of things.[22] The party has taken a strong position against the 'Pol Potist-like terrorist grouping' Sendero Luminoso (Shining Path), of extreme Maoist inspiration. It has been quite critical of other 'ultra-leftist' groups considered to be less than enamoured of following the Soviet line.[23] Finally, though the PCP supports García's confrontation with the International Monetary Fund over the debt issue, it chastises his administration for 'occasionally taking an anti-Soviet and anti-communist stand'.

Taking guidance from Moscow, the PCP treads carefully between critical support for a popular, anti-imperialist president like García, and more sectarian forces on the left which are contemptuous of the Kremlin's 'conservatism'. The party clearly rejects the indiscriminate terrorism of Sendero Luminoso, but has yet to denounce the pro-Castro Tupac Amaru group, of more recent vintage.[24] Committed to legality, the party is in a sense a defender of the system in which it participates, not an outcast; to the extreme left, that may well constitute a crass betrayal. Jorge Del Prado's writings can be relied upon to reflect thinking in the Kremlin, and from that standpoint, it appears that Moscow is satisfied with the PCP's strategy of guarded support for García. Continuing disputes with the People's Republic of China may partially explain the PCP's attacks on Sendero Luminoso, but the party could also hope thereby to create a moderate image for itself. In a nutshell, through its local ally Moscow is well positioned to take advantage of the anti-American attacks of President García, and to be seen as a friend in time of need. Soviet efforts are designed to deepen divisions between Washington and nationalistic democrats in Peru and elsewhere, in the hope of moving some key South American governments toward a more non-aligned posture.

In sum, despite their pro-Soviet orientation and ideological quarrels with revolutionary groups on the extreme left, communist parties in the region are resilient and adapt well to local conditions. Under experienced leadership tested during times of persecution and clandestine activities, Moscow's allies in South America remain loyal to the aims of the international communist movement. Successful transitions to democracy in Argentina, Peru, and Brazil reduce the prospects that communists will come to power, but with their newly acquired legal status, the parties can more easily articulate their own ideas as well as the Kremlin's line. Fealty to the Soviet line is crucial to the parties' strategy, but flexibility and pragmatism, rather than revolutionary romanticism or 'subjectivism', characterise their behaviour in the 1980s.

The formalisation of relations between the Soviet Union and Brazil, Argentina, and Peru, respectively, establishes frameworks through which Moscow collaborates in commercial, political, and diplomatic matters with its South American interlocutors. As will be made clear, Moscow's commercial stake in the region is substantial, and it provides a solid infrastructure for 'collateral diffusion' into more sensitive areas. In addition, the Soviet Union maintains ten embassies, seven trade offices, six civilian technical missions and one military mission (in Peru) in South America, a growing presence that is complemented by multifaceted representation from other East European countries.[25] The Soviet airline Aeroflot provides service to Lima and Buenos Aires, and Soviet delegations travel frequently to the region. In short, the Soviet Union has developed 'an impressive array of trade, cultural and consular establishments [in South America], and it all amounts to a greatly expanded Soviet capability to make contacts at all levels of [South American] governments and societies'.[26] Major South American actors recognise the Soviet Union's superpower status, and demonstrate a willingness to do business with the Soviet state. This is important given Moscow's desire to expand its global reach, particularly into an area formerly considered geopolitically 'off-limits'. Moscow's ability to compete effectively with Washington in the Third World would be dramatically enhanced if it produced major inroads into South America and moved the competition into critical defence and security areas. To be recognised as a bona-fide competitor is important to the Soviet Union, because that would bring it prestige and status, and it could lead to it being perceived as an equal to the United States. Finally, as mentioned earlier, none of the major South American countries perceives the Soviet Union to be a major strategic threat to themselves or the region, or to be a state committed to reckless expansion in South America. This conventional view suits Moscow well, and it reinforces its projection of a 'good international citizen' image as well as its need for acceptance.

THE SOVIET UNION AND ARGENTINA

Stable political and diplomatic relations between the Soviet Union and Argentina in the 1980s strengthen a growing web of trade and commercial ties between both countries, an interactive relationship that is highly beneficial to each partner. Argentina is Moscow's principal trading partner in the region, and two-way trade between the countries amounted to over $1.82 billion in 1983 and $1.58 billion in 1984, but it declined to $1.36 billion in 1985. Soviet imports from Argentina include foodstuffs and agricultural products, and sales to Argentina are mostly industrial goods, machinery and transportation equipment.[27] In 1983 the Soviets bought 9.7 million tons of wheat, corn, and sorghum, as well as large quantities of meat, wool, and hides. In 1985 over 8.0 million tons of cereal grains were purchased by the Soviets, but imports fell off in 1986 because of purchases from other sources and slight improvements in the Soviet Union's own production. This is viewed with some concern in Buenos Aires, because Argentina expects the Soviet Union to adhere to the terms of a trade agreement signed earlier, and because Argentina looks to maintain stable marketing arrangements for its grain.[28] Soviet purchases of grain from Argentina peaked in 1980–82, when the effects of the US embargo were most directly felt; still, total purchases since 1978 add up to more than 55 million tons. Soviet needs in this area are not met with domestic production and, even if shortfalls occur from year to year, it is expected that Moscow will continue looking to Argentina as a principal source of agricultural commodities. In fact, Deputy Foreign Minister V. Ivanov has said that 'Argentina will continue to hold a preferential place in future grain purchases made by the Soviet Union', and that deals in other areas are expected.[29]

Soviet purchases of grain from the European Economic Community (EEC) in 1986 reduced the amount of grain brought from Argentina. Cutbacks are of great concern to Buenos Aires, as is the fact that the trade agreement between the Soviet Union and Argentina covering grain sales is not likely to be renewed in 1990. Finally, there was some doubt as to whether the Soviet pledge to purchase 4.5 million tons of grain in 1987 would be kept; if not, Argentina would have to find other markets.[30]

The Soviet Union and Argentina also collaborate on a number of technical ventures. In 1983 a group of Argentine firms formed a consortium with a Soviet state-owned enterprise to undertake the construction of a hydroelectric plant in Argentina. Agreements have also been signed between Soviet commercial agencies and provincial governments in Argentina, involving in one instance an exchange of trolley buses for Argentine wines.[31] The Soviets are involved in the construction of parts of the rail system in Buenos Aires, and some of their companies competed for contracts for the expansion of the ocean port at Bahía Blanca, several hundred kilometres south of Buenos Aires.[32]

On the other hand, the principal problem in the trade area between the Soviet Union and Argentina is the latter's huge surplus, or to put it differently, the consistently large trade deficits incurred by the Soviet Union in its trade with Argentina. The Soviets have accumulated billions of dollars in deficits since 1980 and have begun to suggest that Argentina increase its imports of Soviet goods in order to bring about a more symmetrical trade relationship.[33] The quality of some Soviet goods is not high, and that clearly affects the desirability of Soviet exports. Soviet technology in some areas also lags well behind that of Western manufacturers. Soviet willingness to supply Argentina with heavy water for the latter's nuclear programme could lead to the supply of other sensitive materials, and to a gradual improvement in the Soviets' balance of trade with Argentina, but major political considerations might also intervene. There is a recognition in Argentina that the Soviets have a real interest in bringing about a more balanced commercial relationship, but somewhat like Japan, Argentina would find it difficult to become a less aggressive exporter.

Robert Evanson argues that it is possible that 'Soviet trade efforts have been designed to facilitate a process' of encouraging Argentina to move toward a more non-aligned posture, and to view Moscow as a mature actor and trading partner.'[34] Need is a second factor, in the sense that Moscow's failures in agriculture force it to depend on large imports of grain in order to satisfy domestic consumption. Third, the institutionalisation of a large trade framework legitimises doing business in other areas; over the long run, this may well be the definitive Soviet objective. For example, a pre-agreement has been reached between the Soviet Union and Argentina establishing joint ventures in the Argentine fishing industry. It will increase the number of Soviet trawlers in Argentine waters (now around 70) and probably add to the Soviets' capability for gathering naval intelligence in the South Atlantic. This illustrates the fact that strategic motivations are as important as the Soviets' willingness to find new trading partners in South America, and that conventional business deals may well have long-term political consequences.

The transition from military to civilian rule in Argentina brought approval from Moscow, despite the latter's relationship with the military regime. The CPSU issued a favourable opinion of President Alfonsín's election, and a Soviet delegation attended Alfonsín's inauguration.[35] Argentina's entry into NAM and its criticism of the International Monetary Fund's (IMF) lending policies are viewed positively in Moscow, though Argentina's foreign and economic policies are not particularly intended to register satisfaction by the Soviets. In fact, Argentina has refused to join those countries (including Cuba and Peru) calling for either repudiation or arbitrary limits on debt payments and has managed to obtain some relief in paying back part of its $50 billion external debt. Clearly, a confrontation between Argentina and Western financial institutions would have some propaganda value for Moscow, but the Kremlin is in no position to offer Argentina any realistic alternatives in this matter. For the Kremlin, episodic confrontations over the debt question are preferable to partial resolution of the issue.

Alfonsín is committed to removing potential sources of East–West confrontation in South America. In trying to assert Argentine and Latin American interests on behalf of regional stability, he has stated: 'What we have to do in Latin America is to learn to raise our own national banners so that our subcontinent doesn't become the ideological battleground of the two superpowers'.[36] Moscow is probably aware of the fact that if it assumes a high security profile in the region, it could complicate relations between Washington and Buenos Aires and, paradoxically, damage its own long-term interests. So far, Moscow has refrained from actively pursuing any sort of a security relationship with Argentina, and the latter has shown no inclination to do otherwise.

On the other hand, the unresolved dispute between Argentina and Britain over possession of the Falkland Islands has the potential to disrupt inter-American relations once again and create new opportunities for Moscow.[37] Early in his term, Alfonsín stated that 'on the Malvinas [Falklands] issue we understand what the return of democracy has meant: to negotiate with Great Britain by peaceful means'.[38] So far, efforts to resolve the dispute have failed, and Britain has improved its military presence on the islands. For London, holding on to the islands involves national honour and resolve, and the dispute still carries deep emotional and psychological connotations for the Argentines. Lastly, the extension by Britain of its security zone around the islands by an additional 150 miles is seen in Argentina as a violation of its own claims over those waters. London's decision came in the wake of the Argentine-Soviet agreement on fishing, and it is clearly an effort designed to cope with a hostile naval presence off the Falklands. The dispute between Britain and Argentina over the Falklands involves East–West (security) as well as North–South challenges (anti-colonialism), and Moscow is clearly on the side of Argentina.

From Moscow's standpoint, a resolution of the dispute would reduce its options and would offer no opportunity to capitalise on the conflict. Still, that would not represent a political, much less a strategic, defeat, because the South Atlantic is not an area of priority for the Soviet Union. Soviet prestige is not involved in the issue, but Moscow would gain if London and Buenos Aires were to renew hostilities. Moscow's response to an outbreak of conflict would be circumspect, but the point is to show that the Soviets are well-positioned to ride the tiger if the dispute goes on, and could gain politically if armed conflict were to break out. In political and diplomatic terms, Moscow favours Argentina and is critical of Britain's efforts to maintain a 'colonial outpost' in the South Atlantic. Soviet ambassador Kvasov declared in 1984 that his country's support for Argentina on the Falklands matter was 'clear, firm and consequent', and that position was reaffirmed during Alfonsín's visit to the Soviet Union.[39]

The fact that the Alfonsín government is popular, that Argentina is no longer ruled by generals, and that the Falklands issue is on the agenda of NAM adds some credibility to Argentina's claims. Lingering doubts regarding Washington's commitment to the security of its Latin American partners are fed by Soviet propaganda, which at times has portrayed the United States as an unreliable ally. Finally, Moscow can afford to sit and wait, because it loses nothing of substance if the matter is settled, and it stands to benefit geopolitically if a flare-up re-occurs. Britain, as the winner of the war in 1982, finds itself today largely on the defensive, and perceived intransigence on its part is of concern to key governments in Europe and Latin America.

One of the consequences of the Falklands War is that attitudes inside the Argentine armed forces regarding perceived threats in the South Atlantic are changing. Carlos Moneta points out that some sectors of the military do not perceive the Soviet Union to be a threat in the region.[40] Argentine military analysts now take account of rifts in the Western bloc, and particularly of what a London–Washington *entente* means for Buenos Aires. The military casts the dispute in a North–South context, and that has led to rethinking of Argentina's security needs. In addition, 'many rising young officers are bitter toward the United States for supporting Britain in the Falklands War', though that has yet to produce sympathies for Moscow in the ranks.[41] If such a reassessment leads to an institutional view of Britain as a hostile power, of the United States as irrevocably committed to its defence priorities in Europe, and of the Soviet Union as a potential strategic ally, that could certainly redound to Moscow's benefit.

There is little evidence that the Soviets have been able to influence political, economic, or security developments to any appreciable degree in Argentina, but it is clear that there is a consensus in Argentina that supports an economic relationship. Moscow values the preservation and expansion of formal political relations, and the Argentines hold a similar view. Argentine Foreign Minister Dante Caputo recently pointed out how important his country considers relations with the Soviet Union to be, and President Alfonsín's visit to

Moscow provides more evidence of that compelling fact.[42] Matters of 'high politics' do not yet occupy a central place in the parameters of the Western security system, and because conditions that would bring about sustained collaboration in sensitive matters do not obtain. After all, Argentina belongs to the Organisation of American States (OAS), subscribes to the Rio Treaty, and maintains a whole array of governmental and non-governmental contacts with the United States.

In conclusion, Argentina does not perceive the Soviet Union to be its opponent, and it is interested in sustaining a very profitable trade and economic relationship with Moscow. Political issues are becoming more salient, and Argentina has elicited favourable Soviet responses on issues such as the dispute over the Falklands, the resolution of the Central American crisis, and bilateral matters. Buenos Aires supports Moscow's calls for the elimination of nuclear weapons by the year 2000, and Argentina expects to do business with the Soviet Union for the foreseeable future without incurring major costs. There may be reason to suspect that Argentina would play 'a Soviet card' in order to gain leverage in its conflict with Britian over the Falklands, but that is far from certain. The potential value of the policy is a strong deterrent to British and US moves in the South Atlantic, but Argentina is unsure of how far Moscow would go in its support. Still, Vacs notes that 'the web of shared interests [between Argentina and the Soviet Union] appears to be solid and destined to expand. The countries' discreet partnership is no longer a matter of temporary convenience but will be a constant in international relations for the foreseeable future'.[43]

THE SOVIET UNION AND BRAZIL

Brazil is the largest and most populous nation in South America. And in addition to its geographic and demographic preeminence, it has the most highly developed economy of the newly industrialising countries. Brazil possesses a wealth of natural resources, an increasingly diverse industrial base, and dynamic export capabilities. For reasons that have to do with Brazil's size, economic potential, and growing assertiveness in international affairs, Moscow is committed to deepening its ties to this nation. As the world's eighth largest free-market economy, Brazil is able to supply a variety of goods needed by the Soviet Union, and the latter finds obvious benefits from establishing a presence in such a huge market.[44]

Ties were preserved during periods of repressive rule by Brazilian military regimes although these regimes persecuted local communists, failed to resume ties with Cuba, and sought the collaboration of other authoritarian regimes in the Southern Cone for the creation of regional bulwarks against communism. During this period Soviet influence in political and security matters was negligible, due to the hostility of the military toward Marxism-Leninism, and because Brazil maintained close ties with Washington. Still, Soviet trade with Brazil in 1971 was higher than with any other Latin American country except Cuba. The Soviets' principal export to Brazil for much of the 1970s was oil. By the end of that decade, the Soviets had sold to Brazil goods valued at $553 million but had imported over $2.5 billion in Brazilian products.[45]

The trend has continued into the present. The Soviets purchase corn, soya, rice, coffee, cacao, and cooking oil from Brazil, while selling chemicals, fertilisers, flour, and limited amounts of petroleum. During 1982–83 the Soviet Commercial Agency V/Prodintorg and the Brazilian Sugar and Alcohol Institute signed contracts covering deliveries of 445 000 tons of crude and 100 000 tons of refined sugar to the Soviet Union.[46] Soviet purchases went from $226 million in 1979 to $864 million in 1983, but declined to $500 million in 1985.[47] Brazil enjoys enormous surpluses in its trade with the Soviet Union, and the latter has let it be known that it wants Brazil to purchase more Soviet goods.

Joint efforts are under way designed to expand the Soviet economic presence in Brazil and bring the large trade imbalance into line. Already involved in large hydroelectric projects, the Soviets are looking for purchases of utility vehicles from Brazil and are interested in participation in a large irrigation project in Pernambuco. At a meeting of the Soviet-Brazilian Inter-Governmental Commission for Commercial and Economic Cooperation held in April 1986, discussions continued on Soviet participation in the installation of a plant to produce cast iron and manganese; joint ventures in the production of refractory bauxite and in the processing of copper ore are also planned.[48] Moscow has also been promoting a trend toward licensing, industrial cooperation, and greater coordination between export and import trade. If this endeavour succeeds, it would strengthen what is clearly an impressive commercial relationship between the communist superpower and South America's most powerful country.

In the political-diplomatic field, Brazil's shift to a more non-aligned posture under former President Joao B. Figueiredo (1979–85), its earlier repudiation of a military treaty with the United States, and its refusal to sign the Nuclear Non-Proliferation Treaty were seen in Moscow as part of Brazil's 'global awakening'.[49] Figueiredo's foreign policy stressed ideological neutrality, and it moved Brazil away from a marked pro-US tilt. Ties with key Third World countries in the Arab world and Africa expanded Brazil's economic influence and created new incentives for Brazilian industrialists, manufacturers, and consumers. Moscow's forays into West Africa and the deployment of Cuban combat forces in Angola raise geopolitical concerns in Brazil's security bureaucracies and in the armed forces, but have yet to be defined as threats to vital Brazilian interests. The armed forces are supplied with mostly US and Western equipment, and likewise benefit from the growth of a domestic arms industry. In 1985 nearly 40 per cent of the requirements in defence material were met from domestic sources, and Brazil exports certain types of weapons to nations in the Middle East and elsewhere.[50] US military doctrines are dominant, and thousands of officers in all three branches of the armed forces have received advanced training in US military establishments. At times, Soviet civilian technicians have been stationed in Brazil, but not in large numbers.

On the other hand, the Soviets do not have a military presence in Brazil, there are no security arrangements between the countries, and Brazil and the Soviet Union compete over arms sales to some Third World countries. Western and US doctrines, not Soviet concepts, pervade strategic thinking, and Brazil subscribes to the Rio Treaty and is a member of the OAS. Anti-communist attitudes in the military and the lack of any substantive desire to antagonise the United States deter effective penetration by the Soviets of sensitive areas. In short, there is little that the Soviets can do to influence security developments in Brazil, because the Soviets lack the instruments to do so, and the government and armed forces can resist overt Soviet penetration.

Political disputes and territorial antagonisms with Suriname, Peru, and other South American countries are handled pragmatically, and the prospects that any of these would create opportunities for Soviet adventurism are remote.[51] Its rivalry with Argentina led Brazil to allow British planes to refuel in bases in southern Brazil during the Falklands War, and to a subsequent reassessment of security interests in the South Atlantic. An assessment of the Argentine-Brazilian rivalry says that a state of 'friendly competition', rather than any sort of hostility prevails, and points out that security tensions in the Southern Cone have subsided since 1978–82.[52] A 'window of opportunity' now exists which could lead both countries to reduce the potential reappearance of geopolitical worries and forestall the initiation of a conventional and nuclear arms race in the area. There is no evidence that Moscow is capitalising on the Brazilian-Argentine rivalry. If it were to do so, it would jeopardise its productive economic relationship with both countries.

Finally, flare-ups of anti-American sentiment in Brazil are isolated and do not provide real opportunities for the Soviets to fan the flames of nationalism and anti-Americanism. Brazil's communists are divided and do not offer a reliable link through which Moscow's influence could be asserted. President Sarney's government is centrist and conservative, and would not look kindly at either internal or external efforts at destabilisation.

In sum, Moscow's ability to exercise effective influence in Brazil's political or security developments is quite limited, and Moscow is probably unwilling to lose what it already has achieved by way of trade in exchange for minor political gains. The Soviets have not acquired any defence burdens in regions that are important to Brazil (e.g. Suriname), so their structure of risks is low. Brazil is not threatened by the Soviet Union and both countries prefer not to raise major East–West issues into their relationship, lest divisions and disagreements complicate profitable economic interactions. Brazil does not wish to antagonise its traditional partners, but it continues to identify with demands for Latin American unity and purposefulness. Improvements in its relations with Cuba are welcomed in Moscow, and may in the long run provide Moscow with wider access.

THE SOVIET UNION AND PERU

In its relations with Peru, the Soviet Union has been through experiences shared elsewhere in South America, namely, a transition to democratic rule in 1980 and the election of a popular nationalist president, Alan García, in 1985; a desire to maintain relations that were established with prior military governments; and the inclusion of communists in the political process. Moscow has learned from the repetition of these experiences and is becoming familiar with the values and norms of societies vastly different from Soviet society. Adaptability and resiliency characterises this relationship, and the Soviets probably view with some optimism the medium- to long-term prospects of widening their penetration in Peru.

President García inherits a military relationship with the Soviet Union, as well as established ties in trade and in some cultural areas. García also faces an intractable insurrectional movement in some regions of Peru, and spasmodic but deadly waves of urban terrorism. His rhetorical flair does not win him any friends in Washington or at the headquarters of western financial institutions, but the Kremlin has shown no inclination to throw its lot in with him. Some scenarios suggest that Peru is becoming increasingly unstable, and there are occasional reports of conspiracies being hatched and coups plotted by disgruntled sectors within the armed forces. The level of violence in the country is at times alarming, and there is some evidence to suggest that the process of democratisation is weakening, though not quite to the point of a reversal.[53]

Peru is the only South American country that has purchased substantial quantities of Soviet weapons; the Soviet military involvement in the country dates back to the early 1970s. The army has in its arsenal Soviet T-54 and T-55 battle tanks; M-46 122 mm and M-54 130 mm howitzers; SA 2 and SA 3 surface-to-air missiles; and M-1938 76 mm AA guns. In turn, the Air Force has acquired fighter aircraft and transports from the Soviet Union, as well as combat helicopters. Peru purchased 36 Sukhoi S-22 fighters, 16 Antonov An-26 transports, and 8 Mi-6 and Mi-8 attack helicopters from the Soviet Union in the 1970s on relatively easy credit terms, and the air force in particular is considered among the best in the region.[54] The value of arms transfers from the Soviet Union to Peru between 1979 and 1983 was $440 million, or nearly 30 per cent of the value from all sources. If one includes purchases made earlier, the total value of Soviet military equipment sent to Peru exceeds $1 billion, surpassed only by the value of equipment provided to Cuba in all of Latin America.[55]

On the other hand, the quality of some weapons leaves something to be desired, and there have been complaints of the manner in which the Soviets comply with maintenance and service agreements. The US State Department contends that Moscow recognises the necessity for in-country overhauls of SU-22 engines. No major purchases have been made recently, but that is largely due to the economic crisis. Major credit has not been available since 1980.

With arms purchases, there came a comprehensive programme of training that sent some 3000 Peruvian military personnel to the Soviet Union, including fighter aircraft pilots. Some 150 Soviet military advisors and technicians are stationed in Peru and provide maintenance and instruction for Soviet-made equipment, but otherwise keep a relatively low profile. This is the only case of a Soviet military advisory presence in South America, but the Soviets have access to Peruvian bases. Soviet fishing vessels off Peru come in for repairs, and at some point the Soviet navy could enlarge its presence in the area.[56] Still, the Peruvian government prefers the status quo in the relationship.

Soviet military involvement in Peru in the 1970s stemmed from the belief that the Peruvian military was ready to reduce US military influence in the country and purchased Soviet arms in order to demonstrate just how independent its foreign policy would be. Arms purchases served immediate political aims for the Velasco and Bermúdez administrations (1968–80) and were in line with other nationalistic measures. Need and relatively easy terms of credit were additional factors, as was the fact that other suppliers could not deliver the goods in the time frame which the government desired. The availability of Soviet weapons partly satisfied Peru's need to seek ties with the East, and do so at marginal costs to its more traditional ties. Finally, by diversifying its sources of supply Peru reduced the 'danger of vulnerability and dependency' on a single supplier. Purchases from the Soviet Union followed a rational calculus of self-interest by Peru and did not damage its standing with the west.[57]

For the Soviets breaking into the South American market was attractive, and it allowed them to display their wares in an area where US and Western suppliers held sway. The Soviets did not expect to replace Peru's traditional sources of supply, but did take advantage of an opportunity provided to them. Over time, they established a credible presence in the country. By agreeing to the request for arms. the Soviets demonstrated more than symbolic support for the anti-imperialist rhetoric of the Peruvian military, but were cautious enough not to go in as deep as they had in Egypt. Soviet military involvement in Peru is a low-cost venture that does not throw up unmanageable risks and is something of a strategic aberration. In retrospect, it could be seen as a case of successful penetration, but it has not spread into other areas of Peruvian society.

The economic consequences of these deals are still felt, and the crisis affecting Peru's ability to pay its debt has forced Moscow to work out innovative payback formulas. Peru owes the Soviet Union over $1 billion, and has made some payments in kind rather than in hard currency. In 1984 the Soviets agreed to take some Peruvian products like fishmeal and textiles instead of the $100 million due to them that year, and have at other times received metals and foodstuffs instead of cash.[58] Part of the debt due in 1983 was refinanced over a new six-year period, as was the case with some payments falling due in 1984. The government is considering a plan whereby Peru would satisfy some of its debt with the Soviet Union by providing certain products to Nicaragua, such as tires, mining equipment, and trucks. It appears that the Nicaraguans initiated the suggestion, and a Peruvian official has been quoted as saying that 'for us, there is no difference in paying to either the Russians or the Nicaraguans'.[59] In effect, Moscow has shown flexibility in its dealings with Peru and does not fail to drive home the point that it treats its clients in a satisfactory manner, unlike rapacious capitalist creditors. This has political value for the Kremlin, because it generates favourable publicity and creates the image of the Soviets helping out a friend in time of need. The rescheduling of Peru's debts by the Soviets has been hailed as a model of a mature economic partnership, and Moscow is likewise showing strong support for President García's 'principled position' in his confrontation with the IMF.[60] Exploiting the debt issue is a natural for Moscow, and deepening rifts between Peru and its capitalist creditors are welcomed by the Kremlin.

The military aspect makes Peru's relationship with the Soviet Union different from Brazil's or Argentina's, as does the fact that Moscow's economic stake in Peru is nowhere as high as in the other two cases. The value of bilateral trade in 1983–85 was well under $100 million – Peru simply does not have the economic wherewithal of the larger countries. The sources of Soviet influence in Peru do not form a coherent matrix and are constrained by indigenous factors and Peru's ties to the West and Latin America. It is unlikely that Soviet analysts can predict where present trends will lead with any more accuracy than US academic or government experts.

CONCLUSION

The Soviet Union has made major inroads into South America in the last decade or so and has established viable frameworks in trade and commerce with key nations. The Soviets have satisfied some of the need for exporting goods for Brazil, Argentina, and Peru, and have incurred a hugh trade deficit in the process. Consumption pressures in the Soviet Union itself are somewhat alleviated through the purchases of grain and other commodities from South America, so Soviet policies in the region have substantial domestic consequences.

In particular, the Soviet Union's relations with Brazil and Argentina have taken on the character of mutually convenient partnerships, but one where the partners choose to cooperate in some areas and not do so in others. The choices are fairly explicit, and there is sufficient leverage on either side to resist unwanted overtures. Argentina, for instance, has not sought clear-cut security arrangements with the Soviet Union despite its continuing conflict with Britain over the Falklands, because for Argentina that would be too risky. The Soviets have themselves refrained from heating up the dispute, but clearly benefit from the absence of a resolution.

The Soviets have failed to establish effective institutional relationships with the military establishments of Brazil and Argentina, and their presence in Peru is subject to specific constraints. Part of the explanation for this lies in the fact that Brazil and Argentina produce some weapons themselves, and that Western countries still dominate the Latin American arms market. The anti-communist attitude of key military establishments in the region reduces the probabilities of collaboration with the Soviets in this area, but there is some evidence from Argentina to suggest that attitudinal and generational changes in the armed forces may lead to a reassessment of Argentina's strategic doctrines. In effect, the Peruvian case has not reproduced itself in the region, and Soviet military involvement elsewhere is seldom felt. Individuals involved in non-military or technical tasks may as part of their role gather information that is useful to the Soviet military, security, and intelligence bureaucracies, but do so on an *ad hoc* basis. Obviously, Soviet intelligence services operate in the region and may well be assisted by Cuban operatives now that several countries (e.g. Brazil) have resumed diplomatic relations with Havana, but the capabilities of Western agencies are still thought to be superior. A Soviet naval presence in the South Atlantic concerns Western planners, as would a potential presence off Peru's Pacific coastline.

The present alignment in all three cases is stable, and is intended to endure in the medium to long term. In each case, the relationship has weathered severe crisis (changes in government; war involving one of the partners; deep economic difficulties), so there is some experience in crisis management. Military and democratic regimes have done business with Moscow, and the latter's revolutionary ideology is not a major factor in shaping relations with influential South American governments. The Soviet model is not emulated, and its failures are well known in the area.

The Soviet presence in the larger Latin American countries does allow Moscow to encourage the anti-American tendencies ever present in the domestic politics of the region, and the competition with Washington reaches into the ideological and cultural spheres. In 1984 over 11 000 students from throughout Latin America (not including Cuba) were being trained in the Soviet Union and Eastern Europe; of these, 1185 were from Peru. In several years, these Soviet-trained students could provide a source of influence for the Soviets. It is probable that some of them are being recruited into Soviet intelligence activities. In effect, being in a position to capitalise on the varied manifestations of anti-Americansim is a strong incentive for the Soviets, because they may reap political gains without being identified as intruders. The area's nationalistic wrath focuses on Washington, not Moscow, and the Soviets do not have to defend a legacy of neo-colonial practices.

To conclude, the strengthening of relations between the Soviet Union and major South American countries in the 1980s is in line with General Secretary Brezhnev's remarks at the 26th Congress of the CPSU that 'the states of Latin America, including Mexico, Brazil, Argentina, and Venezuela are playing a more important role in world affairs', a trend the Soviets have not overlooked. A complex structure of mutual incentives involving commerce and increasingly salient political issues sustains a growing and probably permanent Soviet presence in South America.

Notes

1. This notion is developed in Howard J. Wiarda, 'United States Policy in South America: A Maturing Relationship', *Current History*, vol. 84, no. 499, February 1985, pp. 49–52, 86. See also Riordan Roett, 'Democracy and Debt in South America', *Foreign Affairs*, vol. 62, no. 3, 1984, pp. 695–720.
2. See Heraldo Muñoz and Joseph S. Tulchin (eds), *Latin American Nations in World Politics* (Boulder, CO: Westview, 1984).
3. Consult Augusto Varas, *Soviet-Latin American Relations in the 1980s* (Boulder, CO: Westview, 1986); Cole Blasier, *The Giant's Rival, The USSR and Latin America* (Pittsburgh: University of Pittsburgh Press, 1983).
4. Helan C. Jaworski, 'Peru: The Military Government's Foreign Policy in Its Two Phases', in Muñoz and Tulchin (eds), *Latin American Nations*,

pp. 207–15 (see note 2).

5. A. Ahtamzyan, 'Leninist Principles of the International Policy of the CPSU and the Soviet State', *International Affairs* (Moscow), no. 3, March 1986, p. 16.

6. Augusto Varas, 'Ideology and Politics in Latin American-USSR Relations', *Problems of Communism*, vol. 33, no. 1, January–February 1984, p. 37.

7. Daniel S. Papp, *Soviet Perceptions of the Developing World in the 1980s* (Lexington, MA: Lexington Books, 1985), p. 41. For a summary of the debate regarding the characteristics of the more developed Latin American countries, see Jerry F. Hough, 'The Evolving Soviet Debate on Latin America', *Latin American Research Review*, vol. 16, no. 1, 1981, pp. 124–43.

8. Rodney Arismendi, 'Some Reflections on a History-Making Event', *World Marxist Review*, vol. 29, June 1986, p. 19.

9. Wayne A. Selcher, 'Recent Strategic Developments in South America's Southern Cone', in Muñoz and Tulchin (eds), *Latin American Nations*, p. 101 (see note 2).

10. 'The 27th Congress of the CPSU and Its International Significance', *International Affairs* (Moscow), no. 6, June 1986, p. 7.

11. Aldo César Vacs, 'Soviet Policy toward Argentina and the Southern Cone', *Annals of the American Academy of Political and Social Sciences*, vol. 481, September 1985, p. 163.

12. See the speeches by Alfonsín and Andrei Gromyko in 'In a Friendly Visit', *Pravda*, 14 October 1986, p. 4.

13. Monica Hirst, 'Democratic Transition and Foreign Policy: The Experience of Brazil', in Muñoz and Tulchin (eds), *Latin American Nations*, pp. 225–7 (see note 2).

14. Francis Fukuyama, 'Gorbachev and the Third World', *Foreign Affairs*, vol. 64, no. 4, Spring 1986, p. 726.

15. Sally W. Stoecker, 'R. A. Ulianovsky's Writings on Soviet Third World Policies, 1960–1985', Rand P-7177 (Santa Monica, CA: Rand Corporation, February 1986).

16. Vacs, 'Soviet Policy toward Argentina', p. 161 (see note 11).

17. See Pedro Ramet and Fernando López-Alves, 'Moscow and the Revolutionary Left in Latin America', *Orbis*, vol. 28, no. 2, Summer 1984, pp. 341–63.

18. Data on communist parties taken from Richard F. Staar, 'Checklist of Communist Parties in 1986', *Problems of Communism*, vol. 36, no. 2, March–April 1987, pp. 40–56.

19. Eul-Soo Pang and Laura Jarnagin, 'A Requiem for Authoritarianism in Brazil', *Current History*, vol. 84, no. 499, February 1985, pp. 61–4, 88.

20. Riordan Roett and Scott D. Tollefson, 'The Transition to Democracy in Brazil', *Current History*, vol. 85, no. 507, January 1986, p. 21.

21. Staar, 'Checklist of Communist Parties in 1986' (see note 18).

22. Jorge del Prado, 'A Manifesto of Construction and Peace', *World Marxist Review*, vol. 29, February 1986, p. 20.

23. Jorge del Prado, 'Time for Decisive Changes', *World Marxist Review*, vol. 29, April 1986, p. 16.

24. See David Scott Palmer, 'The Sendero Luminoso, Rebellion in Rural Peru', in Georges Fauriol (ed.), *Latin American Insurgencies* (Washington: Georgetown University Center for Strategic and International Studies and the National Defense University, 1985), pp. 67–96; Cynthia McClintock, 'Sendero Luminoso: Peru's Maoist Guerrillas,' *Problems of Communism*, vol. 32, no. 5, September–October 1983, pp. 19–34.

25. US Department of State, Bureau of Public Affairs, 'Soviet Activities in Latin America and the Caribbean', Current Policy No. 669 (Washington, DC, February 1985).

26. Morris Rothenberg, 'Latin America in Soviet Eyes', *Problems of Communism*, vol. 32, no. 5, September–October 1983, p. 15.

27. 'Soviet Trade with Latin America', *The Latin American Times*, no. 72, 1986, p. 13. The figure for 1985 is from Robert K. Evanson, 'Soviet Economic and Military Trade in Latin America', *World Affairs*, vol. 49, no. 2, Fall 1986, pp. 75–85.

28. 'Importante convenio de granos con Japón', *La Nación* (Buenos Aires), 28 July 1986.

29. *The USSR and the Third World*, vol. 15, no. 2, 1985.

30. 'USSR Disappoints Alfonsín on Grains', *Latin American Weekly Report*, 30 October 1986, p. 5. See also *Southern Cone Report*, 16 October 1986.

31. 'Soviet Trade with Latin America', p. 13 (see note 27).

32. *Southern Cone Report*, 2 August 1986, p. 6.

33. Robert K. Evanson, 'Soviet Political Uses of Trade with Latin America', *Journal of Interamerican Studies and World Affairs*, vol. 27, Summer 1985, pp. 99–127.

34. Ibid., p. 114.

35. *The USSR and the Third World*, vol. 14, no. 1984.

36. 'Argentina's 100 Days of Hope', *Newsweek*, 19 March 1984, p. 45.

37. David Lewis Feldman, 'The United States Role in the Malvinas Crisis, 1982; Misguidance and Misperception in Argentina's Decision to Go to War', *Journal of Interamerican Studies and World Affairs*, vol. 27, Summer 1985, pp. 1–22.

38. 'Argentina's 100 Days of Hope', p. 45 (see note 36).

39. *Southern Cone Report*, 13 April 1984, p. 3.

40. Carlos J. Moneta, 'Fuerzas armadas y gobierno constitucional después de las Malvinas: Hacia una nueva relación civil-militar', *Foro Internacional*, vol. 10, no. 26 October–December 1985, pp. 190–213.

41. Edward Schumacher, 'Argentina and Democracy', *Foreign Affairs*, vol. 62, no. 5, Summer 1984, p. 1092.

42. 'Argentina Looks East', *Insight*, 14 July 1986, p. 39.

43. Vacs, 'Soviet Policy toward Argentina', p. 167 (see note 11).

44. Blasier, *The Giant's Rival*, pp. 32–7 (see note 3).

45. Ibid., pp. 51–3 (Tables 3, 4 and 5).

46. 'Soviet Trade with Latin America', p. 14 (see note 27).

47. Evanson, 'Soviet Economic and Military Trade in Latin America', p. 77 (see note 27).

48. *Latin American Times*, no. 73, 1986, p. 26.

49. Wayne Selcher, 'Brazil's Foreign Policy: More Actors and Expanding

Agendas', in Jennie K. Lincoln and Elizabeth G. Ferris (eds), *The Dynamics of Latin American Foreign Policies* (Boulder, CO: Westview, 1984), pp. 101–23.

50. Adrian J. English, *Armed Forces of Latin America* (London: Jane's, 1984).
51. Selcher, 'Brazil's Foreign Policy', pp. 118–20 (see note 49).
52. Wayne A. Selcher, 'Brazilian-Argentine Relations in the 1980s: From Wary Rivalry to Friendly Competition', *Journal of Interamerican Studies and World Affairs*, vol. 27, Summer 1985, pp. 25–53. This would change if the Falklands dispute heats up.
53. Riordan Roett, 'Peru: The Message from García', *Foreign Affairs*, vol. 64, no. 2, Winter 1985/86, pp. 274–86.
54. English, *Armed Forces of Latin America*, chapter on Peru (see note 50).
55. US Arms Control and Disarmament Agency, *World Military Expenditures and Arms Transfers, 1985* (Washington, DC: US Government Printing Office, 1985).
56. David Jordan, 'Soviet Strategy in Latin America', *World Affairs*, vol. 149, no. 2, Fall 1986, pp. 87–92. Mr Jordan is a former US ambassador to Peru.
57. See Jaworski, 'Peru: The Military Government's Foreign Policy', pp. 211–13 (see note 4).
58. *Andean Group Report*, 18 May 1984; 5 October 1984.
59. 'Perú analiza nueva forma de pago a la URSS', *La Nación* (San José), 10 May 1986, p. 17A.
60. N. Zaitsev, 'Latin America in the Grip of the Foreign Debt', *International Affairs*, no. 3, March 1986, pp. 73–80. The author is Deputy Director of the Institute on Latin America of the Soviet Union's Academy of Sciences.

East and Southeast Asia

6 The Soviet Union and Southeast Asia: The Vietnam Connection
Sheldon W. Simon

INTRODUCTION

The Socialist Republic of Vietnam and the Soviet Union are joined in a symbiotic relationship. Of their own volition, Hanoi's leaders have joined the socialist bloc led by the USSR. Moscow and its CMEA associates have provided the military and economic assistance essential for the Vietnamese military occupation of Cambodia and the maintenance of a viable national economy. In effect, Hanoi has sacrificed its hard won independence from great powers – France and the United States – attained at an incalculable cost of blood and treasure over 35 years and has mortgaged its future to a new mentor. Moscow provides both the material requirements for Vietnam's hegemony over Indochina and protects Hanoi's dominance by deterring Chinese aggression.

In return, the Soviets have acquired the use of Vietnam's US-built naval and air bases at Cam Ranh Bay and Da Nang. These facilities permit the Soviet Pacific Fleet to remain permanently deployed in the South China Sea and Indian Ocean and to monitor US naval and air movements out of the Philippines. These deployments fit into a larger maritime plan for the creation of a full-time presence on all major world ocean routes to protect Soviet international commerce as well as to challenge US forces in the event of a Soviet-American confrontation.

However, the longer the Soviet Union commits its resources to the development of Vietnamese empire, the more isolated the Soviets become in Southeast Asian politics. The region's most important politico-economic group, the Association of Southeast Asian Nations (ASEAN), has ostracised Hanoi because of the latter's invasion and occupation of Cambodia – an action which threatens ASEAN's frontline state, Thailand. Unless the Soviets can promote a resolution of the Cambodian conflict which meets the minimal security needs of ASEAN, Moscow will be unable to establish the broader regional ties it needs to become a genuine competitor for regional influence with the United States.

Similarly, Vietnam must transcend its dependence on the USSR. The Soviets may have provided enough to keep Vietnam afloat but certainly not enough to promote economic development. Only new trade with and investment from the West can inaugurate genuine growth. There are, therefore, incentives for both Moscow and Hanoi to loosen the ties that bind. The trick will be to do so without either side sacrificing its current benefits: for Vietnam, control of Cambodia and Laos; for the Soviet Union, the use of Cam Ranh Bay and Da Nang.

SOVIET GOALS AND SOUTHEAST ASIA

Soviet foreign policy in the Third World is driven by a quest for *security* and *status*. Security is embodied in the goal that no Third World region become the sole preserve of a major adversary; status reflects the USSR's determination to promote its newly acquired position as a world power.

In the 1970s, with the exodus of US arms from Southeast Asia in the wake of the Second Indochina War, Kremlin leaders believed that their view of 'peaceful coexistence' had prevailed. That is, the concept of *détente*, as stated in the Basic Principles Agreement of 1972, opened the way for Soviet-backed transformations in Southeast Asia as part of the new 'correlation of forces'. The Soviet call for US recognition of Moscow's new position in Southeast Asia – as Vietnam's mentor – was meant to demonstrate that the USSR had an equal right to involvement in Third World affairs. Washington's refusal to acquiesce in the Soviets' new politico-military position in Indochina is described by Moscow as a pretext for renewed US military involvement in the region to reverse the process of national liberation.[1] Fear of a revitalised United States challenge to the Soviet presence in Southeast Asia has been reinforced by the build-up of US air and naval assets in the Pacific during the Reagan administration.

If the primary Soviet strategic goal in Southeast Asia is to extend its East Asian presence, then Soviet bases in Vietnam are essential to provide forward deployed elements of the Pacific Fleet and ensure that they need not be contained at the choke points between the Sea of Okhotsk, the Sea of Japan, and the East China Sea. Pacific Fleet elements in Southeast Asia serve both to protect Moscow's own growing merchant trade routes between Europe and the Soviet Far East and to challenge US sea control in the Indian Ocean. If the Soviets develop fixed-wing, catapult-launched aircraft carriers in the 1990s, they will also be able to bring naval air power to bear for the first time in the region. These new Soviet military systems, scheduled for deployment around the turn of the century, will enhance the importance of Vietnamese bases and, therefore, increase Hanoi's political leverage in the relationship. Moreover, a stable Vietnam-dominated Indochina adds to the security of the bases, further cementing Moscow's diplomatic support for Vietnam's insistence that the Heng Samrin government's control of Cambodia is irreversible. (If Hanoi were to agree to a coalition government after a proposed 1990 Vietnamese withdrawal, the Soviet Union could also accept that outcome.)

While the Soviet naval and air build-up at Cam Ranh Bay has increased steadily through the mid-1980s, it does not yet constitute a significant challenge in any hypothetical confrontation with the US Seventh Fleet. In 1987 some 25–30 vessels were stationed in Vietnam, the majority of which were supply ships and submarines. Sixteen TU-16 Badgers, a squadron of Mig-23s, eight TU-95 and TU-142 reconnaissance aircraft are flown in on rotation from the Soviet Far East.[2] The reconnaissance planes and bombers are 1960s technology, relatively old and slow. Similarly, the surface vessels deployed out of Cam Ranh Bay are among the least sophisticated in the navy. They possess primarily 'day-sailing' capability with minimal electronics. The best ships are kept instead near Soviet home waters where they can be protected by land-based aircraft. In turn, these ships protect the homeland from attack.[3]

In sum, Cam Ranh Bay's military value is limited in wartime by its vulnerability to US air attack from Clark field in the Philippines and because both southern and northern access to Cam Ranh Bay is confined to straits controlled by the ASEAN states, Japan, and the United States. Nevertheless, the Vietnam connection is crucial for a variety of Soviet objectives. It is both a political and military counter against China, permitting the Soviets to surround the PRC Navy from both the north and south.

Vietnamese air and port facilities provide a potential threat to regional sea-lane choke points such as the Malacca Strait. A Soviet naval presence ensures that Moscow's interests must be considered in future regional security deliberations. The Soviets also hope to capitalise on anti-China sentiment among the ASEAN states, especially if the United States becomes more deeply involved in the PRC's military modernisation. Finally, a significant Soviet naval presence in Southeast Asia could be used to aid friendly regimes in difficulty and to provide support for future pro-Soviet insurgencies.

The USSR is troubled by an inability to devise a doctrine for East Asia comparable to the Pacific community concept which potentially links the market-oriented economies of the region. Recently, Gorbachev published a refurbished version of the old Asian collective security proposal, originally broached by Brezhnev in 1969. In a May 1985 dinner address to visiting Indian Prime Minister Rajiv Gandhi, the Soviet General Secretary proposed an all-Asian security conference, presumably to capitalise on the USSR's limited *rapprochement* with China and its new political position in Indochina. Gorbachev seems to believe that he can apply the same concept he has proposed for European security to Asia, despite vast differences between the two regions.[4]

Beginning with his July 1986 Vladivostok speech and continuing with an extensive interview on its first anniversary with the Indonesian newspaper *Merdeka*, Gorbachev outlined a Soviet Asian policy which cast the USSR in the role of peacemaker. *Izvestiia* summed up Soviet goals for the region in a 28 July 1987, review of Moscow's worldwide policies:

> Broad opportunities for solving the region's problems are opened up by the Mongolian People's Republic proposals on the conclusion of a convention on nonaggression and the nonuse of force by the Asian and Pacific states, and by the DPRK's proposals on the withdrawal of US troops from South Korea, the country's unification on the basis of peaceful, democratic principles without outside interference, the replacement of the truce agreement with a peace agreement and the drafting of a nonaggression declaration between North and South. The efforts made by Vietnam, Laos, and Cambodia to normalize the situation in their region and the course aimed at establishing good-neighbourly relations, trust, and cooperation with the ASEAN countries, the creation of a zone of peace in Southeast Asia, and the normalization of relations with China on the basis of the principles of peaceful coexistence proceed in the same direction. The struggle of the socialist and nonaligned countries for the speediest convening of an international conference on the transformation of the Indian Ocean basin into a zone of peace is an important avenue of efforts to consolidate peace in Asia.

Gorbachev's *Merdeka* interview stressed Soviet willingness to accommodate both Asian and US nuclear concerns by agreeing to eliminate SS-20s in Asia without insisting upon the removal of US warheads in Korea, the Philippines, and Diego Garcia. He also called upon the United States to agree to a freeze in nuclear-capable aircraft in the North Pacific and to negotiate a naval separation whereby neither side would approach the coastline of the other within range of their on-board nuclear systems.[5] In effect, the General Secretary hoped to thwart the Maritime Strategy by appealing to the nuclear fears of the US's Asian allies.. A limitation on naval manoeuvres would remove the Seventh Fleet from the Sea of Okhotsk and northern Sea of Japan which shelter Russian SSBNs.

The Gorbachev idea is the culmination of several different initiatives which portray the Soviet Union as Asian peacemaker. They include a Mongolian proposal for an Asian mutual non-aggression pact, the Indochinese states' call for establishing good-neighbourly relations with ASEAN, the Indian Ocean peace zone proposal, and the South Pacific Forum call for a non-nuclear zone.[6] Moscow's promotion of peace is contrasted with American warmongering as embodied in the Reagan administration's 'neoglobalism' by which the United States provides 'open support for all counterrevolutionary and all opposition forces that are waging a struggle against lawful regimes wherever they might be'.[7]

The Soviets portray the Pacific community as an effort to NATO-ise Asia, that is, to create 'a closed regional grouping...another militaristic bloc'.[8] What the Soviets appear to fear most, then, is exclusion from a broader community of Asian-Pacific states following export-oriented, market-based policies. The Soviets believe that the United States wants 'to transform the economic structure under creation there into a type of platform or base for stepping up military preparations and military cooperation'.[9]

Soviet officials visiting Southeast Asia in the spring of 1986 lashed out at the Pacific Basin Community idea and warned that Moscow would oppose any moves to forge 'closed economic groupings like the Pacific community'. By contrast the Soviet Union would be willing to participate in an all-Asia security conference 'as a great Pacific nation'.[10]

VIETNAM: A SOVIET FULCRUM

The history of Soviet-Vietnamese communist relations reveals a good deal of the psychological trait of approach-avoidance on Vietnam's part. Proud of Ho Chi Minh's legacy which first proclaimed an independent Democratic Republic of Vietnam in 1945, the Democratic Republic of Vietnam (DRV) was the first communist state in Asia to come into being without substantial Soviet assistance. This sense of independence was reinforced during the First Indochina War. The Kremlin did not provide the Vietminh with material aid on any significant scale. The 1954 Geneva Accord disappointed Ho Chi Minh for Vietminh plans to control all of Indochina were sacrificed to Moscow's European priority at the time: ensuring that the European Defence Community came to naught. Hanoi's independence was eroded, however, in the course of the Second Indochina War during the 1960s. About 80 per cent of North Vietnam's economic aid and two-thirds of its military requirements were met by the USSR. At the same time, the Kremlin demonstrated that Vietnam's interests continued to be subordinated in Soviet policy considerations to strategic concerns regarding the United States. Brezhnev received Nixon in May 1972 during the heaviest US bombing of the war against the North. He also pressured the Vietminh to make concessions at the Paris peace talks to hasten a conclusion to the war.[11]

The Soviet hold over Vietnam was consolidated in mid-1978 when Hanoi obtained membership in the Council for Mutual Economic Assistance (CMEA) and then formed a virtual Soviet alliance in the November Treaty of Friendship and Cooperation, a prelude to the Socialist Republic of Vietnam's (SRV) invasion of Cambodia. In the aftermath of China's subsequent attack on the six northernmost Vietnamese provinces, the Soviets achieved a major breakthrough in Southeast Asia: access to Vietnamese bases at Cam Ranh Bay and Da Nang. Like Cuba, Vietnam had become a full-fledged socialist country on a par with the Eastern European allies. The Vietnam portfolio is handled by the Liaison with Socialist Countries Department within the Central Committee, not its International Department.[12]

Soviet technical assistance to Vietnam began as early as 1959. By 1984 approximately 60 000 Vietnamese had been trained in the Soviet Union: 40 000 as skilled technicians, 18 000 as recipients of university degrees, 2000 as post-graduates, and 70 as Doctors of Science. Soviet-trained students account for 7 per cent of all university graduates in Vietnam and 50 per cent of those holding post-graduate degrees. In 1986 approximately 5000 Vietnamese were studying at tertiary level institutions in the Soviet Union.[13]

Vietnam has become heavily dependent on the Soviet Union and Eastern Europe for the inputs necessary to fuel its economy. Over 80 per cent of the country's petroleum, fertiliser, and metal products come from CMEA and the USSR. In return the SRV ships two-thirds of its exports to the same suppliers.[14] This heavy two-way trade has led to an international division of labour which increasingly organises the Vietnamese economy in accordance with Soviet requirements.. The Vietnamese have accepted the supervision of a joint Soviet-Vietnam committee on aid disbursement, an arrangement the Soviets also negotiated with Laos and Cambodia.[15]

Reflecting the Soviet interest in large prestigious projects, much of the USSR's assistance to Vietnam has gone into building hydroelectric stations, harbours, bridges, and railway construction.[16] In agriculture, the Soviets have encouraged the Vietnamese to plant commercial crops (coffee, tea, tobacco, cotton, rubber, and tropical fruit) that are in demand in the USSR. Over 6000 Soviet advisors operate throughout the economy. Total Soviet aid comes to 20 per cent of Vietnam's GNP.

Because of CMEA trade practices, hardly any money is transferred between Hanoi and Moscow. Rather, trade is conducted on a barter basis while Vietnam's current account deficit grows larger with each passing year. Between 1975 and 1984, Vietnam's trade deficit grew from 110 million roubles to 740 million roubles. Commodity and light industrial exports to the USSR are funded primarily through Soviet buy-back arrangements whereby the Soviet government finances the manufacture of the products in return for a predetermined amount of the output. The Soviets manipulate Vietnam's production policies through differential prices. For those goods in high demand, Moscow offers higher procurement prices and subsidised inputs, thus stimulating Vietnam's gross agricultural output in those commodities. In effect, Vietnam has become a tropical food supplier to the USSR and CMEA.

To ensure that it maintains a dominant trade position in the desired commodities, the USSR has raised its rouble purchase price (offset against Vietnam's debt) to the world level and above in some cases, for example, rubber. Thus, Hanoi's opportunities to diversify markets and obtain hard currency are, to a large degree, preempted.

Vietnam's growing debt to CMEA is also being paid off through the export of labour. Under agreements signed in 1981, Vietnamese workers are sent to the Soviet Union and Eastern Europe for up to six years. According to Soviet publications, approximately 20 000

Vietnamese were working and receiving training in the USSR in 1984. When the number of Vietnamese in Eastern Europe is added, the total for that year reached 60 000 Vietnamese in the USSR, Czechoslovakia, East Germany, and Bulgaria. In accordance with the intergovernmental agreements, 40 per cent of their wages are written off against Vietnam's debts.

While Soviet economic aid supports the commercial sector of Vietnam's economy, military assistance sustains Hanoi's empire in Laos and Cambodia. Estimated by US defence officials to have a military budget of $2 billion per year, the Vietnam People's Army (VPA) has been provided with a Soviet armoury which makes it the largest and most sophisticated in Southeast Asia. Such modern systems as Mi-24 combat helicopters (used in Afghanistan), SU-22 swing-wing fighter aircraft, T-54/55 and 62 type tanks, missile attack boats, and a variety of surface-to-air missiles have been delivered to Vietnam since 1984.[17] The Mi-24s are being used in Cambodia against the Resistance.

The VPA itself is the third largest army in the world with over one million personnel in 1985, up from 700 000 at the end of the Second Indochina War. Its air force consists of 270 combat aircraft – primarily Mig-21s, 135 transports, and 200 helicopters. The navy has acquired six Petya-class frigates and eight OSA-II fast attack coastal craft armed with Styx surface-to-surface missiles. While primarily a coastal defence force, the navy also has some 27 landing craft, four of which are capable of ocean voyages. In sum, the SRV Navy is gradually developing a South China Sea capability.

The Soviet build-up of Vietnamese forces and its dominant position in Vietnam's economy are the price Moscow is willing to pay for its strategic position in Southeast Asia. The security of Soviet naval facilities in southern Vietnam requires stability in Indochina. Therefore, Moscow supports Vietnam's domination of Cambodia. Like Hanoi, Moscow hopes to persuade China and ASEAN that Vietnam's hegemony over Indochina is a *fait accompli* along with the Soviets' new strategic presence. Hence, until 1987 Moscow turned down several Chinese requests to discuss Cambodia because 'discussing that behind the backs of our friends would be treachery'.[18] The Soviets wish to see a Vietnam – China accommodation – but on Hanoi's (and the USSR's) terms. Moscow believes that Sino-Soviet relations will be improved in a situation of Soviet preponderance. Chinese leaders, on the other hand, insist that the animosities of the past can only be overcome with the restoration of an independent, non-aligned Cambodia – a Cambodia beholden neither to Hanoi nor Moscow.

The Soviet Union and ASEAN

Although Indochina has been the recipient of both Soviet largesse and political support, Moscow has not ignored the other Southeast Asia, ASEAN (the Association of Southeast Asian Nations, consisting of the essentially pro-Western market-oriented states of Malaysia, Indonesia, Thailand, the Philippines, Brunei, and Singapore). ASEAN's total combined GNP is over $200 billion, more than 20 times that of Vietnam, with an aggregate population of about 300 million.

Soviet policy toward ASEAN has evolved through several stages. Initially, between 1967 and 1971, the Association was condemned as a tool of Washington, another version of SEATO. The Soviets feared that ASEAN was to be a new military pact led by an anti-communist Indonesia, further excluding the Soviet Union from the region. Between 1971 and 1975, while Soviet suspicions of ASEAN persisted, it was also seen as a potentially useful grouping if it could accelerate the withdrawal of Western forces from the region. The Soviets appeared to be heartened by ASEAN's 1971 Zone of Peace, Freedom, and Neutrality (ZOPFAN) proposal which averred that all foreign bases in Southeast Asia were temporary in nature.

The Soviets were concerned about ASEAN's attempt at better relations with China in the aftermath of Hanoi's military victory in Indochina. Establishment of diplomatic relations by Malaysia, Thailand, and the Philippines nullified Moscow's previous advantage in Southeast Asia, where state-to-state relations with China had been virtually non-existent. The Soviets responded by reversing their earlier posture on ASEAN. From mid-1978 until mid-1979, Moscow commented favourably on ASEAN's role in the non-aligned movement and its efforts toward economic cooperation.[19]

The most recent stage of Soviet-ASEAN relations seems to have retrogressed once again. Moscow's backing of Vietnam's invasion of Cambodia and Hanoi's threat to Thailand constitutes a reversion to its original attitude of hostility toward the Association. Once again ASEAN is portrayed as a pawn in US global strategy and an integral part of its Pacific community concept: '[I]t has been decided also to turn ASEAN, whose countries the Pentagon would like to see at the forefront of the West's global anti-Soviet strategy, into a military group.' Soviet commentators specify that Washington plans to link ASEAN navies to an East Asian air and sea network for purposes of surrounding and containing Soviet actions in East Asia.[20]

In truth, ASEAN states, for the most part, do not welcome the growing Soviet naval presence in Southeast Asia. Malaysia, Thailand, Indonesia, and the Philippines have all turned down Soviet requests for port calls. Additionally, Malaysia, Thailand, Indonesia, and Singapore have cracked down on Soviet espionage in the 1980s, expelling several Soviet citizens between 1983 and 1985.

Political pressure on ASEAN appears equally unavailing. When deputy foreign minister Mikhail Kapista visited Singapore in April 1983 and threatened that Hanoi could supply Southeast Asian insurgencies if ASEAN continued to undermine the SRV's control of Cambodia, ASEAN leaders uniformly condemned him. They also reiterated that ASEAN had no intention of either giving in to blackmail or abandoning the principle it was defending in Cambodia: the unacceptability of military intervention in a neighbouring state.

On balance, Moscow is probably uncomfortable with its current hard line toward ASEAN. Resolution of the Cambodian issue (on Hanoi's terms) would go a long way toward solving Soviet political difficulties in Southeast Asia. If the Khmer resistance could be eliminated, both the political and legal basis for ASEAN's opposition to the Heng Samrin regime in Phnom Penh would be destroyed. The Soviet military presence in the region could then be legitimated since the Soviets could argue that they had been invited by Vietnam in the same way the Americans had negotiated base arrangements in the Philippines.[21] Alternatively, a coalition government in Cambodia following a Vietnamese withdrawal around 1990 could also reduce ASEAN objections to the Soviet-Vietnam bases arrangement.

The Soviets probably benefit from ASEAN's generally relaxed view of their presence. With the exception of the Philippines (discussed below) no ASEAN member faces a significant communist insurgency. Consistent records of economic success beginning in the early 1970s have strengthened the legitimacy of each government. There is, therefore, no equivalent for ASEAN of the Warsaw Pact threat to NATO and, consequently, no felt need to create a common policy against dangers which do not seem real. As a Malaysian specialist recently noted:

1. the Soviet Union does not have a record of direct military aggression in the region;

2. the Soviets are seen as psychologically distant;
3. Vietnam is seen as ultimately planning to reduce its dependence on the USSR;
4. there is no perception that the Soviet Union has vital interests in Southeast Asia (unlike Northeast Asia);
5. there is a perception that the main threats to ASEAN security are internal more than external;
6. in so far as there may be a Soviet challenge, it is seen as basically non-military – possibly subversion but not military conquest;
7. there is a perception that the Soviet Union faces an unfavourable balance of military forces and will be no match for the United States since the US will maintain its technological edge.[22]

At bottom it is difficult for ASEAN specialists to construct convincing scenarios for the limited use of Soviet force confined to Southeast Asia. If the vulnerability of the straits region is discussed, why would the USSR want to block the straits unless a global crisis had occurred? The only genuine military targets in the region are US ships, planes, and bases.[23]

The one exception to a relaxed view of the Soviets is, of course, Thailand. Bangkok's concern is derived from the Soviet-Vietnamese alliance, the growing Soviet presence at Cam Ranh Bay, large numbers of Soviet military advisors in Indochina, and Soviet espionage and efforts to infiltrate the student and labour movements in Thailand. The close political relationship between Bangkok and Beijing seems to make Thailand somewhat of a junior PRC partner in the Sino-Soviet dispute.

The Soviets have tried to exploit differences within ASEAN, particularly over the question of whether China or Vietnam is the greater threat to regional stability. Like Hanoi, Moscow plays upon Indonesia's antipathy toward China and Jakarta's desire to play the major ASEAN role in negotiating a settlement of the Cambodian imbroglio. Thus, in March 1985 Soviet Deputy Foreign Minister Kapitsa chose Jakarta as the location to announce a Soviet willingness to serve as a guarantor of any future ASEAN-Indochina arrangement. Indeed, from the Soviet viewpoint, *rapprochement* between ASEAN and Vietnam would move its 'Asian collective security' plan a giant step forward.

The Soviets stepped up their 'smiling face' diplomacy toward ASEAN in the fall of 1985. Taking advantage of growing discontent caused by falling commodity prices and protectionist sentiment in the

US Congress, Moscow sent high-level delegations to the region offering aid and trade. The Soviets proposed industrial cooperation to Malaysia in tin and copper mining as well as petroleum development. Although Malaysia is the USSR's most important ASEAN trading partner, Kuala Lumpur maintains a heavy surplus of 10:1 in two-way trade. Typically, obstacles to a better Soviet performance reside in goods that are qualitatively inferior to those available in the international market as well as problems in after-sales servicing. Moreover, the Soviet preference for barter arrangements is unattractive to ASEAN.[24]

Thailand has become an important target for Soviet courtship, perhaps in the hope that Bangkok will subsequently accept Soviet good offices in negotiating a *modus vivendi* with Vietnam over Cambodia. The Soviet Trade Commission has promised to settle accounts 'in freely convertible currency' rather than barter. The Soviets have expressed a desire for Thai textiles during a period when US quotas are being imposed against Thai garments.[25] Moscow has also offered to assist in the construction of Thai power plants and agricultural processing factories, proposing payment for these services in traditional Thai exports. The USSR has increased its imports of sugar and rice – most of the latter subsequently trans-shipped to Vietnam.[26]

The Soviet embassy in Thailand is its largest among the ASEAN states with 86 nationals. (By contrast only 10 Thais have diplomatic status in Moscow). Thai intelligence sources believe that 50 of the Soviet personnel are either KGB or GRU (military intelligence) operatives.[27] Bangkok is also concerned about Soviet recruitment of Thai students from rural areas for training in the USSR, particularly since recruitment has been under way over the past few years without notifying the Thai Foreign Ministry.[28]

Soviet policy toward the Philippines has generated considerable controversy. Because Manila has been the only ASEAN member confronting an active and growing communist insurgency, much attention has been paid to whether the USSR is involved in aiding the Philippine communists, and how their fortunes affect Soviet relations with the Philippine government. Some analysts point to indirect Soviet aid to the Philippine communists (CPP) via trade union movement links to the Soviet-controlled World Federation of Trade Unions. A KGB defector, Stanislav Levchenko, also claimed in 1982 that Soviet intelligence officers regularly channelled funds to the CPP through third countries. CPP publications follow the Soviet line on Vietnam,

Mozambique, and Angola. However, with the exception of a single arms shipment in 1981, there is no evidence of direct Soviet military aid to the CPP-led New People's Army (NPA). Moreover, CPP leaders deny having accepted Soviet military aid even though they claim it has been offered.[29]

Publicly, the Soviets deny involvement with the CPP/NPA. Then Soviet Foreign Minister Gromyko assured Imelda Marcos during an October 1985 visit to Moscow that the USSR does not meddle in internal Philippine affairs.[30] Moscow also offered to establish joint ventures to help boost the Philippine economy. Particularly intriguing was a suggestion that Manila expand its ship repair facilities to service Soviet vessels.[31]

Moscow was completely surprised by the successful efforts of the political opposition led by Corazon Aquino, widow of the assassinated Benigno Aquino, to assume power in February 1986. Believing that Marcos would remain in office, the Soviet ambassador was the only diplomat in Manila to congratulate him on his 'electoral victory'. Suspicious of Third World populist movements, the USSR has been very slow to establish good relations with the Aquino government. Indeed, the first open critique of the Marcos years did not appear in the Soviet press until June. The *Pravda* writer spent little time assessing the new government, noting ruefully that 'the removal of Marcos proved a convenient way to release steam and ease the people's anger, while preserving the US strategic and economic positions'.[32]

The numerous military coup attempts against the Aquino government in 1986 and 1987 have perplexed Soviet commentators. They appear unable to decide whether the government's continuation or its overthrow would best serve Soviet interests. In general, the unsuccessful coups are portrayed as US-planned efforts to destabilise the country so that the military will be able to have its way in destroying the Communist Party of the Philippines (CPP) and renewing the US bases agreement in 1991.

While the New People's Army remains a thorn in the Aquino government's side and a source of frustration for the military, a successful CPP revolution is improbable. There is no nationwide mass base. Should the Philippine economy continue to stagnate and the problem of agricultural land reform go unresolved, however, the mass base could develop in the 1990s. Only then might the Soviets risk direct aid to the CPP. However, at that point, the party itself might reject direct assistance, fearing that it would undermine its nationalist credentials.

In sum, with the partial exception of the Philippines, the Soviets continue to invest heavily in government-to-government relations in Southeast Asia. They do not want to be seen backing insurgencies, particularly since such a stigma has hindered China in the development of relations with ASEAN. Sensing possible political benefits in ASEAN's resentment over US commercial protectionist measures, the USSR has stressed the desirability of expanded Soviet trade and joint ventures for ASEAN economies. It links these economic initiatives with broader political goals, including its Asian security conclave and the creation of a nuclear-free zone in Southeast Asia.[33]

VIETNAM'S NEEDS IN THE SOVIET RELATIONSHIP

The Vietnamese-Soviet relationship is symbiotic. For the Soviets, as previously discussed, the 1978 Treaty of Friendship and Cooperation led to Southeast Asian base facilities for its Pacific Fleet, a strategic position to China's south, and general recognition as an East Asian power whose interests must be considered in regional security arrangements. What has Vietnam derived from the Soviet connection other than constraints upon the independence it had achieved at such a high price through three major wars against the Japanese, the French, and the Americans? Have the Vietminh thrown off Western domination only to be newly entrapped by Soviet imperialism? Or are there payoffs, too, for Hanoi in maintaining Soviet ties?

Quite simply, without Soviet economic and military assistance, Hanoi would be unable to sustain what its leaders believe to be the politico-military rights won in 35 years of warfare – hegemony over Indochina. Isolated politically and cut off from Western and Japanese economic assistance because of its 1978–79 invasion of Cambodia, only the Soviet bloc provides the wherewithal for the VPA to remain in Cambodia and Laos.

This is no easy task. Vietnam is one of the world's most poverty ridden countries with an annual national income below $200 per capita and a population of 62 million. Vietnam has one of the highest mean population densities of any agricultural country. As a result of intensive cropping, the soil erodes and the forests shrink. By the mid-1980s one-third of the country's land was barren. Vietnam's own conservation studies predict dire consequences if environmental degradation continues, including the loss of all forests by the turn of the century, accelerated soil erosion, flooding, siltation, and crop failures. Reversing this cycle requires swift action to reduce population growth and a massive reforestation programme to restore the hydrological balance.[34] External assistance is essential if these needs are to be met; and the USSR is the only country both willing and able to provide it.

In addition to specific needs met by the USSR, Vietnam views itself unabashedly as a member of the socialist commonwealth headed by the Soviet Union. Moscow has proved, at least from the time of the Second Indochina War, a reliable friend. Hanoi's security interests are bound up in maintaining a good relationship with the Soviet state. Bureaucratic linkages between the USSR and Vietnam across virtually all areas of the society are designed to ensure the relationship's longevity.[35] An extensive network of both party and government ties has developed.

Most important of all in Hanoi's eyes is strategic necessity. Indochina must be unified or Vietnam cannot be independent. Since the 1960s efforts to encroach on Vietnam have originated with US and Chinese footholds in Laos and Cambodia. Chinese support for the Cambodian resistance is seen by Hanoi as a direct threat to Vietnam's new-found unity, the latest attempt by a great power to encircle and attack Vietnam from the west.[36]

The staunchest advocate of ties to the USSR may be the Vietnam People's Army, which has been a major beneficiary. Not only are Soviet arms, vehicles, aircraft, ships, and petroleum necessary for the prosecution of the war in Cambodia but also for the modernisation of the armed forces. If the VPA is to develop technical standards sufficient to cope with China's PLA, then the Red Army must remain its mentor.

Despite continued Soviet pressure on Vietnam to increase its economic efficiency, there is no indication that Moscow is significantly reducing its support for the SRV's economy. To the contrary, agreements to coordinate the two countries' latest five-year plans (1986–90) have been initialled. These documents project an increase of bilateral trade by 170 per cent, as well as the growth of general economic assistance: 'It is planned to continue deliveries to Vietnam of complete sets of equipment for the construction and equipping of power, transport, machine-building, chemical and mining enterprises, the development of communications, and the expansion of the network of academic, medical, and service institutions'.[37] This largesse will be paid for by Vietnamese commodity and light industrial exports, although the Soviets have also agreed to reschedule Vietnam's $2.3 billion debt repayable over 30 years.[38]

Some fluidity in the relationship could occur around 1990. The Vietnamese claim that they will withdraw their forces from Cambodia by that date, thus establishing a *fait accompli*; that is, the existence of a pro-Hanoi regime in Phnom Penh, operating independently of a Vietnamese military prop. Although outside observers are sceptical that the SRV will, in fact, be able to withdraw by that date, should their forces be removed, the major obstacle to Hanoi's normalisation with ASEAN would also disappear. If ASEAN effects a *modus vivendi* with Hanoi in the early 1990s and the Sino-Soviet detente continues, prospects for Hanoi's developing economic and political ties with Japan and the United States would be greatly enhanced. These new relationships, in turn, would lead to a reduction in economic dependence on the USSR and CMEA. Moreover, changes in Southeast Asia's political relations could also breathe new life into ASEAN's ZOPFAN proposal. A depolarising Southeast Asia could lead to an ASEAN request for both the Americans and Soviets to leave their bases in the Philippines and Vietnam.

VIETNAM AND ITS OPPONENTS

In dealing with its adversaries, Hanoi hopes to split ASEAN (the lesser danger) from China (the greater). Among the ASEAN states, it hopes to separate the anti-PRC contingent (Indonesia and Malaysia) from Thailand and Singapore, which view Beijing as an important 'ally' against the SRV. The Soviet Union has no major objection to this strategy, although Moscow deviates from it in its own recent efforts to effect a *rapprochement* with the PRC. While the Soviets would prefer to see a Sino-Vietnamese *détente*, they have no interest in pressuring Hanoi for concessions on the Cambodia issue which could jeopardise Soviet access to Cam Ranh Bay.

For its part the notion of submitting to Chinese pressure is repugnant to Vietnam. In Cambodia, the Chinese-armed and fanatically anti-Vietnamese Khmer Rouge are seen not only as a threat to national security but also as a challenge to Vietnam's legitimacy as hegemon in Indochina. On the other hand, a *modus vivendi* with ASEAN may be possible. The six members are interested in a political settlement for Cambodia which takes account of both Thai and Vietnamese security interests. Beijing, by contrast, hopes to destroy Hanoi's influence in Cambodia (and subsequently Laos) entirely, thus restoring the region as a traditional Chinese sphere of influence.[39]

Pending that achievement, the PRC prefers to keep on 'bleeding' Vietnam, rendering it weak, dependent, and confining its military actions to Cambodia.

ASEAN has sought a viable relationship with Vietnam since the latter's military victory in 1975. The ASEAN Treaty of Amity and Cooperation has been left open for accession by other Southeast Asian states, specifically with Hanoi in mind. The Zone of Peace, Freedom, and Neutrality (ZOPFAN) concept is also meant to appeal to Vietnam since it would apply to US as well as Soviet bases in the region. Prior to its invasion of Cambodia, Vietnam seemed interested in a *rapprochement* with ASEAN. Hanoi opened prospects for peaceful coexistence in a series of visits to ASEAN capitals. Thus, the sense of betrayal in ASEAN was even stronger when the VPA marched into Cambodia in late 1978. Vietnam's promises of non-intervention rang hollow and served to move ASEAN in the direction of informal security cooperation.[40]

Indonesia, however, has reservations about the ASEAN-Vietnam confrontation. Believing Hanoi to be the wrong enemy and resentful at having to subordinate Jakarta's 'natural leadership' to Thailand's needs as the frontline state, Indonesia has become ASEAN's interlocutor with Vietnam. In some ways, Jakarta also serves as Hanoi's spokesman in ASEAN councils.

General Beni Murdani, Suharto's right-hand man, has been quoted as justifying Vietnam's intervention in Cambodia as 'a question of survival' to protect itself from a Chinese threat.[41] Strains within ASEAN are exacerbated over this issue since, for its own security, Thailand depends on a Chinese threat to Vietnam and acquiesces in Beijing's supplies to the Khmer Rouge. For Bangkok the strategic link to China may seem a better guarantee for its security than Jakarta's preference of conceding some degree of Vietnamese hegemony in Cambodia, thus facilitating Hanoi's role as a buffer against the PRC.

Vietnam's policy toward the United States is based on the need for more diversified foreign aid and a return to the world economy. These goals depend, however, on the withdrawal of VPA forces from Cambodia and the establishment of a reconciliation government for that country that is acceptable to Thailand and China. Since 1985 Hanoi has displayed some sensitivity to US demands. It has set a deadline for troop withdrawals (1990) and even expressed a willingness to consider elections in Cambodia on the condition that the Khmer Rouge not participate.[42] This, of course, continues to be the sticking point since China will not accept a settlement that excludes the

Khmer Rouge. By 1988, Vietnam indicated it would even be willing to accept a coalition government as a successor to the Heng Samrin regime in Cambodia which could include Khmer Rouge elements, providing the Khmer Rouge military had been disbanded.

CONCLUSION

There is little evidence to suggest that the Soviets have overcome their prime difficulties in becoming an important source of influence in Southeast Asia. They remain outside the political, economic, and social networks of the region; and their proposals for entry – most recently an Asian collective security conference – are unrealistic. The hoary 'falling dominoes' thesis never came true. For the ASEAN market-oriented, export-led growth states the Soviets have had no attraction. Moreover, the negative implications of Soviet support for Vietnamese aggression have served only to drive these states together for their own economic and political security, while seeking continued support from the United States, Japan, and other Western states. The more the Soviets and Vietnamese rely on coercion, the less successful they are likely to be in the face of Southeast Asian nationalism.

Moscow's foothold in Vietnam is, nevertheless, important. Vietnam's dependence ensures the USSR continued access to Cam Ranh Bay, a strategic linchpin in its encirclement of China and challenge to US naval dominance in the South China Sea and Indian Ocean. Thus, Moscow will continue to support Hanoi's client government in Cambodia in hopes that ASEAN and China will ultimately accept the new status quo. In all probability, however, Soviet calculations are wrong. As long as Vietnam's position in Indochina remains dependent on Soviet military supplies, ASEAN will continue to oppose both the SRV and the USSR in regional and global diplomacy.

Both Hanoi and Moscow have suggested that the Southeast Asian strategic situation could be frozen as part of an overall settlement. SRV Foreign Minister Nguyen Co Thach has said that Vietnam would be willing to cap the Soviet military presence in Vietnam if the ASEAN states would be willing to do the same for the US military presence.[43] There are three particularly intriguing features of this proposal: (1) it could be a first step toward the realisation of ASEAN's cherished ZOPFAN; (2) it would permit Hanoi to be the arbiter of the Soviet military presence in Vietnam; and (3) it would freeze a regional military balance that is overwhelmingly favourable to the United States.

The Vietnamese (with Soviet encouragement) are offering important incentives to ASEAN and the United States to accept a Hanoi-dominated Indochina. The key question is whether China can also be enticed into a settlement. A freeze on the Soviet naval and air presence to its south would be appealing, particularly since no similar restraints would be imposed on Beijing. Similarly, the maintenance of US military superiority in Southeast Asia is reassuring. These gains would have to be balanced against China's acceptance of a permanent Soviet presence to its south which would serve to guarantee Vietnam's independence. As a medium-term policy – 10 to 20 years – this settlement may be the best Beijing can achieve. It would provide the kind of stable environment the PRC needs to continue its economic and technological modernisation. If this effort is successful, China will have overwhelmed Vietnam as an economic power in the region, and Vietnam – even with Soviet support – will present little threat to Chinese interests in the region.

In sum, the Soviets may well have succeeded in establishing a strategic foothold in Southeast Asia. However, the political importance of that foothold is a diminishing asset as long as both the USSR and Indochina remain outside the dynamic, economic, and social developments which characterise the Pacific Basin, including China. The presence of armed forces in peacetime is no longer the fungible asset it was twenty years ago. The Soviets may discover that they have invested in the wrong instrument of political influence for Southeast Asia.

If Vietnam succeeds in broadening its international contacts after the promised withdrawal of most of its forces from Cambodia in 1990, ties to the USSR could be loosened. Reduced economic dependence on the Soviet bloc would be the first step toward a restoration of some independence in Vietnam's foreign policy. This, in turn, would lead to diminished tensions with China and ASEAN.

Alternatively, the Soviets themselves could break the political log-jam by reducing support for Hanoi in a bid for greater influence with the ASEAN states and as part of a general *rapprochement* with China. This scenario seems less probable, however, given the USSR's commitment to its new air and naval facilities along the South China Sea. If there is to be a dealignment in Soviet-Vietnamese relations, the initiative must come from Hanoi.

Notes

1. An informed discussion of Soviet views of the Third World for Moscow's global strategy is found in S. Neal MacFarlane, 'The Soviet Conception of Regional Security', *World Politics*, vol. 37, no. 3, April 1985, especially pp. 303–7. See also Frances Fukuyama, 'Gorbachev and the Third World', *Foreign Affairs*, vol. 64, no. 4, Spring 1986.
2. These figures are taken from Leszek Buszynski, 'Soviet Foreign Policy and Southeast Asia: Prospects for the Gorbachev Era', *Asian Survey*, vol. 26, no. 5, May 1986, p. 597.
3. For a more extended discussion of Soviet Pacific Fleet deficiencies, see Sheldon W. Simon, 'The Great Powers' Security Role in Southeast Asia: Diplomacy and Force', in Young Whan Kihl and Lawrence E. Grinter (Eds), *Asian-Pacific Security: Emerging Challenges and Responses* (Boulder, CO: Lynne Rienner Publishers, 1986), pp. 91–3.
4. The Gorbachev proposal is assessed in Hiroshi Kimura, 'Soviet Policy toward Asia under Chernenko and Gorbachev: A Japanese Perspective', *Journal of Northeast Asian Studies*, vol. 4, no. 4, Winter 1985, pp. 60–1.
5. *New York Times* excerpts of the *Merdeka* interview, 23 July 1987.
6. *Izvestiia*, 6 December 1985; in FBIS, *Daily Report, USSR*, 10 December 1985, p. CC11.
7. Typical allegations are found in the 'International Situation', broadcast of the Radio Moscow Domestic Service, 3 April 1986; in FBIS, *Daily Report, USSR*, 8 April 1986, pp. CC3-CC4.
8. Soviet Government Statement on the Asia-Pacific Region, *Tass*, 23 April 1986; in FBIS, *Daily Report, USSR*, 23 April 1986, pp. CC1-CC3.
9. 'International Observers Roundtable', Radio Moscow Domestic Service, 27 April 1986; in FBIS, *Daily Report, USSR*, 30 April, 1986, p. CC4. See also *Krasnavia Zvezda Observer*, 4 May 1986; in FBIS, *Daily Report, USSR*, 12 May 1986, p. CC5.
10. Statement by Akil Salimov, deputy president of the Supreme Soviet, in Kuala Lumpur, carried by *Agence France Presse* (AFP), 5 June 1986; in FBIS, *Daily Report, Asia Pacific*, 6 June, 1986, p. 01.
11. Dieter Heinzig, 'The Soviet Union in Southeast Asian Eyes', *Sino-Soviet Affairs*, vol. 9, no. 3, Fall 1985, pp. 10–11. See also David W. P. Elliott, 'Vietnam in Asia: Strategy and Diplomacy in a New Context'. *International Journal*, vol. 32, no. 2, 1983, pp. 292–3.
12. Fukuyama, 'Gorbachev and the Third World', p. 728 (see note 1).
13. These figures are drawn from Carlyle A. Thayer, 'Vietnam and the Soviet Union: "Soviet Studies" and Vietnamese Perceptions', a paper presented to the Workshop on the Soviet Union and the Asia-Pacific Region, East–West Center, Honolulu, 1–5 April 1986, p. 8.
14. Robert C. Horn, 'The USSR and the Region', *Southeast Asian Affairs, 1985* (Singapore: Institute for Southeast Asian Studies, 1985), p. 72.
15. Buszynski, 'Soviet Foreign Policy and Southeast Asia', pp. 600–1 (see note 2).
16. The following discussion on Soviet economic aid, objectives, and controls in Vietnam is drawn primarily from Derek Martin da Cunha, 'Aspects of Soviet-Vietnamese Economic Relations, 1979–1984',

Contemporary Southeast Asia, vol. 7, no. 4, March 1986, pp. 307–13, 315, and 316.

17. International Institute for Strategic Studies, *The Military Balance, 1985–86*, as carried in the *Pacific Defence Reporter*, December 1985/January 1986, p. 160.

18. Discussion with a Soviet specialist on Southeast Asia in Nayan Chanda, 'Cambodia: Straw in the Wind', *Far Eastern Economic Review*, 16 January 1986, p. 21.

19. A good review of Soviet-ASEAN relations is found in S. Bilveer, 'The Soviet Union and ASEAN: Interests, Policies, and Constraints', *Indian Political Science Review*, vol. 38, no. 1, April 1985, especially pp. 95–100.

20. A particularly detailed treatment of these allegations appears in *Kransnaya Zvezda*, 23 May 1986, in an article by Colonel V. Rodon, 'Neoglobalists and ASEAN', in FBIS, *Daily Report, USSR*, 29 May 1986, pp. CC14–CC16.

21. Indonesian Foreign Minister Mochtar took this position in an April 1986 interview. *AFP*, Hong Kong, 28 April 1986; in FBIS, *Daily Report, Asia-Pacific*, 29 April 1986, p. N1.

22. Pacific Forum, *Current Attitudes and Reactions to Soviet Policies in the Asia-Pacific Region* (Honolulu, 1984), p. 5.

23. Ibid., p. 33.

24. James Clad, 'Malaysia: Grinning and Bearing It', *Far Eastern Economic Review*, 28 November 1985, p. 19; Barbara Crossette, 'Soviet Tries to Expand Influence in Southeast Asia', *New York Times*, 8 April 1986.

25. *The Nation* (Bangkok), 31 October 1985.

26. *The Nation* (Bangkok), 8 June 1986; and *Matichon* (in Thai), 9 June 1986; in FBIS, *Daily Report, Asia-Pacific*, 11 June 1986, p. J7.

27. John McBeth, 'Thailand: Wary of the Bear', *Far Eastern Economic Review*, 21 November 1985, pp. 36–7.

28. *The Nation* (Bangkok), 21 October 1985.

29. Further discussion of conflicting evidence concerning alleged Soviet-CPP links may be found in Leif Rosenberger, 'Philippine Communism and the Soviet Union', *Survey*, vol. 29, no. 1, Spring 1985, pp. 134–7; Leif Rosenberger and Marian Leighton, 'The Soviet Union: Meshing Strategic and Revolutionary Objectives', in Kihl and Grinter (eds), *Asia-Pacific Security*, pp. 70–1 (see note 3); Ross H. Munro, 'The New Khmer Rouge', *Commentary*, December 1985, pp. 36–8; and Paul Quinn-Judge, 'Philippine Insurgents are Turning Down Soviet Support', *Christian Science Monitor*, 26 November 1985.

30. Seth Mydans, 'Philippines' First Lady Plays the Soviet Card', *New York Times*, 8 November 1985.

31. *AFP* (Hong Kong), 31 October 1985; in FBIS, *Asia-Pacific*, 1 November 1985, p. 8.

32. V. Ovchinnikov, 'The Philippines since February', *Pravda*, 14 June 1986; in FBIS, *Daily Report USSR*, 19 June 1986, pp. E1–E4.

33. Soviet Deputy Foreign Minister Kapitsa's remarks to President Aquino as reported in the *Manila Bulletin*, 29 April 1986.

34. Summary of the SRV Committee for National Utilization of Natural

Resources and Environment Protection report in Australia–Vietnam Society, *Vietnam Today*, vol. 36, February 1986, pp. 3–6.

35. This last point is emphasised by Thayer, 'Vietnam and the Soviet Union', p. 25 (see note 13).

36. See the discussions in Michael Leifer, 'Obstacles to a Political Settlement in Cambodia', *Pacific Affairs*, vol. 58, no. 4, Winter 1985–86, especially pp. 631–2; and William S. Turley, 'Vietnam/Indochina: Hanoi's Challenge to Southeast Asia's Regional Order', in Kihl and Grinter (eds), *Asian-Pacific Security*, pp. 177–200 (see note 3).

37. *Pravda*, 12 January 1986, in FBIS, *Daily Report USSR*, 13 January 1986, p. E1.

38. Interview with Vice Premier Trang Phuong in the *Far Eastern Economic Review*, 19 December 1985, p. 98.

39. Radio Moscow in Vietnamese, 18 February 1986; in FBIS, *Daily Report, USSR*, 20 February 1986, p. E3.

40. William Bach, 'A Chance in Cambodia', *Foreign Policy*, vol. 64, no. 2, Spring 1986, p. 92.

41. Donald E. Weatherbee (ed.), *Southeast Asia Divided: The ASEAN-Indochina Crisis* (Boulder, CO: Westview, 1985), pp. 8–11.

42. Ibid., p. 20.

43. Nayan Chanda, 'Thach's New Tack', *Far Eastern Economic Review*, 17 April 1986, p. 48. A Soviet Foreign Ministry representative made a similar proposal in the author's presence at a conference on 'Indochina's Future' at the Rockefeller villa in Bellagio, Italy, 2–6 December 1985.

7 The Soviet Union and East Asia
Thomas W. Robinson

INTRODUCTION

In a volume devoted to Soviet relations with the Third World, East Asia is an anomaly. Although both South and North Korea regard themselves as 'Third World' members and each is accepted, to some degree, as such by other states, few take China and Japan as Third World even though China is a 'developing' nation in the objective sense. Japan is an economic superpower; China, a member of the strategic triangle; South Korea, a newly industrialising country; and North Korea, a Marxist hermit kingdom. The development of Soviet policy in this region must therefore be placed in a broader framework, namely, relations with the United States and China in the strategic triangle, Japan as concerns mostly economic matters (with a small security component), North Korea in terms of inter-party relations and Pyongyang's attempts to use Moscow for its own aggressive purposes against the South, and South Korea hardly at all, since diplomatic relations do not exist and trade is almost non-extant. So East Asia provides a contrast with Soviet policy elsewhere outside the orbit of ruling communist parties.

THE BASIS OF SOVIET INVOLVEMENT IN EAST ASIA

None the less, the Kremlin's approach to this region supplies lessons for the subject as a whole and can serve as a base for the broader inquiry, in terms of some of the general motives and regularities of Soviet foreign policy as a whole. The subject is best introduced, therefore, by inspecting the determinants of Kremlin involvement in the area: interests, including the weight of the past; domestic factors; the politics of the strategic triangle; and available policy means, especially military power. Once these determinants are delineated, it will be possible to discuss Soviet relations with the four other states of the region.

Soviet interests in East Asia are what one would expect of a state with a rapidly expanding power base, global ambitions, and a regional territorial presence. Moreover, Soviet policy in the 1980s is overlaid by the legacy of several centuries of international involvement in the region and evaluations of that past. Six interests present themselves, in order of importance.[1] First, defence of the Soviet homeland, including land seized historically from others (in East Asia, from Japan, China, and Mongolia); second, integration of Asian interests into broader Soviet interests and, at the same time, subordination of Asia in Soviet foreign policy to Europe, the Middle East, and global competition with the United States; third, defence of the 'gains of revolution', e.g. regimes and territories both Leninist and 'friendly' to (and usually controlled by) Moscow – in Asia so far limited to Mongolia, North Korea, Vietnam, and Afghanistan; fourth, economic development of Siberia and utilisation of foreign resources for that purpose; fifth, expansion of Soviet influence throughout Asia by both traditional and unconventional means; and, finally, acquisition of technology and industrial goods through trade with Asian countries.

It should be noted that this list excludes others usually normal to most states: broad and friendly interaction for its own sake, trade for mutual advantage, and promotion of regional integration. In that regard, Moscow's approach to East Asia remains pre-modern and marginal to contemporary civilisation. Moreover, the list contains contradictory objectives: territorial defence and defence of the revolution often oppose those dealing with trade and development. Finally, the traditional Russian and Soviet over-concentration on defensibility fails to consider security concerns from any other viewpoint, a malady characteristic of the Kremlin's self-imposed isolation over many decades. Finally, Soviet interests in East Asia are a function of the domestic order in the Soviet Union, which has largely remained constant.[2]

Until very recently, domestic factors have militated against major Soviet involvement in East Asia, except under special circumstances, as at the end of the Second World War. The very character of the Soviet Union constrains it to face west, not east. Its population is concentrated in European Russia, where also is located most of the usable land, heavy industry, and the roots of Russian culture. Siberia and the Soviet Far East, by contrast, are far away, cold, sparsely populated, inhospitable agriculturally, and lacking in a self-sufficient industrial base. Siberia is in fact a colony and a mineral storehouse to be exploited for the benefit of regions to the west. Moreover, most of what assets Soviet Asia does have are concentrated either south of the Trans-Siberian Railroad, and hence quite close to China, or along the Pacific Coast, largely cut off from the rest of the USSR and subject to foreign invasion (as occurred in the early 1920s).[3]

Moscow also finds itself facing many domestic difficulties of fundamental character, longstanding duration, and not subject to easy solution. Many are economic: low growth rates, poor productivity, poor quality of goods, no match between price and supply, inadequacy of food production and distribution, over-direction of the economy from above, low rates of technological innovation, an aging industrial plant, an underdeveloped infrastructure, and an emerging energy shortage. Others are of a social character or are social problems stemming from the very nature of party rule or exacerbated by it: astonishing alcoholism rates, very high rates of labour mobility, gross age and sex imbalances in the countryside, the whole nationality problem, an actual decline in life-span, the decline of ideological belief to near the vanishing point and the consequent rise of other belief systems (especially religion), the double burden on women, the decline of social discipline, and massive defection to Western popular culture. This is compounded by the very nature of the Soviet Communist Party: rigid, over-bureaucraticised, ideologically deterministic, superannuated, sluggish, top-heavy, and caught in the economically self-defeating zero-sum mode of Leninist decision making.[4] The result of these many shortcomings is a nation in crisis, much needful of a respite in the international arena, but at the same time increasingly xenophobic and pugnacious (this in an age of transnationalism and interdependence), over-concerned about its enemies (mostly the product of its own threats and actions), and worried that history may in the end not transpire as Marx and Lenin foretold. These domestic problems and foreign policy attitudes condition the Soviet approach to East Asia as they do to other regions.

The third policy determinant is the structure and processes of the Sino-Soviet-American strategic triangle. Moscow, like Washington and Beijing, is constrained by that system, which has formed the basis of international politics for several decades and will continue to do so to the end of the century. Its operational characteristics are clear: the Soviet-American leg remains the most important but also the most stable; China as the weakest of the three supplies most of the dynamism within the system. The triangle is a balance of power system, primitive though it may be, and obeys all the rules of such a system; and because each of the three are such giant states, much influenced by their respective internal orderings, a close relationship exists between their domestic situations and their foreign policies, on the one hand, and the shape of the triangle and the configuration of international relations as a whole, on the other. The consequence of these forces by the late-1980s is to produce a triangle roughly equilateral in form, with China gradually warming to the Soviet Union and equally carefully distancing itself from the United States; one which for the first time can be called comparatively harmonious; and one which provides – again for the first time – breathing space for Moscow, as well as Washington and Beijing, to devote much needed attention to internal matters.[5]

At the same time, however, changes in the international system outside the triangle, not always susceptible to the influence of intra-triangular relationships, are exerting their own pull on Soviet foreign policy or are developing independently of Soviet activities. Perhaps the most important of these is the rising importance of the international economic system led by the United States, West Europe, and Japan. Many contemporary economic problems cry out for solution: the enormous Third World debt phenomenon, massive job exportation to East Asia and the consequent response of protectionism, roller-coaster oil prices with attendant economic dislocations, the US balance-of-payment deficit, and the very low global rates of growth with all the obvious implications for developing nations.[6] Moscow has little to say about any of these issues. In addition to international economic developments, states increasingly successfully pursue their own policies outside Soviet influence, regions have gained in autonomy, and issues have taken on a life of their own beyond the Kremlin's capability to influence them.[7] These include the Lebanese Civil War, the latter-day phases of the Arab-Israeli dispute, the Iran–Iraq War, the South African crisis, the terrorist activities of Libya and of non-state terrorist organisations, and the Solidarity mass movement in Poland, to name a few.

If these changes are taken into account by Kremlin leaders as well as those in the White House and the Chung-nan Hai, three conclusions become apparent. First, a new stability within the triangle has emerged such that Moscow may find time to deal with its internal problems without having to worry unduly about the winds of international politics. Second, the Soviet Union can, for the first time since the late 1950s, address its relationship with China on the merits of the issues that separate them. And third, Moscow can influence extra-triangular trends and issues less successfully than before (although this conclusion needs to be modified, at least partially, by the vast growth in projectable Soviet military power). To the extent that such trends and issues escape from the Kremlin's ability to influence or control them gradually, Moscow's say in events in East Asia is correspondingly constricted.

SOVIET POWER IN EAST ASIA

The range of Soviet interests in East Asia, domestic determinants of Soviet foreign policy in general, and relations within and outside the strategic triangle are all modulated by the fourth factor determining the Soviet position in East Asia, available national power. Although always an elusive quality, it is clear what the situation is *vis-à-vis* East Asia. The Kremlin possesses enormous military power in the region, both conventional and nuclear. With over 1500 high performance fighter aircraft, 600 bombers, 1200 missiles, 2500 nuclear warheads, 54 ground divisions, 400 warships and power projection vessels, and 133 submarines, the Soviet Union poses a distinct threat to the entire region.[8] Moreover, Soviet strategy, doctrine, and deployments all emphasise offensive operations.[9] Finally, Moscow not only occupies an Asian nation by force but also has an increasingly potent projection capability and a base structure to go with it. If gross national power were reducible to the military component alone, the Soviet Union would easily dominate East Asia. As it is, Moscow's level of military power, even when its agreement to eliminate SS-20 missiles in Asia is factored in, is far beyond that necessary for defence *per se*.

Power is more than force, of course. There is also a diplomatic, or political, component. Moscow maintains alliances with two of the communist states in the region, Mongolia and North Korea. But it long ago lost its formal tie with China, and its threatening posture toward that country, plus Japan and South Korea, is enough to constrain each of them to meliorate their own interrelations, which historically have been highly antagonistic. The diplomatic component is not only the matrix of alliance and alignments. It also concerns attitudes. The Soviets profess to believe that their policies and deployments in the region are strictly defensive when reality indicates otherwise. They then accuse all others of 'imperialism', since (the Kremlin asserts) only Soviet policies can be defensive. They take this posture a step further by declaring it Moscow's innate right to participate in every Asian situation and dispute merely because the Soviet Union is a superpower. From that, it is but a short step to declare the right to project power into the entire region, to sign alliances with states far from

Soviet borders, to insist on participating in regional trade, and even to station military forces throughout the region. It is this attitudinal dualism that constrains other states to conclude that the Kremlin is imperialist in essence while defensive in form and hence untrustworthy.[10]

The economic component of Soviet power is not very helpful to the Soviet cause in East Asia. Trade with Japan is several billions of dollars per annum and the China trade will soon attain similar levels after a quarter century in the doldrums. But the magnitude is not great for Tokyo and buys little or no influence there or in Beijing. Matters will remain such for the foreseeable future. Moreover, Soviet goods, although adequate, are not of the highest quality and not actively sought. Moscow's currency remains inconvertible, and the country is not open to international economic influence and suffers from the consequent lack of competitiveness. East Asia is not, therefore, enormously important to Moscow economically, despite the proximity of the Siberian mineral storehouse, and the USSR is even less attractive to East Asian countries which (with the exception of North Korea) look east and south to develop their trade rapidly within Asia, across the Pacific, and with Europe into a single market of global interdependence, from which the Kremlin is excluded.[11]

The geographic component of Soviet power places Moscow in a somewhat better position. Although suffering from the severe constraints noted earlier, which until quite recently did not permit active Soviet involvement in the region, matters have now begun to change. The completion of the Baikal-Amur Mainland Railroad, construction of many airfields, and the heavy-lift helicopter make access less difficult. The jet aircraft, the earth satellite, and a more efficient radio-telephone net knit the parts of Soviet Siberia together. The million plus troops east of Lake Baikal, the development of the Siberian minerals base, and the small net inflow of population all provide Moscow with the underpinnings of a much more active approach to East Asia. Already results are in hand. Although SS-20 missiles in Siberia no longer are a central element in the Asian military balance, the ground force can still influence political issues thousands of miles away; the Soviet Pacific Fleet based along the Primorskaya, on Kamchatka, and in the Kuriles enables Moscow to project sea and air power far to the east and south. For the first time, the Russians are in Asia to stay, as geography is becoming an advantage, not an obstacle.[12]

INTERESTS PLUS POWER EQUALS SOVIET ASIAN POLICY

The problem is that the Kremlin cannot use its power, mostly military, in Asia. Other Asian states, especially China, are also militarily strong and oppose Soviet expansionism. Moreover, the United States is still a major military power in East Asia, is allied with Japan, South Korea, and (informally) China, and possesses a commanding base structure as well as the nuclear weapon. Any direct Soviet use of force in East Asia would meet with US, Chinese, and Japanese military opposition, as well as bring into the picture other US allies outside the region, including the Philippines, Thailand, Australia, New Zealand (despite recent problems between Auckland and Washington), and even Pakistan. The Asian *balance* of military power thus does not favour the Soviet Union and will probably remain that way.[13] Moreover, the probability of nuclear war, while not negligible, is none the less quite small. The Kremlin does not want such a conflict, whether it were to begin in Asia or elsewhere, since the destruction of the Soviet homeland would follow as would the united opposition of Europe, North America, and most of Asia. But without the prospect of nuclear conflict,[14] and with the likelihood of conventional war in Asia also small (with one exception, Korea, which will be discussed below), Soviet military force is not a usable policy instrument except as a device to threaten the enemy. And since that would tend to draw together the US-led coalition even more closely, the utility even of that device is questionable.

The Kremlin does wish to continue two other long-term quests in Asia. One is to demonstrate its superpower status. With only the military as a viable component of Soviet power in the region, the temptation is ever-present to intervene in some crisis or situation and insist Kremlin viewpoints be taken into account and to deploy, or even use, force to back up a verbal policy. The question then becomes the length to which Moscow would go before its bluff was called and retreat sounded. The other quest is to assist in spreading Marxist-oriented revolutionary movements. But these are in very short supply in Japan and South Korea, while the Marxist governments in Beijing and Pyongyang are distressingly independent. Thus, the Soviet Union is reduced in East Asia (if not in South and Southeast Asia) to a negative policy: defending Pyongyang against an external threat that is not imminent. A part of Moscow's recent melioration of relations with

North Korea and the partial re-equipping of the North's military with Soviet arms can be justified, at least ostensibly, as a counter to US transfer of equipment (F-16s and the like) to Seoul. But such Soviet activities should be placed in the category of balance of power maintenance rather than spreading revolution. Indeed, the Kremlin must be careful not to encourage North Korean aggression, lest it become involved in direct confrontation with the United States. Thus, until very recently, Moscow has withheld the kind of equipment that might prompt Pyongyang to move against Seoul.

SINO-SOVIET RELATIONS

The USSR's relations with each of the nations of East Asia illustrate in detail how these four factors meld together to produce Soviet policy there. This policy centres, of course, on China as the most important regional state and a member of the strategic triangle. Since the late 1950s, when the Sino-Soviet dispute first became public, relations with China have been strained. Differences began in the ideological sphere but quickly spread to state-to-state relations and turned violent by the late 1960s. It is something of a mystery why ties between these two communist nations, so seemingly similar in terms of political philosophy and structure, should have fallen out so soon and so completely. The reasons are complex, being a mixture of differences in style, personal rivalry, level of development, national interests, and many other factors. In the end, however, it comes down to power politics: a rivalry for influence in Asia and in the communist movement, and reciprocal military threats against each others' national territory.[15]

But although the struggle has been two-sided, with each depending on comparative advantages in terms of power, it has been China, largely, that has determined the direction and timing of the dispute. Moscow from the beginning has desired settlement of differences, and its policies have been directed to that end, to disciplining the Chinese for what Moscow considered needless (but sometimes dangerous) transgressions, or to protecting itself (sometimes overdoing it) from what it thinks are predatory Chinese intentions. Because the Soviet Union has a superiority in raw power, the natural policy has been to keep Chinese excesses – as they are perceived in Moscow – in bounds by application of military force, alliance making, and withholding of economic benefits, and then attempting to right things with Beijing through offers to negotiate from the presumed position of strength thereby created. The trouble, of course, is that China has felt no compulsion to come to terms with the Soviet Union. And when the Kremlin turned up the military pressure, Beijing merely lined up the Americans as military insurers and willing suppliers of the economic goods denied by the Soviets. A stalemate thus was ensued in Sino-Soviet relations that lasted to the end of the 1970s.[16]

Accordingly, Moscow had to wait for a change in attitude in Beijing. This could only come after Mao, of course, and after China solidified its new ties with the United States. That meant waiting essentially until 1982, since Sino-American normalisation did not take place until 1979 and some of the remaining sore points in that relationship (e.g. resolving the Taiwan issue in the Reagan administration) were not put aside or cleared up until mid–1982. By then, however, there were enough blips on the screen for the Soviets to decide the time was ripe to move.

The new Kremlin programme was two-pronged, as is the case in many Soviet initiatives. On the one hand, offers were made at the day-to-day end of the scale to improve practical relations a step at a time. Thus, by 1982, some delegations began to be exchanged, trade grew for the first time in many years, and unofficial visits by Soviet China specialists were made. On the other hand and more importantly, high-level official statements by Brezhnev, in Tashkent and Baku, offered to open the way to talks on, and compromise solution to, the major obstacles impeding full-blown *rapprochement*. The Chinese also decided the time was ripe (the 18 August communique on Taiwan arms sales had just been signed with Washington), and therefore received Soviet Vice Foreign Minister Leonid Illichev in October 1982 to resume official talks between the two countries. The two agendas were, to be sure, quite different: Beijing wanted timetables for Soviet withdrawal from Vietnam and Afghanistan, and for the reduction of Siberian troop levels to pre-1965 levels; Moscow desired to avoid such topics (except perhaps the first as part of a package deal on the border question) and instead wanted to work on the details of normalising state-to-state relations.[17]

Movement along both paths continued in 1983. Trade went up another notch, although hardly to dramatic levels. Border trade reopened after more than two decades. Delegations and exchanges increased in volume and frequency. The official talks saw both a spring and a fall round, and the newly promoted Vice Foreign Minister, Mikhail Kapitsa (himself a China specialist), went to China in

September to press Deng and his colleagues for a more formal state treaty to replace the lapsed 1950 defence and trade agreement. Moreover, by agreement, both countries agreed to cease polemics against the other, always a sign that serious developments were in the offing. Progress was slowed somewhat, however, by Brezhnev's passing in late 1982 and the uncertain start (mostly for health reasons, as it turned out) of the Andropov regime to establish itself in Moscow. The new Soviet leader took it as his top priority to begin the long work of reforming the Soviet Union from the inside. He died before much further progress could be made with the Chinese. And the successor Konstantin Chernenko administration was so short-lived that it too could do little on the China question.[18]

One has therefore to wait until the Gorbachev succession to find propitious domestic Soviet conditions for dealing with China. By then, as well, Beijing was ready to deal. Thus, in early 1986, Deng Xiaoping began to hint that the 'Three Obstacles', previously set forth as a package of conditions that must be met if 'fundamental' improvements in Sino-Soviet relations were to take place, could be broken apart or even partially satisfied. That – and a further upturn in more practical ties such as trade and the first agreement since the middle 1950s on Soviet aid to China – sent negotiations into higher gear. Kapitsa made more trips and Ivan Arkhipov, the Council of Ministers Deputy Head, went to Beijing in March to negotiate several new technical agreements. It is true that the Chinese chose not always to hear the notes of optimism streaming from Moscow (for example, in the Gorbachev speech to the 27th Party Congress in February), averring that political relations – as opposed to economic and technical ties – had not yet improved. Beijing feared moving too fast in Moscow's direction lest Washington take umbrage and cut back economic, technological, and military supplies. But the Chinese could hardly turn the other way after reading the Gorbachev Vladivostok speech in late July. There the Soviet leader in essence offered China all disputed Amur-Ussuri riverine islands (including at least part of Hei Hsia-tzu Island, at the confluence of the two rivers and under Soviet control in contravention of treaty since the late nineteenth century) as well as to pull back at least some Soviet troops from Mongolia. This is an offer that China may well take seriously as the basis for final negotiation of a new border treaty and border region arms control agreement. Since there is little discussion concerning the location of the border, if the two countries can seize the opportunity to arrange a *modus vivendi* on the troop issue, the way is open to major improvement in Moscow–Beijing relations.[19]

Presuming such an improvement does transpire, what are the implications for Soviet policy in the region and more generally? Much will depend on the magnitude of the drawdown of Soviet forces stationed in areas adjacent to China. To gain Chinese approval, a border agreement would have to carry significant force reductions, if not to the pre-1965 level of approximately 15 divisions, then surely to less than 30. Much would then depend on what happened to those forces. If they were entirely disbanded – an unlikely prospect to be sure – their equipment would still be available to Soviet forces elsewhere. If they were moved out of Siberia, the Soviet threat to NATO, the Middle East, and Southwest Asia would grow correspondingly. And to the extent that such moves would make defence plans for the United States and its allies more difficult, the Soviet Union could assume a more assertive stance in its relations with all members of the US alliance system, as well as carry on a more forward and confident policy throughout the Third World.[20]

On the other hand, a force drawdown in Siberia and the Soviet Far East would remove at least part of the only effective instrument Moscow possesses to influence East Asian events. Hence, the Kremlin would not be able to negotiate with Japan (presuming it would find the motivation to do so in terms of interests) from a 'position of strength'. Moreover, the remaining components of Soviet military strength in East Asia – the Pacific Fleet and Backfire bomber force – would assume greater relative importance in Soviet regional policy, but at a discounted level with the elimination of Asia-based SS-20 missiles. But backed less with a ground component, their effectiveness would further decline: a ground threat to Japan (cited by some as justification for the build-up of the Japanese Self-Defence Force) would fade, as would Soviet capability to assist Vietnam from a distance by threatening to invade China, if the latter were to take military action against its southern neighbour.[21]

A Soviet-Chinese agreement would have two other effects. First, it would provide Gorbachev with some of the breathing space he needs to work on solutions to Soviet domestic problems. Second, it might encourage the Kremlin to enter more seriously into arms control arrangements with the United States in both nuclear and conventional arenas, although that argument admittedly cuts both ways. Much would depend on the seriousness of the internal problems of the Soviet Union. On balance, a major Sino-Soviet agreement would significantly influence the conduct of Soviet policy everywhere, as well as reshape the very character of world politics. A 'soft landing' in

Sino-Soviet relations, coupled with continued harmony in Sino-American ties (which appears likely) and additional breakthroughs in arms control negotiations between Washington and Moscow, would reconfigure the strategic triangle into a set of more or less harmonious bilateral components that could remain positively inclined for a decade or more. On the other hand, it could lead, though the likelihood is not great, to a pugnacity on the Kremlin's part that would eventuate in US-Soviet confrontation and crisis. In such a case, the meeting ground for superpower tests of strength probably would be in the Third World.[22]

THE KREMLIN AND JAPAN

Soviet policy toward Japan is much easier to analyse. Essentially, Moscow has never had a successful approach toward Japan, at least not since 1945, and the policy issues that divide them are likely to persist into the indefinite future. Moreover, the Soviet Union has no leverage on Japan, since the two countries are so different domestically and since they live in international worlds mutually sealed off from one another. Further, because Japan's foreign policy depends largely on the strength of its ties with the United States, Tokyo must not deviate much, if at all, from US policy leadership. This means that the prospects for succumbing to threats, blandishments, and blackmail from Moscow are minimised. Finally, so long as the Kremlin pursues a policy, however benign it considers that policy to be, of expansion of influence, projection of power, and outright seizure of territory, Japan must be on its guard. Tokyo, therefore, has particular interest in the US-administered series of anti-Soviet measures in Asia and elsewhere, mostly in the security realm. What the Japanese need not fear is the economic power of the Soviet Union. Its self-imposed economic autarchy, currency inconvertibility, and refusal to engage in reciprocally beneficial trade practices under the theory of comparative advantage exclude it from the open international economic system of which Japan is a leader. Thus, Soviet-Japanese trade is poorly developed, and will remain so – at about $5 billion per year, a pittance for both economies – for the indefinite future. Hence, Japan will remain closely tied economically with the United States, and since the United States provides the framework for overall Japanese relations with Moscow, prospects for Japanese investment in Siberia are small as long as US policy toward Moscow is strongly negative.[23]

Given these factors, to say nothing of the innate Japanese attitude toward the Soviet Union – Russians are always last in Japanese public opinions polls, and the increasing Soviet military threat to Japan has only accentuated the feeling – the main issues in Soviet-Japanese relations stand very little chance of solution or even of being addressed on their merits. The most important issue is, of course, Soviet refusal to return the four Northern Islands seized at the end of the Second World War. Moscow has heavily garrisoned these otherwise unimportant pieces of real estate as part of its Kuriles offensive-defensive barrier, which leads Tokyo to abjure from signing a peace treaty, the basis of normal international comity between former enemies. The issue is emotional in Japan, and no Japanese government can afford to accede to the Soviet territorial gain. For its part, the Kremlin dares not return the islands, lest it admit that they were taken illegally and the Pandora's Box of all past Russian and Soviet territorial seizures be opened. Essentially, the matter is frozen and will probably remain so, especially in light of the visit of Eduard Sheverdnadze to Tokyo in early 1986 and the stark omission of any reference to it in Gorbachev's speech at Vladivostok in July.[24]

The second issue is the Soviet military build-up and the proper Japanese response. Since, without a viable military, Japan is defenseless alone against Soviet attack, Tokyo's only hope is common US-Japanese resistance. The policy issue concerns the changing mix of the two countries' contribution. That in turn touches on accurate assessment of the Soviet threat and the kinds of circumstances in which the Kremlin is likely to initiate action. As to the former, the actual Soviet threat to Japan is less than that derived from Soviet order of battle listings alone. A high percentage of the Soviet Pacific Fleet is configured to fight a nuclear conflict with the United States on a global scale or a nuclear-conventional war with China. The residual for possible use against Japan, while still formidable, is much less than the total.[25] The latter resolves itself into three scenarios. First, the Soviets might attack Japan directly. But that would bring on World War III and would lead to destruction of the Soviet homeland. The probability of such action, including the so-called 'Hokkaido scenario' (wherein the Soviets would seize that portion of Japan and then try to negotiate), is thus quite small.

It is the second and the third scenarios that give US and Japanese defence planners concern. One of these would be the spread to Asia of a Soviet-US conflict begun elsewhere. Such a conflict would not even have to be nuclear; indeed, only the *threat* of conflict would have to ensue to guarantee some sort of Japanese involvement. The reason is that the Soviet Far East Fleet is primed to rush for the open waters of the Pacific, and to escape the geographic prison of the Seas of Japan and Okhostk, lest the US Seventh Fleet and associated land-based US units in Japan, Korea, and the Philippines carry out preemptive air attacks against Soviet bases at Vladivostock and Petropavlovsk, and against Soviet submarines in these waters and Backfire bombers throughout the Primoskaya. (That, in fact, is the US strategy of so-called 'forward defence'.[26])

The third scenario involves escalation out of a Korean conflict. Given a Soviet role in supporting a Northern attack (to be discussed below), Moscow could become more deeply involved. Since Japan would have to serve as the staging base and rear area for US forces assisting the South, and since the prospects for nuclearisation of the conflict at an early stage are not low, the probability of some kind of Soviet attack on US facilities in Japan – even on US ships in the Sea of Japan and the Western Pacific – is finite. Even a conflict confined to the Soviets and Japanese, to say nothing of Americans and Koreans, would have the potential for escalation. A Soviet attack against Japan would, of course, bring into play the Japanese-American Security Treaty, and hence World War III. While it might be averred that global conflict is generally a low probability event, given nuclear deterrence, chances rise greatly if a wider confrontation escalates out of a regional conflict like Korea.

The third major policy issue affecting Soviet-Japanese relations is the recent Soviet diplomatic initiative in East Asia, e.g. Gorbachev's attempts to play a more central role. That raises the more general question: what is Japan's place in the Soviets' Asian *weltanschauung*? The Kremlin's historic policy objectives, ratified as recently as the Vladivostok speech of July 1986, are a mixture of China-centered military defence, undifferentiated power projection, avoiding conflicts not of its own choosing, advancing the cause of Soviet-oriented and (hopefully) Soviet-controlled Marxist-Leninist revolution, and promoting the withdrawal of the United States from East Asia. The only possibility the Kremlin sees for Japan concerns the last issue, since all the others have long drawn a blank. Moreover, the Soviets perceive some opportunity stemming from Washington–Tokyo bickerings over economic problems. The question for Moscow is how to enter the game, which has so far been played in a different arena with the Soviets locked out. The best that they can do until they acquire the economic wherewithal is to talk themselves in the door. Thus the

Gorbachev assertion[27] that, just as Japan and the United States are Asian powers and have legitimate interests there, so the Soviet Union has an equal right to participate. It is doubtful, however, that mere declaration will convince Japan, or the United States, that the Soviet Union deserves such a voice in Asian economic and political affairs. In any case, the Kremlin itself resists the universal application of such logic, which would see, for instance, equal US participation in East European affairs.

The Soviet Union also must find concern over the growing Japanese economic role in Asia, particularly in China and Southeast Asia, and over Tokyo's growing military-technological potential. As regards economic matters, Japan is already the giant of the region in every measure: it has a gross national product equal to that of the USSR, dominates trade in all regions of Asia except India-Pakistan, has the major say in Asian international financial institutions, and is the largest purveyor of foreign aid to China and Southeast Asia.[28] A strong Japan closely associated with a strong China and even more closely linked to a strong United States, all anti-Soviet, would freeze the Kremlin out of East Asia. The only way Moscow could then break into the region is by force – generally unlikely, as we have seen – or by a thoroughgoing alteration of the basics of the Soviet system – just as improbable, even under the comparatively forward looking leadership of Mikhail Gorbachev. Just as importantly, Japan is, with the US, the world's leader in technology, perhaps the most important area of all for the future of the Soviet economy. However, with an unappealing economic policy, Moscow can do little to take advantage of Japanese technology. It thus risks falling even further behind, especially damaging in an era when US-Japanese technological cooperation is likely to become the order of the day and sweep Western Europe, North America, and East Asia into a single integrated juggernaut.

Finally, in the military area, a number of developments just over the horizon will probably give the Soviet leaders much worry. The Japanese Self-Defence Force is on the road to becoming a very potent regional force, with strong capability of defending Japan's own territory and airspace, and of projecting power into more distant waters some 1000 miles in all directions from Tokyo Bay. The military budget grows steadily, the one per cent GNP limit has already been crossed, and the quality of Japanese hardware is excellent. And Japan not only has a major space launch capability, but is already cooperating with the United States in Star Wars research.[29] A second development concerns the US-Japanese cooperation in building up

US forces, both conventional and nuclear, mostly at sea on US ships (some of which are home-ported in Japan, others of which are replenished or repaired there) but also including the two US F-16 squadrons at Misawa in Northern Honshu. Both of these forces are part of the latter day US 'forward' strategy.

Third is the use to which the Japanese Maritime Self-Defence Force is to be put in event of US-Soviet conflict. Already US and Japanese fleets exercise together, and the MSDF (Maritime Self Defence Force) patrols far into the Northern Pacific and has agreed to carry out important anti-Soviet military functions in event of conflict or threat of war. Foremost among these are tracking and being ready to help destroy Soviet submarines, and laying mines in the four straits around Japan to prevent Soviet egress to the open Pacific. The United States Navy leans heavily on the MSDF for these tasks. With 40–60 destroyers and many P-3C aircraft, Japan already makes a vital difference to US strategy in East Asia, especially when the Soviet fleet already greatly outnumbers the US Navy, in all measures but aircraft carriers, in the region.[30]

A final development in the military sphere is the growing role of Japan in the construction of a broad, Western, and trans-Pacific security system against Soviet power projection in Asia. Already the MSDF sends ships as far south as Australia for joint exercises. The day may not be far off when, confronted with an obvious Soviet threat none can handle alone (or confidently assume the US can handle alone), the need will be obvious to establish a joint command, supported by a collective defence pact. If present trends continue, Japan may not only be signatory to such an alliance but may also be a leader against the Soviet Union and a principal material contributor. Indeed, it is not impossible, if the need were to arise, to envisage Japanese-Chinese naval cooperation against Moscow, as well as Tokyo–Seoul cooperation, say, in control of the waters and airspace of the Sea of Japan. Further afield, it is wise to consider what Japan's role in regional security might be were the United States to lose use of Clark Field and Subic Bay in the Philippines after 1991. Would, for instance, Japan become more directly involved in the security affairs of Southeast Asia? Asian security is already a seamless web. After the Soviet invasion of Afghanistan in 1979, Tokyo moved to improve its ties with India, economically and politically. Thus the trend is clear: greater Japanese activism in Asia as the Soviet threat increases and as UK defence resources are strained.[31]

A final topic concerning Soviet relations with Japan is how the Japanese rise to global status will affect the Soviet position in the Third World. Although most developing countries do not perceive any

Moscow–Tokyo rivalry, in many cases choices will be made between them. To the extent that that occurs, a sense of rivalry may emerge. For instance, Japan is already the second largest donor of foreign aid (excluding military assistance) to the Third World, after the United States, and Japan's trade with Third World countries is far ahead of that of the Soviet Union. Since Third World nations by definition are vitally concerned with economic development and obtaining the technological, financial, educational, and material means thereto, they look increasingly to Tokyo as a benefactor. Indeed, it is a cardinal principle of Japanese foreign policy to place economic relations with Third World countries in the highest category of priority, second only to such ties with developed countries.

The Soviet Union cannot effectively compete against Japan in these areas. And to the extent that Moscow loses out, its propaganda appeal among the Third World leadership to serve as a role model evaporates. Thus, the Kremlin has much to fear as Japan gathers momentum in these areas. The same is true of Japanese activism in international economic institutions – the World Bank, the International Monetary Fund, the Asian Development Bank, and United Nations agencies. Infusion of Japanese capital has enhanced their economic value to the Third World. The Soviet Union is not even a member of most of these institutions, leaving it even farther behind in the Third World. Moreover, Japanese assistance, with no strings, comes from a former developing country itself which, now being democratic, pacifist, and capitalist, is more likely to be taken as a role model than the Soviet Union, whose aid is always contingent and whose government is the very opposite of democratic, warlike in the extreme, and saddled with a failed form of socialism.[32]

THE SOVIET APPROACH TO KOREA

Korea is the remaining element in Soviet policy toward East Asia. We must concentrate on North Korea, and treat South Korea only as an afterthought, since Soviet policy toward Seoul stems mostly from Moscow's relations with North Korea and the United States.[33]

Moscow has had much difficulty in its relations with Pyongyang since 'liberating' the North in 1945. Since then, relations have ranged from indifferent to poor, as Kim Il Sung sought to free his regime from Soviet overlordship. This was done first by restoring the 'hermit kingdom' status to the North through the so-called 'ju-che' philosophy of self-reliance in all departments, then by balancing between Moscow and Beijing within the system of communist states, and finally by seeking an independent foreign policy through establishing good relations with as many Third World nations as possible. These policies have largely been successful, although costs to North Korea have been high in terms of declining rates of economic growth, militarisation of the people's lives, isolation from the outer world, and attitudes of suspicion on the part of many foreign rulers. North Korea is the last of the communist states to be ruled by its founder-king and now the only one unwilling even to acknowledge the nature of the contemporary world, much less recognise officially, and attempt to work with, the broad variety of states comprising the international system. The core of Pyongyang's policy is to conquer South Korea by force, which it attempted once without success and which it is ready to try again whenever it thinks it can do so without excessive costs.[34]

The Kremlin thus has three problems with Kim. First, it must assure that North Korean proclivities toward aggression against the South are checked, lest the Soviet Union find itself at war with the United States. Second, it must do what it can to maintain contact and reasonably good relations with Kim in order to prevent Pyongyang from siding with Beijing in the Sino-Soviet dispute. And, third, it must reconcile North Korea's independent stance in the Third World with the general direction of Soviet policy there. Moscow has applied various methods and expended a variety of resources to gain these ends, and has been indifferently successful at best. The Stalinist policy of direct domination – through massive economic assistance, arms, advisors, and ideological-organisational control might have succeeded were it not for the Korean War, which gave the North the opportunity, in the midst of defeat and destruction, of bringing in the Chinese to balance off the Soviets. Thereafter, up to the early 1980s Moscow fought a see-saw battle with Beijing – conducted within the confines of intra-communist party-state relations and thus sealed off from the outer world's ability to understand in detail – for influence in Pyongyang. Kim, who soon learned what China already had found out about three-sided international games, adroitly leaned first to one side and then back to the centre and then to the other. At one point, during the 1970s Moscow largely gave up on Kim and adopted a policy of distancing the Kremlin from Kim's palace-residence, thereby showing him what life could be like without Soviet largess and with only the Chinese to talk to. In any case, the phases of Soviet-North Korean relations – some five of them can be noted between 1945 and the end of

1981 – reflect the status of Soviet-Chinese struggles, as well as Kim's ideological-political vacillation. Moscow could do little about this, especially as Kim discovered that through balancing he could gain benefits from both sides simultaneously, thus pushing up the Soviet frustration quotient noticeably at several points.[35]

A further method was to try to buy North Korean support through trade and economic assistance. Although estimates vary, Moscow has in fact put considerable resources into North Korean development, in terms of technology transfer, rouble support, advisors, and plant construction. Indeed, the very base of what economic success Pyongyang has had is much due to Moscow's largess (giving lie, thereby, to Kim's claim of self-reliance; North Korean redevelopment would have been significantly retarded without Russian help). Such assistance, to be sure, has not permitted the Kremlin to dictate how Kim should run his country. On the contrary, the Great Leader has been on the Chinese side of the line more often than the Soviet and sometimes has taken policy tacks internationally (for instance, support of the Kampuchean resistance to the Soviet-supported Vietnamese invaders) that are directly contrary to Soviet policy. But the economic lever has kept Moscow in the game, at least, and provides one of the few instances (all the rest are also in the system of communist states) where economic assistance has led to visible results.

Aside from these modes of influence, Moscow has the military assistance card to play. Pyongyang prides itself on its ability to produce domestically most of the equipment it wants for its prospective invasion of the South, from small calibre weapons through tanks and submarines. That is one area where it can claim policy independence from Moscow. Some items, however, are beyond the North's reach, including high technology radar equipment, precision-guided munitions, recent model missiles, more modern tanks and associated armours, and (especially) high performance jet aircraft. Until very recently, the Kremlin wisely refused to transmit such items to North Korea, either in kind or by rendering the assistance or building the plants necessary for Pyongyang's own production. Because Moscow is the sole source for such equipment – China's capabilities in these areas are inadequate – the North had to forego it. Moscow's denial thus became an important and continuing element in the avoidance of a new Korean war (the US commitment to the South, Seoul's own rising defence capabilities, and China's opposition to Pyongyang's Southern Expedition being the others).[36]

Moscow's policy toward North Korea began to change in 1982 – the year, not coincidentally, when Sino-Soviet relations began to turn. The reasons are still unclear, but appear to be the usual conglomeration of coincidences, reactions, deliberate departures, and accidents. One clear cause was Kim's assessment of Chinese policy directions. Deng and his colleagues by then were well into their series of revolutionary economic changes, with attendant foreign policy consequences – especially the 'open door' to Western investment and the decision to work back toward the centre of the US-Soviet political spectrum. Kim did not like what he saw in China, and also realised that closer Sino-Soviet relations meant less room for manoeuvre between them. Another was Kim's impatience, toward the end of his life, to resolve the North–South separation in his favour. Since Beijing did not appear willing to sponsor the invasion, Kim would have to work up the circumstances himself. Creating disorders in the South and making sure the Americans would be busy with some crisis elsewhere are the two that have to be present simultaneously. Kim could take care of the first, he thought, but would need help on the second. Since China was also strongly opposed to a new war – which would make a shambles of its foreign policy as well as wreck the new economic departures – and since only Moscow could supply the needed equipment as well as create a diversion elsewhere in the globe, Kim began to solicit the Kremlin. Then, finally, a bit of extra risk-taking may have surfaced in Moscow after Brezhnev: with such a heavy expenditure in the military area for over two decades and with a right-wing US administration beginning to rearm and to overtake Moscow's advantage once again, perhaps the time had arrived to teach the Americans that Moscow was a power equal to Washington, and perhaps its superior in some areas. Korea might be one place to exercise a few options, albeit with care and so that a small expenditure of resources on the Kremlin's part would require a disproportionate but wasteful response on the part of the White House.

As in the Chinese case, it took a while for the process to get going. Thus, 1982 and 1983 passed without much overt indication of what was about to pass, largely because of the geriatric instability in the Soviet leadership and the problems created in late 1983 over the Rangoon Incident – when North Korean agents killed much of the South Korean leadership and barely missed then President Chun Doo Hwan – and the KAL 007 incident, in which a South Korean airliner was shot down by a Soviet fighter. Trade (always a reliable barometer of inter-communist political relations), tipped significantly upward during these two years. Events picked up in 1984, when Kim Il Sung went to Moscow (by train, seven days in each direction) for the first time in 23 years. He laid the groundwork for the *modus vivendi* that was to follow. North Korea would obtain Soviet acknowledgement of the legitimacy of the 'royal succession' (in the person of Kim's movie-mogul son, Chong Il), additional economic assistance, higher trade levels, and more and higher quality military aid. Moscow would expect Kim to support it in anti-US operations – such as terrorist training, military assistance, and arms transfers to a range of Third World countries friendly to Moscow, and to move to a position of equidistance between the Soviet capital and Beijing.

These things were done, on both sides. It is true that Kim also visited China in 1984, once officially and publicly and twice secretly (both of these after the Moscow visit). But these trips can probably be attributed to fence-mending after Rangoon. The Chinese were very upset at the outrage, especially when they were also being used by Kim to convey his alleged proposals to improve relations with Washington at the very moment when the Rangoon incident took place. Kim also wanted to reassure Beijing that Pyongyang would not throw the Chinese over in favour of the Soviets.

In 1985 activities went into high gear. The Soviets began to deliver Mig-23s to Pyongyang (totalling by 1986 around 50) and more capable, 230-mile, surface-to-surface missiles. Soviet intelligence overflights also commenced then: Mig-25 high-capability reconnaissance planes now regularly fly down the North Korean East Coast, across the DMZ, around the Yellow Sea, and then back along the same route. The North has received some good information on South Korean air defenses while the Soviets have obtained materials on the Chinese, a nice trade-off. Also, no less than ten protocols were signed during Kim's Moscow visit, ranging from military issues to much increased trade, significantly higher Soviet economic assistance including building new factories and refurbishing old ones, return of many Soviet technicians, and student and cultural interchanges. They were not made public then so as not to disconcert the Chinese or the Americans. They would be allowed to find out gradually.[37]

Besides that, the Soviets made it known that some of the Siberian-based SS-20 mobile missiles were trained on US bases in South Korea and that its Backfire bombers have planned missions in the South. This imparted a new element into the equation, for the

Korean military situation[38] is thereby pulled up into the overall US-Soviet strategic equation. The recent US-Soviet accord to eliminate Asian SS-20s will inevitably reduce the value of the missile component of this equation in the Korean peninsula. Moreover, the Soviets have made no move to foster North–South negotiations or to propose realistic multi-party talks on the question. Obviously, Moscow thinks it can control Kim in Korea by modulating its assistance to him – despite all the evidence of the last two decades. More broadly, the Kremlin appears to consider that in Kim and in Korea it has a means to extend its power into the heart of East Asia at little cost to itself.

Additionally, the Soviets seem to want to stay in the game against China on the peninsula. Indeed, Gorbachev may realise that the Chinese have come close to playing their last card in attempting to keep the North Korean army out of the South. Beijing has moved, since 1982, from stressing that its security treaty with North Korea is a defensive one, to asserting that it will not support aggression against Seoul, to declaring that it will actively oppose the North. China has thus become a security guarantor, of sorts, of South Korea.[39] If this is the case, perhaps the Soviets feel some more direct action of their own is necessary to rein in the North Korean leader.

Finally, the Kremlin probably feels it cannot pass up an opportunity. It supposes it can do with Pyongyang what it did with Hanoi in the late 1970s: make it dependent on Soviet policy and material support. In the case of Vietnam, Moscow did obtain its goal: Cam Ranh Bay and Da Nang as valuable military bases and a major extension of its power into Southeast Asia. The Soviet fleet is already at the North Korean port of Najin, south of Vladivostok; already in 1986 a Soviet flotilla dropped anchor there for the first time since the 1950s. With Kim so desperate to carry out a 'final solution' of the Korean problem before his demise, Moscow wants to repeat its Southeast Asian victory of 1978–79. But Korea is not Southeast Asia and Kim Il Sung is less pliable than Ho Chi Minh's successors. The Kremlin's greed could thus reap a whirlwind by precipitating a new war. Such a conflict would enflame all of Northeast Asia and in all probability escalate upward militarily and out of the region geographically. That would spell disaster not only for both Koreas, Japan, and the United States, but also for the Soviet Union.

Hope appeared in 1987 in the form of the South Korean political miracle. A nation that had been trying for three decades to break the authoritarian hold and take on a solidly democratic form of government appeared, finally, to be achieving success. As usual with the South, the process was disjointed, fraught with danger, and capable at any point of coming apart, evidenced by widespread political protests in South Korea. But it was far enough advanced that a firm popular base for a newly elected government could emerge if President Roe Tae Woo, elected by only a plurality of Korean voters, successfully placates or divides his opposition. That, together with continued South Korean economic growth and military modernisation, could spell the end of Kim Il Sung's hopes to take personal control of the whole peninsula. Along with the expected political-economic opening out of the North after the Kim (or Kims) succession, the Soviet position in Pyongyang could well decline greatly. The threat of war is 'good' for Moscow in the sense that its influence rises in such circumstances; the reality of peace would be 'bad' in the sense that it would have to compete for influence in Korea on terms, mostly economic, in which it had no comparative advantage.

The US-Soviet arms control agreement of 1987, featuring a Soviet pledge to remove all SS-20 mobile missiles east of the Urals, will undoubtedly improve the strategic picture in Asia for all parties, including the Soviet Union. To be sure, Moscow will possess less nuclear striking power in Asia against China, Japan, and US bases there. But the declination will be marginal. More important will be the political effects. First, the Kremlin can argue to China that it has taken a major step to lessen Sino-Soviet tensions and that the Chungnan Hai should respond with a more positive stance in the border talks. This powerful argument could tip the scales toward an overall border location-arms control agreement. Second, Moscow can argue to Japan in favour of a fundamental improvement in Japanese-Soviet relations. If the Gorbachev leadership were wise, it would follow the US agreement with an offer to return the smaller two Northern Islands to Japan. Tokyo would be hard pressed not to assent and such developments could stop the Japanese rearmament programme in its tracks. As for US-Soviet relations in the Pacific, the overall improvement following the new arms control agreement could well open the way to direct discussion of the lateral-vertical escalation threat noted earlier. The upshot of these three changes could therefore be a better chance for the Soviet Union to play a more central role in East Asian affairs, and a more acceptable, peaceable one at that.

Notes

1. This draws on Thomas W. Robinson, 'Soviet Policy in East Asia', *Problems of Communism*, vol. 22, no. 6, November–December 1973, pp. 32–50; and 'Soviet Policy in Asia', in William B. Griffith (ed.), *The Soviet Empire: Expansion and Détente* (Lexington, MA: D. C. Heath, 1975), pp. 285–336.

2. For an elaboration, see Thomas W. Robinson, 'Soviet Policy in Northeast Asia: Determinants, Options, and Possible Changes', *Asiatic Research Service, Korea University, 1977; and* 'The Soviet Union in Asia in 1980', *Asian Survey*, January 1981, pp. 14–30.

3. Allen S. Whiting, *Siberian Development and East Asia: Threat or Promise?* (Stanford: Stanford University Press, 1981), and Thomas W. Robinson, 'Siberian Development and Its Implications for the United States and Japan' (Washington, DC: US Department of State, June 1979).

4. See *inter alia*, Seweryn Bialer, *The Soviet Paradox: External Expansion, Internal Decline* (New York: Knopf, 1986); and Marshall Goldman, *The USSR in Crisis: The Failure of an Economic System* (New York: Norton, 1983).

5. The author's writings on the strategic triangle form the basis of this section, and include: 'Détente and the Sino-Soviet-US Triangle'. in Della Sheldon (ed.), *Dimensions of Détente* (New York: Praeger, 1978); 'American Policies in the Strategic Triangle', in Richard A. Melanson (ed.), *Neither Cold War not Détente* (Charlottesville, VA: University of Virginia Press, 1983); 'On the Further Evolution of the Strategic Triangle', in Ilpyong J. Kim (ed.), *The Sino-Soviet-American Strategic Triangle* (New York: Paragon, 1987); and 'Triple Détente? The Strategic Triangle in the Late Twentieth Century', in Jane Shapiro Zacek (ed.), *The USSR under Gorbachev: Issues and Challenges* (New York: Paragon, forthcoming).

6. In a large but unsatisfactory field, see Victor Argy, *The Postwar International Money Crisis: An Analysis* (London: George Allen & Unwin, 1981); Michael Stewart, *The Age of Interdependence: Economic Policy in a Shrinking World* (Cambridge: MIT Press, 1984); William R. Cline, *International Debt and the Stability of the World Economy* (Washington, DC: Institute for International Economics, 1983); Susan Strange (ed.), *Paths to International Political Economics* (London: Allen & Unwin, 1984); Susan Strange, *Crisis Capitalism* (New York: Blackwell, 1986); and Miles Kahler (ed.), *The Politics of International Debt* (Cornell: Cornell University Press, 1986).

7. Roger Hansen, *Beyond the North–South Stalemate* (New York: McGraw-Hill, 1979); Robert L. Rothstein, *The Weak in the World of the Strong: The Developing Countries in the International System* (New York: Columbia University Press, 1979); Robert O. Keohane, *After Hegemony: Cooperation and Discord in the World Political Economy* (Princeton: Princeton Unviersity Press, 1984); K. J. Holsti, *The Undividing Discipline: Hegemony and Diversity of International Theory* (Winchester, MA: Allen & Unwin, 1985); Robert O. Keohane and

Joseph S. Nye, *Power and Interdependence: World Politics in Transition* (Boston, MA: Little, Brown, 1977); and John G. Ruggie (ed.), *The Antinomies of Interdependence: National Welfare and the International Division of Labor* (New York: Columbia University Press, 1983).

8. *The Military Balance* (London: International Institute for Strategic Studies, annually), and *Asian Security* (Tokyo: Research Institute for Peace and Security, annually).

9. *Soviet Military Thought*, a multi-volume translation series (Washington, DC: Government Printing Office, 1972 *et seq.*); V. D. Sokolovsky, in Harriett Fast Scott (ed.), *Soviet Military Strategy* (New York: Crane, Russak, 1975); Harriet Fast Scott and William F. Scott (eds), *The Armed Forces of the USSR* (Boulder, CO: Westview, 1981); Mark E. Miller, *Soviet Strategic Power and Doctrine: The Quest for Superiority* (Miami: Advanced International Studies Institute, 1982); Joseph D. Douglas, Jr and Amoretta M. Hoeber, *Soviet Strategy for Nuclear War* (Stanford, CA: Hoover Institution, 1979); Colin S. Gray, *Nuclear Strategy and National Style* (Washington, DC: Hamilton Press, 1986); and Helmut Sonnenfeldt and William Hyland, *Soviet Perspectives in Security*, Adelphi Paper No. 150 (London: International Institute for Strategic Studies, 1979).

10. Roman Kolkowicz and Ellen Propper Mickiewicz (eds), *The Soviet Calculus of Nuclear War* (Lexington, MA: D. C. Heath, 1986); John Van Oudenaren, *Deterrence, War-Fighting, and Soviet Doctrine*, Adelphi Paper No. 210 (London: International Institute for Strategic Studies, 1986); and Graham D. Vernon (ed.), *Soviet Perceptions of War and Peace* (Washington, DC: National Defense University Press, 1986).

11. Trade statistics can be viewed in the *Far Eastern Economic Review* Annual. See also John Stephan, 'Asia in the Soviet Conception', in Donald S. Zagoria (ed.), *Soviet Policy in East Asia* (New Haven, CT: Yale University Press, 1982), pp. 29–56; and James W. Morley (ed.), *The Pacific Basin: New Challenges for the United States* (Montpelier, VT: Capital City Press for the Academy of Political Science, 1986).

12. Theodore Shabad, 'Siberian Development and Soviet Policy in East Asia', *Asian Perspective*, Fall–Winter 1982, pp. 195–208; *Defense of Japan* (Tokyo: *Japan Times* for the Japan Self-Defense Agency, annually from 1977); Allen S. Whiting, *Siberian Development and East Asia*; Richard H. Solomon and Masataka Kosaka (eds), *The Soviet Far East Military Buildup* (Dover, MA: Auburn House, 1986).

13. Department of Defense, *Soviet Military Power* (Washington, DC: Government Printing Office, annually from 1982); Anthony H. Cordesman, 'The Military Balance in Northeast Asia: The Challenge to Japan and Korea', *Armed Forces Journal International*, November 1983, pp. 80–81; G. Jacobs, 'Soviet Forces and the Pacific Basin', *Jane's Defense Review*, Spring 1983, pp. 553–7.

14. Thomas W. Robinson, 'Nuclear Weapons and Arms Control in Asia', in Toby Trister Gati and Mike Mochizuki (eds), *Geopolitics and Strategy in East Asia: Testing the US–Japan Alliance* (ms 1987); Harry Gelman, *The Soviet Far East Buildup and Soviet Risk-Taking against China* (Santa Monica, CA: Rand Corporation, August 1982).

15. Donald S. Zagoria, *The Sino-Soviet Conflict, 1956–1961* (Princeton: Princeton University Press, 1962); Alfred D. Low, *The Sino-Soviet Dispute* (Rutherford, NJ: Farleigh Dickenson University Press, 1976); and Oleg Borisov and B. T. Koloskov, *Sino-Soviet Relations, 1945–1970* (Bloomington: Indiana University Press, 1971), are some of many sources.

16. Harry Gelman, 'The Sino-Soviet Dispute in the 1970s: An Overview', in Herbert J. Ellison (ed.), *The Sino-Soviet Conflict* (Seattle: University of Washington Press, 1982), pp. 355–71.

17. C. G. Jacobsen, *Sino-Soviet Relations since Mao* (New York: Praeger, 1981; Seweryn Bialer, 'The Sino-Soviet Conflict: The Soviet Dimension', in Zagoria (ed.), *Soviet Policy in East Asia*, pp. 93–119 (see note 11); *Current Digest of the Soviet Press* (CDSP), 21 April 1982, pp. 6–7, and 27 October 1982, p. 4.

18. Thomas P. Thornton, 'The USSR and Asia in 1983: Staying the Brezhnev Course', *Asian Survey*, January 1984, pp. 1–17; Donald S. Zagoria, 'The USSR and Asia in 1984', *Asian Survey*, January 1985, pp. 21–32; Donald S. Zagoria, 'The USSR and Asia in 1985: The First Year of Gorbachev', *Asian Survey*, January 1986, pp. 15–29; and Chi Su, 'China and the Soviet Union: "Principled, Saluatory, and Tempered" Management of Conflict,' in Samuel S. Kim (ed.), *China and the World: Chinese Foreign Policy in the Post-Mao Era* (Boulder, CO: Westview, 1984), pp. 135–60.

19. William deB. Mills, 'Gorbachev and the Future of Sino-Soviet Relations', *Political Science Quarterly*, vol. 101, no. 4, pp. 535–7. The presence of the 'Three Obstacles' are Soviet forces in Mongolia, Vietnam, and Afghanistan which, Beijing has asserted, must be withdrawn.

20. There is almost no unclassified literature on this important topic. But see Robinson, 'Nuclear Weapons and Arms Control in Asia', Henry S. Rowan, 'Distant Relations: Links Between Asian and European Security', in Solomon and Kosaka, *The Soviet Far East Military Buildup*, pp. 221–35 (see note 12). The need for further work on this subject was dramatised by the agreement between the United States and the Soviet Union at Washington, which saw Soviet willingness to eliminate SS-20 missiles in Asia in December 1987 as part of the overall settlement. See Michael Mandelbaum and Strobe Talbot, 'Reykjavik and Beyond', *Foreign Affairs*, vol. 65, no. 2, Winter 1986/87, pp. 215–35.

21. Thus the Soviet dilemma in its Asian policy: demanding 'participation' in Asia based on no firm means of policy other than threat of force, which in this scenario would decline. Moreover, existing Soviet military units in Soviet Asia would be weighted even more to the global nuclear mission. And in a post-Reykjavik world, even they might lose much of their effectiveness.

22. Implications also follow for Sino-Soviet relations in the Third World. A Moscow–Beijing *rapprochement* would greatly lessen the felt need in both communist capitals to compete for influence in the Third World. And since both policies in that area are found largely, if not completely,

on competition with the other, their respective levels of interest and propensity to invest resources in Third World states would, on margin, decline. Perhaps that would be made up, in the case of heightened Soviet-US tensions, by a tendency in the Kremlin to get on with the job of ousting the United States from these vast areas of the globe. If so, a tendency would arise to draw China back into the fray, as struggle for global primacy shifted to those countries. A kind of equilibrating mechanism would thus be constructed.

23. The best work on Japanese foreign policy is Robert A. Scalapino (ed.), *The Foreign Policy of Modern Japan* (Berkeley, CA: University of California Press, 1977), while a good recent survey of Soviet-Japanese relations is Roger Swearingen, *The Soviet Union and Postwar Japan* (Stanford, CA: Hoover Institution, 1978).

24. John J. Stephen, *The Kurile Islands: Russo-Japanese Frontiers in the Pacific* (Oxford: Clarendon Press, 1979); Japan Ministry of Foreign Affairs, *The Northern Territories Issue: Japan's Position on Unsettled Questions*, (Tokyo: Public Information Bureau, 1968 *et seq*); and Fuji Kamiya, The Northern Territories: 130 Years of Japanese Talks with Czarist Russia and the Soviet Union, Soviet Policy in East Asia, pp. 121–52 (see note 11).

25. Thomas W. Robinson, 'Soviet-Japanese Security Relations' (in Stephen P. Gilbert (ed.), *Security in Northeast Asia*: Approaching The Pacific Century (Boulder, CO: Westview, 1987) pp. 29–52.

26. The so-called Maritime Strategy, adumbrated by the Reagan administration (but having its roots in the late Carter administration) was declassified in a January 1986 Naval Institute pamphlet by that name under the signature of the Chief of Naval Operations, Admiral James D. Watkins. The best review is John J. Mearsheimer, 'A Strategic Misstep: The Maritime Strategy and Deterrence in Europe', *International Security*, vol. 11, no. 2, Fall 1986, pp. 3–57, which lists many sources. See also Captain D. M. Schwartz, 'Contemporary US Naval Strategy: A Bibliography', US Naval Institute *Proceedings*, January 1986, pp. 41–7. As of this writing, no one has drawn the implications of the Maritime Strategy for Asia. But see the author's initial approach to the subjects, 'Nuclear Weapons and Arms Control in Asia', footnote 14.

27. In the so-called Vladivostok speech, 28 July, 1986. In *CDSP*, 27 August, 1986, pp. 1ff.

28. James C. Abegglen, *The Strategy of Japanese Business* (Cambridge, MA: Ballinger, 1984); Robert A. Scalapino *et al.* (eds), *Asian Economic Development – Present and Future* (Berkeley: Institute of East Asian Studies, University of California, 1985); and Robert C. Christopher, *The Japanese Mind: The Goliath Explained* (New York: Simon and Schuster, 1983) are some recent entries attempting to explain Japan's economic 'miracle'.

29. *Defense of Japan*, 1977–(see note 9), and *Asian Security*, 1979–(see note 8) provide details.

30. Mike Mochizuki, 'Japan's Search for Strategy', and Masashi Nishihara, 'Expanding Japan's Credible Defense Role', *International Security*, vol. 8, no. 3, Winter 1983–84, pp. 152–205; Yukio Satoh, *The Evolution of*

Japanese Security Policy, Adelphi Paper No. 178 (London: International Institute for Strategic Studies, 1982); and J. W. M. Chapman *et al.*, *Japan's Quest for Comprehensive Security* (New York: St Martin, 1983) serve as introductions to the subject.

31. Hisahiko Okasaki, 'Japan's Security Policy: A Time for Strategy', *International Security*, Fall 1982, pp. 188–96; Takesugu Tsurutani, *Japanese Policy and East Asian Security* (New York: Praeger, 1981); Robert W. Barnett, *Beyond War: Japan's Concept of Comprehensive National Security* (New York: Pergamon, 1984).

32. For details, see Alan Rix, *Japan's Economic Aid* (New York: St Martin, 1980); Japan Economic Institute, *Japan's Relations with Southeast Asia* (Washington, DC: Japan Economic Institute, August 1981); William L. Brooks and Robert M. Orr, Jr, 'Japan's Foreign Economic Assistance', *Asian Survey*, March 1985, pp. 322–40; and Alexander Caldwell, 'The Evolution of Japanese Economic Cooperation, 1950–70', in Harold Malmgren (ed.), *Pacific Basin Development: The American Interests* (Lexington, MA: D. C. Heath, 1972), pp. 34–5.

33. This despite the fact that, economically, culturally, and politically, South Korea is not only a quintessential Third World nation – formerly colonial, non-Western, developing, foreign trade dependent, democratising only slowly, resource poor, militarily governed, playground of the superpowers, etc. – and that a major plank in Seoul's foreign policy is the notion that it is a Third World nation and wishes to thicken its tie with other such states. Difficulty also stems from the very nature of North Korea: autarchic, self-isolated, rigidly totalitarian, certainly not neutralist, clearly aligned with other communist states, and militarily aggressive, to name a few un-Third World-like qualities. Indeed, it is one of the wonders of the Third World that North Korea can be taken as one of them, even sometimes as a leader, while South Korea is almost entirely excluded. One must conclude that the major criteria for Third World status is apparently political: if a state is aligned with the United States, it is therefore not considered to be Third World; if it is aligned with the Soviet Union, it must be acceptable.

34. The best sources are Byung Chul Koh, *The Foreign Policy Systems of North and South Korea* (Berkeley, CA: University of California Press, 1984), which provides many additional references; Robert A. Scalapino and Chong-sik Lee, *Communism in Korea* (Berkeley, CA: University of California Press, 1972, 2 vols) and Robert A. Scalapino and Kim Jun-yop (eds), *North Korea Today: Strategic and Domestic Issues* (Berkeley, CA: Institute for East Asia Studies, University of California, 1983).

35. Yong-chool Ha, 'Soviet Perceptions of Soviet-North Korean Relations', *Asian Survey*, May 1986, pp. 573–90; Joseph M. Ha, 'Soviet Perceptions of North Korea', *Asian Perspective*, Fall–Winter 1982, pp. 105–31; Lee Such-ho, 'Major Determinants of Soviet Support for North Korea', *Korea and World Affairs*, Spring 1985, pp. 91–115.

36. Ralph N. Clough, 'The Soviet Union and the Two Koreas', in Zagoria, *Soviet Policy in East Asia*, pp. 175–200 (see note 11); Ahn Byung-joon, 'The Soviet Union and the Korean Peninsula', paper presented to

Pacific Forum Workshop on Soviet Policies in the Asia-Pacific Region, May 1984, 33 pages.

37.   Young-whan Kihl, 'North Korea in 1984: The Hermit Kingdom Turns Outward!' *Asian Survey*, January 1985, pp. 65–79. The *Korea Herald*, 1985 and 1986, provides many details.

38.   A 900 000 to 500 000 manpower under arms advantage in favour of the North; an equipment balance on the ground and sea in favour of the North by several hundred per cent in every category; a 100 000 man infiltration force clothed in South Korean uniforms ready to rush through several dozen tunnels under the DMZ or ride several hundred helicopters and hundreds more landing boats into every sector of South Korea; over 70 per cent of the army (some 26 divisions) poised just across the DMZ within a few miles of Seoul; and a warning time down to less than an hour – not enough for the US-South Korean command to react appropriately. This with an extremely volatile political situation in the South. The only ultimate deterrent is the US threat to use nuclear weapons from the outset of conflict, which would guarantee nuclear escalation to the Soviet-American level, especially if the Soviets directly interfere with the US shipping to Korea, as many expect. See Young Choi, 'The North Korean Military Buildup and Its Impact on North Korean Military Strategy in the 1980s', *Asian Survey*, March 1985, pp. 341–55.

39.   Such Chinese sentiments have been conveyed privately, or verbally, to the Americans, as for instance, by Tao Bingwei, Head of Asian and Pacific Studies, Institution of International Studies in Beijing, at a Professors World Peace Academy conference in Los Angeles on the Strategic Triangle, 16 February, 1985; and Ding Shinghao, at the Thirteenth Annual Meeting of the Mid-Atlantic Region of the Association for Asian Studies, Princeton University, 10 November, 1984, both of which statements were noted by the author.

South and Southeast Asia

8 The Soviet Union and South Asia

Stephen P. Cohen

SUMMARY

The Soviet Union has expanded its presence in South Asia since its first approaches to India in the 1950s. However, its influence in the region peaked in 1966–71, when it was a supplier of weapons to both India and Pakistan and entered into a Treaty of Peace and Friendship with India. Except for a continuing arms supply relationship with New Delhi, Moscow has seen its influence decline in the region (except in Afghanistan, where it remains embattled). Indeed, the invasion of Afghanistan has stimulated a regional reaction against the Soviet Union.

It is likely that Soviet economic, ideological, and political influence will continue to decline in South Asia, even in India. New Delhi is especially wary of new Soviet approaches to Beijing, which had been its common interest with Moscow.

This rapidly evolving region now includes two nuclear states and two near-nuclears. The United States is again a regional factor through its assistance relationship with Pakistan and a revived tie with India. However, US policy has yet to grapple fully with the emergence of the regional 'pentagon of power', to fine-tune its policies to South Asian complexities, and to address the growing problem of regional nuclear proliferation.

INTRODUCTION

Much of the relationship between the Soviet Union and South Asia derives from the region's threefold strategic conundrum. First, South Asia is strategically divided between its major military powers, India and Pakistan. The intensity and apparent permanence of the struggle between these two states requires no elaboration here.[1] Second, the region does not contain resources or assets that the Soviets might regard as vital (China is a greater military threat, the Persian Gulf and South Africa are vastly richer in resources, and Japan and Western

Europe are more productive). Third, South Asia is located at the margin of the global competition between the United States and the Soviet Union, and even of the Eurasian competition between the Soviet Union and China.

Ironically, South Asia's peripheral strategic position had its advantages. While not regarded as terribly important by either superpower, India and Pakistan have separately benefited from superpower rivalry – enabling them better to pursue their own harsh competition. Indeed, first India and then Pakistan defined the strategy of non-alignment in terms of this rivalry. Both came to see advantage in pursuing a course more or less (for India, usually less) distant from Moscow than Washington, and both ran little risk since neither superpower thought the stakes to be very great.

However, the strategic marginality of South Asia is changing. While the regional schism between India and Pakistan continues, the Soviet advance into Afghanistan on the one hand, and hints of Soviet normalization with China, on the other, suggest a new entanglement with superpower (and particularly Soviet) concerns. Further, this entanglement will involve both India and Pakistan. While India is clearly the dominant regional power, Pakistan's location next to the Gulf and Afghanistan and its ability to sustain outside support has once again made it a state to reckon with.

Because of Pakistan's reemergence as at least a regional power, we identify an emerging pentagon of power in and around South Asia: a competition for influence and power among the two superpowers, China, and the two regional powers. The fact that all five of these countries are nuclear weapons states or near-nuclears adds a new, and historically unprecedented dimension to their competition.

While Soviet policy in and toward South Asia will be largely shaped by Moscow's interpretation of where its interests rest, other factors are also important, as these shape the response of regional states to Soviet stratagems. History, personality, and ideology have moulded regional perceptions of the Soviet Union, and these will be summarised in the following section. We will then examine in some detail the different dimensions of the Soviet-South Asian relationship. Particular attention will be devoted to major changes in the region due to the Soviet invasion and occupation of Afghanistan which is, after all, as much a South Asian state as it is a Central Asian or Middle Eastern one.

PERCEPTION AND INFLUENCE

The view of the Soviet Union – as seen from South Asia (especially India) – has seven major components. First, few South Asians regard the Soviet Union as a model for political development. Leninism holds little appeal for South Asian elites. Pluralist democracy is legitimate in South Asia, even in those states under military rule. This has baffled the Soviets, who tend to associate a lack of economic development with the need for coercive Leninist structures. One practical implication of rejection of the Soviet model is the complete absence of Soviet assistance to South Asian police and internal security services.

Second, the Soviets benefit from regional anti-Americanism. The United States has long been linked to British imperialism (although the historical record indicates otherwise). More pernicious, many South Asian elites inherited the anti-Americanism of the British Left.[2] As many members of the 'Cambridge Comintern' spied for the Soviets because they despised the Americans, many South Asians of Jawaharlal Nehru's generation also saw the Americans as crude and materialistic – unworthy successors to the British Raj. They feared a link between the raw capitalism of the United States and their own merchant castes and classes.

Third, there has been a perception of the Soviet Union as a developed society. This fast-fading image saw in the Soviet/Socialist model a pattern appropriate to Pakistan or India; had not socialism lifted the Soviet Union from backwardness to the front rank of industrial powers? The fact that the Soviets also purported to be an 'Asian' society was an added attraction. Now, with Soviet-supplied industries in India turning to the West for new technologies and with direct evidence of the inability of the Soviet system to produce a wide range of quality goods, few South Asians take the socialist pattern seriously. Even the left-Communist Chief Minister of West Bengal encourages private investment and his son is a capitalist.

One perception that has not faded is that the Soviets geophysically dominate Asia. This image is exemplified (and reinforced) by the Sovo-centric Mercator projections hanging on the walls of nearly every office in India's Ministry of External Affairs.[3] The image, of course, is false: the Mercator exaggerates the size of the Soviet Union by about 40 per cent and deemphasises the area of countries such as India and China. South Asians tend to imagine a giant, sprawling Soviet Union, looming over Eurasia. The strategic lesson drawn from this image by many South Asians is that the Soviet Union is an Asian power that they must learn to live with – and to accommodate if necessary.

Many South Asians also believe that it is easy to do business with the Soviets. They keep secrets. They do not have an inquisitive press. They are hard bargainers, but deals are kept confidential. Embarrassing concessions never become public. They are expert flatterers, carefully calibrating responses to fit the status of their interlocutors. In the United States, Japan, and Europe, South Asians are part of a general crowd of poor nations seeking help. In contrast, the Soviets are fullsome with praise even when their terms are tough.

Indians and Pakistanis are also confident that the Soviets can be exploited. They have been particularly helpful to India in the UN, and most Indians believe that the Soviets need them more than they need the Soviets. Even the Pakistanis, Bangladeshis, Sri Lankans, and Nepalis have learned, however, that moving closer to the Soviets brings waves of Western and Chinese diplomats offering technology, weapons, money, agricultural cooperation, special quotas, loans, and the other fruits of non-alignment.

Finally, many South Asians regard the Soviets as relatively recent arrivals, and put even the Soviet occupation of a South Asian country (Afghanistan) in a broader historical context. Indians and Pakistanis remember another imperial expansionist power – Britain – which conquered historic Hindu principalities and an Islamic empire. Such strategists as Zbigniew Brzezinski may point to the inexorable expansion of Soviet power to the heart of South Asia, but his arguments carry little weight in India and less than they should in Pakistan.[4]

These impressions and images set South Asians apart from most other developing regions. They demonstrate a mixture of apprehension and self-confidence when dealing with Moscow. They are not interested in Soviet ideology or doctrine, but they do believe that the Soviets can be exploited for material gain – or at least used to enhance their bargaining power *vis-à-vis* either one of Moscow's strategic antagonists. And, with the exception of Afghanistan, most of the South Asian states are so politically and administratively advanced that they do not need Soviet assistance in developing the sinews of their statehood: political parties, police, intelligence and administrative services, and armed forces.

THE SOVIETS IN SOUTH ASIA: INFLUENCE AND PRESENCE

At independence from British colonial rule, there was virtually no important support for the Soviet Union in South Asia except from the pro-Soviet Communist Party of India and a few pro-Soviet elements in the Indian Congress Party. The Communist Party of Pakistan was banned (as it is today) and even then had only a few members. Moscow's influence elsewhere in South Asia was marginal. Although it was to grow in Afghanistan where the local communist party was severely fragmented, the Soviets' greatest success there came in the 1960s with effective penetration of the Afghan military establishment. There has never been any serious Soviet presence in Nepal or Ceylon (now Sri Lanka).

It was not until the mid-1950s that the Soviet Union began to establish significant contacts with South Asia (particularly India), and there is no question that the Soviet presence has greatly expanded. However, the Soviets have not acquired influence in direct proportion to the growth of their presence. Further, neither the Soviet presence nor its influence expanded uninterruptedly during the period 1955–86.

Soviet political influence in South Asia was probably at a peak in 1966–71. The United States had virtually withdrawn from the region, turning a political pentagon into an unstable rectangle (the Chinese, still hostile to India, became Pakistan's chief arms supplier). The Soviets (with US encouragement) presided over the 1966 Tashkent meeting that formally ended the 1965 Indo-Pakistani War; Moscow then found itself supplying weapons to both India and Pakistan, trying to build a position in the former and weaning the latter from US and Chinese influence. The Soviets felt confident enough to float a regional collective security treaty which would embrace India, Pakistan, and other states in a *de facto* encirclement of China. When this received no response they proposed a Treaty of Peace and Friendship to India.[5] New Delhi at first responded slowly to this suggestion, but agreed to it in 1971 as the price they would pay to keep Moscow from supplying further economic and military aid to Pakistan just as the conflict over East Pakistan/Bangladesh was about to reach a crisis. The Indians also received valuable diplomatic support from the Soviets during the 1971 war. The treaty was virtually ignored until ten years later when, ironically, the 1978 communist revolution in Afghanistan and subsequent Soviet invasion brought new external assistance to Pakistan, thereby (according to the Indian view), threatening India. The Indians have since received large amounts of modern equipment from the Soviets on good, but not fully publicised, terms. In turn, they have been reticent when asked to criticise the Soviet operations in Afghanistan. In terms of net gain, this hardly works to Delhi's advantage, since it was about to achieve strategic dominance over Pakistan before the Soviet invasion of Afghanistan transformed regional relations.

One consequence of ten years of close Indo-Soviet relations (and the virtual abandonment of South Asia by the United States) has been the growth in uncritical pro-Soviet attitudes in Indian universities and among Indian intellectuals. Even the Indian press has found it hard to report objectively on the Soviet Union, in part because Moscow cut off access to some journalists who appeared 'unfriendly', i.e. who exercised independent judgement. More alarming has been Soviet penetration of the shadowy world of influence buying. According to several accounts, companies that conduct business with the Soviet Union are obliged to set aside a percentage of profits as contributions to pro-Soviet groups within the Congress Party and perhaps to pro-Soviet labour unions, journalists, newspapers, and on other fronts.[6] Since the total economic flow amounts to billions of dollars, this money has made the Soviet Union a major factor in Indian elections – such funds can be used to pay campaign workers, arrange mass meetings, buy advertising, and purchase other services. Withholding such funds from a candidate is an ironic threat when it comes from the Soviets.

Details of the Soviet role in Indian domestic politics came under public scrutiny after a curious incident in 1983. According to press reports from journalists sympathetic to Indira Gandhi, a member of the Communist Party of India (CPI) known to be one of her supporters carried a letter from her to Yuri Andropov.[7] Mrs. Gandhi was reported to have asked for Soviet support in fighting both the Indian right and left, which had joined hands to oppose her 'progressive' politics. She held a deep fear of links between foreign governments and domestic Indian opponents. Her supporters claim she was able to keep the Soviets in check while at the same time exploiting them (among other tactics she created her own Indo-Soviet friendship group when the Soviet-controlled organisation began to attract too much support).[8] This may have been a personal, not a systemic inclination, since her son and successor, Rajiv Gandhi, has apparently resisted the temptation of drawing heavily upon Moscow for support in domestic matters. However, the Soviets, their money, and their supporters are to be reckoned with.

Despite this penetration of domestic Indian politics, overall Soviet influence is declining both in India and the rest of South Asia. Except for the occupation of Afghanistan and the military arms supply relationship with India, the Soviets are clearly in a weaker position in South Asia today than they were fifteen years ago. Their ideology remains unattractive to all South Asians (even in Afghanistan, where it was sustained by a massive military presence), Soviet economic influence is fading fast in a modernising India, and the Soviet occupation of Afghanistan discouraged Pakistani ethnic minorities from seeking Soviet assistance against the Punjabi and military-dominated central government of Pakistan.

The assessment, then, is one of an increase in presence – largely a military presence – but not an increase in overall Soviet influence. The Soviets cannot even claim to have done this on their own: the absence of a US strategic interest in South Asia from roughly 1965 to 1980 left the field wide open to them. China's post-1965 efforts to support Pakistan ensured that the Soviet role in that country would remain low, but certainly accelerated the growth of Soviet influence in India.

THE VIEW FROM MOSCOW

As seen from Moscow, South Asia possesses three important qualities. First, India has been big enough to serve as a partial counter to Chinese power. This has been the central factor influencing Soviet policy toward India and Pakistan from at least 1959 when Sino-Indian relations began to heat up and the Sino-Soviet dispute reached its muffled crisis. The two conflicts were united when Moscow openly supported India. This was one of the two precipitating factors in the formal break between Moscow and Beijing – the other being the Soviet refusal to assist the Chinese nuclear programme. A corollary of this Indo-centric (and Sino-phobic) axiom of Soviet regional policy has been intermittent Soviet interest in dividing China and Pakistan, a policy that reached a peak in 1967–69 with the provision of arms to Islamabad in the face of strong Indian opposition.

However, Pakistan has an independent standing in Soviet strategic calculations, stemming from its special relationship with the Gulf, the Islamic world, and Afghanistan. This interest in Pakistan has fluctuated greatly over the years, as Pakistani power has risen and fallen and the Soviets' own Southwest Asian interests have shifted. With a hot war on its hands in Afghanistan, with Iran involved in internal revolution and the war against Iraq, and with a limited Soviet presence at the mouth of the Gulf, Pakistan has been at the height of its importance for Moscow.

Finally, Moscow is nervous about any US presence in or cooperation with the states of South Asia. At one time Pakistan did serve as an outpost of US strategic intelligence and lent its territory for both electronic and aerial observation of Soviet military facilities. More recently, there has been public discussion of US-Pakistani cooperation in stabilising vulnerable Gulf states, and certainly the Soviets have vehemently criticised US, Pakistani and Chinese support for the Afghan *mujahidin*.

By emphasising these strategic calculations we do not wish to ignore lesser – or derived, or indirect – motives, nor do we believe that the Soviets give equal weight to each. Certainly, the Soviets would like to see Leninist states established on their borders (although the People's Republic of China is not a happy precedent); certainly they would like to have access to a 'warm water port' (although one wonders how the line of communication would have been sustained through some of the world's most difficult terrain, inhabited by some of the world's most hostile tribes).[9] Certainly, the Soviets are worried about nuclear proliferation in South Asia, although they are unlikely to take positive measures to restrain India, even as they demand that the United States do so in the case of Pakistan. Certainly the Soviets value India's 'third world' credentials (although the Egyptians and Indonesians came before them, and the Cubans, Nicaraguans, and Ethiopians now serve as Soviet surrogates). And, certainly, the Soviets were concerned that the precedent of Afghanistan – a rebellious communist state – must not be allowed to stand, lest other friendly communist countries acquire similar ideas. All of these factors have been important in shaping Soviet policies toward South Asia, but underlying them is a basic strategic calculation which overrides specific economic, ideological, and even bilateral political attractions.

This strategic interest has been, since the late 1950s, the Soviet fear of China. This has led to a persistent attempt to support states with grievances against China (first India, now Vietnam), and a divide-and-rule strategy directed against those with close ties to China, e.g. Pakistan. Thus, the guiding dictum of Soviet policy in South Asia has been not only opposition to China, or even opposition to China allied with a modest regional power such as Pakistan, but opposition to China allied with Pakistan in combination with a large industrial power. A China-Pakistan-US link not only strengthens an unfriendly government in Islamabad it remains an effective counter to the expansion of Soviet power, as evidenced in the successful program of support for the Afghan *mujahidin.*

Because of this importance of China to the Soviets, the latter have intensely cultivated relations with India from the time Sino-Soviet differences became significant. India has a territorial dispute with China that closely parallels that of Moscow, it has a long common border with China and, like Vietnam, it maintains forces along that disputed border in active resistance to perceived Chinese pressures.[10] There is no evidence that the Indians have formally agreed to assist the Soviets against China (and Moscow must be uncertain as to how useful the Indians would be in a real Sino-Soviet crisis), but only India and Vietnam have the capacity and motivation to assist the USSR in containing China. In the case of India, the Treaty of Peace and Friendship would nominally prevent the Indians from assisting China in the course of a new Sino-Soviet conflict.

Framing these strategic calculations is a working relationship between India and the Soviet Union which has often glowed with an aura of permanence. There are many links between Soviet and Indian security bureaucracies, and a number of important Indian civil servants, diplomats, and politicians have forged credible careers out of a pro-Soviet tilt. The Soviets have been coming to India for 25 years, installing and repairing defence facilities and cultural centres, and Indians have been travelling to the Soviet Union for tourism and technology – the relationship is comfortable, and until recently has operated as smoothly as these things can. Yet, the Soviets are capable of switching sides as strategic opportunities open up, and the Indians are as wary of such changes *vis-à-vis* the Soviets as the Pakistanis are *vis-à-vis* their reconstructed US relationship.

INDIA AND THE SOVIET UNION: FRIENDSHIP TO DEPENDENCE

India's current dependence upon the Soviet Union for the projection of its own power and prestige has been ideologically and technically inadvertent. The architect of non-alignment, Jawaharlal Nehru, originally conceived of a high purpose for this policy: nothing less than the melioration of the Cold War between the Soviet Union and the United States. Nehru did not see non-alignment as materially advantageous; he contrasted it with the easy path of formal alliance and often noted that non-alignment would involve sacrifice.[11] Nehru's endorsement of non-alignment was motivated by an unquestionably high vision, and even those who criticised it never doubted his bona fides. India's substantial political weight was in large part moral, not based on its feeble arsenals.

The Soviets must have thought Nehru a gullible idealist. He was invited to come to Moscow in June 1955, immediately after he 'introduced' the Chinese to the world at Bandung. His warm reception was intended in part to balance his strong advocacy of China during his Beijing visit in October 1954. There then followed a change in the Soviet ideological interpretation of India, an offer of a steel mill, and finally, in December 1955, support for India on Kashmir and Goa.[12] At this point the Soviets saw a friendly India as one path out of their international political confinement – even if the path led only to the developing world.

Five years later, after the hardening of their dispute with China, the Soviets were confronted with a difficult choice. After some hesitation the Soviets joined the West in backing India, providing high altitude helicopters and advanced MiG-21 fighter aircraft. New Delhi and Moscow came to see how their border disputes with Beijing paralleled each other; Moscow viewed New Delhi as an important counter to Chinese power; the Indians welcomed Moscow's support, since it also strengthened their hand against Pakistan (US military assistance was provided to India with the proviso that it would not be directed against Pakistan).

The Sino-Indian war shattered Nehru, but did validate his non-aligned strategy in that the United States and the Soviet Union were joined together in a common objective – the defence of India. But Nehru did not live to see another surprising development, which turned his policy inside out, and led to a level of Indian dependency on the Soviets that he would have found intolerable. The development was the departure of the United States from South Asia, as its involvement in Vietnam grew. This departure turned a complicated multilateral diplomacy into a matter of Pakistan plus China vs. India plus the Soviets. To India's dismay, India's by then close ties to the Soviets freed the latter to soften Moscow's position toward Pakistan, first supporting India's position on Kashmir without criticising the Pakistanis, and then actually providing military equipment to Islamabad.

By this time the Indian and Soviet propaganda machines were in full swing, dominated in India by pro-Soviet elements among Indira Gandhi's advisors. Non-alignment was transformed into a justification for virtual alignment with the Soviet Union; India's articulate publicists explained that this maximised support from both superpowers. India thus entered a long twilight of shaping its own diplomacy so as to accommodate important Soviet interests.

Defenders of New Delhi's policy argue that no other power was willing to provide what the Soviets did, and that India gained from the Soviet tie. They miss the point that something fundamental had changed in India's role in the world, and its decline as an independent power can be exactly correlated with its degree of closeness to the Soviets, even though it had more tanks, guns, and airplanes by 1979 than it did in 1950–60. Even more striking was Indian willingness to claim victory for a 'non-alignment' measured in narrow material terms. That this Indian strategy has spread to a hundred other countries is hardly something to boast of.[13]

India's pro-Soviet tilt in the non-aligned movement has proven to be embarrassing, especially when pushed to excess (one recent Indian foreign minister was fired when he carried his anti-American zeal too far). India itself has come under attack from more authentic Soviet clients (such as Cuba and Ethiopia), who went to the extent (in November 1985) of successfully lobbying, in New Delhi, against an India proposal to have the non-aligned 'youth conference' secretariat located in that city, away from direct Soviet control.

On balance, India's diplomatic position in the world has suffered as a result of its willingness to accommodate Soviet sensitivities. The most serious damage occurred around the time of the Soviet invasion of Afghanistan, when Indian public statements on the event shifted from condemnation to cautious approval, before relapsing into silence. India's reputation was hardly enhanced when its diplomats assured the rest of the world that India was not consulted beforehand by the Soviets and that they were thus not in a position to influence Moscow's decision. They also argue that the political liabilities of the Soviet tie are not an adequate measure of the overall value of the relationship to India – and of India's ability to extract benefits from Moscow. This is a correct assertion, and we shall now consider the most important part of the Indo-Soviet link, its military component.

The Military Tie

India is the largest non-bloc recipient of Soviet arms, of which the value for 1979–1983 came to about $3.6 billion. The pace of Soviet shipments to India accelerated after 1980 and Indira Gandhi's return to power, although the Janata party had signed one major deal with

Moscow. India's air force is today 75 per cent Soviet in origin; its tanks, 40 per cent Soviet; and its major ships, 60 per cent Soviet or East bloc in origin.[14] About half of India's aircraft and armor is or will be 'co-produced' in India, and India will sell some spare parts back to the Soviet Union and other users of Soviet equipment.

There are restrictions on Soviet transfers. They do not allow India to export Soviet-designed weapons commercially, nor are the Indians free to produce critical spare parts at will, and certain systems must be returned to the USSR for overhaul. The Soviets have not shared many advanced technologies, and 'co-production' has not led to genuine self-reliance.

Given the expectations of Nehru, Krishna Menon and the Indian military in the 1950s and 1960s, this is a serious failure. Their intention was that India would move to an autonomous design, manufacturing, and export capability at a level roughly matching the value of weapons that would have to be imported. Instead, the best Indian designers work abroad (none in the Soviet Union), very few private Indian firms have been allowed to serve as a conduit for Western defense technology, and the dream of defence autonomy is buried under the fiction that India 'produces' its own aircraft, tanks and ships. Compared with the development of Brazil's defence industry, which lagged behind India's as late as the mid-1960s, India's recent performance has been disappointing.

However, in two other areas New Delhi has not only retained military autonomy, but it shows signs of competing with, and even supplanting, the Soviets. These matters of doctrine and strategy are of potentially greater significance than is dependency on Moscow for military hardware.

Strategic Autonomy

Unlike Afghanistan and other backward developing states, India's military ties to the Soviet Union did not lead to an intimate relationship between the two armed forces, or the subordination of its military doctrine to Soviet strategy. Indian doctrine remains a mix of British, UK, and indigenous sources; the open Indian military literature rarely, if ever, refers to Soviet writings or examples. Undoubtedly, Indian tactics are influenced by the performance and design of Soviet-supplied weapons, and some Indian officers have probably become 'pro-Soviet' because of their contacts with the Soviets, but available evidence points to the continued independence of the Indian armed forces, the autonomy of Indian strategic doctrine, and an Indian willingness to separate Soviet and Western military technologies (a sensitive point for those Americans concerned about technology theft).[15]

At the strategic level India has shown no interest in accommodating Soviet interests, especially in the Indian Ocean and South Asian regions. New Delhi has systematically expanded its naval forces (drawing heavily upon the Soviets for assistance) and now possesses the largest indigenous navy in the Indian Ocean. This navy has been deployed on a number of 'showing the flag' missions designed to enhance Indian, not Soviet, interests, and in at least one case (a deployment to the Seychelles) may have served as a counter to Soviet influence. Indian strategists regard the Indian Ocean region as their natural sphere of influence; while they are particularly concerned with US, British, and French deployments and the Diego Garcia facility, the expanding Soviet navy is also of concern to them. The Indian navy is years away from being able to challenge a superpower force, but long-range Indian plans call for an increasing role in the smaller Indian Ocean island and littoral states, eventually supplanting some outside powers – including the Soviet Union – as the region's dominant naval power.

Finally, there is no evidence of active Indo-Soviet military cooperation, planning, or even sharing of strategic intelligence. While Soviet ships call at Indian ports, their presence is no greater than that of other navies, and they receive no special access. The same is true of Soviet military relations with other South Asian states, although they did once try to establish a foothold in Bangladesh. Generally, Pakistan, Bangladesh, and Sri Lanka share India's reluctance to be seen as offering 'bases' to a superpower, and in any case have military and naval establishments of such competence and Western orientation that intimate cooperation with the Soviets is neither necessary nor attractive.

AFGHANISTAN AND SOUTH ASIA

Besides leading to the virtual destruction of a South Asian state, the Soviet invasion of Afghanistan has had a profound impact on the rest of the region. The impact has not been altogether negative. Pakistan, in particular, has been able to manoeuvre its way skillfully through the debris of Afghanistan, and even turn the situation to its own advantage

– although it also faces unprecedented perils as it directly confronts the Soviets on one border and the Indians on the other (with revolutionary Iran as a third neighbour). The following are some of the important regional consequences[16] of the Soviet invasion and occupation of Afghanistan.

First, Pakistan's strategic importance is newly recognised by the Islamic world, by China, and most importantly, by the two superpowers. Pakistan has taken advantage of this to rebuild its military establishment and to continue work on its nuclear programme –looking ahead to the day when the Afghan crisis will end one way or another. India's past close relationship with the Soviet Union has also made it easier for Pakistan to make the case that it is the only reliable anti-Soviet power in South Asia. There are periodic doubts by Western donors as to whether Pakistan is more interested in obtaining support against India than in resisting the Soviets, but these are allayed by Islamabad's evident support for various Afghan resistance groups. Pakistan supports these groups not because of Chinese, Saudi, or US pressure, but because it cannot allow the Soviet Union to consolidate its position in Afghanistan.

Second, Islamabad has been careful to manage its policies so as to reduce the risks of direct confrontation with Moscow. The Soviet Union is allowed to maintain a large and active mission in Pakistan, it has completed construction on Pakistan's only steel mill, and the two countries have been engaged in a long and tortuous negotiation over Afghanistan conducted under UN auspices. The Soviets, too, do not want to push Pakistan very hard. Even when they presented a threatening *démarche* to Islamabad because of the Pakistani nuclear programme they were careful to stress that their own response would be 'defensive' in nature.[17] Indeed, because the episode took place just before a critical official Pakistani visit to Washington the Pakistanis probably benefited. Rather than drawing criticism because of their nuclear programme, they earned additional support because they were seen to have stood up to the Soviets.

Third, while Pakistan has gained in some ways from the Soviet invasion of its neighbour, it has also paid a heavy price. There is strong Pakistani domestic criticism of the government's policy because of the social, economic, and even military consequences of hosting nearly three million Afghan refugees. Many of the refugees are armed, and one result of the Afghan war has been the wide distribution of weapons inside Pakistan. Student groups regularly brandish Sten guns and Kalashnikovs, and any unexplained murder is readily attributed to the refugee population.

Fourth, a revived Pakistan not only protected India from having to deal with a crumbling Pakistan (and thus itself coming into direct contact with Soviet forces), it has also enabled Islamabad to put forward a number of regional arms control proposals and enter into some limited negotiations with India. Pakistan is certainly not India's equal, but it has been able to deal more confidently with India now that the military and political imbalance between the two states is not as severe as it was in 1973–79.

Fifth, Indian relations with the Soviet Union are again closer to true equality, since the latter became bogged down in an embarrasing war it could not win. All evidence indicates that India has been better able to negotiate with the Soviets on arms, economic, and strategic issues after the invasion of 1979; indeed, it could and did tell the Soviets that they were to blame for India's worsened strategic position, since the invasion of Afghanistan brought new weapons to Pakistan. The Indians now have the options of moving closer to the United States and China, options which did not exist before 1980.

Sixth, the Soviet invasion of Afghanistan once again made the United States a factor in South Asia. Since Washington has no regional territorial ambitions, it is a 'safe' counter for the Indians and Pakistanis against the Soviet Union. An expanded US regional role is also a positive factor for the Pakistanis, whose other strategic partners, the conservative Arabs and the Chinese, also have good US ties; it is even beneficial for the Indians who could use the United States as a channel to China, and who do exploit the new US role to gain leverage over the Soviets.

Finally, the Soviet invasion of Afghanistan stimulated formal regional cooperation among the South Asian states (except Afghanistan). While purportedly limited to economic, cultural, and other non-security issues the new South Asian Association for Regional Cooperation (SAARC) inevitably has strategic implications. It gets the South Asian states into the habit of cooperation; this has already led to joint efforts in such sensitive fields as anti-terrorism and narcotics control. It also moves South Asia closer to a regional cooperative system in which India's natural dominance becomes more apparent and effective through the willing cooperation of its smaller neighbours.

SOURCES AND DIRECTIONS OF CHANGE

The pattern of Soviet involvement in South Asia describes a steady, upward, trajectory. Soviet economic, military, and political engagement in the region has expanded over the years, focusing on India. So far, the Soviets have not acquired influence in the same measure, and India in particular has been able to balance dependence on the Soviet Union for military hardware with an assertion of strategic and military autonomy. There is no serious risk that it or any other South Asian state will undergo the kind of penetration seen in Afghanistan, which resulted first in a communist coup and then in direct Soviet invasion.

In looking for sources of change in the Soviet-South Asia relationship we will not address the implications of a complete Soviet political or military victory in Afghanistan. Neither is likely. A political victory would imply a government in Kabul that was acceptable to the Soviets and the millions of internal and external Afghan refugees. This kind of government is not in sight. A military victory is equally improbable; despite their escalation of the war the Soviets cannot defeat the *mujahidin* as long as the latter receive substantial outside assistance. The most likely outcome is a political solution ultimately *unfavorable* to the Soviet Union some time in 1988 or 1989. The Soviets show signs of settling for a token 'victory' to be followed by a military withdrawal.

Assuming the Soviets will eventually depart from Afghanistan, there are at least four other issues that will shape Soviet involvement in South Asia and the policies of the major South Asian states toward Moscow. These are the Soviet reaction to regional nuclearisation, the evolution of regional strategic cooperation, significant changes in regional domestic politics, and alterations in South Asia's strategic environment.

The Soviets and Regional Nuclearisation

India and Pakistan are within reach of a military nuclear capability. It is not likely they will exercise their nuclear option unless some traumatic event occurs (war between them, the termination of US arms assistance to Pakistan, or a sharp increase in Sino-Indian tensions).[18] In the past the Soviets have been studiously non-committal in criticising India's nuclear programme although they have cooperated with other suppliers in restricting and controlling nuclear assistance to Delhi. The Soviet calculation of interest assumed that a non-nuclear India faced with a hostile, nuclear-armed China would remain dependent upon the Soviets as insurance against a clash with Beijing. Moscow must have concluded, as did the US government in the case of Pakistan, that supplying India with conventional weapons enhances overall Indian security, obviates the need for an Indian nuclear programme, and leads to strategic cooperation in the region and elsewhere.

Public evidence of a Pakistani nuclear programme has completely disrupted this calculation.[19] While India deploys conventional Soviet weapons against Pakistan, it does not want overt Soviet support against Pakistan since this would trigger further United States involvement in South Asia (the US agreement with Pakistan becomes operative against communist threats, not merely a threat from India alone).

Thus, the 1986 Soviet *démarche* against the Pakistani nuclear programme divided Indian opinion. Pro-Moscow elements see an opportunity for further Indo-Soviet cooperation and continue to build up the nuclear threat from Pakistan and the staunch support India has received from the Soviets on this issue. However, the balance of Indian opinion was alarmed by the spectacle of a second superpower attacking a regional nuclear programme. They correctly saw the *démarche* as further evidence of Moscow rethinking its regional South Asia policy and of a revived Soviet interest in regional – not just Pakistani – nuclear proliferation.

Indians are concerned that if Pakistan should reach a point where exercising the nuclear option is easy (a bomb in the 'barsati') then the Soviets would shy away from active support of India for fear of nuclear confrontation with Pakistan. The Indians should also be concerned with the uncertainty of a Soviet response to their overt or covert acquisition of a nuclear weapons capability: this could make the Soviets more eager to maintain good ties with India – hoping to influence Indian targeting decisions so as to provide a nuclear balance to Chinese forces. More likely, the Soviets would view further proliferation on their border with great alarm and see India's move as a major step towards true strategic self-reliance – reminiscent of China's nuclearisation.

Regional nuclear uncertainty thus presents major challenges to Moscow. Neither India nor Pakistan is under firm Soviet (or United States) control; they are antagonists and both, in different ways, are hostile to an expanded Soviet presence in South Asia. If they go nuclear, Moscow would have only a marginal chance of influencing regional nuclear development in ways favouring its interests; more likely, this would trigger nuclearisation elsewhere on the Soviet periphery.

Regional Strategic Cooperation

One other regional development would have a profound impact on Soviet policy – genuine strategic cooperation between India and Pakistan. This is partly dependent upon nuclear events. Should India and Pakistan achieve a stable nuclear relationship (at the pre-weapon stage or some agreed-upon nuclear plateau) they might huddle under a self-erected nuclear 'umbrella' and restore the strategic unity of the Subcontinent. Cynics will argue that this is fanciful – the most likely outcome of a nuclear arms race would be to exacerbate their other conflicts.

There is room for disagreement here.[20] Regional strategists have already conceded the right of possession of nuclear weapons to India and Pakistan, and many have argued that proliferation would not be destabilising. Both countries would be constrained by financial and technical considerations from building a large nuclear force. Neither could become a major nuclear power without substantial external assistance, and that seems to be unlikely. Indeed, the prospect of superpower support for regional nuclear clients (and a regional proxy nuclear arms race) would not be favoured by either Indian or Pakistani elites.

The major incentive for strategic cooperation would seem to be the classic one of external threat. This is tacitly recognised by many Indians and Pakistanis, but was given concrete expression by the late president of Bangladesh, Zia ur-Rahman, who in 1980 first proposed the formation of SAARC. This is not yet a regional strategic forum, but its existence is a sign that strategic cooperation is taken more seriously now than at any time since the Sino-Indian war of 1962. One bit of corroborating evidence is that hawks in India and Pakistan complain of a 'Pakistan lobby' and an 'Indian lobby', respectively.

Strategic cooperation between India and Pakistan is some distance away, but both sides have exercised a measure of restraint over the past six years, and Pakistan has made a number of tension-reduction proposals. While these have been met by some limited Indian responses, it may be that an external Soviet threat cannot overcome purely regional grievances and fears. This suggests that there may be some useful role for sympathetic outside powers.

Genuine regional cooperation might be opposed by the Soviets. Their model remains Tashkent, where they served as the broker between two quarrelling powers and remained influential with both for several years through the supply of weapons to each. The Soviet strategic objective was to reduce further the fading US presence and to balance Chinese influence. When India and Pakistan refused to submerge their differences, the Soviets reverted to the time-honoured strategy of divide-and-rule, pitting India and Pakistan against each other. Indo-Pakistani hostility remains a major diplomatic and propaganda theme of the Soviets; their exposed position in Afghanistan was another good reason they opposed the evolution of regional strategic cooperation, since ridding the region of their presence would be high on the agenda of any such movement.

Domestic Political Developments

Because of a combination of domestic and international trends, the relatively high standing of the Soviet Union in several South Asian states – especially India, but also Pakistan – is likely to deteriorate in the next decade. Both states are in a phase of religious revitalisation, with a resurgence of Islamic ideology dominating Pakistani politics and a resurgence of Sikh, Hindu, and Muslim sentiments threatening the secular structure of India. Marxism-Leninism is a declining intellectual force. This will not be seen immediately in the colleges and universities of South Asia, or in the columns of many popular journalists where there are intellectual and institutional advantages in propagating the Soviet tie. But the intertwined ideologies of pro-Sovietism and anti-Americanism are not so deeply rooted that the next generation of Indian leaders will be unable to independently calculate their own national interest.

That interest will be seen increasingly as tied to the West, to Japan, and to an independent world role. Indian strategists are coming to recognise (as, in some ways, Pakistanis did before them) that their regional security system has evolved into a fluid, complex game in which tight alliances are neither necessary nor advantageous. They are also more aware of India's lack of economic and technological progress. Under Rajiv Gandhi's direction there is an effort to alter the fundamental direction and structure of the Indian economy; this actually began during his mother's last years in office, and it implies a more complicated and flexible international stance. This new departure is motivated partly by the realisation that the hitherto beneficial economic ties with the Soviet Union were not enough to truly modernise the Indian economy and make it internationally (or even regionally) competitive.[21]

One impetus for change has come from the great expansion of Indian (and other South Asian) contacts with the economically advanced world, particularly with the United States. By the end of the century there will be at least one million Americans of South Asian origin resident in the United States; this highly educated and articulate group will become a force for change in their mother countries, even as they thrive abroad.

While India will become a supplier of intermediate technology to the Soviet Union, it is unlikely to ever again receive significant inputs of technology from Moscow. With the exception of weapons, there are few products available in the Soviet Union that public and private Indian firms cannot produce themselves – sometimes of higher quality and at lower cost. As for other regional states, they have become accustomed to a higher standard of consumer and industrial goods than the Soviets can provide, and are willing to import such goods. They are also unlikely candidates for a closer economic (let alone cultural or ideological) relationship with the Soviets.

Changes in the Strategic Environment

The most important event external to South Asia that could affect the Soviet role in the region would be a change in Soviet relations with China. The Indians have been able to ignore Soviet slights on Afghanistan and the jibes of Soviet clients in the non-aligned movement, but they have taken note of changes in Moscow's approach to China, and the implications for their own security.

Soviet rethinking on China was apparent fully a year before Gorbachev's Vladivostok speech of 1 July, 1986. During Rajiv Gandhi's visit to Moscow in May 1985, Brezhnev's Asian Collective Security proposal was modified to explicitly include both of the 'Asian nuclear powers', i.e. China as well as the USSR.[22] The 'Helsinki' model of regional accord was prescribed as an 'all-Asian forum' for Asia, and in rather patronising terms India was described as 'a great power enjoying much prestige and respect both in Asian countries and throughout the world'. A former Indian ambassador to Moscow, Inder Kumar Gujral, concluded that:

[Gorbachev] has notified India that the prospects of friendly relations growing between the Soviet Union and China are bright. Of course he has taken pains to assure us that India occupies an autonomous position in Soviet foreign policy ... All the same, every readjustment between two mighty powers will affect others and we should proceed to examine its fallout on South Asia and on the rest of Asia.[23]

At Vladivostok, Gorbachev again stressed the common ground between the two 'Asian' nuclear powers, Moscow and Beijing, and renewed his call for an Asian Helsinki.[24] His specific references to India were even more disappointing: India was mentioned solely in the context of the non-aligned movement and because of its 'moral authority' and 'traditional wisdom' – not because of a special strategic relationship with the Soviet Union. Similarly, references to Pakistan and Afghanistan were conciliatory, and Indian strategists could not have been pleased at Gorbachev's reference to Moscow's brokering at Tashkent. Finally, through lavish praise of China and Japan, and inclusion of the United States as an Asian power, Gorbachev's remarks implicitly devalued India's importance.

Any softening of Soviet relations with China will have a greater impact on India than on Pakistan. The latter is likely to retain Islamic and United States support even if Beijing were to abandon the Afghanistan issue as one of its three preconditions for normalisation with Moscow. However, India has no comparable alternative source of cheap weapons – and would the United States again be available to support India in a confrontation with China?

If Sino-Soviet normalisation continues, India will be faced with some difficult choices. It could conclude a border deal on China's terms, but this might lead to a domestic backlash and would be opposed by the army, the service most humiliated by the 1962 defeat. It could seek support from the United States (which backed it with arms against China in 1962–64), but this seems very unlikely now. Third, India could itself put pressure on China and attempt to force the Soviets (and the US) to reconsider the normalisation process with China. This is self-evidently risky, but would be feasible if two conditions were met: India'a nuclear programme would have to be close to fruition so that the Chinese could not threaten India with nuclear devastation, and Pakistan would have to be neutralised. The latter could only be accomplished through a generous Indian policy toward Pakistan, since Islamabad now has a restored military capability of its own. Strange things can happen, but Indian generosity seems unlikely. All in all, India will be seriously shaken if the Soviets further normalize their ties with China, leaving New Delhi in an exposed and vulnerable position.

Recent Indian interest in building a military relationship with the United States and Indian nervousness over some minor border disputes with China are South Asian manifestations of strategic changes occurring elsewhere. These are largely beyond India's power to influence, let alone control. In brief, India runs the risk of strategic isolation, and the prospect is all the more worrisome because of its recent extended dependence upon the Soviets. Pakistan, on the other hand, has always pursued a strategy of multiple external partners so it is less vulnerable than India.

Paradoxically, this trend may be good for India. It could again bring New Delhi to a policy of authentic non-alignment in which (like Pakistan) its dependencies were diffused and shared among several outside powers, and (unlike Pakistan but like China) it drew increasingly from its own resources for military security.

CONCLUSIONS

Three primary conclusions flow from our analysis of the Soviet-South Asia relationship. These pertain to the region's revived importance, a strategy for maximising US influence, and the new salience of the nuclear issue.

South Asia's New Importance

South Asia is now a strategically transformed region. It is located at the confluence of four nuclear or near-nuclear powers. It was the site of a major international war involving the Soviet Union, numerous domestic political conflicts, and it has some bearing on US relations with China to the east and important Gulf states to the west. While Indians in particular long for the return of the day when the region was ignored by the outside world (leaving New Delhi as the dominant regional power) this is unlikely to reoccur. Willing or not, the United States is also a player in a newly important South Asia.

The Nature of US Involvement

The United States' regional interest has been, since 1947, to encourage the major South Asian states to work together in ensuring that outside powers do not penetrate the Subcontinent.[25] This means working around the Indo-Pakistani conflict while working with both states to enhance their individual defensive capabilities. This has always been very difficult since support for one is seen as unfriendly (even hostile) by the other. However, the presence of the Soviet Union in South Asia has made it easier to pursue this policy. The alternative, throwing the United States' support behind either India or Pakistan, is unacceptable, and only invites the Soviets to support the neglected party. With the growth of a formal regional organisation, SAARC, US support for regional cooperation is simplified. The United States has a useful role to play in encouraging such efforts and fostering bilateral confidence-building measures and other arms control steps which enhance regional security. There will also be cases where India or Pakistan play a stabilising regional and extra-regional role in smaller states. This is also in the United States' interest: to the degree that these two countries (whose concerns with stability generally parallel the US's) supplant Soviet power and influence, US interests are also served.

The Nuclear Genie

Finally, we need to take a fresh look at the nuclear problem. While the US strategy of deflecting Pakistan's nuclear programme by ensuring its conventional security appears to have worked, it cannot be pursued indefinitely. First, the ambiguity evident in the Pakistani programme may lead the Indians into a nuclear decision of their own; second, it is very expensive, and can be justified only as long as Pakistan is regarded as a critical component of the Afghan struggle. The United States has bought time but not a solution with its regional non-proliferation policy. The 1986 Soviet *démarche* to Pakistan may have been a quirk, but Washington does not want to be in the position of politically (and perhaps physically) defending a covert Pakistani nuclear programme against Soviet attacks.

The best solution to the nuclear question would be a regional one. A time-bound agreement between India and Pakistan not to build nuclear weapons, or to freeze their weapons programmes at an agreed upon plateau could be easily verified. The United States is the most likely broker of such an agreement since it has excellent relations with India and Pakistan and has a strong interest in stabilising the proliferation problem. The Soviet Union is not likely to be an acceptable broker for the Pakistanis, nor could China play such a role in India, but Soviet and Chinese support for a regional nuclear agreement would be necessary at every stage. This is one of those rare issues where great power cooperation is feasible and desirable but cannot alone bring about a solution opposed by two powerful regional states.

Two important developments have occurred since the above was written.

First, the Soviet Union finally recognized the futility of its Afghan venture and has agreed to withdraw its troops. This decision was codified at the UN-sponsored 'proximity' talks, and a formal agreement respectively binding the Soviets, the U.S., Afghanistan, and Pakistan to a phased withdrawal, conditions for support to the *mujahidin*, a neutral status, and a pledge of non-interference was signed on April 14, 1988. The eight-month Soviet withdrawal is to begin May 15, 1988, but it is likely that the Soviets will depart in a rush as the Kabul regime collapses. The Soviets are unlikely to return, nor are they likely to establish a redoubt in hostile northern Afghanistan.

Finally, the Soviets have significantly breached the principles (although not the letter) of the Non-Proliferation Treaty with their lease to India of a nuclear-powered Victor II attack submarine. While this may be part of a larger package involving Soviet power reactors, it also indicates that the Soviets believe that proliferation is coming to South Asia and that they must retain their ties with India, an emerging regional and Indian Ocean power. Since India has itself significantly improved its relations with the U.S., and the Soviets are improving thier ties to Pakistan, we are likely to see a further intensification of South Asia's complex diplomacy.

Notes

This chapter was written while Professor Cohen was a member of the Policy Planning Staff of the US Department of State; the views and opinions in his chapter are Professor Cohen's and do not necessarily reflect the policies of the United States government.

1. An excellent attempt to explain the reason for their tragic enmity is found in Sumit Ganguly, *The Origins of War in South Asia* (Boulder, CO: Westview, 1986).
2. For a provocative interpretation see Nirad C. Chaudhuri, 'My Views of the Real East-West Conflict', *Encounter*, September–October 1985, pp. 7–15.
3. A discussion of the Mercator's distortions and a sample of the alternative Peters projection is found in *South Atlas* (London: South Publications, 1985).

4. See Zbigniew Brzezinski, *Game Plan: How to Conduct the US Soviet Contest* (Boston, MA: Atlantic Monthly Press, 1986), pp. 61–5.
5. There are many surveys of Soviet policy in South Asia. A recent account is S. Nihal Singh, *The Yogi and the Bear: A Study of Indo-Soviet Relations* (New Delhi: Allied, 1986).
6. See Georgie Anne Geyer, 'Vying for India's Favor', *Washington Times*, 11 February, 1986. For documentation of Soviet disinformation efforts see US Department of State, Bureau of Public Affairs, *Soviet Active Measures: An Update*, July 1982, Special Report No. 101.
7. Inder Malhotra, in *Times of India*, 29 September, 1983.
8. Bharat Wariavwalla, 'Domestic Compulsions', *Seminar* (New Delhi), August 1986.
9. The oft-cited will of Peter the Great, advocating Russian acquisition of a warm water port on the Indian Ocean, is a forgery.
10. It should be noted, however, that the Soviets have never fully supported India's border claims with China. Soviet maps have shown parts of Indian-claimed territory as belonging to China for over thirty years, despite many official Indian protests. These maps 'reveal the limits of Indo-Soviet entente', See A. G. Noorani, 'Soviet Maps of India', *Indian Express*, 17 October, 1986.
11. For a summary of Nehru's views see *India's Foreign Policy: Selected Speeches, September 1946–April 1961* (New Delhi: Publications Division, 1961).
12. See Richard Remnek, *Soviet Policy towards India* (New Delhi: Oxford, 1972).
13. For a critique of India's tilting non-alignment by an eminent Indian journalist see Kuldip Nayar, 'NAM and the Frozen Past', *Tribune* (Chandigarh), 4 September, 1986.
14. Figures calculated from International Institute for Strategic Studies, *The Military Balance, 1985–1986* (London: IISS, 1986). For other data see Joseph G. Whelan, *The Soviet Union in the Third World, 1980–1982: An Imperial Burden or Political Asset? The Soviets in Asia, An Expanding Presence* (Washington, DC: Congressional Research Service, Report No. 84-56 S, 27 March, 1984); and Dilip Mukerjee, 'India and the Soviet Union', *Washington Quarterly*, vol. 9, no. 2 (Spring 1986), pp. 109–30.
15. Fear of leakage to the Soviets of US supplied material led a special Defense Department group to brief Indira Gandhi's senior advisors in 1984 on a global US programme to contain such leaks. See Department of Defense, 'The Technology Security Program' – Report to the 95th Congress from Caspar W. Weinberger, Secretary of Defense, February 1985, p. 66. See also Office of the Under Secretary of Defense for Policy, 'Assessing the Effect of Technology Transfer on US Western Security', February 1985; and 'Soviet Acquisition of Militarily Significant Western Technology: An Update' (September 1985).
16. We will deal only with South Asian consequences, which are major. Paradoxically, the impact of the Soviet invasion has been less in the upper Gulf area because of Iran's preoccupation with internal

revolution and its bitter conflict with Iraq. For a useful discussion of the concept of regional security see Barry Buzan, 'A Framework for Regional Security Analysis', in Buzan and Gowher Rizvi (eds), *South Asian Insecurity and the Great Powers* (New York: St Martin, 1986).

17.   For published accounts see the *Washington Post*, 15 July and 21 July, 1986.
18.   A survey of South Asia nuclear development is in Leonard S. Spector, *The New Nuclear Nations* (New York: Vintage, 1985).
19.   See, for example, *Washington Post*, 4 November, 1986, and the claim that Pakistan has tested a triggering device and has enriched uranium to bomb-grade levels.
20.   The linkage between nuclearisation and regionalism is discussed from several angles in Stephen P. Cohen (ed.), *The Security of South Asia: Asian and American Perspectives* (Urbana and Chicago: University of Illinois Press, 1987).
21.   Indo-Soviet trade has been conducted in non-convertible rupees, and must be balanced. Currently, as in the past, there is a surplus on the Indian side due to falling oil prices (the Soviets are a major supplier of oil to India). This is likely to be taken up in the form of additional Indian arms purchases – reducing Indian exports to the Soviet Union puts Indians out of work. The Indians have been displeased with the quality of many Soviet non-military products. See US Department of State, *Warsaw Pact Economic Aid to Non-Communist LDCs, 1984* (Bureau of Intelligence and Research Publication 9345, revised May 1986).
22.   Gorbachev speech at dinner for Rajiv Gandhi, reported in Foreign Broadcast Information Service (South Asia), 22 May, 1985.
23.   I. Gujral, 'The Indo-Soviet Summit', *Indian Express*, 4 June, 1985.
24.   FBIS (USSR), 29 July, 1986.
25.   For the text of early documents describing this interest see US Department of State, Historical Office, *Foreign Relations of the United States*, vol. 3, 1947, and subsequent volumes, especially *FRUS*, vol. 6, Appendix B, 1949 (Washington, DC: US Government Printing Office, 1972 and 1977).

9 The Soviets in Afghanistan: Risks, Costs, and Opportunities
Marvin G. Weinbaum

INTRODUCTION

Soviet decisions on Afghanistan, both prior to and for nearly a decade following the 1979 invasion and occupation, lend support to the view that Moscow's foreign policies, though essentially reactive and cautious, are also opportunistic and embued with a capacity for the relentless pursuit of basic objectives. While Soviet actions in Afghanistan have been marked by a high degree of consistency and continuity, they also furnish a good demonstration of the Soviet leadership's willingness to assume greater risks when the perceived opportunities to be exploited or threats to be contained increase substantially. Acceptance of costly commitments seems most apparent when Soviet dominion over a fraternal socialist state is challenged, either because the regime is threatened by internal foes or undermined by its own incompetence or ineffectiveness.

Beginning with the 1978 Revolution, relations with Afghanistan have to be viewed apart from those between the Soviet Union and most other Third World states. Where once Moscow's policies toward Afghanistan set precedents in Soviet strategy toward the Third World, events so raised the stakes for Soviet security that Afghanistan was transformed from a friend to a client to more nearly a satellite state. As such, Afghanistan passed beyond the point of having the capacity for independent policies, foreign or domestic. Until 1973 and the fall of the monarchy, Soviet policy makers showed considerable sensitivity to Afghan national and Muslim religious feelings and did little to encourage revolutionary activity. But the leadership in Moscow had thrust upon it in the late 1970s opportunities and potential threats that could not be ignored. International pressures and economic burdens have not been inconsequential in forming Soviet policy, but into the late 1980s they have been acceptable and manageable when weighed against the uncertainties in alternative policies, particularly the fear that withdrawal could question Soviet credibility as guarantor of the security and development of socialist states. During this time the Soviets have persisted in their hope that a pacified Afghanistan could be groomed as a model of development for poor countries and an example of the compatability of Marxism and Islam.

IDEOLOGY AND DOCTRINE

With the struggle in Afghanistan already extending far longer than the Soviets' Great Patriotic War and the only time in the post-war period that the Red Army has been committed militarily outside of the East bloc countries, the Afghan conflict carries for the Soviet Union distinctive historical significance. Afghanistan was transformed from a largely representative case of Soviet-Third World relations to a special example of satellite protection and control policy. Until a decade ago Afghanistan was a bona fide non-aligned state, with close trade and military ties to the Soviet Union but with a culture and political institutions that also oriented it to the Muslim world and the West. Soviet leverage over Afghanistan's foreign policy and influence in economic planning and development reflected the country's strong dependence on its northern neighbour. Yet governments in Kabul prided themselves on *bi tarafi* (literally, without sides), a policy of balancing and benefiting from political and economic relations with both the communist East and the United States and its allies. All that has changed. Since late December 1979, Afghanistan has been in the grip of a Soviet occupation, the setting for a conflict that has seen hundreds of thousands of deaths and at least one-third of the population in exile. Until recently time seemed to be on the side of the Soviet forces and their Kabul government in a process that many believed was well on the way to bringing about a Mongolianisation of Afghanistan.

Whatever grand schemes Soviet policy makers had for Afghanistan prior to 1978, they had never conceived of the country as ripe for a socialist revolution and, indeed, their doubts persisted even after the coup that year brought a Marxist regime to power. Well before any approach was formulated toward developing countries and post-independence states, policy makers and ideologues in Moscow viewed Afghanistan as a backward, feudal country which, in its traditional historical role, would stand as a buffer against the West. The socioeconomic underdevelopment of the country made any notion of trying to install a sister socialist state to the south as unwise as it was unorthodox.

Afghan irredentism as much as any factor provided the opening for a more active role by the Soviet government. The decision by Afghan Prime Minister Mohammad Daoud to seek Soviet assistance in the mid-1950s involved little attraction for the Soviets ideologically. The championing of Pushtunistan, a new ethnic state to be carved out of Pakistan's northwest frontier, left the Kabul government no choice but to turn to the Soviets. A reluctance by previous postwar Afghan regimes to form ties that would expose their military to Soviet influence was overcome by the need for arms. The United States, despite repeated requests by Kabul emissaries in 1954 and 1956, refused to equip an Afghan army out of concern that the arms would be used against pro-Western Pakistan. With the periodic closure of the Pakistani border, increased trade with the Soviet Union also offered substitute trade routes critical to the Afghan economy.

The possibility of a Soviet military thrust and occupation of Afghanistan was a much discussed topic during the height of the Cold War and through the early 1960s. It was usually linked with an invasion of Iran or West Pakistan. Observers generally discounted, however, the probability of direct aggression by the Soviets. They cited the almost certain military counter-action by the US-backed Central Treaty Organisation (CENTO) and possible direct US involvement. Nor were the proud and martial Afghans expected to submit peacefully to foreign rule or a puppet regime. Efforts by the Soviets to penetrate Afghan public life with the aim of winning the country over as a political or military ally appeared a far more probable course for the Soviets. But this too was largely dismissed in a period when the Soviets were trying to court non-aligned Third World opinion. As Dupree wrote in 1960, the Soviets seem to regard 'a neutral Afghanistan, antagonistic to Pakistan, as more valuable to Soviet aims than an occupied or satellite, but rebellious, Afghanistan'.[1] Economic penetration offered the easiest and most logical way for the Soviets to influence Afghan institutions and guarantee against antagonistic policies emerging in Kabul.

With Daoud allowing the crisis over Pushtunistan to escalate during the early 1960s, the country was either to deepen further its economic reliance on the Soviets and limit its room to manoeuvre on foreign policy, or else to modify its course. King Mohammad Zahir chose the latter and in 1963 dismissed Daoud. To replace the Pushtun cause, the king assumed the role of patron for Afghanistan's experiment with democracy. A new constitution inaugurated in 1965 was expected to provide wider access for various ethnic and tribal groups to government institutions, and would also create a better climate for attracting domestic and foreign investment in a more balanced economic development.

Political liberalisation permitted the formal organisation of a local communist party. Known as the People's Democratic Party of Afghanistan (PDPA), the party made considerable headway in recruiting students at Kabul University and in reaching recent graduates employed in the middle ranks of government ministries. Particularly important were cells set up in the military ranks among young officers, most of them trained in the Soviet Union. The PDPA suffered along with other parties that formed in the limbo of a quasi-legal existence, for despite free elections and parliamentary politics, the government withheld the legalisation of competing parties. By 1968 the rhetoric from the party's newspaper was too strong for the government, which closed the paper down. But in no small part, because Soviet military supplies and trade remained important, the regime in Kabul allowed communist party leaders to seek office in the parliamentary elections of 1965 and 1969, and several were elected.

By 1967, however, PDPA communists had already split into two rival factions. The differences in the main reflected ethnic and regional antagonisms among activists. Moreover, one of the two groups, Khalq (peoples), came to represent a more independent nationalist, if at the same time also highly orthodox, brand of communism. Both expressed their undaunted support for the Soviet Union, but the second group, Parcham (flag or banner), gained the reputation of total loyalty to Moscow. This included, when required, a pragmatic line in applying doctrine. While Khalq argued for a working-class party subject to the discipline of a vanguard, Parcham disagreed with this traditional, hard-line approach. They were more closely associated with a strategy calling for a broad national front, at least in the first stage of the revolution. Both factions did agree that the monarchy, even if far less autocratic than before, stood in the way of the liberation of Afghanistan from its backwardness. The regime was seen as dominated by an oppressive landowning and a small capitalist class, both in league with foreign economic interests.[2]

Soviet policy makers naturally felt more comfortable with the Parcham group, which was viewed as having a realistic approach and being more inclined to follow instructions. Yet neither faction received the full recognition in Moscow accorded many other national communist parties or the financial support it sought. From an early date the Soviets maintained contacts with both factions and, when they could, assumed the role of mediator in an effort to unify them. Local communists were seen as useful, even necessary, in developing a consciousness among an emerging working class in the cities (still less than 100 000 by the most liberal definition), but the Soviets believed that a hard sell of communism would be counter-productive. Certainly no mass support appeared at hand for a communist system in this still largely rural society. The Parchamis in particular were viewed suspiciously by Pushtun tribal leaders as urban intellectuals and non-believers. The Soviets held to the view well into the 1970s that neither of the parties – together with about 5000 members – was in a position organisationally to seize and hold power.

As a result, the Soviets took no direct hand in trying to destabilise a series of floundering, increasingly criticised governments formed under the constitutional system after 1965. Soviet policy seemed guided by the view that Afghanistan's bourgeois stage of capitalist development ought to be allowed to run its course. However, as Valenta points out, no policy options were ever foreclosed in Afghanistan.[3] Ideology was frequently used to rationalise choices, never to dictate policy. Through 1973, and perhaps late into the Daoud-led republic, Soviet objectives for the region were not seen by Moscow as threatened by or incompatible with Afghan independence and non-alignment. The country took Western economic assistance but, most importantly, had refused to join the regional containment pacts created by the West and allied regimes during the mid-1950s. The Soviet commitment to local communists was never open-ended; the PDPA offered at best a low-cost investment for the future. Only in the late 1970s were the restraints lifted and a revolutionary course encouraged. Until then, what consistently governed Moscow's actions were calculated decisions – not inevitably correct ones – aimed at incremental rather than strategic advantage but leading, just the same, to outcomes that might have far-reaching consequences.

ACTIVE AND REACTIVE POLICIES

There is much to be explained in the effective mortgaging of the country by a communist-led regime. The Soviets' wholesale destruction of provincial urban centres, depopulation of the countryside, and virtual absorption of governing institutions has ended a policy of decades of considerable sensitivity to Afghan nationalism.[4] To understand this change requires a consideration of the factors that motivated decisions taken in Moscow in the 1970s and that continue to influence the leadership's thinking. This comprehension must also take notice of important continuities in the Soviet approach.

At least until the 1979 invasion, the Soviets were in a position of largely reacting to events in Afghanistan, including many developments from the 1950s on that conformed with desired goals and provided economic and political benefits. It was not until the installation of the Babrak Karmal government on the heels of the invasion that the Soviets came fully into a position of creating initiatives. However, until the decision to withdraw from Afghanistan they continued to follow a cautious and, what was deemed a less costly route in pursuit of the war. Even in the decision to invade, the risks in acting forcefully under the deteriorating circumstances in Afghanistan were perceived as fewer than the dangers of taking no decisive action, although Moscow was in retrospect probably oversold on the possible dividends.

Into the early 1970s, the communists were positioning themselves for an opportunity to assume or, at a minimum, to share power when the constitutionally created government finally fell. The principal obstacle to the Left's plan to take the lead in a new regime that abolished the monarchy was, as already mentioned, its narrow popular base and its lack of legitimacy, especially in the countryside. To overcome these handicaps, several military officers, some with Parcham connections, found common cause with the still respected cousin of the king, former Prime Minister Daoud. By 1973 the plotters were ready to act. Still, the timing was not of their choosing and was prompted by what seemed to be an imminent coup against the liberal government by an elite unit in the military headed by the king's son-in-law General Abd al-Wali. The Soviets, from all evidence, played no part in the bloodless overthrow of the monarchy that returned Daoud to power. They welcomed the new republican regime, and had every reason to expect that relations with Afghanistan would further improve economic and military cooperation. By giving its approval for Parcham's formal participation in a coalition government under Daoud, Moscow saw new opportunities through cooperation for communists to increase their influence in the bureaucracy and to be in a position to move slowly into ascendance in the regime, certainly after Daoud's death. (Interestingly, the more active support for the PDPA preceded a period beginning in 1975 when Moscow, after a long hiatus, again began to give aid to communist parties in the Middle

East.) Not all local communists were so pleased or optimistic. The Khalq group balked at taking part in the new government, arguing that Daoud's instincts were in fact unprogressive and that he could not be expected to undertake tough social programmes or attack the country's economic elites.

Fairly early in the life of the republican government, it became clear that President Daoud had no intention of bringing into being the 'national-democratic' regime that Parcham and the Soviets had banked on. By late 1975 Daoud had forced from positions of influence in Kabul nearly all of his recent communist allies. His domestic policies deviated very little from those of his predecessors. He backtracked on implementation of the substantial reforms, including land reform, promised in the first months of the regime. Many key figures in the previous government and royal court were rehabilitated. Even those non-communists who had welcomed the republic in the hope of more rapid economic development through vigorous leadership were in time disillusioned. The President showed little of the determination and political savvy that he had exercised in office two decades earlier. Political liberals of course found it hard to forgive Daoud for destroying the constitution or to approve of a regime that permitted no independent political activity.

The Parchamis had reason to feel betrayed, and Khalq party members felt vindicated. Yet the Soviets hesitated to break with or even openly criticise the Kabul government. President Daoud resisted more obvious Soviet attempts to propagandise through publications and, in general, increase their penetration of Afghan cultural life. In 1976, he had Soviet advisors within the Afghan military reassigned, presumably to reduce their contact with the lower ranks. Economic ties between Kabul and Moscow remained firm, and, in fact, several new agreements between the two governments were negotiated. Daoud did nothing domestically that could be construed as posing a serious threat to Soviet security.[5] As such, Afghan government policy remained within the range of dissent that the Soviet Union was tolerating among its friends and protégés throughout the Third World.

Policy makers in Moscow had reason, however, to treat Afghanistan differently, to set for it higher standards than for other client states. They looked on apprehensively as Daoud moved after 1974 on several fronts, in ways that promised to reduce Soviet leverage in Afghanistan and to make the Kabul government potentially less dependent. Once free of communist participation in his cabinet, Daoud could settle outstanding issues with Iran and greatly improve relations with his long-time adversary, Pakistan. The Shah promised $2 billion in development credits, and Daoud shelved the revived Pushtunistan issue in exchange for promises by Pakistan Prime Minister Zulfiqar Ali Bhutto to grant increased regional autonomy to the Pushtuns. A common market including the three countries seemed in the offing. It was going too far to perceive in these converging interests, as one observer did, the beginnings of a confederation of Muslim states as a bulwark against not only Hindu-dominated India but also Soviet influence.[6] But Afghan non-alignment, with a weaker Soviet tilt, also seemed confirmed by the rapidly growing contacts between Daoud and the rulers of oil-wealthy Arab states that held out promise of major new sources of financial investment. Only in face of these rapidly unfolding, potentially destabilising changes did the Soviets, without giving much public indication of their irritation, begin to look for alternatives to Daoud. They had reason now to take the indigenous communist movement more seriously, both because of what it had accomplished in 1973 and because of the way it continued to infiltrate the military ranks. But Moscow doubted that local communists would be in a position to play a leading role and possibly assume power without greater unity between the PDPA factions. Soviets advisors thus actively encouraged the reconciliation agreement between Khalq and Parcham that took place in mid-1977.

The Soviet Union does not appear to have orchestrated or taken part in the communist-led coup that followed less than a year later. Typically in its policies in the Third World, Moscow does not order local communists to initiate coups. Soviet leaders are likely to be far more critical in the advice and promises they give once friendly forces come to power.[7] Very likely, the Soviets were kept informed of plans to get rid of Daoud and, plainly, they did nothing to save him. The view that Moscow's role was secondary is strengthened by the fact that Hafizullah Amin, a Khalq leader, and not Parcham head Babrak Karmal, set the coup in motion.[8] In fact, there are many observers who believe that the Soviets were apprehensive and hoped to postpone a coup attempt because of their long-standing doubts that local communists were ready and that government forces could be defeated. There was no particular urgency to act. Moscow probably also wanted more time to strengthen its loyalist Karmal. In any event, whatever the Soviets' feeling, the Khalqis could not be deterred from stepping up public agitation or readying a conspiracy within the military.

But once again the timing of the coup against the government was not of the communists' own choosing. It was only because the PDPA sensed the possibility of its own liquidation that they acted. Indeed, when the communists made their move on 27 April, 1978 against the President's palace they did so in self-defence, after Daoud had forced their hand by ordering the arrest of the entire party leadership. Power now passed to a radical clique nurtured on a Stalinist textbook-like model for guiding and managing a revolution. In contrast to communist victories elsewhere in the Third World, the PDPA lacked entirely a mass peasant base and was dominated by ideologues rather than the military. Not surprisingly, its composition and approach left little room for even the pretence of a socialist democracy, and it was to prove as inappropriate as it was repressive and inflexible.

With the April or Saur Revolution, Afghanistan fell for the Soviets into a category of client that had progressed beyond the status of liberation movement or friendly state to the kind of regime character-ised by South Yemen, Angola, and Ethiopia, that is, ideologically conformist, economically linked, and security assisted. As in those countries, the Soviets did not encourage a revolutionary process as much as they adopted the regime and felt obliged to extend help for its programmes and, when necessary, defend its survival once it had passed a certain stage.[9] Afghanistan was to become less distinguish-able from a satellite in the East European mould during the 1980s when integration of its economic, cultural, and political institutions with those of the Soviet Union had proceeded much further. During the late 1970s, however, Afghanistan's leadership was permitted to retain a national communist posture more typical of Moscow's Third World relations.

Although Moscow announced its intention to provide inspiration and more than a little material assistance to the Marxist regime, it welcomed the denial by the government of Noor Mohammad Taraki on assuming power that a communist revolution had taken place or that Afghan sovereignty was in any way diminished.[10] To be sure, the regime's rhetoric contained all the expected Marxist-Leninist jargon, but the early disclaimers about ideology and comforting words about respect for Islam, nationalism, and non-alignment in the new order fit very well with the portrayal by Moscow of Afghanistan as merely a socialist state of the type found elsewhere in the Arab world. Despite the steady increase in Soviet military advisors and support forces, Afghanistan resembled other left-wing nationalist regimes in the Middle East in not permitting the Soviet military full rights to create and maintain bases. The public statements stressing independence also well suited the Soviet belief that until a popular front could be built, the regime was well advised to proceed slowly. The series of economic agreements that were quickly signed between the two countries were not expected to upset the image, for they merely strengthened long established economic arrangements. Economic ties to the West were not expected to be cut.

Soviet plans for Afghanistan continued to rest on cooperation between local communists. But the predictable falling out between the Khalqis and Parchamis was not long in coming, and when Vice-President Karmal and several others in his party, accused of plotting against the regime, were expelled from office by President Taraki and Foreign Minister Amin, the Soviets managed to gain the Parchamis safe passage out of the country to diplomatic exile in East European embassies. There began a steady purge of Parchamis from the bureaucracy as well, and the Soviets, although displeased, concluded that they had no choice but to accept the victors of the power struggle.[11] Nor could Moscow's advisors do much when the Khalq leadership, having consolidated its position, began to push ahead with ambitious agrarian reforms and social policies. Seemingly carried away with revolutionary fervour, they were bent on forcing an accelerated transformation of the society, directly challenging many traditional national and religious practices. The government seemed oblivious to the heavy costs of the reforms and the potential created for political instability. Cautionary warnings from the Soviets and remaining Parchamis were ignored as Amin, in his determination to create a popular following, entirely alienated the still powerful provincial elites and bureaucracy. The idea was to act quickly, sustaining the offensive before reactionary interests had an opportunity to muster counter-revolutionary forces. Afghanistan further paid its dues by siding with the most hard-line Third World Marxist states in international forums.

The more that the Taraki government gained enemies, the greater its dependence on the Soviet Union grew. The regime sought to secure itself against mounting criticism and, more importantly, rebellious groups in the countryside, by calling on the Soviets for additional military and technical aid. Even though Soviet observers not so privately labelled the government programs as 'infantile left-wingism', Moscow met its financial commitments. There was little choice for the time being but to go along lest the government's difficulties be exploited by Islamic militants. The number of Soviet advisors grew to

5000 in the bureaucracy, in large part to replace purged Parchamis. Civilian technicians also arrived in great numbers to take up the jobs left by the thousands from the middle class fleeing to Pakistan. The presence of 3000–4000 military advisors in the country was needed to compensate for the continuous purges and massive desertions in the Afghan armed forces.

By the end of the Taraki–Amin period, only an estimated 1000 of 8000 officers with commissions in the Afghan army in 1978 still remained.[12] The assignment for the first time of Soviet advisors at the platoon level marked the extension of Soviet influence in the Afghan military. Soviet dominance became particularly evident in the air force where in this heavily purged unit they assumed most of the combat and supportive roles. No small token of the increased reliance on Moscow was a peace and friendship treaty signed between the countries in November 1978 that authorised Soviet intervention, if necessary, to defend the revolution. Thus the Soviets became increasingly responsible for a regime in which their stakes had grown considerably, but one that was basically unstable and which resisted Moscow's attempts to exercise fuller political control.

It was under these circumstances that Moscow prepared to undertake some initiatives. The uprising in Herat (in which more than 25 000 Afghans may have died) in March 1979 and the massacre by the insurgents of a Soviet military mission in September were particularly bitter reminders that the Afghan government forces were rapidly deteriorating. Having also come to the conclusion that the conflict could be won only if the right leadership were in place, the Soviets actively manoeuvred to get rid of Amin. For all his demonstrated ideological conformity, Amin, now also Vice-Premier, never shed his streak of independence and arrogance. Because of these personal qualities and his studies in the United States during the 1960s, he was not fully trusted by the Soviets. More specifically, there was resentment in Moscow that Amin had for some time rejected a more visible Soviet military role and rebuffed Soviet demands to build an air base at Shindand near the Iran border. Amin was considered to have broken promises and repeatedly ignored advice from the Soviet ambassador, among others. The regime never really pursued an announced effort to put together 'progressive forces' in a national front. Amin, in particular, appeared incapable of mollifying his domestic opposition, left or right. Above all, it was concluded in Moscow that Amin was the principal source of his country's troubles – utterly ruthless in his systematic elimination of all who disagreed with him. Even with the headaches of involvement, there was no going back. The April Revolution was a net gain for the Soviets but one that had been squandered, in their estimation, by an overly zealous, militarily inept communist government.[13]

A plan was hatched in Moscow with Taraki's approval to have his personal guard kill Amin. When the plot was leaked in Kabul, Amin was ready, and in a gun battle Taraki was captured and later murdered. The Soviets, although they had tried to take matters into their own hands, had still been obliged to act through agents and to watch helplessly as they again lost control of the direction of events. Though Soviet complicity in the plot was practically admitted, they formally at least adopted the government now headed by Amin alone. But knowing that Moscow considered him expendable and that his days were numbered, Amin quietly sought other political options for himself and his regime, making contacts with both Western and Muslim intermediaries. Finding no viable alternatives, Amin agreed to Soviet demands made late in the year to station larger numbers of combat troops in the country.

Moscow had finally decided that if it were to pay the increasingly high costs of saving the revolution, it had better install a more compliant leadership in Kabul and assume directly the job of pacifying the country. The Soviets would have to drop any pretence of non-interference in a Third World country, a concept that it had so long cultivated. In choosing to overthrow a national leader, using its own military, the Soviets had embarked on a course exercised sparingly and previously only against wayward satellites in Eastern Europe. The Soviet demands in Afghanistan for a brand of loyalty and influence over policy that went far beyond mere ideological conformity did not represent so much a turn in Soviet Third World strategy as it underlined how Afghanistan had become a special case.

THE PRICE AND PROMISE OF INVASION

In the aftermath of the Soviet invasion that began on 26 December, 1979, analysts debated at length whether the action was offensive or defensive in nature. To a great extent the discussions reflected the way the observer tended to view broader Soviet international policy. Hard-liners and the more cynical perceived a carefully engineered set of policies set to a well-calculated timetable, all part of a 'grand design' of Soviet expansionism in the march to the warm waters to the south

The bold thrust was taken not only in fulfillment of an old dream but as an extension of Soviet power in a wider global strategy that took form in the 1970s and that had led to a list of new client states in the Third World. Victory in Afghanistan would bring the Soviets closer to controlling the oil resources of the Persian Gulf and in the process undermine Western power and influence throughout the entire region. In this view, *détente* was for most purposes dead, and, anyway, the Soviets had never linked opportunities in the Third World with the conditions needed for reaching strategic global agreements with the United States.

Others detected in the Soviet decision to invade the consequences of years of failures and some ineptitude in dealing with Afghanistan – in short, a desperate act to salvage a policy and a struggling client. The Soviet Union's southern flank was legitimately threatened by Islamic fundamentalism and hostile, anti-communist forces. The risks in acting were decidedly fewer than in trying to remove unfriendly regimes in China, Turkey, and Western Europe. Although events have tended to strengthen the latter interpretation, it is also clear that even a policy aimed at short-term objectives and based on defensive motives cannot be entirely separated from longer-term ambitions and opportunities. By their counter-strategies, the Soviets would affect the regional balance of power. As Bhabani Sen Gupta points out, the military operation in Afghanistan could not help but come at the expense of the United States and its influence in the area.[14]

In the decision to invade there is none the less reason to believe that there was vigorous debate within the Soviet policy-making hierarchy. The various short- and long-term implications of a military operation were examined. The policies that emerged are likely to have been the products of the competing views and interests of the KGB, military establishment, and the Politburo, and within each of these circles there were at times divergent views. Debates were of course less often over strategic objectives than over the best tactical means to realise Soviet goals.

It is possible to reconstruct some of the reasoning involved in the decision to invade. To begin, it apparently was not considered to involve especially high risks for the Soviet Union. There was little likelihood of serious armed Afghan opposition. The Soviets would have the element of surprise and could easily overwhelm with their combat units any Afghan forces that might choose to defend the Amin government. Even that was deemed unlikely, despite Amin's strong links with the military. But just to make certain, Soviet commanders are reported to have disarmed key Afghan units under false pretext just prior to the invasion. An initial strike force of 80 000 troops was felt sufficient to give the Afghan military in subsequent weeks and months the support needed to turn the conflict in progress decisively against the guerrillas. Thus the war was expected to be short. Soviet forces could begin to withdraw in a determined period, and expected Third World and Muslim country criticism would be blunted.

There was little likelihood of outside assistance for the Afghan regime. The United States was not about to seek a confrontation over the reeling in of a Soviet client state and, in any case, the US had no immediate military capability to speak of in the area. Distracted by the hostage-taking in Iran, the United States was not expected to be ready for another crisis or to be able to mount an effective response. Believing that US military action against Iran was itself imminent, Soviet planners expected US protests to be muted. Beyond all this, the pessimistic conclusions reached by Soviet leaders about the immediate future of relations with the United States and China meant that there was little to be jeopardised by a military intervention.[15] Moreover, with Soviet advances through surrogates in Vietnam, Ethiopia, Angola, and Mozambique as recent examples of unchallenged intervention, Moscow could hope to build on the image of the United States as an uncertain, declining superpower in geopolitics.[16]

On the risk-reduction side of the ledger, there was good reason to get on with the invasion at an early date. A complete Soviet takeover was needed if the safety of advisors was to be guaranteed. The mujahidin were not on the verge of winning; indeed, the government had some notable successes in the second half of 1979. But the long-term prognosis was hardly bright, and the war was seen as continuing indefinitely. It was critical that the insurgents not be allowed to capitalise further on the unpopularity of Amin. The danger of setting a precedent for other client socialist states became a major consideration. Ideological affinity in itself would not likely have forced the Soviets to invade despite the declaration by Chairman Brezhnev in 1979 that Afghanistan now qualified as a Marxist-Leninist state. Moscow might have downplayed its socialist obligations, written off the Afghan 'nationalist revolution' as not worthy in view of its failure to gain countrywide support. As Dupree observes, the Khalq government could have been labelled as deviationist as an excuse for withholding full support.[17] Given its inability to institute reforms, the Afghan government provided, after all, a poor showcase for bringing scientific socialism to a Third World country. However, abandonment or benign neglect seems never to have been an option in dealing with neighbouring Afghanistan. There was little likelihood that the Soviets would permit the defeat of this fraternal state by a popular rebellion where it could have repercussions on dissidents in Eastern Europe or, by the victory of 'religious fanatics', leave an impression on Muslims in Soviet central Asian republics.

The installation of Babrak Karmal to replace Amin was viewed as a key to solving the Afghan problem. Still believing that the communists had gone astray and that bridges could be built to non-party intellectuals, tribal heads, and religious leaders, Soviet advisors thought – naively as it turned out – that Karmal's return could mark the opening of a campaign of reconciliation. More moderate social reforms were expected to help to placate the opposition. The presence of Soviet armed forces, by stabilising the country politically and militarily, would buy time for Karmal to consolidate a broadened front. Of course, any government put in office and sustained by the Soviets with their military might would have a formidable struggle to prove its legitimacy in the eyes of Afghan nationalists regardless of orientation. The Soviets badly underestimated the Parchami leader's reputation in Afghan politics for toeing the Moscow line and his unacceptability based on earlier political activities and associations – in spite of what he professed on coming to power about respect for religion and room for non-party views. In banking on Karmal, as it had earlier on Taraki and Amin, the Soviet Union deviated in an important way from other interventions in the Third World: where elsewhere it had aided revolutions based on movements showing indigenous strength, in the case of the Afghan communists, it was faced with an endangered group that could not hope to survive without Soviet personnel and arms.

SUPPORTS AND POST-INVASION GOVERNMENTS

Prior to 1978 generous Soviet material assistance had been given to Afghanistan with virtually no political conditions aside from continuing those non-aligned policies already in effect. Soviet and East bloc aid and trade never precluded sizable aid programmes from the West, most notably those of the United States. In fact, Afghanistan was the first less developed country to receive simultaneously substantial Soviet and US assistance. Over the years, the US and Soviet economic assistance programmes were more nearly complementary than

competitive. Afghan regimes for years managed to attract commitments from both sides by arguing that those programmes gave
assurance that the country would be able to sustain its neutrality
indefinitely. Even under Taraki and Amin, the Kabul government was
not anxious to forfeit its then very modest US support. Whatever the
major powers' motives, with their aid and that of their allies, the
quality of life in Afghanistan, certainly in the major cities, noticeably
improved.

Between 1976 and 1980, Soviet arms deliveries totalled about $450
million.[18] By this time aid and trade with the Soviet Union bore
directly on the defence of the revolution and were contingent on
political performance. A key element in Soviet plans was the
restructuring of the country's security apparatus. However critical the
Soviets' presence in backing up the Afghan military, the Soviets
doubted that the cities could be secured from infiltration without a
more effective intelligence network. In time, under KGB tutelage,
Moscow built the secret police, known as KHAD, into a network of
many thousands of agents. It put Najibullah, who would later succeed
Karmal as party General Secretary, in charge of what soon became
one of the better organised (and dreaded) institutions in the country.

Between 110 000 and 120 000 Soviet troops have been stationed in
the country through the end of 1987. An additional 10 000 to 15 000 are
positioned just north of the border and available for operations on
short notice. Without doubt the material aid together with the
presence of the Soviet military are the mainstays of regime support.
However, the post-invasion strategy goes beyond the simple resort to
force, and methods of cooptation and control are often subtle. The
Soviets have had difficulty abandoning the idea that tribes and
minorities could be won over with the right policies. They also
perceive of these groups as instrumental in coping with the insurgency.
Efforts are made to buy off guerrilla leaders, sometimes with success.
Also, tribal militias are paid to police the border area with Pakistan
and interdict rebels and their supplies.[19] After Karmal resigned in May
1986, his successor announced his intention to bring more minorities
into the government cabinet. The Soviets, based on their own
experience, are believed to have repeatedly pressed for a divide-and-
rule-nationalities policy. Also to broaden the appeal of the pro-Soviet
government, Najibullah, following Moscow's wishes to coax non-
party people to participate, sought out businessmen and professionals
for the country's governing bodies without, of course, relinquishing
any real power. A unilateral cease-fire with the resistance was

declared for a period in early 1987 as the leading piece in an intensified, continuing campaign of national reconciliation, aimed mostly to impress the international community.

Soviet involvement in the Afghan economy and society rapidly increased after the invasion. Almost entirely gone are the bilateral aid programmes of Western countries. Officials in Kabul reported that in 1985 nearly 95 per cent of the aid received came from socialist countries, with the Soviet Union accounting for better than 70 per cent of the total.[20] By the mid-1980s the Afghan government reported that more than 45 per cent of the state budget revenues came from projects built with Soviet assistance, and Soviet-built projects produced 75 per cent of all industrial goods.[21] More than 70 per cent of Afghanistan's foreign trade is now with the Soviet Union. The Soviets heavily subsidise a large part of the Afghan economy. As a policy aimed primarily at winning over the urban population, Moscow keeps the price of food low, subsidising its exports of such essentials as sugar, cooking oil, wheat, and clothing. The transport of Afghan imports from Europe and Japan transiting the Soviet Union is also heavily subsidised.

An accurate estimate of the number of party members is difficult. The government claimed in May 1986 to have 155 000, but has counted among these men serving in the military.[22] The number of Afghans who are sent to the Soviet Union each year is also not precisely known, but it is substantial. A British source maintains that at least 15 000 civil servants are there for training, and 5000 children are sent to camps each year.[23] Within the country technical schools have been established, staffed by Soviet instructors, and the Soviets have provided experts on agriculture, health, transportation, scientific development, and cultural affairs. Soviet advisors have also become essential to the functioning of most of the country's main ministries. Because of the regular purging of the professional civil service in Kabul, unqualified party people are appointed to most of the senior level and middle level jobs.

In almost every sense, Afghanistan has become a dependent state, far more so than the countries of Eastern Europe and Soviet clients in the Third World. As one high Afghan official was quoted as saying, 'We obtain all vital materials and means for the defense of the revolution, that is food, arms, equipment, oil and other material goods – from the USSR'.[24] Although the Soviets have invested heavily and could never expect full repayment, they have also helped to create a deeply economically indebted country. In this and the unequal terms of trade between the countries, in particular the purchase by Moscow of natural gas from Afghan fields at far less than the world price, there is much that resembles what capitalist countries have been accused of pursuing with developing countries in exploitative relationships.

INTERNATIONAL PARAMETERS AND CONSTRAINTS

A full assessment of costs and benefits to the Soviets in the invasion and continuing conflict requires consideration of the responses of the international community. As already observed, the possible repercussions of armed intervention on regional and Western relations as well as the potential effects on Soviet satellites, client states, and Soviet Muslim minorities were no doubt weighed in Moscow's decision to act. In retrospect, the Soviets were both right and wrong in judging the reactions of Western non-aligned states. Moscow correctly guessed that these countries would be unable or unwilling to intercede. Most governments in the Third World were too preoccupied, disinterested, or intimidated to mount anything more than a diplomatic response, even though with few exceptions none took seriously the Soviet argument that its troops had been invited to install a new government. The Soviets probably miscalculated the US reaction, namely the Carter administration's stronger than expected condemnation and subsequent policy decisions aimed at punishing the Soviet Union.

The international outcry had little immediate impact until recently in deterring the Soviets from sustaining their engagement of troops or broken their determination to protect a friendly government in Kabul. The pressures that have been felt were never unacceptably high, and allied states in the Middle East and elsewhere refused to let the Soviet role in Afghanistan get in the way of their cooperation or threaten supply lines. The outrage of many states, including most of the Muslim world, for most of a decade failed to produce the moral, material, and political/diplomatic support for the Afghan resistance groups that would force the Soviet Union to reconsider its role in the fighting or shouldering of support for discredited communist regimes in Kabul.[25]

External reactions in the international community to the Soviet policies have none the less figured in calculations of cost and benefits. Kremlin leaders are apparently reluctant to accede to demands by the Soviet military for the larger combat forces necessary to seal the Pakistan borders, in part no doubt in their unwillingness to approve an escalation that draws greater international attention to the conflict.

Although the Soviets have pursued a scorched earth policy in emptying the countryside of food producers, they remain sensitive to charges of genocide and immoral actions, especially over the issue of the use of chemical warfare. That the Soviets have been content throughout most of the war to secure the major population centres and communications and supply routes is as much a sensible political strategy as a way of minimising casualties and the likelihood of a major confrontation with Pakistan and its allies.

In trying to get international acceptability for their military role, the Soviets never tired of arguing that their limited contingent in Afghanistan was made necessary by the training and equipping by the United States, Egypt, China, and Pakistan of bandits trying to overthrow the revolutionary government. Nor have they dropped the fiction that Afghanistan remains an independent, sovereign country. Moscow hardly relishes the yearly condemnations in the United Nations General Assembly that conclude with lopsided votes calling for an end to foreign (meaning Soviet) intervention in Afghanistan. The five million Afghan refugees in Pakistan and Iran (more than one-third the pre-1978 population) and the international concern they arouse, more than the fighting itself, have kept the Afghan issue in the public view. For all the support that the Soviet Union receives from its Third World client states, none gives unqualified endorsement of the Soviet military role and most support some sort of withdrawal. Eighteen Muslim states have regularly opposed the Soviet Union on Afghanistan and most conceive of Moscow's actions as designed to stifle Islamic resurgence within as well as outside the Soviet Union. The bitterness felt by critical, conservative Arab states over the war has been of deep concern to the Soviets. But at least until recently, Moscow had assumed that it had already paid most of the political price for its tarnished image; on balance, there was more to lose were its surrogates in the Middle East and elsewhere to doubt, in a policy reversal, Soviet reliability. In view of Moscow's history of less than all-out support to its Middle East clients in their periodic military confrontations with Israel, a firm commitment to Kabul's forces was thought necessary to impress, above all, Syria, Libya and Iraq.

The struggle has surely affected relations with Khomeini's Iran. The Islamic Republic is at times strongly critical of the Soviet Union over its role in Afghanistan. No doubt, Moscow's assistance to Iraq in its war with Iran fuels Tehran's anger. All the same, the Khomeini regime has never allowed feelings about the plight of refugees or the killing of fellow Muslims in Afghanistan to occasion a rupturing of trade relations with the Soviet Union. Indeed, those relations strengthened in response to the presence of US military forces in the Persian Gulf beginning in mid-1987. Similarly, for all of Pakistan's significant role as sanctuary for Afghan refugees and insurgents against the Soviets and the Kabul government, policy makers in Pakistan, along with the Soviets, have laboured to keep diplomatic lines open and civil. In their absence, the extended, indirect talks in Geneva between the Islamabad and Kabul governments to find a negotiated solution to the conflict would be impossible.

The Soviets may have reason to regret that their actions in Afghanistan revived a US military and economic aid plan for Pakistan and that, in general, countries in the region and beyond are more conscious of Soviet aggressive capabilities. Any military adventure hatched in Moscow reaching beyond Afghanistan has been made potentially more costly and consequential for a general peace. The dangers of superpower confrontation account for a tacit understanding between Moscow and Washington. Despite generous material aid targeted for the resistance, the United States has always been accused of falling short of what it would take to force the Soviets to alter the character of the war. Until the Stinger ground-to-air missile was introduced in large numbers in 1987 with devastating effect on low-flying fighter aircraft, sophisticated weapons had been regularly denied the insurgents. In large part, this was to placate Pakistan's leaders who want neither great uncontrolled firepower within their territory nor provocation that might increase Kabul-directed sabotage in Pakistan's cities. A hesitation to raise the stakes is above all explained by a desire to avoid pushing the Soviet military into intensifying a conflict that could spill over Afghan borders and conceivably lead to more direct US involvement.

SOVIET PRIORITIES AND FUTURE SCENARIOS

The Soviets operate with a reasonably conscious cost-benefit set of calculations for Afghanistan, though not necessarily a strict economic ledger. The long-term costs of overcoming the major dislocations in the Afghan economy and the price tag for a conflict against the externally financed resistance are increasingly expensive. At a time of growing foreign exchange deficits, Moscow is no doubt anxious to divert some of the resources expended on the war to other areas. Some estimates of the cost of Soviet occupation and economic development support ran as high as \$3 billion yearly by the mid-1980s.[26] But it would be a mistake to assume that Moscow's policies will be dictated solely by economic considerations. Backing for counter-insurgencies in Ethiopia and Angola, and the underwriting of Cuba's economy testify to the Soviets' willingness to assume protracted and expensive commitments in the Third World. Where important political and especially security objectives are involved, economic concerns ordinarily give way. But now that reform in the Soviet Union is a high *political* priority, the costs of the Afghan invasion gain enhanced valuation as an obstacle to internal economic development.

Moscow is anxious not to pay an unnecessarily high political price relative to the returns. The 40 000 or more casualties suffered by Soviet forces, including more than 15 000 deaths, do represent a domestic cost of the policy. The consciousness of war and criticism in some strata has grown in recent years within the Soviet Union. Morale problems and drugs and disease among the troops are becoming well known. The Soviet press, in its exercise of greater openness, now touches on these problems; it has even implied that Afghan veterans are having severe adjustment problems and, like US Vietnam veterans, becoming forgotten. The costs of the war have also risen beyond what Soviet leaders initially calculated as tolerable. Indeed, if the Soviet leadership under Gorbachev should ever do the unexpected and completely desert their Afghan allies and defy the logic of intervention and occupation — as the military withdrawal implies — it will come from the very pragmatic determination that, on balance, Soviet global policy opportunities and internal gains are greater without Afghanistan.

There are several reasons why the Soviets, especially in passing economic reform, have found it difficult to rapidly loosen their grip on Afghanistan. Above all, to do so would be to abandon the local communist party and those who have collaborated or sympathised with the Soviet Union. Put simply, all exposed pro-Soviet elements would be quickly overwhelmed and very probably slaughtered in the event that Soviet protection were quickly withdrawn. Those Afghans who have thrown in their lot with the communist regime probably number more than a half million, with 30 000 or so being highly vulnerable. After what might be a protracted, almost genocidal, war, any resistance-led regime that supplants the present government is likely to be strongly anti-communist. Since a political consensus among opposition groups is unlikely to emerge, especially in victory, there would almost certainly ensue a period of civil war that if allowed to proceed might result in the ascendance of the most militant, fundamentalist Islamic groups. It would, in any event, be a period of high political instability in which no negotiated arrangements for Afghan neutrality or the safety of Soviet sympathisers could be guaranteed. What had until recently been axiomatic in any scenario was that the ascendance of an authentic government in Kabul, one that tilted away from the Soviet Union, would never be acceptable in Moscow. At no time had the Soviet Union ever tolerated, where it could prevent, an unequivocally hostile regime on its borders. Most of all, the Soviets worked to avoid an anti-communist government whose elements would have so many scores to settle against Moscow and its collaborators.

At least until their overtures to withdraw, there had even been reason to doubt that the Soviet leadership would settle for a non-hostile government, on the order of a return to a *status quo ante*. The opportunities created by the occupation, as long as the Soviet position did not become politically untenable, had been thought to be too appealing, given the investment already made and the price already paid. As is sometimes pointed out, why should the Soviets settle for a Finland if they can have a more advantageous arrangement? In any event, many feared that a Finland-like solution was, for several reasons, probably impossible. First, those individuals once prominent in Afghan political life who might have led a restored, neutral government are gone, the most important of them victims of the deadly power struggles after the Marxist coup of 1978. The few other potential claimants lacked a strong constituency either inside or outside Afghanistan. The deposed king, mininally acceptable to the Soviets, might provide the unifying element. But whatever Moscow's actual plans for the monarch, it is apparent that Zahir Shah and his supporters could no more coexist with most of the resistance leaders than they could with the communists that the Soviets hope to leave behind. It is difficult to imagine that any person or group approved by the Soviets would also be agreeable to resistance groups operating out of Pakistan, assuming that they could agree among themselves on the composition of an interim government.

It is also difficult to predict which element among the opposition factions will gain the ascendancy—if any.

Even if a phased Soviet withdrawal can be negotiated, one that includes some protective measures for those who have cooperated, Moscow still has good reason to be wary. In exchange for the West's ceasing of aid to the resistance, the Soviets are expected to demand a withdrawal drawn out long enough to provide for an orderly, safe transition. Yet the precedent of a Soviet disengagement under duress or through compromise on less than ideal terms could have repercussions in the East bloc countries and conceivably among restive Muslim populations in the Soviet Union's Central Asian republics. Much of the credibility of threats that keeps the satellite countries in line rests on a belief in Soviet determination to intervene in the affairs of socialist states and the ability of the Soviet military to prevail over those who would try to reverse what are viewed as revolutionary achievements. Similarly, Moscow has committed far more of its prestige, not to mention material support, here than elsewhere in the Third World.

On the positive side, the Soviets had hoped that Afghanistan would become an attractive model of development and, despite the contradications in values, permit the reconciling of Islam with Marxism.[27] Plainly, neither objective aimed at the Muslim countries could be realised while the fighting continues. However, in a favourable settlement or with the defeat of the resistance, Soviet planners would have the somewhat unique opportunity of directing, with minimum local impediments, the modernisation of one of the globe's more backward states. Favourable economic arrangements with the Soviet Union and its allies could be paraded and presented as an alternative to the penetration of Western private capital and dictates of international creditors. Better than what the Soviet Union can expect to project using its own Islamic people, Afghanistan might have served as a proving ground that a Marxist regime can successfully coexist with conservative as opposed to militant fundamentalism. Such a demonstration, would have softened the image of the Soviet Union in Iran and Pakistan.

The Afghan intervention has had its military benefits. There is little evidence that the drawing down of stocks or the deployment of Soviet divisions has as yet placed severe strains on the country's defensive posture in either the European or Chinese theatres. Even if the war has gone on longer than was expected, it has usefully pointed up serious shortcoming in Soviet organisation, command, and supply and, in general, has given Moscow a more realistic picture of the limits in fighting a guerrilla war. Besides testing equipment, more than 60 000 officers have gained combat experience.

The logistical advantages in having Soviet forces placed closer to the Indian Ocean and on Iran's eastern flank are frequently cited. Except for the Soviet occupation of the Wakhan Corridor, strategically placed between Pakistan and China, the geographic benefits are probably overrated. The presence of Soviet troops below the Amu Darya has no doubt done more to alert the countries in the area to a Soviet threat than was directly gained by their deployment. All the same, Soviet military intervention in Afghanistan has given credibility to political pressures on Pakistan and Iran, and made it more difficult for the United States or anyone else to introduce a fighting force in the area.

The Soviet ability to make decisive gains against the mujahidin as well as to take advantage of regional geostrategic opportunities has hinged to a large extent on the political stability and strength of Pakistan. Here Islamabad proved more stable than many analysts believed. The generosity and cooperation of its Arab friends and China and, most importantly, the United States through its mutual security agreements, improved the preparedness of Pakistan's armed forces, even though Pakistan has reason to be cynical about the US commitment in light of past experiences, notably involving conflicts with India. The Islamabad government's political will to sustain support for the cause of the resistance could be severely tested were Washington to deny economic aid in retaliation for Pakistan's nuclear weapons programme. Domestic factors are certain to be critical. The state of the economy together with the political skills of General Zia and his civilian government, and the ability of the opposition parties to unite will influence the ongoing debate in Pakistan about the domestic costs of support for the refugees and Afghan guerrillas operating from Pakistan. Opposition politicians play on the rising popular resentments caused by the war and the economic impact of absorbing Afghan refugees. The mounting civil disorder in the country is viewed by many Pakistanis as too heavy a price to pay for their Afghan policy and alignment with the United States.

The Soviet withdrawal, if effected, will relax some of these pressures on the Zia government and confirm its judgment to oppose the Soviet invasion and aid the Afghan resistance and refugees.

The Soviet embrace that began in earnest in 1978 and became all consuming after the 1979 invasion appears to be loosening. Until recently, given Kabul's need for both material and regime support, it seemed probable that Afghan independence would be largely compromised, suggesting parallels with the Soviet Union's control over Mongolia. For the longest time Moscow clung to the view that the mistakes made by Taraki and Amin, and to some extent by the Karmal regime, were responsible for the obstacles to a dialogue with contesting social and political forces which were needed to win over most Afghans to the revolution. Irreconcilables would, it was believed, in time lose the will to resist, especially if their Western benefactors and Pakistan tired of the conflict. Despite the resurgence of Islamic fundamentalism, Soviet ideology has not entirely yielded the view that religion in Afghanistan, as in the Soviet Union, is only a passing phenomenon, doomed once the older, reactionary sources of authority are gone. The training of a new generation of Afghans, many of them in the Soviet Union, was expected to give promise of a population socialized and educated to accept a Marxist regime in Afghanistan.

The Soviets (as did most Western analysts) underestimated the residual strength of nationalism in Afghanistan, even among those Afghans largely sympathetic to the revolution. Marxist ideology cannot easily erase the historic image of a free tribal spirit, the invader resisted, and Islam defended. The will of most Afghans to match the Soviet's determination to stay the course has been a defiance found in few if any other countries that the Soviets have confronted and tried to subjugate. But just as Afghanistan seemed to have passed the point where in its political and economic integration with the Soviet Union it could still qualify as an independent Third World state, the future of Soviet-Afghan relations has become problematic. Whatever the outcome, the Afghan intervention illustrates how a superpower may be willing to transform what was previously a client into a satellite if the perceived stakes are sufficiently high, the risks acceptable, and the costs manageable.

POSTSCRIPT

This chapter was essentially written well before the Soviet's signing on 14 April 1988, of an agreement to begin withdrawing armed forces from Afghanistan. Until then, the prevailing, if cynical view was that the Soviets, having concluded the impossibility of a direct military victory, would use the protracted negotiations between the Kabul and Islamabad governments to undermine politically their adversaries, driving a wedge between the Afghan refugees and their Pakistani hosts, between the mujahidin leadership and the rank-and-file refugee community, and between the resistance groups and their international supporters. But with this campaign promising uncertain results, the Soviets undertook a reassessment.

The earlier policy calculus based on stakes, opportunities, and costs still applied. What apparently changed was the Soviet's assignment of evaluative weights to these factors, about which we can only surmise.

In all probability the continuing defense of the Kabul regime was found too costly in view of other attractive foreign policy opportunities, including agreements with China and the United States, and expanded influence within the Muslim states. *Glasnost* and the domestic reforms sought by General Secretary Gorbachev also made it increasingly difficult to suppress criticism of the conflict and ignore its significance for restructuring the economy. Narrowly interpreted, the withdrawal downgraded an endless war to a national liberation struggle that could be supported from a distance. More broadly, the actions in Afghanistan suggest new limits in Moscow's commitment to states heretofore held within its closest orbit. It would appear to challenge the doctrine that only a high degree of control over neighbouring socialist states is compatible with Soviet security, and perhaps signal a fundamental shift in the Soviets' willingness to co-operate with the West in managing regional conflicts. If so, Afghanistan may again become a useful beacon for following the direction of Soviet policy in the Third World.

Notes

1. Louis Dupree, 'Afghanistan's Big Gamble, Part II', *American Universities Field Staff*, vol. 4, no. 4, 2 May, 1960, p. 20.
2. Fred Halliday, 'Revolution in Afghanistan', *New Left Review*, no. 112, November–December 1978, pp. 22–3.
3. Jiri Valenta, 'From Prague to Kabul', *International Security*, vol. 5, no. 2, Fall 1980, pp. 114–41.
4. Marvin G. Weinbaum, 'Soviet Policy and the Constraints of Nationalism in Iran and Afghanistan', in Yaacov Ro'i (ed.), *The USSR and the Muslim World* (London: George Allen & Unwin, 1984), especially pp. 244–58.
5. Francis Fukuyama, 'New Directions for Soviet Middle East Policy in the 1980s: Implications for the Atlantic Alliance', unpublished paper February 1980, p. 14.
6. Hasan Kakar, 'The Fall of the Afghan Monarchy in 1973', *International Journal of Middle East Studies*, vol. 9, no. 2, 1978, p. 210.
7. Fukuyama, 'New Directions', p. 14 (see note 5).
8. Selig S. Harrison, 'Dateline Afghanistan: Exit through Finland?' *Foreign Policy*, no. 31, Winter 1980–81, pp. 166, 169.
9. Halliday, 'Revolution in Afghanistan', p. 40 (see note 2).
10. Louis Dupree, 'The Democratic Republic of Afghanistan, 1979' *American Universities Field Staff*, no. 32, 1979, p. 2.
11. Vladmir Kuzichkin, a former KGB major, in an interview in London

with Frank Melville, reported in *Time*, 22 November, 1982, p. 33.

12. Geoffrey Warhurst, 'Afghanistan – A Dissenting Appraisal', *RUSI*, September 1980, p. 33.
13. Mark Heller, 'The Soviet Invasion of Afghanistan', *Washington Quarterly*, vol. 3, no. 2, Summer 1980, p. 43.
14. Bhabani Sen Gupta, *Afghanistan: Politics, Economics and Society* (Boulder, CO: Lynn Reinner Publishers, 1986), p. 91.
15. Valenta, 'From Prague to Kabul', p. 9 (see note 3).
16. Sen Gupta, *Afghanistan*, p. 24 (see note 14).
17. Louis Dupree, 'Afghanistan: 1980', *American Universities Field Staff*, no. 37, 1980, p. 2.
18. US Arms Control and Disarmament Agency, 'World Military Expenditures and Arms Transfers, 1971–1980', publication 115, March 1983, Table III.
19. Tribal heads are reported to get $50 per month for each fighter under their command in addition to gifts of Kalashnikov rifles. David K. Shipler, 'The Sovietization of Afghanistan', *New York Times*, 4 May, 1986, p. 4.
20. *New Kabul Times*, 23 March, 1985.
21. *Afghanistan Forum*, vol. 14, no. 4, 1986, p. 4. Reprinted from news release by Bakhtar Information Agency, Kabul, 19 April, 1986.
22. Ibid., p. 18. Reprinted from *Middle East Times*, 18–24 May, 1986.
23. *Afghanistan Forum*, vol. 13, no. 2 (1985), p. 21. Reprinted from an article by Nazari Rahmattullah, 'Afghanistan Needs Help against Soviet Holocaust', *St Louis Globe Democrat*, 21–22 July, 1984.
24. Henry S. Bradsher, *Afghanistan and the Soviet Union* (Durham: Duke University Press, 1983), p. 238.
25. Marvin G. Weinbaum, 'International Community and Afghanistan', in Ralph Magnus (ed.), *Afghan Alternatives*, (New Brunswick, NJ and Oxford, GB: Transaction Books, 1985), pp. 107–12.
26. Edward R. Giradet, *Afghanistan: the Soviet War* :London: Croom Helm, 1985), p. 135.
27. Sen Gupta, *Afghanistan*, p. 174 (see note 14).

Middle East and North Africa

10 The Soviet Union, the Persian Gulf, and the Iran–Iraq War
Jerrold D. Green

INTRODUCTION

Soviet policy toward the Persian Gulf can best be understood within the broader context of its general Middle East policy. For the Gulf area in particular, it is argued that the Soviets have been more earnest than successful in extending their influence. Only three Gulf states have diplomatic relations with Moscow (Kuwait, the UAE, and Oman). The Soviets are primarily viewed as an unreliable and even dangerous alternative to the United States. In most cases the Soviets have had to push themselves into the region as there is virtually no pull from within. What we find overall is a series of temporary, pragmatic, and functional relationships. For the most part the Soviets are viewed with distrust as a consequence of significant ideological differences as well as due to Moscow's inability or unwillingness to more effectively champion the Arab cause. This skepticism need not be a permanent impediment to increased Soviet involvement and influence in the region although it is likely to obtain in the near term. Ultimately, however, the Soviets will continue to confront a group of states that is profoundly suspicious about their aims and motives.

BACKGROUND AND OVERVIEW

The influence of the Soviet Union in the Persian/Arabian Gulf area[1] is almost in inverse proportion to the region's perceived significance to the Soviet leadership. A cursory familiarity with the area's geography indicates that the Persian Gulf is far closer to the borders of the Soviet Union than it is to the United States, Western Europe, or Japan. Yet the area is of crucial significance to the latter three because of its huge petroleum reserves. Although the United States imports only 3 per cent of its oil from the Gulf, Western Europe relies for 28 per cent and Japan for more than 50 per cent of its oil imports on the region.[2] Thus,

255

even if the Gulf region were not significant to the Soviets for geographic reasons, the West's need for Gulf oil makes it of major strategic interest to Moscow. In short, the Persian Gulf is an area of vital concern to the West; thus, it is of major importance to Moscow as well.

Soviet policy toward the Gulf can only be understood within the broader context of Soviet Middle East policy. In recent years the record of Soviet accomplishment in the region has been distinguished primarily by failure. To begin with, Moscow can only claim significant degrees of influence with Syria, Libya, and the People's Democratic Republic of Yemen (PDRY). It also has influence with Iraq although, as is shown below, this has declined in recent years and is characterised more by its sporadic nature than by consistency and growth. Soviet influence in the region can profitably be evaluated in comparison with US influence. First, two of the three states with whom the Soviets have significant influence are at the fringes of the Middle East – Libya to the west and the PDRY to the south. In a broad regional context neither is terribly influential or even important. Libya, under the leadership of the mercurial Colonel Qaddafi, is an ally of dubious benefit. Qaddafi is universally distrusted throughout the Middle East due to his megalomaniacal and unfounded self-perception as a potential successor to Egypt's Gamal Abdel Nasser. His attempts to subvert fellow Arab leaders, his support of Persian against Arab in the Iran–Iraq War, his brutal treatment of his opponents both at home and abroad, his aggression toward Chad, and his sponsorship of international terrorism mark Qaddafi as a leader with significant opposition and no meaningful support in virtually every Middle Eastern capital. Given his unreliability and widespread unpopularity, from a Soviet perspective Qaddafi could almost be considered to be the United States' secret weapon in the region.

Soviet support for the PDRY is also of questionable benefit to Moscow. The PDRY is hardly a major regional actor. The recent civil war involving two Marxist factions served to heighten the distrust and skepticism of most Middle Easterners about Marxism, which is viewed as an alien and hostile import rather than an ideology appropriate or desirable for the region. Many have asked whether civil war is the inevitable outcome of Soviet support. Certainly there are those in the Middle East who equate Moscow with instability and subversion. Recent events in the PDRY served to undermine further Moscow's undesirable regional status.

Soviet support for Syria is more beneficial to Moscow and more substantive. Indeed, it is clear that Syria is the Soviet Union's main asset in the Middle East. Given the multitude of problems in the region – the immobilisation of Egypt due to its adherence to Camp David and its economic decline, the paralysis of Iran and Iraq, which continue to be dominated by their endless war, the continuing disintegration of Lebanon, and falling oil prices which have severely affected oil producers throughout the Middle East – Syria's Hafiz al-Assad has emerged as the region's most effective and potentially most influential leader. Syria has virtual veto power in a number of sectors. For example, little if anything can be accomplished in Lebanon without active Syrian involvement. Furthermore, due to its *rapprochement* with Jordan and its devastating attacks on the Palestine Liberation Organisation, Syria has emerged as a dominant force in much of the political life of the region. On one level this is clearly beneficial to the Soviets as it is always useful to back winners. Still, unqualified support for Syria has not led to a dramatic or even a palpable increase in Soviet regional involvement or influence. Indeed, it can plausibly be argued that Moscow needs Damascus at least as much as Damascus needs Moscow.

It is generally assumed that in patron–client relationships the client is dominated by the patron. We must recognise, however, that the obverse may be equally valid. The Soviet Union, as a superpower, keenly feels its responsibility to challenge the United States as well as to provide a viable alternative to US support for those states unwilling or unable to turn to the United States. Obviously this does not obtain in every country of the world for not all states are strategically equal. Still, in regions of crucial significance to one superpower there is likely to be a serious concern or interest by the other. This may lead to one or the other power simply opting out of a situation of rivalry (e.g. the US in Afghanistan, the USSR in Grenada). It also may promote a significant degree of competition between the two and can take the form of direct confrontation (e.g. the Cuban Missile Crisis) or, as is more often the case, indirect contestation through surrogates or allies (e.g. Nicaragua, Angola). This competition has been particularly common in the Middle East but has historically evolved in a fashion that has often embarrassed and plagued the Soviets. It is in these failures that we are able to appreciate why the Soviets need the Syrians just as the Syrians need them.

A natural and obvious entry point for the Soviet Union into the Middle East is as a viable alternative to the United States, which supports Israel. Although the Soviets initially supported the creation of

Israel and even funnelled arms to it during its war of independence in 1948, this support eroded and ultimately culminated in the Soviet Union's break in diplomatic relations with the Jewish state in 1967 and in its shift to the Palestinians. The United States, as Israel's primary supporter, has in a sense disqualified itself from playing a more broad-gauged, balanced, and influential regional role, at least in theory. Because of their unremitting opposition to Israel the Arab states could logically be expected to turn to the Soviets who have historically supported the Arab position while opposing the Israeli-American one.

In practice, the Arabs, for the most part, have refused to turn to Moscow and instead have continued to rely on the United States, the source of their collective humiliation resulting from the United States' unbalanced and overwhelmingly pro-Israel stance. This heavy-handed statement of the problem highlights Moscow's dilemma. It is avowedly committed to the Arab cause yet the Arab world repeatedly turns to the United States, its nemesis, for support, while eschewing involvement with the superpower that is ready and eager to provide 'salvation'. The Arab masses are frequently mystified by and opposed to the close relations their political leaders have with the United States – a country which these same leaders regularly vilify because of its overwhelming commitment to Israel and disregard for the Arab world. Indeed, for a variety of ideological and practical political reasons virtually all Arab leaders are afraid to be seen by their followers as being too pro-American.[3] None the less, this reluctance has not pushed such leaders into Soviet arms. Thus, the more the Soviets are unable to involve themselves in regional politics, the more important those remaining states with whom they have close relations become to them. And given the Reagan administration's exaggerated fears of Soviet power in the Middle East, regional actors have learned how to use Moscow as a means to influence Washington. For example, it was this technique that helped Kuwait convince the United States to reflag Kuwaiti oil tankers in the Gulf as a reaction to Kuwait's chartering of Soviet tankers. Yet being used by regional actors does not automatically help Moscow, and may even hurt it.

Close relations can also be problematic. Issues which continue to plague the Soviets in the Middle East, at times unfairly, include the perceived inferiority of the Soviet Union to the United States. For example, popular and elite perceptions of the Soviet Union by Middle Easterners are hardly enhanced by the Arab military record against Israel. Arab elites are unwilling to indict themselves by talking of

Israeli military superiority in the areas of training and troop performance. It is far easier to talk of inferior Soviet equipment. And indeed, it is generally believed that the Soviet Union is technologically inferior to the United States. As Rashid Khalidi notes:

> The USSR is still seen as an invaluable source of military hardware, particularly for states with the requirement for massive quantities of inexpensive weaponry, such as Iraq and Syria, or which the United States will not supply with weapons. Even from these states, however, there are muted complaints about the technical inferiority of Soviet arms in comparison with those provided by the United States to Israel.[4]

The Soviets are viewed as being excessively cautious, whereas the United States is willing to take risks to help its friends. There is no Soviet-Arab functional equivalent to the US-Israeli relationship. Indeed, as a US analyst in conversation with an Iraqi official was told: 'What we [Iraqis] really must admire about the United States, irrespective of her Middle East policies, with which we disagree, is the steadfastness she displays toward her ally Israel. This despite all that Israel has done to embarrass your government and president.'[5] Such sentiments are not uncommon in the Middle East.

Another development which seriously damaged Soviet prestige in the region was the expulsion of Soviet advisors from Egypt by President Sadat in 1972. The Soviet Union has never fully recovered from this humiliating blow. It suffers from a constant scepticism by Arabs about its willingness to aid the Arab cause. For example, the shock of Israel's walk-over victory in 1967 and the Soviet Union's complete helplessness have never been forgotten nor forgiven in the Arab world. More recently, Israel invaded Lebanon and expelled the PLO from it, bombed Iraq while successfully destroying its nuclear reactors, and has repeatedly defeated a changing constellation of Arab armies in a series of wars and clashes dating from 1948 to the present. Arabs are well aware of the fact that the Soviet Union has been unwilling or unable even minimally to oppose, influence, or affect Israeli policies. The portrait of Israel with its population of three million being able to repeatedly and regularly defeat Soviet clients is etched in the minds of many Middle Easterners who question the strength of the Soviet Union, given its reluctance or inability to challenge tiny Israel. Furthermore, recent Soviet-Israeli negotiations aimed at renewing diplomatic ties between the two states compound the problem by creating the impression that Moscow has all but given up its 'struggle' with Israel. Many Arabs believe that the Soviets do not really help their friends. As Khalidi further notes: 'From a Middle Eastern perspective, the Soviet Union appears to be manifestly unequal to the United States in power, capability, reach and willingness to intervene in the region.'[6]

Another explanation for the Soviet Union's rather undesirable position in the region is that it has little to offer most Middle Easterners. Ideologically, Soviet-style communism is unattractive as it is incompatible with Islam. It is alien and unappealing to all except those few populating the fragmented and small communist parties in the Middle East. There is also suspicion about Soviet aims and ambitions. The Soviet incursion into Iranian Azerbaijan in the 1940s is still remembered by some. Soviet advisors tend to be considered arrogant, racist, and remote wherever they have served although only limited numbers of Arabs have actually been exposed to them. Many in the Middle East view the Soviets as being overtly anti-Islamic. It is widely recognised that the Soviets are perpetrating a brutal war of attrition in Afghanistan and that the USSR itself has a large population of Muslims in Central Asia who are forbidden to live a genuinely Islamic life. In short, there is no intrinsic pull toward closer involvement with the Soviet Union except as an alternative to the United States, and here its record is unimpressive at best.

Despite the many flaws in its policies, the United States is in a preferable regional position. It not only has close ties with Israel and NATO member Turkey, which the Soviets view as a threat in a fashion somewhat akin to US views of Cuba, but with almost every other state in the region. US ties with Morocco and Tunisia are quite good (despite the Israeli attack on Tunis in order to bomb the PLO). Relations are 'correct' if not particularly warm with Algeria. US policy makers still remember the constructive role played by Algiers in the negotiations with the Islamic Republic of Iran on behalf of the hostages from the US embassy.

US-Libyan relations are at an all-time low as a result of Libyan sponsorship of terrorism and the United States' retaliatory bombing in 1986. Yet humiliating a Soviet client in the fashion that the United States did, and a client as unpopular as Libya, subtly enhanced the US's image in the region while weakening that of the Soviets. Although most states in the region publicly and vigorously opposed the US bombing of Libya, virtually no Arab state took action against the United States. Given Qaddafi's unpopularity, many Arab leaders quietly applauded the US's actions although this will never be overtly acknowledged by them.[7] As a conflict between the United States and a Soviet client, the client got the worst of it and the Soviets suffered accordingly. Furthermore, the United States was able to bomb Libya and the Soviets did nothing to help its client. This contributed to the United States' image in the region as well as providing ammunition to those who question Moscow's genuine commitment to its friends in the Middle East. Indeed, Libya's stock has fallen even further, given its lacklustre military performance in Chad. The fact that Chad is currently trying to sell millions of dollars of captured Soviet weaponry does little to enhance Moscow's regional image.

Elsewhere in the region the United States has very close relations with Egypt, although Egypt's deteriorating economic situation might temper this somewhat.[8] The character of US-Sudanese relations is somewhat murky at present because of a recent change in government. In the Gulf region the United States has very close relations with all states, and also in the Fertile Crescent with Jordan. Although King Hussein occasionally threatens trips to Moscow if the United States is not sufficiently sympathetic to his needs, he none the less is locked into close ties with the United States, which seems to take him for granted. His diminishing credibility with the Palestinians tends to foster a certain dependence on the United States and his recent *rapprochement* with Syria can in part be explained by mutual Syrian-Jordanian antipathy toward the PLO and Yasser Arafat in particular. The shift should not be interpreted as Jordan moving toward the Soviet Union, which it is not.

What can be gleaned from this survey is that the United States has a stronger position in the Middle East than does the Soviet Union. The Soviets are restricted to the periphery of the region (Libya, PDRY) and are committed to clients who are either unreliable (Libya) or exceedingly independent (Syria). For there is no evidence to indicate that Syria is a puppet of the Soviets. As Moscow's most successful partner in the region, Syria has no reason to allow itself to be simply a creature of Moscow. Indeed, it can be hypothesised that the Soviet-Syrian relationship is not unlike the US-Israeli one, although in a less intense version. Although Israel is heavily dependent upon the United States, it is a highly independent political actor. As is argued above, patrons can need clients as much as clients need patrons.[9] In the Soviet-Syrian case the relationship could be interpreted as being of unusual import for Moscow. That is, Soviet efforts in the Middle East have not borne fruit in a geostrategically crucial area where the United States continually outreaches the Soviet Union in building influence.

If the Soviets were to 'lose' Syria, where would they be? They would be further restricted to the fringes of the region and would thus be unable to challenge either the United States or Israel. This would be a disastrous blow to Soviet prestige and might deter other states elsewhere from forging close ties with Moscow. Thus, Moscow must tread with care in its dealings with Assad.

THE SOVIET UNION, IRAN, AND IRAQ

Soviet policy towards the Gulf, Iran, and Iraq can best be understood as part of the Soviet Union's broader policies toward the Middle East as a whole. In the early part of this decade Soviet-Iraqi relations were roughly comparable to Soviet-Syrian relations today. That is, the Soviets and the Iraqis closely cooperated in a variety of spheres. Each side needed the other but there was no evidence that Iraq was dominated by the Soviets. Soviet-Iranian relations, on the other hand, were of a dramatically different sort. Iran under the Shah was a major pillar of US foreign and security policy in the Middle East. The United States had carved out a significant role in attempting to guarantee security for the Persian Gulf region. Comprised of small and relatively weak entities, Gulf area oil producers felt themselves to be vulnerable to domestic subversion and external attack. The security of these states was almost as important to the United States as it was to the states themselves, as access to Gulf-produced petroleum provided a source of major strategic dependence for the United States and the Western alliance. A *de facto* agreement emerged in which the oil producers would pump the oil and the United States would share, quietly, responsibility for the security of these states. By helping to protect Saudi Arabia, for example, the United States would also be helping Japan and the NATO alliance.

Unfortunately, an adequate means of ensuring Gulf security eluded Washington. The United States was unwilling to commit large numbers of troops to the Gulf region – memories of Vietnam were too recent for many Americans, who were unwilling to send large numbers of US troops to fight 'other people's wars' in exotic corners of the globe. Fortunately, the Shah of Iran had the resources, both financial and otherwise, to involve himself heavily in Gulf security. Anxious to use Iran's extraordinary oil revenues in order to modernise, industrialise, and 'surpass Sweden by the year 2000', the Shah was eager to develop his military as quickly as possible. This was of direct benefit and interest to the United States as it served as a means to ensure Gulf security while not requiring the presence of US troops.

The military mettle of Iran was tested in Oman where the Shah supported Sultan Qabus against rebel groups based in Dhofar. The Iranian military did not function terribly effectively although ultimately the rebels were suppressed. The Soviet Union was not pleased at the prospect of having a US armed and trained ally on its southern border, but there was little it could do about it. From a United States perspective the Shah's inherent conservatism, his close, albeit quiet, ties with Israel, and his unremitting hostility toward radicalism made him an unusually attractive partner. Furthermore, in terms of his regional involvement the Shah was a realist. Throughout the 1970s he made sincere and significant attempts to minimise Iran's historical tensions with Iraq. For the most part he was successful, and the relative calm enjoyed by the two states allowed the Shah to concentrate his efforts elsewhere, for his desire to be a regional power was only the first step toward seeking a global, mini-power role which, despite its lack of realism, was his true goal. Although then, as now, this seems unrealistic, no one, including the United States, was willing to disabuse the Shah of his absurd notions.

The Shah's *rapprochement* with Iraq was viewed as a mixed blessing in Moscow. On the one hand, a tranquil Middle East with the US-oriented Shah playing a dominant role obviously limited Moscow's influence. On the other, Moscow recognised that Iran was a far more important state to it than Iraq. Iran is larger both geographically and in terms of population than Iraq and shares a significant border with the USSR as well as with Afghanistan. In short, it has historically been quite important to the Soviets. Iran, by seeking improved relations with Iraq, a Soviet ally, allowed Moscow to avoid having to make a difficult choice between a country that was close to it and another with which Moscow hoped to improve relations. If the USSR could at the same time weaken Iran's ties with the United States, so much the better. In any case, Iran's lessening of tensions with Iraq eventually evaporated upon the ascent to power of Ayatollah Khomeini.

Despite naive arguments that the Iran–Iraq War is one of ideology in which pan-Arabism and pan-Islam are struggling for dominance, the war can be more usefully understood as one between Saddam Hussein and Ayatollah Khomeini. Both are exploiting their ideological differences as well as the historical enmity between their countries in a war whose personalistic overtones virtually overshadow other considerations.[10] Hussein is not seen by other Arab leaders as the defender of Arab interests while Khomeini is not widely regarded outside of Iran as some sort of commander of the faithful. Indeed, pan-Arab oriented states such as Libya and Syria have supported Iran, while Islamically oriented states such as Saudi Arabia have opposed it.

From the perspective of Moscow the Iran–Iraq War was a disaster of almost major proportions from its very beginnings in September 1980. The Soviet Union had opposed its client state, Iraq, initiating the war. By choosing to attack Iran anyway, and manifesting its independence from Moscow, Iraq subtly humiliated the Soviets, who appeared to lack control. Furthermore, by going to war with Iran, Baghdad put Moscow into the position of having to make a difficult decision: should Iraq be supported, or Iran, or both, or neither?

The reasons for supporting Iraq, as well as the precedents for such support, were not insignificant factors in Moscow. Iraq and the Soviet Union signed their first arms agreement in 1958, shortly after the Iraqi Revolution. Throughout the 1960s Iraq was reliant on Soviet support due to sporadic conflict with the Kurds, tensions with Syria, and the rise in influence of Iran. In 1972 the two countries signed a Treaty of Friendship and Cooperation. Iraq was the second largest importer of Soviet arms in the Middle East in the years 1963–82. Significantly however, Soviet arms supplied only 58 per cent of Iraq's arms imports as opposed to 84 per cent of Syria's, which received the largest share of Soviet arms. These aggregate figures do not tell the entire story. During the period 1973–77 Iraq was dependent upon the Soviets for 70 per cent of its weaponry; this decreased dramatically in 1978–82 to 50 per cent.[12] The decline was the product of an Iraqi reluctance to be too heavily dependent upon Moscow and Moscow's opposition to Iraq's war with Iran. Moscow, during the war's first two years, opted for neutrality as it was reluctant to support Iraq at the expense of Iran. Given that Iran was being supported by two Soviet clients, Libya and Syria, support for Iraq by Moscow might have proved costly for the Soviets elsewhere. A significant lesson can be learned from Iraq's willingness to initiate a war opposed by the Soviets:

> dependence on the USSR for weapons imports does not necessarily translate into political influence ... the exporter often develops interests in maintaining levels of arms exports that are unrelated to the original objective of increased influence. Middle Eastern clients have demonstrated that they are willing to accept the

consequences of breaking or reducing their dependence on the Soviet Union for arms when they have felt that their autonomy was being compromised.[12]

The willingness of a client to ignore the wishes of its patron is no less relevant for analyses of US involvement in the Middle East. Furthermore, it highlights the analytical problem of ascribing responsibility to a patron for the actions of its client. Attempts to place responsibility on the USSR for each action taken by every one of its numerous clients is no less foolish than laying blame on the United States for every action taken by its partners. It is painfully evident, for example, that the attack by Iraq on Iran placed the USSR squarely in the middle of a major strategic, ideological, military, and political dilemma.

According to Robert Freedman, the Soviets had good reasons for supporting either Iran or Iraq.[13] In the latter case the Soviets were not willing simply to abrogate their Treaty of Friendship with Iraq nor were they able to overlook the fact that they were still Iraq's major arms supplier. Furthermore, support for Iraq would allow the Soviets to demonstrate to the Arab world that it was indeed a strong, decisive, and loyal ally – as mentioned above, attributes that many Arabs felt were in exceedingly short supply in Moscow. Given Iraq's strong and unremitting opposition to the Camp David Accords and its consistent and vocal opposition to the United States, Baghdad was a partner of significant value to the Soviets. Yet arms sales were none the less curtailed during the war's first two years.

The arguments in favour of Soviet support for Iran were no less compelling. Iran, after many years under the Shah, had finally moved out of the US orbit. Khomeini detested the United States just as fervently as the Shah used to embrace it. Indeed, as the hostage crisis in the US Embassy in Tehran deepened so did the humiliation of the United States. Also, the fall of the Shah promoted strategic uncertainty in the Persian Gulf as Iran was no longer the United States' policeman in the strategic waterway. Indeed, from the US perspective Iran, under the rule of Khomeini, quickly moved from being part of the solution to a potential part of the problem. Questions of Gulf security in Washington became as much a question of Iranian as of Soviet force projections. The United States' displacement after years of virtually dominating Iran and the Gulf presented Moscow with an attractive but difficult choice – between two avowedly anti-US powers. Despite Iran's anti-Americanism, however, it was not well disposed towards Moscow either. As Khomeini stated on more than one occasion: 'America is worse than Britain; Britain is worse than America. The Soviet Union is worse than both of them. They are all worse and more unclean than each other!'[14]

Thus, desires to exploit directly Iran's anti-Americanism were more easily expressed than realised by Moscow. Yet normalisation of some sort of relationship with Iran was important to Moscow for other reasons, and this normalisation would have been far more difficult to achieve in the face of heavy and public support for Iraq. It should not be forgotten, for example, that the Soviets share a border with Iran, not with Iraq. Iran also shares its eastern border with Afghanistan where the Soviets are still embroiled in a frustrating and difficult war. Although the Afghan mujahidin were never the beneficiaries of large amounts of Iranian aid, the Soviets obviously hoped that Iran would help the Afghan rebels as little as possible. In short, support for Iran was both tempting and unrealistic to Moscow in roughly equal measures.

As the Iran–Iraq War continued to unfold, Moscow found itself in the potentially dangerous position of being stuck in the middle. Iraq made overtures to the United States which ultimately culminated in the reestablishment of diplomatic ties between the two nations. Indeed, the United States seemed to circumvent its own policy of neutrality and in 1983 appeared to tilt toward Iraq.[15] This became evident somewhat later. In testimony to the House Committee on Foreign Affairs Middle East Subcommittee, Assistant Secretary of State for Near Eastern Affairs Richard Murphy was asked about arms sales to both Iran and Iraq. Despite claims of US neutrality he stated: 'We have tried to stanch the flow of arms to Iran, based on the recognition that it is Iraq that has been suing for 3 years to get to the table and Iran that has been rejecting coming to the table.'[16]

Thus, although the United States claimed neutrality, it is clear that it perceived Iraq in a more positive light than it did Iran. Furthermore, the hearings where Murphy was testifying dealt with questions about the sale to Iraq of Bell helicopters which Murphy could not guarantee would be put to exclusively non-military use. The sale went ahead smoothly and as planned. The Irangate scandal hardly changed this as US arms transfers to Iran were meant to generate funds for the Nicaraguan Contras *and* to promote the release of US hostages in Beirut. It is testimony to the Reagan administration's ineptitude that it could provide arms to Iran while still considering itself to side with Iraq!

In a sense the Soviet Union and the United States found themselves in a roughly comparable situation. Both sought strict neutrality but neither could achieve it. Although the attractions of Iran were considerable to both countries, Khomeini was so intractable that it was virtually impossible to influence him. The United States had been so humiliated by the hostage crisis that it clearly held a serious grudge against Khomeini and the Islamic Republic of Iran. Realistically speaking, a relationship with Iran was both impossible and, given the United States' humiliation, undesirable. Although some pragmatists continue to argue for a renewal of overt relations with Iran, given the outcome of covert dealings, such a renewal remains both impractical and unpopular both in Tehran and Washington.

Iraq was an attractive target for the United States for a variety of reasons. This is not to say that scepticism about Iraq disappeared, but rather that the possibility of establishing a closer relationship with Moscow's ally and second largest arms purchaser in the Middle East was politically very appealing. Although the Iraqis did have some supporters in Washington, the US government was very realistic in its appraisal of what closer relations with Iraq could and could not accomplish. Also, Iraq was the combatant of choice among the United States' friends in the Middle East. While Iran was being supported by Syria and Libya, two US adversaries, Iraq was being championed by Saudi Arabia, the Gulf states, and Jordan. Israel had an early preference for Iran over Iraq although this never seriously affected its ties with the United States as the two confronted far more pressing bilateral issues.

Iran's intractability affected not only Washington but also Moscow. Despite those who claim that Islamic fundamentalists seem to be more opposed to the United States than they are to the Soviet Union, there is no evidence that Moscow has had any more success dealing with these groups than has the United States.[17] In the case of the Islamic Republic of Iran this is clearly the case. Given the Soviet Union's obvious antipathy to Islam and to Islamic political orders, as well as its historical involvement with Iraq, it is hardly surprising that Khomeini did not trust the Soviets. Further, as the US relationship with Iraq continued to prosper, the Soviets realised that neutrality would only alienate both sides. For just as Moscow applauded the United States's loss of Iran, the United States would have been pleased by Moscow's abandonment either of or by Baghdad. This, the Soviets refused to let happen: arms sales to Iraq were resumed after a period early in the war when they cut off arms shipments to the Hussein regime.

Implications of the Iran–Iraq War

In addition to producing an odd realignment of forces within the Middle East, the Iran–Iraq War has presented a major challenge to both superpowers. From the perspective of the Soviets, Libyan and Syrian support for Iran somewhat undercut Moscow's attempts to improve relations elsewhere in the region. Although the Soviets after their initial two-year hiatus returned to support for Iraq, in the eyes of many Middle Eastern leaders the Soviets were also supporting Iran, indirectly, through Libya and Syria. This perception was costly to the Soviets not only in Egypt and Jordan, but also with the combined members of the Gulf Cooperation Council (GCC) which includes Saudi Arabia, Kuwait, Bahrain, Qatar, the United Arab Emirates (UAE), and Oman. Founded in 1981, the GCC was geared to collective security measures and in large part was the product of the Iranian Revolution and the Iran–Iraq War. After the fall of the Shah, President Jimmy Carter forwarded what became known as the Carter Doctrine. This doctrine stated in unambiguous terms that any attempts to exploit or to take advantage of the power vacuum in the Gulf resulting from the fall of the Shah would be resisted, with force, by the United States. The military manifestation of the Carter Doctrine became the Rapid Deployment Force, later termed the Central Command (CENTCOM).

CENTCOM was created as a mobile strike-force whose primary goal was to act as a trip-wire in the event of Soviet force projections into the Gulf area, as well as to bolster the confidence of the GCC members who were skeptical about US security guarantees. Although in a period of sustained combat the United States could not hope to defeat the Soviets, the assumption was that if a Soviet invasion was sufficiently costly or if it was made clear to the Soviets that the United States would not tolerate military activity in the Gulf region, then Moscow would be reluctant to deploy troops in the area. That the Carter Doctrine was promulgated by a president reluctant in the extreme to use military force probably highlighted both to the Soviets and to the members of the GCC that the United States took threats to the Gulf seriously and was indeed committed to ensuring that the Soviets would not take advantage of recent problems there. Indeed, the GCC was created, in part, as an adjunct to the Carter Doctrine. It was definitely an outgrowth of security concerns, and although its military capabilities were hardly commensurate with the concerns that led to its founding, the GCC was none the less a positive step toward promoting unity in an area badly in need of collective security arrangements.

In large part the Carter Doctrine and CENTCOM were reasonable, prudent, and desirable refinements of US Middle East policy. Unfortunately, they never really dealt with the primary threats to the political order(s) prevailing in the Gulf. There is little or no evidence that the Soviets are contemplating any type of military venture in the Gulf region. Those who argue that the Soviet invasion of Afghanistan indicates a willingness on the part of Moscow to project force even further, should also realise that the Soviet's inability to pacify Afghanistan has probably chastened the Soviet leadership somewhat. Given its weak military record in Afghanistan, the Soviet military is unlikely to seek another protracted conflict where the likelihood of success would be even less. For example, as Joshua Epstein has written in reference to one such scenario:

> The invasion of Iran would be an exceedingly low confidence and risky affair for the Soviets ... Given the Soviets' manifest conservatism in the face of possible superpower confrontations, and given the serious risk that a move on Iran would prove far more costly than the returns, it can only be assumed that the Soviets would prefer to secure their ends in the Gulf by other means, by coercive measures short of direct intervention.[18]

Epstein's analysis has been borne out by recent history. Indeed, Moscow's record in Afghanistan indicates such a low level of military accomplishment that a Soviet invasion of Iran as part of a drive to the Gulf is even more unthinkable now than it was five or six years ago.

The Soviets continue to harbour regional aspirations while US interests remain roughly the same – political stability and access to oil. In recent years the situation has changed somewhat. The Iran–Iraq War has lasted far longer than most would have predicted. Concerns about its spilling over into the Gulf region as a whole are more real now than ever. Even the current involvement of the US navy in the Gulf does not change the fact that virtually no one would like a decisive victory by either side. Certainly the members of the GCC realise that a victory by either Iran or Iraq would serve to destabilise the region in different but equally disruptive ways. Combined with these factors we should not lose sight of the drastic drop in oil prices and the implications this has had and will continue to have for the Gulf region. Development plans have been curtailed, projects stopped, and a palpable economic decline become evident. Although for the most part the oil producers do have huge financial reserves outside of the country, issues of political repression, corruption, and generalised mismanagement usually become more acute in periods of economic decline and stagnation.

Indeed, from the perspective of the Soviet Union and the United States, the Carnegie Endowment's assessment of threats to the stability of the Gulf region remains relevant: 'Challenges to American interests [increases in regional instability] in the Persian Gulf are more likely to be political ... than military, and the military threats are more likely to come from within the region than from Moscow.'[19] Given the events that have destabilised the Middle East in recent years, the Carnegie analysts argue that Middle East politics are the product of regional and national developments rather than of Soviet policies or actions. Indeed, such crucial events as the following bear this out: the Iranian Revolution, the Iran–Iraq War, the assassination of Anwar Sadat, the *coup d'état* in Sudan, the takeover of the Grand Mosque in Mecca, the revolt by paramilitary police in Cairo, and the uprising of Iranian pilgrims in Mecca. What is being argued here is not that the Soviets are politically unimportant, but rather that their regional involvement may be more subtle than many think. Furthermore, the Middle East does have a political dynamism wholly separate from the machinations of Washington and Moscow: exaggerating superpower capabilities is as serious as ignoring them.

Certainly one way in which the Soviets might improve their status in the Gulf region would be to work through existing political groupings in the relevant societies. This could be through avowedly pro-Soviet communist groups such as Iran's moribund Tudeh Party. Such Soviet involvement is difficult to predict and to identify. Indeed, the conventional wisdom that argues that the Soviets thrive on regional instability may not be wholly true. One problem experienced by the Soviets is their sense that the United States does not take them sufficiently seriously within the region. On the other hand, this does not necessarily indicate permanent conflict between the superpowers. For example, as Alexander George has noted: 'the two superpowers do have important common interests in the Middle East, which on occasion lead them to operate with restraint or to cooperate with one another ... at times both superpowers must back their local allies, but, at the same time, they must avoid being dragged into war with each other'.[20] Such factors govern the actions of both superpowers and are particularly relevant in the Arab–Israeli conflict. They are also relevant to the Iran–Iraq War, which seems, for the moment at least, to have settled into a pattern which is regularised if not wholly accepted, by both Moscow and Washington. A decisive victory by either Iran or Iraq could prove risky to both superpowers. A unilateral victory might well destabilise the region and could lead to greater superpower involvement with the risks to both conceivably outweighing the benefits.

This brings us back to the question raised above: does the Soviet Union genuinely seek to foment or exploit political instability in order to weaken the position of the United States in what is, after all, an area of US influence? Conventional wisdom argues that the Soviets initiate and exploit such crises. Yet as was indicated earlier, most of the major upheavals and political changes in the Middle East in recent years have been the product of indigenous regional and national political forces and not the result of Soviet machinations. This is not to say that Moscow does not benefit from these changes, but in most of the above instances does so primarily because the United States stands to lose even more. For example, the Iranian Revolution hurt US interests but did not otherwise help the Soviets. Yet to view the interests of one superpower only in relation to those of the other is a serious mistake. The Soviet Union has interests in the Middle East that go beyond its rivalry with the United States. Yevgeny M. Primakov provides an 'official' but none the less commonsensical statement of the Soviet position: 'The U.S.S.R. has always proceeded from the premise that revolutionary situations cannot be exported to other countries and that revolution ripens on the local soil as a result of the development of internal contradictions. As historical experience has shown, attempts to force revolution frequently yield directly opposite results.'[21] The question then is not whether the Soviets are generally supportive of chaos in the Middle East, but rather, under what circumstances are they likely to benefit from it? More specifically, are there instances of domestic instability which the Soviets can exploit? This determination necessitates an analysis of regional and national politics in the Middle East which is beyond the scope of this chapter. Yet, to use Primakov's metaphor, what is needed is an investigation of the local soil to see how hospitable it is to Soviet offers of support. To date, Soviet powers of persuasion have been limited to say the least, although under Gorbachev Moscow has developed a potentially effective strategy which mixes pragmatism with flexibility. Whether this will be effective remains unclear.[22]

Currently only Kuwait, Oman, and the UAE maintain diplomatic ties with Moscow. The other members of the GCC have rejected such ties, although there has been some talk of Saudi Arabia exchanging ambassadors with Moscow. What is significant here is that Moscow is quite interested in a critical area which is unusually sceptical about Soviet aims and aspirations as well as methods. Given this scepticism, we could easily hypothesise that there is nothing that would please Moscow more than a series of coups and revolutions in these states.

Given the extremely limited assets that the USSR can claim in the Gulf, would it not be well served by some sort of upheaval that would weaken the United States' virtual stranglehold on the area?

Although it would be tempting to respond affirmatively to such a hypothetical question, it must also be recognised that not all opposition groups in the Middle East identify with Moscow. Islamic oriented actors and groups, such as Khomeini, Takfir wa-Hijra, and al-Dawa, consider the USSR, the United States, and the various regimes of the Middle East to be equally reprehensible. None the less, it can be assumed that the Soviets are assiduously trying to ingratiate themselves both with the regimes in the region and with their opponents. Both ruling elites and oppositionists are aware of this, and there are no guarantees that the appropriate formula will permanently elude Moscow. We can also assume that upheaval which the Soviets can influence or control is difficult for Moscow to stimulate but will remain an immediate aim of Soviet policy makers. But as the Iran–Iraq War has shown, regional instability can hurt Moscow just as it does the United States, a lesson that appears to be gradually absorbed in Soviet thinking about its prospects in the Persian Gulf.

CONCLUSIONS

To date, the USSR has shown itself unable to respond to the needs of governments and opposition groups in the Gulf region. Moscow's influence has been limited by widespread scepticism about Soviet aims and intentions, the perceived caution and conservatism of the Soviet leadership, and the communist ideology which attracts few admirers among the Muslim peoples of the Gulf states. The Soviets have little to offer other than to serve as a counter to the United States. Yet here the cure may be worse than the disease, for although the United States is held in low regard because of its support for Israel, it is also the key actor in providing for Gulf security. Thus, the Gulf states are obliged to overlook US involvement with Israel in order to benefit from US security guarantees to protect both the conservative monarchies that dot the region and the petroleum industries which provide the revenue to support them.

In terms of Iran and Iraq the situation is somewhat different. Here the Soviets are cautious and risk averse. There is no ideological confluence between Iran or Iraq and the USSR. Relations with Iran are not good, and although this has promoted Soviet support for Iraq in a war which Moscow originally opposed, what we find is a marriage of convenience with little ardour on the part of either partner. The Iraqis accept Soviet support but are not wholly reliant on it; the Soviets provide this support in order to keep a foot firmly planted in the region.

These circumstances could change. But if the Soviet position does improve in the Gulf region it will be a product of the types of functional alliances discussed above. The watchwords here are pragmatism and fluidity – two characteristics more descriptive of current Soviet Middle East policy than that of the United States. Although the Soviet record in the region is not impressive, neither is the United States'. The United States has greater assets in the region and thus has more to lose. The Soviets are unlikely either to be pulled into the region or to push themselves in. What we should be wary of is a combination of the two in which material and political support by Moscow will be provided against a backdrop in which Soviet support can be justified by the recipient to a people historically distrustful of the USSR. Although such a development may now appear to be unlikely, it is hardly impossible.

Notes

1. There is always some controversy surrounding the appropriate appellation of the Gulf. Arabs prefer to call it the Arabian Gulf while Iranians prefer Persian Gulf. I use the two interchangeably although tend toward Persian Gulf because this name is used more commonly. This usage is not meant to reflect any political bias. Indeed, on a recent visit to Kuwait it was facetiously suggested to me by a member of the religious community that the name 'Islamic Gulf' be adopted as a way around the problem!

2. Mark N. Katz, *Russia and Arabia: Soviet Foreign Policy toward the Arabian Peninsula* (Baltimore, MA: Johns Hopkins University Press, 1986), p. 8.

3. For analyses of the relationship between ideology and politics in the Middle East focusing on Arabism and Islam, see Jerrold D. Green, 'Are Arab Politics Still Arab?', *World Politics*, vol. 38, no. 4, July 1986, pp. 611–25; and 'Islam, Religiopolitics, and Social Change', *Comparative Studies in Society and History*, vol. 27, 1985, pp. 312–22.

4. Rashid Khalidi, 'Arab Views of the Soviet Role in the Middle East', *Middle East Journal*, vol. 39, no. 4, Autumn 1985, p. 720.

5. Christine Moss Helms, *Iraq: Eastern Flank of the Arab World* (Washington, DC: Brookings Institution, 1984), p. 203.

6. Khalidi, 'Arab Views of the Soviet Role in the Middle East', p. 720 (see note 4).

7.	This sentiment was conveyed to me privately several times in visits to the Middle East both immediately after the US bombing and several months later.

8.	For an excellent and disturbing analysis of Egypt's current economic decline, see Paul Jabber, 'Egypt's Crisis, America's Dilemma', *Foreign Affairs*, vol. 64, no. 5, Summer 1986, pp. 960–80.

9.	This issue is discussed in David F. Ronfeldt, 'Superclients and Superpowers: Cuba: Soviet Union/Iran: United States', Rand Paper Series (Santa Monica, CA: Rand Corporation, 1978). For a discussion of Syria's foreign policy see Christopher Dickey, 'Assad and His Allies', *Foreign Affairs*, vol. 66, no. 1, Fall 1987, pp. 58–76.

10.	Those who oversimplify the relationship between Arabism/Iraq and Islam/Iran (e.g. the Helms' volume cited in note 5) tend to attribute too much significance to ideologies which rarely stimulate policy but *are* used to justify policies once they have been decided upon.

11.	Alexander J. Bennett, 'Arms Transfers as an Instrument of Soviet Policy in the Middle East', *Middle East Journal*, vol. 39, no. 4, 1985, pp. 745–74.

12.	Ibid., pp. 746–7.

13.	Robert O. Freedman, 'Soviet Policy toward the Persian Gulf from the Outbreak of the Iran–Iraq War to the Death of Chernenko', unpublished.

14.	Imam Khomeini, *Islam and Revolution*, trans. Hamid Algar (Berkeley, CA: Mizan Press, 1981), p. 185, quoted in Daniel Pipes, 'Fundamentalist Muslims between America and Russia', *Foreign Affairs*, vol. 64, no. 5, Summer 1986, p. 939.

15.	See Helms, Iraq, p. 205 (see note 5).

16.	House of Representatives, Committee on Foreign Affairs, Subcommittee on Europe and the Middle East, *Developments in the Middle East, September 1985* (Washington, DC: US Government Printing Office, 1985), p. 41.

17.	See Pipes, 'Fundamentalist Muslims between America and Russia', (See note 14) for an unconvincing attempt to explain why fundamentalists are anti-US when they should be anti-Soviet.

18.	Joshua Epstein, 'The Soviet Threat to Iran and the Deterrent Adequacy of US Rapid Deployment Forces', unpublished, 1981, p. 60.

19.	Staff of the Carnegie Panel on US Security and the Future of Arms Control, *Challenges for US National Security: Assessing the Balance: Defense Spending and Conventional Forces* (New York: Carnegie Endowment for International Peace, 1981), p. 189.

20.	Alexander L. George, 'Mechanisms for Moderating Superpower Competition', *AEI Foreign Policy and Defense Review*, vol. 6, no. 1, 1986, p. 8.

21.	Yevgeny M. Primakov, 'The Soviet Union's Interests: Myths and Realities', in Ibid., p. 28.

22.	For a useful look at Soviet attempts to improve its position in the Middle East see Galia Golan, 'Gorbachev's Middle East Strategy', *Foreign Affairs*, vol. 66, no. 1, Fall 1987, pp. 39–57.

11 The Soviet Union and the Arab-Israeli Conflict
Augustus Richard Norton

INTRODUCTION

As it enters its fifth decade, the Arab-Israeli conflict continues to be an important focus for superpower involvement in the Middle East. The Soviet Union – like the United States – has played a key supporting role in the struggle. Since the creation of the state of Israel in 1948. Moscow has been enmeshed in the Arab-Israeli conflict, initially on the side of Israel and subsequently on the side of several of the Arab belligerents. Yet, if there is any lesson from Moscow's involvement in the conflict, it is that the Soviet Union has been no more successful than the United States – indeed, probably less so – in shaping events in the Middle East to its benefit. Soviet and US policy makers might hope for a Middle East populated by pliant, responsive, and reliable allies. In reality both have often had to deal with obdurate and unpredictable regional powers which, as often as not, act contrary to the wishes and interests of the superpowers. To a degree that many observers might find surprising, the experiences of the two adversaries have had a number of common characteristics. Not unlike their counterparts in Washington, Kremlin decision makers have frequently discovered that their friends and allies in the region refuse to behave like dutiful client states and are quite capable of pursuing self-interested policies, even when doing so complicates, undermines, and jeopardises Soviet policy.

THE GOALS

Soviet policy in the Middle East has been motivated by a number of goals, including the quest for prestige and economic gains, as well as the desire to spread Marxism-Leninism, but there can be little doubt that the primary impetus has been a drive to assure Soviet security. The primacy of the security goal is evident in repeated public statements, as well as in 'private' comments by Soviet officials, academics, and diplomats. The proximity of the Middle East to the

Soviet Union and its geopolitical interests in the Mediterranean Sea, in the Turkish straits, and along its southern border testify to the region's significance for the Soviet Union. One well-known Soviet expert, Yevgeny M. Primakov, refers to the region as the USSR's 'soft-under-belly'.[1]

Even before the enunciation of the Truman Doctrine in 1947, the world witnessed a series of Soviet attempts to balance and negate Western power and influence in the Middle East. Thwarted in its postwar efforts to achieve gains in Greece, Turkey, and Iran, the USSR grasped the opportunity to leapfrog over the northern tier of containment and establish a relationship with republican Egypt in 1955. The initiative in Egypt, as many subsequent Soviet moves, may be viewed as an opportunistic countermove intended to frustrate the containment policy of the United States. 'American actions of the late 1940s and early 1950s – such as the attempts to set up regional defense organizations and above all the permanent stationing in or near the Mediterranean of US naval and air power – could not but be interpreted by Moscow as potential threats to Soviet security.'[2] Not surprisingly, one of the persistent Soviet goals has been the acquisition of military bases and facilities in the region, a goal that has been – from time to time – fulfilled in Egypt, South Yemen, Syria, and Libya.

In addition, Moscow's pursuit of security has yielded economic benefits by virtue of its arms exports to the region. In recent years the Soviets have reaped an impressive harvest of hard currency as a result of their arms sales to Arab buyers (about one-third of all arms imported by Middle Eastern states originate in the Soviet Union or in other Warsaw Pact states). One analyst notes tht arms exports to the region accounted for 9 per cent of total Soviet exports, and accounted for an even larger proportion of hard currency earnings.[3] 'By 1981, an estimated 85 percent of [arms] sales were for hard currency and, for the 1970–81 period, they were contributing about 20 per cent to the USSR's total hard currency exports.'[4]

While the Soviet Union is not dependent upon Middle East oil, the demand for and the value of Soviet oil exports are obviously affected by fluctuation in the market stemming from the decisions and shifts in export capacity of Middle East producers. In recent years domestic needs have been growing in the USSR, and petroleum exports for hard currency have increased, necessitating a revision of the export structure, much to the detriment of the East European states that have depended upon the USSR for at least 15 per cent of their imports. As a result, the East European importers have had to purchase additional oil from Middle Eastern producers to compensate for the declining availability of Soviet oil. Thus, the USSR has a serious, if indirect, interest in the export of oil from the Middle East.

A ZERO-SUM GAME?

The Soviets have been known to fish the troubled waters of the Arab-Israeli conflict, and many observers argue that the USSR has no interest in seeing the conflict brought to a close.[5] However, in this chapter it will be argued that a review of the recent history of Soviet involvement in the region advises a degree of scepticism about such claims. There have been some well-known moments of saber rattling, but, on the whole, the USSR seems to be acutely aware of the dangers that are inherent in a region commonly referred to as a hotbed of tension' by Soviet officials, in which the two major powers on earth compete for influence and position.[6] Not only does the continuation of the conflict engender severe risks of superpower confrontation but, in the view of the Soviets, permanent instability thwarts and preoccupies the revolutionary forces that will inevitably transform the Arab countries.[7] In short, as one careful student of Soviet policy in the Third World argues, the record of Soviet behaviour indicates that the risks are severe enough to lead Moscow to see 'wisdom in restraint'.[8]

Soviet actions in the Middle East have often been on the cautious side and almost always reactive to events within the region 'that it neither caused nor had much ability to control'.[9] This is not to say that Moscow is a benevolent force in the region (its major wedge for involvement continues to be the sale of arms), or that its policies are always non-provocative and danger-free. Moscow has taken major, even if calculated, risks; it has not been deterred by the knowledge that substantial Soviet material support for regional partners has raised the likelihood of armed conflict.[10] Most notably in the 1973 war, Egypt and Syria would have been unable to launch and sustain their attack had it not been for sizable shipments of Soviet arms prior to and during the war. Furthermore, even if its actions have tended to be cautiously opportunistic and reactive, there is no denying that since 1982 the USSR has become entangled in a relationship with Syria that might severely limit its flexibility and substantially increase the chance that the USSR will be drawn directly into the next Arab-Israeli war.

Western observers like to characterise the Soviet engagement in the Middle East as a zero-sum competition with the United States.[1] Certainly a persistent aim of US policy in the region has been the exclusion, or at least the minimization of, Soviet influence in the region.[12] These aims have not only proven durable, but have received renewed emphasis in the Reagan administration.[13] Yet there is no mistaking the Soviet desire to return the favour. There is growing evidence and consensus among US academic specialists – views which this chapter bolsters – that Soviet perceptions have changed significantly since the 1950s. Karen Dawisha argues, for example, that the Soviets have come to recognise that the Arab states need no longer choose between the United States and USSR. They have a number of options in Europe and in the region that may prove as beneficial as ties with Moscow.'As Soviet Orientologist [Yevgeny M.] Primakov frankly admitted in a June 1982 interview, the Middle East is not considered in Moscow a "zero-sum game." A loss for the United States is no longer an automatic gain for the Soviet Union.'[14] The recent upsurge in Islamic radicalism emphasises that both Washington and Moscow may be on the losing end of developments in the region. They may have increasing incentives to cooperate rather than compete to maintain their positions in the region.

THE OPERATIONAL CODE

In recent years much attention has been focused on Soviet relations with Syria, Libya, South Yemen, and the PLO, leading some to conclude that the Soviets are the natural allies of 'radical' or 'rejectionist' Arab states in the region. There is a large measure of truth in this claim. Yet, if the record of post-Second World War policy in the Middle East provides any lesson, it is that the Soviet Union's approach to the Middle East is thoroughly pragmatic. It hardly precludes relationships with non-radical or non-rejectionist Arab states. In other words, the Soviets have been keen to take allies where they can find them and to seize opportunities as they appear, with scant regard for radical credentials. As a result, Soviet ideologues have often had to stretch credulity to justify, in Marxist-Leninist jargon, ties that are transparently grounded in expediency.

A review of the Arab-Israeli conflict since the Second World War reveals an operational code underlying Soviet behaviour and policy toward the region. It marks the Soviet Union as cautiously opportunistic in exploiting the conflicts of the region for its advantage, but above all defensive and pragmatic, not ideological or rigid, in adapting to the contradictory forces and rivalries at play in the region. Soviet policy is sensitive to the divisions within the region and, increasingly as a consequence of experience, mindful of its limited capacity to influence regional events and dictate the outcome of power struggles in favourable ways. The following rules appear to animate Soviet policy.

1. *Avoid armed conflict with the United States*, a first and paramount rule.
2. *Prefer states to political movements.* Syria's anti-PLO actions have sometimes angered and frustrated the Soviets, yet they have consistently adjusted their policies to reflect the greater weight they accord to the state. Thus, Soviet rhetoric supporting the PLO has been only weakly translated into effective defense of the PLO, a reality now well recognised by Palestinian leaders.
3. *Do not get out front on an issue.* The consistent pattern of Soviet policy has been to follow the Arab lead. For instance, little was done to align the Soviet Union with the Palestinian cause until the Arab states had come out in clear support of Palestinian national rights.
4. *Stress the strategic significance of Arab unity, and decry disunity.* In the Soviet view, a disunited Arab world profoundly complicates Soviet policy, and permits the United States to follow a divide-and-rule strategy. Despite their ceaseless hackneyed exhortations, the Soviets have been no more able to reconcile competing Arab aims than has the United States.
5. *Commend revolutionary violence, while condemning terrorism.* Sensational acts of terror-violence committed by elements of the PLO have been criticised with some regularity by the Soviets, who argue that abhorrent acts of violence are counter-productive and indicative of a movement that is less than fully serious about its aims. Simultaneously, the Soviets have frequently accused Israel of committing acts of state-sponsored terrorism. The legitimacy of the Palestinian cause notwithstanding, the PLO's involvement in widely condemned acts of violence has certainly undercut Moscow's support.
6. *Seek the international prestige and influence that derives from playing a role in the peace progress and short-circuit any attempt to deny the USSR that role.* In his speech to the 27th Party Congress in 1986, Gorbachev declared that the Soviet Union is in favour 'of

stepping up a collective search for ways to solve conflict situations in the Near and Middle East ... This is what the interests of universal security insistently demand'.[15] The Soviet role in such a 'search' remains to be fully revealed, but it is obvious that the Soviets have no intention of letting it go forward without their participation.

7. *Provide arms to counter accusations of a lack of support.* The Soviets are in a no-win game. As long as Israel remains the predominant military power in the region, the Arab states will always seek more weapons, and the Soviets will never be able to provide enough. If the Soviet Union genuinely seeks to avoid being drawn into a regional conflict, it is faced with a formidable dilemma. It must either deny the Arab states the military capacity to confront Israel from a position of strength, or risk being sucked into a direct conflict with the United States.[16]

8. *Support communist parties in the Arab states only so long as such support does not jeopardise relations with an Arab state. Raisons d'état* dictate the sacrifice of the local communist parties, however much their abandonment may be lamented in the Kremlin.

EVOLUTION OF THE CONFLICT

The Soviet's operational code may become clearer if we briefly review its shifting, largely reactive response to the Arab-Israeli conflict over its forty-year history. Although the Soviets are now closely linked with Syria, Libya, and the PLO, any discussion of Soviet policy in the Middle East would be incomplete if it ignored the early relationship with Israel.

The 1948 War

The Soviet Union favoured the creation of a binational state in Palestine, but it quickly recognised that such a solution was not feasible given the attitudes of the protagonists. Thus, when the UN partition plan came up for a vote in May 1947, the USSR was one of its supporters. Andrei Gromyko, then USSR representative at the UN, announced the Soviet vote: 'It would be unfair to refuse to reckon with ... or deny the right of the Jewish people to the satisfaction of their aspiration [for the formation of a state in Palestine].'[17]

A number of factors seem to have influenced the Soviet decision to support the creation of Israel. No doubt a desire to facilitate the withdrawal of British forces was high on the list. The progressive potential of the Arabs was not assessed to be high. It did not pass unnoticed that one of the major Arab personalities of the day, Hajj Amin al-Husseini, the Mufti of Jerusalem, was known to have been a Nazi supporter. In contrast, the new Jewish state, with its Labor Zionism underpinnings and ideological links to socialism, must have seemed a much more congenial partner. One leading scholar argues that the Soviet Union aspired to implant a state in the region that would serve as a permanent source of conflict, and thus would serve as a means for continuing Soviet involvement, but this may concede more foresight to Moscow than is justified.[18]

Soviet *de jure* recognition of Israel came promptly on 17 May, 1948, and Soviet-arranged arms shipments were crucial for the victory of the new state over its Arabs foes. Support encompassed arms shipments through Czechoslovakia, including heavy weapons, tanks, and planes. In addition, several groups of Jewish fighters were trained by Czechoslovak officers and were en route to Israel by the end of 1948. As Ben-Gurion was to remark several times, the support of the Soviet Union was quite important: 'It was only the Russians and the Czechs who stood by us from the beginning to the end of the 1948 war without wavering – they had enough of their own reasons, of course, but that was not important for us.'[19] In later years the Soviets were inclined to downplay their early support for Israel, but this hardly diminishes the importance of Soviet support in 1948.

The first Israeli ambassador to the Kremlin, Golda Meir, presented her credentials on 10 September, 1948. The following day she paid a visit to the Moscow synagogue, hence symbolising one of the enduring concerns of Israel: the plight of Soviet Jewry. In this light, it is noteworthy that in Meir's first meeting with the Foreign Ministry's Middle East Department, the question of Jewish emigration was raised. By way of response, an infamous article appeared in *Pravda* on 12 September, announcing that a line was to be drawn between the support of Israel and the question of Soviet Jewry.[20]

Trade agreements between the two countries were signed as early as 1949, but further strains soon emerged in the relationship. For instance, to the annoyance of the Soviets, Israel supported UN action in Korea (as did many Arab states), and there were persistent fears – spurred by the Israeli Communist Party – that Israel would join an anti-Soviet alliance.

On 12 February, 1953, the Soviets severed relations with Israel, after Soviet Jews were alleged to have been involved in the notorious and fabricated Doctors' Plot, and following a bomb explosion at the

Soviet embassy in Tel Aviv. However, the death of Stalin intervened, and the new Soviet leadership arranged a face-saving apology by the Israelis in order to justify a reestablishment of relations on 20 July, 1953. In the prearranged Israeli statement, Israel declared that it 'will not be a party to any alliance or pact aiming at aggression against the Soviet Union'.[21]

Reestablished diplomatic relations did not deter the Soviet Union from seeking other friends in the Middle East, and it did so in Egypt. Initially, the 1952 Free Officers Revolution in Egypt was met by indifference in Moscow, which viewed the deposing of King Farouk as a coup by a reactionary and pro-American officer corps. However, as Gamal Abdel Nasser consolidated his position, it became clear that what had happened in Egypt was anything but a mundane *putsch*. The turning point for the Soviet Union was the Bandung conference of non-aligned states of April 1955, which saw Nasser – acting in league with China, India, Indonesia, and Yugoslavia – declare a policy of positive neutralism and Third World independence. Nasser's *bona fides* was buttressed by his vehement criticism of the US-endorsed Baghdad pact that linked his arch-rival Iraq to Egypt's former imperialist master, Britain. Egypt under Nasser promised to be in the forefront of the struggle to decolonise the Third World, and a relationship with Egypt would not only associate the USSR with the decolonisation movement, but would allow the Soviets to partially neutralise the containment policies of the United States. In short, Nasser must have seemed a made-to-order Soviet client. In September 1955, after the United States had declined to meet Egypt's requests for arms, the Soviets agreed to supply arms to Egypt through an agreement with Czechoslovakia. A similar arrangement to supply arms to Syria followed in 1956.

The 1956 War

In July 1956 the United States, miffed by Egypt's recognition of 'Red China' and deeply suspicious of Nasser's positive neutralism, reneged on its earlier offer to assist in the construction of the Aswan high dam, a central policy goal of Nasser and a keystone of his economic development plan. Nasser reacted on July 26, 1956, by nationalising the Suez Canal, which was then still in British hands. Nasser's action set into motion a chain of events which was to culminate in the joint Israeli-British-French Suez invasion the following fall.

The 1956 war marked a low point in Soviet-Israeli relations. For the first time thinly veiled threats against the very existence of Israel were issued from Moscow. In a now well-known note, Soviet Premier Nikolai A. Bulganin warned his Israeli counterpart, David Ben-Gurion, that the actions of Israel 'are putting a question mark on the very existence of Israel as a state'.[22] Although the Soviets would subsequently castigate Israel and its policies, and characterise it as a vestige and servant of imperialism in the region, the 1956 war remains the only instance when the existence of the Israeli state was brought into question by the USSR.

Although pressure from Washington was undeniably decisive in bringing the tripartite Suez adventure to a close, the Soviets improved their image among the Arabs by boisterously, though belatedly, threatening Paris and London, thereby gaining a degree of popular credit in the Arab world for their role in bringing the attack to an end and in reestablishing the popular Nasser's power.

As it moved to construct its relationship with Egypt, the Soviet Union also embraced Syria. In January 1956 the USSR and Syria signed an arms agreement, which was promptly followed by a series of economic and cultural accords. Yet, Syrian politics were in a tumult well into the 1950s. While the Ba'ath (or Arab Socialist Renaissance) Party was in nominal control by the post-Suez period, the Ba'athists found themselves faced with an array of conservative competitors, as well as a problematic partnership with the Syrian Communist Party, which was led then – as now – by the venerable Khalid Bakdash. By late 1957 the Ba'athists feared being overwhelmed by the communists, whose influence within both government and military was considerable, and growing. Inspired by the imperatives of political survival and legitimated by Ba'athist and Nasserist calls for Arab unity, the Syrian government proposed that Syria and Egypt join together to form a United Arab Republic (UAR).

The UAR came into existence in February 1958. One of Nasser's preconditions for uniting Egypt with Syria was the disbandment of all political parties in Syria, so it was not surprising that Cairo quickly assumed the leading role in the UAR. Egyptian security and military forces promptly became very active in Syria and moved with dispatch to establish order. Although the Soviets had earlier endorsed the goal of Arab unity, when reality dawned they changed their tune. Nasser had not been deterred by his relationship with Moscow from harshly persecuting Egyptian communists. By December 1958 the Egyptian-directed security forces launched a series of arrests of Syrian communists, prompting Bakdash to flee to Iraq (where General Abdul

Karim Kassem had seized power in 1958, thereby deposing the pro-Western regime and removing Baghdad from the Baghdad Pact) Khrushchev was incensed by the clampdown on the communists, and by 1959 was engaged in a stinging exchange of charges and counter-charges with Nasser.[23] For his part, Nasser's anger was no doubt fed by the fact that Moscow was moving enthusiastically to cement a relationship with Egypt's regional rival, Iraq.

When Syria withdrew from the UAR in 1961, the Soviet Union acted quickly to recast its ties with Syria. To the chagrin of Bakdash, Kremlin ideologues coined a new cachet, 'revolutionary democracy', for pro-Soviet states like Syria that were judged to be on the non-capitalist path of development. The new formulation was ambivalent on the role of the communist party in revolutionary democracies. It specifically called for the participation of party members in government as individuals, where official party participation was not feasible. Bakdash's dissatisfaction with the new prescription for communist action, and the endorsement of the Ba'athist regime that was implied, was made plain in a number of articles, but Moscow did not stir from its position.[24] Meanwhile, in 1964 Nasser ordered the release of a number of party members who had been jailed on political grounds, thereby diminishing Soviet ire.

While the Soviets have not been silent when Arab communists have been persecuted, they seem to have reconciled themselves to the fact that the importance of their relations with Syria and Egypt (not to mention Iraq, the most persistent in its drive to eradicate indigenous communists) far outweighs the good health and well-being of local party members. Only when the attacks on communists have been particularly egregious, as in Iraq during the early 1960s, have the Soviets been willing to jeopardise their relations with a regime to demonstrate their distaste for anti-communist repression.

The 1967 War

The 1967 war was to be a turning point for Soviet influence in the Middle East. The virtual destruction of the Egyptian and Jordanian air forces, and the humiliating one-sided defeat of the Syrian, Egyptian, and Jordanian armies by Israel, prompted a massive resupply and reequipment effort by the Soviets, who used the disaster to strengthen their ties with Egypt and Syria. (It should also be remembered that Soviet reports, in May 1967, of a pending attack by Israel upon Syria figured prominently in Nasser's precipitous actions, and more than a few Arabs came to view the USSR with suspicion as a result.[25]

Until 1967 a relationship between the leading Arab states and the USSR was a foreign policy option for the Arab states, but the 1967 war indisputably sealed the virtual dependence of Egypt and Syria. Indeed, by breaking diplomatic ties with Washington Egypt, Syria, and Iraq forfeited any opportunity to play the United States against the Soviet Union, thereby sealing their dependence upon Moscow. Echoing Arab actions, the Soviets severed diplomatic relations with Israel in 1967 – for the second time. That year symbolised the polarisation of the main belligerents in the Arab-Israeli conflict between the United States and the USSR.

The War of Attrition

Various stillborn US-Soviet efforts to bring a close to the Arab-Israeli conflict marked the period from 1967 to 1973, a period that was characterised by low-level combat between Israel and Egypt and by the emergence of the Palestinian fedayeen as an increasingly militant and semi-autonomous movement. With the exception of acts of terror by various component organisations within the PLO, which the Soviets repeatedly dismissed as reckless and counterproductive, the Soviets played a key role in bolstering Egypt in the fighting that occurred during this period. A sizable contingent of soldiers, advisors, and technicians – reaching a total of 20 000 by 1971 – were deployed to Egypt, and General V. V. Okunev was dispatched to command Soviet air defence units.[26] Soviet pilots were directly engaged in the defence of Egyptian airspace, and clashed with Israeli aircraft on several occasions, most notably on 31 July, 1970 when the Israelis downed four Soviet-piloted Mig-21s.[27]

In contrast, during the 1970 Jordan crisis the USSR was credited with adopting a 'cautious policy'. Soviet claims to have helped to still the fighting in Jordan may not, however, be warranted.[28]

The October War

Despite some significant setbacks, notably Anwar Sadat's expulsion of Soviet military advisors from Egypt in July 1972, the Soviets persisted in a diplomacy that vehemently supported the Arabs in their conflict with Israel. In the two years preceding the October war, the USSR was outspoken in its support of the right of Arabs to regain the territories occupied in 1967 by Israel, yet it explicitly declined to endorse Arab calls for Israel's destruction.

The Soviet justification for the stalwart, if circumscribed, support it lent the Arabs against Israel was as follows: Israel committed an act of aggression by launching the 1967 war, and the Soviet Union is committed – indeed, has a 'sacred duty' – to support movements of national liberation. Since Israel's retention of the occupied territories is proof of its aggressive qualities, the struggle to liberate and regain these lands is an act of self-defence. In fact, at the onset of the October war, the USSR claimed that Israel had started the conflict through its aggressive actions.

As the 1973 war drew nearer, Soviet press reports, and broadcasts beamed to the Middle East, took on aura reminiscent of the pre-June war period. The Israelis were accused of massing forces on the Syrian and Egyptian borders in preparation for an attack. This is not meant to imply that the decision to go to war in 1973 was other than an Arab one. Claims by some scholars that the Soviets 'made the decisions that led to the October War' or, more pointedly, that the Soviets 'unleashed' the Arabs betray an incomplete understanding of the realities of the USSR's relationships with the Arab states.[29]. The Soviets proved just as unable to control their Arab allies as the United States has been to control Israel. This is not to say that the Soviet role was unimportant. Soviet technical assistance supported Arab war planning and, of course, without Soviets arms the conflagration could never have been ignited, but the decision to go to war was clearly made by Egypt and Syria.[30]

It is clear that the Soviets had foreknowledge of the war and did nothing to prevent it, despite their obligations to do so in the view of many US observers.[31] Evidence for Soviet foreknowledge includes the evacuation of Soviet dependents from Cairo and Damascus, the launching of observation satellites to monitor the fighting, and the initiation of sizable seaborne shipments, all prior to the outbreak of hostilities on 6 October.[32] During the war it was only when Israeli forces turned the tide of battle that the Soviets began to work actively for a cease-fire. They did so in the context of a well-telegraphed set of signals to the United States, including a threat to intervene militarily to underline Moscow's commitment to its allies. Undeniably, Soviet actions in 1973 represented a calibrated, but dangerous, exercise in diplomacy. Yet it was through US–USSR collaboration that a cease-fire was arranged, a cease-fire doubtless helped along by Soviet expectations of playing a key role in subsequent Middle East peace making.

If the Soviets saw themselves playing a central role in the negotiations that would follow the October war, they were quickly to be disappointed. The Geneva conference, really no more than a ceremony, convened in December 1973 with the Soviets (but not the Syrians) in attendance. If the Geneva conference was to have any meaning, the Arab-Israeli conflict would have to be tackled in its entirety, but this is exactly what Henry Kissinger opted not to do. Instead, the Soviets were obliged to watch impotently while the United States under Kissinger's leadership implemented a step-by-step approach that was designed to reduce the negotiating process to manageable slices or steps. By doing so the United States was able to avoid facing the most difficult aspects of the conflict (viz., the Palestinian questions), and simultaneously deny the Soviets the forum they yearned for and the diplomatic role they coveted. To add insult to injury, Kissinger reports that not only was the United States intent on excluding the USSR from the negotiating process, but Moscow's Syrian ally spurned an opportunity to involve the USSR in the negotiations.[33]

The 1982 War

By the end of the 1970s, the Soviet Union had suffered a series of political humiliations. President Anwar Sadat aligned Egypt with the United States, abrogated the Treaty of Friendshhip and Cooperation with the USSR in 1976, and signed a peace treaty with Israel in 1979. Even before the beginning of the Gulf war in 1980, or the Israeli invasion of Lebanon in 1982, the Soviets were engaged in a tricky juggling act in the Middle East, but the stunt became ever more difficult as time passed and contradictions accumulated. As Michael Simone notes, 'By late 1981, Moscow has publicly committed itself to ... support for Syria, the formation of an anti-imperialist Arab coalition, Soviet participation in a collective settlement that recognizes Israel, an end to the Iran–Iraq slaughter, a strong PLO, and an independent Lebanon. It would become increasingly difficult to juggle all these balls.'[34]

The Israeli invasion of Lebanon in 1982 brought many of the inherent contradictions in Soviet policy to the surface. If a superpower is judged by the performance of its friends, then Soviet leaders must have been chastened by the results of the 1982 fighting in Lebanon. Rather than winning laurels for stalwart support, the Soviet Union was ridiculed for supplying inferior weaponry and technology. Of course, the stunning defeat of the Syrian air force was widely interpreted as a defeat of Soviet military technology. For their part, the Soviets parried complaints with criticisms of Arab disunity and inaction during the Lebanese war and of the fighting effectiveness of Arab armed forces – problems that have dogged the Arab states and Soviet strategists for over a generation.[35]

There is no mistaking the fact that Moscow was anxious to stand back from the cross-fire in Lebanon and to avoid a confrontation with the United States, especially given the quiescence of the Arab world in the face of Israel's invasion. Vadim Zagladin, first deputy chairman of the Central Committee Department for International Relations, revealed that Moscow's support was clearly constrained by the desire to avoid a clash with the West. 'We shun publicity. But I can assure you that our activity during the Lebanese war was very intensive. It is no coincidence that our friend Arafat has said that the USSR did all it could, except for that which could have led to an armed conflict with the West.'[36]

Since the promulgation of the long-sought Treaty of Friendship and Cooperation with Syria in 1980, the Soviets have sold the Assad regime a surfeit of weapons. They also acted relatively quickly to replace the Syrian losses in the 1982 fighting with an array of first-line equipment, including sophisticated surface-to-surface and surface-to-air missiles, aircraft, and tanks. About 5000 Soviet military personnel were sent to Syria to operate, and train the Syrians to operate, the new missile systems.[37] On the other hand, throughout this period, Soviet officials went to some lengths to emphasise that the umbrella of the 1980 treaty did not extend to Lebanon, where Syria was often acting at cross-purposes with Soviet interests.[38]

THE PLO WRANGLE

In the aftermath of the war, the Soviets found themselves faced with a deadly conflict between their ally in Damascus and their allies in the PLO. Soviet relations with the PLO extend back to the early 1970s when, following the lead of the Arab states, Moscow began to lend support to the idea of Palestinian statehood. By 1978 the Soviet Union recognised the PLO as the sole legitimate representative of the Palestinian people, applying the formula that had emerged from the 1974 Arab League conference in Rabat. In 1981 the PLO office in Moscow was accorded full diplomatic status.[39] While profoundly discomfited by the fractiousness of Palestinian politics and the 'reckless adventurism' of some elements of the PLO, the Kremlin apparently concluded that through its support of the PLO it would secure a fail-safe option in the Middle East. So long as the Palestinian question is unresolved it will remain a resonant and emotive issue in Arab political culture, and through its ties with the PLO the Soviet Union can associate itself with the issue and claim credit for its supportive stance. Should the Palestinians win the state that they seek, the Soviets would hope to win a return on their diplomatic investment in the PLO.[40]

However, what Kremlin policy makers failed to anticipate was the unwillingness of Hafiz el-Assad to concede the mantle of PLO leadership to Yasir Arafat, for whom Assad has a hearty personal dislike. The Syrian president was also committed to preventing the PLO under Arafat, or probably under any Palestinian leader, from taking a line independent of Syria. Assad's abiding fear is that the PLO will follow the Egyptian model and pursue a separate peace, either in league with Jordan or alone, thereby leaving Syria isolated. The efforts of Arafat and Hussein to coordinate a negotiating position during 1985 and 1986, in rough accordance with the Reagan proposal of 1982 (which does not even mention Syria or Syrian claims), only increased Assad's suspicions.

Syria's sponsorship of an alternative Palestinian leadership and its direct role in combating Arafatist elements in Lebanon came as an unwelcome complication for the Soviets. Not that the Syrian-PLO clashes since 1983 were without precedent, as illustrated by the 1976 Syrian actions in Lebanon on the side of the predominantly Christian militias against the PLO and its Lebanese allies. In 1976 the USSR sought to distance itself from Syrian actions, and to find a compromise for its relations with Syria and the PLO. It has attempted to do the same thing in more recent clashes since 1985, but with palpably less success. Unlike the situation in 1976, deep and real cleavages have emerged within the PLO. The fighting of a decade ago was relatively short lived, but the same thing may not be said of the current battles. Syria's Lebanese ally is the Shiite Amal movement, which harbours a profound enmity for the PLO. It has proved to be a willing – but not altogether effective – ally of Syria's continuing campaign to quell any attempt by the PLO to establish an independent position in portions of Lebanon that lie outside Syrian influence.[41]

The Kremlin has been reduced to impotence, alternately wringing its hands in frustration, while issuing steady reminders of the need for Arab unity. As Galia Golan notes, the result is a policy that seeks to satisfy all and pleases none, a policy that seeks to support no one, but alienates all.[42] 'At no time since the 1970 civil war in Jordan has the tactical and ephemeral nature of the Soviet commitment to the Palestinians and PLO been so apparent as in the days and months of the Palestinians' most recent struggle in Lebanon.'[43]

By the autumn of 1984 it had become apparent that the Soviets, either through ineffectualness or unwillingness, were not going to weigh in on the side of the PLO. In the communiqué that followed the Assad visit to Moscow of October 1984, there was no reference to reconciliation between the two warring sides, and only a 'thorough exchange of views' on the Palestinian question was noted.[44] Subsequently, Soviet officials have been relatively candid in admitting that Syrian policies do not always coincide with those of the Soviet Union.[45]

Syria is an important ally in the Middle East (one US government analyst asserts that the USSR accords greater importance to its relationship with Syria than with any other Third World state),[46] and when forced to choose, it is hardly surprising that Moscow has favoured Syria over the internally riven PLO.

THE SOVIET FORMULA FOR A SETTLEMENT

Although it may be true that the Soviets have 'not allocated important material or political resources to the search for a negotiated settlement to the Arab-Israeli settlement',[47] one wonders whether this reflects a lack of opportunity or a lack of willingness. What is often meant by such statements is that the Soviet Union has not expended great energy or resources to support a US-designed search for a negotiated settlement. In short, the evidence that the USSR opposes a settlement is hardly compelling, while there is plenty of evidence to suggest that it opposes a settlement on US terms. This point is well made by Dimitri Simes: 'A careful analysis of Soviet behaviour indicates that while initially "no war no peace" strategy indeed dominated Moscow's attitude to the Arab-Israeli dispute, that is no longer the case. Today the Soviet Union does not oppose a settlement per se. Rather, it strongly opposes a settlement arranged without the Kremlin's participation and under the sponsorship of the United States.'[48]

In the view of the Soviets, it is a precondition of settlement that the United States change its attitude toward, and interpretation of, Soviet activities in the region, which Moscow views as a legitimate expression of Soviet security concerns, economic interests, and status as a regional and global power. Soviet commentators argue that because the Middle East poses no direct military threat to the United States, as it does to the USSR, the US fails to understand Soviet sensitivities about developments in the region.

The Soviets have strongly favoured the resurrection of the Geneva conference, or the convening of an alternative international conference with Soviet participation. Nearly all communiqués issued following state visits by Arab leaders to Moscow, or by Soviet diplomats to Arab capitals, have included this demand. A major sticking point in the convening of such a forum is the stipulation that the forum include representatives of the PLO, a feature rejected by Israel, the United States, and, one surmises, even Syria. Meanwhile, Moscow has dismissed the step-by-step approach as no more than an attempt by 'imperialist reaction' (i.e. the US and Israel) to weaken the unity of the Arab countries.

Since 1973 the Soviet formula for a settlement of the Arab-Israeli conflict has remained relatively unchanged. The prime component of any settlement is Soviet participation in the process and in the result. The core components of the Soviet settlement formula are drawn from the 1967 United Nations resolution 242, which the USSR, unlike Syria and the PLO, has accepted as the starting point for a resolution of the conflict. The proffered formula includes:

1. A demand for Israeli withdrawal from all, or nearly all, of the territory occupied in 1967.
2. Recognition of the rights of the Palestinians, and since 1974, the establishment of a Palestinian state.
3. Acknowledgment of the rights of all states in the region to exist in peace.

On the heels of the Reagan proposal of 1 September, 1982, which envisaged a central role for Jordan in shepherding the establishment of a Palestinian autonomous region, Brezhnev announced a revised Soviet plan on 15 September, 1982. It hardly seems coincidental that the Brezhnev plan was taken almost word for word from the plan announced by the Arabs after the Fez conference earlier the same month. The key points are as follows:

1. Palestinian refugees are to have the right to return to a new state of Palestine, or to receive compensation for their property losses.

2. East Jerusalem is to be incorporated into the Palestinian state, with appropriate guarantees for freedom of access to the holy sites for Christians, Jews, and Muslims.
3. The UN Security Council is to provide security guarantees.

On 29 July, 1984, a refinement of the 1982 plan was offered. This proposal discussed the transition period during which the occupied territories would be transferred from Israeli to Palestinian control. During this period – of 'several months' – the Soviets proposed that the United Nations could exercise control.

While the Soviets have opposed the US preference for making Jordan the senior partner of any Palestinian state, they did note, in 1984, that the independent Palestinian state could determine the nature of its relations, 'including the possibility of forming a confederation.'[49] Moscow seemed anxious to make the best of a bad situation: Arafat was seriously flirting with King Hussein and, hence, with the US formula. The problem was how to gain a Soviet role in a process choreographed for Washington's benefit. Hussein's support for an international conference, reflecting his serious doubts about the ability of the United States to play a neutral role in the region, was probably very much on the mind of Kremlin planners as they developed the 1984 proposals. But while Hussein warmly welcomed the new Soviet proposal, as did Arafat, both of them proceeded to attempt to formulate a joint negotiating position in the context of the September 1982 US proposal which foresaw Jordan negotiating on behalf of the Palestinians with the aim of creating an autonomous Palestinian entity within the Kingdom of Jordan. To the obvious satisfaction of the Soviets, as well as the Syrians, Hussein's efforts came to naught.

Bolstering a Weak Hand

Even if the disarray within the PLO is attenuated – a possibility that should not be discounted following the April 1987 session of the Palestine National Council, which saw several of Arafat's main detractors rejoin the fold, apparently with a nudge from Moscow – and even if Syrian and PLO ambitions can be reconciled, the Soviets are left with a weak hand in their campaign to play a key role in any resolution of the conflict. The source of their weakness lies in part in the competing purposes of the Arab states, but it also stems from the simple fact that the Soviet Union lacks diplomatic relations with Israel.

Therefore, Moscow is not an appealing interlocutor to Washington, or to Tel Aviv.

Almost on an annual basis there are rumours that the USSR and Israel will restore diplomatic relations. Soviet and Israeli diplomats meet periodically but discreetly. In 1986 there may well have been significant steps toward the restoration of diplomatic relations with Israel. Breaking with precedent, there was a highly publicised official meeting in Helsinki during August. Although the encounter foundered when the Israeli delegation focused on Soviet Jewry, there were several indications that the dialogue would be continued. Press reports indicated that 'consular matters' (the status of Russian Orthodox properties in Jerusalem) would be pursued between the two sides. In September Prime Minister Shimon Peres met in New York with Soviet Foreign Minister Eduard Shevardnadze, leading to an announcement that the normalisation of relations would remain under consideration. The September meeting was the highest level official contact since the Soviets severed ties in 1967.[50] Then, in October 1986, Poland and Israel agreed to open interest sections in one another's capitals. Hungary followed suit in September 1987. Important meetings between Israeli and Soviet officials continue, as in April 1987 when Foreign Minister Peres met with senior CPSU officials in Rome.

It is not difficult to recognise that the Soviets must play a role in any effective resolution of the Arab-Israeli conflict, but given the narrow range of Soviet ties and the lack of relations with Israel, the Soviet Union has had very little to offer from the US view. For a considerable time, the Soviets have been satisfied with a strategy aimed at fostering the isolation of Israel and the United States, but it now seems that the Soviets have decided to broaden their options in the region. If so, we may witness the sort of dramatic development that could well break the log-jam in the Arab-Israeli conflict, while concurrently signalling a decisive shift in Soviet Middle East policy.

POLITICAL ECOLOGY OF THE REGION

The Middle East is a region of increasing disorder and turmoil, and it is likely that the United States and the Soviet Union will experience ever greater difficulties in implementing their policies in the region. Fundamental social change and growing Palestinian opposition to Israeli rule in the occupied territories; the growing militarisation, and perhaps nuclearisation, of the region; severe uncertainties about regime change in Syria, and maybe Jordan as well; continuing questions about the economic viability of Egypt; and the rising tide of Islamic movements all combine to provide a formidable range of challenges to even the most creative and agile policy maker. Meanwhile, the lingering Arab-Israeli conflict festers with the stubborn potential to ensnare the two superpowers in a clash that both would prefer to avoid. In the remainder of this century, the Soviet Union, already well scarred from its role in the Arab-Israeli conflict, is likely to collect additional bruises in the Middle East. Present and future Soviet policy makers are going to have to be much more inventive than their predecessors if the problems described below are to be managed, if not surmounted.

The Challenge of Islam

Any extra-regional power that is seen as a purveyor of a non-Islamic or, especially, anti-Islamic ideology faces serious problems in a region which has experienced a resurgence of Islam as a culturally authentic idiom of social protest and political action. The United States, the quintessential 'western' power, had already found itself castigated and attacked for its 'anti-Muslim' policies, and the Soviet Union has as well. Marxism-Leninism may legitimate or validate the Soviet state, but it hardly endears it to the peoples of the Middle East. In a region which has given birth to three of the world's great religions, atheism is not an asset. Most of the Islamic militants reject Marxism-Leninism as an alien dogma, and they have not failed to draw very pointed conclusions about the limited value of Soviet support. For instance, Shaikh Said Sha'ban, leader of the Lebanese Tawhid (or unity) movement, noted in 1986: 'The Soviet Union always supports the Arabs before and after the conflicts, but during the war keeps aside. It has shown us this shameful behaviour in all stages and its false attitude is not unknown to anyone.'[51]

The resurgence of Islam, not to mention a worldwide resurgence of religion, has surprised and confounded Soviet policy makers.[52] In general, religion has been viewed as a reactionary and anachronistic social phenomenon. For instance, Leonid Brezhnev, in his speech to the 26th CPSU Congress, conceded that the 'liberation struggle' could develop under the banner of Islam, but noted that 'experience also indicates that reaction [sic] uses Islamic slogans to start counterrevolutionary insurrections'.[53] To this day, many Soviet academics argue that Islamic fundamentalism is a temporary phenomenon; yet the Soviets seem increasingly aware that history is replete with accounts of 'temporary' phenomena that have shifted the course of human events. It may suffice to note that the Afghan mujahidin resisted the Soviet-supported Kabul government and tied down over 100 000 Soviet troops. As the resistance in Afghanistan demonstrates, 'anachronisms' can shoot.

Endemic Violence and Societal Fragmentation

The general breakdown in order, tragically illustrated in Lebanon, has spawned numerous acts of terror that not only threaten the position of the United States and the West, but of the Soviet Union as well. This fact was brought home to the Soviets in Syria during the late 1970s, when Soviet officers and technicians became a favoured prey of Assad's opponents,[54] and, more recently, in Lebanon, where a Soviet diplomat was killed and three others were kidnapped in September 1985 in an incident of terrorism that stemmed from Syria's attempts to impose its authority upon Tripoli, Lebanon.[55]

Arab Disunity

Throughout the period of its involvement in the region, the USSR has often been faced with the difficult task of balancing the contradictions inherent in its relationships with the states of the region. It is simply not possible to buttress competing regional adversaries without eventually paying a price. No doubt the Soviet Union, like the United States, would prefer to escape such predicaments, but they are very much a price of doing business in a Middle East where Arab unity is a popular slogan, but notable for its absence.

For its part, the Soviet Union has consistently exhorted the Arabs to come to a unified position in their confrontation with Israel, just as it has frequently despaired of Arab disunity. Nor is it certain that a concerted Arab stance *vis-à-vis* Israel would redound to the benefit of the Soviet Union. Under such an unlikely circumstance, the Arabs might collectively decide that their interests lie not with Moscow but with Washington, as Egypt did after the 1973 war. Nevertheless, it is not difficult to understand why Arab unity has so preoccupied Soviet policy makers. The task of balancing Arab rivalries has been a persistent one. Regional strife, between Egypt and Syria, Iraq and Syria, Jordan and Syria, Egypt and Libya, and the

PLO and Syria has imposed clear dilemmas of choice on Kremlin policy makers, and will continue to do so.

If the past is prologue, the Soviet Union can be expected to continue to pursue a cautiously opportunistic, defensive, and pragmatic policy in the Arab-Israeli conflict. The missing element has been innovation in the search for a peaceful solution, and it now appears likely that Moscow will attempt such innovation through the restoration of diplomatic ties with Israel. US diplomats with long experience in the Middle East are prone to comment on the ineptness that has long marred Soviet Middle East policy, but, looking at the situation in 1987, those comments may no longer be as apposite as they once were. Recent Soviet moves – ranging from the rescheduling of $3 billion in Egyptian military debt to Moscow's efforts to repair the schisms dividing the PLO internally –have shown deftness and flexibility.

But, even if sustained, Soviet flexibility and innovation may only be a necessary but not a sufficient condition for constructive moves toward peaceful solution of the Arab-Israeli conflict. Granted, were the two superpowers to act in concert their leverage would increase mightily, but such a change, however meritorious, is implausible in the extreme. The intractability and complexity of the problems in the Middle East remain formidable, and the ability of either the United States or the USSR to impose its own designs continues to be circumscribed by the social and political dynamics of the region. As the states of the region have amply proven, superpowers usually enjoy a good deal less respect than they think they deserve. Neither Washington nor Moscow wields the decisive influence that the one sometimes attributes to the other.

Notes

1. Yevgeny M. Primakov, 'The Soviet Union's Interests: Myths and Reality', *AEI Foreign Policy and Defense Review* (American Enterprise Institute, Washington, D.C.), vol. 6, no. 1, 1986, pp. 26–34, quote at p. 30.
2. Oles M. Smolansky, 'The Soviet Union and the Middle East', in *The Soviet Empire: Expansion and Detente, Critical Choices for Americans*, vol. 9 (Lexington, MA: Lexington Books, 1976), pp. 259–84, quote at p. 260. Also see Malcolm E. Yapp, 'The Soviet Union and the Middle East', *Asian Affairs*, vol. 63, new series vol. 7, part 1 (February 1976), pp. 7–18.

3.   Alexander J. Bennett, 'Arms Transfer as an Instrument of Soviet Policy in the Middle East', *Middle East Journal*, vol. 39, no. 4, Autumn 1985, pp. 745–74, see p. 747.

4.   Ibid., p. 769.

5.   For examples see Mark N. Katz, 'The Soviet Union and the Third World', *Current History*, vol. 85, no. 10, October 1986, pp. 329–32, 339–40; and Alvin Z. Rubinstein, 'A Third World Policy Waits for Gorbachev', *Orbis*, vol. 30, no. 2, Summer 1986, pp. 355–64.

6.   See Steven L. Hosmer and Thomas W. Wolfe, *Soviet Policy and Practice toward Third World Countries* (Lexington, MA: Lexington Books, 1983).

7.   Primakov, 'The Soviet Union's Interests', p. 31 (see note 1).

8.   Neil S. MacFarlane, 'The Soviet Conception of Regional Security', *World Politics*, vol. 37, no. 3, April 1985, pp. 295–316, quote at p. 311.

9.   Robert O. Freedman, 'Patterns of Soviet Policy toward the Middle East', *Annals of the American Academy of Political and Social Science*, no. 482, November 1985, pp. 40–64, quote at p. 58.

10.   See Francis Fukuyama, 'Gorbachev and the Third World', *Foreign Affairs*, 64, no, 4, Spring 1986, pp. 715–31.

11.   See Larry C. Napper, 'The Arab Autumn of 1984: A Case Study of Soviet Middle East Diplomacy', *Middle East Journal*, vol. 39, no. 4, Autumn 1985, pp. 733–44. Napper notes 'the Kremlin continues to view its competition with the US in the Third World as a zero-sum game, [and] an improvement of Moscow's relations with Egypt, Jordan, or any other moderate Arab states would be seen as undercutting the American position in the [Middle East]' (p. 734). Freedman, 'Patterns of Soviet Policy', p. 41 (see note 9) makes the same point.

12.   William B. Quandt, former office director for Middle Eastern Affairs on the National Security Council staff, observes: 'The anti-Soviet theme has certainly been a dominant one in American policy in the area.' *Decade of Decisions: American Policy toward the Arab-Israeli Conflict* (Berkeley, CA: University of California Press, 1977), p. 6. Also see Bruce R. Kunniholm, 'Retrospects and Prospects: Forty Years of US Foreign Policy', *Middle East Journal*, vol. 41, no. 1, Winter 1987, pp. 7–25.

13.   The Reagan administration has viewed the Middle East through the lens of US-Soviet rivalry, a perspective easily verified by Secretary of State Alexander Haig's preoccupation with 'strategic consensus', a concept that the Arab states of the region found manifestly irrelevant to their concerns. Moreover, the statements of senior officials, and a consideration of the qualifications of appointees to the National Security Council (NSC) staff, serve to establish the fact that strategic consensus may have been jettisoned in name, but the focus on the Soviet role in the region has continued to be dominant. On the last point, it is striking that prior to 1987 virtually all of the NSC staffs dealing with the Middle East had had little exposure to the region, excepting Israel. Indeed, the NSC Middle East staffs during the Reagan administration were comprised of a series of individuals who could be described as international

relations theorists, national security experts, professional diplomats, or authorities on Soviet foreign policy, but not experts on the Arab world or the Middle East. For instance, Dennis Ross, appointed to the NSC in June 1986, was executive director of the Berkeley/Stanford programme on Soviet International Behavior, and is known for his work on Soviet foreign policy. See his 'Acting with Caution: Middle East Policy Planning for the Second Reagan Administration', *Policy Papers*, no. 1 (Washington, DC: Washington Institute for Near East Policy, 1986). For a representative administration statement see Michael H. Armacost, Under Secretary of State for Political Affairs, 'US-Soviet Relations: Coping with Conflicts in the Third World', at Brown University, 26 September, 1986 (US Department of State, Current Policy No. 879).

14. Karen Dawisha, 'The USSR in the Middle East: Superpower in Eclipse?' *Foreign Affairs*, vol. 61, no. 2, Winter 1982/83, pp. 438–52, quote at p. 444.

15. Michael Simone, 'Soviet Foreign Policy toward Syria since the 26th Party Congress', unpublished paper, Columbia University, New York, May 1986, p. 42.

16. As Cynthia Roberts notes, there is good argument to be made that the Soviet Union has been less likely than the United States to send top-of-the-line equipment to the Middle East: 'A partial qualitative breakdown of the inventories of the major parties to the Arab-Israeli dispute reveals that in crucial categories, the Soviet Union has not transferred the same level of advanced equipment as have the United States or France.' Roberts cites the F-15/F-16 aircraft and early warning aircraft as examples. See 'Soviet Arms-Transfer Policy and the Decision to Upgrade Syrian Air Defenses', *Survival*, vol. 25, July/August 1983, pp. 154–64, quote at p. 160.

17. Surendra Bhutani, *Israeli Soviet Cold War* (New Delhi: Atul Prakashan, 1975), pp. 15–16.

18. Adam B. Ulam, *Expansion and Coexistence: Soviet Foreign Policy, 1917–73*, 2nd edn (New York: Praeger, 1974), p. 584.

19. Quoted in *New Middle East*, June 1969, p. 16.

20. Avigdor Dagan, *Moscow and Jerusalem: Twenty Years of Relations between Israel and the Soviet Union* (New York: Abelard-Schuman, 1970), pp. 36–7.

21. Ibid., p. 73.

22. Excerpts of the note are in ibid., p. 108.

23. See George Lenczowski, *Soviet Advances in the Middle East* (Washington, DC: American Enterprise Institute for Public Policy Research, 1971), pp. 106–9.

24. For example see Khalid Bakdash, 'The National Liberation Movement and the Communists', *World Marxist Review*, vol. 8, no. 12, December 1965.

25. See Charles Yost, 'The Arab-Israeli War: How It Began', *Foreign Affairs*, vol. 46, no. 2, 1968, pp. 304–20; in Irene L. Gendzier (ed.), *A Middle East Reader* (New York: Pegasus, 1969), pp. 366–83, especially pp. 371–2; and Nadav Safran, *From War to War: The Arab-Israeli*

Confrontation, 1948–67 (Indianapolis, IN: Pegasus, Bobbs-Merrill, 1969), pp. 274–8.
26. Hosmer and Wolfe, *Soviet Policy*, p. 47 (see note 6).
27. Quandt, *Decade of Decisions*, p. 102 (see note 12).
28. Ibid., pp. 124–5.
29. Dina Rome Spechler, 'The USSR and Third-World Conflicts: Domestic Debate and Soviet Policy in the Middle East, 1967–1973', *World Politics*, vol. 38, no. 3, April 1986, pp. 435–61, quoted at pp. 440 and 436 respectively.
30. Quandt, *Decade of Decisions*, pp. 297–8 (see note 12).
31. See Foy D. Kohler, Leon Gouré, and Mose L. Harvey, *The Soviet Union and the October 1973 Middle East War: The Implications for Detente* (Miami, FL: Center for Advanced International Studies, University of Miami, 1974).
32. Ibid.
33. Henry Kissinger, *Years of Upheaval* (Boston, Mass.: Little, Brown, 1982), pp. 944–5.
34. Simone, 'Soviet Foreign Policy toward Syria', p. 15 (see note 15).
35. Karen N. Brutents was brutally frank – at the time of Israel's invasion of Lebanon – in depicting the impotence of the Arabs: 'There is no question that Tel Aviv's unceremonious behaviour is also fostered by the extremely weak opposition to Israel in the Arab world, the definitive passivity displayed by many Arab states at this dramatic time in this world and the absence of even the degree of unity that would make an Arab "summit" conference possible. There is no doubt that among other factors this is the result of the Camp David agreements, which took the largest Arab country, Egypt, out of the ranks of the Arab world and created a secure Sinai rear for Israel's aggression.' 'Tragedy of Lebabon', *SShA: Ekonomika, Politika, Ideologiva*, no. 9, September 1982, pp. 5–8, trans. Joint Publication Research Service no. 82551, USSR Report, pp. 3–7, quote at p. 4.
36. Quoted in Galia Golan, 'The Soviet Union and the PLO since the War in Lebanon', *Middle East Journal*, vol. 40, no. 2, Spring 1986, pp. 285–305, at p. 289.
37. Bennett, 'Arms Transfers', p. 758 (see note 3).
38. Pedro Ramet, 'The Soviet-Syrian Relationship', *Problems of Communising*, vol. 35, no. 5 (1986), pp. 40–1.
39. The most current analysis of the PLO relationship with the Soviet Union is John C. Reppert, 'The Soviets and the PLO: The Convenience of Politics', in Augustus R. Norton and Martin H. Greenberg (eds), *The International Relations of the PLO* (Carbondale: Southern Illinois University Press, forthcoming).
40. For additional information on this point see Augustus R. Norton, 'Moscow and the Palestinians', in Michael Curtis, Joseph Neyer, Chaim I. Waxman, and Allen Pollack (eds), *The Palestinians: People, History, Politics* (New Brunswick, NJ: Transaction Books, 1975), pp. 228–48.
41. For background see Augustus R. Norton, *Amal and the Shi'a: Struggle for the Soul of Lebanon* (Austin: University of Texas Press, 1987).
42. Golan, 'The Soviet Union and the PLO', p. 298 (see note 36).

43. Ibid., p. 287.
44. Napper, 'Arab Autumn of 1984', p. 740 (see note 11).
45. See 'Seminar' with Karen N. Brutents, deputy chief of the International Department of the CPSU Central Committee, in *al-Watan* (Kuwait), 4 January,, 1986, pp. 14–16; trans. in FBIS (USSR), 7 January, 1986, pp. H8–H21.
46. Napper, 'Arab Autumn of 1984', p. 734 (see note 11).
47. Ibid., p. 733.
48. Dimitri K. Simes, 'The Soviet Approach to the Arab-Israeli Conflict', in Michael C. Hudson (ed.), *Alternative Approaches to the Arab-Israeli Conflict: A Comparative Analysis of the Principal Actors* (Washington, DC: Center for Contemporary Arab Studies, Georgetown University, 1984), pp. 137–51, quote at p. 138.
49. Golan, 'The Soviet Union and the PLO', p. 295 (see note 36).
50. *New York Times*, 19 August, 1986; ibid., 22 September, 1986; and *Christian Science Monitor*, 30 September, 1986.
51. *Jomhuri-ye Eslami* (Tehran, in Persian), 20 April, 1986, p. 2.
52. This conclusion is based on a reading of Soviet analyses and private comments by Soviet scholars. Also see Carol R. Saivetz, 'Soviet Perspectives in Islam as a Third World Political Force', in Paul Marantz and Blema S. Steinberg (eds), *Superpower Involvement in the Middle East: Dynamics of Foreign Policy* (Boulder, CO: Westview, 1985), pp. 31–49. For an unusually clear-headed Soviet view see A. Vasilyev, 'Islamic Fundamentalism and Egypt', *Azii i Afrika Segodnia* (Moscow), no. 1, January 1986, pp. 22–6.
53. Quoted in Simone, 'Soviet Foreign Policy toward Syria', p. 10 (see note 15).
54. See Augustus R. Norton, 'Militant Protest and Political Violence under the Banner of Islam', *Armed Forces and Society*, vol. 9, Fall 1982, pp. 3–19, especially pp. 6–12.
55. Augustus R. Norton, 'Estrangement and Fragmentation in Lebanon', See *Current History*, vol. 85, February 1986, pp. 58–62, 88–9.

12 Soviet-Maghribi Relations in the 1980s
I. William Zartman

INTRODUCTION

There is little indication that the Soviet Union sees North Africa as much of a region. The term 'Maghrib' or 'Arab Maghrib' is used in Soviet Arabic broadcasts since it is part of the Arabic language, but it is scarcely used in Russian writings and speeches. The Maghrib is seen as part of the regions to which it belongs – the Arab world, Africa, the Mediterranean, and the newly independent formerly colonised developing world, and it is referred to in these terms in Soviet discussions. On the other hand, it is composed of four very different countries, each with its own brand of bilateral relations with the Soviet Union. It is this bilateralism which is dominant, and between it and the broader worlds to which the four countries belong, North Africa as a sub-region loses its significance in Soviet eyes.

In the bilateral relations of the Soviet Union with each of the four countries of the region, what are the strategies and criteria that determine Soviet policies, and how do these policies relate to the Maghribi states' strategies and criteria? More specifically, does the Soviet Union seek special relations with the big countries of a region like North Africa and pay less attention to the smaller ones; do its relations improve the 'more socialist' the country; does it seek to establish beachheads with smaller more vulnerable states; or does it seek to polarise the region on an East–West dimension? The balance sheet for the 1980s, valid for earlier decades as well, shows that the USSR has steadily 'high' relations with Algeria, 'low' with Tunisia, a medium level with greater fluctuations with Morocco, and a rising diagonal' of intensifying relations with Libya. It appears that these relationships are important to the USSR, which goes to some lengths to maintain and to balance them. As such, Soviet understanding of these relations tends to correspond to the general expectations of the Maghribi partner (with some disappointment in Libya's case), and tends to narrow the gap between the reality and image of these relations. But since the relations reflect reality, they also limit the influence one party has over the other.

This chapter will focus on the 1980s, and it will concentrate on Libya, Algeria, and Morocco since they have the most interesting and active relations with the USSR and its satellites. In examining Soviet-Maghribi relations, it will divide the subject matter into three components: foreign policy positions, domestic forms of government, and developmental matters. It will organise its answers to a number of basic questions into four sections: Soviet perceptions of its relations with North African states; Maghribi perceptions; the reality; and the use of influence to change either the perceptions or the reality.

SOVIET PERCEPTIONS

Algeria

Algeria has had historic ties of friendship with the USSR since the national liberation war of 1954–62.[1] Its proclaimed socialist orientation and its dynamic Third World leadership made it attractive in Soviet eyes and a natural partner and 'ally'. In addition, its relative development among the countries of the Group of 77, its feistily independent foreign posture that covered a broad identity of policy positions with the Soviet Union, its dominant state capitalism and its heavy industry option as a basis for development, and its vanguard single party all provided points of commonality and bases for sympathy.

In all of these aspects, the very fact that Algeria's policies and positions are its own and are accompanied by a haughty, prickly attitude toward foreign influence only make Algeria a more attractive associate for Moscow. The only incident which has troubled Soviet-Algerian relations was the overthrow of president Ahmed ben Bella by the Algerian army in 1965, just as Soviet analysts were getting caught up in their own debate about the acceptability of military rule as a source of progressive leadership in the Third World. The fall of ben Bella perplexed Soviet analysts, as did the fall of Kwame Nkrumah in Ghana the following year and Modibo Keita in Mali in 1968. However, events soon showed that the new government of Houari Boumedienne would not have the objectionable Trotskyite advisors of his predecessor, but that it would pursue and even intensify the radical 'Third World' foreign policy positions and would strengthen its oil-fuelled state capitalism. The USSR has viewed Algeria as a reliable partner since then.

Soviet-Algerian friendship is based first of all on Moscow's appreciation of Algeria's anti-capitalist, anti-imperialist, and anti-colonialist foreign policy positions. The Soviet news analyst, N. Andreyev, has observed: 'Algeria is an active member of the Non-Aligned Movement, which has become an important factor in international politics. Algeria contributes to consolidating the movement's anti-imperialist trends and to strengthen its progressive trends. Examining current important issues, we see that the Soviet and Algerian positions on those issues are either identical or close.'[2] Four years later, a visiting Soviet delegation under CPSU Central Committee Secretary B. N. Ponomarev 'noted Algeria's positive contribution to the struggle for freedom, people's independence and peace; affirmed the CPSU's solidarity with the Algerian revolution; and acclaimed Algeria's consistent struggle against imperialism and its allies and against all forms of domination and exploitation'.[3]

More important than simple foreign policy coincidence, however, is the deeper basis of attraction for the Soviet Union in Algeria's domestic orientation. Soviet references to Algeria's socialist development are constant features of the 1980s, covering any evidence that relations have 'quietly soured since the death of Houari Boumedienne' in 1978.[4] In 1981 a CPSU delegation under Sh. R. Rashidov, first secretary of the Uzbek CP central committee, rated highly 'the Algerian people's successes, under the leadership of their vanguard, the FLN [Front de Liberation Nationale], in the struggle to build socialism'.[5] The same year, at the Kremlin dinner honouring President BenJedid, CPSU General Secretary Leonid Brezhnev provided a good summary of Soviet views:

We have a longstanding friendship with Algeria. Its foundations were laid in the difficult years of the Algerian people's heroic struggle for independence. It grew stronger each year, when free Algeria, having chosen in favor of socialism, embarked on the path of profound social transformation in the interests of the masses. We share the Algerian people's joy over its accomplishments in creating modern industry and conducting agrarian reform, in resolving important social and cultural problems. Much also unites us in international policy, where we take a common stand on the vital problems of the present day.[6]

Five years later, during BenJedid's second state visit to Moscow, *Izvestiia* declared, 'Under President C. BenJedid's leadership, Algeria is resolving questions concerning the implementation of building a new society in accordance with the principles of the FLN Charter, and transformations are being implemented for the purpose of strengthening the country's independence and sovereignty, developing the national economy, and solving social problems.'[7] While 'building socialism' was left for the Algerian delegation to articulate, the reference was included in the joint communiqué, and the tone of the speeches and accounts was as fullsome as before. The visit followed on the revision of the National Charter which diluted its socialist rigour and provided scriptural justification for BenJedid's pragmatism and liberalisation. If the new policy is enacted, the socialist basis of Soviet-Algerian cooperation may be weakened, but for the moment it still remains strong.

Building on Soviet approval of the Algerian path of socioeconomic transformation, bilateral cooperation has flourished to tie together the foreign and domestic aspects of relations. Coincidence of views on foreign issues can be paralleled by Soviet support for Algerian economic development measures, and this cooperation can then be justified as Soviet assistance to Algeria's efforts to liberate itself from international capitalism and imperialism and to strengthen its independence and sovereignty, ideas which echo the justifications for state capitalism (not by that name!) in the National Charter itself. As Ya.Ryabov, chair of the USSR State Committee for Foreign Economic Relations, indicated on the anniversary of the Soviet-Algerian cooperation treaty, 'The twenty years of Soviet-Algerian economic cooperation attest to its fruitfulness. Algeria has frequently noted its importance in consolidating the country's economic development, implementing plans for its socio-economic development, and consolidating Algeria's position in the face of the onslaught of the international monopolies.'[8] Soviet-Algerian cooperation is thus perceived as being directed both toward shared goals and against common targets.

Libya

Far from stable, Libyan-Soviet relations have been warming up to a lyric level of amity in recent years.[9] It is ironic that Soviet affinity for Libya has come as a direct result of US pressure and hostility and not of internal impetus from either country. The United States has produced a *casus foederis*. Of the three elements present in Algero-Soviet bilateral relations – domestic socialism, foreign policy agreement, cooperation for development – only the last two are operative in the

Libyan case. The Soviet Union has a longer list of common foreign policy positions with Libya than with any other country in the region, and it has a basis of cooperation against a military as well as an economic enemy.

But the USSR has very little to say about the nature of Libya's domestic system. To be sure, cooperation began with the 1969 military revolution (a coup in the right direction, unlike the overthrow of ben Bella), took a turn for the better in 1974 as the USSR sought a replacement for Egypt, and gradually improved from that good start as the regime developed its revolutionary nature.[10] But Qaddafi chose a path that was explicitly a 'middle way', and from the beginning he was as critical of communism as of capitalism. A freewheeling and eclectic pioneer, borrowing and inventing his way through the problems of life, Qaddafi is scarcely of the type that constitutes a recognisable and reliable fellow traveller for the capital of communist orthodoxy. Yet Libya is referred to as an 'ally', even though its request for a friendship treaty has been repeatedly rebuffed by Moscow, and the ongoing succession of world events give it cause to make common with the Soviet Union to an increasing degree.

Socialism is never invoked in the few Soviet references to the Libyan domestic political system. The junta is referred to as 'Libya's revolutionary leadership' or 'the people's government', and it is occasionally called 'progressive' or 'successful in building a new society' or 'in political and social development', but the path is not identified. In a 1981 radio commentary, Libya was classified among the

> developing countries which have opted for a progressive development path, which are achieving drastic economic and social changes and are actively struggling against imperialism ... Diplomatic relations between [the USSR and Libya] were established ... in 1955 and they gained new content after the September 1969 Revolution which brought down the royalist regime and eliminated the political, military and economic positions of imperialism in the country. Relations then began to develop in the course of the joint struggle against the domination of foreign imperialist monopolies, for the elimination of national and social injustice, and for the establishment of relations among states based on equality and mutual respect.[11]

Following Qaddafi's visit to Moscow two months later, Tass observed, 'Notwithstanding that the USSR and Libya differ one from another in many respects, that there are certain ideological distinctions between them, full mutual understanding has been reached' on many foreign policy issues.[12] At the dinner for Qaddafi, Brezhnev spoke in words not reported from his meetings with BenJedid: 'We are glad to welcome you here again in the Kremlin, Comrade al-Qaddafi ... When representatives of the USSR and Libya address each other as "comrade", this reflects the character of relations that have formed between them – relations of equality, mutual respect, revolutionary solidarity.'[13] Thus, if camaraderie exists, it is in the field of foreign policy, not domestic affairs.

Foreign policy cooperation touches two areas – agreement on positions of both Third World and East–West issues, and support for Libya in its conflict with the United States. The latter has cooperated in the conflict so as to make the Soviet-Libyan position credibly defensive rather than aggressive or revisionist, as it used to be in the 1970s and early 1980s. In both periods, Libya has portrayed itself as seeking to 'achieve its independence against American imperialism' and then to 'stand up against the threats from American imperialism'. The position of Libya in regard to many international issues, as well as its active conflict with the United States, allows the Soviet Union to use joint communiqués to attack the US directly, rather than simply addressing positive principles as it does with Algeria. It also permits frequent reference to military cooperation and supplies, items not mentioned in regard to Algeria.

In addition, Libya's paradoxical position, which combines oil wealth and underdevelopment, provides a broad opportunity for trade and technical assistance from the Soviet Union, 'to assist by all means the revolutionary and independent development of this young Arab country in the interests of the Libyan peoples and the anti-imperialist Arab national liberation struggle'.[14] Current thinking on such relations has kept apace of events; 'the Soviet Union's readiness to develop mutually advantageous and equal economic cooperation with Libya on a long-term basis, to give it assistance in strengthening its defence capability and to cooperate in the international arena for the benefit of peace and security of peoples on the basis of agreed principles was emphasised during the conversation between Mikhail Gorbachev and Abdelsalam Jallud in Moscow after the US air raid.[15] The 'principles' in question were doubtless the five elements of an international 'code of conduct' – domestic sovereignty, territorial integrity, international equality, decolonisation, and non-alignment – which Brezhnev enunciated during the state dinner for Qaddafi at the beginning of the decade.[16]

Morocco

Moroccan-Soviet relations[17] illustrate the diversity that can be found in good bilateral relationships. Morocco is known to be on the opposite end from Algeria and Libya on the spectrum encompassed by the Non-Aligned Movement. Its foreign policy attitudes, military and security relations, and specific activities, as Tunisia's, are associated with the West. Its domestic political and economic systems are characterised by pluralism and free enterprise, operating under monarchial – not socialist – centralism. (On the other hand, unlike Algeria and Libya, Morocco – as Tunisia – has a legal, functioning communist party, although it is a minor player on the political scene, a safety valve for tamed, marginal radicalism.)

There would seem to be little in common between Morocco and the USSR. Yet for that very reason, each has a calculated interest in influencing the activities of the other. Morocco has a policy of keeping its options open, a foreign policy reflection of a basic Moroccan rule of political behaviour to keep ties with all sides and hedge bets.[18] It also has a specific interest in maintaining relations with its neighbour-enemy's ally, and has been remarkably successful in tying down the Soviet Union so that it does not follow its natural tendencies and come out openly in support of the Algerian-supported Saharan rebels. Similarly, the Soviet Union sees an advantage in keeping the best relations possible with Morocco, with its strategic Atlantic position, its dominance of the phosphate trade, and its close relations with the United States. The result is a most ambivalent relationship, whose very contradictions stand as the guarantee of its durability.

Morocco does not figure in Soviet news and activities to anywhere near the extent that Algeria and Libya do. There have been no official visits in either direction in the 1980s and, therefore, no joint communiqués. The two parties congratulate each other on appropriate national holidays. The Soviets' favourite historical event is the Moroccan national liberation movement's struggle for independence. They cannot very well congratulate Morocco anymore on the anniversary of the evacuation of the US bases in 1963, since Morocco signed a new contingency agreement in 1982 on the renewed use of the same facilities in connection with the Rapid Deployment Force, only four years after the last Americans left the jointly-staffed facilities. On national holidays, Moscow points attention to its pro-Arab policy, but there are no shared positions on foreign policy issues.

Similarly, there is little to approve in Morocco's domestic system since it is scarcely progressive, revolutionary, or socialist. Indeed, feature stories in the Soviet press highlight the social problems, economic difficulties, and unenlightened policies of Morocco. The country is portrayed as a backward society whose policies and orientation provide it with only the causes of, not the answers to, its problems. From the descriptions given of the three neighbouring countries, one would not sense that they are similar societies with common conditions of development and parallel problems to overcome. Wrote I. Vorosheykhin in *Pravda*: 'One can see the effects of phenomena which are typical of stagnation, which have touched many branches of the country's economy. And one can see the complexity of the social problems that practically every Moroccan comes in contact with today'.[19] After listing the problems and their implications, the article identifies as a major cause 'the growing expenditures for military needs, particularly for the maintenance of the Army and for the purchase of military technology and various kinds of weapons, primarily in the United States'. The problems are thus laid at the doorstep of US militarism, while skillfully avoiding the Saharan affair for which the military expenditures have been made.

Focus on the negative aspects of the Moroccan system, however, reinforces an important component of Moroccan-Soviet relations. Such negative reporting parallels the analysis of Morocco's loyal opposition parties, the Socialist Union of Popular Forces (USFP) and the Party of Progress and Socialism (PPS) or communist party, and these parties provide the institutional contact with the USSR (or the Soviet Communist Party) as a supplement to government contacts. Neither party is Moscow-directed, and the USFP particularly plays an important role in the Moroccan political system, to the point of being an occasional government partner and potential government leader.[20] Through these contacts, however, Morocco keeps in touch with the USSR, and the USSR legitimises its views of Moroccan society.

Yet all is not negative. Barred from any coincidence of views on foreign policy and disparaged for its internal system, Morocco can none the less enjoy the third element of good relations with the Soviet Union – cooperation against jointly-deplored economic ills. Indeed, it is the very weakness of the domestic economy (as well as the imbalance of Morocco's political relations) that allows the two countries to enter so wholeheartedly into cooperative relations. As long as Rabat is willing not to let its close ties with the West stand in the way of cooperative relations with the USSR and Moscow is willing not to permit the unprogressive domestic system in Morocco to prevent closer exchanges, the two sides can enter into mutual cooperative relations. The 1984 *Pravda* article again let progressive Moroccan politicians express this sentiment, which it quoted with approval:

> It is necessary to maintain a course toward the expansion of reciprocal trade both with the capitalist countries and the socialist countries, and, in consideration of that, to approach the development of Moroccan-Soviet cooperation ... Moroccan communists proceed from the hypothesis that cooperation with the USSR is an important factor in Morocco's development, and that Moroccan-Soviet business ties are a substantial element in guaranteeing their homeland's sovereignty and national independence ... The Moroccans themselves realize this.[21]

Emphasis on this third component of bilateral relations is not something that must be subtly discerned by analysts; it is periodically referred to quite explicitly by Soviet spokesmen, who deny 'tendentious comments of certain circles' that the lack of foreign policy harmony or domestic progressiveness stand in the way of good relations based on cooperation for mutual benefit.[22] Both for Morocco and for the USSR, fish and phosphates are the basis of good relations.

Intra-Regional Relations

To some, there is another state in North Africa, the Saharan Arab Democratic Republic (SADR), the store-front organisation run by the Popular Front for the Liberation of Saqiet el-Hamra and Rio de Oro (*Polisario Front*) and recognised by the OAU as a member in order to clear the agenda of an item that was nearly fatal to the organisation.[23] Since the Polisario fights Morocco, the successor state to Spain in the territory, with Soviet arms supplied by Libya from 1975 to 1984 and by Algeria before and afterward, the Saharan conflict is of concern to the USSR. However, rather than regarding the territory as another state in the region, it is better to look at it as part of multilateral regional relations and examine Soviet attitudes under that heading.

Intra-regional relations pose a delicate challenge to the Soviets since, as the review of Soviet bilateral relations has shown, they seek to maintain good relations with the major antagonists of the regional conflicts. By seeking both to sympathise with and encourage the approved attitudes and conduct of its associates in the region but also to maintain ties with other states, the USSR finds a compelling reason to avoid polarising relations in the region. The implications for international relations – and specifically for the interaction between East–West and North–South relations – are significant. Under what conditions would it be considered in the Soviet interest to seek polarised East–West relations in a Third World region, and under what conditions would it seek diffused or non-polarised relations? Paradoxically, nearly any characterisation that one could make of the region – from bipolarised conflict to cooperation within an ethos of unity – could apply to current relations with the Maghrib, making it difficult to posit verifiable hypotheses to answer the question. Therefore, before returning to explanations, it is important to undertake descriptions of relations in the region.

From its policy of avoiding polarisations, the Soviet Union emphasises measures of harmony in North African relations whenever possible. This involves, more precisely, support for principles of cooperation and for principles of settlement in issues of conflict. It is preferable if both sets of principles accord with the views of the states that the USSR favours, but such support from the Soviets must be expressed in such a way as not to offend the other parties to the conflict. A good example of principles of cooperation covers the Algerian friendship treaty with Tunisia, and then with Mauritania, of 1983. Soviet comments stressed nothing but the positive aspects of the relations, which involved neighbourly cooperation, mutual security, openness to all other states of the region, and a promise of conciliation among the states. What the statements did not bring out was the bipolar split which the treaty brought to North Africa through its exclusion of Morocco and Libya, which then signed a friendship and unity agreement of their own the following year at Oujda. Moscow was rather silent on the Oujda treaty, which unites an 'approved' and 'unapproved' state, whereas it greeted the Algerian treaty positively even though it contains the same mix of members.

A good example of the principles of settlement can be drawn from the Saharan conflict. There the Soviet Union has long followed the principles of support for UN resolutions and for self-determination and even armed liberation struggles. However, open support and recognition of the Polisario would have led to a rupture of relations by Morocco, leaving the USSR with a reduced margin of manoeuvrability. Algeria has long pressed for open support for the Polisario in its joint communiqués with the Soviet Union, but has never gotten further than a reiteration of the right of self-determination and support for the relevant UN and OAU resolutions.[24] When the OAU adopted this solution and tried to give it various, and conflicting, operational forms in 1981 (referendum) and 1983 (negotiation), the USSR was able to ignore the details and emphasise its support for the OAU-adopted principle of self-determination. Since Morocco itself accepted the 1981 version, the Soviet position could be enunciated without offending Rabat.

Needless to say, the Soviet Union is uninterested in a more active role of mediation or conciliation, since that would necessarily carry it beyond the mutually acceptable principles into the dangerous manoeuvring about their implementation.[25] There is no evidence that the USSR has any interest in the conflict itself or in the Polisario, which it has not recognised and which spouts a woolly sort of Marxism and would be an unreliable ally. The conflict does marginally increase Algeria's military dependence on the Soviet Union and hence also increases the utility of good Soviet relations for Morocco. But since it is a very destabilising condition in North Africa relations and not something that the Soviets can control, they have more interest in keeping it within bounds or in eliminating it altogether, rather than in seeing it escalate. Furthermore, the Saharan conflict increases Morocco's dependence on the United States (while also posing frictions of miscomprehension between the two dependent partners, to be sure) and hence tends to work more against than for Soviet interests. The result is a retreat to principles, as seen, and avoidance of polarising positions.

This appreciation of Soviet regional perceptions also helps an understanding of a further aspect of Soviet relations. The USSR – at least in the Maghrib – avoids taking sides among the parties of the region. Any military assistance it gives is explicitly unrelated to regional conflicts and is not directed against any other party in the region. Such aid is related to the normal needs of states to arm and defend themselves, or it is more specifically related to their need to defend themselves against 'US aggression, imperialism or adventurist militarist provocations'. Algeria is an example of the first, Libya of the second.

As for the Western Sahara, the Soviet Union has never identified with the Polisario war against Morocco nor claimed the Polisario as 'its contras' nor admitted to their using its weapons. The evil force in connection with the conflict is of course 'imperialism and its agents', which 'have tried to take advantage of the dispute ... to divide this organization [the OAU] which contributes so importantly to the struggle for independence and genuine freedom in Africa.'[26] It is not at all clear in that just who has caused what; the conflict seems to have an uncaused life of its own, on which external imperialism capitalises. 'The Soviets ... will continue as before to support the struggle of the peoples of northwest Africa in favor of a just and peaceful settlement of the Western Sahara against the manoeuvres of imperialism and neo-colonialism.'[27] The forces of good and evil on a global level are clearer in this picture than are the sides – or even the causes – on the regional level.

A similar picture is present in Chad, where the Soviet Union viewed the Libyan presence with a blind eye in 1981 but neither then nor at any other time approved of Libyan policy or claims on the country (or parts of it). The Chadian conflict serves no Soviet interest and any stand would alienate some African countries, so Chad is never mentioned in Soviet-African communiqués, even as an unresolved problem or as a national liberation movement. The omission is not the most important of Libya's disappointments in its relations with the Soviet Union and so is not a likely subject for pressure from Tripoli.

Much has been made in the 1980s of the Soviet Union's decreased emphasis on socialism as a precondition for good relations, and indeed of the contrary conclusion that socialism might not even be possible or desirable as a proximate stage of development for Third World countries.[28] The spectrum of Soviet relations with North Africa must be seen within this context. As noted, the domestic system is only one of three elements on which good relations are based, foreign policy views and economic exchanges being equally important. Morocco's free enterprise and Libya's idiosyncratic polity do not disqualify them for various relations based on other elements of mutual interest, but by the same token Algeria's growing pragmatism is likely to be less disquieting to the USSR than are its efforts to effect an opening toward the United States. The Soviet Union's own ideological pragmatism allows it to view bilateral relations in the non-zero-sum global and regional context, as a great power rather than as an ideological leader.

MAGHRIBI PERCEPTIONS

Perceptions of Soviet-Maghribi relations vary on each side of the relationship. The North African countries are neither Marxist nor developed nor are they world powers. None owes its independence to the USSR. If Moscow had some role in the decolonisation of any of them, it was secondary in importance and, if anything, gave rise to all the greater a desire on the part of the new nation to assert its autonomy. Each of the Maghribi states aspires to some form of Third World leadership, which depends on its ability to show both its independence from, and its good relations with, the superpowers. There is no Cuba in North Africa. This may change if Libya continues to be under direct US pressure, but even in the extreme Qaddafi will have to perform a thorough denial of himself to establish Libya as a Soviet satellite. However, if perceptions of the bilateral relations are not common, they are at least complementary, in varying ways.

Algeria

The specificness of the Algerian experience is perhaps the basic theme that underlies the otherwise often diverse thinking of all Algerian presidents, from ben Bella through Boumedienne to BenJedid. Algeria's socialism is its own, not Marx's or Lenin's nor Moscow's or Beijing's, and its tenets are revised as the evolution of Algerian society demands. This occurred most recently in the extraordinary party congress of December 1985, when the National Charter was revised in a more liberal, pragmatic direction (while still keeping its references to things socialist).[29]

Algerian specificness also means underdevelopment, and the need and calling to lead other Third World nations to a New International Economic Order. If the Group of 77, as the Non-Aligned Movement, inveighs against neo-colonialism and imperialism, it is because it shares a common history, not because it identifies a priori with the opposing camp. Algeria is troubled by the North in general and its great power aspects, as much as it seeks to maintain its autonomy from East and West. Thus, *détente* is welcomed, but when it leads to *entente* between the superpowers in an imposed solution in the Middle East, for example, against the interests of the Palestinian people, then it is to be combated.

Being neither equidistant from both superpowers nor aligned with either leaves Algeria in an ambiguous position on occasion. On the one hand, Algeria speaks for the South, a third point of view in a bipolarised world. BenJedid's speech in Moscow on 9 June 1981 at the banquet given by Brezhnev was a masterpiece of enunciated common positions with the Soviets without once evoking the West as the enemy. Although Israel was the most specifically cited source of evil, the main cause of troubles in the world was 'international tensions', a bipolar not a one-sided matter. In the 1986 presidential visit, the two parties seem to have spent much time reciting their domestic and foreign positions and accomplishments to each other, rather than actually moving toward a common position. Commonality came only in marginal overlap rather in any basic coincidence of views.[30]

On the other hand, the Algerian political language, through which all Algerians are socialised in their political thinking, leaves no doubt that the enemy is imperialism, along with Zionism, and trains its readers and listeners to see the world in radical Manichaean terms. To some extent this is a factional matter within the post-Boumediennist elite, with the radical language of a 'Boumediennist' faction covering more pragmatic and liberal actions by the president and his closer followers. Yet the two positions meet on another level, since the refusal to name names in favour of more conceptual explanations and descriptions of world conditions is essentially an ideological position, of a kind more familiar to Soviet ears than to the pragmatic, non-ideological West.

Algeria has a number of more specific issues and themes that complement Soviet positions. Algeria offers strong principled support to national liberation movements, translated into careful support for the Palestine Liberation Organisation (PLO), the African National Congress (ANC), and the Southwest African People's Organisation (SWAPO), and it has made a major diplomatic campaign in favour of the Polisario. It favours the elimination of non-Mediterranean and nuclear naval forces from the Mediterranean. Since these, and others like them, are all positions on which the Soviet Union has a similar but not always identical point of view, there is a possibility of working out joint communiqués. But underlying specific benefits on specific points is the more general advantage that accrues to the broad position of both parties. When the purported leader of the Eastern bloc and the purported leader of the Southern group can work out common declarations, it strengthens the position of both of them.

Libya

Libya's (or more specifically, Qaddafi's) image of Soviet relations is more simple, direct, flamboyant, and operational than that of Algeria. Qaddafi has come a long way since the beginning of the previous decade when he began working on his third universal theory, based on rejection of both capitalism and communism and on a search for a specifically Libyan, Arab authentism. His relations with the USSR were tempestuous and often hostile during the first half of the 1970s.[31] It was the pro-US swing of Egypt, the failure of Qaddafi's merger schemes with other Arab countries, and his increasing isolation from mainstream Arab politics along with his association with the Steadfastness Front of Syria, South Yemen, and the PLO that led him to make his 'pact with the devil' and seek support from the Soviet Union.

During the second half of the decade Qaddafi would lecture the Soviets on correct policy – as he would do as late as 1982 when he castigated the USSR for its weak support and inaction during the siege of Beirut. But as isolation increased and Libya became more beleaguered in its own positions, with even the Steadfastness Front collapsing, while US military pressure escalated, Libya needed a closer alliance. The distinctions between the Green Book and the red books became less important, even if they did not disappear. In 1978 Qaddafi threatened to join the Warsaw Pact. But it was more of a threat directed against the West than a promise to the East, and in any case he was neither invited nor accepted. A more earnest effort to gain a friendship treaty with the USSR began in the early 1980s.

Qaddafi's simple direct message to Moscow is 'help', repeated in many ways during visits and speeches. It may take the form of a call for Soviet support in communiqués, for active Soviet efforts in a given direction (as in Beirut), or for new arms and protection. Over the 1980s the message has increasingly become one of proclaiming identity of views and calling for active engagement as a consequence – a simple syllogism presented in dramatic rhetoric. A comparison of passages from Qaddafi's speeches in Moscow in 1981 and 1985 well illustrates the progression from an alliance between the Third Way and the communist way to close similarity of views in a bipolar world. In 1981 Qaddafi declared:

> My country and the Steadfastness and Confrontation Front are aware of the benefit of friendship with your country and the socialist community at the bilateral and international levels. We have never felt that our friendship with you and our developing bilateral cooperation have been at the expense of any of our social or political values, which are connected with our national independence and our unionist and nationalist Arab endeavors to affirm our neutrality, our social choices and our spiritual beliefs ... My country declares to the world that it maintains neutrality and resists any attempt to reduce or cancel its international role through the

creation of a situation that might compel neutral states to relinquish their neutrality.[32]

Five years later, there were dramatic differences:

[O]ur joint struggle is one and against this one enemy and this joint struggle will go on as long as imperialism exists ... Thus, the imperialists and the Israelis are in one camp but the Soviet Union, the Jamahiriya, and progressive forces are on the other side. The contradiction between the Soviet Union and the Israelis is not only political but also deeply ideological ... Why does Libya come to the Soviet Union? Because there are mutual objectives. Libya and the Soviet Union are fighting on the same side ... [33]

Libya's enemies are also clearly expressed in the US-Israel tandem as direct, identifiable actors, not ideological forces. Libya calls on the Soviet Union to see the world in the same way by simply asserting that it does so. 'But analysis is not enough', as Qaddafi says several times in his 1985 speech. 'Although these forces were and are still being condemned by the United Nations and the whole world and their hostile policies exposed, they persist in their expansion, aggression and recklessness.' Action is needed.

Libya must be disappointed with the results. Reports on the effect that the US raids had on Qaddafi indicate a stunned leader, although not one disillusioned with his Soviet ties.[34] Instead, Jallud immediately travelled to Moscow to press again for action, in the form of arms and assurances, only to be rebuffed with a sermon on the value of not rocking the international boat. The perception of the benefits of the Soviet alliance apparently remains unshaken, whatever temporary dulling effects might have on the brashness of Libyan policy.

Morocco

Morocco's perceptions of its bilateral relations with the USSR are simpler still, in a different direction. Hassan II is the ultimate realist, a politician and tactician rather than an idealist or an ideologue. He makes and unmakes pacts with devils, although in Moroccan politics there are no devils, only momentary allies and enemies. At the same time, Hassan resolutely identifies himself with the West, a rare Arab leader to do so, and he holds clear ideas about who can call himself a Muslim and who cannot (notably Khomeini).[35] On the way to his clear goals, notably the recovery of the Sahara, King Hassan will seize on a deal when he can find one. His alliance with Libya in 1984 and his phosphate agreement with the USSR in 1978 are two useful marriages of convenience in this regard. In his speeches and interviews, King Hassan practically ignores the Soviet Union. When he does refer to it, it is in the context of identifying world communism as the threat to the West (including Morocco).[36] With the USSR, Morocco has no common enemies, only common projects.

THE REALITY OF RELATIONS

In general, the perceptions that both sides hold of their bilateral relations between Soviets and North Africans are realistic. Since perceptions and reality are mutually determining, and eventually come into balance, this means that that balance is a short-range rather than a long-range realisation. Perceptions make sustainable changes in reality, by creating particular events in bilateral relations that can be lived up to by both sides. Reality in turn makes sustainable changes in perceptions so that the parties see events and possibilities as they really are rather than opening themselves up to surprises of shortfall or overflow.

Discerning the gap between perception and reality is very difficult, all the more so since there always must be a gap if relations are to have any movement or dynamism (change or potential for change) in them. Official parties do not often express their disappointments in inter-state relations, and if they do express their hopes, they tend to be public relations icing rather than the real cake. Unofficial spokesmen are more vocal in their hopes and disappointments, but as an attempt to influence reality and official perceptions, rather than to reflect them. The greatest gaps seem to occur in the area of political support. Libya wants more active Soviet military protection, which Moscow is reluctant to extend or even to promise. Algeria would like more open Soviet support for the Polisario. Even the Soviet Union hopes for a more orthodox evolution of Maghribi societies and polities, in line with Soviet doctrine and objectives, and it revises its orthodoxy from time to time to take recalcitrant reality into account.[37] But in order to ascertain the gap, one must first ascertain the reality.

Security

Security relations between the Soviet Union and North African countries are formalised by no treaty. The closest thing to a formal relationship came in 1983 when, after a number of years of badgering by Libya, Moscow agreed in principle to a friendship and security treaty during a visit by Jallud in March 1983, following the joint US-Egyptian military exercises near the border the previous month.[38] The 'preliminary agreement' had been preceded by discussions two years earlier, also with Jallud, on coordination and support in the event of an attack on Libya.[39] However, neither has been formalised by a regular treaty of friendship such as those enjoyed by Ethiopia, Angola, Mozambique, Congo, and formerly Somalia and Egypt. When the chips were down in the US raid of April 1986, the Soviets sat on their ship offshore, much as they had done during the Libyan conflict with Egypt in 1977. Qaddafi announced his intention to join the Warsaw Pact but never received an invitation. Libya has carried out joint naval exercises with Soviet units – in November 1982, July 1983, and December 1985 – and has given the Soviets virtual basing rights for air and naval units.

It is doubtless Qaddafi's refusal to grant formal facilities, which would compromise his own view of a non-aligned status, plus his penchant for irresponsible adventures, as in Chad, Uganda, or London, that underlie Soviet reluctance to sign a friendship treaty. However, the military relationship is only recent, growing out of Qaddafi's visit to Moscow in April 1981,[40] and the escalation of US pressure in 1986 could lead to the next step of a formal security relationship. It apparently did lead to the unfreezing of a particularly large arms supply agreement, which had been in suspension in Moscow since Qaddafi's visit in 1985 and was revived by Jallud in May 1986.[41] Soviet naval units make port calls in Algeria (and in Tunisia) but there are no formal agreements or military relations. The days of Western concern over the possible Soviet use of Mers el-Kebir at Oran in Algeria (or of Bizerte in Tunisia) are well past.[42]

None the less, there are a number of indicators of military cooperation between the USSR and both Algeria and Libya. Various sources list the number of East German and Soviet military technicians and advisors in Algeria at 250 and 1000, respectively, in 1983;[43] 790 total in 1984,[44] and 1300 in 1985[45]; and in Libya at 400 and 1800, respectively, in 1983; 2800 together in 1984; and 2000 in 1985. Soviet and East German advisors reportedly assisted Libyan troops in the operation of equipment in the Chad invasion of 1981.[46] Over 3500 Algerian military personnel have trained in the Soviet Union since Algerian independence (until 1984), and over 7600 Libyans since Qaddafi's coup.[47] The political effects of such an experience are ambiguous, as usual. In Algeria, for example, some Soviet-trained officers comprise a radical 'Boumediennist' group in the army opposed to the dilution of Soviet ties, whereas others are part of the very group that looks to greater diversification under BenJedid. There is still a good deal of military coordination, with exchanges of visits by general officers between the USSR and the two Maghrib countries. It should be noted as well that Libyan military security has been organised by the East Germans, and has consequently been effective in discovering and overcoming some attempted coups. In sum, military cooperation on many fronts is a feature of Algerian-Soviet and Libyan-Soviet relations. It has been constant since the early years of independence in the first case, with perhaps a slight decline in the BenJedid 1980s, and on the rise in the second case, particularly since the beginning of the 1980s, exceeding the Algerian level.

The basis of cooperation over military 'software' – training, visits, exercises, consultation – is the use of common hardware. Both Libya and Algeria, and with much lesser quantities, Morocco and Tunisia, regard their arms acquisitions from the Soviet bloc as commercial transactions, to be paid with their oil revenues, and the Soviet Union and its allies agree, since the revenues are in hard currency. But there are obviously deeper political or alignment implications as well. Algeria, the second largest African arms purchaser in the decade ending in 1983 and the fourth largest in the Arab world, purchased nearly all its imported weapons from the Soviet Union.[48] Libya was the largest African arms purchaser in the decade and the largest Arab purchaser in the first half of the decade. By the second half, it had slipped to third (even though its absolute total had doubled). Three-quarters of Libya's purchases in the first half, and the same amount but representing barely a half of its purchases in the second half, came from the Soviet Union, with the substantial increase coming from lesser providers in the East and West blocs and the Third World.

Both countries make heavy arms investments because of the general leadership position which they see for themselves in regional politics and because of the immediate security problems on their borders. Algeria is locked in an active military rivalry with Morocco and to a less avowed extent with Libya itself, while extending its power and protection over its other, weaker neighbours. Libya is engaged in its own rivalry with Egypt and to a lesser extent Algeria, while still occupying the Aouzou Strip of northern Chad and infiltrating and pressuring its other three weaker neighbours. Yet the relations of Algeria and Libya to Soviet sources of military hardware are different, even paradoxically so.

Algeria is 90 per cent dependent on the Soviet Union for its military supplies, and it renews that dependency every seven years or so when it remodernises its military. Although there is currently much discussion of Algeria's desire to diversify its sources of arms,[49] that diversification, while real, is only symbolic. It will take a major reorientation to effect a balanced arms supply programme or to unhook Algeria from its Soviet dependency. Since the latest rounds of modernisation came in 1980–81 and again in 1986, in part as a reward to the army for its support for the new president, and since the mid-1980s have brought Algeria a serious revenue shortfall because of falling oil prices, meaningful diversification is unlikely in the near future. Algeria's armaments, while considerable for a developing country (and one not directly at war), are geared to its status as a leadership claimant in the Arab and African regions.[50]

Libya is only 50 per cent dependent on the USSR for arms, and perhaps some 60 per cent dependent when Eastern Europe is added. Libya turned to the Soviet Union for its arms supplies in 1970, but purchases started doubling annually in the years of the mid-1970s and peaked at the end of the decade. New arms agreements were made with the USSR in June 1981 at levels of over $2 billion per year (equal to the 1979 level) and then again in May 1986 at reportedly substantially higher levels.[51] Libya sought to expand its diversification in the early 1980s, as its money ran short and as the Soviets began to have second thoughts about Qaddafi's adventuresome policies. However, both reasons also came to limit other suppliers, as France, Italy, and others came to suspend their contracts and deliveries in the mid-1980s.

The fact is that Libya is extravagantly overarmed. Much of the over-supply is stocked as a collection, saved from immediate deterioration only by the dry Libyan climate but still gradually out of maintenance. Libya has more main battle tanks than all its neighbours combined; yet its army is a tenth their combined size and its population a twentieth. Other weapons furnish similar comparisons; there is simply not the manpower in the Libyan military establishment to utilise the hardware collected in the various parks. The rest of the over-supply – particularly in smaller arms – is distributed to various insurgent groups throughout the world. The Polisario itself, to cite a prominent example, is also overarmed, and has been essentially running on its stockpiles since 1984 when Libyan arms supplies ceased.

The Soviets are steadfastly silent both on the use of their arms outside of Libya and on endorsement of the causes which they advance. Yet Soviet agreements with Libya do not contain the standard restrictions on the re-export of arms or on their use outside the purchaser's territory. Arms sales under these conditions seem to be a support for good Soviet-Libyan relations rather than for specific causes and aims of Libyan policy. Libya's goals, like its arms supplies, are far more expansive than Algeria's: Libya seeks not only to defend its national territory, but also to stock up for a massive assault on Israel, to underwrite the efforts of progressive national liberation movements in the Arab and Muslim world and beyond, and to extend harassment and control over surrounding land, sea, and airspace.[52] Yet its dependency on the Soviet Union in the accomplishment of these aims – or, to put it differently, the degree of Soviet endorsement of them – is much less than in the case of Algeria and its more conventional objectives.

The cost of these security ties is unknown. Although the USSR initially offered Algeria weapons under generous terms and grants, after 1975 it tended to furnish arms on commercial terms and in exchange for hard currency.[53] Similarly, in the case of Libya, the possibility of obtaining hard currency in exchange for arms is generally considered to be a major, if not the primary, motive for the Soviet supplies.[54] Libyan debts are not reported along with those of other countries. The external debt to the USSR is sometimes estimated at $9 billion, compared with its debt to Western commercial banks of $10 billion in 1985, and how much of the Soviet debt is for military goods is less certain. Debt there is, however, and it is repaid in part by permitting Libya to export twice as much to the Eastern bloc as it imports; Libya at the beginning of the 1980s was estimated to be supplying 10 per cent of the Soviet Union's hard currency earnings.[55] One of the results of the US raids of April 1986 may have been a Soviet agreement to reschedule Libya's debt, possibly in exchange for greater control over Qaddafi's adventures.[56]

Development

Development relations with the Soviet Union, covering economic, social and technical matters, are important for Morocco as well as for Algeria and Libya. There are over 70 000 technical assistants in North Africa (1984) from the East bloc and Cuba, half of the world total. Over 1 per cent of the resident Libyan population, or 53 800 people, were East bloc technicians.[57] Although the Libyan figure is the world's largest, the Algerian figure of 10 750 is the world's third largest (after Iraq), a significant number compared to the French; in addition, there are 275 Cubans. Morocco's figure is 2325 for the same year (and Tunisia's 415). In the same year, 2375 Algerians were in higher education establishments in the Eastern bloc, the tenth highest figure in the world, on the level with Madagascar, Mozambique, Sudan, Colombia, Iraq, and India. There were half that number of Moroccans and a quarter as many Libyans as Algerians, and 30 Sahrawis.[58]

Rank orders change in regard to official development assistance (ODA) or economic aid and investment. There Morocco leads North Africa and ranks fourth in the world (after Afghanistan, India, and – barely – Iraq) in aid granted by the Soviet Union between 1954 and 1984. Compared to Morocco's $2.1 billion figure is Algeria's $1.345 billion; figures for Libya are unknown and Tunisia has received $125 million over the period. Aid to Algeria is an ongoing matter, amounting to $315 million in 1980, $50 million in 1981, $250 million in 1983, etc. whereas Morocco and Tunisia have not received Soviet ODA in the 1980s. Morocco's peak year was in 1978 when it signed the 'contract of the century', according to King Hassan II – a $2 billion aid agreement to develop a plant to produce phosphates which it would then sell to the USSR, plus $300 million to develop Morocco's fishing and fish canning facilities. In addition to the Soviet aid, Algeria has received $775 million from Eastern Europe over the three-decade period, including $250 million in 1981, and Morocco received $215 million prior to the current decade.

The Soviet Union operates its economic and technical assistance through three frameworks – individual projects, two-year plans, and bilateral commissions on economic, scientific, technical, and cultural cooperation. Algeria held the eleventh meeting of its Commission in June 1986; it generally meets annually in one capital or the other. The Libyan Commission, which also meets annually, appears to have been established by treaty in 1972. Tunisia's Commission first met in February 1986, and Morocco does not appear to have a commission.

All countries organise their bilateral cooperation through joint two-year 'plans'; however, aid figures do not seem to be announced at the time the plan is negotiated. Examples of projects of Libya include the development of high voltage power mains as the basis for an integrated national power system, construction of a metallurgical plant in Misurata, plants for processing fertilisers, magnesium, and chlorine, and protein, and a nuclear research station near Tripoli and a nuclear power plant with desalinisation facilities as well. Algeria has received Soviet assistance in building a Saharan gas pipeline, in expanding the el-Hadjar and Annaba steel mills, in building an aluminium plant at Msila, in creating the University of the Sciences at Annaba, in mineral prospecting in the Hoggar and in developing the iron ore deposits at Gara Jebilet, in establishing the National Hydrocarbons Institute at Boumerdes, and the construction of dams in the Kabylia and wells in the Aures and the Sahara.[59]

Even Tunisia has enjoyed a number of projects, such as the Jumin, Tin, Duimis, and Mellah river dams, naval training and repair for the Tunisian merchant marine, irrigation complex at Sidi al-Barak, and others. Beyond the fisheries and phosphates projects, there is no record of other examples of Soviet cooperation with Morocco in the economic field, and its biennial plans are limited to cultural and scientific cooperation. North–South economic aid and cooperation is a business filled with high hopes and many shortfalls. On this rocky road, the Soviet record does not seem any better or worse than any other developed donor. Weak technology, commercial competition, repayment rigidities, cultural frictions, intrusive or competing interests are all present, no less but probably no more than elsewhere.

In trade relations with the East bloc and the Soviet Union, as in everything else, each North African country shows a different pattern, and each peculiarity contributes to explain the general relations.[60] In the 1980s Morocco and Algeria have both shown a trade deficit with the East bloc. However, Morocco's deficit tends to be smaller and its imports and exports to the bloc a much larger percentage of its total trade than is the case with Algeria, for almost the same amount of combined imports and exports with the bloc. Thus, East bloc trade is more important for Morocco than Algeria, and both are of similar importance to the bloc – Algeria perhaps a bit more so because it is a slightly larger market for bloc goods. In regard to the USSR alone, most of Morocco's bloc trade is with the Soviet Union whereas Algeria's bloc trade is much more diversified. Also, Morocco's trade balance with the USSR is consistently in deficit, whereas Algeria's trade is more nearly in balance. Again, Morocco's and the Soviet Union's trade is more important to each other than is the case with Algeria. (Tunisia is in a similar but lesser position on all counts – a small percentage of its trade is with the bloc and the USSR, both balances are in deficit, and smaller figures are involved.)

Libya has had a positive balance in recent years in its dealings with the East bloc, with totals that tend to be slightly larger than Algeria's but that represent a smaller percentage of its total exports and imports than is the case with Morocco and almost the same percentage of its imports but a larger percentage of its exports than is the case with Algeria. Thus, Libya, while a growing customer of the bloc, is not a markedly better customer than either Morocco or Algeria. Trade is at best the consequence but certainly not the cause of their warming relations. Since arms are not included in this balance, it is surprising that the non-arms balance is not more favourable to Libya in order to cover the larger arms deficit. The other surprising element is the unimportance of Soviet-Libyan trade among all bloc trade with Libya. Libya exports nothing to the USSR and generally imports even less than does Algeria.

Politics

Political relations are a less tangible but no less important aspect of reality. Since they often involve nothing more than the delivery of words, measured against other, contingent words, it is hard to find an appropriate measure. One indicator that does express some important features of political relations is the exchange of visits.[61]

Although not too much should be read into such figures, two propositions may be asserted, of the most simple nature: the higher the level of the visit, the more important the relationship to the visitor (but not necessarily the friendlier the relationship); and the more frequent the visit, the more important the relationship to the visitor. Thus visits may be used as a rough indicator of the balance of perceived importance as well as an aspect of reality; balanced visits between two countries would indicate a shared appreciation of bilateral relations. Probably not much can be read directly into figures about interstate visits.

The results would seem to indicate that Soviet-Algerian and Soviet-Libyan relations are at about the same level of importance, and that the Soviet Union is somewhat more important to the two North African countries than the reverse. Qaddafi has travelled to Moscow nearly every year of the 1980s and Jallud every year. BenJedid has gone every five years. Brezhnev and his successors have never been to North Africa.

An interesting case is presented by Morocco, which is not in the visiting business. One Soviet political delegation was received in 1982 and 1984, and two economic delegations in 1982, in exchange for no Moroccan visits. But in 1982 and 1983, two additional Soviet delegations went to Morocco each year to visit with Moroccan loyal opposition parties, not only the communists (PPS) and socialists (USFP) but also the conservative fundamentalist Istiqlal. In all cases, party ties with the CPSU were openly discussed. On the other hand, a 'treaty' of cooperation was signed in 1984 between the CPSU and the Algerian ruling single party, the FLN, and the latter has been very active throughout the 1980s in exchanging visits with its Soviet counterpart and in conferring on party, foreign policy and other policy matters. Thus both Algeria and Morocco use their own party structures to nurture relations with the Soviet Union. (Moscow somewhat rosily reported that 'many positive changes in Tunisia political life' have occurred in the three years since the Tunisian Communist Party was legalised.[62])

PERCEPTION, REALITY, AND INFLUENCE

Each of the three North African states has its own type of bilateral relationship with the Soviet Union involving varying degrees of cooperation and consultation on various fields of activity. All three countries are strongly committed to their own ways of doing things, ways which vary considerably from the Soviets' in the case of Morocco and much less so in the cases of Algeria and Libya. Libya under attack has made efforts to show the coincidence of the two different ways which came from different sources, whereas Algeria has insisted on the separate identity of two different ways coming from the same common sources. But none of the states is a satellite of the Soviets. Algeria has a limited dependency, in military supplies, and Libya has a broader dependency, in military supplies and political support, to the point where it might be termed a Soviet client state, with all the connotations of complementarity and mutuality rather than dominance that term carries.[63]

The point is that these are *bilateral* or dyadic relationships, not a multilateral network, probably not even in the Soviet mind. They are simply neither broad enough nor reliable enough individually to be part of a centralised operation. It seems totally inaccurate to claim that 'one may speak of a multilateral system of military cooperation among progressive regimes which consists of an inner and an outer circle (including Algeria and Libya) ... In comparison, the coordination of military policies in the Third World among western powers is on a much lower level.'[64]

It has been seen that there is a rough equivalence between perception and reality in each of the three dyads and also a rough equivalence between the two parties' perceptions of the nature of the relationship. Dissonance is probably greatest in the Libyan-Soviet dyad, where the Libyans expect more out of a relationship that only they see as symmetrical and where the Soviets only expect not to know what to expect. Soviets and Moroccans have no illusions about each other, knowing that their general relationship is cordially hostile but that specific deals can be struck on the side. Algerians and Soviets have rather realistic, fulfilled expectations of their relationship based on constant positive performance in the past, although the Soviets are a bit wary about the degree of philandering that will be practiced by the new Algerian regime in search of meaningful diversification and liberalisation. Thus the efforts of Moroccans and Algerians, and of Soviets, within their two dyads, bear primarily on influencing each other on specific policy issues and, residually, on maintaining the relationship as it is. The Libyans and Soviets, on the other hand, place that second consideration first, trying to work out a mutually acceptable, stable relation, while at the same time so working on particular policy positions.

Since the means by which groups of people seek to influence each other are not infinitely variable, one may separate out two categories of methods – verbal persuasion and trade-offs. If national styles of persuasion can be epitomised, one can say that Algeria explains and consorts; Libya exhorts and consorts; and Morocco declares and debates. Beyond their regular ambassadorial contacts, Algerian and Soviet delegations visit each other on specific policy issues and seek to move each other closer to preferred positions. Similar ideological language facilitates persuasion, as do common perceptions and interests in areas such as the Mediterranean, Middle East, and South Africa. In June 1982, for example, the two countries' foreign ministers conferred on the Lebanese situation at the UN in New York, but the Algerians got little more than verbal support from the Soviets. In March 1983 Algerian envoys carried a message to Moscow coordinating policy on the Middle East. There do not appear to be any striking examples in the 1980s in which *démarches* of this type produced major changes in either country's policy.

Similarly, Libya tries to get the Soviets to see Zionism as an evil and an enemy of equal importance with imperialism ('The alliance of imperialism with Zionism is a natural thing ideologically ... Zionism is the movement of the rich, imperialist and interest-earning Israelis.

The Zionist ideology is the natural contradiction of Marxism and Jamahiri theory').[65] A well-trained Marxist would recognise the form but not the content of Qaddafi's analyses, which therefore does not always lead to the desired praxis. In 1982 Qaddafi tried to obtain Soviet involvement in the defence of Beirut by threatening a serious review of Arab relations with Moscow if action were not forthcoming, but the threats were no more influential than Algerian persuasion had been. In 1981 Qaddafi received support from Moscow for his claim that he had no territorial designs on Chad and that Libyan troops had not crossed the Chadian border, but two years later Moscow found these contentions hard to accept against continued evidence of Libyan adventures; in 1985 Moscow ridiculed Western charges that Libya had anything to do with terrorism. Presumably, these instances of persuasion were accomplished by convincing assertions of 'fact'; it is not known what facts were offered by the Soviet side in exchange.

From Morocco, the most interesting example of persuasion is Rabat's ability to keep Moscow from following its natural instincts and openly supporting the Polisario and its government in exile. Instead, as recently as 4 April 1986, the Soviet ambassador in Rabat declared that 'the USSR recognises neither the Polisario nor the SADR'.[66] Algerian-Soviet communiqués mention only the Saharan people and their self-determination, not the guerrilla organisation. The Soviet position has been bought by Morocco with fish and phosphates rather than with trade-offs in positions on other foreign policy issues. It was precisely the USSR's interest in signing a fishing treaty with Morocco to gain access to the rich waters off the Canary coast that led it to agree to recognise that coast 'as defined in internal Moroccan legislation' and thus it became the only country to recognise Morocco's Saharan claim. But beyond that exchange, the USSR appears to consider the entire relationship to be a valuable commodity and does not want to jeopardise it with a position that is less valuable to it.

Polarising is a consideration in Soviet-Libyan relations as well, introducing a final example of influence. By some reports, trade-offs were involved in determining the nature of the current bilateral relationship after the US raids. Libya wanted greater protection, in a package including defence, arms, and a treaty. The Soviet Union was unconvinced of the reliability of its would-be protégé, particularly after the Libyans had ordered fire on US ships and planes in the previous Gulf of Sirte incident. The compromise reached seems to have exchanged protection for control, with the Libyans not getting as much protection as they wanted and the Soviets not getting as much control.[67] The control would be used, not to take over Libya but to restrain it, reining in a proclivity for adventure which the Soviets see as a liability. The situation is one of countervailing attempts at influence in order to find a mutually acceptable relationship.

CONCLUSION

Can one say that the Soviet Union has chosen a pattern of non-polarised relations along the southern shore of the Mediterranean, or has such a pattern been forced on it? Could Libya become a South Yemen? Conversely, is US policy preventing the Yemenisation of Libya or encouraging it? Because human situations are often resolutely non-dichotomous, clear answers to these questions are difficult and possibly unreal. It has been seen that US policy of badgering Libya – whatever Libya's faults – is pushing Tripoli and Moscow into closer relations, but that does not necessarily mean that the same policy might not also be raising the cost of a complete takeover beyond the point of its worth to the USSR. If the cost of an internal takeover by a more reliable Soviet client leader were not high, Qaddafi's adventures might well provide the impetus for such an action, after having previously provided the impetus for closer relations.

Since the Soviets do not view the Northern African region as a region (at least publicly), the whole is only the sum of its bilateral parts. Thus Moscow enjoys the same sort of position in Morocco (and Tunisia) that the West enjoys in Libya, a position of economic relations and little else – with Algeria holding a more neutral stance in between. The USSR is probably as pleased with the Libyan relationship with the West, since the USSR cannot satisfy all Libya's economic needs, as it is with Morocco's and Tunisia's relations with the USSR, since they provide an entrée into Western turf. Given the world of recent times, Moscow has done rather well in the Maghrib and, paradoxically perhaps, in many ways which do not disadvantage the West. A shift from client to satellite relations with Libya would put that situation in jeopardy, and that might be a bigger hindrance for the Soviets than any United States policy response.

Notes

1. On Algerian foreign policy, see John Entelis, *Algeria: The Revolution Institutionalized* (Boulder, CO: Westview, 1986); Nicole Grimaud, *La politique étrangère de l'Algerie* (Paris: Karthala, 1984); Bahgat Korany, 'The Foreign Policy of Algeria', in B. Korany and Ali Dessouki (eds), *The Foreign Policies of Arab States* (Boulder, CO: Westview, 1984).
2. N. Andreyev, Moscow radio in Arabic, 17 March, 1981.
3. B. N. Ponomarev, Moscow radio, 11 October, 1984.
4. R. Craig Nation, 'Soviet Engagement in Africa: Motives, Means, and Prospects', in R. Craig Nation and Mark Kauppi (eds), *The Soviet Impact in Africa* (Lexington, MA: Lexington Books, 1984), p. 44.
5. *Pravda*, 28 March, 1981.
6. Ibid. 9 June, 1981.
7. *Izvestiia*, 25 March, 1986.
8. Ya. Ryabov, *Pravda*, 27 December, 1983.
9. On Libyan foreign policy, see I. William Zartman and A. G. Kluge 'The Foreign Policy of Libya', in B. Korany and A. Dessouki (see note 1); I. William Zartman and Aureliano Buendia (eds), *Foreign Policies of Arab States* 'La politique étrangère', in Maurice Flory et al. (eds), *La Libye nouvelle*, (Paris: CNRS, 1975).
10. See Robert Freedman, *Soviet Policy toward the Middle East*, 3rd edn (NY: Praeger, 1983), pp. 163ff.
11. Moscow radio, 19 February, 1981.
12. Tass, 30 April, 1981.
13. Ibid., 27 April, 1987.
14. A. Timoshkin, Moscow radio, 24 April, 1981.
15. Vdemya, 27 May, 1986.
16. Tass, 27 April, 1981; Robert Freedman, 'Moscow and the Middle East', *Middle East Contemporary Survey 1985* (New York: Holmes & Meier, 1986).
17. On Moroccan foreign policy, see John Damis, 'The Impact of the Saharan War' and Mark Tessler, 'Myths and Realities', in I. William Zartman (ed.), *The Political Economy of Morocco* (New York: Praeger, 1987); Damis, *The Moroccan Dimension* (Washington: National Council on US–Arab Relations, 1986); George Vedel (ed.), *Edification d'état moderne*, part IV (Paris: Albin Michel, 1986); I. William Zartman, The Role of Islam in Moroccan Foreign Policy', in Adeed Dawisha (ed.), *Islam in Foreign Policy* (London: Cambridge University Press, 1985).
18. Lawrence Rosen, *Bargaining for Reality* (Chicago: University of Chicago Press, 1984), p. 108.
19. I. Vorosheykhin, *Pravda*, 27 August, 1984.
20. See I. William Zartman, 'The Opposition as Support for the State', in Adeed Dawisha and I. William Zartman (eds), *The Durability of the Arab State* (London: Croom Helm, 1987).
21. *Pravda*, 27 August, 1984.

22. Y. Andreyev, Moscow radio, 2 March, 1981; N. Andreyev, Moscow radio, 1 March, 1984).

23. On the Saharan war, see Damis, 'Impact of the Saharan War' (see note 17); John Damis, *Conflict in Northwest Africa* (Stanford: Hoover Institute, 1983); I. William Zartman, *Ripe for Resolution: Conflict and Intervention in Africa* (New York: Oxford University Press, 1985). See also Carol Saivetz, 'Periphery and Center: The Conflict in the Western Sahara and Soviet Policy in the Middle East, paper presented to the American Association for the Advancement of Slavic Studies, Kansas City, October 1983.

24. Tass, 28 March, 1981; *Pravda*, 11 October, 1984; Tass, 28 March, 1986.

25. Zartman, *Ripe for Resolution*, pp. 28f (see note 23).

26. Moscow radio, 15 July, 1983.

27. Ibid.

28. Elizabeth Valkenier, 'Revolutionary Change in the Third World: Recent Soviet Assessments', *World Politics*, vol. 38, no. 3, April 1986, pp. 415–34; Jerry Hough, *The Struggle for the Third World: Soviet Debates and American Options* (Washington, DC: Brookings Institution, 1986).

29. 'Algeria', in *Africa Contemporary Record 1985–86* (New York: Holmes & Meier, 1986).

30. Tass, 28 March, 1986.

31. John Cooley, *Libyan Sandstorm* (New York: Holt, Rinehart & Winston, 1982), pp. 83, 245–7.

32. Voice of the Arab Homeland, 27 April, 1981.

33. JANA, 12 October, 1985.

34. *Jeune Afrique* 1339, September 3, 1986, pp. 30–5.

35. See Zartman, 'Role of Islam in Moroccan Foreign Policy'. For an insightful view of Qaddafi, see Hassan II, *Discours et interviews* (Rabat: Information Ministry, 1984), p. 177: interview with *Figaro*, 24 February, 1984.

36. See Hassan II, *The Challenge* (London: Macmillan, 1979).

37. Valkenier, 'Revolutionary Change', (see note 28).

38. Tass, 18 March, 1983; radio Moscow, 21 March, 1983.

39. Radio Moscow, 26 June, 1981; *Izvestiia*, 30 June, 1981.

40. John Wright, *Libya: A Modern History* (Baltimore, MD: Johns Hopkins University Press, 1982), p. 202.

41. Kuwait radio, 27 May, 1986; Abu Dhabi radio, 27 May, 1986.

42. Grimaud, *La politique étrangère*, pp. 114–42 (see note 1).

43. Ruth Leger Sivard, *World Military and Social Expenditures 1983* (Washington, DC: World Priorities, 1983).

44. Department of State, *Warsaw Pact Economic Aid to Non-Communist LDCs 1984* (Washington, DC: US Government Printing Office, 1986), p. 20.

45. Department of State, *Atlas of US Foreign Relations* (Washington, DC: US Government Printing Office, 1985).

46. David E. Albright, 'The Soviet Union in Africa', in Colin Legum (ed.), *Africa Contemporary Record* (New York: Africana, 1981).

47. Department of State, *Warsaw Pact Economic Aid 1984*, p. 21.
48. Arms Control and Disarmament Agency, *World Military Expenditures and Arms Transfers 1970–1979* (Washington, DC: US Government Printing Office, 1982), pp. 127ff; *World Military Expenditures 1985* (Washington, DC: US Government Printing Office, 1985), p. 131ff.
49. Entelis, *Algeria*, p. 202f (see note 1).
50. Grimaud, *La politique étrangère*, pp. 130–4 (see note 1).
51. For analysis up to 1982, see I. William Zartman, 'Arms Imports – The Libyan Experience', in *World Military Expenditures 1971–1980*, pp. 15–22 (see note 48).
52. See Zartman and Kluge, 'Foreign Policy of Libya' (see note 9); Mary-Jane Deeb, 'Qaddafi's Calculated Risks', *SAIS Review*, vol. 6, no. 2, Summer–Fall 1986, pp. 161–62.
53. Grimaud, *La politique étrangère*, p. 132 (see note 1); Alexander Bennett, 'Arms Transfers as an Instrument of Soviet Policy in the Middle East', *Middle East Journal*, vol. 39, no. 4, Autumn 1985, pp. 745–74.
54. Zartman, 'Arms Imports', p. 19 (see note 51).
55. Lisa Anderson, 'Qadhdhafi and the Kremlin', *Problems of Communism*, vol. 34, no. 5, September–October 1985, pp. 29–44, at p. 37.
56. *Al-Bayan*, 2 May, 1986.
57. Department of State, *Warsaw Pact Economic Aid 1984*, p. 16. If the 'other' in the North Africa table refers to the Polisario (camps), then the 3575 Cuban technical assistants represent from 5 per cent to 10 per cent of the population, depending on estimates.
58. Department of State, *Warsaw Pact Economic Aid 1984*, p. 17.
59. *Ekonomicheskaia Gazeta*, vol. 51, December 1983, p. 21; see Grimaud, *La politique étrangère*, pp. 134–9, for evaluation (see note 1).
60. Figures are found in IMF, *Direction of Trade Statistics Yearbook* (annual).
61. Steven J. Brams, 'The Structure of Influence Relationships', in James N. Rosenau (ed.), *International Politics and Foreign Policy*, revised edn. (New York: Free Press, 1969), pp. 583–9.
62. Radio Moscow, 9 September, 1984.
63. See Luigi Graziano (ed.), 'Political Clientelism and Comparative Perspectives', *International Political Science Review*, vol. 4, no. 4; Christopher Shoemaker and John Spanier, *Patron-Client State Relations* (New York: Praeger, 1984); Elise Pachter, 'Dissonance and Clientelism: US–Zaire Relations' (Washington, DC: Johns Hopkins, SAIS doctoral dissertation, 1987).
64. Joachim Krause, in Kauppi and Nation (eds), *The Soviet Impact*, p. 138 (see note 4).
65. Qaddafi, JANA, 12 October, 1985.
66. *Jeune Afrique*, 1336, 13 August, 1986, p. 72.
67. *La Repubblica*, 16 April, 1986.

Sub-Saharan Africa

13 The Soviet Union, The Horn, and Tropical Africa

F. Seth Singleton

INTRODUCTION

Times have changed since the 1975–79 period of Soviet intervention in Africa. The 1980s have been a period of Soviet consolidation and adjustment to the difficulties of the African situation. In Ethiopia and Angola the Soviets are committed to communist state building and protection of the Marxist regimes. Elsewhere involvement has been very cautious. The Soviets gain little from their African allies, and their commitments to Africa are difficult and costly to fulfill and often unproductive.

Africa actually consists of three separate regions: the Mediterranean littoral and the Horn, tropical Africa, and southern Africa. Only the first has any direct relevance to Soviet security, hence the establishment of naval facilities on Ethiopia's Dahlak Islands and at Aden and efforts to gain access in Madagascar and elsewhere on the Indian Ocean approaches to the Gulf. Military facilities in tropical Africa are not directly relevant and not worth the cost or risk.

In the 1980s Soviet prestige in Africa has been restored by the combination of non-intervention, support for allies in Angola and Ethiopia, and association with African positions on South Africa and other issues. Promises have been scaled back, then fulfilled.

African leaders seeking development of peasant economies tied to Western markets and trade are less inclined to see 'socialism' as a solution to their problems; nor do Africans wish to emulate an unsuccessful Soviet economy. Gorbachev has reiterated that the Soviet Union will not provide much help to Africa. Thus, the Soviet Union will be largely irrelevant to Africa's greatest needs and concerns – investment capital and rural development – for the foreseeable future.

Soviet policy thus retreats to consolidation of gains in Angola and Ethiopia and anti-American propaganda, although a South African revolution may change that. By amplifying the concerns of Africans –

333

South Africa, debt repayments, Western military threats – the Soviets successfully promote anti-American attitudes. This is a resource accumulated toward a time when Soviet power may again be sufficient for expansion.

ETHIOPIA, THE HORN, AND SUDAN

Ethiopia: Africa's First Communist Country

In September 1979, on the fifth anniversary of the Ethiopian revolution, Alexei Kosygin dedicated Lenin Square opposite Africa Hall in Addis Ababa. On the tenth anniversary, in September 1984, Politburo member Grigorii Romanov helped inaugurate the Workers Party of Ethiopia – a ruling communist party. The Ethiopian leaders seemed committed to the establishment of a communist system, even at high economic and social cost. Social Affairs Minister and Politburo member Berhanu Bayih said that the government would collectivise the entire peasantry – some 38 million people and 90 per cent of the population. Or as Chairman Mengistu had said in 1981: 'there are some who have forgotten that the sole basis for our revolutionary struggle was the ideology and politics which we follow ... who tend to neglect political and ideological issues, taking the priority we have given to economic reconstruction as a reason'.[1]

In examining Soviet relations with Ethiopia it is important to recall that national communism is not necessarily conducive to Soviet influence. Tito and Mao were communists, although their policies differed significantly from those of Moscow. Like Vietnam, Ethiopia is an ally but not a satellite. Ethiopia's culture is distinct and, like China, the country has successfully resisted foreign domination for thousands of years. Currently Soviet influence depends on the policies of Ethiopian leaders and has not resulted primarily from Soviet initiatives. Paul Henze concluded in 1983:

> Ethiopia itself is an open question. Its revolution is far from consolidated. Basic political questions are as unsolved as they were in 1975. Mengistu's capacity to maintain himself in power remains to be demonstrated. Ethiopian nationalism has been strengthened by the defeat of the Somalis and the Eritrean rebels, but this very nationalism may prove to be a serious problem for the Russians. They are going to have to continue providing not only economic aid

but increasing quantities of economic aid. The full price for Ethiopia is far from being paid.[2]

The Workers Party of Ethiopia

After five years of dallying by COPWE, the Commission to Organise the Party of the Workers of Ethiopia, the Workers Party of Ethiopia (WPE) was inaugurated in September 1984. The WPE structure is an almost exact copy of the Soviet communist party: General Secretary, Politburo, Central Committee, Secretariat, Party Congress, Central Control Commission. Branches are to be formed in workplaces and army units throughout the country. Mengistu plans to establish party schools beyond the central party school now operating in Addis Ababa.

The formalities can be misleading. The former ruling junta, the Standing Committee of the Provisional Military Advisory Council (PMAC), transformed itself into the Politburo. The PMAC was not abolished, but continues to operate in tandem with the WPE. Mengistu is both WPE General Secretary and PMAC Chairman. (Soviet sources always list the WPE first, but use both titles.) Most of the first eleven full and six candidate members of the WPE Politburo were also PMAC standing committee members. Regional administrators also have been left in place. As in most Soviet-model systems, the key institution may be the central Secretariat of the WPE.

The crucial power issue in Ethiopia concerns the relationship between party and army. The army must fight in Eritrea and Tigre and may be used to force peasants into collectives. Most of the soldiers are themselves peasants with little or no education, and Army leadership is likely to be more cautious than that of the top leaders and party officials.[3] A newly created political branch, modelled after the Soviet Main Political Administration of the Armed Forces, is responsible for ideology and loyalty. At the inaugural WPE Congress General Mesfin Gebre Kal, himself a Central Committee member, took an oath of loyalty on behalf of the army. Defence Minister and Politburo member Lieutenant General Tesfaye Gebre Kidian also mentioned the creation of the first party cells in the armed forces.[4]

The economy is managed by a Central Planning Supreme Council created in 1978, and Soviet and East German advisors have pushed centralisation and collective farms. The rapidly growing economic bureaucracy apparently is staffed largely by economic ideologues out of touch with local and peasant realities. This is both a communist problem and a more general African one: bureaucracies of secondary school and university graduates imposing unrealistic forms of 'social-ism' on peasants have existed in Guinea, Tanzania, and other countries.

Like other African 'vanguard parties', the WPE is a small, elite organisation. Soviet emphasis on 'vanguard parties' in Africa became the cornerstone of policy in the late 1970s, when the Soviets apparently believed that an increasing number of 'socialist oriented' African states could be transformed into communist ones by Soviet-Cuban-East German internal system-building. The Soviets always said that new 'vanguard parties' had to develop real roots among the people – and then found that in African conditions this was very difficult to accomplish.[5] In September 1985 the Ethiopian party had only 900 'cells' and a total membership of perhaps 15 000, although 30 000 members were claimed.[6] This represents about one of every thousand adult Ethiopians. In 1981 COPWE, the party forerunner, had a membership which consisted of 95 per cent 'teachers, officials, members of the army and other sectors of society' while workers comprised 2.9 per cent of party membership and peasants 1.2 per cent. In 1982 the percentage of workers (a flexible classification in which bureaucrats may be included) reportedly reached 21.7 per cent and peasants 3.3 per cent; the intelligentsia was now only(!) 75 per cent of total membership.[7] WPE ties to the people are obviously very weak. The army, not the party, is the only real transmission belt connecting rulers and ruled, and Ethiopia remains a military regime with a new party label. The task for Mengistu and the Soviets is to maintain control of the army, while developing party institutions.

Cadre training – preparation of the future Ethiopian elite – is especially important in this context. In 1984 Romanov mentioned that 3000 Ethiopians were training in the USSR;[8] others are in East Germany. This seems a small number given Ethiopia's total popula-tion of 42 million people and its importance in Soviet policy.

The Soviet Interpretation of Ethiopia

In spite of the enthusiasm for Ethiopia's top leadership and for the shift from army rule to that of a 'fraternal party', Soviet spokesmen are cautious when speaking of the future. Politburo member Romanov deliberately introduced scepticism and uncertainty about Ethiopia's prospects in his speech to the founding WPE Congress:

A distinguishing feature of Comrade Mengistu's report is the combination of revolutionary aspiration for the future and the consideration of the real situation ... The WPE talks honestly and openly about difficulties and unresolved problems. It rightly stresses that much effort and time are still needed to extricate the country from their clutches of a backwardness inherited from the past.

Moreover, Romanov was wary of the Ethiopian leadership:

> success in building socialism can only be achieved by a party that does not lose its bearings, or backslide ... There is no doubt that under party leadership Ethiopia's movement forward along the chosen path will be even more assured and purposeful.[9]

The party is not accepted as Marxist-Leninist, but only as 'a party guided by the ideals of Marxism-Leninism.' In relations with the Soviet Union, 'on the whole, the potential and reserves of mutual cooperation are considerable and its prospects are good'. In Soviet language, a 'potential' which is 'good' 'on the whole' means that serious problems exist.

During his visit to Moscow in November 1985 Mengistu met at length with Prime Minister Nikolai Ryzhkov to discuss economic questions, presumably the Ethiopian problem in repaying its Soviet debt and other matters concerning Soviet and CMEA economic aid. The details of the Ethiopian debt are not known, but like other Soviet allies, Ethiopia is expected to repay its loans. Since coffee exports to the West are the only major source of hard currency earnings and since prices have been low, the Ethiopians are currently having difficulties making these payments. Soviet aid during the famine of 1984 and 1985 was highly touted by the Ethiopians, although it consisted only of trucks (probably sent for military purposes) and of air transport. The real aid came from the United States and Western Europe. The economic talks in Moscow resulted in no new agreements. As usual, speeches and communiqués praised the importance of party-to-party ties and the Soviet-Ethiopian friendship treaty – and mentioned only 'the desire to further deepen their economic ties'.[10]

While in Moscow Mengistu himself acknowledged the existence of 'bitter ideological struggle' within the Ethiopian elite and said that 'the decisive transitional period of the Ethiopian revolution' is now at hand.[11] Such language has an ominous ring, reminiscent of the Stalin purges. He also announced 'preparations to proclaim The People's Democratic Republic of Ethiopia', that is, taking a communist state name. He reaffirmed the classical Leninist formula of building 'organs of people's power' – the party and secret police and political cells within the army – before undertaking economic change. This follows the policy of 'socialist orientation' in place since 1975 and is in line with Soviet efforts to convince new allies to concentrate on political control, on control of the army and bureaucracy, and incidentally, of the masses. Only when the leadership is secure against coups and rebellions should backward economies be transformed. Radical attempts to change society must wait until power is firmly consolidated; otherwise, it may be lost. As Soviet generals have said, the task of the army in this period is to repress and suppress everyone who resists, including the peasant majority.[12] The policy of control first follows the Soviets' own experience during 1917–28.

Mengistu's Moscow trip came just after President Reagan's speech at the United Nations in which he mentioned Ethiopia (along with Afghanistan, Cambodia, Angola, and Nicaragua) as a pro-Soviet regime. In response, Mengistu employed some virulent anti-American rhetoric, while Gorbachev accused the United States of taking 'societal revenge' against Soviet-linked countries. He contrasted the 'provocative military maneuvers' of Washington with Soviet proposals for an African nuclear-free zone and an Indian Ocean Zone of Peace (presumably to exclude US carrier forces and SLBMs from as much of the area as possible). Sounding another constant Soviet theme, Gorbachev contrasted claimed Soviet and Ethiopian support for the Organisation of African Unity (which Ethiopia chaired in 1984–85) with 'the imperialist policy of dividing African states'.[13]

The Soviet-Ethiopian communiqué issued at the end of Mengistu's visit claimed 'complete identity of views' on all world issues. This is stronger language and indicates a closer relationship than was evident in the May 1986 Soviet communiqué with Angola, and much closer than 1986 communiqués with Mozambique, Libya, and Algeria.

Marx against the Peasant – Again

Party and peasant, city and countryside, food production and land tenure are key issues in Ethiopia, as in all twentieth-century revolutions. Lenin knew that the revolution would be secure only when the peasants were under control; Stalin broke that resistance by force, deporting several million to concentration camps. The Ethiopian leaders seem utterly Stalinist in their policies toward the peasantry: 'We believe 100% collectivization will work and is the only way to develop the rural areas of our country.'[14]

The Ethiopians have apparently taken advantage of the famine to bring rebellious peasants into camps and either control or deport them. Those unwilling to submit become refugees dumped on impoverished neighbours in Sudan and Somalia. Whether this policy can be extended to 38 million peasants is questionable. Gorbachev congratulated the Ethiopians for surviving the famine and for moving peasants to 'new areas that are most favorable in which to live and work'.[15] The Soviet leader thus endorsed Ethiopia's resettlement schemes.

Ethiopian peasants traditionally live in scattered farmsteads and, as part of current government policy, must be relocated to consolidated villages. The 1984 development plan anticipated collectivisation of half the peasantry by 1995. In 1984 no more than two percent of the land was in cooperatives; the rest was still individually controlled.[16] The land reform of 1975 redistributed large estates to the peasants and created peasant associations. We know little about what goes on in the Ethiopian countryside, but do know that peasant smallholders are notoriously resistant to losing their land. Prices paid to peasants have been low and controlled, which has kept food production down.[17] These policies, which run counter to the movement toward a free market in much of Africa, exacerbated the famine of 1983–85.

In 1983–85 the regions of Ethiopia hardest hit by famine were Eritrea and Tigre, where most of the countryside is in rebel hands. Tigre was expected to produce only 30 per cent of its food needs in 1985–86. The 1985 national harvest of 5.5 million tons of food production was 12 per cent below normal, and in 1986 Ethiopia needed to import 1.08 million tons of food for six million hungry people. However, in summer and fall 1985 food shipped to Ethiopia piled up on the docks, and the Ethiopian army refused to use military trucks for food distribution in the north. Many who came to government camps were 'resettled' to the south, perhaps as many as 600 000 in 1985. The French *Medecins sans Frontières* claimed that 100 000 people may have died during 'resettlement'.[18]

Soviet sources are generally silent about the problems of Ethiopia's peasants, and about periodic peasant rebellions, except to denounce 'imperialism's attempts to politicize and ideologize the hunger problem ... using it against the forces of social and national liberation'.[19] Ethiopia is now treated like Afghanistan by the Soviets – i.e. by saying little about the reality of developments unfavourable to their clients.

The National Question and the Rebellions

Since 1978 the Ethiopian government has said that it will resolve the nationalities issue along Soviet lines, by allowing some autonomy and cultural independence.[20] However, this can happen only after all national territory is reconquered and resistance ends. In the Soviet view, the ongoing rebellions are caused by the United States:

> Because of the strategic location of Ethiopia reaction and international imperialism are actively opposing the revolution there and using nationalism as a means of their subversive policy. Separatist organizations ... draw generous aid in return for their waving of the flag of nationalism and serve as a tool to carry out the strategic designs of imperialism and reaction.[21]

Of the several rebellions, that in the Ogaden has been brought under control, with a large portion of the local population driven into exile in Somalia. The Western Somali Liberation Front still exists, but creates little trouble for the Ethiopian army. The Oromo areas are also largely quiet. The Eritrean People's Liberation Front (originally Marxist and Cuban-trained) and the Tigrean People's Liberation Front remain strong and troublesome. The EPLF and TPLF have sanctuary in and a supply route from Sudan; perhaps as many as 500 000 refugees fled to Sudan in 1984 and 1985, and food for Tigre enters via Sudan. The EPLF and TPLF are distinct revolutionary organisations, and disputes between them have interrupted supplies.

The national conflict in Ethiopia is not based entirely on the split between Christian and Muslim. Eritreans and Oromos and Somalis are Muslim, but Tigreans, whose language is spoken throughout the north, are Christian. Tigreans resent the continued dominance of Shoan Amharas in positions of power, a situation which has intensified since the revolution. The TPLF aims to free Ethiopia from 'Soviet lackeys', who represent only the narrow ethnic interests of the Shoans.

Before the famine the Ethiopian army had made little progress against the Eritreans, and the Tigreans were growing stronger. In 1983 Ethiopia introduced compulsory military service for all men between the ages of 18 and 30, with reserve obligations to age 50. However, Ethiopian offensives in 1983 and 1984 failed to clear the province. In March 1984 Eritreans claimed that they had routed 'thousands of Ethiopian troops' in a counter-attack.[22] Although the Soviet model of counter-insurgency relies on staying power rather than quick victory, the strength of the insurgency must have been worrisome.

Despite defections from the Ethiopian army and continuing military problems faced by the Ethiopian government, about half of the Cuban troops serving in Ethiopia since the 1978 Ogaden war were withdrawn in early 1984. Cost, estimated at some $6 million per year,[23] may be one reason for the withdrawal, for it is usual Soviet practice to require the hosts to pay for Socialist Community troops quartered in the country. Another reason may have been the decision to transfer Cuban troops to Angola, without increasing the total size of Cuba's African expeditionary forces. The 5000 Cuban soldiers remaining in Ethiopia appear to serve as a special protective force for the PMAC/Politburo leaders. They can hold an airport as a bridgehead if the Soviet Union decides to intervene against a coup – maintaining 'socialist orientation', as in Afghanistan.

A usual Soviet rule is that Soviet or other communist-bloc troops may fight foreign attackers, but not internal insurgents. Once a country becomes part of 'socialism', however, intervention is justified, as in Hungary or Czechoslovakia. The rule was broken in Afghanistan, but so far has been upheld in Ethiopia; in 1977–78 Cubans fought the Somalis, external invaders, but not the Eritreans. Whether the Soviets would consider direct intervention in Ethiopia obviously depends on circumstances. But given Gorbachev's announced priority for domestic economic reform and the experience of Afghanistan – and the scepticism of Soviet experts about the benefits of building socialism in faraway backward countries – intervention against the Ethiopian army is unlikely to be undertaken in the near future. Soviet influence, as well as the communist future of Ethiopia, depends on politics within the leadership, including the army.

Ethiopia: Regional Influence
Ethiopia is now the centre of dissident politics and a guerrilla sanctuary for groups from two neighbouring countries, Somalia and Sudan. It has also become a location for training camps for South Africa's African National Congress (ANC) and of the ANC radio – conveniently out of reach of the South African military. Ethiopia is already a multiethnic empire with pretensions to regional dominance and continental influence. Socialist Ethiopia inherits both the country's symbolic role as mentor of free Africa and the headquarters of the OAU and the UN Economic Commission for Africa. Pan African influences touch the Ethiopian leadership, and the revolution is watched by a crowd of international bureaucrats.

The official Soviet-Ethiopian line is that Ethiopia seeks 'good-neighbourliness' with all nearby countries.[24] The conditions for neighbourly relations, however, include Sudan's eliminating supplies to the Tigreans and Eritreans, and Somalia's renunciation of claims to the Ogaden. Ethiopian support for the southern Sudan rebellion and the Somali dissidents could be negotiated. For the present, Ethiopia and the Soviets take the high moral ground of advocating territorial integrity and offering *détente* while pursuing the military reconquest of the borderlands.

Somalia

When the Soviet Union switched sides in late 1977 during the Somali-Ethiopian war over the Ogaden, policy makers in Moscow hoped to bring the warring countries together under Soviet tutelage. At Aden in March 1977 Fidel Castro had personally tried to reconcile the Ethiopians, Eritreans, and Somalis. The Somalis walked out. The Soviets made no decision to reject Somalia. Convinced of the waning power of the United States, they tried to benefit from the US decision to reject those who had overthrown Haile Selassie. In November 1977 Somalia abrogated its Soviet Friendship Treaty, broke relations with Cuba, and expelled all Soviet military and civilian advisors. The Soviets left without a fuss. Soviet officers then directly crossed the border to join the Ethiopian soldiers fighting the Somali army that they had armed and trained. Cubans fought against the Somalis in the Ogaden but refused combat against the Eritreans whose leaders they had helped.

Africans reacted warily to the Soviet-Cuban intervention in Ethiopia and the betrayal of Somalia. Most African leaders sided with Ethiopia in the dispute over the Ogaden, favouring the principle of territorial integrity lest Africa become the scene of numerous secessionist and territorial wars. But Soviet behaviour in Ethiopia was typical imperialism in which a greater power took sides in a quarrel among Africans for its own advantage. Cuba's image also suffered, for Cuban troops fought as a result of a Soviet decision – as proxies, not independent allies – and they opposed those they had formerly helped. Thus two years before the Soviet invasion of Afghanistan, the Soviet and Cuban image had begun to sour in Africa.

From the experience on the Horn the Soviets gained greater understanding of the ethnic and national feelings of Africans, but never regretted their choice for the larger and regionally dominant country with its long symbolic leadership of African self-determination. Soviet facilities lost at Berbera could be rebuilt on Ethiopia's Dahlak Islands, not to mention the use of the port at Aden. The United States, for its part, gained use of the Soviet-built facilities at Berbera, but these were not very extensive. The entire 1977 affair and its aftermath illustrate the relative unimportance of particular military facilities and the extent to which local animosities dominate great power allegiances.

The increasingly unpopular Somali dictatorship of Siyaad Barre remains Soviet and socialist in form, but anti-Soviet in content. Not only is reconquest of the Ogaden out of the question, but the Ethiopians are able to invade Somali territory at will. Forays by the Ethiopian army across the border at points where the Somali north, formerly British Somaliland, might be cut from the formerly Italian south are undertaken on occasion to make the point. Addis Ababa hosts two Somali dissident groups, the more radical Democratic Front for the Salvation of Somalia and the more conservative Somali National Front. Few educated Somalis, at home or in exile, are active supporters of the regime. Some military officers and others educated in the Soviet Union retain nostalgia for the good old days of the Soviet alliance, but this has nothing to do with ideology. Rather, Somalis have resented limited US military aid. They understandably prefer their position in the mid-1970s as a strong and growing regional force, with Soviet arms, to their present (but more natural) role as a backwater.

The natural role for Somalia in Soviet (and perhaps Ethiopian) thought would be as three regions, north, south, and Ogaden, included separately in a Greater Ethiopian Federation ruled from Addis Ababa. Serious thoughts of this sort will await the end of the present rebellions in Ethiopia. The Somali dissident movements may be stockpiled to await a more propitious time.

Sudan

Sudan is a strategically located African country: it borders eight other states and the Red Sea. It is also one of the world's poorest countries, severely affected by drought and famine which affected an estimated six million people in 1985. Sudan remains on the list of countries needing emergency food (along with Angola, Mozambique, and Ethiopia) in spite of a record grain harvest of 4.6 million tons in 1985. In the rebel held countryside of the south, a million people may be hungry – the result of rebel action against food convoys to government controlled areas, as well as of government unconcern and inefficiency.

Sudan hosts an estimated five million refugees. Some three million are in rebel held areas; 75 per cent are from Ethiopia and Eritrea, the others from Uganda and Chad. In addition, Sudan cannot meet the interest payments on its $9 billion debt, resulting in a decision by the International Monetary Fund (IMF) in early 1986 to cut off further credit. Government efforts to control imports and black market currency trade have failed, as anyone who has visited the market in Khartoum will well understand.

The changes since the army coup that toppled General Nimeiri in April 1985 – anti-American agitation, the March 1986 agreement with Libya, some warming of relations with Ethiopia and the Soviet Union – are driven by the internal politics of Islamic fundamentalism. Nimeiri had made himself highly unpopular, and the country was in desperate economic straits. Nimeiri tried to forestall renewed rebellion in the non-Muslim provinces of the south by administrative reorganisation and political deals. Nevertheless, by early 1984 the rebels, successors to the An'yanya rebellion of 1959–72, controlled much of the south. Southern leaders sought control of oil revenues and an end to the uprooting of people to accommodate the Jonglei canal project. Egyptian and US connections were too close for some nationalist army officers who resented Sudan's participation in US-sponsored Bright Star exercises, while Libyan planes occasionally bombed Khartoum. Nimeiri tried to save his position by a coalition with one of the two Islamic movements, the Muslim Brotherhood. The Brotherhood's price for joining the government in September 1983 was nationwide imposition of *sharia* (Islamic law), which inflamed the smouldering rebellion in the non-Islamic south. At the same time Nimeiri imprisoned the popular leader of the rival Ansar movement, Sadiq el-Mahdi. By early 1984 Nimeiri had lost almost all sources of domestic support.

The elections of April 1986, after a year of military rule under General Siwardahad (Siwar el-Dahab), brought to power Sadiq el-Mahdi and his Umma (Islamic unity) party, political front for the Ansar. Sadiq is charismatic, British-educated, an orator, and an administrator. He is descended from *the* Mahdi who led the Islamic resistance to the British in the 1880s and who founded Ansar. The National Islamic Front, party of the Brotherhood, received 20 per cent of the vote.

The Sudan Communist Party, one of the traditional communist parties of the Arab world, emerged from underground to contest the elections. Although it was important in Sudanese politics in the 1950s and 1960s, it had been suppressed after the Nimeiri coup of 1969. Evidence of its lack of importance in Sudan today is provided by the fact that the CP won very few votes and only a few seats in the 1986 elections.[25] The Soviets take little interest in the Sudan CP, or in African or Arab communist parties generally, and show no sign of attributing prestige or devoting resources to it.

Changes in Sudan's foreign relations are of some limited benefit to the Soviets. Sudan's absence from the 1985 and 1986 Bright Star exercises helped disrupt US military planning in the Middle East. The dramatic change was Sudan's decision to normalise relations with Libya and to drop the special security arrangement with Egypt. In July 1985 Libya held out a promise to end all supplies to the southern rebellion, an issue of importance in Khartoum. On 14 March, 1986, in Tripoli, Sudan Defence Minister Mohammed signed a military cooperation agreement with Libya. Libya promised military aid and training – use of the Tupolevs which had recently bombed Khartoum to bomb the southerners! On 31 March 1986 Sudan dissolved the 1982 ten-year integration agreement with Egypt.

Such changes are common among Arab states, where integration agreements come and go quite regularly. The interesting part is that Libya, whose African policy is not linked to the Soviet Union, is now cooperating with Sudan against the southern insurgency, which is aided by Soviet client Ethiopia. All this makes perfectly good sense if one realises that in this region the primary divisions are Islamic-Christian or Arab-African, not East–West, and that the superpowers get drawn in on the principle that 'the enemy of my enemy is my friend'.

Also in March 1986 Prime Minister Sadiq told a Khartoum rally that Sudan had 'decided to put all its resources at the disposal of the Libyan people in the face of savage US aggression.'[26] In April a US diplomat was shot in Khartoum, and another anti-American rally was held. Former Vice President Omer Muhamed el-Tayeeb, once head of the secret police, was convicted of treason for his part in the airlift of Ethiopian Jews to Israel and, incidentally, for cooperation with the CIA. A Sudan military mission visited Moscow in March 1986, and Prime Minister Sadiq visited in August, although party chief Gorbachav did not meet with him.[27] Sudan has also restored diplomatic relations with Ethiopia.

None of this can be viewed as necessarily pro-Soviet or 'leftist' behaviour. Rather, it is based on a revival of Islamic nationalism, led by the army and the Ansar, with the objective of asserting Sudan's independence from Egypt, moving out of the US orbit, and trying to cope with the burning issue of the southern rebellion. As in other cases, Sudan's shift away from one superpower is not a gain for the other.

In the south the Sudan People's Liberation Movement, led by John Garang (an alumnus of Grinnell College and Iowa State University), controls the countryside. The SPLM is based on the Dinka people. Although it has tribal rivals, all oppose *sharia* law and Arab rule from Khartoum. Garang's forces, numbering perhaps 15 000, have training camps and a radio station in Ethiopia. Garang claims that his goal is a united Sudan ruled by socialist principles.[28] Nevertheless, his movement is the direct successor to the An'yanya separatist rebellion of 1959–72. SPLM rhetoric about unity and socialism may have more to do with keeping Cuban and Ethiopian backing than with a real policy decision.

The SPLM refused to participate in the April 1986 elections, and no elections were held in half of the southern districts. Garang had met with Sudanese officials in Ethiopia in March, with no results. His conditions for a cease-fire include an end to *sharia* law, the elimination of military ties with Egypt *or* Libya, and a new constitution. Sadiq and the army cannot meet these conditions, for they are faced with rising Islamic sentiment, as evidenced by the burning of a Christian church in Port Sudan.

The Soviet Union provides support to the southern rebellion indirectly, via Ethiopia, for open support would alienate the Arab countries. What would best serve Soviet purposes in Ethiopia would be to trade support for the SPLM for a Sudanese cut-off of supply and sanctuary to the Eritreans. One suspects that encouragement of Garang was undertaken as a bargaining chip for Eritrea. But the Sudanese cannot end the Eritrean rebellion any more than the Soviets or Ethiopians can change the local roots of southern Sudanese dissent.

Soviet analysis, realistic as usual, says that Nimeiri fell because he had become a personal tyrant supported only by privileged bureaucrats. His effort to co-opt 'the Islamic wave' failed. That the successor military government let communists and others out of jail is good, in the Soviet view, but the 'democratically inclined army' is not ready to 'achieve a transfer of power directly into the hands of [communist] representatives of the people's movement'. Sadiq and Umma are passed off as 'conservative' and 'representing a privileged minority'.[29]

These comments by Georgii Mirskii, leading Soviet analyst of Arab military coups, are essentially correct. Mirskii also hints at a thwarted conspiracy. He says that unspecified Radical Free Officers in the army 'see Garang's movement as a central element of the process of revolutionary transformation which for the time being awaits further development as a result of the preventative coup of the generals'. Mirskii quotes the Cuban paper *Granma* as saying that the Free Officers are 'an organic part of the Sudan national liberation movement including Garang'.[30] A Sudan takeover by military radicals, possibly Cuban connected, who accept Garang will have to wait, and may wait a very long time.

TROPICAL AFRICA

Significance in Soviet Policy

The area between the western part of the Middle East (the Maghrib, Egypt, Sudan, and the Horn) and southern Africa is referred to by the Soviets as 'tropical Africa'. Unlike the Mediterranean littoral and the Horn, it is not important to Soviet military security. The tropical African countries do not have the potential as an 'anti-imperialist' cause comparable to Namibia and South Africa; nor can they help the Soviet economy. Political turmoil in tropical Africa offers opportunities for influence, but to what end? The Soviets are consummate realists and expect that expenditures of the scarce resources of money, attention, and political capital should produce commensurate results.

Soviet experts now accept the view that Africa will remain tied to the Western economy for the foreseeable future.[31] Furthermore, the effort to create an entire African tier of Soviet-linked countries 'of socialist orientation', undertaken in the late 1970s by the CPSU International Department, has either failed or, where it succeeded as in Angola and Ethiopia, has cost so much and caused so much trouble that the benefits are questionable.[32] Given the internal demands on Soviet resources, the Soviets are not likely to make new commitments to clients in areas not of strategic importance to them.

Among Africans the great discovery of the last decade has concerned the general irrelevance of ideology for economic development – especially socialist ideology, which ignores peasants, depresses crop prices, and substitutes bureaucratic controls for market incentives. The Soviet market has simply not been important to the economies of most African countries. Even Ethiopia and Angola conduct more than 80 per cent of their trade with the West. Even if it endures, the recent improvement in Soviet economic performance will not produce for a generation the surplus over domestic needs that a policy of real aid to Africa would require. Soviet spokesmen continue to insist that Africa's economic problems are a colonial legacy, and therefore the Soviet Union and its allies cannot be expected to provide significant amounts of aid.[33]

Soviet connections are useful to African leaders almost exclusively for military or security reasons. The Soviets may supply arms. More important, they and their Cuban and East German allies can provide needed technical assistance in training and controlling the army and the bureaucracy and, thus, keep the regime in power. But the Soviets are not now eager to spare the resources for more commitments in unpredictable African circumstances. The result is a Soviet policy that is limited to encouraging anti-Americanism (primarily concerning the issue of South Africa, where it is successful) and to building long-term friendships and diplomatic connections for use in some future era when the USSR will have established itself as a truly global force.

Poverty and Soviet Influence: Six Brief Cases

Nigeria

The Soviet Union regards Nigeria as a major regional power, worthy of cultivation as are other regional capitalist powers such as India, Brazil, or Mexico. Nigeria is the only country in tropical Africa in which the Soviets maintain significant industrial aid projects. Relations have been friendly since the Soviets provided military support to the central government during the Biafran War of 1967–70; these friendly relations continue in spite of successive Nigerian governments and coups. Nigeria was the largest African trading partner of the USSR in 1981–83, although its total trade has recently been surpassed by that of Ethiopia. No evidence points to Soviet efforts to meddle in internal affairs in Nigeria. Rather, the Soviets wish to gain a long-term diplomatic foothold as part of their 1980s policy of general friendship with all of Africa. Nigeria's dominance within West Africa, its role as an oil supplier to the United States, and its leading role in pan-African diplomacy make connections welcome. Because of its importance, Nigeria is perhaps the one country of tropical Africa where the Soviets might be tempted to make a commitment to a revolutionary regime if invited to do so, in spite of the cost. However, such an evolution of Nigerian politics seems highly unlikely.

Like most other Africans, educated Nigerians reject US African policy, particularly its presumed patronage of South African apartheid, and consider the West led by the United States to be the source of many of Africa's troubles. This does not make the Soviet Union more attractive, however. Tight party dictatorship has little appeal to Nigeria's spirited politicians, and the freewheeling capitalists big and small see little to copy in the Soviet economy. Americans are potential close friends to be censured for bad behaviour. Soviets are occasionally useful, but only if kept at a distance.

Ghana

The military dictatorship of Jerry Rawlings is intensely anti-American.[34] People's Defence Committees rule the neighbourhoods and villages, and militia march in Accra's streets. The rhetoric is socialist, and in March 1986 Ghana signed a cultural agreement with Moscow for cooperation in radio, television, and publishing. Yet by early 1986 the Ghanian left was accusing Rawlings of selling out to capitalism, because Ghana signed an agreement with the IMF to help rescue its destitute economy. With an IMF loan and some investment from Europe the economy has revived. Ghana perhaps best illustrates the combination of Soviet disinterest and African economic need which prevents Soviet involvement in even highly favourable political circumstances. The Soviets in Ghana and elsewhere will concentrate on propaganda and anti-Americanism, while leaving concern for the economy to the West.

Congo

Congo adopted a policy of 'socialist orientation' before the term was invented by declaring itself a 'people's republic' in 1969. Cubans, Soviets, and Chinese had been active in Brazzaville since 1964. Brazzaville then was the coordination point for aid to the unsuccessful rebellion in eastern Zaire; in 1975–77 it was the entrepôt for Cuban-Soviet aid to the MPLA. In the 1960s and 1970s Congo experienced a half dozen coups by competing army, militia, and youth organisations and leaders. All contenders claimed to be Marxist-Leninist! When the country settled down under Denis Sassou-Nguesso (1978–) and the Congolese Labour Party, the Soviets went forward with economic and party agreements and a friendship treaty (1980). The party agreement, like others of its kind, provided for cadre training and political-military officer training and coordination of propaganda.

The friendship treaty, like those with Vietnam, Angola, Ethiopia, Mozambique, and South Yemen, included a clause (Article 10) which allows intervention by mutual consent if the regime is threatened. This made Congo a fully 'socialist-oriented' country like Angola, Ethiopia, or Mozambique, presumably on its way to eventual socialism and admission into the Soviet camp.

Congo, however, is rich by African standards and closely tied economically to the West. Its offshore oil, adjacent to Angola's Cabinda fields, is under the management of the French firm Elf Aquitane, now joined by the Italian firm AGIP and Getty Oil.[35] Per capita income is the third highest in tropical Africa. The Congolese never left the franc zone or the IMF; they were original participants in the Lomé conventions linking European trade to Africa, and in general never changed either their French cultural affiliations or their European economic ties. In the 1980s economic prosperity and the elimination of a military threat from Zaire through French mediation has made Congo much like other Francophone African countries in politics, economy, and culture in spite of formal Soviet connections. The national language is French, and TV and radio programs are packaged in France or received from neighbouring Zaire.

Uganda

The current leader of Uganda, Yoweri Museveni, started his political career in 1970 as a thoroughgoing Leninist. Sixteen years later Museveni entered Kampala with his National Resistance Army, which fought the marauding troops of former Presidents Idi Amin and Milton Obote. He announced an end to the killing, in which some half million Ugandans in the south had been killed by the northern soldiers under Amin and Obote during 1970–86. He brought moderates from the conservative Baganda tribe into his military government and encouraged peasant smallholder production. A decade and a half of chaos in Uganda, Libyan aid to Amin, the economic failure of peasant socialism in neighbouring Tanzania, and living with Ugandan villagers terrorised by government soldiers had their effect on Museveni's views. His government will be authoritarian and non-aligned, but Uganda needs fewer guns and more food. Chaos in Uganda did not produce Soviet influence; rather, it undermined the existing Soviet position.

Madagascar

After 1974 the Ratsiraka military government followed the socialist economic pattern of low food and cash crop prices paid to farmers, the restriction of imports, and state controlled trade. By 1983 the economy was kept afloat only by French subsidies. Outlying areas, including the north near the superb harbour of Diego Suarez, were close to rebellion. Under Ratsiraka Madagascar's Soviet bloc connections included arms deliveries, East German training of the security police, and an agreement which allowed Soviet and East German censorship of unfavourable information. Soviet officials alienated many Malagasy by their imperious behaviour. In 1984 a political turn toward Western Europe and the United States occurred. Clearly, the missing element in the Soviet presence and influence was the most important one –effective economic advice and aid. For this reason, Madagascar, much like Congo, has not evolved into a Soviet client, and the harbour at Diego Suarez has not become a Soviet base.

Guinea

According to the hypothesis that Soviet expansion is based on local instability and the Soviet provision of arms, Guinea should now be a Soviet ally. Soviet-trained military officers seized power in April 1984 after the death of long-time dictator Sékou Touré. Touré had already accustomed Guineans to repression and arbitrary rule. The economy was socialist, state managed, and included a Soviet-built bauxite mining complex, although Touré had been cool toward the Soviets, as he built his cult of personality.

The first acts of the Guinean military council were to announce an end to arbitrary police power and to free political prisoners. Since the coup Guinea has loosened some of the less rational extensions of state socialism and shows no sign of an interest in a Soviet alliance. The point, perhaps clearer in this case than in any other, is that African leaders, whether military or civilian, increasingly realise that too much state socialism, too much dictatorship, and too much arbitrary rule simply do not work. They do not grow food, nor increase the leaders' popularity. Guinean colonels, led by Moussa Traore, are well aware of their country's needs and of what they must do to be successful. Neither a Soviet alliance nor a replication of Soviet economic or governmental structures fits those needs.

Postscript: The French Connection

France, not the United States, is the most important Western power in Africa.[36] France manages Western economic aid to many African countries and maintains military forces in Africa to support African allies. It is also tropical Africa's largest source of weapons. While Soviet propaganda and diplomacy in Africa are directed against the United States, good bilateral relations with France are a Soviet objective. France exerts influence in Angola and Mozambique. In Guinea, Mali, Congo, Madagascar, Benin, and other places where the Soviets are present, the French are more influential than the Soviets. Because they do not wish to alienate France, the Soviets must tread lightly in Africa. French policy has been to strengthen their cultural and economic connections, while not worrying overmuch about Soviet political influence or arms shipments. Soviet anti-American propaganda is of little concern to them. French policy has succeeded in Congo, Madagascar, Guinea, Mali, and Benin – all countries of Soviet influence and presence but now tending toward the West.

CHARACTERISTICS OF SOVIET AFRICAN POLICY

Soviet Analysis of African Conditions

By the 1980s the Soviets had discovered a real Africa rather different from the one that the International Department had expected would join the 'Socialist Community'. The Soviets found ethnic politics which often used ideology as a cover, serious economic problems for which socialist solutions were unfit, ruling cliques in the capital with little or no effective contact with the often hungry and goods-starved peasant majority, strong pan-Africanist sentiment and resistance to joining any European imperialist grouping against another except for temporary tangible advantage, local conflicts with long-standing historical roots that have nothing to do with Soviet or US pretensions to world leadership.

Recent Soviet analysis is similar to that of Western and African scholars. African societies are seen as 'backward' and dominated by 'pre-capitalist' peasants who resist socialist economic organisation. Elites comprise a 'bureaucratic bourgeoisie', and national policy depends on the views and decisions of those few who hold power. The urban working class is small, disorganised, and unable to provide a social base for socialism or a communist party.[37] The army is the key instrument of social control. It is divided into a few top commanders, middle-rank officers (colonels and majors), and the 'noncoms' and soldiers. Military coups occur either when the army as a whole, led by the commanders, overthrows the regime, or when the colonels and majors stage a coup against the loyalist top commanders. In either case, while a seemingly radical military government may result, the long-term effects are likely to be unfavourable to Soviet interests. The army commanders have no class base and will backslide into nationalism and a pro-Western orientation.[38]

The only way to build communism from a military regime, as in Ethiopia, is to create a 'vanguard party' which takes over power. In the meantime one must control the army along Soviet lines, by establishing political-military cadres and by using political education among the soldiers, as well as by creating a strong security police force. Implementation of this policy takes much effort and may fail in any case. Other than the long, difficult road of creating a Leninist vanguard party with real roots among the people – a task accomplished nowhere in Africa[39] – the Soviets offer no solutions to the pressing problems of the continent. Suppression of ethnic movements, as in Ethiopia, does not change the ethnic and tribal mentality of Africans.

In the 1970s Soviet policy makers were optimistic that their guidance, combined with 'the changing world correlation of forces', could transform African regimes into communist ones. This is no longer the Soviet view. Organisation of communist parties in Africa is now seen as premature. The task of communists is to encourage the 'national-democratic revolution' – anti-Western nationalism – while working inside existing parties and governments.[40]

Two events in the late 1970s registered in Moscow the importance of ethnic and religious conflicts in Africa. The first was the failure to bridge Somali and Eritrean conflicts with Ethiopia in 1977 and 1978 through Fidel Castro's personal mediation. Subsequently the Somalis, Eritreans, and the Sudanese all adopted a Saudi-Egyptian-US orientation. The fact that the Soviets had trained the entire Somali officer corps and that the Cubans had trained Eritrean political cadres meant nothing. The second event was the Zimbabwe election of 1980, in which the Shona majority voted for Mugabe and ZANU, while the Ndebele minority supported Nkomo and ZAPU. Earlier Soviet military aid to ZAPU had no influence on the outcome.

Soviet arms transfers to Africa have been concentrated in Angola, Ethiopia, and throughout southern Africa, although other African countries now dependent on Soviet arms include Congo, Cape Verde, Guinea, Guinea-Bissau, and Mali. Mozambique falls closer to Zambia and Tanzania than to Angola in its proportion of arms from the USSR. Neither the Soviets nor the Africans expect much to come of most of these military connections. The Somali experience was painful and instructive for the Soviets. Guinea's 1984 coup, carried out by military officers trained in the Soviet Union, did not put that country into Moscow's camp. Guinea-Bissau has been moving away from its Soviet orientation since a military coup in 1980, while Congo, Madagascar, and Mozambique among the 'socialist oriented' have loosened Soviet connections in favour of stronger economic ties with Western Europe. The number of Africans trained in the Soviet Union is not a reliable guide to future orientation.[41]

Soviet Progress First: No New Poor Clients and Limited Aid

Building socialism and finding reliable allies in Africa is difficult for the Soviets. Tropical Africa is not a source of profitable trade for them and will continue to develop within the Western economic system. Soviet priorities for the use of scarce resources put the Third World low, and tropical Africa last, on the list of Soviet global priorities.

In early 1986 General Secretary Gorbachev told the 27th Party Congress that Soviet resources should be committed primarily to domestic needs. He said that the Soviet Union's own progress, not military adventurism, would determine Third World choices: 'We are watched by the huge heterogeneous world of developing nations. It is looking for its choice, and what this choice will be depends to a large extent on socialism's successes.' The single key sentence of the report recognised that Soviet world power depends on its economic base: 'In short, comrades, acceleration of the country's economic development is the key to *all* our problems; immediate and long term, economic and social, political and ideological, domestic and foreign.'[42] Gorbachev also left no doubt that the Soviet Union has a long way to go before its successes will be highly attractive to others.

Since the early 1980s economists at the Institute for the Economy of the World Socialist System and others have argued against wasting money on Third World adventures.[43] In Africa new clients in search of money or 'hard goods' need not apply; even the truly socialist-oriented have been informed that they are expected to pay for Soviet support. Only Angola and Ethiopia receive Soviet aid, although Angola pays for most of its imports from its oil revenues. This policy makes close Soviet connections unattractive to African countries.

The only new adventures which the Soviet Union might undertake in tropical Africa are those promising high military-security gains at low cost and low risk, or truly major changes in the world correlation of forces, but still at low risk. Invitations from strategically placed mini-states (e.g. Cape Verde or Mauritius) might qualify. So might revolution in Nigeria, which is unlikely. Support and sustenance of a regionally dominant ANC government of South Africa would certainly qualify. In that event, all other predictions for Africa are off.

Low Level of Attention and Concern

Third World issues received little attention in Gorbachev's 27th Party Congress report. Apart from concerns which span the Asian borders of the USSR, China, and Afghanistan, specific references to the Third World were covered in a single sentence, a mention of 'the Middle East, Central America, and Southern Africa' as areas of crisis needing attention. Attention to Africa in Party Congress reports was highest in 1976, when Brezhnev touted the Angolan victory as a model for what was to come and as proof that *détente* would accelerate, not impede, 'the changing correlation of forces'. The distribution of articles in Soviet journals such as *World Marxist Review* also show less attention to Africa, with the exception of South Africa. In the early 1980s focus shifted toward Latin America, and WMR now features European and Asian issues.[44]

Lack of public attention does not always mean lack of Soviet interest. Counter-insurgency and consolidation of communism in Angola and Ethiopia are best pursued, as in Afghanistan, outside the limelight. In southern Africa, too, the Soviets wish to downplay their involvement.

Uphold Existing Commitments in Angola and Ethiopia

Soviet prestige and credibility are now tied to the preservation and success of the MPLA in Angola and of Socialist Ethiopia. Gorbachev's policy may put new commitments last, but it puts maintaining Soviet prestige very high among its priorities. Ethiopia and Angola are treated as candidate members of the world Socialist Community. In both countries Soviets, Cubans, and East Germans are deeply engaged in the internal building of communist institutions – the ruling party, police, political control in the army, economic planning. This internal involvement separates Soviet policies of diplomatic friendship, as in India or Nigeria, from efforts to create new communist countries. Ethiopia and Angola have received a Soviet commitment of protection, and the Cuban troop presence in these (and no other African) countries is both a symbol and a guarantee of that protection. Mozambique remains a borderline case which, like the rest of southern Africa, awaits developments in South Africa. The Soviets are not deeply politically involved with, and have refused to make the commitments requested by, the Mozambicans.

Anti-Americanism

The struggle to influence hearts and minds is very important in Africa. From experience Africans have come to view the West, not the Soviet Union, as the most dangerous imperialist threat. By 1980 this perception had shifted. Soviet and Cuban interventions, particularly in Ethiopia, increased African scepticism about Soviet motives. In the 1980s the Soviets have tried to dispel African distrust by correct, friendly, pro-African behaviour. They avoid new interventions and try to pin the 'imperialist' label on the United States.

As Soviet policy has shifted from expansion to consolidation, Soviet propaganda and diplomacy avoid mention of Soviet 'might' and 'the changing correlation of forces'. Throughout Africa and at such forums as the United Nations, the Organisation of African Unity, and the Non-Aligned Movement, the Soviets describe the United States as a dangerous military imperialist and as the patron and ally of South African racism and apartheid. The Soviets hope to instill anti-American attitudes for future political advantage. On the occasion of state visits to Moscow by African leaders, Mr Gorbachev has said at various times that 'the US Administration [is] the strangler of the freedom and independence of the peoples'; that Africans must cope with 'the imperial bandit face of neocolonialist policy'; that the United States 'is bleeding them white while shedding crocodile tears over the economic difficulties of its victims'.[45] Soviet propaganda themes include South Africa, arms to UNITA, attacks on Libya, and other aspects of the 'Reagan doctrine'.

Globalist Initiatives

Finally, a new Soviet motif connects peace and disarmament with world poverty and debt. In the 27th Party Congress report Gorbachev claimed that US military spending was paid for by Third World debtors.[46] The proposed remedy is a world conference which would persuade the United States to reduce military spending and give the savings to Third World debtor countries. The Soviet Union bears no responsibility for either poverty or the arms race; both can be ended by a simple humane policy of Washington that would divert the cost of weapons into debt forgiveness.

Notes

1. Quoted in John Cohen, 'Agrarian Reform in Ethiopia', Harvard Institute for International Development, discussion paper no. 164, April 1984.
2. Paul B. Henze, *Russians and the Horn* (European-American Institute for Security Research, 1983), p. 50.
3. A large body of Soviet literature documents the tendency of African national armies to 'backslide' from radical 'revolutionary democracy' toward more conservative and anti-Soviet nationalism. Egypt, Somalia, and Sudan are cited with other countries.
4. *Krasnaia Zvezda*, 12 September, 1984. According to General Tesfaye, 'servicemen who are party members are beacons whom the rest strive to emulate'.
5. Eduardo dos Santos of Angola bluntly described the difficulties of party building in 'Avangardnaia rol' partii na nyne ishnem etape Angol'skoi revoliutsii', *Kommunist*, no. 5, March 1985, pp. 88–98. Dos Santos said that 'The majority of party organs ... in the localities ... are not capable of fulfilling their leading role' and 'the number of party officials is excessively high compared to the number of members'. These comments apply throughout Africa.
6. *Pravda*, 4 September, 1984, and *Problems of Communism*, vol. 34, no. 2, March–April 1985, p. 92. The authorities in Addis Ababa probably do not have an accurate count of party membership.
7. Olga Kapeliuk, 'Reforme agraire inachevée en Ethiopie', *Le Monde Diplomatique*, April 1984, p. 11.
8. Romanov's speech is published in *Pravda*, 9 September, 1984.
9. Ibid.
10. *Izvestiia*, 12 November, 1985.
11. *Pravda*, 3 November, 1985.
12. Soviet General Samoilenko wrote in an unpublished paper (Uppsala, 1978) that 'The internal function of armies of countries of socialist orientation is to oppress organized and non-organized resistance of those social forces which are interested in preserving pre-capitalist socioeconomic structures or in the development of capitalist relations.' Major-General Mozolev, 'Rol' armii v razvivaiushchikh stranakh', *Voenno-Istoricheskii Zhurnal*, no. 4, 1980, p. 62 has an almost identical formulation.
13. Radio Addis Ababa, 31 October, 1985.
14. Berhanu Bayih, quoted in *Africa Research Bulletin*, March 1986, p. 8113.

15.   *Pravda*, 3 November, 1985.
16.   Kapeliuk, 'Reforme agraire' (see note 7).
17.   See Cohen, 'Agrarian Reform in Ethiopia' (see note 1). Peasant Associations must sell much of their crop to the state Agricultural Marketing Corporation at fixed prices. AMC also buys the entire state farm output.
18.   *Africa Research Bulletin*, Economic Report, 28 February, 1986, p. 8079.
19.   In 'Hunger in Asian and African Nations', *World Marxist Review*, no. 2. February 1986, pp. 51–63, Ethiopian Windwassen Hailu mentions 580 000 peasants 'resettled'. He criticised the United States for attempting to use the provision of food to support the Eritrean rebels: 'A ship carrying food for famine victims set out for Ethiopia from Australia. It was demanded that the food be distributed according to the wishes of the supplier. Ethiopia replied that it would be happy to receive assistance, but if the country's sovereignty and unity were made a condition for that assistance Ethiopia did not need it. Of course it is hard to turn down food aid when people are going hungry. But firmness must be shown' (p. 59).
20.   See Berhanu Bayih in *World Marxist Review*, no. 4. April 1978, p. 62. To reconquer the borderlands first and grant some self-rule later was also Bolshevik policy in 1918–21.
21.   Radio Moscow, 7 September, 1984.
22.   *New York Times*, 17 May, 1984; *African Research Bulletin*, 1984, p. 7183.
23.   *New York Times*, 25 January, 1984, p. A2.
24.   'The Soviet Union and Socialist Ethiopia confirmed their well known position in favor of creating an atmosphere of peace and good-neighborliness in the region ... [for] inviolability of frontiers, non-interference in internal affairs, and renunciation of all territorial claims.' Soviet-Ethiopian communique, *Izvestiia*, 12 November, 1985.
25.   The Sudan CP election platform is found in *Information Bulletin: Documents of the Communist and Workers Parties*, June 1986, pp. 28–9. See also ibid., April 1986, pp. 38–9 for a pre-election statement. Both documents skirt the key issues of *sharia* law and southern autonomy.
26.   *Africa Research Bulletin*, Pravda, 19 August, 1986.
28.   Text of SPLM manifesto in *Africa Contemporary Record*, 1983–84, pp. C32–38.
29.   Georgii Mirskii, 'Konets chernoi epokha', *Aziia i Afrika Segodniia*, no. 1, January 1986, pp. 27–31.
30.   Ibid., p. 28.
31.   See Jerry Hough, *The Struggle for the Third World: Soviet Debates and American Options* (Washington, DC: Brookings Institution, 1986), particularly chs 4 and 6.
32.   Boris Ponomarev, 'The Communists and Our Day's Pressing Problems', *World Marxist Review*, no. 2, February 1985, pp. 5–12. Ponomarev, recently retired chief of the International Department, mentions 'difficulties that arose in the course of construction for a number of countries, the belated tackling of pressing problems, and

some negative phenomena'. 'The socialist oriented countries... have innumerable problems, some of which have no analog in either the past or the present.' 'Inter-state conflicts (for instance, the war between Iran and Iraq) and separatist movements have become a painful phenomenon.' Compare this 1985 view to Ponomarev's enthusiasm for 'socialist orientation' in *Kommunist*, no. 2, January 1979.

33. At a spring 1986 UNCTAD meeting the Soviets said: 'The reasons for the extremely difficult economic condition of the least developed nations lie in their colonial past, their unequal position in the system of the world capitalist economy, and in the present neo-colonial policy of the imperialist powers... The Soviet Union cannot agree in principle with the idea that the socialist countries should equally share with the industrial capitalist states the demand [for aid].' *Foreign Trade*, no. 4, April 1986, pp. 40–41.

34. In spring 1986 a ship purportedly carrying arms to Ghana, with a crew including US citizens, was seized by Brazalian authorities. The 1983 plot was later shown to be an East German forgery. See *Africa Research Bulletin*, 15 April, 1986, pp. 8009–10.

35. For information on the West African oil belt see David Underwood, *West African Oil: Will It Matter?* (Washington, DC: Center for Strategic and International Studies, Georgetown University, 1983).

36. Helen Kitchen makes this point in *US National Interests in Africa*, Washington Papers, no. 98 (Beverly Hills, CA: Sage, 1983), p. 25.

37. Soviet writers can be condescending about Africa: 'The economic, social, and cultural level of development in African countries is extremely low. That is why implanting in people's minds the goals of socialist orientation is a very complex task.' N. Gavrilov, 'The New Africa Emerging', *International Affairs* (Moscow), no. 7, July 1980, p. 37.

38. See Mozolev, 'Rol' armii v razvivaiushchikh stranakh' (see note 12); also E. Mel'nikov, 'Rol' armii v osvobodiashchikh stranakh Afriki', *Voenno-Istoricheskii zhurnal*, no. 6, June 1982, pp. 55–61.

39. Yu. Irkhin, 'Strany sotsialisticheskoi orientatsii', *Kommunist Vooruzhennikh Sil*, no. 7, April 1982, p. 88, includes data for vanguard parties as follows: MPLA (Angola): 30 000 members, some 1300 party cells, most members are government officials; FRELIMO (Mozambique): 35 000 members; PCT (Parti Congolais du Travail, Congo): 7000 members; WPE (Ethiopia): 30 000 members, mostly officials. These are 0.4, 0.3, 0.1, and 0.4 per cent of the population, respectively. See also Dos Santos, 'Avangardnaia rol' partii' (see note 4).

40. For guidance to African communists see 'For the Freedom, Independence, National Revival and Social Progress of the Peoples of Tropical and Southern Africa', a manifesto published in New Delhi in 1978 by several unnamed 'communist and workers parties' of Africa. The language includes phrases obviously translated from Russian, hence a Soviet role.

41. Based on conversations in Africa with officers and others who had been educated or trained in the USSR, it appears that training in the Soviet Union may, in fact, induce some anti-Soviet reactions. Many Africans

compare relative Soviet poverty to the affluence of the West, and resent Soviet efforts at political indoctrination.

42. Gorbachev's report in *Information Bulletin*, 27th Congress of the CPSU, September 1986, quotes on pp. 28 and 90.

43. See Thomas Zamostny, 'Moscow and the Third World: Recent Trends in Soviet Thinking', *Soviet Studies*, vol. 36, no. 2, April 1984, pp. 223–35.

44. Among indicators of lack of attention to Africa, a survey article in *Miroviia Ekonomika i Mezhdunarodnaia Otnosheniia* ('Tekushchie problemy mirovoi politiki', January 1986) listed 'regional conflicts' last among 'pressing problems', and mentioned only South Africa after Nicaragua and the Middle East. The most recent articles on Africa in the two military-political journals, *Kommunist Vooruzhennikh Sil* and *Voenno-Istoricheskii Zhurnal*, appeared in 1983. The new editor of *Aziia i Afrika Segodniia*, Grigorii Kim, is an Asian specialist.

45. Gorbachev speeches for Samora Machel of Mozambique, Chadli BenJedid of Algeria, and Eduardo dos Santos of Angola, in *Pravda*; 7 May 1986, and 1 April, 1986.

46. In the 27th Congress report: 'There is an irrefutable causal connection between the trillion-sized debt of these countries and the more than trillion-sized growth of military expenditures in the past ten years. The 200-odd billion dollars that are being annually pumped out of the developing countries and the practically equal size of the US military budget in recent years, are no coincidence.' *Information Bulletin*, September 1986, p. 23.

14 Soviet Prospects in Southern Africa: Great Opportunity or Growing Frustration?

John Seiler

INTRODUCTION

Southern Africa remains a region of potential opportunity and corresponding risk for the Soviet Union at a time when its relationships in most other parts of the world have stabilised and when its domestic economic priorities argue for an overall reduction in any commitment of money, arms, and political energy to major regional interventions.

For the Soviets, the temptation is an entire region supportive of its international diplomatic priorities, inclined toward its ideology, and amenable to its strategic and economic requirements. That tempting goal is achievable if the present pattern of regional disintegration continues unabated. South African policies encourage that prospect: destabilising military and economic intervention in the region generally and growing repression at home. The avowedly Marxist-Leninist regimes in Angola and Mozambique already require additional military aid from Moscow, and other regional governments – especially Zimbabwe, and perhaps Botswana and Zambia – may find Soviet arms necessary. In addition, as Pretoria struggles to control domestic unrest, the Soviet Union will be asked to increase its modest military support for the African National Congress (ANC) in South Africa and for the South West Africa People's Organisation (SWAPO) in Namibia.

But the risk is substantial. The South African military could easily defeat the combined armies of its neighbours. Even the outcome of a large-scale encounter between the South African Defence Force (SADF) and the Cuban contingent in Angola is not predictable; so that while the Soviets and the Cubans cannot afford a defeat of their Angolan and Mozambican clients, they remain reluctant to be drawn into battle with the SADF.

Another element in Soviet caution is their growing recognition of the intricacies of elite and ethnic politics in most regional states. The Soviets have been repeatedly frustrated in Angola, Mozambique, and Zimbabwe by misperceptions and resultant miscalculations about political dynamics. They see Angolan and Mozambican scepticism about Soviet ideology and aid and the resultant overtures to the West for aid and to socialist supporters in Western Europe and Canada for fresh ideas about economic and political development.

In addition, as Soviet analysts turn their attention to recent South African developments, they show increasing sensitivity to political complexities and to the hazards posed for either prediction or commitments. Without forsaking their allegiance to the ANC, they have shown a willingness to talk with representatives from other black groups, including Gatsha Buthelezi's *Inkatha*. The Soviet Union also has a major economic reason for avoiding confrontation with Pretoria: for some years, its diamonds and gold have been sold internationally by South African directed marketing mechanisms that effectively provide the stability of cartels for all major producers.

Since the goal of effective regional preponderance involves so much risk, the Soviet Union is more likely to adhere to its tacit policy of building on stalemates in regional conflict. Although Moscow argues publicly that it seeks peaceful resolution of these conflicts and has repeatedly offered its services to achieve Namibian independence and to end the fighting in Angola, it appreciates that, given the growing attraction of Western economic involvement in the region, its own influence depends on continued dependence for arms purchases by Angola and Mozambique (and, potentially, by Zimbabwe and other regional governments).

The South African government's growing belligerence in the region provides the greatest challenge to this tacit Soviet policy. Pretoria has always been sure that Moscow directs a pervasive international challenge to its own regional prosperity and communal survival. Since the recent imposition of Western sanctions, the South African government has become more sure of its perception and of its ability to deal effectively with this threat.

Could US policy help to constrain Soviet regional prospects? While Reagan administration policy has effectively supported South African regional goals, a reversal of that approach would not easily curb growing South African aggression. A new policy from Washington could end aid to União Nacional para a Independência Total de Angola (UNITA) and grant diplomatic recognition to Luanda, thus reducing UNITA's chances for military success and the Angolan government's need for more Soviet arms. Renewing US contributions to UN programmes for SWAPO and ANC might promote contacts with these parties, a first step toward ending the Soviet monopoly of political influence with them. But no US policy – politically feasible in domestic politics – would end the Angolan and Mozambican civil wars or get South Africa out of Namibia, until those wars have come near their conclusion or Pretoria has decided on its own to withdraw from Namibia.

Thus, the most likely prospect for regional conflict is a stalemate between the Soviets and Cubans, on one side, and the South African government, on the other. Regional black regimes and the black people of Namibia and South Africa will have little influence on this stalemated conflict but will continue to suffer its consequences. A change for the better might come for Namibia and for its neighbours, if Pretoria is forced to concentrate its security resources more fully within South Africa. As a corollary, the Soviet Union would then lose some regional influence. But pending such a retrenchment, the overall stalemate will continue, with the abiding mutual misperceptions risking escalation in regional conflict, with even more loss of lives and greater destruction of fragile socioeconomic institutions.

REGIONAL CONFLICT AND SOVIET INVOLVEMENT: CHANGING DYNAMICS

The Marxist concept of readiness for revolution has been honoured more in the breach than in the observance since the Russian Revolution. Soviet involvement in South Africa during this century reflects no exception to this pattern. During the 1920s and 1930s, the region was dealt with abstractly by Moscow's ideological chiefs. At first, South Africa in particular was conceived in terms of embryonic class conflict, but in 1928 the Sixth Comintern Congress announced blithely that the political goal for South Africa was 'a workers' and peasants' government with full, equal rights for all races, black, coloured and white'. The South African Communist Party (SACP), a small and mostly white group, was outraged at the negative impact this directive would have on its effectiveness among white workers but had no influence on the ruling.[1]

Active regional involvement began in the 1950s on two distinct fronts. Within South Africa, the SACP took an active role in ANC campaigns against the imposition of apartheid legislation by the

National Party government that had come to power in 1948. In the rest of the region, Moscow responded to initiatives by black nationalists. From the start, difficult choices had to be made or tacitly avoided among individuals and organisations with woefully inadequate information about the overall political context and with nothing more than abstract ideological principles as guidelines. As the South Africa government took increasingly effective steps to stifle the ANC and the Pan-Africanist Congress (PAC), the Soviet Union became more preoccupied with black nationalism in the Portuguese colonies of Angola and Mozambique and in the fledgling Central African Federation (CAF), where the United Kingdom was trying to weld together a white settler community (Southern Rhodesia, later Zimbabwe), with black colonies in Northern Rhodesia (Zambia), and with Nyasaland (Malawi). Nationalist fighting started in these territories in the 1960s. Appeals for Soviet aid came willy-nilly. Opportunity, or the Soviet perception of it, was the determinant factor. Analyses of ideological readiness for Marxism-Leninism were made well after the fact of commitment and even then on the bases of flimsy evidence and self-serving arguments.

This pattern of Soviet opportunism has obscured Moscow's potential for advantage in those regional states that gained their independence from the United Kingdom with minimal resistance. The protectorates of Bechuanaland, Basutoland (now Botswana, Lesotho), and Swaziland were granted independence in the 1960s in haste and with almost no infrastructure or political preparation, in order to avert South African appeals for their incorporation into the Republic as prototypical ethnic homelands. The UK mandate in Tanganyika (now Tanzania) ended much the same way. Julius Nyerere had begun a modest nationalist movement, but the UK's alacrity in conceding his leadership meant that independence came without extensive political organisation and with little discussion of the country's future. In Zambia and Malawi, black nationalism had been organised, but its focus was the Federation, not UK colonialism, so that the UK decision to grant independence to both territories outside the CAF framework left Kenneth Kaunda and Hastings Banda with no meaningful focus for political organisation or debate.

Since independence, only Tanzania has had even a semblance of public debate about development goals and tactics. For the other five countries, despite a great range in official rhetoric, these issues remain unarticulated, except within tiny groups of intelligensia at impoverished universities, by officials whose economic well-being depends on government favouritism, and by miners (especially in Zambia, but also on a modest scale in Botswana), whose income gives them elite status in poor societies. Without public debate, these economies and societies have moved fitfully from various traditional forms toward capitalist ones, stimulated by South African economic ties and (to a modest extent) by US economic aid.

The absence of discussion about societal goals in itself contributes to political instability in states whose structures of allegiance depend in large part on economic rewards rather than traditional allegiances. To compound this tendency, none of these new regimes has been hospitable to public criticism, tending to perceive its very articulation as 'radical' or even 'subversive'. In this repressive attitude, they have been encouraged by South Africa and in the 1960s by the United Kingdom and the United States. In Malawi, Banda's heavy-handed destruction of potential opposition was aided by intelligence from the CIA and British counter-intelligence on the grounds that Malawian dissidents were tied to Soviet bloc governments or the PRC. When a radical party seemed ready to take over Zanzibar, Washington (with Frank Carlucci, then a junior official, playing a pivotal role) squelched its initiative and encouraged Julius Nyerere to bring the island into union with mainland Tanganyika – opting for Nyerere's 'African Socialism' over the expressed Marxism-Leninism of the Zanzibaris.[2]

What prospects does the Soviet Union have in these states? While Tanzania, Botswana, and Swaziland have managed peaceful leadership transitions since independence, Tanzania has profound economic problems and Botswana's relatively successful agricultural development encourages large-scale livestock holdings achievable only by well-to-do officials and businessmen, with growing frustration for Tswana peasantry. Swaziland will probably remain calm because of the unusual degree of support for its monarchy.

Lesotho is far less stable. At Pretoria's suggestion, Chief Leabua Jonathan's long-lived government (itself put in place with Pretoria's help after independence to forestall an electoral victory by a popular nationalist) was deposed in 1986 by Lesotho's tiny army. Only the titular monarch and the churches have any hold on Sotho political support, so it will take gifted military rule to keep Lesotho from slumping into further instability.

Both Malawi and Zambia are nearing succession crises, with Banda and Kaunda old and in poor health, and with no preliminary development of potential successors. Malawi's economic success, especially in agriculture, makes a violent succession struggle less likely; but Zambia has endured since independence conflict between its privileged class of officials and miners and a growing impoverished peasantry. Thus, opportunities will probably occur, but in deciding whether to act on them, the Soviet Union will consider its repeated disappointments with the nationalists and subsequent governments in Angola, Mozambique, and Zimbabwe.

In the face of growing South African pressures, the regional black states have acted with striking consistency. By and large, they have limited ANC and SWAPO activities to minimise Pretoria's excuses for intervention. At the same time, rather than acquiescing in South African economic predominance, they have made substantial strides through the SADCC (Southern African Development Coordination Conference) toward the goal of ending all resort to South African rail and port facilities by 1990. None the less, in the next few years Pretoria will maintain an insurmountable economic leverage against its neighbours; for example, the 1986 order that Mozambican miners could no longer work in South Africa had a painful impact on the Mozambican economy. Of course, South Africa can be hurt by some of its own punitive steps; although surplus black labour in the Republic cushions the shock of this action, SADCC cuts in use of the South African infrastructure or in imports of South African foodstuffs and industrial products could seriously hurt Pretoria as sanctions shrink its traditional European and North American markets.

Angola

Angolan nationalists, much like their French African counterparts, were exposed in the metropole during visits or longer education stays to a vigorous, intellectual left-wing politics uncommon in the United Kingdom and Scandinavia. Of course, given Salazar's repression of all dissent, Portuguese left-wing politics tended to be abstruse and dogmatic, unrelated to calculations of opportunity or marginal advantage. None the less, it excited the small numbers of mestizos and blacks who were exposed to it and who, on their return to Luanda, nurtured it in various discussion groups.[3]

Only in 1960, when the Belgians granted a precipitous independence to the Congo, providing simultaneously a prototype for Angola and an escape route from security police arrests, did Angolan nationalists see a realisable end to their own political aspirations. Luanda political activities flourished, despite police actions, and most of the Angolan students still in Portugal fled in early 1961. Their original intention was to seek scholarships in the Soviet Union, but when the US embassy in Geneva learned of their transit an urgent cable to Washington secured President Kennedy's personal endorsement of US scholarships as a counter to bloc offers. The student programme was handled by the African-American Institute (AAI) and the money for the first batch of students came from the CIA (to AAI's chagrin, when it found out, because its ties with black Africa were threatened), because no other funds were available on such short notice. Cold War competition for influence among Angolan nationalists had begun.[4]

From its origins Angolan nationalism was repeatedly divided by personal and factional conflicts. Personal rivalry for leadership and prospective power, coming from both principled men and knaves, was common. Some conflict was class based. The mestizos were urban middle-class and intelligentsia combined. They were uninformed about life in rural Angola and often dismissive, if not outright racist, in their judgements of blacks. The few blacks who held power in the MPLA (Movimento Popular de Libertação de Angola) were suspicious of mestizo motivation. They were more sympathetic to rural interests and to the urban poor (the *poder populares*), and more determined (for this conviction they are often termed 'radical') that extensive political organisation and an armed struggle should be prerequisites for nationalist success.[5] Some conflict was ethnically based, not as a motive for conflict among nationalist leaders, but as a political device used by some of them – Jonas Savimbi most effectively among the Ovimbundu – to build a political base as a underpinning for broader leadership.[6]

Political changes in neighbouring countries also influenced conflict among Angolan nationalists. The MPLA gained during Lumumba's brief rule in Leopoldville, but a series of conservative governments there shifted support to the FNLA (Frente Nacional de Libertação de Angola). On the other hand, when the Marxist officer, Massamba-Debat, took over Congo–Brazzaville in August 1963, MPLA fortunes were strengthened.[7]

From 1961 on, these overlapping conflicts made it very difficult for prospective sponsors – whether the Soviet Union, the United States, individual African states, or the African Liberation Committee of the OAU – to decide where to give political and military support and whether to press for a merger of the two major organisations. In 1963 US diplomats in Africa recommended that some aid be given to both groups and that the United States not be perceived as choosing one or the other.[8] At first, following African equivocation about which to support, the Soviet Union took a similar approach.

The MPLA and the FNLA themselves were opportunistic in their search for foreign support. The FNLA's Holden Roberto had early success in the United States, because of his ties with the Methodist Church (whose missions in northern Angola had been attacked by Portuguese policy and military units) and support given by the American Committee on Africa.[9] MPLA leaders had already established strong ties with West European socialists (MPLA relations with the Portuguese Communist Party were strained by Moscow's tendency through the 1960s to encourage the PCP to win modest political changes from Lisbon at a time when the MPLA was increasingly committed to independence from Portugal as the only way to win genuine freedom).[10] By the time MPLA's Agostinho Neto made his first US visit in 1963, Roberto's support in the small circle interested in African nationalism was firm. Neto could not even get a hearing with Kennedy or senior officials, because Cuba had given Marxism a negative image and because behind the scenes the Kennedy administration had modified its criticism of Portuguese colonialism in order to keep military access to the Azores bases.[11]

Because no arms aid was forthcoming from Washington, Roberto turned quickly for help to the Soviet Union, Cuba, and the PRC.[12] Savimbi, after being rebuffed in a bid for FNLA leadership, gained enough support from Algeria to evoke a PRC offer of military aid. Then, when Zambia gained independence in 1965, Kaunda's tacit endorsement gave Savimbi the prospect of an escape and entry route to central Angola. With this backing, he left the FNLA and started UNITA in March 1966.[13]

By 1964 the OAU African Liberation Committee gave the bulk of its modest military support to the MPLA. The Soviets followed the OAU line from 1964.[14] But despite considerable arms and training, no effective military action took place in Angola. Instead, byzantine disputes grew in the MPLA exile communities in Algiers, Brazzaville, and Lusaka, with the resort to shootings frequent.[15] In 1972 the Soviets were disgusted enough at MPLA inactivity to end *all* military aid – resuming it only in August 1974.[16] By 1972 total Soviet aid to the MPLA came to about fifty million dollars, while US aid had gone mostly to the FNLA and came to only a few million dollars.[17]

In April 1974, when the Portuguese coup took place, none of the three Angolan nationalist organisations had proved its effectiveness.

The FNLA had little impact even in Roberto's Bakongo home-base. The MPLA had some influence in Luanda's slums, and UNITA had begun organisation among the Ovimbundu. No patron could be optimistic about prospects or enthusiastic about appeals for increased support. Indeed, when the Soviet Union resumed aid to the MPLA in August 1974, it did so as an endorsement of the PCP officers who were momentarily directing the Portuguese coup.[18] As an immediate result, by early 1975 the Soviets had sent enough arms to equip 6000 men, up from 1500. They also supplied additional weapons for untrained militants in Luanda – the *poder populares*, who played a decisive role in the MPLA rout of FNLA forces in mid-1975 and provided the rationalisation for the Portuguese withdrawal that November in favour of the MPLA.[19]

An upsurge in US aid to the FNLA in early 1975 brought a sharp increase in Soviet support for the MPLA. However, US aid had accelerated more rapidly than Soviet aid, and by October 1975 was equal to the overall Soviet level – $80 million.[20] At the end of 1975, Soviet aid increased again in response to the SADF intervention, and Cuban troop numbers went from 1500 to over 10 000 by mid-1976.[21]

In retrospect, whatever the difficulty of proving whose intervention triggered others, it is clear that none of the intervening governments –particularly the Soviet Union, the United States, and South Africa – gave any serious attention to alternative policies for Angola. Each backed a single party to a complex nationalist dispute in a large, hard-to-administer multi-ethnic nation, and in doing so each projected perceptions of international politics that had very little to do with Angola and which, taken together, imposed disastrous human and economic consequences still being played out in that increasingly shattered land.[22]

Not long after independence in 1976, without effective military or political control of the countryside, without trained cadres, and despite an uneducated rural population totally uninformed about even the rudiments of Marxism, the MPLA Central Committee decided to hold its first party congress in 1977 and at that congress to launch the MPLA as 'a party guided by Marxism-Leninism, the ideology of the proletariat'.[23] With that decision made, naivete on the MPLA side was presumably matched by that on the Soviet side, and the two governments signed a Treaty of Friendship and Cooperation in October 1976.

Some MPLA leaders warned against a premature definition of a Marxist-Leninist party as self-delusion and counter-productive to those massive organisational and educational efforts still necessary for effective political development. One critic, Nito Alves, now considered a pro-Moscow figure often critical of MPLA overtures toward the West, was particularly strenuous in his criticism of the Central Committee action. In an effort to limit his influence, he was removed from a party post, but not from the Central Committee. Later, in May 1977, Alves and Jose Van Dunem were expelled from the Central Committee and imprisoned; but on 27 May their supporters released them and began a short-lived coup attempt. Although the Soviets probably knew in advance of the Alves coup, they did not warn Neto until 5 June when Neto forces had clearly reestablished control. The Cubans, on the other hand, may not have known of the impending coup, but did provide crucial military support to Neto as soon as the coup attempt began.[24] In any case, Luanda demanded the recall of both the Soviet and Cuban ambassadors.[25]

The Alves coup was the first test for Soviet involvement in Angola after independence. The Soviets failed that test and kept their pivotal role afterward in large part because the MPLA had no feasible alternative for large-scale military aid. Since a peak in good relations in late 1975 and during 1976, it seems evident that the Angolan government has grown increasingly disgruntled at the Soviet presence; indeed, the growth in that presence has contributed to Luanda's negative appraisals.

Of course, each succeeding SADF raid against SWAPO bases in Angola since the first one in 1978 has resulted in Angolan requests for more arms from the Soviet Union, but the Soviets have never been generous in their supply. To the contrary, until recently, Soviet terms of sale were harsh: hard currency and short-term repayments. Total arms purchases have come to $1–3 billion; the Angolan government has had to divert half of its Cabindan oil income to pay for Soviet arms and for Cuban troop maintenance.[26]

The Angolan military has been frustrated by the poor quality of Soviet arms and the inadequacy of Soviet help in devising maintenance and training programmes.[27] Finally, and most disturbing to Luanda, Soviet advisors have repeatedly constrained the Angolans from attacks on UNITA, presumably from a concern about an SADF reaction, by withholding, until recently, SAM-8s and other components of a sophisticated air defence system and by not permitting Angolan Migs to attack UNITA trucks or its Jamba headquarters.[28]

Faced by a growing UNITA challenge, the Angolan government has been increasingly torn. On the one hand, its need for arms can be met only by the Soviet Union; on the other, economic aid and investment are far more likely from Western Europe and North America. In late 1981, when Neto made his first overtures to the West, pro-Moscow members of the MPLA Central Committee resisted strenuously. To strengthen their position, Moscow made a pro forma pledge of $2 billion of economic aid over ten years (there are no signs of its delivery, even in part), warned Luanda about the risks of economic ties with the West, and sent officials to Luanda to reiterate its concern. Aside from concern that arms supplies might not be available, even for sale, the Angolan government could not have taken the Soviet action very seriously: only 2 per cent of its exports and 7 per cent of its imports involved it with CMEA members. The United States was Angola's largest trade partner, despite its prolonged refusal to grant Luanda diplomatic recognition.[29]

Angolan economic moves toward the West were slowed in 1983 when UNITA won a major victory at Cangamba and Luanda was impelled to buy more arms from the Soviet Union. The battle was in August; major arms shipments arrived as early as September.[30] In a coordinated response, the Cubans increased their troop levels to 35 000 – a new peak total – shifting at least 5000 men from Ethiopia.[31]

In 1984, encouraged by Kaunda and the Reagan administration, the Angolan government took a bold political risk in striking an agreement with the South African government. In return for a staged withdrawal of SADF forces that had maintained *de facto* bases in southern Angola, Luanda promised to keep SWAPO north of a buffer zone in that same area. In an extraordinary step, joint South African-Angolan military patrols began to monitor the SWAPO removal and, on several occasions, Angolan soldiers fired on SWAPO guerrillas. For Luanda, the intangible cost of turning against SWAPO must have been great; but in taking this step, the Angolan government must have hoped that SADF withdrawals would lead in turn to an end of South African support for UNITA, with some hope for a return to stability in southern and central Angola. In fact, the agreement broke down well before the end of 1984, with Pretoria arguing that the continued presence of SWAPO in small numbers in southern Angola necessitated the return of their own troops.[32]

The Soviets knew nothing of this short-lived agreement until it was announced in February 1984. They were dismayed that Angola could take such a basic initiative without informing them. They could hardly have been pleased by the weakening of SWAPO and the tacit acknowledgement of South African regional policy. None the less, to put the best face forward on a *fait accompli*, the Soviet government reluctantly acknowledged the agreement while taking every opportunity to remind Luanda that neither Pretoria nor Washington could be trusted.[33]

Momentarily heartened by the failure of the Angolan-South African agreement, the Soviet Union must have been disturbed by the SADF's willingness to take greater risks in its 1985 campaign. In the September battle by UNITA for Mavinga, 2000 UNITA troops were airlifted 500 miles by C130s to minimise the risk of Angolan ground attack and to maximise surprise – although, at the same time, the SADF was cautious enough not to use its fighter-bombers as protection for the C130s, in fear of generating the first Angolan resort to their Soviet Migs and their first use of their strengthened air defences.[34]

Despite its deepening dependence on Soviet arms, the Angolan emphasis on pragmatic economic policies grew markedly during 1985. Even before its second party congress in December 1985, the government had decided (but not announced) its willingness to apply for IMF and IBRD membership, a prospect that made Western banks more receptive to easing repayment on outstanding loans at a time when oil revenues were dropping sharply.[35]

At the party congress the leadership called for 'realism' in economic policies and stressed the need for grassroots participation in the shaping and implementation of party policies. Some of the mestizo leadership uncomfortable with economic pragmatism were replaced by blacks more sympathetic to President dos Santos's initiatives.[36] Given the absence of effective party organisation and policy at independence, and the dampening impact of the war with UNITA on party activities since, the decisions of the 1985 party congress might best be seen not as a reshaping of an orthodox Marxist-Leninist party but as first steps toward its effective political and economic organisation – something that Alves had counselled in 1977, although he remained opposed to strengthening economic ties with the West.[37]

The February 1986 decision by the Reagan administration to give 'covert' aid to UNITA slowed Angolan economic pragmatism and recharged Angolan and Soviet concern about the level of fighting in the country. In a series of meetings culminating in dos Santos's state visit to Moscow in May 1986, and in various published articles, the Soviets attributed the US initiative to a resurgence of 'neo-globalism'.[38] General Secretary Gorbachev pledged to dos Santos that the Soviet Union would fulfill its commitments under the 1976 Treaty of Friendship and Cooperation. In a joint statement made at the end of the dos Santos visit, the two governments referred to the 'explosive situation... in which racists in the US administration [are]... conniving at attempts by the Pretoria racists to destabilize the "front-line" states and ... encouraging the undeclared war that the racists have unleashed against the People's Republic of Angola and the People's Republic of Mozambique'.[39] Although nothing was said specifically about increases in Soviet arms or Cuban troops, in June 1986 the Soviets warned that SADF air raids on Soviet and Cuban vessels in the Angolan port of Namibe were 'acts of international terrorism ... [that] cannot go unpunished'.[40]

During mid-1986 US aid began to flow to UNITA via Zairean channels. As UNITA activity increased in northern Angola and near Cabinda, the Angolan army increased its activities and hinted that it might strike at UNITA bases and supply lines within Zaire.[41] At the same time the numbers of Cuban troops assigned to defend the Cabindan perimeter were increased substantially. In mid-1987 another Angolan attack on UNITA's Mavinga base was repelled with substantial casualties.[42]

With these spurts of escalation, however modest each one is, Angola becomes less governable, and the Angolan government becomes less free to reduce its military dependency on the Soviets and the Cubans. The human costs also grow. Even UNITA, with its longstanding commitment to sustaining political support among the Ovimbundu, has begun mining peasant fields and roads around its bases to protect against government attack – but with mounting casualties among its own civilian supporters.[43]

The economic incentives point Luanda westward. There is little Soviet economic activity, but in those economic sectors with some Soviet involvement relations have been awkward. The Soviet approach to Angolan fisheries is one example – nothing short of blatant plundering; so that even a recent Soviet agreement to sell more of the fish it catches within Angola has not reversed Luanda's judgement that other arrangements would be preferable. As fishing contracts between the two countries expire, they are not renewed; instead, new contracts have been made with Spanish companies.[44]

Although Luanda has not yet applied for IMF and IBRD membership, the Angolans (like the Mozambicans) recently accepted the Berlin clause in the Lomé Convention – to the DDR's chagrin – and at this late date, a belated invitation to join the CMEA would have little chance of wooing them away from the West.[45]

Even if the Angolans made a major shift in economic orientation, as the second party congress suggests they are determined to do, reducing the impact of Soviet, Cuban, and other bloc advisors in the military and in other government departments would be far more difficult. Given Soviet ineptness in inter-racial relations, and the accumulating frustrations for the Angolans of the military and economic connections, Luanda might make an effort toward this end – if the drain of the war is reduced and the need for arms also drops, and if the US government shifts its policy to one that underpins the extensive involvement of US companies and banks by offering diplomatic recognition and a broader acknowledgement of the Angolan (and black African) view of regional destabilisation by Pretoria.

As for the Soviets, they must understand by now the fragility of their influence on Angola. Only with a continued regional stalemate will Luanda need more Soviet arms, but with that stalemate goes the growing risk of potential victory by UNITA over the Angolan forces. That defeat cannot be accepted by the Soviets, partly because of their ideological commitment to Angola and partly because no African government, whatever its ideological position, would be comfortable with the implications of having UNITA, backed by white South Africa, in charge in Luanda. To avert such a defeat might require the commitment to battle of Cuban troops, something that neither the Soviets nor the Cubans are eager to do.

Recent Soviet doctrine argues that Western capitalism may have an inevitable role in the development of new states, even those professedly socialist.[46] But there is not yet a Soviet doctrine to rationalise a military defeat and political counter-revolution in a state to which Moscow has committed itself so extensively. The Soviet Union may soon have hard choices to make about Angola, even though it will do whatever it can to avert such choices; in the meantime, every other aspect of Moscow's policy and behaviour in Southern Africa is affected by its Angolan quandary.

Mozambique and Zimbabwe

Mozambique and Zimbabwe demand more and more to be considered in relationship to each other as their political, military, and economic prospects become increasingly intertwined. The strongest sign of the growing ties is the presence of 12 000 Zimbabwean troops stationed along the Beira corridor of Mozambique since the end of 1986 to serve the security interests of both countries. They represent a rare instance among African governments of military cooperation across shared borders. (It was far less risky to their own internal security in the 1960s when Nigeria and other West African states sent contingents to the Congo under the UN aegis.)

Because these Zimbabwean troops are well-trained by UK advisors, they cannot be ignored. On one side, the MNR (Moçambique Resistencia Nacional) and the SADF must take them into account when planning Mozambican operations. The United Kingdom and the United States must consider whether to add to their present modest support for these contingents in order to stabilise the Mozambican government and reduce MNR prospects. The Soviet Union must consider how to aid them – since it has the same security goals for Mozambique that the United Kingdom and the United States now tentatively support. For the Soviets, military aid to Zimbabwe's more competent army would be more effective than the same level of aid to FRELIMO (Frente de Libertação de Moçambique); but, despite Robert Mugabe's strenuous efforts during 1986 and 1987 to secure the purchase of a Mig-29 squadron, the negotiations remain unresolved, because the Soviet Union and some senior Zimbabwean military leaders agree that such a major commitment would provoke a destructive SADF reaction.[47] Finally, for other regional black regimes, Mozambican-Zimbabwean military cooperation suggests that their own modest contributions (after several decades of ineffective rhetoric in favour of it) might actually work to deter South African regional aggression.

The ties between Mozambique and Zimbabwe go back well before their independence. Even while FRELIMO was still fighting the Portuguese, Mugabe's small cadre of Zimbabwean African National Union (ZANU) guerrillas was given access to FRELIMO camps in southern Tanzania and northern Mozambique. (ZANU relations with Kaunda's Zambia were far less stable, and Kaunda's support for Joshua Nkomo's Zimbabwean African People's Union (ZAPU) has not been forgotten by Mugabe.[48]) Once Mozambique gained independence in 1975, it closed its border with white-ruled Rhodesia and denied Salisbury access to Beira and Ncala harbours at considerable economic cost and some military risk.[49] Mozambican bases were made available to ZANU for training and support, as it launched major raids into northeastern Rhodesia and quickly built its primary base of political support among the Shona in that region.

Although FRELIMO repeatedly sought reconciliation between ZANU and ZAPU, it grew frustrated at Nkomo's unwillingness to commit his men to battle. At first, Samora Machel asked the Soviet Union to give arms to ZANU, in addition to its continuing support for ZAPU. When that request was spurned, Machel gave ZANU arms from his own stocks and from Tanzanian sources.[50] Later, Machel played a crucial role in getting Mugabe to take part in the 1979 Lancaster House constitutional talks that led to ZANU's electoral victory and to Zimbabwean independence in 1980.[51]

In turn, small numbers of Zimbabwean troops aided FRELIMO in operations against the MNR as early as 1981. By the end of 1986, that number had grown to 12 000, entrenched along the entire length of the Beira railroad-pipeline corridor from the Zimbabwean border to the sea.[52]

Most significantly, given the close personal ties between Machel and Mugabe, it is certain that Machel's mounting disappointment with Soviet economic and military aid was conveyed to Mugabe and probably was a crucial factor in shaping the guarded Zimbabwean attitude toward Soviet involvement in that country.[53]

Mozambique

The pattern of Soviet relations with Mozambique was impelled by factors considerably different from those at work in Angola, offering Moscow less opportunity at the start, but with similarly discouraging results over time.

At its origins in 1962, FRELIMO brought together the significant embryonic nationalist groups in Mozambique under the strong leadership of Eduardo Mondlane, thus providing a degree of unity never achieved in Angola.[54] Mondlane, US-educated, was eclectic in his ideological orientation and turned primarily to the People's Republic of China for ideas about political organisation during guerrilla warfare. More practically, the Chinese provided training and arms for FRELIMO.[55] Only toward the end of 1974, FRELIMO turned to the Soviet Union for heavy armaments not available from the Chinese, but not with any accompanying ideological shift, although Mondlane was disappointed at the PRC support for the FNLA against the MPLA, FRELIMO's sister movement.[56]

At independence in November 1975, FRELIMO began with a foundation of rural support in northern and central Mozambique.[57] Raids by Rhodesian-backed MNR groups so disrupted these areas that in 1977 FRELIMO decided to re-orient party organisation from a Chinese-model emphasis on peasant participation to central party control. This understandable, if misguided, practical reaction was formalised that same year at the third party congress by the announcement that FRELIMO had become a Marxist-Leninist party despite the total absence of the customary prerequisites. In the next several years, notably unsuccessful efforts were made to implement centralised agricultural and industrial policies.[58]

After Zimbabwean independence in 1980, the MNR campaign took a sharp upturn, as its white Rhodesian and Portuguese patrons moved to South Africa and gained support from SADF elements. In time, the SADF took control of the venture.[59] The SADF raid on alleged ANC facilities in a Maputo suburb in January 1981 marked another upturn in the fighting. Pretoria threatened further reprisals unless Mozambique ended ANC raids from its territory.[60] FRELIMO turned to the Soviets for increased aid. At that time, there were 500 bloc and 1000 Cuban advisors in the country, with DDR advisors running the security police.[61] The Mozambicans could reasonably hope for help, even if they had to pay for it on the demanding terms set for previous arms purchases. But the Soviets provided little beyond the empty consolation of public threats of reprisal against further SADF attacks, a hint of Cuban troop relocation from Angola, and several visits to Maputo by senior military officials. In fact, Soviet arms sales in 1982 fell below the 1980–81 level and stayed at this lower level through 1983.[62]

In the meantime, the scope of MNR activities continued to grow. SADF support became more evident.[63] More extensive raids added to the impact of a prolonged nationwide drought; the agricultural economy was crippled. Mozambique made a final effort for Soviet economic aid. It requested full membership in the CMEA, and may have had DDR support for its application, but the Soviet Union rejected it, suggesting publicly that a minimum level of political readiness and domestic effort were prerequisites lacking in Mozambique.[64] Thoroughly frustrated, Machel started cautious overtures to the West. In 1982 he made contacts with Portuguese businessmen and officials, accepted the Berlin clause as a precondition for economic links with the FRG, began negotiations with the EEC toward participation in the Lomé Convention, and announced an agreement with Portugal for the training of FRELIMO troops.[65]

At FRELIMO's fourth party congress in April 1983, the rethinking of economic policy was made formal by a number of policy changes, whose essence was a shift from large-scale ventures to more modest ones and from central control to the introduction of market incentives.[66] Further steps were taken in 1984 to encourage foreign investment; in September 1984 Mozambique joined the IMF and became eligible for IBRD membership.[67]

From Machel's perspective, political-security problems needed resolution to secure these economic initiatives. He first hinted at them in 1982 and then in 1983 began the extended negotiations with South Africa that led to the March 1984 signing of the Nkomati Accord.[68] The Soviets may have had private warnings of the impending agreement, although the mixed nature of their first public reactions suggests some surprise – these ranged from sympathetic appreciation of Mozambique's plight to scepticism about South African and US motives to defensiveness about their own economic aid to Mozambique.[69] During 1984 they made some effort to demonstrate continued support, but the steps taken were modest and even ironic: an increased barter of consumer goods for Mozambican agricultural products (preserving Mozambique's scarce foreign currency reserves); and a one-time donation of fish, presumably stock from the massive despoliation by Soviet ships working Mozambican waters.[70]

Since Nkomati, Mozambique's security and economic circumstances have worsened rather than improved. After an abortive attempt by South African Foreign Minister R. F. Botha to mediate between FRELIMO and the MNR, SADF support for MNR was expanded in a substantial and blatant fashion.[71] Then, in October 1986 President Machel and a number of senior advisors were killed in a plane crash returning from Zambia to Maputo. Machel's successor, former foreign minister Joaquim Chissano, has pledged continuation of FRELIMO support for sanctions against South Africa and the struggle against the MNR, but the expanded MNR raids have apparently brought a renewal of the widespread starvation common in the late 1970s.[72] The security of the Beira corridor is the key requirement for Mozambique. If the Zimbabwean troops can reduce MNR effectiveness, the SADCC plan to end regional dependence on South African railroads and ports by mid-1989 might succeed.[73] Meanwhile, Mozambique had no choice but to renew the Nkomati Agreement in August 1987.[74]

For the Mozambican government disappointment with Soviet support is evident. Arms were never given. They had to be purchased, under difficult repayment terms; and, unlike Angola, Mozambique had no major export income from which to get the required currency. Post-sales maintenance was inadequate. Soviet training was often poor and irrelevant to the unconventional warfare demands of

Mozambique. Soviet barter arrangements do conserve precious foreign exchange reserves but make any change in trade patterns very difficult. Up to 85 per cent of Mozambican fish supplies have been taken by Soviet vessels.[75] In addition, as early as 1980 FRELIMO became distrustful of Soviet advisors, who seemed desirous of taking control of Mozambican government agencies, and of Soviet ideology, which appeared rigid and not applicable to Mozambican development problems.[76] Most basically, FRELIMO understands now that the Soviets will not risk a confrontation with South Africa either by shifting Cuban troops to Mozambique or by substantially increasing the level of Soviet arms sales.

From the Soviets' perspective, their present commitment and mixed influence are the most they can hope for. A larger economic commitment cannot be justified, given Soviet domestic priorities. Mozambique cannot afford to buy more arms, although Moscow would be willing to sell arms to Zimbabwe for use in Mozambique. The Soviet Union probably appreciates, although it is unlikely to publicly acknowledge, that increased Western economic and military aid to Mozambique and Zimbabwe serves its interest in the preservation of the FRELIMO regime. As long as apartheid survives in South Africa and as long as the SADF carries out raids in the region, the Soviet Union will remain a useful political ally for Mozambique. In return, Mozambique need do little more than give general support to Moscow's broader international interests. Aside from a 1984 vote in the UN General Assembly against the Soviet position on Kampuchea, Mozambique shows no signs of shifting from this general level of support.[77]

Zimbabwe

Soviet relations with Zimbabwe have not recovered from Moscow's inept premature commitment to ZAPU during the Zimbabwean war for independence. As a first result, only a low-level Politburo member was permitted to attend independence celebrations, and it was some months before a Soviet embassy began operations in Harare.[78]

Since independence, the Soviets have won no noticeable advantage with Mugabe, despite his growing bitterness about Reagan administration regional policy and the cancellation of US economic aid in 1986 after a Zimbabwean cabinet member criticised US policy at the US embassy's Fourth of July reception attended by former president Jimmy Carter.[79] When Mugabe needed assistance in military training to put down unrest in Matabeleland instigated by former ZAPU guerrillas, he turned first to the North Koreans and then (when his troops committed numerous atrocities) to the United Kingdom, which now provides training for the entire Zimbabwean army.[80]

In the longer run, Zimbabwean receptivity to increased Soviet ties rests on an intermingling of its diverse elite values and immediate needs. ZANU has a far larger base of university educated people than either the MPLA or FRELIMO: most were educated in Western Europe and in the United States, a smaller number in the Soviet bloc, and the smallest proportion in pre-independent Rhodesia. Despite this range in educational experience, most began schooling in Rhodesian church schools with parallel encounters with racism and humanism – the common paradox of missionary education in black Africa. Mugabe and a few other senior leaders spent long years in detention, during which time they completed university degrees by correspondence and devoted much attention to the application of Marxist principles to Zimbabwean circumstances. Those younger, usually less educated, Zimbabweans who actually fought as guerillas bring still another perspective to bear. They hold firm commitments to rural development and tend to be sceptical about those Zimbabweans who did not fight and who have urban backgrounds and middle-class pretensions. They are impatient with the pace of the movement toward a single-party regime and with the continued economic primacy of white farmers and private enterprise. They are 'radical' about the pace of change, but, lacking coherent ideological backgrounds, are not necessarily likely to push ZANU toward closer ties with the Soviet Union. In any case, for the foreseeable future, Mugabe's austere personal example and resourceful control of ZANU, the military, and the government have kept these potentially divisive perspectives under control.[81]

Two circumstances might break this stability. The first would be a revival of Matabeleland unrest, always a temptation to Pretoria (the Fourth of July speech was prompted by Zimbabwean suspicion that the United States was aiding Pretoria in encouraging Ndebele dissidents). If put down harshly, with resultant social unrest and economic difficulties throughout Matabeleland, hard-line ZANU elements might push for greater power.[82] The second would be a series of military defeats for Zimbabwean troops in Mozambique. In either instance, Mugabe might want additional military aid. As things stand, he would turn first to the United Kingdom or even to the United States before he would ask the Soviet Union for aid.

SWAPO

Soviet relations with SWAPO are circumscribed by the nature of SWAPO's war against South African control of Namibia. Never a large-scale operation, SWAPO activities have diminished considerably since their peak in the late 1970s. Now, often no more than once each year, SWAPO contingents of 300–800 men cross into northern Namibia from Angola. They are monitored closely by SADF planes and trackers. Usually the largest number are turned back to Angola after an initial skirmish; a few are killed or captured. A modest number (in 1983 it was some 50 of an original 800) make their way to Ovambo or Kavango rural hamlets where they hide their weapons and stay until persuaded that SADF sweeps have ended. Dependent on the goodwill of the hamlet's residents for shelter, food, and their lives, they seldom engage in active political education. From their retreats, they sometimes move out singly or in groups of two or at most three to lay mines on roads or at electric pylons. (In 1984 they left a limpet mine at a gas station which inadvertently killed two Americans assigned to the US Liaison Office in Windhoek.) Less than a handful of times SWAPO has fired hand-launched rockets at SADF bases with no damage or injury. In a few instances in the 1970s, small groups of guerrillas penetrated southward from the operational area into the vast, open white farms of north-central Namibia. After surprise attacks on one or two adjoining farms, with some white deaths, they were quickly tracked down and killed, captured, or scattered back toward the north. Only two or three times since the mid-1970s has SWAPO placed mines in south-central Namibian towns – twice in the capital, Windhoek, and once in Swakopmund.[83]

Thus, SWAPO's military impact has been negligible. Despite this, its prospects for eventual victory have grown. Contrary to the SADF conviction that its civil administration in northern Namibia is 'winning hearts and minds', tacit support for SWAPO is widespread among Namibian blacks who feel South African racism at work in the tightening security measures imposed on the territory and who are painfully aware of the incompetence and corruption endemic among the black administrative officials appointed by Pretoria.[84]

For the Soviet Union, its present modest level of military training and arms (given, not sold) provides a substantial return in SWAPO goodwill. Because the stock of educated blacks left northern Namibia for Angola and Zambia in 1974, recent recruits into SWAPO have been relatively uneducated. Their ability to proceed beyond a very basic military training to either military leadership training or ideological education is limited. Perhaps in recognition of the limited utility of actual combat, educated Namibians tend to remain in Lusaka, where they work at or around the Namibia Institute, or a few represent SWAPO in the Soviet bloc, Western Europe, and the United States.[85]

No marked change in the near-dormant level of Namibian warfare is imminent. If a change does come, it will not be from a SWAPO military initiative, but because Pretoria finds itself under so much pressure at home that it needs to withdraw increasing numbers of its permanent force and national service (short-term active duty) soldiers and its security police contingents. If that happens, Pretoria has trained replacement forces: some 7000–8000 mostly black troops in what is called the South West Africa Territorial Force (SWATF) and a small number of SWA security police. Both contingents depend on the white South African officers who would remain. With modest SADF assistance – technicians and a few pilots – the present very small air defence and air force could be maintained. SWAPO incursions from Angola could be monitored and contained with almost as much efficiency as now – although the sheer manpower of national servicemen would be missed, but the present pattern of SADF preemptive raids into Angola would end for want of manpower and, in time, the very low quality of SWATF troops and their doubtful loyalty if required to take part in sustained combat would take a powerful negative effect.[86]

These modest changes would offer very little opportunity for Soviet involvement, so that even if SWAPO should ask for increased arms or some form of Cuban-Soviet technical support involving them directly in SWAPO attacks, it seems unlikely that the Soviet Union would respond favourably.

The ANC and South African Black Nationalism

Given the Namibian stalemate, Soviet attention has turned more to focus on the volatile political situation within South Africa. Until late 1984 the Soviets probably endorsed the astute analyses of South African black nationalism emanating from South African Communist Party circles in black Africa and in London which stressed the long-term nature of the struggle.[87] Given this view, it was adequate for the Soviet Union to provide a modest amount of arms, military training, and political indoctrination for prospective guerrilla leaders.

The ANC recruits, who began with a very high level of education and sophistication about technology, were acknowledged to be competent soldiers. They received their basic training from northern Angolan bases, and some selected cadres went to Eastern Europe or to the Soviet Union for advanced military and political training.[88]

Since the November 1984 East Rand rent riots, which triggered an endless round of black unrest throughout South Africa, Soviet opportunities and risks have grown enormously and have demanded a re-analysis of the prospects for black nationalism.

On the face of it, those prospects might seem bleak. During 1985 the South African government began a massive repression of the ANC, the United Democratic Front (UDF), and a myriad of local organisations. More than 20 000 people were detained, and about 2000 killed, most by the police. Black nationalism has been strengthened, in resistance, and government security resources have been strained far more seriously and more quickly than either Pretoria or the ANC could have imagined.[89] In fact, rock bottom has already been reached: since late 1986 black constables have been brought into service in black townships after only six-weeks' training, compared to the minimum of six months' previously required. Their introduction to ongoing security work has already resulted in increased reports of brutality.[90] In turn, this will bring increased community reprisals. Although adequate supervision seems very difficult, if the government should want to attempt it, white police officers now on dury in Namibia would need to be called home to supplement the limited number of officers now available for supervision in South Africa.

The Soviets have approached this current phase of South African politics with caution and flexibility. Without forsaking their commitment to the ANC, and obviously following the ANC's careful endorsement of the UDF (although the UDF gave its support to the ANC at its inception in August 1983, there are no signs that the ANC directed the establishment of the umbrella organisation), the Soviets have acknowledged that the UDF is a legitimate expression of black nationalism.[91] They have gone further. Soviet diplomats talked with Gatsha Buthelezi during his 1982 visit to Washington, even though there were already signs of friction between him and the ANC.[92] The Soviets's appreciation of the present diversity of motives and priorities among black nationalists is offset by their substantial concern that the ensuing stages of the revolution will not be controllable.[93] These careful responses suggest a parallel caution about making a larger commitment of military aid to the ANC, although Oliver Tambo returned from a November 1986 trip to Moscow hinting at major increases in arms supplies.[94]

The Soviet Union has other reasons for caution. Its reluctance to put Cuban troops into battle against the SADF anywhere in the region is now widely apparent, although Soviet diplomats at the UN reportedly told their South African counterparts after one SADF incursion into Angola that there were limits to their forbearance about such raids.[95] Also significant is Moscow's economic dependence on South Africa: Soviet gold and diamonds are marketed internationally by the South African corporate cartel that wields absolute power in maintaining high prices for both products. It is a mechanism the Soviets could not easily replicate and are therefore unlikely to challenge – or risk being forced out as reprisal by Pretoria for some regional initiative.[96]

The Impact of South African Policy

South Africa is the predominant power in Southern Africa. Its leadership knows this. Its black neighbours know it all too bitterly. The Soviet Union and the United States recognise it tacitly, and both are reluctant to commit the resources necessary to test South African power effectively.

US sanctions in 1986 emphasised for the South African government –and for most Afrikaners and many English-speaking whites – that their isolation from the United States is irreversible. While not forsaking continuing ties with more conservative governments in the UK and the FRG, Pretoria has probably given up its long-held notion that it could convert its Western trading partners to its own righteous and warped world view. That view, based on three centuries of grappling with an unfriendly land, resistant blacks, and an overbearing British colonial administration, sees Afrikaners as uniquely chosen to carry on a constructive Christian morality for the betterment of Africa. Now, they will do it alone, confronting a vast, multi-faceted international threat led by the Soviet Union, with the full cooperation of the Soviet bloc and Marxist regimes elsewhere, but enhanced (with varying degrees of awareness) by a panoply of related social forces common to the West – socialism, liberalism, humanism, secularism, permissiveness, and materialism. (Here, Afrikaners, who bow to no one in their enthusiasm for the good life, mean not the possession of worldly goods but the absence of belief in a metaphysical reality.[97])

This underlying complex of attitudes, common among Afrikaners despite urbanisation and international travel, has been augmented increasingly by a very practical calculation focused on Southern Africa: modest amounts of intervention can win complete success for South African regional policy – the installation of regimes acquiescent to Pretoria's interests. The blatant display of SADF support for the MNR since the Nkomati Accord attests to the dominance of this ruthless pragmatism. What was in the early 1970s a minority view in the SADF became by 1983 a dominant military view, especially in Military Intelligence, which provides the South African government with its 'objective' analyses of regional political dynamics. Most of the regional regimes pose almost no difficulties at all when seen in terms of economic coercion and, if required, military pressure. Lesotho succumbed. Swaziland is compliant. Botswana is constrained. Zambia could easily be dealt with. There is little to halt an MNR win in Mozambique. Zimbabwe and Angola pose some challenge, but those senior SADF officers who recall the original 1975 Angolan campaign dismiss the Cuban fighting potential, partly on the basis of a single, small encounter then and partly on current intelligence assessments whose data cannot be evaluated independently.[98] This interventionist impulse is widely supported within the South African government: there is no obvious military-civilian split over either its regional or (equally ruthless) domestic counter-insurgency implications.[99]

External appeals to the South African government to act with self-restraint have never been successful. The only likely constraint is the growing shortage of manpower and funds, but, as in other states in self-perceived siege, South Africa is likely to devote larger shares of its overall resources to security needs. It may not recognise the need to limit its regional interventions in order to meet domestic security requirements; or if it does, it might decide quick crushing attacks in the region to be better than prolonged support of surrogate forces. It might even decide to use this approach in domestic counter-insurgency, resorting to larger-scale attacks on intransigent black townships or even the apocalyptic use of its few atomic weapons against its own black people.[100]

CONCLUSION

The central fact of growing South African belligerency poses serious policy challenges for both the Soviet Union and the United States.

Neither is prepared to face them. More immediately, the Soviets are likely to maintain their present prudent regional policy, doing everything they can to avoid confrontation with South African military forces. In turn, the United States could reduce somewhat the Soviet influence with the regional black regimes and contribute to the insulation of those states against South African aggression by modest adjustments to its present policy: recognition of the MPLA government and the halting of 'covert' aid to UNITA; economic support for SADCC; military aid in modest amounts if requested by these same states; increased contacts with the ANC and SWAPO and, as long as feasible, financial support for black-run projects within South Africa and Namibia. Central to this modest policy shift is an acceptance of 'radical' regimes as impelled by a sense of urgency about human development. Beyond the grasp of such a US policy is the rising bloodshed within South Africa and the recurrent risks of South African regional intervention.[101]

Notes

1. Kurt M. Campbell, *Soviet Policy towards South Africa* (New York: St. Martin, 1986), pp. 30–4.
2. In various declassified documents from the Johnson Presidential Library, including Carlucci's Embtel 212, 26 March, 1964 (NSF:CO Zanzibar Cables, vol. II); Embtel 600, 17 May, 1964, and Embtel 25, 7 July, 1964 (both from NSF:OO:URTZ, Cables, vol. I). Also see Deptel 1291, 18 April, 1964 (NSF:OO:Zanzibar Cables, vol. II); and from Dar es Salaam, Embtel 1835, 23 April, 1964, and Embtel 1918, 29 April, 1964 (both in NSF:OO:URTZ, Cables, vol. I); and CIA Special Memorandum nos 12–64, 'Implications of Growing Communist Influence in URTZ', 29 September, 1964 (NSF:OO:URTZ, memos and misc., vol. I).
3. John Marcum, 'Bipolar Dependency: The People's Republic of Angola', in Michael Clough (ed.), *Reassessing the Soviet Challenge in Africa*, Policy Papers in International Affairs, no. 25 (Berkeley: Institute of International Studies, University of California, 1986), pp. 13, 14.
4. John Marcum, *Angolan Revolution*, vol. I: *The Anatomy of an Explosion* (Cambridge, MA: MIT Press, 1969), p. 184; also John Seiler, 'The Formulation of US Policy toward Southern Africa, 1957–1976: The Failure of Good Intentions' (PhD dissertation, University of Connecticut, 1976), pp. 181–4.
5. Marcum, *Angolan Revolution*, vol. I, ch. 1, for origins of Angolan nationalism; also, Marcum, 'Bipolar Dependency', p. 19 (see note 3).

6. John Marcum, *Angolan Revolution*, vol. II: *Exile Politics and Guerrilla Warfare (1962–1976)* (Cambridge, MA: MIT Press, 1978), regarding Savimbi's role in the origins of UNITA, pp. 160–9.
7. Ibid., pp. 121–3.
8. Ibid., pp. 14–18; also Marcum, 'Bipolar Dependency', p. 16, second footnote (see note 3.)
9. Marcum, *Angolan Revolution*, vol. I, pp. 55, 62–4; 69; 228–32 (see note 5).
10. Marcum, *Angolan Revolution*, vol. II, pp. 252–5 (see note 6); and 'Bipolar Dependency', p. 14 (see note 3).
11. Marcum, *Angolan Revolution*, vol. I, pp. 201, 269–77 (see note 5); *Angolan Revolution*, vol. II, pp. 101, 127, 128 (see note 6); and 'Bipolar Dependency', pp. 15, 16 (see note 3). See also John Seiler, 'Kennedy's "Dual Policy" toward Portugal and Its African Territories', International Conference Group on Modern Portugal, June 1979.
12. Marcum, *Angolan Revolution*, vol. II, pp. 130–3 (see note 6).
13. Ibid., pp. 160–9.
14. Ibid., p. 171.
15. Ibid., pp. 156, 157, 181, and 182; also his 'The Exile Condition and Revolutionary Effectiveness: Southern African Liberation Movements', in Christian P. Potholm and Richard Dale (eds), *Southern Africa in Perspective*, (New York: Free Press, 1972).
16. Ibid., p. 201, 229.
17. Marcum, 'Bipolar Dependency', p. 16 (see note 3).
18. Arthur Jay Klinghoffer, *The Angolan War: A Study in Soviet Policy in the Third World* (Boulder, CO: Westview, 1980, pp. 31ff.
19. Marcum, *Angolan Revolution*, vol. II, pp. 252, 253, 260, 261 (see note 6).
20. Ibid., p. 263.
21. Ibid., pp. 272–5, also Christopher Stevens, 'The Soviet Role in Southern Africa', in John Seiler (ed.), *Southern Africa since the Portuguese Coup*, (Boulder, CO: Westview, 1980), p. 49.
22. Marcum, 'United States Options in Angola', *CSIS Africa Notes*, no. 52, 20 December, 1985, p. 2; and *Angolan Revolution*, vol. II, pp. 275, 280, 281 (see note 6).
23. Marcum, 'Bipolar Dependency', pp. 20, 21 (see note 3).
24. Ibid., p. 19; also Klinghoffer, *Angolan War*, pp. 128–31 (see note 18); and William M. LeoGrande, *Cuba's Policy in Africa, 1959–1980*, Policy Papers in International Affairs, no. 13 (Berkeley, CA: Institute of International Studies, University of California, 1980), p. 25. Klinghoffer and LeoGrande refer to Cuban aid to Neto, but Marcum suggests both governments abstained from telling Neto of the impending coup or helping him to squelch it.
25. Marcum, 'Bipolar Dependency', footnote, p. 19 (se note 3).
26. Gillian Gunn, 'The Angolan Economy: A Status Report', *CSIS Africa Notes*, no. 58 (30 May, 1986), p. 3; also Marcum, 'Bipolar Dependency', p. 25 (see note 3), and 'United States Options in Angola', p. 4 (see note 22).
27. Marcum, 'United States Options in Angola', p. 7 (see note 22).

28. Marcum, 'Bipolar Dependency', p. 26 (see note 3).
29. Peter Clement, 'Moscow and Southern Africa', *Problems of Communism*, vol. 34, no. 2, March–April 1985, pp. 32, 33; also, Marcum, 'United States Options in Angola', p. 5 (see note 22); and Gunn, 'Angolan Economy', p. 6 (see note 26).
30. Clement, 'Moscow and Southern Africa', p. 34 (see note 29).
31. Ibid., p. 34; also W. Raymond Duncan, 'Cuban-Soviet Relations: Directions of Influence', Chapter 3 of this volume, p. 65.
32. Clement, 'Moscow and Southern Africa', pp. 35, 36 (see note 29).
33. Ibid.
34. Patrick E. Tyler, 'Rebel Success Turns on South African Aid', *Washington Post*, 30 July, 1986 (Department of State: AF Press Clips [*AFPC*], vol. 21, no. 32, 22 August, 1986, p. 7); also, Kurt M. Campbell, 'Gorbachev and the Third World', *Christian Science Monitor*, 8 April, 1986. For a report that gives less weight to Angolan air defence capability and suggests greater SADF involvement, see Marcum, 'United States Options in Angola', pp. 5, 6 (see note 22).
35. Gunn, 'Angolan Economy', p. 5 (see note 26).
36. Ibid., pp. 5, 6; and Marcum, 'Bipolar Dependency', pp. 28, 29 (see note 3).
37. For the dual emphasis on strengthening political organisation, see Eduardo dos Santos, 'Vanguard Role of the Party at Today's Stage of the Angolan Revolution', *Kommunist*, no. 5, March 1986, pp. 88–98.
38. For Soviet statements and actions: *Pravda*, 31 January, 1986, p. 4; ibid., 3 February, 1986, p. 5 (*Current Digest of the Soviet Press* [*CD*], vol. 38, no. 5, 5 March, 1986, p. 24); ibid., 2 April, 1986, p. 5 (*CD*, no. 13, 30 April, 1986, p. 17); ibid., 15 April, 1986, p. 4 (*CD*, no. 15, 14 May, 1986, p. 19); and ibid., 7 May, 1986, p. 2 (*CD*, no. 19, 11 June, 1986, pp. 15–17). On the slowing of economic pragmatism, Jonathan Friedland, 'Observers Say Angola Would Turn to Eastern Bloc', *The Sun* (Baltimore), 20 August, 1986 (*AFPC*, vol. 22, no. 32, 22 August, 1986, p. 7); but for a more sanguine view, Gunn, 'Angolan Economy', p. 6 (see note 26).
39. *Pravda*, 11 May, 1986, p. 1; *Izvestiia*, 11 May, 1986, p. 4; both in *CD*, no. 19, 11 June, 1986, pp. 15–17.
40. *Pravda*, 9 June, 1986, p. 1; *CD*, no. 23, 9 July, 1986, p. 19.
41. David B. Ottoway and Patrick E. Tyler, 'Superpowers Raise Ante as Fighting Intensifies', *Washington Post*, 30 July, 1986 (*AFPC*, vol. 22, no. 29, 1 August, 1986, p. 9); James Brooke, 'Angolan Leader Warns Zaire on Sheltering Rebels', *New York Times* [*NYT*], 27 November, 1986, p. 17; and 'CIA Said to Send Rebels in Angola Weapons via Zaire', *NYT*, 1 February, 1987, p. 1.
42. James Brooke, 'Cubans Guard US Oilmen in Angola', *NYT*, 24 November, 1986, p. A3; and 'Cuba's Strange Mission in Angola', *NYT Magazine*, 1 February, 1987, p. 24. For the 1987 campaign, see Michael Parks, 'Two Major Clashes Reported in Angola', *Washington Post*, 29 July, 1987 (*AFPC*, 23, vol. no. 30, 31 July, 1987, p. 1); David B. Ottoway, 'Angola, Savimbi Forces Clash Anew', *Washington Post*, 11 September, 1987 (*AFPC*, vol. 23, no. 36, 11 September, 1987, p. 6);

John D. Battersby, 'Angola Lags in Drive on US-Backed Rebels', *NYT*, 14 September, 1987, p. A1; and caption for photo, 'Angolan Rebels Display Wreckage of Soviet Aircraft', *NYT*, 4 October, 1987, p. 3.
43. James Brooke, 'Angolan Leader Warns Zaire', *NYT*, 27 November, 1986, p. A17.
44. Noel C. Koch, 'Some Observations on US Security Interests in Africa', *CSIS Africa Notes*, no. 49, 19 November, 1985, p. 4; also, Gunn, 'Angolan Economy', p. 6 (see note 26); and Clement, 'Moscow and Southern Africa', p. 31 (see note 29); also, Blaine Harden, 'Angola Reports Hunger is Widespread', *Washington Post*, 14 August, 1987, and Michael Parks, 'Angola Sacrifices a Bit of Ideology to Boost Economy', *Los Angeles Times*, 16 August, 1987, both in *AFPC*, vol. 23, no. 33 (21 August, 1987), pp. 8, 9.
45. Gunn, 'Angolan Economy', p. 6 (see note 26); for President dos Santos's decision to seek IMF membership, see Blaire Harden, 'Angola's Economy Oiled by Beer Cans', *Washington Post*, 30 August, 1987, in *AFPC*, vol. 23, no. 35 (4 September, 1987), p. 6. Continued economic pressure led Angola to propose an end to UNITA's role in Angola in return for a phased withdrawal of Cuban troops. See Claire Robertson, 'Angolan Proposal on Cuban Issue Studied', *Washington Post*, 11 August, 1987, in *AFPC*, vol. 23, no. 32 (14 August, 1987), p. 2; and 'Crocker Visits Luanda to Air Exit of Cubans', *Washington Post*, 11 September, 1987, in *AFPC*, vol. 23, no. 26 (11 September, 1987), p. 1.
46. Elizabeth K. Valkenier, 'Revolutionary Change in the Third World: Recent Soviet Reassessments', *World Politics*, vol. 38, no. 3, April 1986, pp. 424–6; also, Jerry F. Hough, *The Struggle for the Third World: Soviet Debates and American Options* (Washington, DC: Brookings Institution, 1986), pp. 98–103.
47. David B. Ottoway, 'Zimbabwe Seeks Advanced Soviet Jets', *Washington Post*, 14 April, 1987 (*AFPC*, vol. 23, no. 25, 17 April, 1987, p. 5); 'Zimbabwe Denies Reports Country Bought 12 Mig-29s', *NYT*, 15 April, 1987, p. A3; and Kurt Campbell, 'The Case of the Migs and Zimbabwe's New Soviet Tilt', *Christian Science Monitor*, 7 May, 1987.
48. Michael Clough, 'Moscow and Africa: A 1986 Balance Sheet', *CSIS Africa Notes*, no. 55, 21 March, 1986, p. 3.
49. Keith Middlemas, 'Independent Mozambique and its Regional Policy', in Seiler (ed.), *Southern Africa since the Portuguese Coup* pp. 213–33 (see note 21).
50. David Martin and Phyllis Johnson, *The Struggle for Zimbabwe: The Chimurenga War* (New York/London: Monthly Review Press, 1981), pp. 316, 317; also, Robert Jaster, 'A Regional Security Role for Africa's Front-Line States', in Robert Jaster (ed.), *Southern Africa: Regional Security Problems and Prospect* (London: International Institute for Strategic Studies, 1985), p. 95.
51. Jaster, 'A Regional Security Role', pp. 101–3 (see note 50).
52. Ibid., p. 124; Allister Sparks, 'Harare Stepping Up Rebel Fight', *Washington Post*, 19 November, 1986 (*AFPC*, vol. 22, no. 45, 21 November, 1986, p. 8); and 'Africa Route Revival Faces Many

Problems', *Washington Post*, 1 December, 1986 (*AFPC*, vol. 22, no. 47, 5 December, 1986, p. 7).
53. Clough, 'Moscow and Africa', p. 3 (see note 48).
54. Marcum, *Angolan Revolution*, vol. I, pp. 283, 284 (see note 5).
55. Middlemas, 'Independent Mozambique' (see note 49).
56. Ibid.
57. Gillian Gunn, 'Post-Nkomati Mozambique', *CSIS Africa Notes*, no. 38, 8 January, 1985, pp. 4, 5.
58. Middlemas, 'Independent Mozambique' (see note 49); also, John S. Saul (ed.), *A Difficult Road: The Transition to Socialism in Mozambique* (New York: Monthly Review Press, 1985), pp. 138, 139.
59. Allen F. Isaacman, 'Mozambique: Tugging at the Chains of Dependency', in Gerald J. Bender, James S. Coleman, Richard L. Sklar (eds), *African Crisis Area and US Foreign Policy* (Berkeley and Los Angeles: University of California Press, 1985), pp. 141–8; also, Martin Lowenkopf, 'Mozambique: The Nkomati Accord', in Clough (ed.), *Reassessing the Soviet Challenge in Africa* pp. 60–64 (see note 3).
60. Jaster, 'Regional Security Role', p. 109 (see note 50).
61. Lowenkopf, 'Mozambique: The Nkomati Accord', p. 55 (see note 59).
62. Clement, 'Moscow and Southern Africa', p. 40 (see note 29); Jaster, 'Regional Security Role', p. 109 (see note 50) and Winrich Kuhne, 'What Does the Case of Mozambique Tell Us about Soviet Ambivalence toward Africa?', *CSIS Africa Notes*, no. 46, 30 August, 1985), p. 4.
63. Glen Frankel, 'War of Attrition Hits Mozambique's Poor', *Washington Post*, 12 May, 1986 (*AFPC*, vol. 22, no. 18, 16 May, 1988, p. 8); and Allen F. Isaacman, 'The Malawi Connection', *Africa Report*, vol. 31, no. 6, November–December, 1986, pp. 51–4.
64. 'Is the USSR Losing Out in Mozambique?', *Soviet Review*, vol. 1, no 8, September, 1985 (University of Stellenbosch, Institute for the Study of Marxism), p. 9; Kuhne, 'Case of Mozambique', p. 3 (see note 62); Lowenkopf, 'Mozambique: The Nkomati Accord', p. 56 (see note 59); Saul, *A Difficult Road*, pp. 128, 129 (see note 58).
65. Jaster, 'Regional Security Role', p. 109 (see note 50); Kuhne, 'Case of Mozambique', p. 3 (see note 62).
66. Gunn, 'Post-Nkomati Mozambique', p. 6 (see note 57); Kuhne, 'Case of Mozambique', p. 3 (see note 62).
67. Kuhne, 'Case of Mozambique', p. 3 (see note 62).
68. Clement, 'Moscow and Southern Africa', p. 41 (see note 29).
69. Ibid., pp. 42, 43; Kuhne, 'Case of Mozambique', p. 1 (see note 62).
70. 'Is the USSR Losing Out in Mozambique?', p. 11 (see note 64); also, Henrik Bering-Jensen, 'Still Struggling with Independence', in *Los Angeles Times*, *Insight* section, 26 May, 1986 (*AFPC*, vol. 22, no. 21, 6 June, 1986, p. 7).
71. Frankel, 'War of Attrition' (see note 63).
72. Serge Schmemann, 'Mozambique Jet Crash Still a Mystery', *NYT*, 27 January, 1987, p. A6; and 'Mozambique Seeks US Investment', *NYT*, 28 January, 1987, p. A3; also Sheila Rule, 'A War and Drought Extend the Famine in Mozambique', *NYT*, 9 November, 1986 (*AFPC*, vol. 22,

no. 44, 14 November, 1986, p. 8); 'Mozambicans Trying to Flee War Horrors', *NYT*, 8 December, 1986, p. A9; Frankel, 'War of Attrition' (see note 63); and Alan Cowell, 'Top Mozambican Accuses Pretoria', *NYT*, 5 December, 1986, p. A11.
73. Allister Sparks, 'South Africa's Neighbors Forge a Link to the Sea', *Washington Post*, 28 September, 1986 (*AFPC*, vol. 22, no. 28, 3 October, 1986, p. 10); ibid., 'Harare Stepping Up Rebel Fight' and 'Africa Route Revival Faces Many Problems' (see note 52); and Serge Schmemann, 'Black Nations' Trade Route Seeks to Bypass South Africa', *NYT*, 3 February 1987, p. A1.
74. John D. Battersby, 'Mozambique and Pretoria Renew Nonaggression Pact', *NYT*, 7 August, 1987 (*AFPC*, vol. 23, no. 32, 14 August 1987, p. 2).
75. Alan F. Isaacman, 'After the Nkomati Accord', *Africa Report*, vol. 30, no. 1, January–February 1985, pp. 10,11; Bering-Jensen, 'Still Struggling with Independence' (see note 70).
76. Isaacman, 'After the Nkomati Accord', p. 11 (see note 75); Saul, *A Difficult Road*, pp. 136–147 (see note 58).
77. 'Is the USSR Losing Out in Mozambique?', p. 10 (see note 64).
78. Clough, 'Moscow and Africa', p. 3 (see note 48).
79. Glen Frankel, 'Moscow's Gains in Africa', *Washington Post*, 25 May 1986 (*AFPC*, vol. 22, no. 20, 30 May, 1986, p. 11), notes the bitterness but goes on to suggest Soviet gains without giving any examples.
80. Clough, 'Moscow and Africa', p. 3 (see note 48).
81. Glen Frankel, 'Zimbabwe Wrestles with Its Ghosts', *Washington Post*, 7 July 1986 (*AFPC*, vol. 22, no. 26, 11 July 1986, pp. 7ff).
82. David Martin and Phyllis Johnson, 'Africa: The Old and the Unexpected', *Foreign Affairs*, vol. 63, no. 3, 1985, pp. 609, 610; Clement, 'Moscow and Southern Africa', p. 45 (see note 29); concerning the upsurge in anti-regime killings in Matabeleland during 1987 see Sheila Rule, 'Rise in Killings in Zimbabwe Brings New Curbs on Opposition', *NYT*, 12 October, 1987, p. A3; and concerning MNR incursions into Zimbabwe see Sheila Rule, 'Zimbabwe Farm: Tea and Mayhem', *NYT*, 7 October 1987, p. A10.
83. Interviews with SADF and Security Police officers in Pretoria, Windhoek, and northern Namibia, September–October, 1983.
84. Ibid.; also, Seiler, 'What to Do about Namibia?', *Africa Report*, vol. 29, no. 2, March–April, 1984.
85. I. William Zartman, *Ripe for Resolution: Conflict and Intervention in Africa* (New York: Oxford University Press, 1985), p. 167; Christopher Coker, 'South Africa: A New Military Role in Southern Africa, 1969–1982', in Jaster (ed.), *Southern Africa*, pp. 142–50 (see note 50); 'The Role of the Soviet Union, Cuba, and East Germany in Fomenting Terrorism in Southern Africa', Hearings before the US Senate Subcommittee on Security and Terrorism of the Committee on the Judiciary, 97th Cong., 2nd session, 22, 24, 25, 29, and 31 March 1982, vol. 1, especially pp. 699–706.
86. *Beeld* (Johannesburg), 28 August 1986 (*South African Digest*, 5 September 1986, p. 806).

87. *South African Communists Speak 1915–1980* (London: Inkulukelo Publications, 1981).

88. Steven Mufson, 'The War for South Africa', *Washington Post*, 14 December 1986 (*AFPC*, vol. 22, no. 49, 19 December 1986, p. 8).

89. Allister Sparks, 'South Africa's Violence Shifts Pattern', *Washington Post*, 6 October 1986 (*AFPC*, vol. 22, no. 39, 10 October 1986, p. 3); Alan Cowell, 'Pretoria Imposes Harsh New Rules Aimed at Unrest', *NYT*, 12 December 1986, p. A1; ibid., 'Pretoria Orders a Sweep on Foes in Security Move', *NYT*, 13 December 1986, p. A1; and 'Pretoria's New Line', *NYT*, 14 December 1986, p. 26.

90. *The Citizen* (Johannesburg), 22 September 1986 (*SA Digest*, 26 September, 1986, p. 881); *NYT*, 22 September 1986, p. A10); and Alan Cowell, 'Black Police Units in South Africa Accused of Wide Rights Abuses', *NYT*, 11 December 1986, p. A1.

91. Clement, 'Moscow and Southern Africa', p. 46 (see note 29).

92. Campbell, *Soviet Policy towards South Africa*, p. 45 (see note 1).

93. Boris Bogdanov, 'Cracks in the "Monolith"', *Asia and Africa Today* (Moscow), no. 4, July–August 1986, pp. 66–9; and 'South African Liberation is Drawing Near', round-table discussion, *Asia and Africa Today*, no. 3, May–June 1986, pp. 22–9. For recent outstanding Western analyses of South African black nationalism, see especially Thomas G. Karis, 'South African Liberation: The Communist Factor', *Foreign Affairs*, vol. 65, no. 2, Winter 1986/87, pp. 267–87; Mark A. Uhlig, 'Inside the African National Congress', *NYT Magazine*, 25 January 1987, p. 37ff; and Anthony Lewis, 'Realism in Africa', *NYT*, 26 January 1987, p. A35. According to an Afrikaner academician who visited Moscow in August 1987, Gorbachev went much further in a discussion that same month with Mozambique's President Chissano by suggesting that it would be against Soviet interests for the inevitable collapse of apartheid to be followed by 'something worse'. (John D. Battersby, 'Easing of Soviet Policy on South Africa is Seen', *NYT*, 27 September 1987, p. 19.)

94. *NYT*, 7 November 1986, p. A3; *Washington Times*, 7 November 1986 (*AFPC*, vol. 22, no. 43, 7 November 1986, p. 5).

95. Clough, 'Moscow and Africa', p. 4 (see note 48).

96. Kurt M. Campbell, 'The Soviet-South African Connection', *Africa Report*, vol. 31, no. 2, March–April 1986, pp. 72–5.

97. *NYT*, 22 November 1986; p. 3; Breyten Breytenbach, *The True Confession of an Albino Terrorist* (New York: Farrar Strauss Giroux, 1983), p. 46; also, John Seiler, 'South African Perspectives and Responses to External Pressures', *Journal of Modern African Studies*, vol. 13, no. 3, September 1975, pp. 447–68.

98. Interviews, Pretoria, Windhoek, northern Namibia, September–October 1983; *The Economist*, 25 October, 1986 (*AFPC*, vol. 22, no. 42, 31 October 1986, p. 4); Allister Sparks, 'Moves by Botha Telegraph Pullback from Compromise', *Washington Post*, 17 August 1986 (*AFPC*, vol. 22, no. 32 22 August 1986).

99. John Seiler, 'South Africa's Evolving State Security System', IPSA Study

Group on Armed Forces and Society, West Berlin, September 1984.
100. Two related speculative issues are involved here: whether South Africa already has nuclear weapons or at least the capability to produce them quickly; and whether such weapons would be used against black South Africans. Strong circumstantial evidence suggests South Africa (probably with Israeli cooperation) tested a nuclear device in the South Atlantic in 1979. More recently, preparations for a similar test at Upington were aborted after Soviet satellite observation led to a joint US-Soviet démarche to Pretoria. Also, in 1983 Pretoria acted with great speed to expel two US military attachés after they flew a light plane over the Palabora atomic facility with the intent of taking photos of that off-limits installation. On this point, see Richard Leonard, *South Africa at War: White Power and the Crisis in Southern Africa* (Westport, CN: Lawrence Hill, 1983), pp. 131, 145, 146, and 158. Also, on this point and for an insightful analysis of South African regional security policies, see Christopher Coker, *South Africa's Security Dilemmas*. (New York: Praeger Publishers, with The Center for Strategic and International Studies, Washington, *The Washington Papers*, no. 126, 1987).

There is no question that the Afrikaner definition of *volk* (community, people, nation) excludes all blacks and even non-Afrikaner whites. South Africans outside the *volk* may be useful if they give unalloyed support to Pretoria's policies but in dissent they are most often lumped among 'South Africa's enemies'. Thus, the present resort to increasing conventional force to put down dissent and unrest in black townships generates little guilt among Afrikaners. But any resort to nuclear weapons would come only if officials believed an ultimate threat to Afrikaner survival was underway. Although there has been no recent discussion of this question, Lukas D. Barnard, before he became director of the National Intelligence Service in 1980, wrote a book and a number of articles in which he explored nuclear strategic doctrine and justified the use of nuclear weapons in dire circumstances. See his 'Die Afskrikkingstrategie van Kernwapens', *Journal for Contemporary History and International Relations* (Bloemfontein), vol. 2, no. 2, September 1977, pp. 74–97; and his book *Konflik en Orde in Internasionale Verhoudinge* (Cape Town: Perskor, 1978). On the significance of his appointment, see Martin Schneider, 'New DONS Chief Backs the Bomb', *Rand Daily Mail* (Johannesburg), 15 November, 1979, p. 1. For the most recent informed, although still speculative, analysis of South African nuclear capabilities and intentions, see Kurt M. Campbell, 'Marching for Pretoria', *Boston Globe Magazine*, 1 March 1987, p. 16.
101. Michael Clough, 'Conclusion: Coming to Terms with Radical Socialism', in Clough (ed.), *Reassessing the Soviet Challenge in Africa* pp. 69–90 (see note 3); Anthony Lake, *Third World Radical Regimes: US Policy under Carter and Reagan* (New York: Foreign Policy Association, Headline Series, no. 272 (January/February 1985); and *US Policy and Radical Regimes*, report of a Vantage Conference, 25–27 September 1986 (Muscatine, IA: Stanley Foundation, 1986).

Gorbachev's decision to pay all back UN contributions led the *NYT* to suggest editorially 16 October 1987, p. A38) that a feasible first step in superpower cooperation to constrain regional conflict might be taken in Southern Africa to curb South African regional aggression.

Part III

Conclusions

15 Reassessing Soviet Doctrine: New Priorities and Perspectives
Roger E. Kanet

INTRODUCTION

The preceding chapters have detailed the limitations of Soviet power in the developing world. The impressive military prowess and the revolutionary message and diplomacy of the Soviet Union have succeeded in establishing important beachheads for Moscow around the globe. Much of these gains which the USSR appears determined to retain obscure the shaky economic and technological base on which they rest. Some Soviet-backed regimes, like those in Afghanistan and Angola, are under siege. Soviet leaders and analysts of Third World relations appear increasingly sensitive to the material and political burdens incurred in holding Soviet salients in the developing world. They also appear to be concerned about the costs and risks of expanding Soviet commitments and influence in these areas, not only because of the dim prospects of long-term success of such a policy, but more importantly because of its potentially deleterious implications for efforts to reform the economic and socio-political structure of the Soviet Union. Reform will take decades to accomplish with no assurance that it will succeed even without the distractions and dissipation of resources that an expansionist Third World policy suggests. The encrustations of the past and strong resistance to change from conservative elements in Soviet society – not to mention deep social and ethnic splits within the USSR – hang heavy on Soviet leaders, either inhibiting the practical implementation of these reforms (most of which have yet to be tested) or distorting and weakening their effect when they are applied.

In this chapter we examine the emerging perceptions and assessments of the Soviet leaders and influential analysts of Soviet-Third World relations to determine their sensitivity to the limitations of power and the dubious prospects of Soviet expansion among developing countries. Moreover, we will explore the growing ascendancy of proposals in Soviet policy circles directed at adapting the long-term interests and aims of the Soviet Union to an increasingly polycentric international system. Also reviewed is evidence for any links between growing Soviet awareness of the constraints, burdens, and risks of an aggressive policy in the developing world with its potentially damaging impact on the reform efforts now underway.

The reassessment of Soviet policy in the Third World is part of a broader reevaluation of the foundations of Soviet foreign policy under the rubric 'New Political Thinking' in which the Soviet leadership under Gorbachev has questioned the continued heavy reliance on military power and pointed to the existence of international security problems that require collaboration with the West for their resolution. The innovative concepts introduced into the Soviet discussion on foreign and security policy have been complemented by the restructuring of the major party and state organs involved in policy making and policy implementation, as well as with personnel changes that are meant to facilitate greater central control over foreign policy and modification in the major lines of Soviet policy. The ultimate purpose is to provide the Soviet Union with the respite needed to refurbish its domestic economy as an essential prerequisite for increasing its ability to compete with the United States in non-military areas, as well as to close the technological gap with the West that threatens Soviet military gains of the recent past.

Since Gorbachev assumed the leadership of the CPSU, Soviet foreign policy has been characterised by renewed activism; in the Third World this has included important efforts to expand the range of contacts with non-Marxist governments and continuing support for established clients.

For the forseeable future the Soviets are not likely to resume aggressive policies in the Third World, given the perceived need in Moscow for a respite in tension with the West as a precondition for success in restructuring the Soviet economy. Should the Soviets succeed in their efforts, a revitalised Soviet Union armed with economic and political capabilities to match its military strength would in many ways be a more formidable opponent of US interests in the Third World than it has been to date.

SOVIET REASSESSMENTS OF THE THIRD WORLD

The Party Programme of 1961 spoke with great optimism about prospects for liberation and the role of the USSR in supporting the liberation struggle. The new programme approved at the 27th CPSU

Congress[1] in early 1986 emphasized the revitalised role of neo-colonialism and imperialism in the Third World and noted only that the 'CPSU supports the just struggle waged by the countries of Asia, Africa and Latin America against imperialism' and that the 'Soviet Union is on the side of the states and peoples repulsing the attacks of the aggressive forces of imperialism and upholding their freedom, independence and national dignity.' Progressive states were informed that the tasks of building a new society are primarily their own responsibility, although the 'Soviet Union has been doing and will continue to do all it can to render the peoples following that [socialist-oriented] road assistance in economic and cultural development, in training national personnel, in strengthening their defences and in other fields.'[2]

As mentioned in Chapter 2, the three major concerns that appear in Soviet writing and statements on current developments in the Third World relate to the escalating costs borne by the Soviet Union in supporting its clients, to the poor record of these clients after independence in creating stable political systems and functioning economies, and to the negative impact that involvement in the Third World has had on other Soviet foreign policy concerns – in particular relations with the United States.

Building on arguments that had already been developed quite extensively in Soviet academic publications,[3] Brezhnev's first successor as general secretary, Iurii Andropov, argued that the primary source of economic development had to come from Third World socialist countries themselves:

> Socialist countries express solidarity with these progressive states, render assistance to them in the sphere of politics and culture, and promote the strengthening of their defense. We contribute also, to the extent possible, to their economic development. But, on the whole, their economic development, just as the entire social progress of those countries can, of course, be only the result of the work of their peoples and of a correct policy of their leadership.[4]

This theme dominated Soviet writing and pronouncements during 1984 and 1985. For example, writing on 'Real Socialism and the Liberated Countries', Boris Ponomarev, then head of the International Department of the Central Committee, noted the importance of past Soviet economic aid, but concluded that

> the Soviet Union fundamentally rejects the demands [of the developing countries] that, on a par with the imperialist countries, it

allocate for aid to the developing countries a fixed part of its gross national product ... One cannot agree with the point of view that it is only an influx of resources from without that can guarantee the resolution of the burning problems of the developing countries.[5]

Thus, by the time of the 27th Party Congress early in 1986 the official Soviet position was quite clear: although the Soviets have provided assistance in the past and will continue to do so, primary responsibility for economic growth rests with developing countries themselves. The most important task to be carried out by the USSR is to provide a model, as a developed socialist society, for socialist developing countries.[6] While aid will continue to be provided, the Soviet Union will not expand commitments and permit the development of what one Soviet writer has referred to as 'parasitical attitudes in connection with obtaining aid from the socialist countries'.[7]

The Soviets have also questioned the long-term economic and political viability of some of their client states. During the 1970s, while continuing efforts to expand contacts with key non-Marxist developing states, the Soviets gave special attention to the promotion of Marxist-Leninist vanguard parties.[8] As S. Neil MacFarlane has argued, 'in the early and mid-1970s, the USSR faced an environment in the Third World in which important constraints limiting its activities had been removed or weakened, important stimuli for such activity had emerged or re-emerged, and its capabilities to undertake such activities had increased.'[9] The end result was an optimism about the prospects for revolutionary change in the Third World that went far beyond Soviet expectations of the late 1960s. In this period the Soviets envisioned the growth of vanguard parties and socialist states in the Third World as part of the 'changing international correlation of forces' and the establishment of a 'socialist international division of labor' that would eventually replace Western economic dominance. This view was expressed officially by Premier Alexei Kosygin at the 24th Congress of the CPSU in 1971, when he claimed that Soviet economic relations with developing countries were 'acquiring the nature of a stable division of labour, counterposed in the sphere of international economic relations to the system of imperialist exploitation'.[10] Other Soviet writers noted that the creation of 'revolutionary democratic' regimes enhanced 'cooperation with the socialist countries to a new level and deliberately promote the expansion of such cooperation'.[11]

In the 1980s the Soviets have been far less optimistic about the prospects for Marxist-Leninist vanguard parties and states and have been critical of the policies of some of these parties. Among the more important of those who have voiced second thoughts has been Rostislav Ul'ianovskii, long-time (but recently retired) deputy director of the International Department of the CPSU and originally one of the strongest proponents of the model of 'revolutionary democracy'. Ul'ianovskii now emphasises the long and tortuous path that the building of socialism will entail.[12]

A clear statement of Soviet concerns about the status of Third World national liberation movements appears in an article by Aleksandr Bovin, a prominent Soviet analyst. According to Bovin

The roads of freedom are difficult, agonizingly difficult. And in some measure, to some extent, these difficulties are inevitable. Because, as historical experience shows, the transition from the old to the new and the rise of society to higher levels of civilization have never been easy, smooth or free of collisions, losses and sometimes tragic zigzags.[13]

Although the Soviets do not openly admit that many of their Third World clients face domestic insurgencies, prominent in their writings and statements in recent years has been commentary about the rejuvenated role of imperialism in the Third World and the challenge to newly-liberated countries presented both by capitalist economic domination and US military intervention.[14] When added to the questions posed about the seriousness of the commitment to Marxism-Leninism of some of their allies and the errors in their policies, Soviet comments about US intervention provide evidence of growing Soviet concern about the appropriateness of the past emphasis on vanguard Marxist-Leninist parties.

Closely related to the stated Soviet concerns about the lack of progress in Third World vanguard party states is the growing realisation of the difficulty, if not impossibility, of building a socialist world economy in the foreseeable future, given the revitalisation of capitalism in the Third World. Already in the late 1970s analysts such as Karen Brutents and Evgenyi Primakov pointed to the real economic progress occurring in capitalist developing countries and the positive impact that Western capitalism was having on economic growth in some of these countries.[15] In fact, by 1986 views on the relative importance of capitalist versus socialist developing states had been modified to the point that the revised party programme notes the existence of 'a realistic basis for cooperation of those young states that are following the capitalist road of development 'resulting from' a sharpening contradiction between the interests of the[ir] peoples and the imperialist policy of *diktat* and expansion.'[16] This point follows directly from the argument of Brutents, a deputy director of the International Department, who emphasises the greater long-term value for the Soviet Union of the establishment and strengthening of relations with capitalist countries in the Third World. He notes the positive aspects of their foreign policies and emphasises the growing importance of their relations with the Soviet Union.[17] As Elizabeth Valkenier has argued, in the economic realm:

> [W]hat has emerged since 1975 is an implicit admission in government circles and the academic community that the establishment of an alternate, worldwide economic order, patterned on integration arrangements set up in the CMEA, is both an impossible and impractical proposition. To one extent or another, Soviet officials and scholars now admit that the Socialist countries have to act in a world that resists bifurcation.[18]

Concern about the negative implications of greater Soviet activism in the Third World for the core area of Soviet foreign policy – relations with the United States – has been evident, not only in the writings of Soviet academics, but also in the statements of Soviet leaders. For example, speaking to a plenary session of the Central Committee in 1983 General Secretary Iurii Andropov referred to the implications of the risk of conflict with the United States for the entire communist movement: 'the preservation of peace on earth is both today and in the foreseeable future the pivotal problem of the foreign policy of our party. And not only of our party. The threat of nuclear war hanging over the world induces one to reevaluate the basic concept of the activities of the entire communist movement'.[19]

Responding to the more activist policy pursued by the United States in the Third World since the late 1970s, Soviet commentators have emphasised the threat to 'progressive' forces emanating from Washington and the fact that the resolution of regional conflicts everywhere is difficult because, in the words of Dmitrii Volskii, a prominent Soviet analyst, of 'unwillingness of the imperialist quarters to recognise the principle of the equality of states and peoples, the striving of some countries to dominate others, to exploit their natural resources and to use their territory for their own strategic purposes'.[20] Volskii sees close connections among US acts of 'aggression' in various parts of the world:

> It is hardly a coincidence that at the very time that the wide-scale incursion into Nicaragua was started, the threat of aggression against countries like Syria and Angola also increased. All these add up to a chain of interconnected operations prepared and carried out for the time being through the agency of others ... Meanwhile the chain of conflict situations created by Washington's imperial policy encircles the whole globe at the equator.[21]

Elsewhere, Volskii has also asserted that 'those who are bombing and shelling Third World countries are hatching militarist designs primarily targeted at the Soviet Union and other countries of the socialist community'.[22] The gist of this aspect of the Soviet argument is the claim that the United States has initiated a much more active effort to slow the movement toward socialism and is willing to resort to military means to accomplish this objective. The increased 'bellicosity' of the United States in the Third World means a heightened danger of the possible escalation of local wars into regional, and even global conflicts, especially in the Middle East.[23]

Moreover, Bovin has argued (in the article cited above) that the Soviet ability to support national liberation movements is at least partially contingent on the state of US-Soviet relations. In periods of heightened global confrontation, he maintains, the Soviets are less able to provide economic and other support to developing countries that are suffering from Western economic domination.[24] His argument fits well with that of more highly-placed analysts, such as Boris Ponomarev and Karen Brutents, both of whom have noted that the exacerbation of the international situation and the expansion of the arms race reduce the possibility of expanded Soviet assistance to developing countries.[25]

At least at the level of public pronouncement Soviet academic analysts and highly-placed officials have presented a much less optimistic and more complex interpretation of the Third World in recent years than that which characterised the expectations expressed a decade ago. Yet, the question remains whether this reassessment represents mere tactical modification in Soviet doctrine, or whether it is the external manifestation of a learning process in which the Soviet leadership is increasingly aware of its basic inability to mould the international environment to meet its own objectives. Before attempting to respond to this question, however, it still remains to relate the reassessment in Soviet stated perceptions of the Third World to the broader reconsiderations of foreign policy that are incorporated in Gorbachev's 'new political thinking'.

'NEW POLITICAL THINKING' AND SOVIET FOREIGN POLICY

The Soviet reassessment of both the reality of developments in the Third World and of the nature of its policies toward those countries is but part of a much broader reexamination of Soviet foreign policy referred to by General Secretary Gorbachev as 'new political thinking'. Gorbachev opened his Political Report to the 27th Congress by asserting that:

> for a number of years the deeds and actions of Party and government bodies trailed behind the needs of the times and of life ... The problems in the country's development built up more rapidly than they were being solved. The inertness and fossilization of the forms and methods of administration, the decline of dynamism in our work and an escalation of bureaucracy – all this was doing no small damage.[26]

With these words Gorbachev began an extended litany of problems in Soviet society and the call for the 'new thinking' and 'openness' that have come to characterise his tenure as leader of the party. Turning to the international arena, Gorbachev continued with the demand for rethinking the policies of the past:

> The situation has come to a turning point not only in internal but also in external affairs. The changes in the present world are so deep-going and significant that they require a reappraisal and comprehensive analysis of all factors. The situation created by the nuclear confrontation calls for new approaches, methods and forms of relations between the different social systems, states and regions.[27]

Throughout this speech and in numerous public statements since the Party Congress Gorbachev and other Soviet leaders have argued that the agenda for reform encompasses not only domestic but foreign policy as well. Obviously the essential question, from the perspective of the analyst (and from the perspective of the argument outlined in the present volume), concerns the degree to which the reevaluation of

Soviet foreign policy is more than mere rhetorical updating of Soviet policy and, thus, likely to influence actual Soviet behaviour. Although it is not possible to provide a conclusive answer to this question, the evidence indicates that Gorbachev's call for 'new thinking' in the foreign policy area is more than mere rhetoric meant for propaganda purposes.

In his report to the 27th Party Congress Gorbachev gave some indication of the content of the 'new political thinking' when he raised issues not discussed publicly by Soviet political leaders in the past. The major points that he mentioned include:

1. a recognition of the existence of 'global problems, affecting all humanity' the resolution of which requires 'cooperation on a worldwide scale ... close and constructive joint action by the majority of countries';[28]
2. explicit stress on the interdependence of states, for the 'dialectics of present-day development consists in a combination of competition and confrontation between the two systems and in a growing tendency towards interdependence of the countries of the world community. This is precisely the way, through the struggle of opposites, through arduous effort, groping in the dark as it were, that the contradictory but interdependent and in many ways integral world is taking shape';[29]
3. the argument that 'it is no longer possible to win an arms race, or nuclear war for that matter' and that 'the striving for military superiority can, objectively speaking, bring no political dividends to anybody'. A continuation of the arms race will increase the mutual threat to a point 'where even parity will cease to be a factor of military-political deterrence';[30] and
4. strong criticism of the '"infallibility" complex' and the 'inertness and conservatism' that characterised previous Soviet policy.[31]

In referring to global problems and the growing interdependence among states, Gorbachev has introduced concepts that differ significantly from those that characterised the statements of his predecessors. Most significant is the stress that he placed on interdependence and the need for international cooperation. This is most evident in the security sphere where, he argues, 'the character of present-day weaponry leaves no country with any hope of safeguarding itself solely with military and technical means ... To ensure security is increasingly seen as a political problem, and it can only be resolved by political means.'[32] The security of the Soviet Union and the United States can be maintained only if it is mutual; moreover, although the US military-industrial complex is the 'locomotive of militarism', it is important to recognise that its interests are not identical with 'the actual national interests of that great country'. Finally, the world is dynamic and 'it is not within anybody's power to maintain a perpetual status quo in it. It consists of scores of countries, each having its own perfectly legitimate interests'.[33]

Not all of the specific elements of the 'new political thinking' on foreign policy outlined by Gorbachev at the 27th Party Congress were incorporated in the resolutions approved at the conclusion of the Congress, nor are they included in the Party Program approved at the new thinking' has been a dominant theme in the party press.[35] The most authoritative expansions on Gorbachev's description of the elements of the 'new thinking' can be found in articles by Anatolii Dobrynin, the new secretary of the Central Committee who heads the International Department, and by Evgenyi Primakov, successor to Politburo member Aleksandr Iakovlev as Director of the Institute of World Economics and International Relations.

Both Dobrynin and Primakov repeat, and expand upon, Gorbachev's arguments that the 'interdependence of survival' is crucial in the nuclear age; that the principle of 'equality and equal security' must be observed while reducing the level of military confrontation; that security through military-technical means alone is impossible; that the national security of the USSR can be assured only if US security is also maintained; that the success of Soviet domestic reforms requires a reduction in military expenditures; and that the resolution of problems of international security requires a complex approach to foreign policy that includes military, political, economic, and humanitarian elements.[36]

The 'new political thinking', as presented in the most authoritative Soviet sources, contains three basic components. The first is a revitalisation of Soviet foreign policy by rejecting aspects of Brezhnev's foreign policy and by appealing for greater flexibility in the implementation of foreign policy. The second is the introduction of at least two new concepts or issues on the foreign policy agenda of the top leadership – global problems and interdependence. The third is a reevaluation of the sources of national security which leads to the following conclusions: (1) parity will soon cease to be a factor of political-military restraint; (2) national and international security have become indivisible; and (3) a multifaceted approach to problems of international security must be employed. As Charles Glickham has pointed out, 'the introduction of "the new political thinking" into the lexicon of Soviet foreign relations has meant, if nothing else, a marked change in the way in which the Soviet leadership discusses several basic issues of foreign and security policy'.[37]

As noted earlier in the survey of reassessments of Soviet views of the Third World, academic analysts began discussing a number of years ago most of the issues that have now been placed on the agenda of the top political leadership. For example, since the mid-1970s a number of academic writers as well as some party officials had developed the arguments concerning growing interdependence in the contemporary world, especially in the area of security, and the importance of 'global problems' the solution of which requires increased cooperation.[38]

Also relevant to understanding the background of Gorbachev's 'new political thinking' has been what William Odom has called 'the third revolution' in Soviet military affairs.[39] This 'revolution' has involved a major reassessment of the relevance of nuclear weapons in maintaining security or accomplishing policy objectives. Chief among those who have pointed to the catastrophic consequences of nuclear war and, therefore, the need to overcome the 'inertia of thought and a stubborn, mechanical, unthinking attachment to the old ways'[40] has been Marshal N. V. Ogarkov, former Chief of the Soviet General Staff. Ogarkov and others have presented this argument in order to buttress their call for the resources needed to take advantage of recent technological developments to modernise the conventional military capabilities of the USSR. However, their depiction of the limited military and political utility of nuclear weapons is directly relevant to aspects of the 'new political thinking' advocated by Gorbachev, who has argued that an arms race cannot be 'won' and will likely increase mutual threats to the point that nuclear parity will no longer guarantee deterrence.

This review of recent Soviet writing and statements concerning the place of the Third World in Soviet foreign policy and of the calls for 'new political thinking' demonstrates that the new political leadership in Moscow (at least General Secretary Gorbachev and some of his key supporters) is committed to a new approach to foreign policy. This new approach is based on a more complex view of the international system and appears to take into account the fact that in the contemporary world no country, including the USSR, is able to impose its view of order on the international system. At least at the rhetorical level the Soviet leadership appears to understand some of the realities of the international system in which it is operating.

By no means does this imply that Gorbachev faces no opposition or that his views on foreign policy – or domestic policy, for that matter – will necessarily win out in the long run. Assuming Gorbachev's basic success in implementing his own policy preferences, the crucial question that remains to be answered concerns the impact that his 'new thinking' has had, or is likely to have, on actual Soviet foreign policy behaviour. This is the issue that will concern us in the remainder of this chapter.

THE IMPACT OF THE 'NEW POLITICAL THINKING' ON SOVIET POLICY

In responding to the question of the relationship between the 'new political thinking' and actual Soviet foreign policy behaviour we shall first touch briefly on the broader aspects of Soviet policy, before surveying recent developments in policy toward the Third World. The major elements of Gorbachev's reassessment of Soviet foreign policy include: (1) greater flexibility in making and implementing policy, (2) the introduction of several innovative ideas onto the agenda for consideration by the top leadership, and (3) a reexamination of the sources and requirements for Soviet national security in the nuclear age.

Flexibility in making and implementing policy requires a decision-making process that permits a rapid and effective response to change in both the internal and external environment. Since Gorbachev's assumption of the leadership role three years ago major efforts have been made in Moscow to streamline and reinvigorate the Soviet foreign policy establishment. Substantial reorganisation has occurred within the Ministry of Foreign Affairs, the Central Committee International Department, and the foreign trade sector. By September 1986 one-third of all Soviet ambassadors had been replaced, and only one deputy minister of foreign affairs remained from the Brezhnev era. (The Foreign Minister, his two First Deputy Ministers and seven Deputy Ministers had been replaced by Gorbachev.[41]) In addition, a new directorate has been created within the Ministry to centralise oversight of all arms control and disarmament considerations.[42] It appears that the primary purpose of these staffing and organisational changes within the Ministry is to reassert party control over decision making and, thus, to ensure the introduction of the new policy line advocated by Gorbachev and his supporters.

Given the important oversight and advisory role played by the Central Committee's International Department, changes in that body facilitate the introduction of 'new thinking' into the foreign policy process. The new head of the International Department, the seasoned diplomat Anatolii Dobrynin, is one of the major advocates of revitalisation of Soviet foreign policy. Six of the current nine deputy chiefs of the Department have been appointed under Gorbachev.[43] Of the other three Karen Brutents is among those who have most vigorously called for change in Soviet policy. Moreover, a new section for arms control has been established within the Department.

Substantial change has also occurred in other areas of relevance for Soviet foreign relations. As of 1 January 1987 the foreign trade apparatus of the Soviet Union underwent a major overhaul aimed at eliminating the Ministry of Foreign Trade's monopoly over foreign trade and improving the ability of the USSR to conduct more efficient trade relations. The objective is to introduce greater efficiency in Soviet trade, but also to add a degree of competitiveness into the Soviet economy. As such, it is directly linked to Gorbachev's campaign for economic reform.[44]

Although these and other administrative and personnel changes introduced during the past three years do not guarantee changes in actual Soviet policy, they do appear to represent a first step toward streamlining the policy-making process and, thus, facilitating a more flexible approach to policy making.

Innovative ideas are also essential to any changes in actual Soviet behaviour. Gorbachev and some of his supporters do seem to understand the need to reconsider the underlying assumptions of some aspects of past Soviet policy and have called for innovative thinking in the foreign policy area. Crucial to the successful implementation of such innovation will be support for that thinking within the Soviet foreign policy establishment. Among the new appointees to top positions within both the Ministry of Foreign Affairs and the Central Committee, as well as to other important advisory posts, are individuals who have been associated with the 'new thinking' – in some cases, even before Gorbachev's rise to the post of General Secretary. They include figures already mentioned, such as Foreign Minister Shevardnadze, Party Secretary Dobrynin, International Department Deputy Chief Brutents, and Director of the Institute for World Economy and International Relations Primakov, long-time advocate of precisely the views on foreign policy now espoused by Gorbachev.[45] Another who could be cited in this list is Vladimir Petrovskii, one of the new deputy foreign ministers.[46]

What is evident from recent personnel changes is the fact that Gorbachev is staffing key positions within the state and party foreign policy apparatus with individuals who support his views and who, in some cases, advocated these views before they were incorporated in Gorbachev's thinking. Although this will not assure that policies based on the concepts of 'global problems' and 'interdependence' will be implemented in future Soviet policy, it does mean that Gorbachev will find advice and support if he attempts to introduce such policies.

The *concept of national security* has undergone modification, as well, in the recent pronouncements of the Party leadership. Soviet security, as conceived of by Gorbachev, depends increasingly on political and economic, as well as a military factors, and cannot be guaranteed unilaterally by a mere increase in Soviet military capabilities.[47] Recent shifts in the Soviet position on arms control negotiations – especially concerning verification – and the creation of sections responsible for arms control within the Ministry of Foreign Affairs and the International Department seem to indicate a new commitment to negotiation that coincides with this broadened view of security. It is possible that, in line with his plans for revitalising the economy, Gorbachev will begin to transfer resources from the military to the civilian sector. To date the only evidence to support such an assertion is circumstantial and based on remarks made by Gorbachev that indicate that he is not about to increase military spending, so that he can accomplish political and economic gains which, over the long run, promise to enhance Soviet security.[48] Most important is the need to rebuild and modernise the economic base of the Soviet Union.

Although none of these developments yet provides conclusive evidence that the Soviets under Gorbachev are about to restructure their foreign and security policies, they indicate an understanding of the failures of past policy and the need for internal reform and, by implication, a slowdown in the arms race and a reduction in military spending, if the USSR is to establish a more effective policy in the future. During the past three years growing evidence suggests that actual Soviet behaviour has been undergoing change of a sort consistent with the 'new political thinking'. In virtually all areas of their relations with the outside world the Soviets have attempted to revitalise their role, and that 'revitalisation' has not merely been based on 'more of the same', in the sense of merely emphasising support for radical groups or regimes or focusing exclusively on the conflictual relationship with the United States.

The importance of Gorbachev's new thinking about Soviet foreign and security policy results partially from the recognition that the US position in the world is not based exclusively on military capabilities, as important as they are for the US role as a superpower. If the Soviet Union is to become a full-fledged global power, it must be able to compete with the United States economically and diplomatically, as well as in the military sphere. However, only by very basic, long-term changes can the Soviet Union keep up in the scientific and technological race and thereby retain the hope of becoming an economic superpower. Thus, the major efforts to restructure the Soviet domestic economic (and political) system are meant, in part, to strengthen the economic base from which the USSR can operate in the future. The strategy of interdependence is meant to move the Soviet economy toward joining the world market for the dual purposes of gaining greater benefits for the USSR itself and of expanding Soviet influence in international economic affairs.[49] Moreover, unless the Soviets are able to keep pace with technological developments in the West, the military capabilities of the USSR will likely fall behind those of the United States by the end of the century.

The success of Gorbachev's efforts to restructure the Soviet economy and to close the existing (and growing) technological gap requires a relaxation in the arms race and a reduction in policies likely to result in confrontation and tension with the West.[50] Before examining recent Soviet activities in the Third World, we shall point to some of the new initiatives in Soviet policy toward the United States, the other Western industrial states and China – the areas of primary concern in overall Soviet foreign policy.

RECENT SOVIET INTERNATIONAL BEHAVIOUR

One of the most visible characteristics of Soviet international behaviour since Gorbachev assumed the leadership of the CPSU two years ago has been its renewed activism. In virtually all areas of importance to the Soviet Union – from relations with the United States and China to developments in the Middle East – the new Soviet leadership has demonstrated, in the words of Dimitri Simes, 'a new sense of purpose, a new realism and a new creativity'.[51] Gorbachev's primary objective has been to reverse the decline in both the effectiveness and the credibility of Soviet policy that had been set in the final years of the Brezhnev leadership and to regain the initiative in international affairs.

Of primary concern has been the state of Soviet-US relations which had deteriorated dramatically since the late 1970s. More important, however, than the mere fact of the increased hostility in relations with the United States was the renewed vigour with which the United States pursued its international interests. In the Third World President Reagan, in effect, had declared war on a number of Soviet clients and made clear that the Soviets would not be permitted to make additional gains comparable to those of the mid-1970s. In other words, despite obtaining strategic parity in the military area, the Soviets were not accepted by the United States as an equal in the international political system. Moreover, the revitalised US arms build-up, symbolised most dramatically in the Strategic Defense Initiative, threatened to vitiate past Soviet efforts to gain strategic parity with the United States.

Under Gorbachev the Soviets have made dramatic overtures in the attempt to facilitate nuclear arms control negotiations with the United States – including a willingness to agree to the elimination of intermediate- and shorter-range missiles in Europe and Asia, proposals to cut strategic weapons by 50 per cent and to place a complete moratorium on testing, acceptance of intrusive on-site verification, and an offer to negotiate major reductions in conventional and tactical nuclear weapons and manpower in Central Europe.[52] Although one of the Soviet objectives is no doubt a desire to project the image of having a stronger commitment to arms control than the United States has for propaganda purposes, a broader purpose appears to be based on the realisation that a renewed arms race with the United States would undermine the attempts to commit resources to the revitalisation of the domestic economy and to domestic reform. Moreover, and probably of greatest importance, as Seweryn Bialer and Joan Afferica have argued, 'are Soviet security concerns. These include the widening American technological preponderance, the accelerating American offensive nuclear arms program, and the tension and danger inherent in a new arms race. Even more important than fear of the known is fear of the unknown, the terrible uncertainties concealed in America's grandiose Strategic Defense Initiative.'[53]

In their relations with the major allies of the United States the Soviets appear to be motivated primarily by the desire to convince these countries of their good intentions and to influence them to put pressure on the United States to negotiate with the USSR.[54] The argument that they have been making is that, despite the problems in US-Soviet relations, the mutual benefits derived from the *détente* of the 1970s by all European states can and should continue. A case in point has been the recent effort to expand trade relations and to play a more active role in the international economic system. With this objective in mind the Soviets have applied for observer status at the GATT, shown a willingness to deal more fully with the European Economic Community, and reorganised significantly their foreign trade institutions.[55]

When we turn to an examination of recent Soviet policy in the Third World, the evidence indicates, as well, revitalised efforts, including a number of innovative initiatives, to reestablish or consolidate their role as a major world actor.

Since Gorbachev took over as head of the CPSU in early 1985 the Soviets have attempted to reestablish their position in the Middle East – the Third World region of primary importance for their long-term security interests. In line with prior policy, they have made new commitments of military aid to both Syria and Libya[56] and have continued to support Iraq in its war against Iran, while simultaneously working to normalise relations with the latter. However, they have also expanded their efforts to reach out to more moderate Arab states – such as Egypt, Jordan, and Kuwait – and even to open up discussions with Israel. Since 1986, for example, they have mediated a reconciliation of competing factions of the Palestine Liberation Organisation, initiated talks with Egypt concerning a possible Middle East peace conference, responded to Kuwaiti requests for protection of their oil tankers against Iran by leasing three tankers, held various informal discussions with Israel, and signed economic agreements with Iran.[57]

In Afghanistan the Soviets under Gorbachev continued their attempts to pacify the country by conquest, but have now agreed to withdraw their troops by early 1989. Relations with India, the single most important non-communist developing country for the USSR, have been reinvigorated by mutual visits of Rajiv Gandhi and Mikhail Gorbachev and by new Soviet credits for military and civilian purchases. The Soviets are well aware of the fact that, unless they can continue to remain 'relevant' for the primary Indian concerns – security against Pakistan (and China) and economic development – relations are likely to stagnate.[58] In Southeast Asia the Soviets have mounted increasing efforts to expand both diplomatic and economic contacts with the members of ASEAN – although largely without success to date.[59] In Africa the Soviets have expanded support for their embattled clients in Angola and Ethiopia. In fact, the increase in US assistance to UNITA in Angola has resulted in expanded Soviet military aid and even greater Angolan dependence on the Soviets and their Cuban allies.[60] Moreover, the Soviets have also discussed the possibility of supplying Zimbabwe – whose relations with the USSR have been cool since independence – with a 12-plane squadron of Mig-29 jet interceptors to enhance that country's ability to respond to South African military incursions.[61]

Finally, Foreign Minister Eduard Shevardnadze's official visits to Latin America in early fall 1987 gave evidence of the Soviets' desire to expand diplomatic and economic relations with major Latin American countries. Economic concerns and a wide range of other international issues were on the agenda during discussions with leaders in Brazil, Argentina, and Uruguay. Most important, however, was Shevardnadze's effort to project the image of a Soviet Union concerned about the problems of the region.[62]

Thus, Soviet policy in the Third World has not undergone any dramatic change in recent years, despite the reassessments of the role of the Third World in Soviet policy that were described above. What is evident is a greater degree of flexibility in Soviet initiatives, as in the Middle East, but not an abandonment of past commitments. Moreover, the Soviets appear to be distinguishing between those Third World clients to whom they have made firm commitments – such as Afghanistan, Angola and Ethiopia – and others, such as Nicaragua and Mozambique, where their past commitments have been more limited and where long-term prospects for stable, pro-Soviet regimes are less promising.[63] If this is an accurate assessment of actual Soviet behaviour, what implications does it have for the questions posed earlier in this chapter concerning the degree to which the Soviet leadership has recognised the limitations placed on its ability to structure the world to its own ends and the amount of 'learning' that has been actually occurring in Moscow? In the concluding section we shall attempt to address these questions more fully.

THE 'NEW POLITICAL THINKING' AND THE FUTURE OF SOVIET POLICY

We return now to the questions posed earlier in this chapter concerning the meaning and implications of the debate on 'New Political Thinking' for the future of Soviet foreign policy, in particular in the developing world. Does the debate portend a substantive shift in Soviet policy, or does it merely concern the tactics to be employed to pursue more effectively policies long in place?

In responding to this question it is important first to outline what in fact are the guidelines for Soviet policy that emerge from the discussions in Moscow. The first essential point is Gorbachev's recognition that significant improvement in the Soviet economy is the indispensable basis for future Soviet power in the world. He and his associates recognise that the positive assessment (from a Soviet perspective) of the 'international correlation of forces' that dominated Soviet thinking in the 1970s was premature, at best. It overestimated the role of military power in the ability of the Soviet Union to accomplish its foreign policy objectives and greatly underestimated the ability of the United States effectively to renew its military, political, and economic challenge to the USSR. What is required, if the Soviet Union is to become a full-fledged superpower in the twenty-first century, is a vital and vibrant Soviet society with an economic base from which to challenge continued US predominance. Thus, for the foreseeable future the Soviets will give priority to domestic economic reform and to the political and social 'restructuring' necessary to accomplish this goal.

In order to accomplish these objectives, however, the Soviets require a period of respite from the global conflict and confrontation that have characterised much of the past decade. An upsurge in international tension and an increase in military expenditures would exacerbate the difficulties of economic reform and dim the prospects for significant improvement in Soviet economic performance. Thus, for the foreseeable future the Soviets will pursue policies aimed at reducing international crisis and improving relations with the West – in other words, a policy of retrenchment or Thermidor that will provide a breathing space in competition with the United States and permit the Soviets to devote their resources and attention to domestic concerns.

Yet this retrenchment will not result in renewed isolationism or in a withdrawal from the international gains of the past. Rather, competition with the United States will continue, with different emphases and even with increased intensity, as we have witnessed since Gorbachev's appointment as General Secretary. One of the major objectives of what can only be viewed as a reinvigorated Soviet diplomacy is to refurbish the image and credibility of the Soviet Union as a global power and, concomitantly, to undermine those of the United States. Soviet initiatives in the arms control area have already tended to force the United States on the defensive, as have the broadened Soviet diplomatic initiatives in the Middle East and the Persian Gulf region. Essential to current Soviet policy as well are more relaxed US-Soviet relations which would bring with it numerous benefits for the Soviet leadership. Most important would be the reduction of external pressure on the Soviet leaders at a time when they are concerned primarily with overcoming the long-neglected problems that challenge their domestic social and economic system. In addition, although Gorbachev has made it quite clear that he will not pursue foreign economic policies that would result in dependence on the West, he does expect that the Soviet economy will benefit from increased trade, expanded competition, investment in the form of joint ventures, and technical know-how from the West.

A policy of retrenchment, or Thermidor, does not mean either abandonment of gains already made in the Third World or of the use of force when threats arise to valued clients or national interests. The Soviets will attempt to retain the gains of the past, even if this involves the use of military force as in Afghanistan, Southeast Asia, Ethiopia, etc. Yet, pressures on the West can also be maintained through indirect means, principally by taking advantage of conflicts between the industrial states and the developing world. Expansion of political and diplomatic contacts with key non-communist developing states might bring far greater long-term benefits for the Soviets than their past emphasis on radical Marxist-Leninist regimes such as those in Angola and South Yemen. A policy of Thermidor implies the creation of alignment structures tilted against the United States that would incorporate a growing range of developing countries, while direct military competition with Washington essentially marks time. These alignments could build on the inherent anti-Americanism widespread in the developing world, including in countries currently closely tied to the United States,[64] and would aim at shifting the burden of 'containing' the United States to Soviet clients and to states opposed to US policies, even though they might be capitalist and firmly within the Western sphere of influence. A Soviet Union which saw itself as an integral part of the existing international system – rather than as the besieged centre of a competing alternate system – would likely be even more pragmatic in its search for allies and friends and in the policies that it pursued than the USSR has been to date. Moreover, it would probably be more successful in establishing the type of global role that has thus far eluded the Soviet leadership.

The lines of future Soviet policy that emerge from the recent Soviet discussions, as well as from Soviet behaviour, appear to go beyond mere tactical modifications in past policy. Agreement on a substantial reduction of the Soviet nuclear arsenal, expanded efforts to establish contacts with non-Marxist regimes in the Third World that are not based primarily on security relations – such moves are more than mere tactical modifications of past policy. Yet, even if these changes are meant only as tactical modifications on existing strategy, they can have longer term implications for the evolution of Soviet policy. Given that the motivation for the 'new thinking' in Moscow is based on the desire to rebuild Soviet economic capabilities and to refurbish the USSR's international image and claims to superpower status, this process is likely to be an extended one, as Gorbachev himself has admitted. Yet, a long-term policy of the type outlined above may bring with it the seeds of a more fundamental change in Soviet domestic and foreign policy.[65] One result might be over time the lessening of the overt military threat posed by the Soviet Union and the emergence of Soviet international behaviour more in line with that of a traditional great power.

By no means does this imply that US-Soviet competition will lessen in the developing world or that the Soviets will cease to challenge US interests. In fact, a revitalised Soviet Union armed with economic and political capabilities to match its military strength would in many ways be a more formidable opponent of US interests than it has been to date. It would be more capable of benefiting from the conflicts between the West and the developing world were it not viewed as a potential security threat by many Third World leaders and were it able to provide economic alternatives to the West.

The Soviets would present a more variegated and more complex challenge to US interests in the developing world – one that continued, though on a reduced basis, to employ its military might to accomplish important goals, but also that could count on stable alignments with non-Marxist governments. Yet that challenge would be less fraught with the dangers of military confrontation between the two superpowers.

Notes

1. The present discussion has benefited from a number of important recent treatments of changing Soviet interpretations of the Third World. These include, especially, Francis Fukuyama, *Moscow's Post-Brezhnev Reassessment of the Third World* (Santa Monica, CA: Rand Corporation, 1986), Report No. R-3337-USDP; Francis Fukuyama, 'Gorbachev and the Third World', *Foreign Affairs*, vol. 64, no. 4, 1986, pp. 715–31; Jerry F. Hough, *The Struggle for the Third World: Soviet Debates and American Options* (Washington, DC: Brookings Institution, 1986); Daniel S. Papp. *Soviet Perceptions of the Developing World in the 1980s: The Ideological Basis* (Lexington, MA/Toronto: Lexington Books, 1985); Elizabeth Kridl Valkenier, *The Soviet Union and the Third World: An Economic Bind* (New York: Praeger, 1983); Elizabeth Kridl Valkenier, 'Revolutionary Change in the Third World: Recent Soviet Reassessments', *World Politics*, vol. 38, no. 3, 1986, pp. 415–34; and Thomas J. Zamostny, 'Moscow and the Third World: Recent Trends in Soviet Thinking', *Soviet Studies*, vol. 36, no 2, 1984, pp. 223–35. In a perceptive review essay George W. Breslauer examines these and several other publications; see 'Ideology and Learning in Soviet Third World Policy Today', *World Politics*, vol. 39, no. 3, 1987, pp. 429–48.
2. 'Programma Kommunisticheskoi Partii Sovetskogo Soiuza. Novaia Redaktsiia', *Pravda*, 7 March 1986, p. 7; translated as 'The Programme of the Communist Party of the Soviet Union. A New Edition', *New Times*, no. 12, 1986, p. 43. The previous party programme, published in 1961, had spoken of 'mighty wave of national liberation revolutions' that were 'sweeping away the colonial system and undermining the foundations of imperialism'. 'Programma Kommunisticheskoi Partii Sovetskogo Soiuza', *Pravda*, 2 November 1961, p. 3.
3. See, for example, Iurii Novopashin, 'Vozdeistvie real'nogo sotsializma na mirovoi revoliutsionnyi protesess: methdologicheskie aspekty', *Voprosy Filosofii*, no. 8 (1982), pp. 3–16.
4. 'Rech' General'nogo Sekretaria TSK KPSS Tovarishcha Iu. V. Andropova', *Kommunist*, no. 9 (1983), pp. 14–15. See also Andropov's earlier article entitled 'Pod znamenem Lenina, pod voditel'stvom Partii', *Izvestiia*, 23 February 1979, p. 2. The party programme approved in 1986 used virtually the same wording as that of Andropov when it noted that 'every people creates, mostly by its own efforts, the material and technical base necessary for the building of a new society, and seeks to improve the well-being and cultural standards of the masses'. 'Programma Kommunisticheskoi Partii', p. 7 (see note 2).
5. Boris Ponomarev, 'Real Socialism and the Liberated Countries', *Slovo Lektora*, no. 3, 1984, translated in *Foreign Broadcast Information Service*, 3, 14 June 1984, pp. 2–6 (annex). Similarly, Politburo member Gaidar Aliev had noted in a speech in Hanoi that 'in helping our Vietnamese friends develop their economy, the Soviet people have to share things that they need themselves'. See 'Pravdnik narodov-pobratimov: miting Sovetskogo-V'etnamskogo druzhby', *Pravda*, 1 November 1983, p. 5.

6. This argument has been developed most clearly by Novopashin, 'Vozdeistvie real'nogo sotsializma' (see note 3). It was repeated by Ivan Kapitonov, former party secretary in charge of the Department of Light Industry, who stated: 'The party is guided by Lenin's deep insight that we exert our main influence on the world revolutionary process by our economic policy. Our every success in improving the developed socialist society, in further fortifying the strength of the Soviet state is of international significance and serves the common cause of world socialism and the people's struggle against imperialism, and for democracy, national freedom, and social progress.' 'A Working Class Party, The Whole People's Party: 80th Anniversary of the Second Congress of the RSDLP', *World Marxist Review*, vol. 26, no. 7, 1983, p. 8.

7. L. N. Lebedinskaia, 'Narody byvshego kolonial'nogo mira i real'nyi sotsializm', *Rabochii Klass i Sovremennyi Mir*, no. 4, 1982, p. 24.

8. For a discussion of this policy in the African context, see Daniel R. Kempton and Roger E. Kanet, 'Soviet Policy in Africa: Prospects and Problems for Model and Ally Strategies', in Jane Shapiro Zacek (ed.), *The Gorbachev Generation*, Vol. II *Major Foreign Policy Issues Facing the New Leadership* (New York: Paragon, forthcoming). See also David E. Albright, 'Vanguard Parties in the Third World', in Walter Laqueur (ed.), *The Pattern of Soviet Conduct in the Third World (New York: Praeger, 1983), pp. 208–25*.

9. S. Neil MacFarlane, *Superpower Rivalry and Third World Radicalism: The Idea of National Liberation* (Baltimore, MD: Johns Hopkins University Press, 1985), p. 140.

10. Alexei Kosygin, 'Direktivy XXIV S'ezda KPSS po piatiletnemu planu razvitiia narodnogo khoziaistva SSSR na 1971–1975 godu', *Pravda*, 7 April 1971, p. 6.

11. Rostislav Ul'ianovskii, 'O natsional'noi i revol'iutsionnoi demokratii: puty evol'iutsii', *Narody Azii i Afriki*, no. 2, 1984, p. 16.

12. Cautioning his readers against over-optimism concerning developments in the Third World Ul'ianovskii notes that the transition to socialism will be lengthy and 'the fact that one party or another proclaims itself to be Marxist-Leninist and its revolution socialist does not change the essence of the matter' (ibid.). For a comprehensive examination of the evolution of Ul'ianovskii's thinking, see Sally W. Stoecker, *R. A. Ulianovsky's Writings on Soviet Third World Policies, 1960–1985* (Santa Monica, CA: Rand Corporation, February 1986), No. P-7177.

13. A. Bovin, 'Difficult Roads of Freedom', *Izvestiia*, 12 November 1984, p. 5, translated in *Current Digest of the Soviet Press*, vol. 36, no. 48, December 26 1984, p. 2. More recently Bovin has stated that 'In a number of countries of a socialist orientation, the situation remains unstable, fraught with the possibility of regression.' A. Bovin, 'Perestroika i sud'by sotsializma', *Izvestiia*, 11 July 1987, p. 6.

14. For an examination of recent Soviet literature related to this topic see Roger E. Kanet, 'Soviet Propaganda and the Process of National Liberation', in Albert L. Salter with the assistance of William J. Colligan (eds), *Contemporary Soviet Propaganda and Disinformation*

(Washington, DC: Department of State Publication No. 9536, 1987), especially pp. 228–42. A recent article of this type is Vladimir Krestyaninov, 'Neoglobalism: The Doctrine for Export of Counter-Revolution', *International Affairs*, no. 3, 1987, pp. 30–9.

15. Karen Brutents, 'Imperializm i osvobodivshiesia strany', *Pravda*, 10 February 1978, pp. 3–4; Evgenyi Primakov, 'Nekotorye problemy razvivaiushchikhsia stran', *Kommunist*, no. 11 (1978), pp. 81–91.

16. 'Programma Kommunisticheskoi Partii', p. 7. See, also, 'Political Report of the CPSU Central Committee to the 27th Congress of the Communist Party of the Soviet Union, Delivered by General Secretary of the CPSU Central Committee Comrade Mikhail Gorbachev', *New Times*, no. 9 (1986), p. 18, where Gorbachev discusses the conflicts between imperialism and the developing countries.

17. Karen Brutents, 'Sovetskii Soiuz i osvobodivshiesia strany', *Pravda*, 2 February 1982, p. 4. See also his 'Osvobodivshiesia strany v nachale 80kh godov', *Kommunist*, no. 3, 1984, especially p. 108, where he notes the existence of growing contradictions between imperialism and some of the developing 'states of capitalist orientation'.

18. Valkenier, *The Soviet Union and the Third World*, p. 26 (see note 1).

19. Andropov, 'Rech' General'nogo Sekretaria', p. 15 (see note 4).

20. Dmitry Volsky, 'Local Conflicts and International Security', *New Times*, no. 5, 1983, p. 5.

21. Dmitry Volsky, 'The Face of Imperial Policy', *New Times*, no. 16, 1983, p. 9.

22. Dmitry Volsky, 'The Washington Plot against the Third World', *New Times*, no. 10, 1984, p. 5.

23. See Volsky, 'Local Conflicts', pp. 5–7 (see note 2).

24. Bovin, 'Difficult Roads of Freedom', p. 3 (see note 13).

25. Ponomarev, 'Real Socialism', p. 3 (see note 5); Karen Brutents, 'Dvizhenie neprisoedineniia v sovremennon mire', *Mirovaia Ekonomika i Mezhdunarodnye Otnosheniia*, no. 5, 1984, p. 33.

26. Gorbachev, 'Political Report', p. 13 (see note 16). The present discussion of the meaning and importance of Gorbachev's Political Report has benefited greatly from Charles Glickham's 'New Directions for Soviet Foreign Policy', *Radio Liberty Research*, Supplement 2/86, 6 September 1986, pp. 1–26; and from Gerhard Wettig's 'Das' neue Denken' in der UdSSR – ein Abrücken von alter Klassenpolitik?', *Berichte des Bundesinstituts für ostwissenschaftliche und internationale Studien*, no. 12, 1987, pp. 1–27.

27. Gorbachev, 'Political Report', p. 13 (see note 16). See also Heinz Timmermann, 'Gorbatchows aussenpolitische Leitlinien: Die internationalen Beziehungen Moskaus auf dem 27. Parteitag der KPdSU', *Berichte des Bundesinstituts für ostwissenschaftliche und internationale Studien*, no. 13, 1986, pp. 1–30; and Abraham Becker, Seweryn Bialer, Arnold Horelick: Robert Legvold, Marshall Shulman, *The 27th Congress of the Communist Party of the Soviet Union: A Report from the Airlie House Conference* (Santa Monica, CA: Rand/UCLA Center for the Study of Soviet Behavior; New York: W. Averell Harriman Institute for Advanced Study of the Soviet Union, 1986), pp. 1–82. For

a commentary by a noted Soviet analyst see Shalva Sanakoyev, '27th Congress on Soviet Foreign Policy Main Directions', *International Affairs*, no. 19, 1986, pp. 9–20.

27. Gorbachev, 'Political Report', p. 14 (see note 16).
28. Ibid., p. 19.
29. Ibid.
30. Ibid., p. 36.
31. Ibid., p. 41.
32. Ibid., p. 36.
33. Ibid.
34. See 'Rezoliutsii XXVII s"ezda Kommunisticheskoi Partii Sovetskogo Soiuza po politicheskomu dokladu Tsentral'nogo Komiteta KPSS', *Kommunist*, no. 4, 1986, pp. 81–98 and 'Programme of the Communist Party', pp. 23–7, 43–5.
35. For a listing of some of these articles see Glickham, 'New Directions', pp. 19–20 (see note 26).
36. A. Dobrynin, 'Za bez"iadernyi mir, navstrechu XXI veku', *Kommunist*, no. 9, 1986, especially pp. 22–5; E. Primakov, 'Novaia filosofiia vneshnei politiki', *Pravda*, 10 July 1987, p. 4. See also excerpts of an interview with Primakov in Paul Quinn-Judge, 'Soviet Shift in World Policy', *Christian Science Monitor*, 16 July 1987, pp. 1, 10. In an article concerning conflicts within the capitalist world, Aleksander Iakovlev, Secretary of the Central Committee and Candidate Member of the Politburo (and reportedly a close associate of Gorbachev), repeats some of these points concerning the need for a new approach to foreign policy. See A. Iakovlev, 'Mezhimperialisticheskie protivorechiia – sovremennyi kontekst', *Kommunist*, no. 17, 1986, pp. 3–17. See also the article by Bovin, 'Perestroika i sud'by sotsializma', p. 6 (see note 13); and the discussion of the implications of the 'new thinking' for the ultimate goal of world revolution in E. G. Plimak, 'Novoe myshlenie i perspektivy sotsial'nogo obnovleniia mira', *Voprosy filosofii*, no. 6, 1987, pp. 73–89.
37. The entire paragraph, including the citation, borrows from Glickham, 'New Directions', p. 7 (see note 26).
38. . See, for example, Anatolii Gromyko and Vladimir Lomeiko, *Novoe myshlenie v iadernyi vek* (Moscow: Mezhdunarodnye otnosheniia, 1984). See also Anatolii Gromyko and Vladimir Lomeiko, 'New Way of Thinking; New Globalism', *International Affairs*, no. 5, 1986, pp. 15–27; G. Kh. Shakhnazarov, 'Logika politicheskogo myshleniia v iadernuiu eru', *Voprosy filosofii*, no. 5, 1984, pp. 63–74; G. L. Smirnov, 'Za reshitel'nyi povorot filosofkhikh issledovanii k sotsial'noi praktike', *Voprosy filosofii*, no. 9, 1983, pp. 3–19; M. Maksimova, 'Vsemirno khoziaistvo, nauchno-tekhnicheskaia revoliutsiia i mezhdunarodnye otnosheniia (chast' vtoraia)', *Mirovaia ekonomika i mezhdunarodnye otnosheniia*, no. 5, 1979, pp. 21–33; S. M. Men'shikov, 'Global'nye problemy i budushchee mirovoi ekonomiki', *Voprosy filosofii*, no. 4, 1983, pp. 102–15. It is important to point out that these writings of the early 1980s concerning global problems and interdependence represented a minority, but expanding, view among Soviet analysts. The

dominant position remained that of virtually total hostility and conflict between the USSR and the United States. For a discussion of the early Soviet 'debate' on these issues see Walter C. Clemens, Jr, *The USSR and Global Interdependence: Alternative Futures* (Washington, DC: American Enterprise Institute for Public Policy Research, 1978).

39.   William E. Odom, 'Soviet Force Posture: Dilemmas and Directions', *Problems of Communism*, vol. 34, no. 4, July–August 1985, pp. 6–14.

40.   N. V. Ogarkov, 'Pobeda i sovremennost'', *Izvestiia*, 9 May 1983, p. 2. For a comprehensive examination of the views of Marshal Ogarkov and of other Soviet military analysts who argue for a renewed emphasis on conventional military capabilities see Mary C. FitzGerald, 'Marshal Ogarkov on the Modern Theater Operation', *Naval War College Review*, vol. 39, no. 4, 1986, pp. 6–25.

41.   See Alexander Rahr, 'Winds of Change Hit Foreign Ministry', *Radio Liberty Research*, RL 274/86, 16 July 1986. See also Jan S. Adams, 'Institutional Change and Soviet National Security Policy', unpublished paper presented at a seminar on 'A Third Revolution in Soviet National Security Policy?' Session II: 'Military Doctrine, Institutional and Economic Factors', sponsored by the Mershon Center and the Hudson Institute, Indianapolis, IN, 6–7 February 1987.

42.   See the interview with Victor Karpov, in which he is described as 'chief of the arms limitation and disarmament division of the USSR Ministry of Foreign Affairs', in *New Times*, no. 28, 1986, p. 4.

43.   See Alexander Rahr, 'The Apparatus of the Central Committee of the CPSU', *Radio Liberty Research*, RL 136/87, 10 April 1987.

44.   Philip Hanson, 'Reforming the Foreign-Trade System', *Radio Liberty Research*, RL 104/87, 19 March 1987.

45.   See, for example, E. Primakov, 'Put'' v budushchee', *Pravda*, 22 January 1986, p. 4; and E. Primakov, 'Filosofiia bezopasnosti', *Pravda*, 17 March 1986, p. 6. For references to Primakov's earlier views see Hough, *Struggle for the Third World*, *passim* (see note 1).

46.   See Rahr, 'Winds of Change Hit Foreign Ministry' (see note 41). For Petrovskii's views see his 'Magistral'nyi put'' k bezopasnomu miru', *Mirovaia ekonomika i mezhdunarodnye otnosheniia*, no. 6, 1985, pp. 3–17.

47.   For a perceptive analysis of Gorbachev's views on security that relates these views to actual policy initiatives see Matthew Evangelista, 'The New Soviet Approach to Security', *World Policy Journal*, vol. 3, no. 4, 1986, pp. 561–99.

48.   On verification see Gorbachev, 'Political Report', p. 37 (see note 16); on military spending, ibid., p. 35, where Gorbachev states that: 'Today we can declare with all responsibility that the defence capability of the USSR is maintained on a level that reliably protects the peaceful life and labours of the Soviet people.' Compare this with comments by former General Secretary Brezhnev, made shortly before his death: 'We should tirelessly strengthen the defenses of our country and be vigilant ... the level of combat readiness of the army and navy should be even higher.' Leonid Brezhnev, 'Soveshchanie voenachal'nikov v Kremle', *Pravda*, 28 October 1982, p. 1. The replacing of Defence Minister Marshal

Sergei Sokolov by the relatively unknown and politically unconnected General Dmitri Iazov in June 1987 (supposedly because of inadequacies in the Soviet air defence system exposed by the flight of a small private plane from Finland to Moscow) may be the beginning of a house-cleaning in the military, comparable to those which have already occurred in the party leadership, that will enhance Gorbachev's decision-making flexibility. See 'Marching Orders', *Newsweek*, 15 June 1987, pp. 34–6.

49. See John P. Hardt, 'Changing Perspectives toward the Normalization of East–West Commerce', in Gary K. Bertsch (ed.), *Controlling East-–West Trade and Technology Transfer: Power, Politics, and Policies* (Durham, NC: Duke University Press, forthcoming).

50. However, virtually no Western analyst believes that, even with the best of luck, the Soviets will be able to accomplish the stated goal of closing the technology gap with the West by the end of the century. The policies being advocated by Gorbachev are based on a strategy that includes mobilising productions reserves in the labour pool through greater discipline and efficiency, modernisation of the capital stock of the Soviet economy, and reform and restructuring of the economy in order to facilitate the implementation of the first two aspects of the strategy. Essential to the success of the entire programmes is an increase in the amount of investment funds available. Given already high levels of investment in the Soviet economy, it is very doubtful that they can be increased without at least a short-term reduction in military expenditures. For an excellent overview of current Soviet economic strategy see Dieter Lösch, 'The USSR's Economic Strategy up to the Year 2000: Aims, Methods and Chances of Success', *Intereconomics: Review of International Trade and Development*, vol. 21, no. 4, 1986, pp. 203–9. For other discussions of the Soviet domestic economic reform see Hans-Hermann Höhmann, 'The Place of Economic Policy Objectives on the List of Soviet Political Priorities', and Ronald Amann, 'The Political and Social Implications of Economic Reform in the USSR', in Hans-Hermann Höhmann, Alex Nove and Heinrich Vogel (eds), *Economics and Politics in the USSR: Problems of Interdependence* (Boulder, CO–London: Westview Press, 1986), pp. 41–57, 125–45.

51. Dimitri K. Simes, 'Gorbachev: A New Foreign Policy?', *Foreign Affairs*, vol. 65, no. 3, 1987, p. 491.

52. For discussions of recent Soviet policy on arms control see Evangelista, 'The New Soviet Approach to Security' (see note 47); Sigurd Boysen, 'Gorbatschows Abrüstungsvorschläge: Politische und militärische Bewertung der sowjetischen Abrüstungsinitiativen 1985/86', *Berichte des Bundesinstituts für ostwissenschaftliche und internationale Studien*, no. 1, 1987, pp. 1–70; Gerhard Wettig, 'A New Soviet Approach to Negotiating on Arms Control', *Berichte des Bundesinstituts für ostwissenschaftliche und internationale Studien*, no. 2, 1987, pp. 1–19; and Charlotte Saikowski, 'Does Soviet Offer Reflect Historic Change?', *Christian Science Monitor*, 1 May 1987, p. 5.

53. Seweryn Bialer and Joan Afferica, 'The Genesis of Gorbachev's World', *Foreign Affairs*, vol. 64, no. 3, 1986, pp. 642–3.

54. Although recent Soviet policy has not emphasised efforts to split the US

from its allies, the Soviets have not abandoned the view that 'contradictions' between the United States and its allies are growing and can be exploited by the USSR. See, for example, A. Iakovlev, 'Mezhimperialisticheskie protivorechiia – sovremennyi kontekst', *Kommunist*, no. 17, 1986, pp. 3–17; see, also, Gorbachev, 'Political Report', p. 17 (see note 16). Moreover, current Soviet policy toward Western Europe can well serve the dual function of putting pressure on the United States while also exacerbating differences between the United States and its major European allies.

55. See Vladimir Sobell, 'The USSR and the Western Economic Order: Time for Cooperation?', *Radio Free Europe Research, RAD Background Report*/128 (East–West Relations), 15 September 1986; and Roger E. Kanet, 'Commentary [on Soviet Foreign Economic Policy]', in John P. Hardt and Richard F. Kaufman, (eds), *Gorbachev's Economic Plans*. Study Papers Submitted to the Joint Economic Committee, Congress of the United States. (Washington, DC: U.S. Government Printing Office, 23 November 1987). Vol. 2, pp. 542–49.

56. See Wayne Brown, 'Soviet Union Promises Syria and Libya More Military Aid', *Radio Liberty Research*, RL 212/86, 30 May 1987.

57. John Kifner, 'Soviet Acts to Win Back Influence in Mideast', *New York Times*, 11 May 1987, pp. 1, 6; Bill Keller, 'USSR Expands Contacts with Third World', *New York Times*, 25 May 1987, pp. 1, 4; Joseph C. Harsch, 'Kuwait, the US and Moscow', *Christian Science Monitor*, 2 June 1987, p. 15; Claude van England, 'Iran Set to Pipe Oil through Soviet Union', *Christian Science Monitor*, 12 August 1987, p. 1; Daniel Abele, 'Recent Soviet Moves in the Persian Gulf Region', *Radio Liberty Research*, RL 307/87, 10 August 1987.

58. For two perceptive articles on Soviet-Indian relations see Jyotirmoy Banerjee, 'Moscow's Indian Alliance', and Dilip Mukerjee, 'Indo-Soviet Economic Ties', *Problems of Communism*, vol. 36, no. 1, January–February, 1987, pp. 1–12 and 13–25, respectively.

59. See Daniel Abele, 'The Soviet Diplomatic and Trade Offensive among the ASEAN Countries', *Radio Liberty Research*, RL 333/86, 12 August 1986.

60. See Robert M. Press, 'Soviets Lead Angola Buildup', *Christian Science Monitor*, 7 April, 1987, pp. 1, 8; Jill Joliffe, 'Rising Tension in Angola Heightens Nation's Reliance on Soviets', *Christian Science Monitor*, 4 May, 1987, pp. 18, 19; Bohdan Nahaylo, 'Recent Soviet Policy towards Southern Africa', *Radio Liberty Research*, RL 196/86, 20 May, 1986, especially pp. 2–5.

61. See Kurt M. Campbell, 'The Case of the MIGs and Zimbabwe's New Soviet Tilt', *Christian Science Monitor*, 7 May 1987, p. 22. As John Seiler notes above in chapter 14, the agreement has still not been finalized.

62. See, for example, Julia Michaels, 'Shevardnadze's Visit to Brazil Brings Talk of Apples and Oranges – and Increased Trade', *Christian Science Monitor*, 1 October 1987, pp. 7, 8; *US News & World Report*, 12 October 1987, p. 50.

63. See, for example, Peter Ford, 'Nicaragua Looks to Latin America as Soviets Appear to Limit Aid', *Christian Science Monitor*, 8 June 1987, pp. 1, 11; Nahaylo, 'Recent Soviet Policy towards Southern Africa', pp. 5–6 (see note 60); Sam Levy, 'Though Marxist, Mozambique is Shifting toward the West', *Christian Science Monitor*, 6 August 1985, p. 14.

64. For a compehensive treatment of the breadth and sources of anti-Americanism see Alvin Z. Rubinstein and Donald E. Smith (eds), *Anti-Americanism in the Third World: Implications for US Foreign Policy* (New York-Westport, CT-London: Praeger, Greenwood Press, for the Foreign Policy Research Institute, 1985).

65. For an innovative and provocative discussion of the possibility of change and learning in Soviet ideology as the framework within which Soviet policy is formulated, including both the stimuli and the impediments to change, see Breslauer's review article, 'Ideology and Learning in Soviet Third World Policy' (see note 1).

16 Soviet Prospects in the Developing World: Implications for US Policy
Edward A. Kolodziej

This chapter summarises the limitations of Soviet power, discussed in detail in the preceding chapters, and how they generate incentives for a Thermidor in the superpower conflict in the developing world. A respite, if extended, could conceivably moderate the inclinations of the superpowers to intervene militarily abroad and lead to a redefinition of their struggle from one characterized principally by force and threats to one driven primarily by political and soci-economic competition.

The second main section defines what is meant by Thermidor and how it might evolve. A period of Thermidor is also contrasted with what the Soviet Union and the West understood and expected from *détente* in the 1970s. It also suggests how the United States and the West might benefit from a period of restrained competition within the developing world. A final section casts the superpower conflict within the framework of the modernisation processes that have been sweeping the globe for over four centuries. The United States and the Soviet Union are themselves products of these political, economic, and social processes. Conversely, both have an interest, albeit divergent and clashing, in shaping these processes to their own liking, but short of catastrophic war.

LIMITS OF SOVIET POWER

Military Impasse: Nuclear Balance and Conventional Stalemate

While the absolute power of the Soviet Union has grown, particularly since the Second World War, its relative power in the global society, paradoxically, has not correspondingly enlarged. First, its military power is checked by the nuclear power and by the formidable, if not superior, conventional military capabilities of the West. The Soviet Union can neither disarm the United States in a first strike nor attack NATO without running the grave risk of its own destruction, nor even confidently expect to defeat the West solely with its non nuclear forces. Second, the economic and technological resources at the disposal of the West vastly surpass those available to the Soviet Union and its bloc partners. There is no likelihood that this gap will be closed in the near future. Third, Soviet efforts to enlist the developing world in its struggle with the West have not been successful. Its regional position around the globe is tenuous. In some instances, as in East Asia, the expansion of Soviet influence has coalesced countervailing pressures to contain its spread. The Soviet Union's mixed experience in the developing world has sobered its expectations about its prospects. Under the Gorbachev regime (and even before) there is evidence that the Soviet Union is wary about overcommitting itself in the Third World. Careful attention is being given to the costs, risks, and dubious benefits of projecting Soviet resources and power abroad or of intervening directly with military force in regional affairs. A brief review of the Soviet position in the developing world highlights the weakness of Soviet influence, when viewed against the broad background of the world society with all its profoundly different regional variations rather than from the narrow perspective of the specific but by no means spectacular gains that the Soviet Union has achieved in several parts of the globe.

Assessing Soviet success and prospects in the developing world requires both a worm's eye and a bird's eye view. Much of this volume has been devoted to the former. The pace and direction of global modernisation, the focus of the last section of this summation, are fundamentally shaped by diverse regional conditions arising from the different historical evolution, varied geographic location, and the differential rates of socioeconomic and political development of the peoples of the globe. The superpower competition is mediated through these pre-existing material and social fabrics. Inevitably the East–West struggle has to be adapted to the particular forces operating within each region, to the lines of conflict peculiar to the area, and to the demands and needs made by local actors on the superpowers and their bloc partners. The Soviet Union has established several enclaves around the globe – Cuba in the Caribbean, Ethiopia in Africa, and Vietnam in Asia. But as its grip on these states tightens, its hold in the larger and more important reaches of the globe slips. Where its power is engaged – in Nicaragua, Angola, Mozambique, and Afghanistan – it is being contested by significant local forces.

A Thermidor in the Soviet quest for greater influence and an expanded role in regional affairs around the globe looks inviting. Its attractiveness is underscored by the questionable success, tenuous position, and dubious prospects of a significant break-out of the Soviet Union from the redoubts to which it is confined in the absence of a greater commitment of resources than are either currently available or politically feasible to engage.

The Soviet Union in the Developing World: Questionable Success and Dim Prospects

Central and Latin America

Cuba is the Soviet Union's *point d'appui* in Central America and the Caribbean. As Raymond Duncan and Howard Wiarda make clear, the Soviet success was more a prize presented by Fidel Castro than a revolution instigated and executed by Moscow. Cuba serves as a valuable military and intelligence base and as a springboard for the projection of Soviet military and political influence throughout the region. The Soviet Union, as Havana's benefactor and protector, also indirectly benefits from the enormous prestige reaped by Cuba as a small Caribbean state that has defied US power and got away with it. Cuban military forces insured the consolidation of the Mengistu regime in Ethiopia and provided invaluable protection against attacks from Somalia. Its forces now sustain the Marxist government in Angola. All this has been accomplished without the commitment of Soviet forces.

On the downside, the Soviet subsidy for Cuba is substantial, estimated to be $4–5 billion each year. Cuban militancy has also pushed a cautious Moscow to become more deeply involved and at a faster pace than it might have wished in Grenada and Nicaragua. These revolutions, as Wiarda indicates, were Cuban projects. The US intervention into Grenada was a clear setback for Havana and cautioned Moscow from challenging the United States directly in a region where the latter was militarily dominant. The Soviet Union has extended military and economic assistance to the Sandinista government, but it has been reluctant to go beyond its current level of support – witness reports of curtailed oil subsidies – or to extend to Nicaragua the same security guarantees enjoyed by Cuba.

As for the remainder of Central America, Soviet influence depends more on the US response to the socioeconomic and political forces seeking change in the region than on its use of force or assistance to insurgents or groups pressing for reform. Armed intervention may in the short-run block these reformist elements, but it also breeds resentment and countervailing revolutionary fervour over time. Feudal economic practices and authoritarian political regimes, resting on strong military control dedicated to preserving the privileged, invite revolution, as in Nicaragua and El Salvador, and prepare the ground for Cuban intervention on the side of what at the outset is popular sentiment. Where socioeconomic reform has gone forward, matched by an open political system in which pluralist interests can freely compete for power, as in Costa Rica, Cuban overtures have not received a sympathetic hearing. The Soviet presence in Latin America has notably expanded from what it was only a few years ago. The Soviet Union, a major trading partner of Argentina, earned good will in siding with Buenos Aires over London during the Falklands War. Whether it can fulfill its economic commitments to buy grain and to close its current trade deficit with Argentina is an open question. Toward Brazil, the Soviet Union also presents itself as a reliable economic partner and as a trustworthy political partner. Its pragmatic approach there contrasts with its image projected in Central America or in Leftist circles as a force for revolutionary change.

There is no doubt, as Juan M. del Aguila argues, that the United States faces stiff political competition and a modest economic challenge from the Soviet Union in Latin America. It cannot block Moscow's access to the region. As elsewhere in the Western Hemisphere, Moscow profits from deep feelings of anti-Americanism, while presenting itself in a favourable light as a responsible state bent on improving relations in the region to the mutual advantage of all partners.

Enhanced Soviet presence and prestige cannot be identified with a corresponding setback for the United States. The growing self-esteem and national will evidenced by Latin American states, particularly the most powerful among them, are effective barriers to Soviet expansion. These factors also set limits to US influence in the region.

In adapting to Latin American national sentiments and self-interest, the Soviet Union must downplay and deny its revolutionary pretensions in the region. It must choose between political gains made with key states, like Brazil and Argentina, over those with the smaller states of Central America. It must decide whether it wishes to conform to expected international behaviour or continue to pursue a revolutionary course, intervening in the domestic affairs of other states and disrupting normal diplomatic and economic relations. Until now, Moscow has chosen the first path. Communist or Leftist elements have not been accorded preferred treatment. It has demonstrated a willingness to deal with the previous military regimes in Argentina, Brazil, and Peru. It has been no less willing to accommodate itself to budding democracies in Argentina and Brazil. These democratic trends are additional guarantees of a Latin America capable of fending for itself in dealing with the Soviet Union, with little or no help from the United States. Soviet pressure and influence are checked in Latin America in spite of often heavy-handed US efforts to contain Moscow, which incur Latin American animosities and reinforce anti-American sentiments in the region.

East and Southeast Asia

Nothing succeeds like failure. The US withdrawal from Vietnam had the paradoxical result of strengthening Moscow's position in Southeast Asia while weakening its overall position in East Asia. US military engagement on the Vietnamese salient had the perverse effect of uniting China and the USSR and of galvanising Third World resistance to US intervention. US military disengagement on the ground, offset by continued US naval and air presence in the region, has quieted concerns about United States expansionist intentions while bolstering regional states in their efforts to contain Vietnam's expansion in Cambodia and Laos. China threatens Vietnam's hold on the peninsula and limits its military spread through the region. As Sheldon Simon suggests, ASEAN owes much of its organisational unity and coherence to the vacuum left by the US departure. With little US initiative, the ASEAN states banded together to protect their national economic and security interests. ASEAN's explicit aim of economic cooperation masks an implicit strategic objective of checking Vietnamese aggression.

The Soviet Union is largely confined to its Vietnamese enclave in Southeast Asia. The Vietnamese-Soviet arrangement blocks better relations between China and the Soviet Union and inhibits the latter's access to the ASEAN states. Indonesia is not an exception. If its anti-Chinese stance disposes it to Vietnam, with which it has closer ties than do its ASEAN partners, its economic ties with ASEAN and with the West as well as its purchase of Western arms keep it firmly within the Western orbit. The naval base at Cam Ranh Bay is a Soviet asset, but its military utility can be exaggerated. United States and allied naval forces are a match for the relatively small and exposed Soviet

Pacific fleet. A Soviet military base, on the other hand, increases fears and scepticism about Soviet aims among the regional states.

North Korea provides another base for the Soviet Union, although it is less reliable than Vietnam. Moscow must also compete for favour with Beijing and keep in check Pyongyang's inclination to assert its independence from Moscow's direction. The inability of North Korea to gain sufficient assistance from the Soviet Union to defeat South Korea is likely to be a source of tension as long as the Kim Il Sung regime harbours an expansionist aim. The prospects of defeating South Korea do not appear promising since the military and economic power of Seoul continues to grow despite serious internal upheaval and US military forces underscore the US security guarantee. Democratizing trends in South Korea which are likely to reinforce social and political cohesion over time should not be confused with any notion of reduced opposition to North Korean expansion or to any form of Communist rule.

The economic weight of the Western Pacific basin heavily favours the West. A dynamic Japan has made state-centered capitalism work in Asia and in world markets. China's open-door policy toward Western trade, credits, and technology dilutes much of what may remain of Soviet influence to shape regional affairs, even if Beijing assumes a more orthodox Marxist position after the departure of the Deng leadership. Nationally assertive and increasingly more powerful Asian countries, militarily and economically, offer limited prospects for Soviet aspirations in the region.

South and Southwest Asia

The Soviet Union's major asset in the region is India. The USSR is New Delhi's largest arms supplier and, with some lapses, has been its principal supporter in its clashes with Pakistan and in balancing Chinese influence in the subcontinent. Stephen Cohen's analysis suggests, however, that the Soviet Union's influence in the region may have peaked in the early 1970s in the wake of the Indo-Pakistan war. Its long-term prospects do not appear to be rising. India is the dominant military power in South Asia, and its fear of Pakistan, while real enough, has inevitably lessened with Pakistan's division, when compared to the early years after independence. A nuclear Pakistan would certainly increase concerns, leading very likely to an Indian decision to develop a nuclear military programme and a delivery system for its weapons. It does not appear that such a development is favoured by or in the interest of Moscow. In any event, a nuclear subcontinent is not likely to encourage closer Soviet-Indian ties since Moscow will then have an incentive to qualify its security commitments in the region.

As Moscow moves to curry favour with China and Pakistan, it inevitably risks the further loosening of its ties and attractiveness to New Delhi. Conversely, its intervention in Afghanistan hindered better relations with Beijing and Islamabad. Pakistan's importance has grown in Soviet eyes, since it is a critical funnel for arms to the Afghan rebels, a link to the Islamic forces in the Middle East, and a bridge to the Persian Gulf. Efforts to increase Soviet influence in Pakistan or China offset Soviet access to India.

Meanwhile, India and the other nations of the region look to the West, not to the Soviet Union, to spur economic growth, technological development, and internal modernisation. In India the Soviet Union is not a model either for economic progress or for military doctrine and practice. India, Pakistan, and the other smaller states of South Asia, in contrast to Afghanistan, have advanced their political modernisation to the point that they are not dependent for outside assistance to develop their political systems and political parties, police, intelligence services, or civil administration. The religious revival within the region – Islamic, Sikh, and Hindu – is incompatible with the anti-religious sentiments and secular message of the Soviet Union. The strong currents of national feeling coursing through the region and the self-confidence of local governments to use and manipulate the Soviet Union for their own purposes set limits on Soviet power and bargaining leverage. Both India and Pakistan can use the Soviet Union's quandary in Afghanistan to their respective advantage. New Delhi can at any time break its silence by raising criticism of Soviet military operations in Afghanistan, ease Pakistan's two-front security problem, or reconcile its differences with Washington or Beijing – or do all three. Pakistan's assistance to rebel forces and hosting of millions of Afghan refugees within the country make Pakistan a key player in any resolution of the conflict. Since an end to the fighting is not in sight, the Soviet Union erodes its position on all sides. Unless it is willing to compromise on the Kabul regime, as now seems likely, it has little with which to bargain in the region.

Africa: South of the Sahara

There are several Africas south of the Sahara. The Soviet Union is clearly entrenched in the Horn. Ethiopia under the Mengistu regime has been elevated to the status of a fraternal Marxist-Leninist state.

Counter-balancing the gain in Ethiopia is of course the loss of Somalia. The long-term socioeconomic underdevelopment of Ethiopia, debilitating civil war, chronic internal strife, and periodic famine raise questions about the tangible benefits of Ethiopia as a strategic asset or as a model for socialist development in Africa, despite its potential as a major military base.

The Soviet Union's inroads into Francophone Africa have been modest. With Guinea's recent turnabout and the relaxation of the Marxist-Leninist structure in Benin, the Soviet Union's hold is slipping. Congo Brazzaville is in the Soviet sphere, but it maintains an open posture toward the West. It remains in the franc zone and is dependent on Western and Japanese markets and investments for its economic vitality.

As for the rest of Africa, French military and, increasingly, European Community economic influences are strong. While French security forces are spread thin through the region, they continue to play a key role in maintaining peace in the region and, more importantly, in ensuring regime stability, evidenced most recently by the intervention in Togo in 1986. The Soviet Union has shown little interest in directly challenging French influence. France enjoys the implicit support of its European Community partners and the United States for the security role that its forces play in the region. Washington has sent military aid to the regime of Hassène Habré in Chad to assist successful French efforts to contain Libyan expansion. Qaddafi's intervention does not appear either to have been instigated or actively encouraged by the Soviet Union. As the Francophone states evolve and modernise internally, French influence is likely to diminish, but very likely to the credit of the European Community. The need of Francophone Africa for socioeconomic development orients it to the West. The Lomé accords, favouring African products, position the European states to profit from an enlargement of West African ties with the outside. Parallel to European penetration in the region is Japan's presence as a major trading and world investment partner.

Anglophone Africa, principally centered in Eastern Africa, with the exceptions of Nigeria and Ghana, offers little opportunity for long-term Soviet growth. Because of its large population, size, resources, and key geographic position, Nigeria is by far the most important nation in West Africa and among the Anglophone states. Official Nigerian policy is more even-handed toward the West and East than in the past, although opposition to the United States and the

West European states still runs strong within a large and important segment of Nigeria's elites. Grievances, real and imagined, arising from the colonial and decolonisation experience, the civil war of the 1960s, and Western tolerance of South African apartheid still place the West and the United States on the defensive. Time and presumably a more responsive anti-apartheid policy will diminish the force of these resentments and the obstacles they place to better relations with the West. A pluralistic, politically open system appears better suited to the tribal divisions of Nigerian society than does a one-party state. Here again the West is a better model to follow than the Soviet Union. Like other developing states, once their internal political security needs have been satisfactorily addressed, Nigeria is also turning toward the West in constructing its long-term economic policies. The West may lose Nigeria, but the Soviet Union is ill-positioned to win it.

Other key Black African states of the British Commonwealth – Kenya, Tanzania, Zambia, and Zimbabwe – are also oriented toward the West. The Soviet Union miscalculated in supporting the force of Joshua Nkomo in Zimbabwe's fight for independence over Chinese-backed Robert Mugabe. It has staged a comeback, but again is hampered by its poor showing in making assistance available either in meeting Zimbabwe's needs or those of the other Anglophone states. The principal stumbling block for the West is South Africa's apartheid system. Unless the United States and the Western states respond to African demands for more effective opposition to South African apartheid and its repeated incursions into Black Southern African states to protect its White-dominated system, the currently ascendant position of the West may erode in Moscow's favour.

Lusophone Africa presents a mixed picture. The Angolan Civil War is at an impasse. Lines of conflict and interest are confusing. The Marxist government in Luanda, backed by Cuban troops, controls the capital but not the countryside, where large segments are under the sway of Jonas Savimbi's UNITA forces. Washington's support for Savimbi is offset by the substantial oil revenues pumped into Angola by Shell Oil, a so-called imperialist multinational capitalist corporation, whose installations are guarded by Cuban troops. Luanda, Havana, and Shell form a triangle of interest that supports the economy as well as the government's war efforts against rebel forces and South African attacks. Meanwhile UNITA, linked to South Africa, prevents rail shipments of minerals from Zaire, a Western stronghold, from reaching the Angolan port of Benguela. The Soviet Union and Cuba will not be easily dislodged from Angola. They protect Luanda, whose security needs in the near term take precedence over its long-term socioeconomic development. Once the former have been met in some fashion – an accord with UNITA and South Africa cannot be ruled out – Angola will very likely orient its internal development towards the West as it has already signaled, following the example of its Lusophone partner, Mozambique. Trends in Mozambique offer little comfort to Moscow or Havana. Even before his death, Samora Machel had compromised his government's differences with South Africa in the US-sponsored accord at Nkomati in 1984 to stop support for the rebellion mounted by the Mozambican National Resistance against FRELIMO. His successors pursue his economic reorientation toward the West and the United States. They hope to secure Western help to resolve the civil war in their favour, to open a key rail line to the ocean which has been under constant rebel attack, and to sustain a faltering civil economy.

Whether the Soviet Union will profit from turmoil in South Africa depends more on what the West fails to do than on Soviet ability or resources to shape events. In the long term, apartheid cannot stand, nor can total White rule. The transition to Black government, as recent events attest, will be neither easy nor bloodless. But the Soviet Union did not create the racial conditions that have led to civil strife. As in other independence movements in Africa and elsewhere in the developing world, the Soviet Union has much to offer in arms and military assistance to speed popular demands for change. Along with its European allies, particularly East Germany, the Soviet Union can help shaky regimes in erecting internal security systems to prevent counter-revolutions and to quell domestic opposition. Western influence with these Soviet-dependent states will not be great as long as their internal power is threatened and they remain dependent on the Eastern bloc for support. Even under these conditions Western economic and cultural influence as the long-term prerequisite for political penetration can be exercised in a way to weaken the Soviet presence. The Mozambique and Zimbabwe cases provide evidence for guarded optimism, although Soviet influence in Maputo remains strong and its stock is slowly rising in Harare. Yet Moscow's economic weakness sets clear limits on its possibilities for extensive penetration.

Middle East and North Africa
The Soviet Union is not in an enviable position in the region. Egypt and Israel, the key players in the Arab-Israeli conflict, depend on the United States for economic and military assistance. The moderate

Arab states also look primarily to the United States and to the West for their protection at home and to advance their interests abroad. Syria is the Soviet Union's only notable client in the region. While it has an important veto power over the Palestinian issue and over proposals to resolve civil strife in Lebabon, it cannot dictate solutions for either problem. Much less can it alone regain its territories lost to Israel through its own military initiatives. The value of Syria as a base for terrorist activities cuts two ways for the Soviet Union. Terrorism may disrupt Western interests, undermine moderate Arab influence, and hinder Western access to the region, but as a strategem of the weak, it will not be decisive as an instrument of anti-Western policy. Syrian-backed terrorism adds a measure of unpredictability to Soviet policy in the region. In this game, Syria is by no means the only player. Its impotence in interceding on behalf of US and European hostages held by the terrorist groups suggests the limit of its influence. Its attack on Shiite elements in Lebanon in February 1987 draws it into conflict with Iran, its presumed ally in the war against Iraq. Soviet diplomatic feelers to Israel and improved relations with Egypt indicate Soviet recognition of the limited utility of the Syrian ploy in promoting Soviet interests in the Middle East. Syrian efforts to improve its relations with Western Europe and the United States also imply a more independent course by Damascus and a corresponding weakening of Soviet ties.

The USSR, like the United States, has drawn little benefit from the Iran–Iraq War. The superpowers have hedged their bets with the belligerents, although in support of different domestic and foreign interests. Despite a long-term security relationship with Iraq, as its major supplier of arms, Moscow has also sent assistance to Iran or acquiesced in the transfer of arms there by Soviet clients. These reactions parallel those in the United States and Israel: both have sent arms to Tehran, partly in secret collaboration. A re-awakening of Muslim religious fervour spells trouble for Moscow's control of its Muslim population, one of the largest in the world. Iraq, meanwhile, has had to turn to the West for credits and arms to pursue the war. As the West and East take out insurance policies against a possible Iranian victory, both have an interest in a stalemate. While the Gulf conflict is not the doing of either superpower, both have been thrust uncomfortably into the same political predicament. The West has little leverage over the war and even less to say about the political evolution within Iran. The Soviet Union appears similarly impotent. The absence of a viable communist party or secular Left in Iran, decimated by the Khomeini reign of terror, also leaves no ready mechanism for

Soviet intervention as it did in Afghanistan. Neither superpower faces palatable choices in the Persian Gulf. Iran may not win the war, but given its edge in population and revolutionary commitment, it cannot lose the conflict. Iraq cannot win the war, and may well succumb to Iran's strategy of attrition.

North Africa, somewhat like Latin America, appears to be a zone more of superpower political and economic competition than of military or strategic contest between clearly identified opponents. Qaddafi's Libya, which defies easy classification, is only a partial exception. Soviet supplies of arms imply neither diplomatic support for Tripoli's capricious interventions abroad nor defence against attack, as evidenced in Moscow's prudent profile in the aftermath of the US military strike against Libya in 1986. Algeria depends on Soviet arms, but relies on Western technology and economic ties to spur its development. The United States is a major trading partner and Algiers plays an interlocutory role in the Middle East and in Iran in the service of Western needs, including negotiating for hostages under the control of state-sponsored terrorist groups. Tunisia and Morocco are in the Western camp. Rabat, however, has an important phosphate accord with the Soviet Union, estimated to be worth $2 billion. Soviet economic assistance indirectly aids Morocco against the Polisario rebels, who have received Soviet arms from Libya and Algeria. These confusing lines of interests will not be sorted out in the near future. Neither ideological nor even regime orientation provides a reliable guide to North African politics. The Soviet Union is present in the region and also exerts influence, not all of which is negative with respect to Western interests, as its relations with Morocco suggest. It has not been able, nor has it actively sought, to dictate events. As William Zartman's informed analysis suggests, Soviet gains in North Africa do not automatically equate to Western losses. Like Latin America, North Africa is a laboratory for the 'new political thinking' of the Gorbachev regime and for the politics of competitive interdependence between East and West.

A SUPERPOWER THERMIDOR IN THE DEVELOPING WORLD: EXTERNAL AND INTERNAL INCENTIVES

The Soviet Union appears at least partially blocked in the developing world; its experience has been mixed and its record, hardly brilliant; its regional positions are tenuous; its prospects for significant gain at acceptable cost and risks are dim; the arms race with the West at all levels is at an impasse; and national-minded developing states oppose interference or intervention in their affairs and dispose growing economic and military means to resist either Soviet threats or blandishments. The Soviet Union as a model for socioeconomic or political development has receding attraction. Despite the West's heavy colonial legacy and its sometimes mindless and self-defeating policies, not to mention its internal rivalries, it appears to offer greater long-run opportunities for spurring the modernisation process in the developing world than does the communist bloc. As Chinese policy suggests, developing states appear to have learned the lesson that aid is likely to come more by cooperating with the West than by attacking it.

Limitations on Soviet power and prospects generate compelling incentives for a Thermidor in the superpower competition in the developing world. These incentives are reinforced by powerful imperatives for internal socioeconomic and political reform. Moscow needs a relaxation of the pace and scope of its competition with the West if its domestic reform programme is to succeed. To speed its economic and technological advance, it needs to cut the costs of the arms race and its resource commitments abroad. It also needs access to Western markets, resources, credits, and know-how. The stimulus of a capitalist economy is needed additionally to break the dismal cycle of slow economic growth and patchy technological development. Centralisation and bureaucratisation are to be combatted at home by opening them partially to the rigours of international competition. The conservative farmers of the Midwest, the enterprising machine tool firms of West Germany, and the captains of Japanese capitalism are expected to spur Soviet economic development. Stable access to Western goods and know-how cannot be assured in the absence of some relaxation of tensions with the West.

Distinguishing Thermidor from *Détente*

Thermidor should not be equated with *détente* – or at least with those notions of *détente* widely held in the West in the 1960s and 1970s. To cite a Gaullist slogan of the early Fifth Republic, *détente* was supposed to lead to ever broader East–West *entente* and eventually to cross-bloc cooperation.[1] The Nixon–Kissinger policies of the 1970s, leading to the Berlin accords and to SALT I and II, were essentially buoyed by the same expectations of a satiated Soviet Union progressively moderating its revolutionary aims and its inclinations to use or threaten force to promote them. This optimism bore little fruit in the 1970s. The Soviet Union expanded and modernised its nuclear forces beyond levels expected by US policy makers in the 1970s, although these were essentially conducted within the limits of SALT II. Soviet SS-18 heavy missiles threatened US ground-based nuclear systems and its SS-20s placed NATO forces at risk. It bolstered its conventional and tactical nuclear forces in Europe and those of its Warsaw bloc allies. It also expanded its long-range air and sea forces, projecting them to all major regions of the globe, some for the first time, as in Vietnam, Ethiopia, Angola, and Afghanistan. It rejected, too, any notion that Western conceptions of *détente* implied a relaxation of its hold on Eastern Europe.

Nor did *détente* imply renunciation of an expanded role for the Soviet Union on a par with that of the United States or denial of an enhanced Soviet presence in every major region of the world.[2] Even less did it signify an abandonment by the Soviet Union of its revolutionary aspiration to transform the international system. After years of struggle, *détente* simply signified to Soviet leaders that the Soviet Union had been finally accepted as the equal of the United States. The Soviet Union's special sphere of influence in Eastern Europe was seen to be implicitly legitimated, along with the borders between Poland and Germany that had been substantially redrawn by the Soviet military victory in the Second World War. Conversely, strategic and political parity merely underscored the obvious – a shift in the world's correlation of forces progressively favouring a socialist order. *Détente* was not a resting point. It was more than a consolidation of power and a codification of rules for competition with the West. It was also a process leading along a still arduous path but inevitably toward a socialist international system led by an ascendant Soviet Union.

The economic reforms now underway in the Soviet Union appear principally aimed at expanding the Soviet Union's narrow resource base in order to enable Soviet leaders not only to improve living standards at home, (partly as a desirable aim in itself and partly as a way to elicit measured worker efficiency and productivity), but also to have more power to project abroad in the future in more measured and effective forms and at times and places of the Kremlin's choosing than can be done today. Internal reform and long-term external expansion are not necessarily at odds. How else to overcome the limits of Soviet power abroad than by reform and Thermidor?

Thermidor does not imply Soviet abandonment of those regimes to which it has made a substantial material commitment or a rapid withdrawal from all areas where its power is currently engaged in the Third World. While the level, focus, and modalities of its support may shift, the Soviet Union will be reluctant to withdraw aid to hard-core Marxist-Leninist regimes. Its aid may actually increase to meet new stresses confronting its clients. In the mid-1980s, for example, Soviet aid to Angola, principally in the form of military assistance, expanded, even as the Gorbachev regime, announcing its own version of the Nixon Doctrine, placed primary responsibility for socialist development on local states. The enclaves of Cuba, Vietnam, Ethiopia, and South Yemen are likely to be retained within the Soviet orbit. The withdrawal of Russian troops from Afghanistan would weaken but might not eliminate its presence and influence in Kabul in the same way that US power collapsed in Southeast Asia after the American military pullout. Ending the Afghan conflict would enhance Soviet standing with Muslim opinion in the Middle East. But Soviet influence in disputed areas like Angola, will not be easily dislodged, partly because of the staying power of Cuban military forces.

A Thermidor may even advance Soviet power. It promises to strengthen Soviet diplomacy in efforts to split the West, to pit Western populations against their own governments, and to incite states in the developing world against the United States and its allies. Soviet campaigns against the Strategic Defense Initiative (SDI) and against deployment of missiles in Europe, and calls for a complete ban on nuclear testing illustrate efforts by Soviet diplomacy to arouse popular support in the West and in the developing world for Soviet arms control and peace moves. There is likely to be no moratorium on these kinds of initiatives. The human rights conference held in Moscow in February 1987 and the selective release of well-known dissidents and the raising of restrictions on others – the Sakharov case being the most prominent – are parts of a Soviet offensive to garner global and Western support for a respite in East–West and superpower competition, but not at the expense of its present global position or at the cost of weakening internal Communist party rule.

The Soviet Union can also be expected to take advantage of targets of opportunity in the developing world when they arise, although the automatic engagement of Soviet diplomacy or the commitment of resources cannot be assumed. Soviet past behaviour suggests as much. Thanks to the Arab-Israeli crisis, the Soviets extended their influence in the Middle East in the 1950s. After Egypt was lost and when Iraq's reliability wavered as a favoured client, Syria loomed larger in Soviet calculations and support. As for the Qaddafi regime, as long as Moscow is not obliged to defend Tripoli, it is willing to supply arms (for hard currency) if Libya disrupts Western interests. The Ethiopian revolution and Portuguese withdrawal presented additional opportunities for Soviet advances in the Horn and in southern Africa. Similarly, Nicaragua and, for a time, Grenada afforded tempting possibilities for Soviet gains at what appeared to be reasonable costs and risks. Given the profound differences between the United States and the Soviet Union, a period of Thermidor in the struggle does not preclude Moscow from seizing on opportunities – e.g. civil war in South Africa – for tactical advantage.

On the other hand, Thermidor implies a breathing space in the superpower competition. It suggests a less strident and apocalyptic rhetoric in conducting the competition, a gradual reduction in the resources devoted to the struggle, and a lesser immediate priority assigned by both governments to its pursuit. It assumes a slower pace in nuclear and conventional arms races between the superpowers at global and regional levels. The slowdown is susceptible to regulation through mutual arms control accords verified by on-site inspection and agreement on common measures to assess military power, elements already defined in the superpower treaty to eliminate intermediate- and shorter-range missiles in Europe and Asia.

Several other signs of a Thermidor can also be expected. A major increase in the engagement of Soviet economic and military resources or an enlargement in political commitments abroad – either in the number or in the scope of existing arrangements – are not anticipated. While the Soviet Union cannot be expected to relinquish hard-won gains, commitments undertaken in the past are subject to revision, being either narrowed (e.g. Libya and Mozambique) or subject to selective reduction (e.g. Iraq). The developing world will be approached in a more concrete, pragmatic fashion and not as an undifferentiated whole, as was the tendency in the past. The projection of Soviet power and resources is likely to proceed, but only after a careful weighing of costs, risks, and benefits. The caution already marking Soviet behaviour in Afghanistan, Central America and in southern Africa – current hot spots – is likely to continue. More clearly articulated rules for conducting regional conflict – e.g. Moscow's acceptance of the 'no-Migs' rule for Nicaragua – will serve as further litmus tests of a fully working Thermidor. Zones of non-coercive superpower competition can also be expected to grow. The Soviet

Union may also adopt a more cooperative posture in areas where its power and prestige are now engaged, as in Afghanistan. Predictions of Soviet behaviour will be harder because it will not be mindlessly pushed by ideology but by power and cost-benefit calculations at the margin.

Exploiting the Potential Advantages of Thermidor: Short- and Long-Term Western Strategies

Why should the West respond favourably to a Thermidor if Soviet global and revolutionary aims are not explicitly abandoned and if a pursuit of Thermidor may actually bolster long-term Soviet prospects? And if the West cooperates in a Thermidor in the East–West struggle, how can it turn that Thermidor to its advantage in the long-run?

Several considerations prompt a positive reply to the first question. First, Western popular opinion appears keen on a respite in the superpower struggle and is unwilling to shoulder greater burdens to pressure the Soviet Union for concessions, even if these might be forthcoming. Political support for more expenditures on arms has peaked in the West. Support for insurgencies against Marxist governments in Nicaragua, Afghanistan, and Angola is at too low a level to overthrow these regimes, and more resources and support are not likely to be readily available. The result is stalemate. Counter-Marxist forces will not prevail, but Soviet-backed governments in power will be unable to exercise control over their territories and large segments of their populations.

Second, greater pressures on the Soviet Union – either by quickening the pace of the arms race or by stepping up armed regional opposition to Soviet and communist encroachments – are not likely to work, even if more resources and public support were available. The Soviet Union is not about to collapse despite the frailties of its external position and internal situation. The political hold of Soviet leaders on their own populations and bloc partners cannot be expected to diminish. An uninhibited arms race and greater Western intervention abroad will be likely to incite opposition in the United States and abroad. It is also important to resist exaggeration of the Soviet threat. Measured by capabilities and by the constraints imposed by a decentralised international system, Soviet power, while formidable, is not overwhelming. The Soviet threat should be measured by its grasp, and not its reach. The Soviet Union does best within a militarised Cold War. Its grip tightens in times of tension. Its hold is weakest when it is forced to compete with the West on the battleground of socioeconomic development and human rights.

Third, a break in the superpower struggle will permit the West and the United States to focus on their own economic development and on many of the long-deferred social and ecological problems besetting their societies. A slowdown in the arms race will free resources to meet internal demands for more welfare; to address, particularly in the United States, serious governmental, commercial and financial deficits; and to adapt to the rigours of fierce international economic competition. Serious conflicts divide the West over trade, investment, and employment practices. Time, attention, and resources are needed to relax, if not resolve, these conflicts if the West is to prevail in the long-run within an inhospitable global environment. As George Kennan observed over a generation ago, the West's control over its own productive resources and human talent is the principal guarantee of its own survival, as well as the precondition for the flourishing of its values and interests in an otherwise fractured and refracted world society.[3]

Whether the Western core will hold depends critically, but only partially, on the US use and threat of force and on the development of a global military strategy sensitive to the differentially pursued aims and interests, as well as the preferred policy instruments, that each of the liberal democracies is willing to employ in dealing with the developing world. There is a need, therefore, for some agreement about the likely evolution of the world society and the distribution of power within it and how that evolution might be influenced and directed in support of Western preferences. Some notion of modernisation provides guidelines for the use or threat of military force and other policy instruments in creating a world environment supportive of Western values and interests. The greater economic and technological resources available to the West, when contrasted with the Soviet bloc, and the dynamism and resourcefulness of open societies favourably position the Western states within the world environment for the foreseeable future. They have the means and the know-how to lead the modernisation process in preferred ways. The limits of the Soviet Union's power, its tenuous regional position, and its need for Thermidor and freer access to the West underscore the West's staying power if it holds together.

MODERNISATION: CHALLENGES TO THE WEST AND WHAT TO DO ABOUT THEM

Since the breakdown of Medieval Europe and the split in Western Christendom, the world society has been engaged in fundamentally reforming its governing institutions, in developing novel means and mechanisms for producing and distributing wealth, and in defining new notions of social and personal worth and utility. The first of these processes of modernisation is coterminous with the rise of the nation-state and its globalisation in this century as the primary unit for the political organisation of the world society. The second is represented by the gradual broadening of popular demands, first in the Western world, including imperial Russia, and then around the world for greater national welfare, economic growth, and a more equitable distribution of global wealth. The third, and closely associated with these two preceding processes of modernisation, is the search for a new definition of social and personal worth and principles of political legitimacy consistent with national self-determination and the creation of new modes and organisational mechanisms for the production and distribution of wealth.

The following discussion broadly stretches the dimensions of these systemic forces and their implications for Western and US global strategy. The long-term prospects of the West depend on its response to the challenge of global disorder, economic disarray, and the struggle to define human rights and political legitimacy in ways congenial to its aims and interests. The Soviet Union is only the immediate problem; the longer and more difficult and momentous struggle is within the world society itself.

Globalisation of the Security Dilemma

The nation-state, as the principal vehicle for the political organisation of the world society, is, paradoxically, both the provisional solution to the problem of global order and a major obstacle to its achievement. The nation-state triumphed in Europe for several reasons. Its appeals were more broadly based than the personal loyalties underlying feudalism as a political and socioeconomic system. It also transcended communal differences based on religious beliefs. It enlisted the rising entrepreneurial classes whose wealth derived from commerce, finance, and urban manufacture in support of the state. In turn, state military power extended the economic activity of these new economic interests to distant colonies.[4] The state's appeal widened further to artisans and small landowners, and absorbed the energies and talents of reform minded segments of the aristocracy, such as those in England and in Prussia, alert to a growing sense of national consciousness, a rising capitalist class, and the stirring of popular sentiment urging enlargement of political participation and governmental responsibility for social and economic welfare.

The French Revolution exemplified the new tide of national feeling which had been developing for several centuries under the crown and aristocratic rule. It proved strong enough, when combined with the demands of a rising bourgeoisie for greater participation and power in state affairs, to topple the monarchy itself and the *ancien régime*. As de Tocqueville well understood, the authoritarian rule of the crown and aristocratic privilege blocked the full expression of nationalism and of demands for greater equality and liberty in internal governance.

The nation-state, as it initially emerged in Europe under monarchial and aristocratic aegis and later under imperial and popular-based governments in Europe, proved more successful than its opponents in mobilising material and human resources to establish authoritative political rule, to propel economic growth, and to conduct war more efficiently than had the medieval system. As Michael Howard observes: 'The growing capacity of European governments to control, or at least tap, the wealth of the community, and from it to create mechanisms – bureaucracies, fiscal systems, armed forces – which enabled them yet further to extend their control over the community, is one of the central developments in the historical era, which, opening in the latter part of the seventeenth century, has contributed to our own time.'[5]

The victory of the nation-state in Europe led to its extension around the globe. The struggle for dominion in Europe, arising from continental wars, drove the European states to organise the emerging world society to suit their economic and military needs. The result was a Eurocentric system that prevailed until the Second World War. In the search for security, economic prosperity, and political dominion, the imperial struggles of the European states played the unwitting historical role of organising the world community on nationally based principles of power and legitimacy. In over five centuries to the present era, first Spain and Portugal, and then Holland, Austria, France, and Britain, and subsequently Germany successively competed for European and global hegemony. Empires were the instruments of the struggle. But since the struggle was based on national interest and purpose, it was inevitable that the colonial empires would collapse from their own internal contradictions. The developing states, driven now by the same national forces that propelled Europe to world domination, were at once Europe's legacy and its undoing.

The superpowers' competition may be viewed as simply the lineal descendant of the European state struggle for continental and global hegemony. Their conflict speeded the decolonisation process and ensured the victory of the globalised nation-state. Despite lapses in US traditional opposition to imperialism in having supported British and French colonial policies immediately after the Second World War, the dominant long-run thrust of US policy has favoured national self-determination and opposition to imperial economic preferences in the developing world. No less has the Soviet Union pursued such a course in its support of progressive national regimes in spite of its ideological bias favouring a socialist world order. The Suez crisis, where the superpowers were aligned against Britain and France, signalled their shared, if divergently motivated, interest to be on the side of national political and economic self-determination in the developing world.

The continuing superpower struggle within an incipiently anarchical nation-state system poses several sets of problems in resolving the globalisation of the security dilemma. First, there is the danger that the superpower struggle will draw the other nation-states of the globe into its vortex. There is a tendency on the part of the United States and the Soviet Union to assume that the expansion of one will occur at the expense of the other. As postwar experience suggests, the East–West competition is then transformed into a North–South competition for clients and allies. The appeals made by each superpower, as a global actor, transcend narrow national self-interest as each rival advances fundamentally different solutions to the problems posed by modernisation: liberal democratic versus centralised socialist principles of rule to legitimate political authority; market versus collectivist mechanisms to organise the means of production and to distribute wealth; and divergent conceptions of personal worth and social merit.

While neither has, nor in the foreseeable future will have, the military means to impose its solutions on the other or on the world system, for the many reasons already sketched above, neither superpower can be expected to abandon its effort to foster a global system favouring its views and national interests. Building on the blocs in Europe, the superpower conflict first spread to Northern Asia in

China and Korea – then shifted to the Middle East and subsequently to South and Southeast Asia. The struggle has now extended to Southwest Asia, the Horn of Africa, and Southern Africa as well as to Central America and the Caribbean basin, with tentacles reaching as far as Latin America. The non-aligned movement itself can be understood as a product of the superpower competition, wherein developing nations assume fundamentally contradictory stances, alternately striving to insulate themselves from the costly and risky elements of the superpower conflict while bargaining for benefits in exchange for superpower strategic assets and diplomatic support.

Regional rivalries may be magnified to a global level as local governments appeal for assistance to one or the other of the superpowers. Unable to achieve their objectives alone, local states view superpower assistance as an attractive solution to gain and hold the upper hand in a regional conflict. The struggles in South Asia and the Middle East illustrate the process of client appeal to a superpower for assistance to support regional interests and aims under the guise of blocking the expansion of the rival superpower. A democratic India is the ally of the Soviet Union and an authoritarian Pakistan sides with the United States, largely because of the assistance each local state receives from its superpower patron. Given the political and economic stakes at issue, both superpowers are deeply engaged in the Middle East to bolster the relative power positions of their allies and clients in the region and repeatedly run the risk of being drawn into these regional conflicts.

Third, the vulnerability of many Third World regimes, because of their inability to control their own populations or their failure or unwillingness to respond to internal socioeconomic demands for internal reform, invites foreign intervention. Lebanon and Southeast Asia illustrate this dual problem of external and internal penetrability. Syria and Israel, respectively, have had a significant impact on Soviet and US policy toward Lebanon in the efforts of these regional states to impose their preferred solutions on communal and ideological strife in that country and to gain control over the Palestinian Liberation Organisation. As the Lebanese case suggests, local rivals, however much they depend for assistance on external powers, still preserve a remarkable degree of autonomy in pursuing their own strategic plans and military and terrorist operations.

South Vietnam could neither control its own population nor respond to their needs and win their loyalties. These weaknesses not only aided Hanoi in eliminating its Saigon competitor, but the thirty-year war in Southeast Asia also contributed decisively to the internal collapse of traditional tribal and communal units within the region. Vietnamese intervention paralleled US, Chinese, and Soviet counter-moves as well as the marginal participation of US allies (the Philippines, South Korea, and Australia) and the ASEAN states to determine the political organisation of the region. From a global perspective, the issue was the political composition and orientation of Southeast Asia within world society: whether it would be Western, communist, or non-aligned. Southeast Asia served as the terrain on which this issue was to be resolved in much the same way as Spain in the 1930s although many of the actors had changed as well as the national and ideological stakes of the struggle.

The fourth area of concern of the global security dilemma is simply war itself. Whereas it was a solution to state quarrels in the past – and remains a valued state instrument – its costs and risks, particularly if Third World conflict sparks a superpower clash, posit the need for clearer rules and understandings to guide and limit superpower competition if crises erupt. Arms control negotiations between the superpowers perform this function, however imperfectly and tenuously, at the nuclear level. The tests of strength and resolve between Western and communist forces in Europe over forty years have also led to a body of explicit and implicit rules of engagement that have transformed Europe as the most volatile centre of the Cold War struggle to one of the most stable regions in the East–West confrontation.

Guidelines for Responding to the Security Dilemma in a Decentralised International System

The security of the United States and its allies lies as much in the division of their adversaries as in the strength of their military establishments. With Soviet power counter-balanced to the point that it cannot defeat the United States or the West militarily without risking its survivability, the task confronting the United States is to prevent a hostile coalition in the developing world from emerging either collectively in direct conflict with the United States, or under the Soviet aegis. Given the military power of the United States and the Western bloc, the issue effectively confronting the Western states is retaining access to these areas to support their socioeconomic and political systems rather than an immediate concern about a military defeat of the kind represented by the global struggles of the First and

Second World Wars. The conditions of access will admittedly continue to be partially dependent on Western and United States military capabilities, but the degree to which access will be dependent on force or diplomatic coercion can be easily exaggerated. Israel's survival, the availability of Arab oil, and the retention of South Korea within the Western orbit are currently underwritten by favourable local balances and the insurance provided by US military might and presence. However critical these military requirements may be, they are only necessary, not sufficient, conditions for the desirable evolution of reliable Third World relations. There are also resource limits to militarisation and the West must reckon with the reactions of the communist bloc and the developing world to Western or US efforts to gain military superiority or hegemony.

Since decolonisation, the West has scored its greatest successes when it has been sensitive at a regional level to national sensibilities. It is precisely such a fluid international system of national states that favours the West over the Soviet system which attempts to harness non-aligned nations into a united bloc. The transformation of the Sino-American conflict from an ideological struggle to one of cautious cooperation between hitherto antagonistic national states sets major limits to the possibilities of Soviet expansion in Asia and throughout the developing world. US withdrawal from Southeast Asia freed local national rivalries to work for the United States and the West. Egypt's ouster of Soviet military advisors in 1972 exemplified Soviet failure to recognise Egyptian demands for national self-determination and control over its own territory. The Camp David accords solidified Egypt's reorientation toward the West. In regaining its lost territories and in being granted substantial US economic and military assistance, Egypt addressed (if not fully met) its immediate security and socioeconomic needs. Dividing the Arab camp bolstered Israel's security and reduced the threat of a multi-front war similar to the 1967 and 1973 conflicts. By extension, Western and US security interests, defined by the split in Arab ranks and the preservation of moderate Arab regimes in the Middle East, were advanced. These gains were more the result of effective diplomacy than of military victory.

As this volume has sought to demonstrate, Moscow does not have a firm hold on the developing world, especially on those countries with weight in regional politics. Indonesia is no longer closely aligned with the Soviet Union. Meanwhile, adding to the counterflows of an increasingly multipolar global society, with an enlarging number of centres of diverse forms of power, Jakarta appears strongly resistant to

Chinese communist influence while cautiously acting as Hanoi's interlocutor in ASEAN. The Indian-Soviet alignment appears to be one of convenience and is susceptible to relaxation and reversal as the Pakistani threat recedes (i.e. if Pakistan is prevented from going nuclear) and as Indian interest in socioeconomic development becomes more prominent. Nigerian ties with the West have grown stronger since the civil war, in oil and trade as well as in arms sales. Argentina and Brazil have cordial relations with Moscow, with Buenos Aires hinting briefly of closer ties during the Falklands War, but these emerging Latin American giants, now tentatively groping toward democratic rule, remain within the Western sphere. ASEAN, while non-aligned, is also implicitly a response to Vietnamese expansion. As Moscow's surrogate, Vietnam delimits Soviet possibilities in the region.

Two security tasks therefore seem paramount for the West and the United States. Negatively, the division of the international system can be used to favour Western interests. As a corollary, direct confrontation should be avoided where nationalist demands are at issue. US hostility aimed at Communist China until the Nixon visit in 1972 forced Beijing and Moscow together, although the split between them had begun to occur almost twenty years before. Except perhaps for Christian factions within Lebanon, all others, including rival Muslim elements and PLO forces, could agree on opposition to US military intervention. Similarly, the build-up of US military forces in the Middle East, first against opponents in Lebanon, and later in the Persian Gulf, pits Washington against local forces motivated by deeply felt, uncompromising religious and national sentiment. Long-term US and Western interests, in principle, are better served by drawing advantage from local conflicts and by resisting either direct intervention to resolve deep differences or uncompromising support for any one belligerent.

Positively, the West has an interest in preserving access to those states which now have or will have valuable power capabilities: military forces, natural resources, developed markets for trade and investment, and propitious conditions for the development of popular regimes. Such a mixed coalition of Western and developing state interests is likely to be volatile and shifting in its internal and external alignment structure. Specific alignment shifts are of less importance than the maintenance of a supporting coalition of states, whose primary aims are to ensure Western access to needed resources, material and political, and to prevent the emergence of a dominant anti-Western grouping. Membership of a particular economic or military alignment can be expected to change over time as ties with the West – not just those with the United States – are likely to ebb and flow with circumstance and the conjunctural needs of governments and peoples in the developing world. Conflict outcomes unfavourable to the West at the margin, where Soviet gains appear to have been made (e.g. Ethiopia or Angola), do not necessarily signify a fatal flaw in the Western global position, nor need they be considered a definitive loss any more than were Nasser's Egypt or Sukarno's Indonesia or Mao's China. What is crucial is preventing a united, hostile coalition, an occurrence of low probability, given the current division within the international system.

Welfare and Modernisation

Whether US and Western interests and aims will prevail and flourish also depends critically on how well the non-communist developed states respond to the second driving force of modernisation: the demand of populations everywhere for greater material welfare and a more equitable division of global resources and wealth. Since the Second World War, the West has been on the defensive in the Third World. There was first the colonial burden. Opposition to European domination was identified with a rejection of capitalist modes of ownership of the means of production and of market mechanisms for the distribution of goods and services, for investment priorities, and for returns on capital investment and labour. After decolonisation Third World attacks focused on the United States as capitalism's champion. The United States incurred the animosities and suspicions previously directed toward former European colonial rulers. The United States further engendered the opposition of many Third World countries in projecting its military power abroad, in the Middle East, Southeast Asia, and Central America, in attempts to block perceived Soviet and communist expansion. In mounting a global containment policy, the United States often found itself unwittingly opposed to local demands for self-determination and regime autonomy as well as to long unmet calls for greater welfare and socioeconomic reform. Soviet assistance for wars of national liberation solidified anti-American sentiment in many developing countries, as the United States sided with conservative forces in losing civil wars. It impeded, not speeded, the pressures propelling the modernisation process. US alignments with authoritarian, non-reformist governments, as barriers to Soviet and communist expansion, had the unsought effect of often facilitating Soviet aims, while deepening resentment and resistance to US influence.

To many local regimes collectivist economic solutions to underdevelopment seemed best suited to maintain themselves in power and to preclude counter-revolutionary reactions and coups. State control of national economic resources provided a way to concentrate scarce internal resources on targeted development as well as to distribute land and wealth of former colonial powers and of the ruling regime's domestic opponents. The United States, as the wealthiest nation in the world, was the natural object of Third World ire and was condemned – and still is in many quarters – as the principal support of a global economic system that is perceived as distributing the wealth and productive resources of the globe inequitably and with particular disadvantage to Third World peoples.

Response to the Socioeconomic Demands of the Developing World

The West and the United States are in a vastly superior position relative to the Soviet Union and the communist bloc to respond to Third World socioeconomic needs, at least at a level to ensure their access to needed raw materials and to investment and to outlets for products. In 1983 OECD states accounted for $7.73 trillion of the world's production of wealth against $2.46 trillion by the Warsaw Pact, measured in constant 1982 dollars.[6] This is roughly a three-to-one advantage for the West. The Soviet Union has traditionally been more effective in supplying military arms than economic and technical assitance to Third World states. Slow economic growth in the Soviet Union and in the Warsaw bloc is likely to prevent any immediate change in Moscow's disadvantaged position. This imbalance is not likely to shift in the near future, a condition that potentially gives the West leverage in competing with the Soviet bloc in the developing world.

The Soviet model for socioeconomic development has progressively lost its attractiveness in the southern hemisphere. Communist China, while dedicated to socialist principles, is now experimenting with market-oriented mechanisms to spur productivity, to improve the quality of goods and services, and to increase the efficiency of their distribution. As the Chinese case suggests, the creation of a socialist regime does not bar Western access to a country. The case of Algeria offers additional support for the proposition that the West and its commitment to capitalist principles and modes of operation are not necessarily at risk if some developing states opt for some form of socialist economic system. Following the example of Algeria, whose oil and gas exports are principally to the West, both the West and the states of the developing world can gain from pragmatically tested mixed solutions to diverse and divergent developmental problems.

For Western economic and military strategic needs, the nature of the ruling regime in a particular country is less important than continued access of the Western states to its territory and productive resources. Maintaining such access will depend on Western cooperation regarding a wide range of trade, investment, labour, and monetary issues. These include terms of competition (e.g. subsidies, as well as protectionist measures, for agriculture and industry), concessionary arrangements with developing countries (e.g. the Lomé Convention between the European Community and a large group of Third World states), and more coordinated economic and financial assistance efforts. The West's failure to meet these challenges will have an inevitably negative impact on its immediate security needs in the developing world. While a successful assault on North–South economic issues will not ensure a strengthened Western position, since the developing world is demanding not only more wealth but more power,[7] progress in responding to Third World economic needs is a necessary if not sufficient requirement of long-term Western security and ascendancy, if not domination, in the global system.

Modernisation and Human Rights

A brief word should also be said about the quest of the world's populations for a greater measure of human rights. These may be divided into social and personal claims. Social rights refer to a sense of recognition accorded a group. National self-determination is one of the most powerful of these social rights. Demands by groups for greater recognition of their worth and identity, as ethnic, tribal, religious, or racial entities, further illustrate claimed social rights that attach to the group *per se*. There is normally some notion of deprivation associated with the demand for recognition. For example, the search for a Palestinian, Kurdish, or Sikh homeland – for an independent political state or for greater political autonomy – falls within the realm of social rights, the denial of which challenges the legitimacy of regional or global power arrangements. The demand by Blacks in South Africa for an end to apartheid and for a share in government equal to their numbers illustrates a powerful assault on the legitimacy of the international system. The struggle for Black rule, justified by majoritarian principles, but yet quite distinct and independent as a socio-political force, will persist as long as the deprivation continues.

Personal rights, on the other hand, are defined and interpreted in diverse ways, depending on the different histories and cultures of the world's population and on the stage of a country's political and socioeconomic development. Western values – identified with the freedoms of expression, association, and religion and with the right to vote in open elections for freely competing rivals and parties, as well as the right to own and dispose of private property – clash with other views about personal rights based on demands for greater material welfare or, paradoxically, on the preservation of traditional local mores and practices. Islamic law, for example, stipulates elaborate rules for personal behaviour and defines in great detail the rights and duties of the members of a Muslim society to each other. Hindu practices similarly define personal status and worth and the relations between diverse groups and individuals within the society. Western notions of personal worth are at serious odds with these rival conceptions of individual integrity based on entirely different cultural and historical experiences as well as social principles.

Depending on their interpretation – restrictive or broad – religious and ethnic codes conflict with or complement new notions of personal status and rights associated with national self-determination, industrialisation, an international commercial economy, and the spread of science and technology. Modernity also establishes criteria for the acquisition of power, privilege, and position. These are based more on personal talent and social and economic performance than on claims linked to familial or tribal inheritance, blood, traditional notions of ascription, or proven loyalty to an ideological code or leader. As socioeconomic modernisation spreads, opening new avenues of advancement for previously disadvantaged groups or new opportunities for personal self-expression, 'the traditional distribution of status along a single bifurcated structure characterized by dispersed inequalities [will give] way', as one widely recognised student of modernisation observes, 'to pluralistic status structures characterised by dispersed inequalities'.[8] But greater pluralism in ideological expression cannot be equated with world order, economic development, or democracy. It is more a framework within which Western values and interest can survive and flourish at less cost and risk than in a bipolar global system dominated by a superpower military confrontation.

Several implications for United States and Western security interests flow from the disputed claims of social and personal rights held by different peoples around the globe with differential capacities to protect and promote them. First, the legitimacy of the international system is fundamentally provisional. As suggested earlier in this volume, there appears to be no likelihood that rival ideological positions can be reconciled in the foreseeable future to define a common, universally acceptable set of principles to guide authoritative political decisions to regulate conflict and settle disputes within the international political society. Almost all groups and states will have to live with a global system that, in varying degree, they consider illegitimate and confronted by rivals bent on transforming local or global power arrangements to their liking.

Second, US and Western values will depend for their preservation on uncomfortable alignment with groups and nations subscribing to different conceptions of social and personal values. Saudi Islamic practices, Chinese socialism, and a wide array of authoritarian regimes throughout the developing world – Suharto's Indonesia, Buhari's Nigeria, Zia's Pakistan, and Mobutu's Zaire – form an intricate web of alignments that in varying measure serve useful purposes in meeting the current needs of the West, although they are inconsistent with its professed value system. Those alignments that pose a challenge to the preservation of the West's overall system of supportive alignments with developing nations, like Western support for the White regime in South Africa, cannot be sustained without eroding the West's security interests and threatening its long-term welfare position. Coping with these contradictions is potentially easier for the West than for the communist bloc, which requires closer conformity and centrally directed control by Moscow. The benefits of Arab oil and Chinese accessibility appear to outweigh the inconveniences and embarrassments of supporting regimes and of tolerating internal practices (e.g. deprived women's rights in Saudi Arabia or aggressive abortion policies in China) at odds with Western preferences. On the other hand, indifference to Black insistence for an end to apartheid and for more power in South Africa severely strains the Western global position and puts it on what is the losing side of history in this century.

Because of the crucial importance of the rival claims of social and personal legitimacy as a determiner of global and regional power structures, the definition of Western security interests must be defined broadly enough to confront the problem of deciding what human rights issues to pursue and at what cost or gain in the overall power alignments, supportive of core Western values and interests. What is clear is that it is not sufficient to define security merely in military or even in socioeconomic terms. But broadening the definition of security to include the requirement of addressing the claims of legitimacy of rival groups, however necessary, begs the question of what values and groups to support. The choice is usually between greater or lesser and not always clearly perceived evils.

There is a host of difficulties confounding the definition of a satisfactory political answer to the alignment question. By their very nature, the values at stake are absolute. Compromise between regimes holding antagonistic moral visions of the future – e.g. a Khomeini's Iran and any American administration – will not be easy or necessarily possible. Gaining broad domestic support for repugnant regimes in conflict with Western values – Pinochet's Chile or Mobutu's Zaire – is evidently no less problematic nor easily defensible on political or moral grounds. Even if the moral and political issues could be resolved in building internal consensus on the construction of what appears to be a viable and reliable external set of global alignments, it is by no means clear which values of what groups will prevail, whatever the validity of their moral position or claims. Who could have predicted the revival of religious fundamentalism around the globe? Or the rate of change toward Black rule in South Africa? Modernisation itself does not move at a uniform rate or conform to a single definition, but is given particularly inflected national and ethnocentric meaning depending on local circumstances. What is critical at one point in time to a state – say socialist purity in Mao's China – may be fundamentally redefined at another point in time, as in Deng Xiaoping's China where socioeconomic reform has been ascendant but where pressures for greater political modernisation are resisted. Settling communal rivalries in Lebanon and ensuring a Shiite victory in the Persian Gulf may also take a back seat to economic growth as regime objectives.

CONCLUSIONS: GUIDELINES FOR A LONG-TERM WINNING COALITION

First, Western security interests and aims will depend on creating and maintaining an internally contradictory set of military, economic, and political alignments with developing country regimes and peoples.

These alignments must square with elite and popular demands for national self-determination and self-expression, as well as with socioeconomic development, leading to greater material welfare and a more equitable distribution of wealth within the global system as a whole and within the developing states themselves. These alignments must also be sensitive to the power claims of rival groups, pressing opposed principles of political legitimacy without the West falling into the trap of identifying tolerance with moral obtuseness or indifference to the outcome of political and ideological conflict in the developing world. The Iranian case and the Sandinista betrayal of the revolution against the Somoza regime caution vigilance.

Second, making and manipulating alignments is instrumental to Western purposes, not an end in itself. Coalitions of otherwise contending and contentious states makes sense only if defined by Western interests and values. Whether commitments should be made or assistance provided to a Third World state should be evaluated on the strength of an assessment of the net long-term contribution to the international support structure needed to ensure the Western position and to hold the Western core together. It can be expected that the receiving state will also bargain hard for what it needs. What one can expect then is an interlocking web of national interests, the best guarantee in all likelihood of long-term Western security, understood in the broad terms of the globe's continued modernisation, but under conditions of continuing internal division and decentralisation of political authority.

Third, at a minimum, no anti-Western coalition should be allowed to crystallise in the developing world. The division of the developing world against itself, increasingly structured by the diffusion of military power around the globe, facilitates the maintenance of a fluid international system and the creation of a natural barrier to Soviet expansion. The West has the military and economic resources, as well as a political heritage of tolerance for divergent points of view, that equip it to compete effectively with the communist bloc and to tailor its policies to the differential and not always internally coherent or consistent needs of the developing states. Not all conflict outcomes in the developing world spell serious losses for the West. The Soviet enclaves of Ethiopia, South Yemen, Afghanistan, and even Vietnam and Cuba are dubious assets. The extension of the Soviet sphere of influence to these areas is not necessarily fatal or serious as long as the global system remains essentially open and not arrayed against the West.

Fourth, the construction of reliable long-term ties between key regional actors in the developing world and Western states will be critical for the security and vitality of the West. Among others that can be cited, it is important that the West retain access and influence in China, India, Brazil, Nigeria, and the ASEAN states. Success here will depend on the West's response to the diverse, changing, and ethnocentrically defined modernisation needs of these states. Initiative need not always come from the West, nor is the principal responsibility for maintaining a favourable long-term Western position solely a task of Western diplomacy. Political and socioeconomic trends are not all negative, partly because of forces and groups at work that are implicitly in league with the West. Thanks to internal pressures, more than to Western demands or aid, political and economic reforms are moving previously authoritarian states – Argentina, Brazil, Spain, and Portugal – to the centre of the Western camp. The West also has more to offer than the communist bloc for many developing state regimes. Beijing opened China to the West without Western prompting or pressure and in spite of serious policy differences with the United States.

Fifth, Western cooperation with the Soviet Union and the communist bloc in the developing world is neither impossible nor damaging to Western interests. Stemming the nuclear arms race and proliferation interests both superpowers. Agriculture within the West depends partly on developing world markets and on continued Soviet purchases. At different times both superpowers have played a moderating role in Middle East conflicts and in Indian-Pakistan clashes. Witness, too, Soviet warnings to Libya, prompted by US intelligence disclosures, that Russian mines not be transferred to Iran to threaten Persian Gulf shipping. There are obvious limits to superpower cooperation in regulating conflict in the developing world. Based on the record to date and the profound differences in aims, interests, and ideology between the United States and the Soviet Union, expectations of cooperation must be modest and sober, but need not be ruled out.

Sixth, Western interests may also be served by progressive superpower acceptance of more pluralistically and pragmatically defined relations between themselves and regional states where neither cooperation nor mutually damaging conflict are implied. Gains for the Soviet Union in Latin America and in North Africa, for example, have not been necessarily at the expense of the United States or the West. Conversely, Socialist Algeria's improved relations with

Washington and with the European Community have not injured Soviet interests. Both superpowers have learned – and are learning – to tolerate each other in selected regions of the globe, each profiting from a different mix of bilateral relations largerly defined by the mutual interests of the regional state and those of the superpower in question. Except for a state like Libya, which has its own revisionist and revolutionary agenda to pursue, respective bilateral relations of Moscow and Washington with the other states of the Maghrib, by and large, have served the mutual advantage of the parties and have not been couched in terms aimed directly at weakening the position of either superpower or of its regional partner where a common interest has been defined. Morocco's case warrants close examination. Morocco's improved ties with Moscow, Washington, and even Libya suggest the possibilities of what might be termed complex bilateralism where the superpowers have neither cooperated nor clashed yet both have bolstered Rabat's position without noticeable loss to either superpower. It is conceivable, if Thermidor can be transformed into a true *détente* between the superpowers in the developing world, that the pattern of complex bilateralism sketched in the Maghrib and emerging in Latin America might be extended to areas where superpower competition is currently more intense and where the mental set of a zero-sum game persists.

Seventh, the response to the developing world must be Western, not just American, drawing on the full resources of the United States, the non-communist European states, and Japan. The tasks of integrating the developing world into a Western-tilted, but not necessarily Western-dominated, system is beyond the capacity of any one Western power. Certainly the military requirements of such a strategy cannot be met by any one state or even by all of the Western states in concert. Much remains to be done to husband scarce Western resources, to share military, economic, and diplomatic burdens, and to distribute spheres of primary political responsibility in a coordinated and coherent fashion. Internal conflict and competition within the West currently precludes the development of a global strategy satisfactory to all Western partners in the near term. But either they will all hang together in the developing world or they will hang separately.

Whether the West meets the dual challenges of a disordered world, divided by rival notions of political legitimacy and in economic disarray, will depend finally on the willingness of its diverse peoples to support costly policies and inevitably contradictory stances in fashioning a coalition of global forces favourable to long-term Western interests and aims. The problem is made all the more difficult by obvious and well-articulated splits within each Western state and within the Western coalition about how these aims and interests should be concretely defined as well as about how the distribution of burdens and risks that the peoples and nations of the West should bear. One of the West's most precious assets, often greater in value than its productive capacity, material resources, and human talent, is its capacity for self-criticism. It is an invaluable political instrument with which to adapt domestic needs and competitive claims to exterior imperatives and to exploit opportunities when they arise. It must be left to open, free, and vigorous debate within the West to extract those elements of the Soviet need for a Thermidor for its own advantage – and not necessarily at the expense of the Soviet Union.

Vacillating belief in its own principles and a hesitant will to put them into practice impede the West's response to the global challenge posed by a Moscow on the move. For decades Western leaders trumpeted the virtues of self-determination, open, democratic institutions, opposition to military intervention, cooperation in solving international problems, greater pluralism and tolerance in regulating domestic and foreign strife, and rapid socioeconomic development for the Third World. Now 'new thinking' in the Soviet Union has adopted the West's political lexicon as if it were its own creation in addressing its own and the world's problems while the West continues to react, conditioned by over forty years of Cold War, to a perceived Soviet military threat that no longer appears convincing to many in the West – and even less so to most people in the developing world.

In a dramatic reversal, Gorbachev's Moscow admits past failures – note Bukharin's rehabilitation – and pledges reforms through remedies that strongly resemble, at least in form, those championed in the West: an end to the arms race; less spending on the military and more on social needs and economic growth; relaxation of political tensions; greater reliance on market mechanisms to spur economic production and facilitate efficient and equitable distribution of wealth; the expansion of human rights; and more sensitivity and succor in meeting the needs of the disadvantaged. Meanwhile, the West is portrayed as resistant to the demands of developing nations for a greater say in running their affairs and for increased assistance from the developed North in an increasingly interdependent world, only recently discovered by Moscow. A caring Soviet socialism, using Western ways, proposes to solve its own problems and those of the world without abandoning its collectivist principles, Communist party rule, or its imperial holdings. Like a skilled wrestler, Moscow draws on the West's strengths to its advantage while relying on its own dismal performance – in the perverse logic of Newspeak – to identify its aspirations for more power and wealth with the disenfranchised and downtrodden of the world.

Despite the psychological dissonance and inevitable internal political upheaval occasioned by the process of adjusting to a post Cold War world, the West should welcome a less war-prone world in which the East–West struggle gradually shifts from coercive to non-coercive means of competition. Such a world favours the West, however much it may also benefit the Soviet Union. The Soviet need for Thermidor in its continued quest to be a global power underscores its weaknesses, not its strength. These lie deep within the Soviet system. To compete with the West it has to introduce Western practices into its economic system, to relax tensions in order to facilitate access to Western resources and know-how, and to rely on Western competitiveness to jar lagging domestic performance and to support long-delayed social and political reforms. Emulation is the highest form of flattery. As it embarks on reform, the Soviet regime faces serious dilemmas. An intractable international system compels moderation of its revolutionary aims. Internal reform threatens central party control at home while increasing pressures within the Soviet empire for greater measures of national autonomy and self-expression. The West does not face these dilemmas. It tolerates diversity. It can well survive without having to impose a universal system on the globe, an aim ruled out in any event by the resistance of its own populations to assume the costs and risks of so ambitious and inevitably self-defeating an objective.

The different and divergent interests of the East and West converge toward a Thermidor in the North–South struggle. All that remains is the political will by both sides to negotiate its direction, scope, and modalities.

Notes

1. See Edward A. Kolodziej, *French International Policy under De Gaulle and Pompidou: The Politics of Grandeur* (Ithaca, NY: Cornell University Press, 1974).
2. See, for example, Henry Trofimenko, 'The Third World and US-Soviet

Competition: A Soviet View', *Foreign Affairs*, vol. 59, no. 5, Summer 1981, pp. 1021–40.

3. George Kennan, *Realities of American Foreign Policy* (Princeton, NJ: Princeton University Press, 1954).

4. See William H. McNeill, *The Pursuit of Power* (Chicago, IL: University of Chicago Press, 1982). While scholars appear to agree on the period when modernisation began, there is a wide disparity of views about the causal relation between capitalism and the state. Marxists see the two phenomena as causally related, with capitalism as the motor force of the modern state. See Immanuel Wallerstein, *The Modern World System*, vol. I (New York: Academic Press, 1974) and *Modern World System*, vol. II (New York: Academic Press, 1980). For a similar interpretation of contemporary international relations, consult Mary Kaldor and Ashborn Eide (eds), *The World Military Order* (London: Macmillan, 1979). The classical statement is, of course, that of V. I. Lenin: *Imperialism, the Highest State of Capitalism* (New York: International Publishers, 1939). War is treated as a derivative of underconsumption, which is ascribed to capitalism as one of its essential failures.

Other writers see the state arising from primordial concerns tied to personal and collective security. The territorial nation-state met those needs more satisfactorily than did the feudal system. See John H. Herz, *The Nation-State and the Crisis of World Politics* (New York: McKay, 1976). Herz's theme of the conflict-prone character of the nation-state system is elaborated in Kenneth Waltz, *A Theory of International Relations* (Reading, MA: Addison-Wesley, 1979). One of the most penetrating rejoinders to the Marxist analysis of the state remains Joseph Schumpeter, *Imperialism* (New York: Meridian Books, 1955). This discussion treats the nation-state and capitalism as separate but interdependent instruments of modernisation responding to two fundamentally different, but universally experienced, humans needs and demands: security and welfare to which the nation-state and capitalism are, respectively, provisional solutions.

5. Michael Howard, *War in European History* (London: Oxford University Press, 1976), p. 49.

6. US Arms Control and Disarmament Agency, *World Military Expenditures and Arms Transfers, 1985* (Washington, DC: US Government Printing Office, 1985), pp. 50–1.

7. See, for example, Stephen Krasner, *International Regimes* (Ithaca, NY: Cornell University Press, 1983).

8. Samuel P. Huntington, Jr, *Political Order in Changing Societies* (New Haven, CT: Yale University Press, 1968), p. 32, partially quoting Robert Dahl, *Who Governs?* (New Haven, CT: Yale University Press, 1961), pp. 85–86.

Selected Bibliography
Compiled by Daniel R. Kempton and Kanti Bajpai

I. THE SOVIET UNION AND THE DEVELOPING COUNTRIES

A. The Soviet Union and the Developing World

ADOMEIT, HANNES, *Soviet Risk-Taking and Crisis Behaviour: A Theoretical and Empirical Analysis* (London: George Allen & Unwin, 1982).

ALEXIEV, ALEXANDER R., *The New Soviet Strategy in the Third World* (Santa Monica, CA: Rand Corporation, 1983).

AYOOB, MOHAMMED (ed.), *Conflict and Intervention in the Third World* (New York: St Martin, 1980).

BARROWS, WALTER L., and VINCENT D. KERN, 'Superpower Statecraft in the Third World', *Harvard International Review*, vol. 8 (1986), pp. 7–10.

BIALER, SEWERYN (ed.), *The Domestic Context of Soviet Foreign Policy* (Boulder, CO: Westview, 1981).

BIALER, SEWERYN, *The Soviet Paradox: External Expansion, Internal Decline* (New York: Knopf, 1986).

BROWN, ARCHIE, and MICHAEL KASER (eds), *Soviet Policy for the 1980s* (London: Macmillan, 1982).

BRUTENTS, KAREN N., *National Liberation Revolutions Today: Some Questions of Theory* (Moscow: Progress Publishers, 1977).

BRZEZINSKI, ZBIGNIEW, *Game Plan: How to Conduct the US-Soviet Contest* (New York: Atlantic Monthly Press, 1986).

CALDWELL, DAN C. (ed.), *Soviet International Behavior and US Policy Options* (Lexington, MA: Lexington Books, 1985).

CASEY, FRANCIS M., 'Soviet Strategy for the Third World: Wars of National Liberation', *Journal of East Asian Affairs*, vol. 2, Spring/Summer 1982, pp. 152–69.

CLARKSON, STEPHEN, *The Soviet Theory of Development: India and the Third World in Marxist-Leninist Scholarship* (Toronto/Buffalo: University of Toronto Press, 1978).

CLAWSON ROBERT W. (ed.), *East–West Rivalry in the Third World: Security Issues and Regional Perspectives*. New York: Scholarly Resources, 1986.

COPPER, JOHN F., and DANIEL S. PAPP (eds), *Communist Nations' Military Assistance* (Boulder, CO: Westview, 1983).

DIBB, PAUL, *The Soviet Union: The Incomplete Superpower* (Urbana: University of Illinois Press, 1986).

DONALDSON, ROBERT H., 'The Soviet Union and the Third World', *Current History*, vol. 81, no. 477, October 1982, pp. 313–17.

'DONALDSON, ROBERT H. (ed.), *The Soviet Union in the Third World: Successes and Failures* (Boulder, CO: Westview, 1981).

DONALDSON, ROBERT H., KAREN DAWISHA, ELIZABETH KRIDL VALKENIER, EVGENI M. PRIMAKOV, ROBERT O. FREEDMAN, NILS H. WESSELL, RHODA PEARL RABKIN, JIRI VALENTA, HELEN DESFOSSES, 'Soviet-American Competition in the Third World', *Journal of International Affairs*, vol. 34, no. 2, Fall–Winter 1980–81, pp. 219–393.

DUIGNAN, PETER, 'The World-Wide Threat of Soviet Communism', *Journal of East Asian Affairs*, vol. 2, Fall/Winter 1982, pp. 234–59.

DUNCAN, W. RAYMOND (ed.), *Soviet Policy in Developing Countries*. 2nd edn (Huntington, NY: Robert W. Krieger, 1981).

DUNCAN W. RAYMOND, *Soviet Policy in the Third World* (New York: Pergamon, 1980).

DZIAK, JOHN D., 'The Soviet Union and the National Liberation Movements: An Examination of the Development of Revolutionary Strategy', PhD dissertation, Georgetown University, 1971.

EFRAT, MOSHE, *The Political Economy of Soviet Arms Transfers to the Third World* (Lexington, MA: Lexington Books, 1981).

FEUCHTWANGER, E. J. and PETER NAILOR (eds), *The Soviet Union and the Third World* (New York: St Martin, 1981).

FRANCIS, SAMUEL T., *The Soviet Strategy of Terror* (Washington: The Heritage Foundation, 1985), rev. edn.

FUKUYAMA, FRANCIS, 'Gorbachev and the Third World', *Foreign Affairs*, vol. 64, no. 4, Spring 1986, pp. 715–31.

FUKUYAMA, FRANCIS, *The Military Dimension of Soviet Policy in the Third World* (Santa Monica, CA: Rand Corporation, 1984).

FUKUYAMA, FRANCIS, *Moscow's Post-Brezhnev Reassessment of the Third World*. Report No. R-3337-USDP (Santa Monica, CA: Rand Corporation, 1986).

FUKUYAMA, FRANCIS, *Soviet Civil—Military Relations and the Power Projection Mission* (Santa Monica, CA: The RAND Corporation, 1987).

GARTHOFF, RAYMOND L., *Detente and Confrontation: American-Soviet Relations from Nixon to Reagan* (Washington, DC: Brookings Institute, 1985).

GELMAN, HARRY, *The Soviet Union in the Third World: A Retrospective Overview and Prognosis*. Occasional Paper OPS-006 (Santa Monica, CA: Rand/UCLA Center for the Study of Soviet International Behavior, March 1986).

GEORGE, ALEXANDER L., *Managing US-Soviet Rivalry* (Boulder, CO: Westview, 1983).

GOREN, ROBERTA, *The Soviet Union and Terrorism* (London/Boston: George Allen & Unwin, 1984).

GOWA, JOANNE, and NILS H. WESSELL, *Ground Rules: Soviet and American Involvement in Regional Conflicts* (Philadelphia: Foreign Policy Research Institute, 1982).

GRIFFITH, WILLIAM E. (ed.), *The Soviet Empire: Expansion and Detente* (Lexington, MA: D. C. Heath, 1975).

GRIFFITH, WILLIAM E., *The Superpowers and Regional Tensions: The*

USSR, the United States, and Europe (Lexington, MA: Lexington Books, 1982).

GRIFFITHS, FRANKLYN, 'The Sources of American Conduct: Soviet Perspectives and Their Policy Implications', *International Security*, vol. 9, no. 2, Fall 1984, pp. 3–50.

HARKAVY, ROBERT E., *Great Power Competition for Overseas Bases: The Geopolitics of Access Diplomacy* (New York/Oxford: Pergamon, 1982).

HASELKORN, AVIGDOR, *The Evolution of Soviet Security Strategy, 1969–75* (New York: Crane, Russak and Co., 1978).

HOFFMANN, ERIK P. and FREDERIC J. FLERON (eds), *The Conduct of Soviet Foreign Policy*, 2nd edn (New York: Aldine, 1980).

HORELICK, ARNOLD L., A. ROSS JOHNSON, and JOHN D. STEIN-bruner, *The Study of Soviet Foreign Policy: Decision-Theory-Related Approaches* (Beverly Hills: Sage, 1975).

HOSMER, STEPHEN T. and THOMAS W. WOLFE, *Soviet Policy and Practice toward Third World Conflicts* (Lexington, MA: Lexington Books, 1983).

HOUGH, JERRY F., *The Struggle for the Third World: Soviet Debates and American Options.* (Washington, DC: Brookings Institution, 1986).

JACKSON, RICHARD L., *The Non-Aligned, the UN and the Superpowers* (New York: Praeger, 1983).

JACOBSEN, CARL G., *Soviet Strategic Initiatives: Challenge and Response* (New York: Praeger, 1979).

JONSSON, CHRISTER., *Superpower: Comparing American and Soviet Foreign Policy* (New York: St Martin, 1984).

KANET, ROGER E. (ed.), *Soviet Foreign Policy in the 1980s.* New York: Praeger, 1982.

KANET, ROGER E. (ed.), *The Soviet Union and the Developing Nations* (Baltimore/London: Johns Hopkins University Press, 1974).

KANET, ROGER E. (ed.), *The Soviet Union, Eastern Europe and the Developing World* (Oxford/New York: Oxford University Press, 1987).

KANET, ROGER E. and DONNA BAHRY (eds), *Soviet Economic and Political Relations with the Developing World* (New York/London: Praeger Publishers, 1975).

KAPLAN, STEPHEN S. et al. *Diplomacy of Power: Soviet Armed Forces as a Political Instrument* (Washington, DC: Brookings, 1981).

KATZ, MARK N. 'Soviet Policy toward the Third World', *Washington Quarterly*, vol. 9, no. 4, Fall 1986, pp. 159–63.

KATZ, MARK N., 'The Soviet Union and the Third World', *Current History*, vol. 85, October 1986, pp. 329–32, 339–40.

KATZ, MARK N., *The Third World in Soviet Military Thought* (Baltimore, MD: Johns Hopkins University Press, 1982).

KIM, G., 'The National Liberation Movement Today', *International Affairs* (Moscow), vol. 4, April 1981, p. 28.

KIM, G., 'Social Development and Ideological Struggle in the Developing Countries', *International Affairs* (Moscow), vol. 4, April 1980, p. 65–77.

KLINGHOFFER, ARTHUR JAY, *The Soviet Union and International Oil Politics* (New York: Columbia University Press, 1977).

KORBONSKI, ANDRZEJ and FRANCIS FUKUYAMA (eds), *The Soviet Union and the Third World: The Last Three Decades* (Ithaca, NY/London: Cornell University Press 1987).

LAQUEUR, WALTER, (ed.), *The Pattern of Soviet Conduct in the Third World* (New York: Praeger, 1983).

LISKA, GEORGE, *Russia and the Road to Appeasement: Cycles of East–West Conflict in War and Peace* (Baltimore: Johns Hopkins University Press, 1982).

LISKA, GEORGE, *Russia and World Order: Strategic Choices and the Laws of Power in History* (Baltimore: Johns Hopkins University Press, 1980).

LITWAK, ROBERT S. and SAMUEL F. WELLS, JR. (eds), *Superpower Competition and Security in the Third World* (Cambridge, MA: Ballinger Publishing Co., 1987).

LUTTWAK, EDWARD, *The Grand Strategy of the Soviet Union* (London: Weidenfeld & Nicolson, 1983).

MACFARLANE, S. NEIL, *Superpower Rivalry and Third World Radicalism: The Idea of National Liberation* (Baltimore: Johns Hopkins University Press, 1985).

MAURER, JOHN H., and RICHARD H. PORTH (eds), *Military Intervention in the Third World: Threats, Constraints and Options* (New York: Praeger, 1984).

MENON, RAJAN, *Soviet Power and the Third World* (New Haven/London: Yale University Press, 1986).

MENON, RAJAN, 'The Soviet Union, the Arms Trade and the Third World', *Soviet Studies*, vol. 34, no. 3, July 1982, pp. 377–96.

MITCHELL, R. JUDSON, *Ideology of a Superpower: Contemporary Soviet Doctrine on International Relations* (Stanford, CA: Hoover Institution Press, 1982).

NEUMAN, STEPHANIE G. and ROBERT E. HARKAVY (eds), *Arms Transfers in the Modern World* (New York: Praeger Publishers, 1979).

PAPP, DANIEL S., *Soviet Perceptions of the Developing World in the 1980s: The Ideological Basis* (Lexington, MA: Lexington Books, 1985).

PAPP, DANIEL S., *Soviet Policies Toward the Developing World During the 1980s: The Dilemmas of Power and Presence* (Maxwell Air Force Base, AL: Air University Press, 1986).

PINEYE, DANIEL, 'The Bases of Soviet Power in the Third World', *World Development*, vol. 11, 1983, pp. 1083–95.

PIPES, RICHARD, *US-Soviet Relations in the Era of Detente* (Boulder, CO: Westview, 1981).

PORTER, BRUCE D., *The USSR in Third World World Conflicts: Soviet Arms and Diplomacy in Local Wars 1945–1980* (New York/London: Cambridge University Press, 1984).

PRIMAKOV, YEVGENY M., 'The Soviet Union's Interests: Myths and Realities', *AEI Foreign Policy and Defense Review*, (American Enterprise Institute, Washington), vol. 6, no. 1, 1986, pp. 26–34.

RA'ANAN, URI, FRANCIS FUKUYAMA, MARK FALKOFF, SAM C. SARKESIAN, and RICHARD H. SHULTZ, JR., *Third World Marxist-Leninist Regimes: Strengths, Vulnerabilities and US Policy* (New York: Pergamon, 1985).

RA'ANAN, URI, ROBERT L. PFALTZGRAFF, JR., RICHARD H. SHULTZ, JR., ERNEST HALPERIN, and IGOR LUKES (eds), *Hydra of Carnage: International Linkages of Terrorism and Other Low-Intensity Operations. The Witnesses Speak* (Lexington, MA/Toronto: Lexington Books, D. C. Heath, 1986).

RADU, MICHAEL (ed.), *Eastern Europe and the Third World* (New York: Praeger Publishers, 1981).

RUBINSTEIN, ALVIN Z. (ed.), *Soviet and Chinese Influence in the Third World* (New York: Praeger, 1975).

RUBINSTEIN, ALVIN Z., 'Superpower Rivalry in the Third World', *Orbis*, vol. 27, no. 1, Spring 1983, pp. 28–34.

RUBINSTEIN, ALVIN Z., 'A Third World Policy Waits for Gorbachev', *Orbis*, vol. 30, no. 3, Summer 1986, pp. 355–64.

SAIVETZ, CAROL R., and SYLVIA WOODBY, *Soviet-Third World Relations* (Boulder, CO: Westview, 1985).

SCHMID, ALEX P. *Soviet Military Interventions since 1945* (Edison, NJ: Transaction Books, 1985).

SCHULMAN, MARSHALL D. (ed.), *East–West Tensions in the Third World* (New York: Norton, 1986).

SIMONIYA, N., 'The Current Stage of the Liberation Struggle', *Aziya i Afriki Segdnya*, vol. 5, May 1981, p. 15.

STERLING, CLAIRE, *The Terror Network: The Secret War of International Terrorism* (New York: Holt, Rinehart and Winston and Reader's Digest Press, 1981).

STEVENSON, RICHARD W., *The Rise and Fall of Detente: Relaxations of Tension in US-Soviet Relations, 1953–84* (Urbana: University of Illinois Press, 1985).

STREMLAU, JOHN J. (ed.), *Soviet Foreign Policy in an Uncertain World* (Beverly Hills, CA: Sage, 1985).

TABORSKY, EDWARD, *Communist Penetration of the Third World* (New York: Robert Speller & Sons, 1973).

THOMPSON, W. SCOTT, *Power Projection: A New Assessment of US and Soviet Capabilities* (New York: National Strategy Information Center, 1978).

TROFIMENKO, HENRY, 'The Third World and US-Soviet Competition: A Soviet View', *Foreign Affairs*, vol. 59, no. 5, Summer 1981, pp. 1021–40.

ULYANOVSKY, ROSTISLAV, *National Liberation: Essays on Theory and Practice* (Moscow: Progress Publishers, 1978).

ULYANOVSKY, ROSTISLAV, 'A Theory Implemented: V. I. Lenin and the Problems of National Liberation and Attitudes toward Nationalism', *Novaia i Noveishaia Istoriia*, vol. 2, 1982, pp. 20–2.

US CONGRESS, *Report on Soviet Policy and United States Response in the Third World* (Washington, DC: US Government Printing Office, 1981).

US CONGRESSIONAL RESEARCH SERVICE, *The Soviet Union and the Third World: A Watershed of Great Power Policy?* A Report to the Committee on International Relations, House of Representatives (Washington, DC: US Government Printing Office, 1977).

US CONGRESSIONAL RESEARCH SERVICE (JOSEPH G. WHELAN and MICHAEL J. DIXON), *The Soviet Union in the Third World,*

1980–1982: An Imperial Burden or Political Asset? (Washington, DC: US Government Printing Office, 1983).

US DEPARTMENT OF STATE, *Soviet and East European Aid to the Third World* (Washington, DC: US Government Printing Office, 1981).

US DEPARTMENT OF STATE, *Warsaw Pact Economic Aid to Non-Communist LDCs 1984* (Washington, DC: US Government Printing Office, 1986).

VALENTA, JIRI, and WILLIAM POTTER (eds), *Soviet Decisionmaking for National Security*, pp. 218–36 (London: George Allen & Unwin, 1984).

VALKENIER, ELIZABETH KRIDL, 'Revolutionary Change in the Third World: Recent Soviet Assessments', *World Politics*, vol. 38, no. 3, April 1986, pp. 415–34.

VALKENIER, ELIZABETH KRIDL, *The Soviet Union and the Third World: An Economic Bind* (New York: Praeger, 1983).

WHEELER, JACK, 'Fighting the Soviet Imperialists: The New Liberation Movement', *Reason*, vol. 17, June–July 1985, pp. 36–44.

WHELAN, JOSEPH G. *et al.*, *Soviet Policy and United States Response in the Third World*. Report prepared for the Committee on Foreign Affairs, U.S. House of Representatives (Washington: US Government Printing Office, 1981).

WHELAN, JOSEPH G. and MICHAEL J. DIXON, *The Soviet Union in the Third World: Threat to World Peace?* (Washington/New York/London: Pergamon-Brassey's International Defense Publishers, 1987).

WHETTEN, LAURENCE L. (ed.), *The Present State of Communist Internationalism* (Lexington, MA: Lexington Books, 1983).

WHITE, GORDON, ROBIN MURRAY, and CHRISTINE WHITE (eds), *Revolutionary Socialist Development in the Third World* (Lexington, MA: University Press of Kentucky, 1983).

WILES, PETER (ed.), *The New Communist Third World* (New York: St Martin, 1982).

WILES, PETER and MOSE EFRAT, *The Economics of Soviet Arms* (London: Suntory Toyota International Centre for Economics and Related Disciplines (London School of Economics and Political Science, 1985).

WOLF, CHARLES, JR., K. C. YEH, E. BRUNNER, JR., A. GURWITZ, and M. LAWRENCE, *The Costs of Soviet Empire*. No. R-307311-NA. (Santa Monica, CA: Rand Corporation, 1983).

ZACEK, JANE SHAPIRO (ed.), *The USSR under Gorbachev: Issues and Challenges* (New York: Paragon, forthcoming).

ZAMOSTNY, THOMAS J. 'Moscow and the Third World: Recent Trends in Soviet Thinking', *Soviet Studies*, vol. 36, no. 2, April 1984, pp. 223–35.

ZWICK, PETER, *National Communism (Boulder, CO: Westview, 1983)*.

B. The USSR and Latin America and the Caribbean

ASHBY, TIMOTHY, *The Bear in the Back Yard: Moscow's Caribbean Strategy* (Lexington, MA: Lexington Books, 1987).

BARK, DENNIS L. (ed.), *Red Orchestra: Instruments of Soviet Policy in*

Latin America and the Caribbean (Stanford, CA: Hoover Institution Press, 1986).

BLASIER, COLE, *The Giant's Rival: The USSR and Latin America* (Pittsburgh: University of Pittsburgh Press, 1983).

BLASIER, COLE, and CARMELO MESA-LAGO (eds), *Cuba in the World* (Pittsburgh: University of Pittsburgh Press, 1979).

CLEMENT, PETER, 'Moscow and Nicaragua: Two Sides of Soviet Policy', *Comparative Strategy*, vol. 5, no. 1, 1985, pp. 75–91.

CLISSOLD, STEPHEN (ed.), *Soviet Relations with Latin America* (London: Oxford University Press, 1970).

CROSS, SHARYL, 'Constraints on Expansion: An Analysis of the Soviet-Cuban Dimension Regarding the Present Central American Revolutionary Cauldrum', *Global Perspectives*, vol. 2, Spring 1984, pp. 30–46.

DOMINGUEZ REYES, EDMÉ, 'Soviet Relations with Central America, the Caribbean, and the Members of the Contadora Group', *Annals of the American Academy of Political and Social Science*, vol. 481 (September 1985), pp. 147–58.

DUNCAN, W. RAYMOND, 'Castro and Gorbachev: Politics of Accommodation', *Problems of Communism*, vol. 35, no. 2, March–April 1986, pp. 45–57.

DUNCAN, W. RAYMOND, *The Soviet Union and Cuba: Interests and Influence* (New York: Praeger, 1985).

ERISMAN, H. MICHAEL, *Cuba's International Relations: The Anatomy of a Nationalistic Foreign Policy* (Boulder, CO: Westview, 1985).

EVANSON, ROBERT K., 'Soviet Political Uses of Trade with Latin America', *Journal of Interamerican Studies and World Affairs*, vol. 27, Summer 1985, pp. 99–127.

FALK, PAMELA, S., *Cuban Foreign Policy: Caribbean Tempest* (Lexington, MA: Lexington Books, 1986).

GERSHMAN, CARL, 'Soviet Power in Central American and the Caribbean: The Growing Threat to American Security', *Foreign Policy and Defense Review*, vol. 5, no. 1, 1984, pp. 37–46.

GONZALEZ, EDWARD, 'The Cuban and Soviet Challenge in the Caribbean Basin', *Orbis*, vol. 29, no. 1, Spring 1985, pp. 74–94.

GOTTEMOELLER, ROSE E., *The Potential for Conflict between Soviet and Cuban Policies in the Third World* (Santa Monica, CA: Rand Corporation, 1981).

GOURÉ, LEON, and MORRIS ROTHENBERG, *Soviet Penetration of Latin America* (Coral Gables, FL: Center for Advanced International Studies, 1975).

HOUGH, JERRY F., 'The Evolving Soviet Debate on Latin America', *Latin American Research Review*, vol. 16, no. 1, 1981, pp. 124–43.

KATZ, MARK N., 'The Soviet-Cuban Connection', *International Security*, vol. 8, no. 1, Summer 1983, pp. 88–112.

KRUSZEWSKI, ZBIGNIEW ANTHONY, and WILLIAM RICHARDSON, *Mexico and the Soviet Bloc: The Foreign Policy of a Middle Power* (Boulder, CO: Westview, 1987).

LEIKEN, ROBERT S., 'Fantasies and Facts: The Soviet Union and Nicaragua', *Current History*, vol. 83, no. 495, October 1984, pp. 314–17.

LEIKEN, ROBERT S., *Soviet Strategy in Latin America*. Washington Papers, no. 93 (New York: Praeger, 1982).

LEVESQUE, JACQUE, *The USSR and the Cuban Revolution: Soviet Ideological and Strategic Perspectives* (New York: Praeger Special Studies, 1982).

LEVINE, BARRY B. (ed.), *The New Cuban Presence in the Caribbean* (Boulder, CO: Westview, 1983).

LUERS, WILLIAM H., 'The Soviets and Latin America: A Three Decade US Policy Triangle', *Washington Quarterly*, vol. 7, no. 1, Winter 1984, pp. 3–32.

MASTNY, VOJTECH, 'The Soviet Union and the Falklands War', *Naval War College Review*, vol. 36, 1983, pp. 46–55.

MICHEL, JAMES H., 'Soviet Activities in Latin America and the Caribbean', *Department of State Bulletin*, vol. 85, 1985, pp. 80–5.

MUJAL-LÉON, EUSEBIO (ed.), *USSR-Latin American Relations* (Princeton: Princeton University Press, 1987).

RAMET, PEDRO, and FERNANDO LOPES-ALVES, 'Moscow and the Revolutionary Left in Latin America', *Orbis*, vol. 28, no. 2, Summer 1984, pp. 341–63.

ROSENBERG, ROBIN, 'Soviet Support for Central American Guerrilla Movements as a Strategic Initiative', in *Soviet Armed Forces Review Annual 1983–1984* (1985), pp. 343–89.

ROTHENBERG, MORRIS, 'Latin America in Soviet Eyes', *Problems of Communism*, vol. 32, no. 5, September–October, 1983, pp. 1–18.

SHEARMAN, PETER J., 'Soviet Foreign Policy in Central America', *Global Perspectives*, vol. 1, 1983, pp. 8–22.

SHEARMAN, PETER J., 'The Soviet Union and Grenada under the New Jewel Movement', *International Affairs* (London), vol. 61, no. 4, Autumn 1985, pp. 661–73.

SHUL'GOVSKII, A. F. (eds), *Sovremennye Ideologicheskia techeniia v Latinskoi Amerike*. (Moscow: Nauka, 1983).

SMITH, WAYNE, S., 'Dateline Havana: Myopic Diplomacy', *Foreign Policy*, no. 48, Fall 1982, pp. 157–74.

'SOVIET TRADE WITH LATIN AMERICA', *Latin American Times*, vol. 72, 1986, p. 13.

TELLIS, ASHLEY, J. 'The Geopolitical Stakes in the Central American Crisis', *Strategic Review*, vol. 13, 1985, pp. 45–56.

THEBERGE, JAMES D., *The Soviet Presence in Latin America* (New York: Crane, Russak & Co., 1974).

US DEPARTMENT OF STATE, 'Cuban Armed Forces and the Soviet Military Presence', *Department of State Bulletin*, vol. 83, 1983, pp. 71–89.

US DEPARTMENT OF STATE, BUREAU OF PUBLIC AFFAIRS, 'Soviet Activities in Latin America and the Caribbean', Current Policy No. 669. Washington, DC, February 1985.

US DEPARTMENTS OF STATE AND DEFENSE, *The Soviet-Cuban Connection in Central America and the Caribbean*. Washington, DC, 1986.

VACS, ALDO CÉSAR, *Discreet Partners: Argentina and the USSR since 1917* (Pittsburgh, PA: University of Pittsburgh Press, 1984).

VACS, ALDO CÉSAR, 'Soviet Policy toward Argentina and the Southern

Cone', *Annals of the American Academy of Political and Social Science*, vol. 481, September 1985, pp. 159–71.

VALENTA, JIRI, 'Soviet and Cuban Responses to New Opportunities in Central America', in Richard Feinberg (ed.), *The International Aspects of the Crisis in Central America* (New York: Holmes & Meyer, 1982).

VALENTA, JIRI, 'Soviet Strategy in the Caribbean Basin', *Proceedings of the US Naval Institute*. May 1982.

VALENTA, JIRI, 'The USSR, Cuba and the Crisis in Central America', *Orbis*, vol. 25, no. 2, Summer 1981, pp. 353–67.

VALENTA, JIRI, and HERBERT J. ELLISON (eds), *Grenada and Soviet/Cuban Policy: Internal Crises and US/OECS Intervention* (Boulder, CO: Westview, 1986).

VALENTA, JIRI and VIRGINIA, 'Leninism in Grenada', *Problems of Communism*, vol. 33, no. 4, July–August 1984, pp. 1–23.

VARAS, AUGUSTO, 'Ideology and Politics in Latin American-USSR Relations', *Problems of Communism*, vol. 33, no. 1, January–February 1984, pp. 35–47.

VARAS, AUGUSTO, *Soviet-Latin American Relations in the 1980s* (Boulder, CO: Westview, 1986).

VOLSKY, GEORGE, 'The Soviet-Cuban Connection', *Current History*, vol. 80, no. 468, October 1981, pp. 325–328+.

WESSON, ROBERT (ed.), *Communism in Central American and the Caribbean* (Stanford, CA: Hoover Institution Press, 1982).

WIARDA, HOWARD J. and MARK FALCOFF, *The Communist Challenge in the Carribean* (Washington, DC: University Press of America, 1987).

WIARDA, HOWARD J. (ed.), *Rift and Revolution: The Central American Imbroglio*. (Washington, DC: American Enterprise Institute, 1984).

C. The USSR and East Asia

ALEXANDROV, I., 'On Soviet-Chinese Relations', *International Affairs* (Moscow), vol. 7, July 1982, pp. 16–19.

BILVEER, S., 'The Soviet Union and ASEAN: Interests, Policies, and Constraints', *Indian Political Science Review*, vol. 38, no. 1, April 1985, pp. 95–100.

BROWN, WILLIAM A., 'The Soviet Role in Asia', *Department of State Bulletin*, vol. 83 (December 1983), pp. 13–17.

BUSZYNSKI, LESZEK, *Soviet Foreign Policy and Southeast Asia* (London/Sydney: Croom Helm, 1986).

BUSZYNSKI, LESZEK, 'Thailand, the Soviet Union and the Kampuchean Imbroglio', *World Today* (London), vol. 38, no. 2, February 1982, pp. 66–72.

CHUNG, CHIN-WEE, 'North Korea in the Sino-Soviet Dispute', *Journal of Northeast Asian Studies*, vol. 2, no. 3, 1983, pp. 67–85.

CLINE, RAY S., JAMES ARNOLD MILLER, and ROGER E. KANET (eds), *Asia in Soviet Global Strategy* (Boulder, CO/London: Westview Press, 1987).

CLOUGH, RALPH, N., 'The Soviet Union and the Two Koreas', in Donald

S. Zagoria *Soviet Policy in East Asia* (New Haven, CT: Yale University Press, 1982).

DALLIN, ALEXANDER, *Black Box: KAL 007 and the Superpowers* (Berkeley, CA: University of California Press, 1985).

DIBB, PAUL, 'Soviet Strategy towards Australia, New Zealand and the Southwest Pacific', *Australian Outlook*, vol. 39, no. 2, August 1985, pp. 67–76.

ELLISON, HERBERT J. (ed.), *The Sino-Soviet Conflict: A Global Perspective* (Seattle: University of Washington Press, 1982).

ELLISON, HERBERT J. (ed.), *Japan and the Pacific Quadrille: The Major Powers in East Asia* (Boulder, CO/London: Westview Press, 1987).

GARRITY, PATRICK J., 'Soviet Policy in the Far East: Search for Strategic Unity', *Military Review*, vol. 62, December 1982, pp. 26–38.

GELMAN, HARRY, 'Andropov's Policy toward Asia', *Journal of Northeast Asian Studies*, vol. 2, no. 2, June 1983, pp. 3–11.

GELMAN, HARRY, 'Continuity versus Changes in Soviet Policy in Asia', *Journal of Northeast Asian Studies*, vol. 4, Summer 1985, pp. 3–18.

GELMAN, HARRY, *The Soviet Far East Buildup and Soviet Risk-Taking against China* (Santa Monica, CA: Rand Corporation, August 1982).

GRIFFITH, WILLIAM E., 'Sino-Soviet Rapprochement?' *Problems of Communism*, vol. 32, no. 2, March–April 1983, pp. 20–9.

HA, YONG-CHOOL, 'Soviet Perceptions of Soviet-North Korean Relations', *Asian Survey*, vol. 26, no. 5, May 1986, pp. 573–90.

HA, JOSEPH M., 'Soviet Perceptions of North Korea', *Asian Perspective*, vol. 6, no. 2, Fall–Winter 1982, pp. 105–31.

HART, THOMAS, G., 'Sino-Soviet Relations 1969–1982: An Attempt at Clarification', *Cooperation and Conflict*, vol. 18, no. 2, June 1983, pp. 79–99.

HIRAMATSU, SHIGEO, 'A Chinese Perspective on Sino-Soviet Relations', *Journal of Northeast Asian Studies*, vol. 2, no. 3, September 1983, pp. 51–65.

HORN, ROBERT C., 'The Soviet Challenge in East Asia', *Asian Affairs* (New York), no. 2, Spring 1983, pp. 1–18.

HSIUNG, JAMES C. 'Soviet-Chinese Detente', *Current History*, vol. 84, no. 504, October 1985, pp. 329–33.

JACOBSEN, C. G., *Sino-Soviet Relations since Mao* (New York: Praeger, 1981).

JUKES, GEOFFREY, *The Soviet Union in Asia* (Berkeley/Los Angeles: University of California Press, 1975).

KELEMAN, PAUL, 'Soviet Strategy in Southeast Asia: The Vietnam Factor', *Asian Survey*, vol. 24, March 1984, pp. 335–48.

KIM, ILPYONG, J. (ed.), *The Strategic Triangle: China, the United States and the Soviet Union* (New York: Paragon House Publishers, 1987).

KIMURA, AKIO, 'Sino-Soviet Relations: New Developments and Their Limits', *Journal of Northeast Asian Studies*, vol. 2, no. 1, March 1983, pp. 17–37.

KIMURA, HIROSHI, 'The Conclusion of the Sino-Japanese Peace Treaty (1978): Soviet Coercive Strategy and Its Limits', *Studies in Comparative Communism*, vol. 18, no. 2–3, Summer–Autumn 1985, pp. 151–80.

KIMURA, HIROSHI, 'Soviet Policy toward Asia under Chernenko and Gorbachev', *Journal of Northeast Asian Studies*, vol. 4, no. 4, Winter 1985, pp. 45–66.

MCBETH, JOHN, 'Thailand: Wary of the Bear', *Far Eastern Economic Review*, 21 November 1985, pp. 36–7.

MCLANE, CHARLES B., *Soviet–Asian Relations* (London: Central Asia Research Centre; distributed by Columbia University Press, 1973).

MEDVEDEV, ROY, 'The USSR and China: Confrontation or Detente?', *New Left Review*, no. 142, November–December 1983, pp. 5–29.

MENON, RAJAN, 'China and the Soviet Union in Asia', *Current History*, vol. 80, no. 468, October 1981, pp. 329–33.

MILLS, WILLIAM DEB, 'Gorbachev and the Future of Sino-Soviet Relations', *Political Science Quarterly*, vol. 101, no. 4, 1986, pp. 535–57.

MORLEY, JAMES W. (ed.), *The Pacific Basin: New Challenges for the United States* (Montpelier, VT: Capital City Press for the Academy of Political Science, 1986).

NAKAJIMA, MINEO, 'China May Return to the Soviet Bloc', *Japan Quarterly*, vol. 30, no. 2, April–June 1983, pp. 181–7.

NOBILO, MARIO, 'Prospects of Sino-Soviet *Rapprochement*', *Review of International Affairs*, vol. 34, (20 December 1983), pp. 16–18.

OLSEN, EDWARD A. 'Asian Perceptions of the US-Soviet Balance', *Asian Affairs*, vol. 8, May–June 11981, pp. 262–80.

PALMER, NORMAN D., 'Soviet Perspectives on Peace and Security in Asia', *Asian Affairs*, vol. 8, September–October 1981, pp. 1–19.

PAPP, DANIEL S., *Vietnam: The View from Moscow, Peking, Washington* (Jefferson, NC: MacFarland, 1981).

PARK, JAE KYU and JOSEPH M. HA. (eds), *The Soviet Union and East Asia in the 1980s* (Seoul, Korea: The Institute for Far Eastern Studies, Kyung Nam University; distributed by Westview Press, Boulder, CO., 1983).

PETROV, VLADIMIR, 'Gorbachev Looks at Asia', *Journal of Northeast Asian Studies*, vol. 4, 1985, pp. 26–44.

PIKE, DOUGLAS, *Vietnam and the Soviet Union: Anatomy of an Alliance* (Boulder, CO/London: Westview Press, 1987).

QUESTED R. K. I. *Sino-Soviet Relations: A Short History* (London: George Allen & Unwin, 1984).

ROBINSON, THOMAS W., 'American Policies in the Strategic Triangle', in Richard A. Melanson (ed.), *Neither Cold War nor Detente* (Charlottesville: University of Virginia Press, 1983).

ROBINSON, THOMAS W., 'Detente and the Sino-Soviet-US Triangle', in Della Sheldon (ed.), *Dimensions of Detente* (New York: Praeger, 1978).

ROBINSON, THOMAS W., 'Soviet Policy in East Asia', *Problems of Communism*, vol. 22, no. 6, November–December 1973, pp. 32–50.

ROBINSON, THOMAS W., 'The Soviet Union in Asia in 1980', *Asian Survey*, vol. 21, no. 1, January 1981, pp. 14–30.

ROBINSON, THOMAS W., 'Triple Detente? The Strategic Triangle in the Late Twentieth Century', in Jane P. Shapiro Zacek (ed.), *The USSR under Gorbachev: Issues and Challenges* (New York: Paragon, forthcoming).

ROSENBERGER, LEIF, 'The Soviet-Vietnamese Alliance and Kampuchea', *Survey*, vol. 27, Autumn–Winter 1983, pp. 207–30.

ROZMAN, GILBERT, 'China's Soviet Watchers in the 1980s: A New Era in Scholarship', *World Politics* (Princeton), vol. 37, no. 4, July 1985, pp. 435–74.

ROZMAN, GILBERT, 'Moscow's China Watchers in the Post-Mao Era: The Response to a Changing China', *China Quarterly*, no. 94, June 1983, pp. 215–41.

RUPEN, ROBERT A., 'Mongolia: Pawn of Geopolitics', *Current History*, vol. 81, no. 475, May 1982, pp. 215–18.

SEGAL, GERALD (ed.), *The China Factor: Peking and the Superpowers* (London: Croom Helm, 1982).

SEGAL, GERALD, *The Great Power Triangle* (New York: St Martin, 1982).

SEGAL, GERALD, 'Sino-Soviet Relations: The Road to Detente', *World Today* (London), vol. 40, no. 5, May 1984, pp. 205–12.

SEGAL, GERALD (ed.), *The Soviet Union in East Asia: Predicaments of Power*, Boulder, CO: Westview Press; (London: Heinemann, 1983).

SIMON, SHELDON W., 'The Great Powers' Security Role in Southeast Asia: Diplomacy and Force', in Young Whan Kihl and Lawrence E. Grinter (eds), *Asian-Pacific Security: Emerging Challenges and Responses* (Boulder, CO: Lynne Rienner, 1986).

SOLOMON, RICHARD H. and MASATAKA KOSAKA (eds), *The Soviet Far East Military Buildup: Nuclear Dilemmas and Asian Security* (Dover, MA: Auburn House, 1986).

STUART, DOUGLAS T. and WILLIAM T. TOW (eds), *China, the Soviet Union, and the West: Strategic and Political Dimensions in the 1980s* (Boulder, CO: Westview, 1982).

SU, CHI, 'China and the Soviet Union', *Current History*, vol. 83, no. 494, September 1984, pp. 245–7.

SU, CHI, 'China and the Soviet Union: "Principled, Saluatory, and Tempered" Management of Conflict', in Samuel S. Kim (ed.), *China and the World: Chinese Foreign Policy in the Post-Mao Era* (Boulder, CO: Westview, 1984), pp. 135–60.

SU,CHI, 'Soviet China-Wathcers' Influence on Soviet China Policy', *Journal of Northeast Asian Studies*, vol. 2, no. 4, December 1983, pp. 25–49.

SUCH-HO, LEE, 'Major Determinants of Soviet Support for North Korea', *Korea and World Affairs*, vol. 9, no. 1, Spring 1985, pp. 91–115.

THORNTON, THOMAS PERRY, 'The USSR and Asia in 1983: Staying the Brezhnev Course', *Asian Survey*, vol. 24, no. 1, January 1984, pp. 1–16.

TILMAN, ROBERT O., *Southeast Asia and the Enemy Beyond: ASEAN Perceptions of External Threat* (Boulder, CO/London: Westview Press, 1987).

VAN DER KROEF, JUSTUS M., *Communism in South-East Asia* (Berkeley, CA: University of California Press, 1980).

VAN DER KROEF, JUSTUS M., 'The East–West Conflict and the Cambodian Problem', *Crossroads*, no. 18, Autumn 1985, pp. 1–21.

WALLACE, WILLIAM V. 'Sino-Soviet Relations: An Intrepetation', *Soviet Studies*, vol. 35, no. 4, October 1983, pp. 457–70.

WHITING, ALLEN S., 'Sino-Soviet Relations: What Next?', *Annals of the American Academy of Political and Social Science*, vol. 476, November 1984, pp. 142–55.
ZAGORIA, DONALD S. 'Gauging the Sino-Soviet Thaw', *New Leader*, vol. 65, 29 November 1982, pp. 3–5.
ZAGORIA, DONALD S., 'The Moscow-Beijing Detente', *Foreign Affairs*, vol. 61, no. 4 Spring 1983, pp. 853–73.
ZAGORIA, DONALD S. (ed.), *Soviet Policy in East Asia* (New Haven, CT: Yale University Press, 1982).
ZAGORIA, DONALD S., 'Soviet-American Rivalry in Asia', *Proceedings of the Academy of Political Science*, vol. 36, no. 1, 1986, pp. 103–115.
ZAGORIA, DONALD S., 'The USSR and Asia in 1984', *Asian Survey*, vol. 25, no. 1, January 1985, pp. 21–32.
ZAGORIA, DONALD S., 'The USSR and Asia in 1985: The First Year of Gorbachev', *Asian Survey*, vol. 26, no. 1 January 1986, pp. 15–29.

D. Soviet Policy in South and Southwest Asia

ARNOLD, ANTHONY, *Afghanistan: The Soviet Invasion in Perspective* (Stanford, CA: Hoover Institution Press, 1981).
AYOOB, MOHAMMED, 'India, Pakistan and Superpower Rivalry', *World Today* (London), vol. 28, no. 5, May 1982, pp. 194–202.
BHATIA, VINOD (ed.), *Indo-Soviet Relations: Problems and Prospects* (New Delhi: Panchsheel Publishers, 1984).
BRADSHER, HENRY S., *Afghanistan and the Soviet Union*, 2nd edn (Durham, NC: Duke University Press, 1986).
CANFIELD, ROBERT L., 'Soviet Gambit in Central Asia', *Journal of South Asian and Middle Eastern Studies*, vol. 5, no. 1, Fall 1981, pp. 10–30.
CHEKHANIN, B., 'Soviet-Indian Friendship and Cooperation', *International Affairs* (Moscow), vol. 5, May 1982, pp. 14–20.
COHEN, STEPHEN P. (ed.), *The Security of South Asia: Asian and American Perspectives* (Urbana and Chicago: University of Illinois Press, 1987).
COLLINS, JOSEPH J., *The Soviet Invasion of Afghanistan: A Study of Force in Soviet Foreign Policy* (Lexington, MA: Lexington Books, 1985).
DAWISHA, KAREN, 'Moscow's Moves in the Direction of the Gulf – So Near and Yet So Far', *Journal of International Affairs*, vol. 34, no. 2, Fall–Winter 1980–81, pp. 219–33.
DONALDSON, ROBERT H., *The Soviet-Indian Alignment: Quest for Influence* (Denver, CO: Graduate School of International Studies, University of Denver, 1978.
DONALDSON, ROBERT H., *Soviet Policy Toward India: Ideology and Strategy* (Cambridge: Harvard University Press, 1974).
DUNN, KEITH, 'Constraints on the USSR in Southwest Asia: A Military Analysis', *Orbis*, vol. 25, no. 3, Fall 1981, pp. 607–29.
GIRADET, EDWARD R., *Afghanistan: The Soviet War* (London: Croom Helm, 1985).
GEORGIEV, V., 'Soviet-Indian Cooperation: Tangible Results and Broad Prospects', *International Affairs* (Moscow), vol. 8, August 1985, pp. 23–9.

GRIFFITH, WILLIAM, E., 'The USSR and Pakistan', *Problems of Communism*, vol. 31, no. 1, January–February 1982, pp. 38–44.

HAMMOND, THOMAS, T., *Red Flag over Afghanistan: The Communist Coup, the Soviet Invasion and Their Consquences* (Boulder, CO: Westview, 1983).

HARRISON, SELIG S., 'A Breakthrough in Afghanistan?', *Foreign Policy*, no. 51, Summer 1983, pp. 3–26.

HARRISON, SELIG S., 'Dateline Afghanistan: Exit through Finland?', *Foreign Policy*, no. 41, Winter 1980/81, pp. 163–87.

HORN, ROBERT C., *Soviet-Indian Relations: Issues and Influence* (New York: Praeger, 1982).

HORN, ROBERT C., 'The Soviet Union and Sino-Indian Relations', *Orbis*, vol. 27, no. 4, Winter 1984, pp. 889–906.

HYMAN, ANTHONY, *Afghanistan under Soviet Domination, 1964–81* (New York: St Martin, 1982).

JAIN, RAJENDRA KUMAR (ed.), *Soviet-South Asian Relations, 1947–1978* (Atlantic Highlands, NJ: Humanities Press, 1979), 2 volumes.

KAPUR, K. D., *Soviet Strategy in South Asia: Perspectives on Soviet Policies towards the Indian Subcontinent and Afghanistan* (New Delhi: Young Asian Publications, 1983).

KARP, CRAIG M. 'The War in Afghanistan', *Foreign Affairs*, vol. 64, no. 5, Summer 1986, pp. 1026–47.

KHALILZAD, ZALMAY, *The Return of the Great Game: Superpower Rivalry and Domestic Turmoil in Afghanistan, Iran, Pakistan and Turkey* (Santa Monica, CA: California Seminar in International Security and Foreign Policy, 1980).

LITWAK, ROBERT, SHAHRAM CHUBIN, and TIMOTHY GEORGE (eds), *India and the Great Powers* (London: Grower, 1984).

MAPRAYIL, CRIAC, *The Soviets and Afghanistan* (London: Cosmic Press, 1982).

MONKS, ALFRED L., *The Soviet Intervention in Afghanistan* (Washington/London: American Enterprise Institute for Public Policy Research, 1981).

NAIK, J. A. (ed.), *India and the Communist Countries* (Atlantic Highlands, NJ: Humanities Press, 1981).

NEWELL, NANCY PEABODY, and RICHARD S. NEWELL, *The Struggle for Afghanistan* (Ithaca, NY: Cornell University Press, 1981).

POULLADA, LEON, B., 'The Failure of American Diplomacy in Afghanistan', *World Affairs*, vol. 145, Winter 1982/83, pp. 230–52.

ROSE, LEO E., 'United States and Soviet Policy toward South Asia', *Current History*, vol. 85 1986, pp. 97–100.

RUBINSTEIN, ALVIN Z. 'Afghanistan: Embraced by the Bear', *Orbis*, vol. 26, no. 1, Spring 1982, pp. 135–53.

RUBINSTEIN, ALVIN Z., 'The Last Years of Peaceful Coexistence: Soviet-Afghan Relations, 1963–1978', *Middle East Journal*, vol. 36, no. 2, Spring 1982, pp. 165–83.

SAIKAL, AMIN, 'Soviet Policy Toward Southwest Asia', *Annals of the American Academy of Political and Social Science*, vol. 481, September 1985, pp. 104–16.

SEN GUPTA, BHABANI, *The Afghan Syndrome: How to Live with Soviet Power* (London: Croom Helm, 1982).

SEN GUPTA, BHABANI, 'Communism and India: A New Context', *Problems of Communism*, vol. 30, no. 4, July–August 1985, pp. 33–45.

SEN GUPTA, BHABANI, *Soviet-Asian Relations in the 1970s and Beyond: An Interperceptional Study* (New York/Washington/London: Praeger Publishers, 1976).

SIKORSKI, RADEK, *Moscow's Afghan War: Soviet Motives and Western Interests* (London: Alliance Publishers, 1987).

SINGH, S. NIHAL, 'Why India Goes to Moscow for Arms', *Asian Survey*, vol. 24, no. 7, July 1984, pp. 707–20.

SINGH, S. NIHAL, *The Yogi and the Bear: A Study of Indo-Soviet Relations* (Delhi: Allied, 1986).

SMOLANSKY, S. M., 'Soviet Policy in Iran and Afghanistan', *Current History*, vol. 80, no. 468, October 1981, pp. 321–4+.

SOLOMON, RICHARD H., *Choices for Coalition-Building: The Soviet Presence in Asia and American Policy Alternatives* (Santa Monica, CA: Rand Corporation, 1981).

THOMAS, RAJU G. C. (ed.), *The Great-Power Triangle and Asian Security* (Lexington, MA/Toronto: Lexington Books, 1983).

US HOUSE COMMITTEE ON FOREIGN AFFAIRS, *The Soviet Role in Asia*. Hearings on 19 July–19 October 1983).

US DEPARTMENT OF STATE, 'Afghanistan: Four Years of Occupation', *Special Report no. 122* (Washington, DC: US Government Printing Office, December 1982).

US DEPARTMENT OF STATE, 'Afghanistan: Three Years of Occupation', *Special Report no. 106* (Washington, DC: US Government Printing Office, December 1983).

WATKINS WEBB, KATHI, *Soviet Policy Toward the Asean Nations: A Historical Review* (Santa Monica, CA: California Seminar on International Security and Foreign Policy, 1987).

WEINBAUM, MARVIN G., 'Soviet Policy and the Constraints of Nationalism in Iran and Afghanistan', in Yaacov Ro'i (ed.), *The USSR and the Muslim World* (London: George Allen & Unwin, 1984).

WOLPERT, STANLEY, *Roots of Confrontation in South Asia: Afghanistan, Pakistan, India and the Superpowers* (Oxford: Oxford University Press, 1982).

YODFAT, ARYEH, Y., *The Soviet Union and Revolutionary Iran* (London/Canberra: Croom Helm; New York: St Martin's Press, 1984).

ZIRING, LAWRENCE, 'Soviet Policy on the Rim of Asia: Scenarios and Projections', *Asian Affairs* (New York), vol. 9, January–February 1982, pp. 135–46.

ZIRING, LAWRENCE, *The Subcontinent in World Politics: India, Its Neighbors and the Great Powers*, 2nd edn (New York: Praeger, 1982).

E. The USSR and the Middle East and North Africa

ALIBONI, ROBERTO, *The Red Sea Region: Local Actors and the Superpowers* (London: Croom Helm, 1985).

AMERICAN ENTERPRISE INSTITUTE, 'The Superpowers in the Middle East', *AEI Foreign Policy and Defensive Review*, vol. 6, no. 1 (1986).

ATHERTON, ALFRED I. JR., 'The Soviet Role in the Middle East: An American View', *Middle East Journal*, vol. 39, no. 4 Autumn 1985, pp. 688–715.

BADOLATO, COLONEL E. V., 'A Clash of Cultures: The Expulsion of Soviet Military Advisors from Egypt', *Naval War College Review*, vol. 37, no. 2, sequence 301, March/April 1984, pp. 69–81.

BAR-SIMAN-TOV, YAACOV, *Israel, the Superpowers, and the War in the Middle East* (New York/Westport, CT/London: Praeger Publishers, 1987).

BENNETT, ALEXANDER J., 'Arms Transfers as an Instrument of Soviet Policy in the Middle East', *Middle East Journal*, vol. 39, no. 4, Autumn 1985, pp. 745–74.

BHOKARI, IMTIAZ H., 'Soviet Military Challenge in Gulf', *Military Review*, vol. 65, August 1985, pp. 50–62.

CAMPBELL, JOHN C., 'Soviet Strategy in the Middle East', *American-Arab Affairs*, no. 8, (Spring 1984), pp. 74–82.

CAMPBELL, JOHN C., 'The United States and the USSR, Rivals in the Middle East', *Korea and World Affairs*, vol. 8, Summer 1984, pp. 343–64.

CHUBIN, SHAHRAM, 'Gains for Soviet Policy in the Middle East', *International Security*, vol. 6, no. 4, Spring 1982, pp. 122–52.

CHUBIN, SHAHRAM, 'The Soviet Union and Iran', *Foreign Affairs*, vol. 61, no. 4 Spring 1983, pp. 921–49.

CIGAR, NORMAN, 'South Yemen and the USSR: Prospects for the Relationships', *Middle East Journal*, vol. 39, no. 4, Autumn 1985, pp. 775–95.

DAWISHA, ADEED, and KAREN DAWISHA (eds), *The Soviet Union in the Middle East: Policies and Perspectives* (London: Heinemann Education Books, 1982).

DAWISHA, KAREN, *Soviet Policy toward Egypt* (New York: St Martin, 1979).

DAWISHA, KAREN, 'The USSR in the Middle East: Superpower in Eclipse', *Foreign Affairs*, vol. 61, no. 2, Winter 1982/83, pp. 438–52.

DUNN, MICHAEL COLLINS, 'Soviet Interests in the Arabian Peninsula: The Aden Pact and Other Paper Tigers', *American-Arab Affairs*, no. 8, Spring 1984, pp. 92–8.

FREEDMAN, ROBERT O., 'Moscow and a Middle East Peace Settlement', *Washington Quarterly*, vol. 8, no. 3 Summer 1985, pp. 143–61.

FREEDMAN, ROBERT O., 'Moscow, Damascus and the Lebanon Crisis', in Moshe Ma'oz and Avner Yaniz (eds), *Syria under Assad: Domestic Constraints and Regional Risks* pp. 224–47 (New York: St Martin, 1986).

FREEDMAN, ROBERT O., 'Patterns of Soviet Policy toward the Middle East', *Annals of the American Academy of Political and Social Science*, 482, November 1985, pp. 40–64.

FREEDMAN, ROBERT O., *Soviet Policy in the Middle East since 1970*, 3rd edn (New York: Praeger, 1983).

FUKUYAMA, FRANCIS, 'Nuclear Shadowboxing: Soviet Intervention in the Middle East', *Orbis*, vol. 25, no. 3, all 1981, pp. 579–605.

FUKUYAMA, FRANCIS, *The Soviet Threat to the Persian Gulf* (Santa Monica, CA: Rand Corporation, 1981).

FUKUYAMA, FRANCIS, *The Soviet Union and Iraq since 1968* (Santa Monica, CA: Rand Corporation, 1980).

GLASSMAN, JON D., *Arms for the Arabs: The Soviet Union and War in the Middle East* (Baltimore: Johns Hopkins University Press, 1975).

GOLAN, GALIA, 'The Soviet Union and the PLO since the War in Lebanon', *Middle East Journal*, vol. 40, no. 2 (Spring 1986), pp. 285–305.

GOLAN, GALIA, *The Soviet Union and the Palestine Liberation Organization* (New York: Praeger, 1980).

GOLAN, GALIA, *Yom Kippur and After: The Soviet Union and the Middle East Crisis* (Cambridge: Cambridge University Press, 1977).

GRAYSON, BENSON LEE, *Soviet Intentions and American Options in the Middle East* (Washington, DC: National Defense University Press, 1982).

HALLIDAY, FRED, 'The Arc of Crisis and the New Cold War', *Middle East Research and Information Project Reports*, vol. 11, October–December 1981, pp. 14–25.

HALLIDAY, FRED, 'Current Soviet Policy and the Middle East: A Report', *Middle East Research and Information Project Reports*, vol. 13, June 1983, pp. 18–22.

HALLIDAY, FRED, *Soviet Policy in the Arc of Crisis* (Washington: Institute for Policy Studies; Amsterdam: Transnational Institute, 1981).

HANSEL, HOWARD M. 'Moscow's Perspective on the Fall of the Iranian Monarchy', *Asian Affairs*, 14, 1983, pp. 148–59, 297–311.

HAZAN, BARUCH, A., *Soviet Propaganda: A Case Study of the Middle East Conflict* (Jerusalem: Israel Universities Press; New Brunswick, NJ: Rutgers University Press, 1976).

HEIKAL, MOHAMED, *The Sphinx and the Commissar: The Rise and Fall of Soviet Influence in the Middle East* (New York/London: Harper and Row, 1978).

JABBER, PAUL, 'Egypt's Crisis, America's Dilemma', *Foreign Affairs*, vol. 64, no. 5, Summer 1986, pp. 960–80.

JAHANPOUR, FARHANG, 'Iran: The Rise and Fall of the Tudeh Party', *World Today* (London), vol. 40, no. 4, April 1984, pp. 152–9.

KARSH, EFRAIM, *The Cautious Bear: Soviet Military Engagements in Middle East Wars in the Post-1967 Era* (Boulder, CO: Westview, 1986).

KARSH, EFRAIM, 'Soviet-Israeli Relations: A New Phase?', *World Today* (London), vol. 41, no. 12, December 1985, pp. 214–17.

KASS, ILANA, *Soviet Involvement in the Middle East: Policy Formulation, 1966–1973* (Boulder, CO: Westview Press; Folkstone, ENGL: William Dawson and Sons, 1979).

KATZ, MARK N., *Russia and Arabia: Soviet Foreign Policy toward the Arabian Peninsula* (Baltimore: Johns Hopkins University Press, 1986).

KATZ, MARK N., 'Soviet Policy in the Gulf States', *Current History*, vol. 84, no. 498, January 1985, pp. 25–28+.

KAUPPI, MARK V. and R. CRAIG NATION (eds), *The Soviet Union and the Middle East in the 1980s: Opportunities, Constraints and Dilemmas* (Lexington, MA: Lexington Books, 1983).

KHALIDI, RASHID, 'An Arab View of Containment', in Terry L. Deibel and John Lewis Gaddis (eds), *Containment: Concept and Policy*, vol. 2 (Washington, DC: National Defense University Press, 1986, pp. 414–21.

KHALIDI, RASHID, 'Arab Views of the Soviet Role in the Middle East', *Middle East Journal*, vol. 39, no. 4, Autumn 1985, pp. 716–32.

KHALIDI, RASHID, *Soviet Middle East Policy in the Wake of Camp David* (Beirut: Institute for Palestine Studies, 1979).

KHALIDI, RASHID, *The Soviet Union and the Middle East in the 1980's* (Beirut: Institute for Palestine Studies, 1980).

KHALIZAD, ZALMAY, 'Islamic Iran: Soviet Dilemma', *Problems of Communism*, vol. 33, no. 1, January–February 1984, pp. 1–20.

KHALIZAD, ZALMAY, 'Soviet Dilemmas in Khomeini's Iran', *Australian Outlook*, vol. 38, no. 1, April 1984, pp. 1–8.

KLINGHOFFER, ARNOLD JAY, with JUDITH APTER, *Israel and the Soviet Union: Alienation or Reconciliation?* (Boulder, CO: Westview, 1985).

KRAMMER, ARNOLD, *The Forgotten Friendship: Israel and the Soviet Bloc, 1947–1953* (Urbana, IL: University of Illinois Press, 1974).

LANDIS, LINCOLN, *Politics and Oil: Moscow in the Middle East* (New York: Dunellen Publishers, 1974).

LEDERER, IVO J. and WAYNE S. VUCINICH (eds), *The Soviet Union and the Middle East: The Post-World War II Era* (Stanford, CA: Hoover Institution Press, 1974).

LEITENBERG MILTON and GABRIEL SHEFFER (eds), *Great Power Intervention in the Middle East* (New York/Oxford: Pergamon Press, 1979).

MANGOLD, PETER, *Superpower Intervention in the Middle East* (London: Croom Helm, 1978).

MARANTZ, PAUL, and BLEMA S. STEINBERG (eds), *Superpower Involvement in the Middle East: Dynamics of Foreign Policy* (Boulder, CO: Westview, 1985).

MATHESON, NEIL, *The 'Rules of the Game' of Superpower Military Intervention in the Third World 1975–1980* (Washington: University Press of America, 1982).

MCLANE, CHARLES B., *Soviet-Middle East Relations* (London: Central Asia Research Centre; distributed by Columbia University Press, 1973).

NAPPER, LARRY C., 'The Arab Autumn of 1984: A Case Study of Soviet Middle East Diplomacy', *Middle East Journal*, vol. 39, no. 4, Autumn 1985, pp. 733–44.

NOVIK, NIMROD, *On the Shores of Bab al-Mandab: Soviet Diplomacy and Regional Dynamics*. (Philadelphia: Foreign Policy Research Institute, 1979).

OLCOTT, MARTHA BRILL, 'Soviet Islam and World Revolution', *World Politics* (Princeton), vol. 34, no. 4, July 1982, pp. 487–504.

PAGE, STEPHEN, 'Moscow and the Arabian Peninsula', *American-Arab Affairs*, no. 8, Spring 1984, pp. 83–91.

PAGE, STEPHEN, *The Soviet Union and the Yemens: Influence in Asymmetrical Relations* (New York: Praeger, 1985).

PIPES, DANIEL, 'Fundamentalist Muslims between America and Russia', *Foreign Affairs*, vol. 64, no. 5, Summer 1986, pp. 939–59.

POLLOCK, DAVID, 'Moscow and Aden: Coping with a Coup', *Problems of Communism*, vol. 35, no. 3, May–June 1986, pp. 50–70.

QUANDT, WILLIAM B., 'Riyadh between the Superpowers', *Foreign Policy*, no. 41 Fall 1981, pp. 37–56.

RAFAEL, GIDEON, 'Divergence and Convergence of American-Soviet Interests in the Middle East: An Israeli Viewpoint', *Political Science Quarterly*, vol. 100, no. 4, Winter 1985/86, pp. 561–74.

RO'I, YAACOV, *Soviet Decision Making in Practice: The USSR and Israel 1947–1954* (New Brunswick, NJ/London: Transaction Books, 1980).

RO'I, YAACOV (ed.), *The USSR and the Muslim World: Issues in Domestic and Foreign Policy* (Winchester, MA: Allen & Unwin, 1984).

ROSS, DENNIS, 'The Soviet Union and the Persian Gulf', *Political Science Quarterly*, vol. 99, no. 4, Winter 1984/85, pp. 615–35.

ROSS, DENNIS, 'Soviet Views toward the Gulf War', *Orbis*, vol. 28, no. 3, Fall 1984, pp. 437–47.

RUBINSTEIN, ALVIN Z., 'Soviet Policy in the Middle East: Perspectives from Three Capitals', in Robert H. Donaldson (ed.), *Soviet Union and the Third World: Successes and Failures* (Boulder, CO: Westview, 1981), pp. 15–160.

RUBINSTEIN, ALVIN Z., *Red Star on the Nile: The Soviet-Egyptian Influence Relationship since the June War* (Princeton: Princeton University Press, 1977).

RUBINSTEIN, ALVIN Z., 'Soviet Presence in the Arab World', *Current History*, vol. 80, no. 468, October 1981, pp. 313–16+.

RUBINSTEIN, ALVIN Z., 'The Soviet Union and Iran under Khomeini', *International Affairs* (London), vol. 57, no. 4, Autumn 1981, pp. 599–617.

RUBINSTEIN, ALVIN Z., 'The Soviet Union's Imperial Policy in the Middle East', *Middle East Review*, 15 (Fall 1982–Winter 1982/83), pp. 19–24.

RUBINSTEIN, SANDRA MILLER, *The Communist Movement in Palestine and Israel, 1919–1984* (Boulder, CO: Westview, 1985).

SAIVETZ, CAROL R., *The Soviet Union and the Gulf in the 1980s* (Boulder, CO: Westview, 1988).

SELLA, AMMON, *Soviet Political and Military Conduct in the Middle East* (New York: St Martin, 1981).

SEZER, DUYGA B., 'Peaceful Coexistence: Turkey and the Near East in Soviet Policy', *Annals of the American Academy of Political and Social Science*, vol. 481, September 1985, pp. 1159–71.

SIMES, DIMITRI K., 'The Soviet Approach to the Arab-Israeli Conflict', in Michael C. Hudson (ed.), *Alternative Approaches to the Arab-Israeli Conflict: A Comparative Analysis of the Principal Actors* pp. 137–51, (Washington, DC: Center for Contemporary Arab Studies, Georgetown University, 1984).

SMOLANSKY, OLES M., *The Soviet Union and the Arab Middle East under Khrushchev* (Lewisburg, PA: Bucknell University Press, 1974).

SPECHLER, DINA ROME, *Domestic Influences on Soviet Foreign Policy* (Washington: University Press of America, 1978).

SPECHLER, DINA ROME, 'The USSR and Third-World Conflicts: Domestic Debate and Soviet Policy in the Middle East, 1967–1973', *World Politics*, vol. 38, no. 3, April 1986, pp. 435–61.

ST JOHN, RONALD BRUCE, 'The Soviet Penetration of Libya', *World Today* (London), vol. 38, April 1982, pp. 131–38.

TREVERTON, GREGORY (ed.), *Crisis Management and the Super-Powers in the Middle East* (Montclair, NJ: Allanheld, Osmun, & Co.; Westmead, Engl.: Gower Publishing, 1981).

UNITED STATES NATIONAL DEFENSE UNIVERSITY, *Soviet Intentions and American Options in the Middle East* (Washington, DC: US Government Printing Office, 1982).

VOTH, ALDEN, H., *Moscow Abandons Israel for the Arabs: Ten Crucial Years in the Middle East* (Lanham, MD: University Press of America, 1980).

WELLS, JR., SAMUEL F. and MARK BRUZONSKY (eds), *Security in the Middle East: Regional Change and Great Power Strategies* (Boulder, CO/London: Westview Press, 1987).

YODFAT, ARYEH, Y., *Arab Politics in the Soviet Mirror* (Jerusalem: Israel Universities Press; New York: Halsted Press, 1973).

YODFAT, ARYEH, Y., *The Soviet Union and the Arabian Peninsula: Soviet Policy toward the Persian Gulf and Arabia* (New York: St Martin, 1983).

YODFAT, ARYEH Y., *The Soviet Union and Revolutionary Iran* (New York: St Martin, 1984).

YODFAT, ARYEH Y., 'The USA, USSR, China and the Arab-Israeli Conflict', *International Relations* (Tel Aviv), vol. 20, Summer 1981, pp. 85–93.

F. The USSR and Sub-Saharan Africa

ALBRIGHT, DAVID E. (ed.), *Communism in Africa* (Bloomington: Indiana University Press, 1980).

ALBRIGHT, DAVID E., *The USSR and Sub-Saharan Africa in the 1980s*. Washington Papers, vol. 40, no. 101 (New York: Praeger, 1980).

AMOS, JOHN W., 'Libya in Chad: Soviet Surrogate or Nomadic Imperialist?' *Conflict* (New York), vol. 5, no. 1 (1983), pp. 1–18.

ANDERSON, LISA, 'Qadhdhafi and the Kremlin', *Problems of Communism*, vol. 34, no. 5, (September–October 1985), pp. 29–44.

ARLINGHAUS, BRUCE (ed.), *Arms for Africa: Military Assistance and Foreign Policy* (Lexington, MA: Lexington Books, 1983).

BELFIGLIO, VALENTINE J., 'The Soviet Offensive in Southern Africa', *Air University Review*, vol. 34, July–August 1983, pp. 80–6.

BIENEN, HENRY, 'Soviet Relations with Africa', *International Security*, vol. 6, Spring 1982, pp. 153–73.

BISSELL, RICHARD E., 'How Strategic is South Africa', in Richard E. Bissell and Chester A. Crocker (eds), *South Africa into the 1980s* pp. 209–32 (Boulder, CO: Westview, 1979).

BISSELL, RICHARD E., *South Africa and the United States: The Erosion of an Influence Relationship* (New York: Praeger, 1982).

BISSELL, RICHARD E., 'Union of Soviet Socialist Republics', in Thomas H. Henriksen (ed.), *Communist Powers and Sub-Saharan Africa* (Stanford, CA: Hoover Institution Press, 1981), pp. 1–19.

BRIND, HARRY, 'Soviet Policy in the Horn of Africa', *International Affairs* (London), vol. 60, no. 1, Winter 1983/84, pp. 75–95.

CAMPBELL, KURT M., 'Soviet Policy toward South Africa', PhD dissertation, Oxford University, 1984.

CAMPBELL, KURT M., *Soviet Policy Towards South Africa* (London: Macmillan Press, 1986).

CAMPBELL, KURT M., 'The Soviet-South African Connection', *Africa Report*, vol. 31, no. 2, March–April 1986, pp. 72–5.

CLOUGH, MICHAEL (ed.), *Changing Realities in Southern Africa: Implications for American Policy* (Berkeley, CA: Institute for International Studies, University of California, 1982).

CLOUGH, MICHAEL (ed.), *Reassessing the Soviet Challenge in Africa.* Policy Papers in International Affairs, no. 25 (Berkeley, CA: Institute of International Studies, University of California, 1986).

COKER, CHRISTOPHER, *NATO, the Warsaw Pact and Africa* (New York: St Martin, 1985).

COLLINS, ROBERT F. 'Soviet Influence in Sub-Saharan Africa', *Military Review*, vol. 65 April 1985, pp. 46–57.

CROCKER, CHESTER A. 'US and Soviet Interests in the Horn of Africa', *Department of State Bulletin*, vol. 86, 1986, pp. 29–32.

DAMIS JOHN, *Conflict in Northwest Africa: The Western Sahara Dispute* (Stanford, CA: Hoover Institution Press, 1983).

GANN, L. H., and THOMAS H. HENRIKSEN, *The Struggle for Zimbabwe: Battle in the Bush* (New York: Praeger, 1981).

GAVSHON, ARTHUR, *Crisis in Africa: Battleground of East and West* (New York/Harmondsworth, Engl.: Penguin Books, 1981).

GORMAN, ROBERT F., 'Soviet Perspectives on the Prospects for Socialist Development in Africa', *African Affairs*, vol. 83, April 1984, pp. 163–87.

GREY, ROBERT D., 'Leninism, the Soviet Union, and Party Development in Cuba and Ethiopia', *Northeast African Studies*, vol. 2, no. 3 (1980–1981) and vol. 3, no. 1 (1981), pp. 171–81.

GREY, ROBERT D., 'The Soviet Presence in Africa. An Analysis of Goals', *Journal of Modern African Studies*, vol. 22, no. 3, 1984, pp. 511–27.

GROMYKO, ANATOLY, *Konflict na Iuge Afriki: Mezhdundnarodny Aspekt* (Moscow: Idea, 1979).

GROMYKO, ANATOLY, 'Soviet Foreign Policy and Africa', *International Affairs* (Moscow), vol. 2, February 1982, pp. 33.

HAHN, WALTER F. and ALVIN J. COTTRELL, *Soviet Shadow over Africa* (Coral Gables, FL: Center for Advanced International Studies, University of Miami, 1976).

HELDMAN, DAN C., *The USSR and Africa: Foreign Policy under Khrushchev* (New York: Praeger, 1981).

HENRIKSEN, THOMAS H. (ed.), *Communist Powers and Sub-Saharan Africa* (Stanford: Hoover Institution Press, 1981).

HENZE, PAUL B., 'Communism and Ethiopia', *Problems of Communism*, vol. 30, no. 3, May–June 1981, pp. 55–74.

HODGES, TONY, 'How the MPLA Won in Angola', in Colin Legum and Tony Hodges (eds), *The War over Southern Africa* pp. 45–64 (New York: Africana Publishing, 1976).

IBRAHIM, S. R. MSABASHA, and TIMOTHY M. SHAW (eds), *Confrontation and Liberation in Southern Africa: Regional Directions after the Nkomati Accords* (Boulder, CO: Westview, 1986).

INSTITUTE FOR THE STUDY OF CONFLICT, *Soviet-African Trade: The Western Business Response* (London: The Institute for the Study of Conflict, 1980).

IVANOV, A. A., *Sotsialisticheskii Vybor v Afrike i ideologichesaia Borb'a* (Moscow: Mezhdunarodnye Otnosheniia, 1984).

JASTER, ROBERT S., *Southern Africa in Conflict: Implications for US Policies in the 1980s* (Washington, DC: American Enterprise Institute for Public Policy Research, 1982).

KELLER, EDMOND J. and DONALD ROTHCHILD (eds), *Afro-Marxist Regimes: Ideology and Public Policy* (Boulder, CO/London: Lynne Rienner Publishers, 1987).

KEMP, JACK, 'The Reagan Doctrine in Angola', *Africa Report*, vol. 31, no. 1, January–February 1986, pp. 12–14.

KHAPOYA, VINCENT B., and BAFFOUR AGYEMAN-DUAH, 'The Cold War and Regional Politics in East Africa', *Conflict Quarterly*, vol. 5, Spring 1985, pp. 18–32.

KITCHEN, HELEN, 'Six Misconceptions of Africa', *Washington Quarterly*, vol. 5 (1982), pp. 167–74.

KITCHEN, HELEN, *US Interests in Africa*. Washington Papers, no. 98 (New York: Praeger, 1983).

KLINGHOFFER, ARTHUR JAY, *The Angolan War: A Study in Soviet Policy in the Third World* (Boulder, CO: Westview, 1980).

KLINGHOFFER, ARTHUR JAY, 'The Soviet Union: Superpower Rivalry in Africa', in Bruce Arlinghaus (ed.), *African Security Issues: Sovereignty, Stability and Solidarity* (Boulder, CO: Westview, 1984).

KLINGHOFFER, ARTHUR JAY, 'US-Soviet Relations and Angola', *Harvard International Review*, 8, January–February 1986, pp. 15–19.

KORN, DAVID A., *Ethiopia, the United States and the Soviet Union* (London/Sydney: Croom Helm, 1986).

KUHNE, WINRICH, *Die Politik der Sowjetunion in Afrika* (Baden-Baden: Nomos Verlag, 1983).

LAIDI, ZAKI, 'Stability and Partnership in the Maghreb', *Annals of the American Academy of Political and Social Science*, vol. 481, September 1985, pp. 127–37.

LEGUM, COLIN, 'The Role of the Big Powers', in Tony Hodges and Colin Legum (eds), *After Angola: The War over Southern Africa* (New York: Africana, 1976), pp. 1–44.

LEGVOLD, ROBERT, 'The Soviet Threat to Southern Africa', in Robert I. Rotberg, Henry S. Bienen, Roberg Legvold, and Gavin G. Maasdorp (eds), *South Africa and Its Neighbors: Regional Security and Self-Interest* (Lexington, MA: Lexington Books, 1985), pp. 27–54.

LEOGRANDE, WILLIAM M., *Cuba's Policy in Africa, 1959–1980* (Berkeley, CA: Institute of International Studies, University of California, Berkeley, 1980).

LILLEY, ROBERT J. 'Constraints on Superpower Intervention in Sub-Saharan Africa', *Parameters*, vol. 12, no. 3, September 1982, pp. 63–75.

MCLANE, CHARLES B., *Soviet-African Relations* (London: Central Asia Research Centre; distributed by Colombia University Press, 1974).

MARKAKIS, JOHN and MICHAEL WALLER (eds), *Military Marxist Regimes in Africa* (London/Totowa, NJ: Frank Cass & Co., 1986).

MBOUKKU, ALEXANDRE, 'Angola/Congo/Zaire: An African Triangle', *Africa Report*, vol. 27, no. 5, September–October 1982, pp. 39–44.

MESA LAGO, CARMELO and JUNE S. BELKIN (eds), *Cuba in Africa* (Pittsburgh: Center for Latin American Studies, University of Pittsburgh, 1982).

MILENE, CHARLES, *The Soviet Union and Africa: The History of the Involvement* (Washington, DC: University Press of America, 1980).

NAPPER, LARRY C., 'The African Terrain and US-Soviet Conflict in Angola and Rhodesia: Some Implications for Crisis Prevention', in Alexander L. George (ed.), *Managing US-Soviet Rivalry: Problems of Crisis Prevention* (Boulder, CO: Westview, 1983).

NATION, R. CRAIG, and MARK V. KAUPPI (eds), *The Soviet Impact on Africa* (Lexington, MA: Lexington Books, 1984).

NOLUTSHUNGU, SAM C., 'African Interest and Soviet Power: The Local Context of Soviet Policy', *Soviet Studies*, vol. 34, no. 3 (July 1982), pp. 397–417.

NOLUTSHUNGU, SAM C., 'Soviet Involvement in Southern Africa', *Annals of the American Academy of Political and Social Science*, vol. 481, September 1985, pp. 138–46.

OTTAWAY, MARINA, *Soviet and American Influence in the Horn of Africa* (New York: Praeger, 1982).

OTTAWAY, MARINA and DAVID OTTAWAY, *Afrocommunism* (New York: Africana Publishing House, 1987) 2nd edn.

PACHTER, ELISE, 'Dissonance and Clientelism: US-Zaire Relations', PhD dissertation, Johns Hopkins University, 1987.

PAPP, DANIEL S., 'Angola, National Liberation, and the Soviet Union', *Parameters*, vol. 8, no. 1, March 1978, pp. 26–39.

PETRAS, JAMES F. and MORRIS H. MORELY, 'The Ethiopian Military State and Soviet-US Involvement in the Horn of Africa', *Review of African Political Economy*, September 1984, pp. 21–31.

RA'ANAN, GAVRIEL, *The Evolution of the Soviet Use of Surrogates in Military Relations with the Third World, With Particular Emphasis on Cuban Participation in Africa* (Santa Monica, CA: The Rand Corporation, 1979).

REMMEK, RICHARD B., 'Soviet Military Interests in Africa', *Orbis*, vol. 28, no. 1, Spring 1984, pp. 83–102.

ROSBERG, CARL G., and THOMAS M. CALLAGHY (eds), *Socialism in Sub-Saharan Africa: A New Assessment* (Berkeley, CA: Institute of International Studies, University of California, 1979).

ROTBERG, ROBERT I., 'South Africa and the Soviet Union: A Struggle for Primacy', in Robert I. Rotberg, Henry S. Bienen, Robert Legvold, and Gavin G. Maasdorp (eds), *South Africa and Its Neighbors: Regional Security and Self-Interest* (Lexington, MA: Lexington Books), pp. 55–68.

ROTHENBERG, MORRIS, *The USSR and Africa: New Dimensions of Soviet Global Power* (Washington, DC: Advanced International Studies, 1980).

SAMUELS, MICHAEL A., CHESTER A. CROCKER, ROGER W. FONTAINE, DIMITRI K. SIMES, and ROBERT E. HENDERSON, *Implications of Soviet and Cuban Activities in Africa for U.S. Policy* (Washington: The Center for Strategic Studies, Georgetown University, 1979).

SEEGERS, ANNETTE, 'Revolution in Africa: The Case of Zimbabwe (1965–1980)', PhD dissertation, University of Chicago, 1984.

SOMERVILLE, KEITH, 'Angola: Soviet Client State or State of Socialist Orientation', *Millenium*, vol. 13, no. 3, Winter 1984, pp. 292–310.

STEVENS, CHRISTOPHER, 'The Soviet Role in Southern Africa', in John Seiler (ed.), *Southern Africa since the Portuguese Coup* (Boulder, CO: Westview, 1980).

STEVENS, CHRISTOPHER, *The Soviet Union and Black Africa* (New York: Holmes and Meier, 1976).

THOMPSON, W. SCOTT, and BRETT SILVERS, 'South Africa in Soviet Strategy', in Richard E. Bissell (ed.), *South Africa into the 1980s* (Boulder, CO: Westview, 1979), pp. 133–58.

TOKO, GAD W., *Intervention in Uganda: The Power Struggle and Soviet Involvement* (Pittsburgh: University Center for International Studies, University of Pittsburgh, 1979).

ULYANOVSKY, ROSTISLAV, *Present-Day Problems in Asia and Africa: Theory, Politics, Personalities* (Moscow: Progress Publishers, 1980).

US HOUSE COMMITTEE ON FOREIGN AFFAIRS, SUBCOMMITTEE ON AFRICA. *The Possibility of Resource War in Southern Africa.* Hearing, 8 July 1981.

US SENATE COMMITTEE ON THE JUDICIARY, SUBCOMMITTEE ON SECURITY AND TERRORISM. *Soviet, East German and Cuban Involvement in Fomenting Terrorism in Southern Africa.* Report, 1982.

VALENTA, JIRI, 'Soviet Decision-Making on the Intervention in Angola', in David E. Albright (ed.), *Communism in Africa* (Bloomington: Indiana University Press, 1984), pp. 93–117.

VALENTA, JIRI, 'Soviet-Cuban Intervention in the Horn of Africa: Impact and Lessons', *Journal of International Affairs*, vol. 34, no. 1, Fall–Winter 1980/81, pp. 343–67.

WEINSTEIN, WARREN, and THOMAS H. HENRIKSEN (eds), *Chinese and Soviet Aid to African Nations* (New York: Praeger, 1980).

WHEELER, JACK, 'Fighting the Soviet Imperialist: UNITA in Angola', *Reason*, vol. 15, no. 12, April 1984, pp. 22–30.

II THE UNITED STATES AND THE DEVELOPING COUNTRIES

A. US Foreign Policy

ALTERMAN, ERIC R, 'Thinking Twice: The Weinberger Doctrine and the Lessons of Vietnam', *Fletcher Forum*, vol. 10, no. 1, Winter 1986, pp. 93–109.

'AMERICA AND THE WORLD 1981', *Foreign Affairs*, vol. 60, no. 3 (1982), pp. 465–752.

'AMERICA AND THE WORLD 1982', *Foreign Affairs*, vol. 61, no. 3 (1983), pp. 489–744.

'AMERICA AND THE WORLD 1983', *Foreign Affairs*, vol. 62, no. 3 (1984), pp. 485–804.

'AMERICA AND THE WORLD 1984', *Foreign Affairs*, vol. 63, no. 3 (1985), pp. 441–704.

'AMERICA AND THE WORLD 1985', *Foreign Affairs*, vol. 64, no. 3 (1986), pp. 393–674.

'AMERICA IN THE WORLD', *Harvard International Review*, vol. 7 (1985), pp. 3–23.

'AMERICA'S DEFENSE DILEMMAS', *Public Interest*, Spring 1984, pp. 3–75, and Summer 1984, pp. 3–60.

'AMERICA'S NATIONAL SECURITY', *Wilson Quarterly*, vol. 7, Winter 1983, pp. 98–141.

ANDERSON, WILLIAM D., and STERLING J. KERNEK, 'How 'Realistic' is Reagan's Diplomacy?', *Political Science Quarterly*, vol. 100, no. 3, Fall 1985, pp. 389–409.

ARBATOV, G., 'American Policy in a Dream World', *Current Digest of the Soviet Press*, August 1982.

'ARMS AS A DIPLOMATIC TOOL – REAGAN'S SHIFT', *US News and World Report*, vol. 92, 1982, pp. 27–28.

ARON, RAYMOND, 'Ideology in Search of a Policy', *Foreign Affairs*, vol. 60, no. 3, 1981, pp. 503–24.

ARON, RAYMOND, *The Imperial Republic: The United States and the World 1945–1973* (Lanham, MD: University Press of America, 1981).

AVERY, WILLIAM P., and DAVID P. RAPKIN, *America in a Changing World Political Economy* (New York: Longman, 1982).

AYRES, ROBERT L., 'Breaking the Bank', *Foreign Policy*, no. 43, Summer 1981, pp. 104–20.

BARILLEAUX, RYAN L., *The President and Foreign Affairs: Evaluation, Performance and Power* (New York: Praeger, 1985).

BARILLEAUX, RYAN L., 'The President, 'Intermestic' Issues, and the Risks of Policy Leadership', *Presidential Studies Quarterly*, vol. 15, Fall 1985, pp. 754–67.

BARROWS, WALTER L., and VINCENT D. KERN, 'Superpower Statecraft in the Third World', *Harvard International Review*, vol. 8, January/February 1986, pp. 7–10.

BELL, CORAL, 'From Carter to Reagan', *Foreign Affairs*, vol. 63, no. 3, 1984, pp. 490–510.

BERES, LOUIS RENE, *Reason and Realpolitik: US Foreign Policy and World Order* (Lexington, MA: Lexington Books, 1984).

BERES, LOUIS RENE, 'Understanding "Destabilization": The United States Imperative', *Policy Studies Review*, vol. 3, May 1984, pp. 383–9.

BIALER, SEWERYN, and JOAN AFFERICA, 'Reagan and Russia', *Foreign Affairs*, vol. 61, no. 2, Winter 1982/83, pp. 249–71.

BODE, WILLIAM R., 'The Reagan Doctrine', *Strategic Review*, vol. 14, Winter 1986, pp. 21–9.

BOZEMAN, ADDA B., 'US Foreign Policy and the Prospects for Democracy, National Security and World Peace', *Comparative Strategy*, vol. 5, no. 3, 1985, pp. 223–67.

BREWER, THOMAS L., *American Foreign Policy: A Contemporary Introduction* (Englewood Cliffs, NJ: Prentice-Hall, 1986).

BROWN, HAROLD, *Thinking about National Security: Defense and Foreign Policy in a Dangerous World* (Boulder, CO: Westview, 1983).

BROWN, SEYOM, *The Faces of Power: Constancy and Change in United States Foreign Policy from Truman to Reagan* (New York: Columbia University Press, 1983).

BUCKLEY, JAMES L., 'Arms Transfers and the National Interest', *Department of State Bulletin*, vol. 81, July 1981, pp. 51–3.

BUNDY, MCGEORGE, 'The United States Government and the Population Problem Abroad', *Population and Development Review*, vol. 10, September 1984, pp. 505–10.

BUNDY, WILLIAM P., 'The Conduct of American Foreign Policy: A Portentous Year', *Foreign Affairs*, vol. 62, no. 3, 1984, pp. 482–520.

BUNDY, WILLIAM P., 'The National Security Process', *International Security*, vol. 7, no. 3, Winter 1982–83, pp. 94–109.

BUNDY, WILLIAM P., 'Priorities and Strategies in Foreign Policy: 1985–1989', *Presidential Studies Quarterly*, vol. 15, Spring 1985, pp. 244–60.

CALLEO, DAVID P., *The Imperious Economy* (Cambridge, MA: Harvard, 1982).

CARLETON, DAVID, and MICHAEL STOHL, 'The Foreign Policy of Human Rights: Rhetoric and Reality from Jimmy Carter to Ronald Reagan', *Human Rights Quarterly*, vol. 7, May 1985, pp. 205–29.

CHURBA, JOSEPH, *The American Retreat: The Reagan Foreign and Defense Policy* (Chicago: Regency Gateway, 1984).

CLEVELAND, HARLAN, 'Coherence and Consultation: The President as Manager of American Foreign Policy', *Public Administration Review*, vol. 46, March/April 1986, pp. 97–104.

CLINE, RAY S., 'Geopolitical Perceptions of the World Today', *Political Communication and Persuasion*, vol. 2, 1984, pp. 235–249.

COHEN, BENJAMIN J., 'International Debt and Linkage Strategies: Some Foreign Policy Implications for the United States', *International Organization*, vol. 39, Autumn 1985, pp. 699–727.

COKER, CHRISTOPHER, *US Military Power in the 1980s* (London: Macmillan, 1983).

CRABB, CECIL V., JR., *The Doctrines of American Foreign Policy: Their Meaning, Role, and Future* (Baton Rouge: Louisiana State University Press, 1982).

DALLEK, ROBERT, *The American Style of Foreign Policy: Cultural Politics and Foreign Affairs* (New York: Knopf, 1983).

DEIBEL, TERRY L., 'Why Reagan is Strong', *Foreign Policy*, no. 62, Spring 1986, pp. 108–25.

DENNIS, ROBERT D., 'Human Rights Policy: A Call for a New Sense of Realism', *Global Perspectives*, vol. 3, Spring 1985, pp. 4–22.

DENNY, BREWSTER C., *Seeing American Foreign Policy Whole* (Urbana: University of Illinois Press, 1985).

DESTLER, I. M., LESLIE H. GELB, and ANTHONY LAKE, *Our Own Worst Enemy: The Unmaking of American Foreign Policy* (New York: Simon and Schuster, 1984).

EVAN, ERNEST, 'The Reagan Administration's Policy toward Revolutionary Movements', *Conflict Quarterly*, vol. 3, Fall 1982, pp. 55–61.

FELD, WERNER J., *American Foreign Policy: Aspirations and Reality* (New York: Wiley, 1984).

FORSYTHE, DAVID P., *Human Rights and World Politics* (Lincoln: University of Nebraska Press, 1983).

'FORUM: REAGAN'S FOREIGN AND DEFENSE POLICIES', *Orbis*, vol. 25, no. 3, Fall 1981, pp. 487–510.

FRANK, RICHARD A., 'Jumping Ship', *Foreign Policy*, no. 43, Summer 1981, pp. 121–38.

GARTEN, JEFFREY E., 'Gunboat Economics', *Foreign Affairs*, vol. 63, no. 3, 1985, pp. 538–59.

GELB, LESLIE H. and ANTHONY LAKE, 'Four More Years: Diplomacy Restored?' *Foreign Affairs*, vol. 63, no. 3, 1984, pp. 465–89.

GIFFORD, PROSSER (ed.), *The National Interests of the United States: Seven Discussions at the Wilson Center* (Washington, DC: University Press of America, 1981).

GILPIN, ROBERT, *US Power and the Multinational Corporation* (London: Macmillan, 1976).

GOLDSTEIN, MARTIN E., *America's Foreign Policy: Drift or Decision* (Wilmington, DE: Scholarly Resources, 1984).

GRAEBNER, NORMAN A., *America as a World Power: A Realist Appraisal from Wilson to Reagan* (Wilmington, DE: Scholarly Resources, 1984).

GRAVES, ERNEST, and STEVEN A. HILDRETH (eds), *US Security-Assistance: The Political Process* (Lexington, MA: Lexington Books, 1985).

GREEN, NANCY, 'Administration Puts First Focus on World Bank: Reagan Policy Shift Prompts Skepticism', *Congressional Quarterly Weekly Report*, vol. 43, 5 October 1985, pp. 1999–2003.

GRUNWALD, HENRY, 'Foreign Policy under Reagan II', *Foreign Affairs*, vol. 63, no. 2, Winter 1984/1985, pp. 219–39.

HAIG, ALEXANDER M., JR., 'American Power and American Purpose', *Department of State Bulletin*, vol. 82, June 1982, pp. 40–4.

HAIG, ALEXANDER M., JR., *Caveat: Reagan, Realism and Foreign Policy* (New York: Macmillan, 1984).

HAIG, ALEXANDER M., JR., 'International Trade', *Department of State Bulletin*, vol. 81, September 1981, pp. 19–21.

HAIG, ALEXANDER M., JR., 'A New Direction in US Foreign Policy', *Atlantic Community Quarterly*, vol. 19, Summer 1981, pp. 131–37.

HARKAVY, ROBERT E., *Great Power Competition for Overseas Bases: The Geopolitics of Access Diplomacy* (New York: Pergamon, 1982).

HOFFMAN, STANLEY, *Dead Ends: American Foreign Policy in the New Cold War* (Cambridge, MA: Ballinger, 1983).

HOFFMAN, STANLEY, *Primacy or World Order: American Foreign Policy since the Cold War* (New York: McGraw Hill, 1978).

HOFFMAN, STANLEY, *Security in an Age of Turbulence: Means of Response*. Adelphi Papers, no. 167. London: IISS, 1981.

HOFFMAN, STANLEY, and CYRUS VANCE, *Building the Peace: US Foreign Policy for the Next Decade* (Washington, DC: Center for National Policy, 1982).

HOYT, EDWIN C., *Law and Force in American Foreign Policy* (Lanham, MD: University Press of America, 1985).

HUNTER, ROBERT E., *Presidential Control of Foreign Policy: Management or Mishap?* (New York: Praeger, 1982).

HUNTER, ROBERT E., 'The Relevance of American Power', *SAIS Review*, vol. 5, no. 1, Winter–Spring 1985, pp. 11–24.

HYLAND, WILLIAM G., 'US-Soviet Relations: The Long Road Back', *Foreign Affairs*, vol. 60, no. 3, 1982, pp. 525–50.

IRWIN, WALLACE, JR., *America in the World: A Guide to US Foreign Policy* (New York: Praeger, 1983).

JACOBY, TAMAR, 'The Reagan Turnaround on Human Rights', *Foreign Affairs*, vol. 64, no. 5, Summer 1986, pp. 1066–86.

KEAL, PAUL, *Unspoken Rules and Superpower Dominance*. London: Macmillan, 1983.

KEGLEY, CHARLES W., JR. and EUGENE R. WILTKOPF, 'The Reagan Administration's World View', *Orbis*, vol. 26, no. 1, Spring 1982, pp. 223–44.

KENNAN, GEORGE F., 'Morality and Foreign Policy', *Foreign Affairs*, vol. 64, no. 2, Winter 1985/86, pp. 205–18.

KEOHANE, ROBERT, *After Hegemony* (Princeton: Princeton University Press, 1984).

'KIRKPATRICK AND HER CRITICS', *Society*, vol. 22, March/April 1985, pp. 3–30.

KIRKPATRICK, JEANE J., 'Dictatorships and Double Standards', *Commentary*, vol. 68, no. 5, November, 1979, pp. 34–45.

KIRKPATRICK, JEANE J., 'Doctrine of Moral Equivalence', *Department of State Bulletin*, vol. 84, August 1984, pp. 57–62.

KIRKPATRICK, JEANE J., 'Establishing a Viable Human Rights Policy', *World Affairs*, vol. 143, Spring 1981, pp. 323–4.

KIRKPATRICK, JEANE J., 'The Superpowers: Is There a Moral Difference?', *World Today*, vol. 40, no. 5, May 1984, pp. 177–88.

KOMER, ROBERT W., 'Maritime Strategy vs. Coalition Defense', *Foreign Affairs*, vol. 60, no. 5, Summer 1982, pp. 1124–44.

KORB, LAWRENCE J. and LINDA P. BRADY, 'Rearming America: The Reagan Administration Defense Program', *International Security*, vol. 9, no. 3, Winter 1984–85, pp. 3–18.

KRASNER, STEPHEN D., *Defending the National Interest: Raw Materials Investments and US Foreign Policy* (Princeton: Princeton University Press, 1978).

LAYNE, CHRISTOPHER, 'The Real Conservative Agenda', *Foreign Policy*, no. 61, Winter 1985/1986, pp. 73–93.

LEFEVER, ERNEST W., 'The Trivialization of Human Rights', *Policy Review*, no. 3, Winter 1978, pp. 11–26.

LENCZOWSKI, JOHN, 'A Foreign Policy for Reaganauts', *Policy Review*, no. 18, Fall 1981, pp. 77–95.

LENS, SIDNEY, *The Maginot Line Syndrome: America's Hopeless Foreign*

Policy (Cambridge, MA: Ballinger, 1982).

LISKA, GEORGE, *Russia and the Road to Appeasement: Cycles of East–West Conflict in War and Peace* (Baltimore, MD: Johns Hopkins University Press, 1982).

LISKA, GEORGE, 'From Containment to Concert', *Foreign Policy*, no. 62, Spring 1986, pp. 3–23.

LORD, CARNES, 'American Strategic Culture', *Comparative Strategy*, vol. 5, no. 3, 1985, pp. 269–93.

MANDELBAUM, MICHAEL, 'The Luck of the President', *Foreign Affairs*, vol. 64, no. 3, 1986, pp. 393–412.

MAYNES, CHARLES W., 'Lost Opportunities', *Foreign Affairs*, vol. 64, no. 3, 1986, pp. 413–34.

MCFARLANE, ROBERT C., 'US-Soviet Relations in the Late Twentieth Century', *Department of State Bulletin*, vol. 85, October 1985, pp. 34–8.

MCFETRIDGE, CHARLES D., 'Foreign Policy and Military Strategy: The Civil-Military Equation', *Military Review*, vol. 66, April 1986, pp. 22–30.

MCMAHAN, JEFF, *Reagan and the World: Imperial Policy in the New Cold War* (London: Pluto Press, 1984).

MELANSON, RICHARD A. (ed.), *Neither Cold War Nor Detente? Soviet-American Relations in the 1980s* (Charlottesville: University Press of Virginia, 1982).

MELANSON, RICHARD A., 'A Neo-Consensus: American Foreign Policy in the 1980s', in Richard A. Melanson (ed.), *Neither Cold War Nor Detente: Soviet-American Relations in the 1980s* Charlottesville, VA: University Press of Virgina, 1982.

MILLER, LINDA B., 'The Foreign Policy of Reagan II', *World Today*, vol. 41, no. 4, April 1985, pp. 71–4.

MITCHELL, NANCY, 'Vigilance as Metaphor: The Foreign Policy of Ronald Reagan', *SAIS Review*, vol. 5, no. 2, Summer–Fall 1985, pp. 133–8.

MODELSKI, GEORGE, 'The Long Cycle of Global Politics and the Nation State', *Comparative Studies in Society and History*, vol. 20, no. 2, 1978, pp. 214–38.

MODELSKI, GEORGE, 'Long Cycles, Kondratieffs and Alternating Innovations: Implications for US Foreign Policy', in Charles W. Kegley and Pat McGowan (eds), *The Political Economy of Foreign Policy Behavior* (Beverly Hills, CA: Sage, 1981).

MODELSKI, GEORGE, 'Long Cycles of World Leadership', in William R. Thompson (ed.), *Contending Approaches to World System Analysis* (Beverly Hills, CA: Sage, 1983).

MULCAHY, KEVIN V., 'The Secretary of State and the National Security Adviser: Foreign Policymaking in the Carter and Reagan Administration', *Presidential Studies Quarterly*, vol. 16, no. 2, Spring 1986, pp. 280–99.

NADELMANN, ETHAN A., 'International Drug Trafficking and US Foreign Policy', *Washington Quarterly*, vol. 8, no. 4, Fall 1985, pp. 86–104.

NATHAN, JAMES A., and JAMES K. OLIVER, *United States Foreign Policy and World Order* (Boston: Little, Brown, 1981).

NATHAN, JAMES A., and JAMES K. OLIVER, *Foreign Policy Making and the American Political System* (Boston: Little, Brown, 1983).

NAU, HENRY, 'Where Reaganomics Works', *Foreign Policy*, no. 57, Winter 1984–85, pp. 14–37.

NELSON, ALAN C., 'Immigration Policy and Foreign Affairs: The Reagan Perspective', *World Affairs Journal*, vol. 4, Summer/Fall 1985, pp. 9–16.

'THE NEW TRADE STRATEGY: Reagan Tries to Contain Protectionist Fires, But It May Be Too Late', *Business Week*, October 7, 1985, pp. 90–6.

NUECHTERLEIN, DONALD E., *American Overcommitted – United States National Interests in the 1980s* (Lexington, MA: University of Kentucky Press, 1985).

OLSON, ROBERT K., *US Foreign Policy and the New International Economic Order: Negotiating Global Problems, 1974–1981* (Boulder, CO: Westview, 1981).

OSGOOD, ROBERT E., 'American Grand Strategy: Patterns, Problems and Prescriptions', *Naval War College Review*, September/October 1983, pp. 5–17.

OSGOOD, ROBERT E. (ed.), *Containment, Soviet Behavior and Grand Strategy* (Berkeley: Institute of International Studies, 1981).

OSGOOD, ROBERT E., 'The Revitalization of Containment', *Foreign Affairs*, vol. 60, no. 3, 1982, pp. 465–502.

OYE, KENNETH A., 'International Systems Structure and American Foreign Policy', in Kenneth Oye, Robert Lieber, and Donald Rothschild (eds), *Eagle Defiant* (Boston, MS: Little, Brown, 1963).

OYE, KENNETH A., ROBERT J. LIEBER, DONALD ROTHSCHILD, *Eagle Defiant: United States Foreign Policy in the 1980s* (Boston, MS: Little, Brown, 1983).

PASTOR, ROBERT A., 'Spheres of Influence: Seal Them or Peel Them?', *SAIS Review*, vol. 4, no. 1, Winter–Spring 1984, pp. 77–90.

PAYNE, RICHARD J., 'US Foreign Policy at Sea: National Security on the Seabed', *World Today* (London), vol. 39, no. 10, October 1983, pp. 393–9.

PRANGER, ROBERT J. (ed.), 'Dimensions of US Foreign Policy in the 1980s', *AEI Foreign Policy and Defense Review* (American Enterprise Institute, Washington DC), vol. 4, no. 5/6, 1984, pp. 1–87.

QUESTER, GEORGE H., *American Foreign Policy: The Lost Consensus* (New York: Praeger, 1982).

RA'ANAN, URI, and CHARLES M. PERRY (eds), *Strategic Minerals and International Security* (Elmsford, NY: Pergamon, 1985).

RASHISH, MYER, 'Approach to Foreign Economic Issues', *Department of State Bulletin*, vol. 81, October 1981, pp. 40–46.

RASHISH, MYER and ROBERT D. HORMATS, 'US Trade and Foreign Policy', *Department of State Bulletin*, vol. 81, December 1981, pp. 44–8.

'REAGAN'S FOREIGN POLICY: His No. 1 Aide Speaks Out', Interview with William Clark President's National Security Advisor. *US News and World Report*, vol. 84, 9 May 1983, pp. 35–6+.

RECORD, JEFFREY, 'Jousting with Unreality: Reagan's Military Strategy', *International Security*, vol. 8, no. 3, Winter 1983–84, pp. 3–18.

REUTER, PETER, 'Eternal Hope: America's Quest for Narcotics Control', *Public Interest*, no. 79, Spring 1985, pp. 79–95.

RODMAN, PETER W., 'The Dilemmas of Conservatism: Reagan the Diplomat', *American Spectator*, vol. 15, March 1982, pp. 7–12.

ROTHSTEIN, ROBERT L., 'Condemned to Cooperate: US Resource Diplomacy', *SAIS Review*, vol. 5, no. 1, Winter–Spring 1985, pp. 163–77.

SANDERS, JERRY W., 'Breaking Out of the Containment Syndrome', *World Policy Journal*, vol. 1, Fall 1983, pp. 101–25.

SANDERS, JERRY W., *Peddlers of Crisis: The Committee on the Present Danger and the Politics of Containment* (Boston, MS: South End Press, 1983).

SARKESIAN, SAM C. (ed.), *Presidential Leadership and National Security: Style, Institutions, and Politics* (Boulder, CO: Westview, 1984).

SCHLESINGER, ARTHUR, JR., 'Foreign Policy and the American Character', *Foreign Affairs*, vol. 62, no. 1, Fall 1983, pp. 1–16.

SCHLESINGER, ARTHUR, JR., 'The Logic of Reaganomics', *Wall Street Journal*, vol. 198, 18 November 1981, p. 30.

SCHLESINGER, JAMES R., 'The Eagle and the Bear: Ruminations on Forty Years of Superpower Relations', *Foreign Affairs*, vol. 63, no. 4, Summer 1985, pp. 937–61.

SCHLESINGER, JAMES R., 'Maintaining Global Stability', *Washington Quarterly*, vol. 8, no. 3, Summer 1985, pp. 53–8.

SERFATY, SIMON, *American Foreign Policy in a Hostile World: Dangerous Years* (New York: Praeger, 1984).

SHULTZ, GEORGE P., 'Foreign Aid and US National Interests', *Department of State Bulletin*, vol. 83, April 1983, pp. 25–31.

SHULTZ, GEORGE P., 'Foreign Aid and US Policy Objectives', *Department of State Bulletin*, vol. 84, May 1984, pp. 17–22.

SHULTZ, GEORGE P., 'A Forward Look at Foreign Policy', *Department of State Bulletin*, vol. 84, December 1984, pp. 5–10.

SHULTZ, GEORGE P., 'The Future of American Foreign Policy: New Realities and New Ways of Thinking', *Department of State Bulletin*, vol. 85, March 1985, pp. 13–20.

SHULTZ, GEORGE P., 'Human Rights and the Moral Dimension of US Foreign Policy', *Department of State Bulletin*, vol. 84, April 1984, pp. 15–19.

SHULTZ, GEORGE P., 'New Realities and New Ways of Thinking', *Foreign Affairs*, vol. 63, no. 4, Spring 1985, pp. 705–21.

SHULTZ, GEORGE P., 'Power and Diplomacy in the 1980s', *Department of State Bulletin*, vol. 84, May 1984, pp. 12–15.

SHULTZ, GEORGE P., 'US Foreign Policy: Realism and Progress', *Department of State Bulletin*, vol. 82, November 1982, pp. 1–9.

SHULTZ, GEORGE P., "US-Soviet Relations in the Context of US Foreign Policy', *Department of State Bulletin*, vol. 83, July 1983, pp. 65–72.

SIMES, DIMITRI K., 'America's New Edge', *Foreign Policy*, no. 56, Fall 1984, pp. 24–43.

VAN SLYCK, PHILIP, *Strategies for the 1980s: Lessons of Cuba, Vietnam, and Afghanistan* (Westport, CT: Greenwood Press, 1981).

STEVENSON, RICHARD W., *The Rise and Fall of Detente: Relaxation of Tension in US-Soviet Relations, 1953–1984* (London: Macmillan, 1985).

STRANGE, SUSAN, 'Still an Extraordinary Power: America's Role in a Global Monetary System', in Raymond Lombra and Willard Witte (eds), *Political Economy of International and Domestic Monetary Relations* (Ames: Iowa State University Press, 1982).

TALBOTT, STROBE, *The Russians and Reagan* (New York: Vintage, 1984).

TATU, MICHAEL, 'US-Soviet Relations: A Turning Point?' *Foreign Affairs*, vol. 61, no. 3, 1983, pp. 591–610.

TAYLOR, WILLIAM J., JR., STEVEN A. MAARANEN, GERRIT W. GONG (eds), *Strategic Responses to Conflict in the 1980s* (Lexington, MA: Lexington Books, 1984).

THOMPSON, KENNETH W. (ed.), *Moral Dimensions of American Foreign Policy* (New Brunswick, NJ: Transaction Books, 1984).

TONELSON, ALAN, 'Human Rights: The Bias We Need', *Foreign Policy*, no. 49, Winter 1982/1983, pp. 53–74.

TROFIMENKO, HENRY, 'The Third World and US-Soviet Competition', *Foreign Affairs*, vol. 59, no. 5, Summer 1981, pp. 1021–40.

TUCKER, ROBERT W., 'America in Decline: The Foreign Policy of "Maturity"', *Foreign Affairs*, vol. 58, no. 3, 1980, pp. 449–84.

TUCKER, ROBERT W., 'In Defense of Containment', *Journal of Contemporary Studies*, vol. 6, Spring 1983, pp. 29–49.

TUCKER, ROBERT W., 'Foreign Policy: Thoughts on a Second Reagan Administration', *SAIS Review*, vol. 5, no. 1, Winter–Spring 1985, pp. 1–10.

TUCKER, ROBERT W., *The Inequality of Nations* (New York: Banz Books, 1977).

TUCKER, ROBERT W., *The Purposes of American Power: An Essay on National Security* (New York: Praeger, 1981).

ULAM, ADAM B., 'Forty Years of Troubled Coexistence', *Foreign Affairs*, vol. 64, no. 1, Fall 1985, pp. 12–32.

US DEPARTMENT OF STATE, *Realism, Strength, Negotiation: Key Foreign Policy Statements of the Reagan Administration* (Washington, DC: US Department of State, May 1984).

US DEPARTMENT OF STATE, BUREAU OF PUBLIC AFFAIRS, OFFICE OF THE HISTORIAN, *American Foreign Policy: Current Documents, 1982* (Washington, DC: Superintendent of Documents, US Government Printing Office, 1985).

US HOUSE COMMITTEE ON BANKING, FINANCE AND URBAN AFFAIRS, Subcommittee on International Development Institutions and Finance. 'Dealing with Debt, Rekindling Development: The US Stake in the Performance of the World's Development Banks'. Report, October 1985. Washington, DC: 1985.

US HOUSE COMMITTEE ON ENERGY AND COMMERCE, 'The United States in a Changing World Economy: The Case for an Integrated Domestic and International Commercial Policy'. Staff Report, September 1983. Washington, DC: 1983.

US HOUSE COMMITTEE ON FOREIGN AFFAIRS, 'Problems of the International Debt.' Hearings, 1 and 8 August 1984. Washington, DC: 1984.

US HOUSE COMMITTEE ON FOREIGN AFFAIRS, 'Review of US Foreign Policy.' Hearing, 12 November 1981. Washington, DC: 1981.

US HOUSE COMMITTEE ON FOREIGN AFFAIRS, Subcommittee on Human Rights and International Organizations. 'Review of US Human Rights Policy.' Hearings, 3 March–21 September 1983. Washington, DC: 1984.

US HOUSE COMMITTEE ON FOREIGN AFFAIRS, Subcommittee on International Economic Policy and Trade. 'US International Economic Influence: Agenda for the Future.' Hearing, 24 February 1981. Washington, DC: 1981.

US HOUSE COMMITTEE ON FOREIGN AFFAIRS, Subcommittee on International Security and Scientific Affairs. *Changing Perspectives on US Arms Transfer Policy* Report, 25 September 1981. Washington, DC: 1981.

'US POLICY TOWARD THE INTERNATIONAL LENDING AGEN-cies; pro and con', *Congressional Digest*, vol. 60, 1981, pp. 259–88.

US SENATE COMMITTEE ON ENERGY AND NATIONAL RESOUR-ces, 'Geopolitics of Strategic and Critical Materials.' Hearings, 19 May–22 July, 1983. Washington, DC: 1983.

US SENATE COMMITTEE ON FOREIGN RELATIONS, 'International Security Policy.' Hearing, 27 July 1981. Washington, DC: 1981.

US SENATE COMMITTEE ON FOREIGN RELATIONS, 'The United States in a Global Economy.' Hearings, 27 February–6 March 1985. Washington, DC: 1985.

VINCENT, R. J., 'The Reagan Administration and America's Purpose in the World', in *Yearbook of World Affairs, 1983* (Boulder, CO: Westview, 1983), pp. 25–38.

WALLERSTEIN, IMMANUEL, 'The Three Instances of Hegemony in the History of the Capitalist World Economy', *International Journal of Comparative Sociology*, vol. 24, pp. 100–108.

WALLOP, MALCOLM, 'US Covert Action: Policy Tool or Policy Hedge?', *Strategic Review*, vol. 12, Summer 1984, pp. 9–16.

WEINTRAUB, SIDNEY, 'US Foreign Economic Policy and Illegal Immigra-tion', *Population Research and Policy Review*, vol. 2, October 1983, pp. 211–31.

WELLS, SAMUEL F., JR., 'A Question of Priorities: A Comparison of the Carter and Reagan Defense Programs', *Orbis*, vol. 27, no. 3, Fall 1983, pp. 641–66.

WILDAVSKY, AARON (ed.), *Beyond Containment: Alternative American Policies toward the Soviet Union* (San Francisco: ICS Press, 1983).

WOLFE, ALAN, 'Crackpot Moralism, Neo-Realism, and US Foreign Policy', *World Policy Journal*, vol. 3, no. 2, Spring 1986, pp. 251–75.

WOLFSON, ADAM, 'The World According to Kirkpatrick', *Policy Review*, no. 31, Winter 1985, pp. 68–71.

YOCHELSON, JOHN N. (ed.), *The United States and the World Economy: Policy Alternatives for New Realities* (Boulder, CO: Westview, 1985).

B. The United States and the Developing Countries

CHUBIN, SHAHRAM, *The United States and the Third World: Motives, Objectives, Policies*. Adelphi Papers, no. 167. London: IISS, 1981.

CLAWSON, ROBERT W. (ed.), *East–West Rivalry in the Third World:*

Security Issues and Regional Perspectives (Wilmington, DE: Scholarly Resources, 1986).

CLEMENS, WALTER C., 'The Superpowers and the Third World: Aborted Ideals and Wasted Assets', in Charles W. Kegley, Jr and Pat McGowan (eds), *Foreign Policy USA/USSR* (Beverly Hills: Sage, 1982).

CONGRESSIONAL RESEARCH SERVICE, *Soviet Policy and United States Response in the Third World*. (Report prepared for the Committee on Foreign Affairs, US House of Representatives.) (Washington, DC: US Government Printing Office, 1981).

DAM, KENNETH W., 'Europe vs. Asia: Is Diplomacy a Zero-Sum Game?' *Department of State Bulletin*, vol. 84, October 1984, pp. 33–6.

FEINBERG, RICHARD E., *The Intemperate Zone: The Third World Challenge to U.S. Foreign Policy* (New York: Norton, 1983).

GIRLING, JOHN, 'Reagan and the Third World', *World Today* (London), vol. 37, no. 11, November 1981, pp. 407–13.

GOHEEN, ROBERT F., 'Problems of Proliferation: US Policy and the Third World', *World Politics*, vol. 35, no. 2, January 1983, pp. 194–215.

GOWA, JOANNE, and NILS H. WESSELL, *Ground Rules: Soviet and American Involvement in Regional Conflicts* (Philadelphia, PA: Foreign Policy Research Institute, 1982).

HAGERTY, RANDY, and ROGER E. KANET, 'US and Soviet Involvement in the Third World', *Harvard International Review*, vol. 8, January/February 1986, pp. 11–14.

HAIG, ALEXANDER, M., JR, 'Peaceful Progress in Developing Nations', *Department of State Bulletin*, vol. 81, July 1981, pp. 8–9.

HANSEN, ROGER D., ALBERT FISHLOW, ROBERT PAARLBERG, JOHN P. LEWIS, *US Foreign Policy and the Third World: Agenda 1982* (New York: Praeger, 1982).

HASELAR, STEPHEN, *The Varieties of Anti-Americanism: Reflex and Response* (Washington, DC: Ethics and Public Policy Center, 1985).

JOHNSON, ROBERT H., 'Exaggerating America's Stakes in Third World Conflicts', *International Security*, vol. 10, no. 3, Winter 1985/1986, pp. 32–68.

KOLODZIEJ, EDWARD A., 'Implications of Security Patterns among Developing States', *Air University Review*, vol. 33, no. 6, September/October 1982, pp. 2–22.

KRASNER, STEPHEN D., *Structural Conflict: The Third World against Global Liberalism* (Berkeley, CA: University of California Press, 1985).

LAKE, ANTHONY, *Third World Radical Regimes: US Policy under Carter and Reagan* (New York: Foreign Policy Association, 1985).

LEWIS, JOHN P. and VALERIANA KALLAB (eds), *US Foreign Policy and the Third World: Agenda 1983* (New York: Praeger, for the Overseas Development Council, 1983).

MADISON, CHRISTOPHER, 'Reminder from Reagan: He Remains a Conservative on Third World Aid', *National Journal*, vol. 15, 24 September, 1983, pp. 1948–50.

MAURER, JOHN H. and RICHARD H. PORTH (eds), *Military Intervention in the Third World: Threats, Constraints, and Options* (New York: Praeger, 1984).

NEWFARMER, RICHARD (ed.), *From Gunboats to Diplomacy* (Baltimore, MD: Johns Hopkins University Press, 1984).

NEWFARMER, RICHARD, 'A Look at Reagan's Revolution in Development Policy: Aid to the Third World Based on Spurs to Private-Sector Growth, with Political and Military Strings Attached, Ignores the Key Problems – Absolute Poverty and Income Distribution', *Challenge*, vol. 26, September/October 1983, pp. 34–43.

OLSON, WILLIAM J., 'Global Revolution and the American Dilemma', *Strategic Review*, vol. 11, Spring 1983, pp. 48–53.

PETERZELL, JAY, *Reagan's Secret Wars* (Washington, DC: Centre for National Security Studies, 1984).

PETRAS, JAMES F. and MORRIS H. MORLEY, 'The New Cold War: Reagan Policy towards Europe and the Third World'. *Studies in Political Economy*, Fall 1982, pp. 5–44.

RA'ANAN, URI, FRANCIS FUKUYAMA, MARK FALCOTT, SAM C. SARKESIAN, RONALD H. SHULTZ, JR., *Third World Marxist-Leninist Regimes: Strengths and Vulnerabilities and US Policy* (Elmsford, NY: Pergamon, 1985).

RASHISH, MYER, 'US International Economic Policy and Its Impact on LDCs', *Department of State Bulletin*, vol. 81, October 1981, pp. 46–9.

ROTHSTEIN, ROBERT L., *The Third World and US Foreign Policy: Cooperation and Conflict in the 1980s* (Boulder, CO: Westview, 1981).

RUBINSTEIN, ALVIN Z. and DONALD E. SMITH, 'Anti-Americanism in the Third World', *Orbis*, vol. 28, no. 3, Fall 1984, pp. 593–614.

RUBINSTEIN, ALVIN Z. and DONALD E. SMITH (eds), *Anti-Americanism in the Third World: Implications for US Foreign Policy* (New York: Praeger, 1985).

SEWELL, JOHN W., RICHARD E. FEINBERG and VALLERIANA KALLAB (eds) *US Foreign Policy and the Third World: Agenda 1985–86* (New Brunswick, NJ: Transaction Books, 1985).

SEWELL, JOHN W. and JOHN A. MATHIESON, *The Third World: Exploring US Interests* (New York: Foreign Policy Association, May/June 1982).

SHULTZ, GEORGE P. 'US Foreign Policy and the Developing Countries', *Graduate Woman*, vol. 77, May/June 1983, pp. 20–3.

SOLARZ, STEPHEN J., 'Promoting Democracy in the Third World: Lost Cause or Sound Policy?', *SAIS Review*, vol. 5, no. 2, Summer–Fall 1985, pp. 139–53.

'SOVIET-AMERICAN COMPETITION IN THE THIRD WORLD', *Journal of International Affairs*, vol. 34, Fall/Winter 1980/81, pp. 219–393.

'SUPERPOWER RIVALRY IN THE THIRD WORLD', *Harvard International Review*, vol. 8, January/February 1986, pp. 3–21.

TEXAS UNIVERSITY, LYNDON B. JOHNSON SCHOOL OF PUBLIC AFFAIRS, *United States Policy and the Third World: A Report by the United States Policy and Third World Policy Research Project* (Austin, TX: Texas University, 1982).

THOMPSON, W. SCOTT (ed.), *The Third World: Premises of US Policy* (San Francisco: Institute for Contemporary Studies Press, 1983).

'WHAT US WILL – AND WON'T – DO FOR THIRD WORLD COUNTRIES', Interview with M. Peter McPherson, Administrator, Agency for International Development. *US News and World Report*, vol. 91, 26 October 1981, p. 24.

C. The United States and Latin America and the Caribbean

ALLMANN, T. D., *Unmanifest Destiny: Mayhem and Illusion in American Foreign Policy from the Monroe Doctrine to Reagan's War in El Salvador* (New York: Dial Press, 1984).

BALOYRA, ENRIQUE, *El Salvador in Transition* (Chapel Hill, NC: University of North Carolina Press, 1982).

'THE BASES OF POLICY: The State Department's Appraisal of the Latin American Situation, Spring 1985', *Inter-American Economic Affairs*, vol. 39, Summer 1985, pp. 79–92.

BONIOR, DAVID E., 'Reagan and Central America', *SAIS Review*, no 2, Summer 1981, pp. 3–11.

BOSWORTH, STEPHEN W., 'Grenada', *Department of State Bulletin*, vol. 82, October 1982, pp. 75–77.

BRIGGS, EVERETT E., 'The United States and Mexico', *Department of State Bulletin*, vol. 81, July 1981, pp. 4–7.

BUSH, GEORGE, 'Nicaragua: A Threat to Democracy', *Department of State Bulletin*, vol. 85, May 1985, pp. 22–4.

CALVERT, PETER, 'Latin America and the United States During and After the Falklands Crisis, *Millenium*, vol. 12, no. 1, Spring 1983, pp. 69–78.

'CARIBBEAN BASIN INITIATIVE: Message to the Congress', *Weekly Compilation of Presidential Documents*, vol. 18, 22 March 1982, pp. 323–27.

CASTANEDA, JORGE G., 'Don't Corner Mexico!' *Foreign Policy*, no. 60, Fall 1985, pp. 75–90.

CHACE JAMES, *Endless War: How We Got Involved in Central America – And What Can be Done* (New York: Vintage Books, 1984).

CIRINCIONE, JOSEPH (ed.), *Central America and the Western Alliance* (New York and London: Holmes and Meier, for the Carnegie Endowment for International Peace and IISS, 1985).

COLEMAN, KENNETH M. and GEORGE C. HERRING (eds), *The Central American Crisis: Sources of Conflict and the Failure of US Policy* (Wilmington, DE: Scholarly Resources, 1985).

CORTADA, JAMES N., and JAMES W. CORTADA, *US Foreign Policy in the Caribbean, Cuba and Central America* (New York: Praeger, 1985).

CRAIG, RICHARD B., 'Illicit Drug Traffic and US-Latin American Relations', *Washington Quarterly*, vol. 8, no. 4, Fall 1985, pp. 105–24.

DEALY, GLEN C., 'The Pluralistic Latins', *Foreign Policy*, no. 57, Winter 1984/1985, pp. 108–27.

DICKEY, CHRISTOPHER, 'Central America: From Quagmire to Cauldron?' *Foreign Affairs*, vol. 62, no. 3, 1984, pp. 659–94.

DOMÍNGUEZ, JORGE I., *Interests and Policies in the Caribbean and Central America* (Washington, DC: American Enterprise Institute, 1982).

DOMÍNGUEZ, JORGE I. (ed.), *Economic Issues and Political Conflict:*

US-Latin American Relations (Woburn, MA: Butterworth, 1982).

DOUGLAS, H. EUGENE, 'The United States and Mexico: Conflict and Comity', *Strategic Review*, vol. 13, Spring 1985, pp. 21–30.

ENDERS, THOMAS O., 'Brazil and the United States Today', *Department of State Bulletin*, vol. 81, November 1981, pp. 87–9.

ENDERS, THOMAS O., 'A Comprehensive Strategy for the Caribbean Basin: The US and Her Neighbors', *Caribbean Review*, vol. 11, Spring 1982, pp. 10–13.

ENDERS, THOMAS O., 'Dealing with the Reality of Cuba', *Department of State Bulletin*, vol. 83, February 1983, pp. 73–8.

ENDERS, THOMAS O., 'US Relations with Brazil', *Department of State Bulletin*, vol. 82, October 1982, pp. 72–5.

ENDERS, THOMAS O. and RICHARD R. BURT, 'US Arms Transfer Policy toward Latin America', *Department of State Bulletin*, vol. 81, December 1981, pp. 72–5.

ERISMAN, H. MICHAEL (ed.), *The Caribbean Challenge: US Policy in a Volatile Region* (Boulder, CO: Westview, 1984).

ERISMAN, H. MICHAEL, and JOHN D. MARTZ, *Colossus Challenged: The Struggle for Caribbean Influence* (Boulder, CO: Westview, 1982).

FALCOFF, MARK, *Central America and US Domestic Politics* (Washington, DC: Ethics and Public Policy Center, 1984).

FALCOFF, MARK, 'Central America: A View from Washington', *Orbis*, vol. 28, no. 4, Winter 1985, pp. 665–73.

FEINBERG, RICHARD E. (ed.), *Central America: International Dimensions of the Crisis* (New York: Holmes & Meier, 1982).

FEINBERG, RICHARD E., 'Central America: No Easy Answers', *Foreign Affairs*, vol. 59, no. 4, Summer 1981, pp. 1121–46.

FEINBERG, RICHARD E., 'The Kissinger Commission Report: A Critique', *World Development*, vol. 12, August 1984, pp. 867–76.

FELLON, JOHN, 'On Central America Aid, the Bargaining Begins', *Congressional Quarterly Weekly Report*, vol. 42, 25 February 1984, pp. 443–7.

FISHLOW, ALBERT, 'The United States and Brazil: The Case of the Missing Relationship', *Foreign Affairs*, vol. 60, no. 4, Spring 1982, pp. 904–23.

GOULET, DENNIS, 'Mexico and the US: Discord among Neighbors', *Worldview*, vol. 27 (January 1984), pp. 7–10.

GRAEBNER, NORMAN A., 'American Foreign Policy after Vietnam', *Parameters*, vol. 15, no. 3 (Autumn 1985), pp. 46–57.

GRAYSON, GEORGE W., *The United States and Mexico: Patterns of Influence* (New York: Praeger, 1984).

HALLIDAY, FRED, 'Cold War in the Caribbean', New Left Review, no. 141, September/October 1983, pp. 5–22.

HAYES, MARGARET D., 'United States Security Interests in Central America in Global Perspective', in Richard E. Feinberg (ed.), *Central America: Dimensions of the Crisis* (New York: Holmes & Meier, 1982).

KENWORTHY, ELDON, 'United States Policy in Central America: A Choice Denied', *Current History*, vol. 84, no. 500, March 1985, pp. 97–100+.

LEFEBER, WALTER, *Inevitable Revolutions: The United States in Central America* (New York: Norton, 1984).

LEFEBER, WALTER, 'The Reagan Administration and Revolutions in Central America', *Political Science Quarterly*, vol. 99, no. 1, Spring 1984, pp. 1–25.

LEIKEN, ROBERT S. (ed.), *Central America: Anatomy of Conflict* (Elmsford, NY: Pergamon, 1984).

LEIKEN, ROBERT S., 'Potential Conflict in Central America', in William J. Taylor and Steven A. Maaranen (eds), *The Future of Conflict in the 1980s* (Lexington, MA: Lexington Books, 1982).

LEOGRANDE, WILLIAM M., 'Cuban Policy Recycled', *Foreign Policy*, no. 46 (Spring 1982), pp. 105–119.

LEOGRANDE, WILLIAM M., 'Through the Looking Glass: The Kissinger Report on Central America', *World Policy Journal*, vol. 1, Winter 1984, pp. 251–84.

LEOGRANDE, WILLIAM M., 'A Splendid Little War: Drawing the Line in El Salvador', *International Security*, vol. 6, no. 1, Summer 1981, pp. 27–52.

LEOGRANDE, WILLIAM M., 'The United States and Latin America', *Current History*, vol. 85, no. 507, January 1986, pp. 1–4.

LOWENTHAL, ABRAHAM F., 'Threat and Opportunity in the Americas', *Foreign Affairs*, vol. 64, no. 3, 1985, pp. 539–61.

MACDONALD, SCOTT B., 'The Future of Foreign Aid in the Caribbean after Grenada: Finlandization and Confrontation in the Eastern Tier', *Inter-American Economic Affairs*, vol. 38, no. 4, Spring 1985, pp. 59–74.

'MARE NOSTRUM: US SECURITY POLICY IN THE ENGLISH-SPEAKING CARIBBEAN', *Report on the Americas*, vol. 19, July/August 1985, pp. 13–48.

MENGES, CONSTANTINE C., 'Central America and the United States', *SAIS Review*, no. 2, Summer 1981, pp. 13–33.

MOTLEY, LANGHORNE A., 'Aid and US Interests in Latin America and the Caribbean: With the State Department Taking the Lead, the Reagan Administration Put Forth Strong Arguments for Massive Economic and Military Aid for Central America and the Caribbean Basin', *Carribean Today*, vol. 2, no. 2, 1985, pp. 25–31.

MOTLEY, LANGHORNE A., 'The Need for Continuity in US Latin American Policy', *Department of State Bulletin*, vol. 85, April 1985, pp. 67–73.

PASTOR, ROBERT A., 'Continuity and Change in US Foreign Policy: Carter and Reagan on El Salvador', *Journal of Policy Analysis and Management*, vol. 3, Winter 1984, pp. 175–90.

PASTOR, ROBERT A., 'Explaining US Policy towards the Caribbean Basin: Fixed and Emerging Images', *World Politics*, vol. 38, no. 3, April 1986, pp. 483–515.

PASTOR, ROBERT A., 'Sinking in the Caribbean Basin', *Foreign Affairs*, vol. 60, no. 5, Summer 1982, pp. 1038–58.

PASTOR, ROBERT A. and RICHARD FEINBERG, *US Latin American Policy: A Marshall Plan for the Caribbean?* (Washington, CT: Center for Information on America, 1984).

PURCELL, SUSAN K., 'Mexico-US Relations: Big Initiatives Can Cause Big Problems', *Foreign Affairs*, vol. 60, no. 2, Winter 1981/1982, pp. 379–92.

PURCELL, SUSAN K., 'War and Debt in South America', *Foreign Affairs*, vol. 61, no. 3, 1983, pp. 660–74.

REAGAN, RONALD, 'Saving Freedom in Central America', Address by President Reagan before the International Longshoremen's Association, 18 July 1983, Bureau of Public Affairs, Department of State, Current Policy No. 499.

REAGAN, RONALD, 'United States Policy in Central America', *Weekly Compilation of Presidential Documents*, vol. 20, 14 May 1984, pp. 676–82.

Report of the National Bipartisan Commission on Central America (Kissinger Commission) (Washington, DC: US Government Printing Office, January 1984).

ROGERS, WILLIAM D., 'The United States and Latin America', *Foreign Affairs*, vol. 63, no. 3, (1985), pp. 560–80.

ROGERS, WILLIAM D. and JEFFREY A. MEYERS, 'The Reagan Administration and Latin America', *Caribbean Review*, vol. 11, Spring 1982, pp. 14–17.

RONFELDT, DAVID F., *Geopolitics, Security and US Strategy in the Caribbean Basin* (Santa Monica, CA: Rand Corporation, 1983).

RONFELDT, DAVID F., 'Rethinking the Monroe Doctrine [in the Caribbean Basin]', *Orbis*, vol. 28, no. 4, Winter 1985, pp. 684–96.

SCHOENLALS, KAI P. and RICHARD A. MELANSON, *Revolution and Intervention in Grenada: The New Jewel Movement, the United States, and the Caribbean* (Boulder, CO: Westview, 1985).

SCHROEDER, RICHARD C., 'Decision on Nicaragua', *Editorial Research Reports*, 28 February, 1986, pp. 147–64.

SCHULZ, DONALD E., 'The Strategy of Conflict and the Politics of Counterproductivity', *Orbis*, vol. 25, no. 3, Fall 1981, pp. 679–713.

SHULTZ, GEORGE, P., 'US Approach to Problems in the Caribbean Basin', *Department of State Bulletin*, vol. 82, September 1982, pp. 28–9.

SHULTZ, GEORGE, P., 'US Efforts to Achieve Peace in Central America', *Department of State Bulletin*, vol. 84, June 1984, pp. 67–74.

SIGMUND, PAUL E., 'Latin America: Change or Continuity?', *Foreign Affairs*, vol. 60, no. 3, 1982, pp. 629–57.

SMITH, WAYNE S., 'Dateline Havana: Myopic Diplomacy', *Foreign Policy*, no. 48 (Fall 1982), pp. 157–74.

'SUMMARY OF KISSINGER COMMISSION REPORT', *Congressional Quarterly Weekly Report*, vol. 42, 14 January 1984, pp. 64–6.

TELLIS, ASHLEY, J., 'The Geopolitical Stakes in Central American Crisis', *Strategic Review*, vol. 13, Fall 1985, pp. 45–56.

TREVERTON, GREGORY, F., 'Making Sense of Central America: In Search of a Strategic Vision', *Worldview*, vol. 27, June 1984, pp. 10–12.

TREVERTON, GREGORY F., 'US Strategy in Central America', *Survival*, vol. 28, March/April 1986, pp. 128–89.

ULLMAN, RICHARD H., 'At War with Nicaragua', *Foreign Affairs*, vol. 62, no. 1, Fall 1983, pp. 39–58.

US HOUSE COMMITTEE ON FOREIGN AFFAIRS, 'Concerning US

military and Paramilitary Operations in Nicaragua.' Markup, 18 May–7 June 1983, on H.R. 2760. Washington, DC: 1983.

US HOUSE COMMITTEE ON FOREIGN AFFAIRS, 'Issues in United States-Cuban Relations.' Hearing, 14 December 1982, before the Subcommittee on International Economic Policy and Trade and the Subcommittee on Inter-American Affairs. Washington, DC: 1983.

US HOUSE COMMITTEE ON FOREIGN AFFAIRS, 'Latin America in the World Economy.' Hearings, 15 June–21 July 1983, before the Subcommittees on International Economic Policy and Trade and on Western Hemisphere Affairs. Washington, DC: 1983.

US HOUSE COMMITTEE ON FOREIGN AFFAIRS, 'United States Policy toward Guatemala and El Salvador.' Report, 5 April 1983, of a Study Mission to Guatemala and El Salvador, 20–26 February 1983. Washington, DC: 1983.

US HOUSE COMMITTEE ON FOREIGN AFFAIRS, SUBCOMMITTEE ON INTER-AMERICAN AFFAIRS, 'The Caribbean Business Policy.' Hearings, 14–28 July 1981. Washington, DC: 1981.

US HOUSE COMMITTEE ON FOREIGN AFFAIRS, SUBCOMMITTEE ON INTER-AMERICAN AFFAIRS, 'Honduras and US Policy: An Emerging Dilemma.' Hearing, 21 September 1982. Washington, DC: 1982.

US HOUSE COMMITTEE ON FOREIGN AFFAIRS, SUBCOMMITTEE ON INTER-AMERICAN AFFAIRS, 'US Policy Option in El Salvador.' Hearing and Markup, 24 September–19 November 1981, on H. Con. Res. 197; H. Con. Res. 212. Washington, DC: 1981.

US HOUSE COMMITTEE ON FOREIGN AFFAIRS, SUBCOMMITTEE ON INTER-AMERICAN AFFAIRS, 'United States Policy toward Grenada.' Hearing, 15 June 1982. Washington, DC: 1982.

US HOUSE COMMITTEE ON FOREIGN AFFAIRS, SUBCOMMITTEE ON INTER-AMERICAN AFFAIRS, 'United States-Brazilian Relations.' Hearing, 14 July 1982. Washington, DC: 1982.

US HOUSE COMMITTEE ON FOREIGN AFFAIRS, SUBCOMMITTEE ON INTER-AMERICAN AFFAIRS, 'United States-Mexican Relations: An Update.' Hearing, 10 June 1981. Washington, DC: 1981.

US HOUSE COMMITTEE ON FOREIGN AFFAIRS, SUBCOMMITTEE ON WESTERN HEMISPHERE AFFAIRS, 'Central America: The Ends and Means of US Policy.' Hearing, 2 May 1984. Washington, DC: 1984.

US POLICY IN CENTRAL AMERICA,' *Fletcher Forum*, vol. 8, no. 1, Winter 1984, pp. 1–44.

US SENATE COMMITTEE ON FOREIGN RELATIONS, 'Central America: Treading Dangerous Waters.' Staff Report, November 1983. Washington, DC: 1983.

US SENATE COMMITTEE ON FOREIGN RELATIONS, 'National Bipartisan Report on Central Ameerica.' Hearings, 7–8 February 1984. Washington, DC: 1984.

US SENATE COMMITTEE ON FOREIGN RELATIONS, 'The Situation in El Salvador.' Hearings, 18 March–9 April 1981. Washington, DC: 1981.

US SENATE COMMITTEE ON FOREIGN RELATIONS, 'US Policy toward Nicaragua and Central America.' Hearing, 12 April 1983.

Washington, DC: 1983.

WESSON, ROBERT (ed.), *US Influence in Latin America in the 1980s* (New York: Praeger, 1982).

WIARDA, HOWARD J., 'United States Policy in South America: A Maturing Relationship?', *Current History*, vol. 84, no. 499, February 1985, pp. 49–52.

WINKELMAN, COLIN K., and A. BRENT MERRILL, 'United States and Brazilian Military Relations.' *Military Review*, vol. 63, June 1983, pp. 60–73.

D. The United States and East Asia

ATLANTIC COUNCIL OF THE US COMMITTEE ON CHINA POLICY. *China Policy for the Next Decade: A Report* (Boston: Oelgeschlager, Gunn and Hain, 1984).

BARNETT, A. DOAK, *US Arms Sales: The China-Taiwan Tangle* (Washington, DC: Brookings Institute, 1982).

BELLO, WALDEN, 'Edging toward the Quagmire: The United States and the Philippine Crisis', *World Policy Journal*, vol. 3, Winter 1985–86, pp. 29–58.

BELLO, WALDEN, 'Reflections on a New Era in the Philippines: 'Third Force' Myths and Realities,' *Christianity and Crisis*, vol. 46, 7 April 1986, pp. 111–13.

BETTS, RICHARD K., 'Southeast Asia and US Global Strategy: Continuing Interests and Shifting Priorities', *Orbis*, vol. 29, no. 2, Summer 1985, pp. 351–85.

BIERMEIER, JENS D., 'America's Shifting Emphasis to the Pacific', *Intereconomics*, vol. 20, September/October 1985, pp. 245–50.

BULLARD, MONTE R., 'The US-China Defense Relationship', *Parameters*, vol. 13, no. 1, March 1983, pp. 43–50.

BURNS, WILLIAM J., 'The Reagan Administration and the Philippines', *World Today*, vol. 38, no. 3, March 1982, pp. 97–104.

BUSZYNSKI, LESZEK, 'The US and East Asia: The Case for Realism', *Harvard International Review*, vol. 6, April 1984, pp. 6–11.

CHANG, PARRIS H., 'US-China Relations: From Hostility to Euphoria to Realism', *Annals of the American Academy of Political and Social Science*, vol. 476, November 1984, pp. 156–70.

CHIA, HUNGDAH, 'The Failure of US-Taiwan Relations', *Asian Affairs*, vol. 9, September/October 1981, pp. 20–30.

COOPER, MARY H., 'China: Quest for Stability and Development', *Editorial Research Reports*, 13 April 1984, 271–88.

COPPER, JOHN F., 'Sino-American Relations: Reaching a Plateau', *Current History*, vol. 81, no. 476, September 1982, pp. 241–5+.

CURTIS, GERALD L. and SUNG-JOO HAN (eds), *The US-South Korean Alliance: Evolving Patterns in Security Relations* (Lexington, MA: Lexington, 1983).

DAVIDSON, FREDERIC, 'Strategic Engagement and Sino-American Trade', *SAIS Review*, Summer 1981, pp. 131–40.

DE PAUW, JOHN W., *US-Chinese Trade Negotiations* (New York: Praeger,

1981).

DOWNEN, ROBERT L., 'Reagan Policy of Strategic Cooperation with China: Implications for Asian-Pacific Stability', *Journal of East Asian Affairs*, vol. 2, Spring/Summer 1982, pp. 43–69.

FALK, RICHARD, 'Views from Manila and Washington', *World Policy Journal*, vol. 1, Winter 1984, pp. 419–32.

FEENEY, WILLIAM R., 'US Strategic Interests in the Pacific', *Current History*, vol. 81, no. 474, April 1982, pp. 145–9+.

FEINTECH, LYNN D., *China's Four Modernizations and the United States* (New York: Foreign Policy Association, 1981).

FEINTECH, LYNN D., *China's Modernization Strategy and the United States* (Washington, DC: Overseas Development Council, 1981).

FELTON, JOHN, 'New Slate, New Problems for the Philippines', *Congressional Quarterly Weekly Report*, vol. 44, 1 March 1986, pp. 483–8.

FRANCIS, CORRINA-BARBARA and GUOCANG HUAN, 'Sino-American Ties and Asian Security', *Millenium*, vol. 14, no. 3, Winter 1985, pp. 272–91.

GARVER, JOHN W., 'Arms Sales, the Taiwan Question, and Sino-US Relations', *Orbis*, vol. 26, no. 4, Winter 1983, pp. 999–1035.

GARVER, JOHN W., *China's Decision for Rapprochement with the United States, 1968–1971* (Boulder, CO: Westview, 1982).

GILBERT, STEPHEN P., 'Reagan's Asian Policy: The Past Is Prologue', *Asian Perspective*, vol. 7, no. 1, Spring/Summer 1983, pp. 51–72.

GOLDSTEIN, STEVE, 'Sino-American Relations: Building a New Consensus', *Current History*, vol. 83, no. 494, September 1984, pp. 241–44+.

GORDON, BERNARD K., 'Asian Angst and American Policy', *Foreign Policy*, no. 47, Summer 1982, pp. 46–65.

GORDON, BERNARD K., 'The United States and Asia in 1983: Putting Things into Perspective', *Asian Survey*, vol. 24, no. 1, January 1984, pp. 17–27.

GREENE, FRED, 'The United States and Asia in 1981', *Asian Survey*, vol. 22, no. 1, January 1982, pp. 1–12.

GREGOR, A. JAMES, 'US Interests in Northeast Asia and the Security of Taiwan', *Strategic Review*, vol. 13, Winter 1985, pp. 52–60.

HAN, SUNG-JOO, 'South Korea's Policy toward the United States', *Journal of Northeast Asian Studies*, vol. 2, no. 3, September 1983, pp. 23–34.

HEATON, WILLIAM R., 'America and China: The Coming Decade', *Air University Review*, vol. 35, January/February 1984, pp. 18–29.

HOLDRIDGE, JOHN H., 'US-Dialogue with ASEAN and ANZUS', *Department of State Bulletin*, vol. 82, October 1982, pp. 29–32.

HOLDRIDGE, JOHN H., 'US Interests in the Pacific Island Region', *Department of State Bulletin*, vol. 82, February, 1982, pp. 59–62.

HSIUNG, JAMES C., 'Reagan's China Policy and the Sino-Soviet Detente', *Asian Affairs*, vol. 11, Summer 1984, pp. 1–11.

HUAN, XIANG, 'On Sino-US Relations', *Foreign Affairs*, vol. 60, no. 1, Fall 1981, pp. 35–53.

JOHNSON, CHALMERS, 'East Asia: Another Year of Living Dangerously', *Foreign Affairs*, vol. 62, no. 3, 1984, pp. 721–45.

KREISBERG, PAUL H., 'The United States and Asia in 1984', *Asian Survey*, vol. 25, no. 1, January 1985, pp. 1–20.

KWAK, TAE-HWAN, 'US-Korea Security Relations', *Journal of East Asian Affairs*, vol. 2, Fall/Winter 1982, pp. 260–78.

LASATER, MARTIN L., 'Future Fighter Sales to Taiwan', *Comparative Strategy*, vol. 5, no. 1, 1985, pp. 51–73.

LUKIN, VLADIMIR, 'Relations between the US and China in the 1980s', *Asian Survey*, vol. 24, no. 11, November 1984, pp. 1151–56.

MANNING, ROBERT A., 'Reagan's Chance Hit', *Foreign Policy*, no. 54, Spring 1984, pp. 83–101.

MONJO, JOHN C., 'US-Philippine Relations after the Aquino Assassination', *Department of State Bulletin*, vol. 83, November 1983, pp. 32–4.

MORLEY, JAMES W. (ed.), 'The Pacific Basin: New Challenges for the United States', *Proceedings of the Academy of Political Science*, vol. 36, no. 1, 1986, pp. 1–173.

NIMMO, ELIZABETH M., 'United States Policy Regarding Technology Transfer to the People's Republic of China', *Northwestern Journal of International Law and Business*, vol. 6, Spring 1984, pp. 249–74.

OKSENBERG, MICHEL, 'A Decade of Sino-American Relations', *Foreign Affairs*, vol. 61, no. 1, Fall 1982, pp. 175–95.

OLSEN, EDWARD A., 'Changing US Interests in Northeast Asia', *World Affairs*, vol. 143, no. 4, Spring 1981, pp. 346–65.

PALMER, NORMAN D., 'The United States and the Western Pacific: Understanding the Future', *Current History*, vol. 85, no. 510, April 1986, pp. 145–8.

PARK, KYOUNG-SUH, 'ROK–US Relations in the 1980s', *Korea and World Affairs*, vol. 5, Spring 1981, pp. 5–17.

POLLACK, JONATHAN D., *The Lessons of Coalition Politics: Sino-American Security Relations* (Santa Monica, CA: Rand Corporation, 1984).

PORTER, GARETH, 'The United States and Southeast Asia', *Current History*, vol. 83, no. 497, December 1984, pp. 400–4+.

PYE, LUCIAN W., *Redefining American Policy in Southeast Asia* (Washington, DC: American Enterprise Institute, 1982).

ROBINSON, THOMAS W., 'The United States and China in the New Balance of Power', *Current History*, vol. 84, no. 503, September 1985, pp. 241–4+.

ROSS, ROBERT S., 'International Bargaining and Domestic Politics: US-China Relations since 1972', *World Politics*, vol. 38, no. 2, January 1986, pp. 255–87.

SALONGA, JOVITO R., 'The Aquino Assassination and US-Philippine Relations', *World Affairs Journal*, vol. 2, Fall 1983, pp. 50–9.

SCALAPINO, ROBERT A., 'Uncertainties in Future Sino-US Relations', *Orbis*, vol. 26, no. 3, Fall 1982, pp. 681–96.

SCHIRMER, DANIEL B., 'Those Philippine Bases', *Monthly Review*, vol. 37, March 1986, pp. 21–31+.

SOLOMON, RICHARD H. (ed.), *The China Factor: Sino-American Relations and the Global Scene* (Englewood Cliffs, NJ: Prentice Hall, 1981).

SOLOMON, RICHARD H., 'East Asia and the Great Power Coalitions', *Foreign Affairs*, vol. 60, no. 3, 1982, pp. 686–718.

STANLEY, PETER W., 'Toward Democracy in the Philippines', *Proceedings of the Academy of Political Science*, vol. 36, no. 1, 1986, pp. 129–41.

TOW, WILLIAM T. and WILLIAM R. FEENEY (eds), *US Foreign Policy and Asian-Pacific Security: A Transregional Approach* (Boulder, CO: Westview, 1982).

US HOUSE COMMITTEE ON FOREIGN AFFAIRS, 'Reconciling Human Rights and US Security Interests in Asia.' Hearings, 10 August–15 December 1982, before the Subcommittee on Asian and Pacific Affairs and on Human Rights and International Organizations. Washington, DC: 1983.

US HOUSE COMMITTEE ON FOREIGN AFFAIRS, 'US Aid Programs in Asia.' Report of a Staff Study Mission to Thailand, Indonesia and Sri Lanka, 7 October–1 November, 1984. Washington, DC: 1985.

US SENATE COMMITTEE ON FOREIGN RELATIONS, Subcommittee on East Asia and Pacific Affairs, 'US Policies and Programs in Southeast Asia.' Hearings, 8 June–15 July 1982, on US Policies and Programs in Southeast Asia. Washington, DC: 1982.

US SENATE COMMITTEE ON FOREIGN RELATIONS, 'United States Relations with ASEAN, Hong Kong and Laos.' Report, March 1982. Washington, DC: 1982.

US SENATE SELECT COMMITTEE ON INTELLIGENCE, *The Philippines: A Situation Report* A Staff Report, 1 November 1985. Washington, DC: 1985.

WOLFOWITZ, PAUL D., 'Developments in the Philippines', *Department of State Bulletin*, vol. 86, January 1986, pp. 49–52.

WRIGGINS, HOWARD, 'United States-Soviet Relations across the Arc of Rimland Asia.' *Asian Survey*, vol. 23, no. 8, August 1983, pp. 901–12.

ZAGORIA, DONALD S., 'Soviet-American Rivalry in Asia.' *Proceedings of the Academy of Political Science*, vol. 36, no. 1, 1986, pp. 103–15.

ZHANG, JIA-LIU, 'The New Romanticism in the Reagan Administration's Asian Policy: Illusion and Reality', *Asian Survey*, vol. 24, no. 10, October 1984, pp. 997–1011.

E. The United States and South and Southwest Asia

ARMACOST, MICHAEL H., 'South Asia and US Foreign Policy', *Department of State Bulletin*, vol. 85, February 1985, pp. 25–8.

AYOOB, MOHAMMED, 'India, Pakistan and Superpower Rivalry', *World Today* (London), vol. 38, no. 5, May 1982, pp. 194–202.

AZIZ, M. A., 'Bangladesh in United States Foreign Policy', *Asian Affairs*, vol. 9, March/April 1982, pp. 218–27.

GALBRAITH, PETER, *United States-Indian Relations*. A Report to the Committee on Foreign Relations, United States Senate (Washington, DC: US Government Printing Office, 1982).

HARDGRAVE, ROBERT L., JR, 'Why India Matters: The Challenge to American Policy in South Asia', *Asian Affairs* (New York), vol. 11, no. 1, Spring 1984, pp. 45–56.

JONES, RODNEY W., 'Regional Conflict and Strategic Challenge in Southwest Asia', in William J. Taylor and Steven A. Maaranen (eds), *The Future of Conflict in the 1980s* (Lexington, MA: Lexington Books, 1982).

KHAN, RAIS A., 'America's Role and Interests in South and Southwest Asia', *Asian Affairs*, vol. 9, March/April 1982, pp. 208–17.

MUSTAFA, ZUBEIDA, 'Pakistan-US Relations: The Latest Phase', *World Today*, vol. 37, no. 12, December 1981, pp. 469–75.

PALMER, NORMAN D., *The United States and India: The Dimensions of Influence* (New York: Praeger, 1984).

ROSE, LEO E., 'United States and Soviet Policy toward South Asia', *Current History*, vol. 85, March 1986, pp. 97–100.

SMITH, LOUIS J., 'The United States and Afghanistan', *Department of State Bulletin*, vol. 82, March 1982, pp. 1–12.

THOMAS, RAJU G. C., 'Prospects for Indo-US Security Ties', *Orbis*, vol. 27, no. 2, Summer 1983, pp. 371–92.

THORNTON, THOMAS P., 'American Interest in India under Carter and Reagan', *SAIS Review*, vol. 5, no. 1, Winter–Spring 1985, pp. 179–90.

US HOUSE COMMITTEE ON FOREIGN AFFAIRS, 'Proposed US Assistance and Arms Transfers to Pakistan.' An Assessment; Report, 20 November 1981, of a Staff Study Mission to Pakistan and India, 30 September–17 October, 1981. Washington, DC: 1981.

US HOUSE COMMITTEE ON FOREIGN AFFAIRS, 'Security and Economic Assistance to Pakistan.' Hearings and Markup, 17 April–19 November 1981, before the Subcommittees on International Security and Scientific Affairs, or International Economic Policy and Trade and on Asian and Pacific Affairs, on H. Con. Res. 211. Washington, DC: 1982.

US SENATE COMMITTEE ON FOREIGN RELATIONS, 'Aid and the Proposed Arms Sales of F-16s to Pakistan.' Hearings, 12 and 17 November 1981. Washington, DC: 1981.

US SENATE COMMITTEE ON FOREIGN RELATIONS, 'United States Security Interests in South Asia.' Staff Report, April 1984. Washington, DC: 1984.

US SENATE COMMITTEE ON FOREIGN RELATIONS, 'United States-Indian Relations.' Report, March 1982. Washington, DC: 1982.

ZIRING, LAWRENCE (Ed.), *The Subcontinent in World Politics: India, its Neighbors, and the Great Powers* (New York: Praeger, 1982).

F. The United States and the Middle East and North Africa

ABURDENE, ODEH, 'US Economic and Financial Relations with Saudi Arabis, Kuwait and the United Arab Emirates', *American-Arab Affairs*, no. 7, Winter 1983/1984, pp. 76–84.

AL-AWAJI, IBRAHIM MOHAMMED, 'US-Saudi Economic and Political Relations', *American-Arab Affairs*, no. 7, Winter 1983–84, pp. 55–9.

ANDERSON, LISA, 'Libya and American Foreign Policy', *Middle East Journal*, vol. 36, no. 4, Autumn 1982, pp. 516–34.

ARURI, NASEER H., 'The United States and Israel: That Very Special Relationship', *American-Arab Affairs*, no. 1, Summer 1982, pp. 31–42.

ATHERTON, ALFRED L., JR, 'Arabs, Israelis and Americans: A Reconsideration', *Foreign Affairs*, vol. 62, no. 5, Summer 1984, pp. 1194–209.

BALL, GEORGE, 'America in the Middle East: A Breakdown in Foreign Policy', *Journal of Palestine Studies*, vol. 13, Spring 1984, pp. 4–15.

BERGER, ELENA, 'Dealing with Libya', *Editorial Research Reports*, 14 March 1986, pp. 187–204.

BINDER, LEONARD, 'United States Policy in the Middle East', *Current History*, vol. 84, no. 498, January 1985, pp. 1–4+.

BINDER, LEONARD, 'United States Policy in the Middle East: Toward a Pax Sandiana', *Current History*, vol. 81, no. 471, January 1982, pp. 1–4+.

BOWMAN, LARRY W. and JEFFREY A. LEFEBVRE, 'US Strategic Policy in Northeast Africa and the Indian Ocean', *Africa Report*, vol. 28, no. 6, November/December 1983, pp. 4–9.

CAMPBELL, JOHN C., 'The Middle East: A House of Containment Built on Shifting Sands', *Foreign Affairs*, vol. 60, no. 3, 1982, pp. 593–628.

COKER, CHRISTOPHER, 'Has Reagan Made America Stronger?' *World Today*, vol. 41, no. 2, February 1985, pp. 34–7.

'The Deadly Connection: Reagan and the Middle East,' *Middle East Research and Information Project Reports*, vol. 14, November/December 1984, pp. 3–34.

DEUTSCH, RICHARD, 'Dealing with Gaddafy', *Africa Report*, vol. 27, no. 2, March/April 1982, pp. 47–53.

'DEVELOPMENTS IN US MIDDLE EAST POLICY', *American-Arab Affairs*, no. 13, Summer 1985, pp. 1–22+.

EHRNMAN, BRUCE R., 'Syria and the United States: The Awkward Relationship', *Middle East Insight*, vol. 4, no. 4/5, 1986, pp. 14–20.

FELTON, J., 'Arms and the Middle East: Middle East Arms Bazaar: Weighing the Costs', *Congressional Quarterly Weekly Report*, 2 November 1985, p. 2241+, and 26 October 1985, pp. 2136–9.

'FORUM: US-POLICY TOWARD THE MIDDLE EAST', *Orbis*, vol. 26, no. 1, Spring 1982, pp. 25–34.

'THE "FRESH START" INITIATIVE', *American-Arab Affairs*, no. 2, Fall 1982, pp. 1–50.

FRY, MICHAEL G., 'United States Policy in the Middle East: Lebanon and the Palestinian Question', *Arab Studies Quarterly*, vol. 7, Winter 1985, pp. 27–35.

GARFINKLE, ADAM M., 'America and Europe in the Middle East: A New Coordination?' *Orbis*, vol. 25, no. 3, Fall 1981, pp. 631–48.

GROISSER, PHILIP L., *The United States and the Middle East* (Albany: State University of New York Press, 1982).

HAIG, ALEXANDER M., JR, 'Peace and Security in the Middle East', *Department of State Bulletin*, vol. 82, July 1982, pp. 44–7.

HAIG, ALEXANDER M., JR, 'Saudi Security, Middle East Peace and US Interests', *Department of State Bulletin*, vol. 81, November 1981, pp. 60–3.

HAKKI, MOHAMMED I., 'US-Egyptian Relations', *American-Arab Affairs*, no. 6, Fall 1983, pp. 28–33.

HAMDOON, NIZAR, and THOMAS STOUFFER, 'The United States, Iraq and the Gulf War', *American-Arab Affairs*, no. 14, Fall 1985, pp. 95–116.

HUDSON, MICHAEL C., 'Reagan's Policy in Northeast Africa', *Africa Report*, vol. 27, no. 2, March–April 1982, pp. 4–10.

HUDSON, MICHAEL C., 'United States Policy in the Middle East: Opportunities and Dangers', *Current History*, vol. 85, no. 508, February 1986, pp. 45–52+.

INBAR, EFRAIM, 'The American Arms Transfer to Israel', *Middle East Review*, vol. 15, Fall 1982/Winter 1982/1983, pp. 40–51.

JOYNER, CHRISTOPHER C. and SHAFGAT ALI SHAH, 'The Reagan Policy of 'Strategic Consensus' in the Middle East', *Strategic Review*, vol. 9, Fall 1981, pp. 15–24.

KHAPOYA, VINCENT B. and BALFOUR AGYEMAN-DHAH, 'The Cold War and Regional Politics in East Africa', *Conflict Quarterly*, vol. 5, no. 2, Spring 1985, pp. 18–32.

KLIEMAN, AARON, 'Origins and Assumptions of the Reagan Middle East Initiative', *Crossroads*, no. 10, Spring 1983, pp. 5–38.

LAIPSON, ELLEN, 'US Policy in Northern Africa', *American-Arab Affairs*, no. 6, Fall 1983, pp. 48–58.

LUSTICK, IAN S., 'Israeli Politics and American Foreign Policy', *Foreign Affairs*, vol. 61, no. 2, Winter 1982/83, pp. 379–99.

LYMAN, PRINCETON, 'Libyan Involvement in Sudan and Chad', *Department of State Bulletin*, vol. 82, January 1982, pp. 27–9.

MADISON, CHRISTOPHER, 'Reagan Links Middle East Disputes to Global East–West Struggle', *National Journal*, vol. 16, 28 January 1984, pp. 158–63.

MARANTZ, PAUL and BLEMA S. STEINBERG (eds), *Superpower Involvement in the Middle East: Dynamics of Foreign Policy* (Boulder, CO: Westview, 1985).

MCNAUGHTER, THOMAS L., 'Balancing Soviet Power in the Persian Gulf: How Could Soviet Forces Threaten US Interests in the Region', *Brookings Review*, vol. 1, Summer 1983, pp. 20–4.

MILLER, LINDA B., 'America and the Middle East: Holding the Center', *World Today*, vol. 39, January 1983, pp. 16–21.

MURPHY, RICHARD W., 'US Interests in Lebanon', *Department of State Bulletin*, vol. 84, March 1984, pp. 54–6.

NEUMANN, ROBERT G., 'The Search for Peace in the Middle East: A Role for US Policy', *American-Arab Affairs*, no. 1, Summer 1982, pp. 3–12.

NEUMANN, ROBERT G., 'United States Policy in the Middle East', *Current History*, vol. 83, January 1984, pp. 1–4+.

NEWSOME, DAVID D., 'America Engulfed', *Foreign Policy*, no. 43, Summer 1981, pp. 17–32.

NEWSOME, DAVID D., 'Miracle or Mirage: Reflections on US Diplomacy and the Arabs', *Middle East Journal*, vol. 35, no. 3, Summer 1981, pp. 299–313.

PIPES, DANIEL, 'Breaking All the Rules: American Debate over the Middle East', *International Security*, vol. 9, no. 2, Fall 1984, pp. 124–50.

QUANDT, WILLIAM B., 'Reagan's Lebanon Policy: Trial and Error', *Middle East Journal*, vol. 38, Spring 1984, pp. 237–54.

RAFAEL, GIDEON, 'Divergence and Convergence of American-Soviet Interests in the Middle East: An Israeli Viewpoint', *Political Science Quarterly*, vol. 100, no. 4, Winter 1985–86, pp. 561–74.

'READY TO FIGHT FOR THE MIDEAST: The Reagan Team Will Risk a War if Necessary to Avoid Another Iran', *Business Week*, 19 October 1981, pp. 40–2.

'REAGAN MIDDLE EAST POLICY: A Midterm Assessment', *American-Arab Affairs*, no. 4, Spring 1984, pp. 1–69.

REICH, BERNARD, *The United States and Israel: Influence in the Special Relationship* (New York: Praeger, 1984).

REICH, BERNARD, 'United States Middle East Policy in the Carter and Reagan Administrations', *Australian Outlook*, vol. 38, no. 2, August 1984, pp. 72–80.

RUBIN, BARRY, 'Middle East: Search for Peace', *Foreign Affairs*, vol. 64, no. 3, 1986, pp. 583–604.

RUSTOW, DANKWART A., 'Realignments in the Middle East', *Foreign Affairs*, vol. 63, no. 3, 1985, pp. 581–601.

SAUNDERS, HAROLD H., ANTHONY CORDESMAN, HANNA BATATU and ISMAIL SERAGELDIN, 'Changing Relations between the United States and the Middle East', *AEI Foreign Policy and Defense Review*, (American Enterprise Institute, Washington DC), vol. 4, no. 5/6, 1984, pp. 37–49.

SEELYE, TALCOTT W., 'The PLO and the United States', *Arab Perspectives*, vol. 5, September/October 1984, pp. 11–14.

SEGAL, AARON, 'The United States and North Africa', *Current History*, vol. 80, no. 470, December 1981, pp. 401–4+.

SHAW, HARRY J., 'Strategic Dissensus', *Foreign Policy*, no. 61, Winter 1985–86, pp. 125–41.

SHULTZ, GEORGE P., 'Promoting Peace in the Middle East', *Department of State Bulletin*, vol. 84, January 1984, pp. 32–5.

SISCO, JOSEPH J., 'Middle East: Progress or Lost Opportunity?' *Foreign Affairs*, vol. 61, no. 3, 1983, pp. 611–40.

STERNER, MICHAEL, 'Managing US-Israeli Relations', *American-Arab Affairs*, no. 6, Fall 1983, pp. 15–23.

TOWELL, PAT, 'Military Strikes against Libya Receive Capital Hill Support: Some Concerns on War Powers', *Congressional Quarterly Weekly Report*, vol. 44, 29 March 1986, pp. 699–702.

US CONGRESS JOINT ECONOMIC COMMITTEE, 'The Persian Gulf: Are WE Committed? At What Cost? A Dialogue with the Reagan Administration on U.S. Policy.' Washington, DC: 1981.

US HOUSE COMMITTEE ON FOREIGN AFFAIRS, 'The Crisis in Lebanon: US Policy and Alternative Legislative Proposals. Hearings, 1–2 February 1984. Washington, DC: 1984.

US HOUSE COMMITTEE ON FOREIGN AFFAIRS, 'Proposed Sale of Airborne Warning and Control Systems (AWACS) and F-15 Enhancements to Saudi Arabia.' Hearings and Markup, 28 September–7 October 1981, before the Subcommittees on International Security and Scientific Affairs and on Europe and the Middle East, on H. Con. Res. 194. Washington, DC: 1981.

US HOUSE COMMITTEE ON FOREIGN AFFAIRS, 'The Situation in Lebanon: US Role in the Middle East.' Hearing, 9 September 1982. Washington, DC: 1982.

US HOUSE COMMITTEE ON FOREIGN AFFAIRS, 'US Policy toward the Conflict in the Western Sahara.' Report of a Staff Study Mission to Morocco, Algeria, the Western Sahara and France, 25 August–6

September 1982. Washington, DC: 1982.
US HOUSE COMMITTEE ON FOREIGN AFFAIRS, 'US Security Interests in the Persian Gulf.' Report, 16 March 1981 of a Staff Study Mission to the Persian Gulf, Middle East and Horn of Africa, 21 October–13 November 1980. Washington, DC: 1981.
US HOUSE COMMITTEE ON FOREIGN AFFAIRS, Subcommittee on Europe and the Middle East. 'Developments in the Middle East, August 1983.' Hearing, 3 August 1983. Washington, DC: 1983.
US HOUSE COMMITTEE ON FOREIGN RELATIONS, 'Persian Gulf Situation.' Hearing, 17 September 1981. Washington, DC: 1981.
US HOUSE COMMITTEE ON FOREIGN RELATIONS, 'Policy Options in Lebanon.' Hearing, 11 January 1984. Washington, DC: 1984.
US HOUSE COMMITTEE ON FOREIGN RELATIONS, 'Situation in Lebanon.' Hearing, 1 December 1982. Washington, DC: 1983.
VAN HOLLEN, CHRISTOPHER, 'Don't Engulf the Gulf', *Foreign Affairs*, vol. 59, no. 5, Summer 1981, pp. 1064–78.
VELIOTES, NICHOLAS A., 'US Policy toward the Persian Gulf', *Department of State Bulletin*, vol. 82, June 1982, pp. 65–7.
WEINBAUM, MARVIN G., 'Politics and Development in Foreign Aid: US Economic Assistance to Egypt, 1975–1982', *Middle East Journal*, vol. 37, no. 4, Autumn 1983, pp. 636–55.
WRIGHT, CLAUDIA, 'Journey to Marrakesh: US-Moroccan Security Relations', *International Security*, vol. 7, no. 4, Spring 1983, pp. 163–79.
WRIGHT, CLAUDIA, 'Libya and the West: Headlong into Confrontation?', *International Affairs*, vol. 58, no. 1, Winter 1981–82, pp. 13–41.
WRIGHT, CLAUDIA, 'Shadow on Sand: Strategy and Deception in Reagan's Policy towards the Arabs', *Journal of Palestine Studies*, vol. 11, Spring 1982, pp. 3–36.

G. The United States and Sub-Saharan Africa

ANDERSON, DAVID, 'America in Africa, 1981', *Foreign Affairs*, vol. 60, no. 3, 1982, pp. 658–85.
BISSELL, RICHARD E., *South Africa and the United States: The Erosion of an Influence Relationship* (New York: Praeger, 1982).
BULL, HEDLEY, 'The West and South Africa', *Daedalus*, vol. 111, no. 2, Spring 1982, pp. 255–70.
CLOUGH, MICHAEL (ed.), *Changing Realities in Southern Africa: Implications for American Policy* (Berkeley, CA: Institute for International Studies, 1982).
CLOUGH, MICHAEL, 'Beyond Constructive Engagement', *Foreign Policy*, no. 61, Winter 1985–86, pp. 3–24.
CLOUGH, MICHAEL, 'Mozambique: American Policy Options', *Africa Report*, vol. 27, no. 6, November/December 1982, pp. 14–17.
CLOUGH, MICHAEL, 'United States Policy in Southern Africa', *Current History*, vol. 83, no. 491, March 1984, pp. 97–100+.
COKER, CHRISTOPHER, *NATO, the Warsaw Pact and Africa* (New York: St Martin, 1985).
COKER, CHRISTOPHER, 'Neo-Conservatism and Africa: Some Common

American Fallacies', *Third World Quarterly*, vol. 5, April 1983, pp. 283–99.

COKER, CHRISTOPHER, 'Reagan and Africa', *World Today*, vol. 38, no. 4, April 1982, pp. 123–30.

COKER, CHRISTOPHER, 'The United States and South Africa: Can Constructive Engagement Work?' *Millenium*, vol. 11, no. 2, Autumn 1982, pp. 223–41.

COOPER, MARY H., 'Angola and the Reagan Doctrine', *Editorial Research Reports*, 17 January 1986, pp. 23–40.

CROCKER, CHESTER A., 'The African Private Sector and US Foreign Policy', *Department of State Bulletin*, vol. 82, February 1982, pp. 27–30.

CROCKER, CHESTER A., 'Reagan Administration's Africa Policy: A Progress Report', *Department of State Bulletin*, vol. 84, January 1984, pp. 38–44.

CROCKER, CHESTER A., 'US and Soviet Interests in the Horn of Africa', *Department of State Bulletin*, vol. 86, January 1986, pp. 29–32.

DE ST JORRE, JOHN, 'Constructive Engagement: An Assessment', *Africa Report*, vol. 28, no. 5, September/October 1983, pp. 48–51.

DUGARD, JOHN, Silence is Not Golden', *Foreign Policy*, no. 46, Spring 1982, pp. 37–48.

FISHER, SCOTT, *Coping with Change: US Policy toward South Africa* (Washington, DC: National Defense University Press, 1982).

'FORUM: US POLICY TOWARD SUB-SAHARAN AFRICA', *Orbis*, vol. 25, no. 4, Winter 1982, pp. 853–79.

GILPIN, SUSAN, 'US/Africa: Minerals and Foreign Policy', *Africa Report*, vol. 27, no. 3, May/June 1982, pp. 16–22.

JACKSON, HENRY F., 'Reagan's Policy Rupture', *Africa Report*, vol. 26, no. 5, September/October 1981, pp. 9–13.

JASTER, ROBERT S., *Southern Africa in Conflict: Implications for US Policies in the 1980s* (Washington, DC: American Enterprise Institute, 1982).

KITCHEN, HELEN, 'Africa: Year of Ironies', *Foreign Affairs*, vol. 64, no. 3, 1986, pp. 562–82.

KITCHEN, HELEN, *US Interests in Africa* (Washington Papers, no. 98. New York: Praeger, 1983).

KITCHEN, HELEN and MICHAEL CLOUGH, *The United States and South Africa: Realities and Red Herrings* (Washington, DC: Significant Issues Series, Centre for Strategic and International Studies, 1984).

LEVY, SAM, 'US-Mozambique: Broken Promises? Over the Past, the Reagan Administration Has Sought to Repair Relations with Mozambique, Encourage Its Economic Reforms, and Reduce Its Dependence on Soviet Bloc Assistance', *Africa Report*, vol. 31, no. 1, January/February 1986, pp. 77–80.

LIEBENOW, GUS, 'American Policy in Africa: The Reagan Years', *Current History*, vol. 82, no. 482, March 1983, pp. 97–101+.

LYMAN, PRINCETON, 'US Export Policy toward South Africa', *Department of State Bulletin*, vol. 83, May 1983, pp. 25–9.

MANNING, ROBERT A., 'Reagan's African Aid Agenda', *Africa Report*, vol. 30, no. 3, May/June 1985, pp. 73–7.

MARSHALL, HARRY R., JR., 'US Nuclear Policy toward South Africa', *Department of State Bulletin*, vol. 83, May 1983, pp. 66–9.

OTTAWAY, MARINA, *Soviet and American Influence in the Horn of Africa* (New York: Praeger, 1982).

SHULTZ, GEORGE P., 'The US and Africa in the 1980s', *Department of State Bulletin*, vol. 84, April 1984, pp. 9–15.

THOMPSON, W. SCOTT, 'US Policy toward Africa: At America's Service?', *Orbis*, vol. 25, no. 4, Winter 1982, pp. 1011–24.

UNGAR, SANFORD J. and PETER VALE, 'South Africa: Why Constructive Engagement Failed', *Foreign Affairs*, vol. 64, no. 2, Winter 1985/86, pp. 234–58.

US HOUSE COMMITTEE ON FOREIGN AFFAIRS, SUBCOMMITTEE ON AFRICA, 'Africa: Observations on the Impact of American Foreign Policy and Development Programs in Six African Countries.' Report on a Congressional Study Mission to Zimbabwe, South Africa, Kenya, Somalia, Angola, and Nigeria, 4–22 August 1981. Washington, DC: 1981.

US HOUSE COMMITTEE ON FOREIGN AFFAIRS, SUBCOMMITTEE ON AFRICA, 'Economic Sanctions and Their Potential Impact on US Corporate Involvement in South Africa.' Hearing, 31 January 1985. Washington, DC: 1985.

US HOUSE COMMITTEE ON FOREIGN AFFAIRS, SUBCOMMITTEE ON AFRICA, 'Enforcement of the United States Arms Embargo against South Africa.' Hearing, 30 March 1982. Washington, DC: 1982.

US HOUSE COMMITTEE ON FOREIGN AFFAIRS, SUBCOMMITTEE ON AFRICA, 'The Impact of US Foreign Policy on Seven African Countires.' Report, 9 March 1984, of a Congressional Study Mission to Ethiopia, Zaire, Zimbabwe, Ivory Coast, Algeria, and Morocco, 6–25 August 1983 and a Staff Study Mission to Tunisia, 24–7 August 1983. Washington, DC: 1984.

US HOUSE COMMITTEE ON FOREIGN AFFAIRS, SUBCOMMITTEE ON AFRICA, 'US Policy toward Namibia: Spring 1981.' Hearing, 17 June 1981. Washington, DC: 1981.

US HOUSE COMMITTEE ON FOREIGN AFFAIRS, SUBCOMMITTEE ON AFRICA, 'United States Policy toward Southern Africa: Focus on Namibia, Angola and South Africa.' Hearing and Markup, 16 September 1982 on H. Res. 214; H. Con. Res. 183. Washington, DC: 1983.

'US POLICY TOWARD SOUTH AFRICA: PRO AND CON,' *Congressional Digest*, vol. 64, October 1985, pp. 225–56.

US SENATE COMMITTEE ON FOREIGN RELATIONS, 'Famine in Africa', Hearing, 17 January 1985. Washington, DC: 1985.

WHITAKER, JENNIFER S., 'Africa Beset', *Foreign Affairs*, vol. 62, no. 3, 1984, pp. 746–76.

WINSTON, HENRY, 'South Africa and the Reagan Factor', *Political Affairs*, vol. 65, February 1986, pp. 7–11.

ZARTMAN, I. WILLIAM, *Ripe for Resolution: Conflict and Intervention in Africa* (New York: Oxford University Press, 1985).

Index

Abu Dhabi, 29
Aeroflot, 131
Afferica, Joan, 412
Afghanistan
  communism in, 230–1, 232–3, 234,
    235, 236, 238, 247
  democracy in, 229, 231
  international response to Soviet
    domination of, 244–6
  nationalism in, 230, 231, 235, 240,
    251
  and Pakistan, 28, 213, 214, 234, 246
  refugees from, 245
  resistance movement in, 295, 442
  Soviet commitment to, 227, 235,
    241–4, 246–52
  Soviet influence in, 10, 20, 28, 30,
    38, 42, 56, 172, 205, 207,
    227–8, 230–1, 232, 233, 234,
    236–7, 238, 244–5, 322, 338,
    339, 341, 413, 414, 416, 427,
    428, 432, 439, 457
  Soviet invasion of, 55, 57, 74, 87,
    113, 179, 186, 201, 202, 204,
    205, 206, 213–15, 216, 228,
    229, 232, 238–41, 260, 269
  Soviet withdrawal from, 216,
    250–2, 440
  superpowers in, 250
  and UN, 245
  US assistance to, 14, 229, 240,
    241–2, 243, 246, 257
African-American Institute (AAI),
  367
African National Congress (ANC),
  South African
  activities of, 363–4, 366, 377
  Algerian support for, 314
  Ethiopian training camps for, 341
  Soviet support for, 355, 361, 362,
    382–4
  US support for, 363
AGIP, and Congolese oil reserves,
  350
Albania, 43, 129

Alfonsín, Raúl, 123, 127, 128, 133,
  134
Algeria
  and Cuba, 322
  in Group of 77, 302, 313
  an intermediary, 28
  and Mauritania, 310
  in Non-Aligned Movement, 303
  and Polisario, 310, 317
  self-determination in, 30
  Soviet arms sales to, 309, 311,
    319–20, 321, 437
  Soviet relations with, 301, 302–4,
    306, 311, 313–14, 317,
    318–19, 321–3, 324, 325, 326,
    328, 338
  support for ANC, 314
  and Tunisia, 310
  US relations with, 260, 437, 452,
    458
Alianza Popular Revolucionaria
  Americana (APRA), Peruvian,
  125–26, 129
Aliev, Gaidar, 418n.5
Allende, Salvador, 45, 128
Alliance for Progress, 105
Alves, Nito, 370, 372
American Committee on Africa, 368
Amin, Hafizullah, 234, 236, 237–8,
  239, 240, 241, 251
Amin, Idi, 27, 350
Amin al-Husseini, Hajj, 281
Andreyev, N., 303
Andropov, Yuri (or Iurii), 180, 206,
  399, 402
Angola
  Cuban intervention in, 27, 40, 65,
    70, 72, 74, 75, 76–7, 78,
    79–80, 87, 127, 341, 355, 361,
    369, 370, 371, 373, 374, 385,
    414, 435
  famine in, 343
  French influence in, 352
  internal political problems in, 56,
    434–5

514